# Contents at a Glance

- **61** Rate Music Tracks
- **62** Remove Audio from the Library
- **63** Search for Songs
- **64** Copy Audio Files to a Central Location
- **65** About iPod
- **66** Set iPod Preferences
- **67** Sync Playlists with iPod
- **68** Manually Update iPod
- **69** Customize View of Song List

## CHAPTER 9: Listening to Sound Files

- **70** About Internet Radio
- **71** Listen to Internet Radio
- **72** Load New Internet Streaming Audio Sites
- **73** Store Favorite Internet Radio Sites
- **74** Randomize Songs Being Played Back
- **75** Adjust Sound Level of Music Library
- **76** About Equalizers
- **77** Equalize the Sound
- **78** Save Equalizer Settings
- **79** Apply an Equalizer Preset to an Individual Song
- **80** Create Fades Between Audio Files
- **81** Use Visual Effects with Audio Files
- **82** Shuffle Songs by Album

## CHAPTER 10: Creating Music CDs

- **83** About CD Burners
- **84** Adjust CD Burning Speed
- **85** Set Pauses Between Audio Files on CD
- **86** Burn an Audio CD
- **87** Burn an MP3 CD
- **88** Burn a CD with Segmented Audio Files
- **89** Create a Backup of Your Music Library

## PART III: iMOVIE

### CHAPTER 11: Importing Video Clips

- **90** About Connecting a Digital Video Camera
- **91** Capture Digital Video
- **92** Import Video Files from Other Sources
- **93** About Importing Nondigital Video
- **94** Set Clip Breaks for Importing

### CHAPTER 12: Working with Video Clips

- **95** About the Monitor
- **96** Name a Clip
- **97** Split a Clip
- **98** Crop a Clip
- **99** Set the Direction of a Clip
- **100** Create a Freeze Frame Image

### CHAPTER 13: Creating Movies

- **101** About the Timeline Elements
- **102** About Rendering
- **103** Add Clips to the Timeline
- **104** Set the Speed of a Clip
- **105** Add Photos from iPhoto
- **106** Adjust Display Time of a Photo
- **107** Add Motion to a Photo
- **108** Add a Still Image from Another Application
- **109** Trim Clips in the Timeline
- **110** Add Bookmarks to Your Movie

### CHAPTER 14: Adding Visual Effects to a Movie

- **111** Insert a Transition Between Video Clips
- **112** Create a Movie Title
- **113** Add an Effect
- **114** Apply an Effect Over Time
- **115** Modify Applied Transitions
- **116** Add Movie Credits

### CHAPTER 15: Adding Sound to a Movie

- **117** About Audio Tracks and Audio Formats
- **118** Incorporate Sound Effects into a Movie
- **119** Add Music from iTunes
- **120** Add Music from a CD
- **121** Create Voiceover Effects
- **122** Extract Audio from Video
- **123** Split an Audio Clip
- **124** Adjust the Volume of a Clip
- **125** Mix Audio Track Levels
- **126** Fade Audio
- **127** Lock Audio Clip to Video Clip

### CHAPTER 16: Sharing a Movie

- **128** Preview the Completed Movie in iMovie
- **129** About Movie Export Formats
- **130** Store the Movie on DV Tape
- **131** Create a QuickTime Movie from iMovie
- **132** Add Chapter Markers
- **133** Create an iDVD File
- **134** Put a Movie on the Web

*Continued on next page*

# Contents at a Glance

*Continued from previous page*

## PART IV: iDVD

### CHAPTER 17: Laying Out a DVD

- 135  About DVDs
- 136  Select a DVD Theme
- 137  Add a Movie to the DVD Menu
- 138  Use Movie Folders
- 139  Create a Menu from a Movie with Chapter Markers
- 140  About Drop Zones
- 141  Add Images to Drop Zones

### CHAPTER 18: Customizing the DVD

- 142  Customize the Image or Movie in the Drop Zone
- 143  Remove Images from the Drop Zone
- 144  Create a Custom Background
- 145  Create a Custom Motion Menu
- 146  Change Menu Title
- 147  Change Text of Buttons/Titles
- 148  Set the Start Frame for a Motion Button
- 149  Change Image Displayed on the Button
- 150  Change Button Locations
- 151  Create a Custom Button
- 152  Move Buttons to Other Menus
- 153  Change the Audio that Plays for the DVD Menu
- 154  Save a Custom Theme
- 155  Remove the Apple Watermark

### CHAPTER 19: Adding a Slideshow to a DVD

- 156  Create a Slideshow Using an iPhoto Album
- 157  Manually Create a Slideshow Using the Media Pane
- 158  Create a Slideshow in iDVD with the Finder
- 159  Add Audio to a Slideshow in iDVD
- 160  Reorganize Images in a Slideshow
- 161  Control Slideshow Advancing

### CHAPTER 20: Creating a DVD

- 162  Add an Autoplay Movie to the DVD
- 163  Preview the DVD Content
- 164  Control the Playback Quality
- 165  Burn a Test Version on a DVD-RW
- 166  Burn a DVD

## PART V: GARAGEBAND

### CHAPTER 21: Creating a New Song

- 167  About Synthesized Music and Loops
- 168  Build a Song from Loops
- 169  Adjust the Repeat Length of a Loop
- 170  Add a New Music Track
- 171  Record a Track Using a MIDI/USB Keyboard
- 172  Record a Track Using the Virtual Keyboard
- 173  Record a Live Guitar or Voice Track
- 174  Play Using a Metronome
- 175  Repeat (Cycle) Part of the Song Forever

### CHAPTER 22: Fine-Tuning Your Song

- 176  Change the Song's Title, Time Signature Measurement, Tempo, and Key
- 177  Rename Your Loops and Tracks
- 178  Transpose a Track Up or Down in Pitch
- 179  Mix Your Song's Tracks
- 180  Add Audio Effects to a Track
- 181  Modify an Existing Loop's Notes
- 182  Fix the Timing on a Live Software Music Track
- 183  Add an External Audio Track
- 184  Copy a Track from One Song to Another

### CHAPTER 23: Sharing Your Song

- 185  Customize Your Export Information
- 186  Export the Song to iTunes
- 187  Convert the Song to MP3 or AAC Format
- 188  Locate the Audio File in the Finder

# iLife™ '04

Jinjer Simon

Sams Publishing, 800 East 96th Street, Indianapolis, Indiana 46240 USA

## iLife in a Snap

Copyright © 2004 by Sams Publishing

All rights reserved. No part of this book shall be reproduced, stored in a retrieval system, or transmitted by any means, electronic, mechanical, photocopying, recording, or otherwise, without written permission from the publisher. No patent liability is assumed with respect to the use of the information contained herein. Although every precaution has been taken in the preparation of this book, the publisher and author assume no responsibility for errors or omissions. Nor is any liability assumed for damages resulting from the use of the information contained herein.

International Standard Book Number: 0-672-32577-2

Library of Congress Catalog Card Number: 2003092927

Printed in the United States of America

First Printing: April 2004

07   06   05   04      4   3   2   1

## Trademarks

All terms mentioned in this book that are known to be trademarks or service marks have been appropriately capitalized. Sams Publishing cannot attest to the accuracy of this information. Use of a term in this book should not be regarded as affecting the validity of any trademark or service mark.

## Warning and Disclaimer

Every effort has been made to make this book as complete and as accurate as possible, but no warranty or fitness is implied. The information provided is on an "as is" basis. The author and the publisher shall have neither liability nor responsibility to any person or entity with respect to any loss or damages arising from the information contained in this book.

## Bulk Sales

Sams Publishing offers excellent discounts on this book when ordered in quantity for bulk purchases or special sales. For more information, please contact

> U.S. Corporate and Government Sales
>
> 1-800-382-3419
>
> corpsales@pearsontechgroup.com

For sales outside of the U.S., please contact

> International Sales
>
> 1-317-428-3341
>
> international@pearsontechgroup.com

**Acquisitions Editor**
Betsy Brown

**Development Editor**
Alice Martina Smith

**Managing Editor**
Charlotte Clapp

**Project Editor**
Matt Purcell

**Copy Editor**
Seth Kerney

**Indexer**
Chris Barrick

**Proofreader**
Tonya Fenimore

**Technical Editor**
Max Muller

**Team Coordinator**
Vanessa Evans

**Designer**
Gary Adair

# About the Authors

**Jinjer Simon** has been actively involved in the computer industry for nearly 20 years. Her involvement in the industry has included programming, providing software technical support, end-user training, developing written and online user documentation, creating software tutorials, developing Internet Web sites, creating digital video productions, and writing technical books.

She has written several computer-related books for the retail market, covering topics related to programming, Web development, Microsoft Office, and digital video. Her most recent books include *Teach Yourself Visually Digital Video*, *Word 2003: Top 100 Simplified Tips and Tricks*, and *Excel Programming: Your Visual Blueprint for Creating Interactive Spreadsheets*.

Jinjer is also a contributing author on various computer books, including *Microsoft FrontPage 2002 Unleashed* and *Sams Teach Yourself JavaScript in 21 Days*.

Jinjer and her husband, Richard, live in Coppell, Texas, with their two children and two Jack Russell Terriers. Jinjer currently works as a consultant providing Web site development, writing online documentation, and creating video productions for distribution both over the Internet and on DVD.

**Brian Tiemann** is a freelance technology columnist and software engineer who has written extensively in online magazines about the Macintosh, Apple software, and the philosophy of user-friendly design that has always been synonymous with them. A creative professional in the graphic arts and Web design world as well as in networking and software quality, he uses Mac OS X because of its Unix-based stability underlying the powerful built-in creative tools that let him bring his graphics, music, movies, and photography to life.

Having been a Mac user for nearly twenty years, Brian has observed Apple's growth from a maker of simple personal computers to the powerhouse of film production, digital music, online lifestyle, and publishing that it is today. A graduate of Caltech, the coauthor of *FreeBSD Unleashed*, and the author of *Mac OS X Panther In a Snap*, Brian enjoys iLife, animation, motorcycles, technological gadgets, the outdoors, and writing about them all. He lives in Silicon Valley with Capri, the collie.

# Acknowledgments

I would like to thank my husband, Richard, and our children, Alex and Ashley, for all their love, support, and patience during this project. I would also like to thank my husband for sparking my interest in digital video and photography a few years ago, and for all his great pointers during the development of this book.

I have really enjoyed working with the group from Sams Publishing. This has been a really enjoyable book to write, and I want to thank Betsy Brown for giving me the opportunity to do so. I would also like thank the other people at Sams Publishing who were involved with the editing, layout, and production of the book, specifically Matt Purcell, Alice Martina Smith, and Seth Kerney. They have all been wonderful to work with and have done a fantastic job in their positions to ensure that everything was complete for this book.

I also want to thank my Technical Editor, Max Muller. His technical expertise with iLife, especially iTunes, was invaluable. I really appreciate all the great comments and tips he provided.

Finally, I want to thank Brian Tiemann for his work on the GarageBand chapters.

# Tell Us What You Think!

As the reader of this book, *you* are our most important critic and commentator. We value your opinion and want to know what we're doing right, what we could do better, what areas you'd like to see us publish in, and any other words of wisdom you're willing to pass our way.

You can fax, email, or write me directly to let me know what you did or didn't like about this book—as well as what we can do to make our books stronger.

*Please note that I cannot help you with technical problems related to the topic of this book, and that due to the high volume of mail I receive, I might not be able to reply to every message.*

When you write, please be sure to include this book's title and author as well as your name and phone or fax number. I will carefully review your comments and share them with the author and editors who worked on the book.

Email: consumer@samspublishing.com

Mail:  Mark Taber
       Associate Publisher
       Sams Publishing
       800 East 96th Street
       Indianapolis, IN 46240 USA

# Reader Services

For more information about this book or others from Sams Publishing, visit our Web site at www.samspublishing.com. Type the ISBN of this book (excluding hyphens) or the title of the book in the Search box to find the book you're looking for.

# 1
# ✔ Start Here

Think about the reasons why you purchased your computer. Most likely, at least one of those reasons is to work with digital media files, specifically audio, video, and photos. For example, you might want to download photos from your digital camera to print out on your photo printer, or you might want to import the audio from your music CDs so that you can create MP3 files for your iPod or other MP3 player. You have probably even considered creating your own family movies with video you recorded with your own digital video camera. Whatever the reason you purchased your computer, thanks to the recent advances in computer hardware and storage, your digital media needs are only a click away.

**http://www.store.apple.com**

## WEB RESOURCE
You can order a copy of iLife directly from the Apple Web site. It can also be purchased from most computer stores.

## What Is iLife?

If you have looked at the programs installed on your Apple computer, you have probably been unsuccessful in locating a program called *iLife*. That is because iLife does not refer to a specific program; it identifies a group of multimedia programs also referred to as the *Digital Hub*. You have probably noticed several other programs whose names start with

## Start Here

**NOTE**

Mac OS X provides iTunes, iMovie, GarageBand, and iPhoto as part of the operating system with newly purchased computers. iDVD comes installed on Macintosh computers built with a SuperDrive. If you do not have iDVD 3.0 or later installed on your machine, you can get a copy by purchasing the iLife suite.

**NOTE**

GarageBand was added to iLife '04.

**NOTE**

Screen burn-in does not occur as frequently with the flat-screen LCD monitors popular today as it does with the older CRT monitors.

the letter *I*, including iTunes, iMovie, iPhoto, and iDVD. These programs plus GarageBand make up what Apple has dubbed iLife.

iTunes, iMovie, iPhoto, and iDVD have been integrated so that although they are separate programs, you can share the media among the programs. For example, you can use the audio files in your iTunes library in a movie you create in iMovie, a slideshow in iPhoto, or even as part of the audio for your DVD menu in iDVD. This seamless integration between the four applications is what makes the iLife programs so appealing.

The iLife programs have been referred to as the Apple Digital Hub because each one is designed to work with digital media. You use iTunes to handle all your audio files, iMovie to import movies from digital video cameras and other sources, and iPhoto to work with photos. You can burn DVDs that can be viewed by others using iDVD. Although each program has a distinct functionality, they all integrate by sharing their libraries of digital media.

### Screensavers

One of the features of the Mac OS X operating system (most operating systems have this feature) is the ability to activate a screensaver automatically when your computer sits idle for a specific amount of time. It doesn't matter if the computer is performing a specific task, such as importing video or burning a DVD; the screensaver activates if you have not touched the keyboard or moved the mouse for a length of time.

Screensavers help extend the life of your monitor by making sure that the same image does not remain displayed on the screen for an extended amount of time. If your screen displays the same image for an extended amount of time, the image might "burn in" to the screen. This means that a shadow of the image will be displayed on the screen even when you change what is displayed on the screen. By having a screensaver load after a specific amount of time, you reduce the chances of getting burn-in.

Mac OS X also permits you to put the computer to sleep. This process actually puts the machine in an inactive mode until you want to use it again. Mac OS X allows you to set the time frame before the monitor and the computer go to sleep. When your monitor goes to sleep, the screen goes blank.

Unfortunately, screensavers and the sleep mode can cause problems with tasks you might leave running on your computer while you are not sitting there. For example, if a screensaver kicks in while you are importing video from a digital video camera to your computer, the import might stop or might not import correctly. You can also have problems burning CDs or DVDs if the screensaver kicks in while these processes are running.

To alleviate problems when importing large files or burning DVDs, you should adjust the screensaver activation settings and the settings for putting your monitor and computer to sleep. You need to use the **System Preferences** window to change these settings. Within **System Preferences**, set the screensaver activation time on the **Activation** tab of the **Desktop & Screen Saver** option. Set the sleep activation options on the **Energy Saver** option.

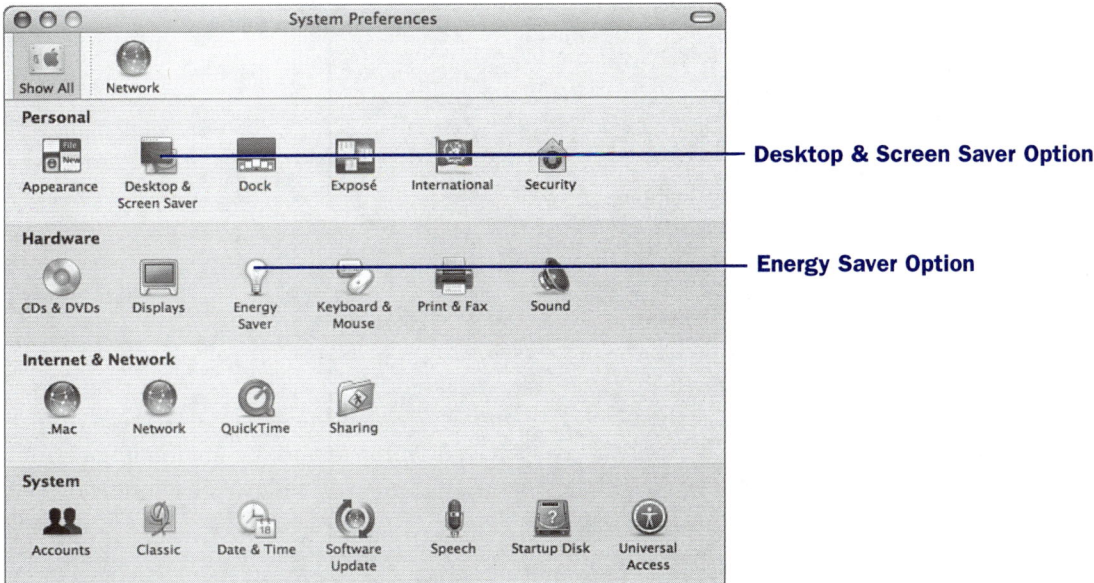

Options in the **System Preferences** application let you control how your computer behaves while you're using iLife.

✓ **Start Here**

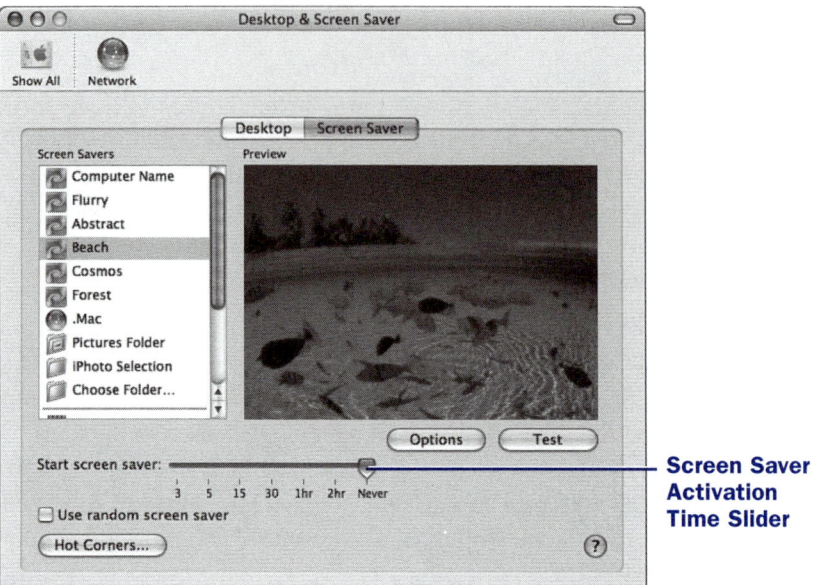

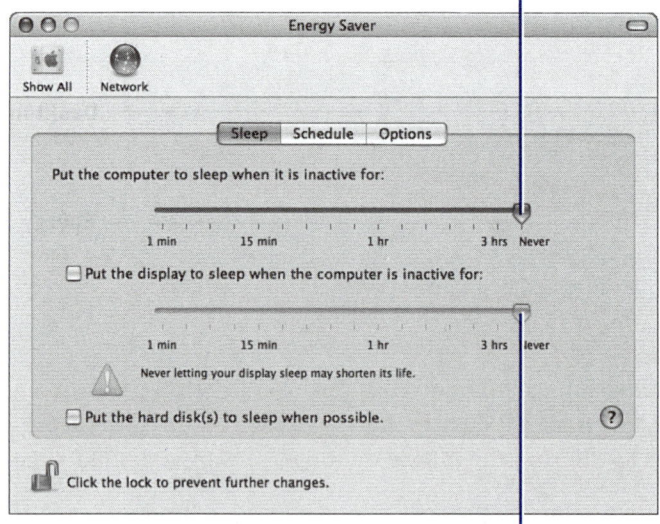

*Turn off screensavers and eliminate automatic sleep settings when importing or burning DVDs and CDs.*

When you are planning to import video or burn a DVD or CD, check the screensaver and sleep settings. If possible, set the **Start screen saver** slider to **Never** during the process. When the process is complete, you can set the screensaver activation time back to the previous selection. You should also set both the **Computer Sleep Slider** and the **Monitor Sleep Slider** to **Never** until the process is complete. After the import or burning process is complete, you can reset your options for the screensaver and sleep modes.

# iPhoto

You can use iPhoto as your electronic photo album. By placing all your digital photos in iPhoto, you can organize them in albums to make them easy to locate and view. For example, you can create an album for all the photos from your summer vacation to the beach or your child's fifth birthday. You can take the same photo album and create a slideshow of the photos to share with others.

iPhoto can import photos directly from many different digital cameras. You can also add photos from other sources, such as Web sites and scanners. After you have imported the photos into iPhoto, you can make minor modifications to each photo. For example, iPhoto allows you to remove red-eye from a photo and convert a color photo to black and white. Although iPhoto does not provide all the advanced photo editing features of more sophisticated photo editing software packages, the features provided work well for customizing most photos you import into iPhoto.

iPhoto is not only an excellent way to organize photos, you can also use it to create slideshows, print photos, email photos, create screensavers, and order custom photo books.

## iPhoto Interface

As with all iLife programs, iPhoto has a simple user interface. The layout of the iPhoto window makes it easy to quickly access and perform nearly all functionalities by clicking the mouse button to select the desired option.

There are actually four different modes in iPhoto; you access them by clicking the four **iPhoto Mode** buttons at the bottom of the iPhoto window. As you click each button, the iPhoto window changes to reflect the selection.

**TIP**

If you want to use the more advanced photo editing features of another program, you can have iPhoto automatically open your photos in that software program whenever you select a photo to edit. For example, you can have iPhoto open Adobe Photoshop as the photo editor when you click a specific photo in the library.

 **Start Here**

- **Import mode**—Provides the ability to import photos from a digital camera connected to your computer. If the camera is properly connected, the camera information displays at the bottom of the iPhoto window. iPhoto can not only detect the camera connection, but also the number of photos on the camera available for importing.

- **Organize mode**—The default iPhoto mode provides options for creating albums and adding photos to an album. The bottom portion of the window displays buttons for sharing your selected photos with others. You can print photos, create a slideshow with them, send them in email messages, place them on a Web site, or create a photo CD with them using the options available in **Organize** mode.

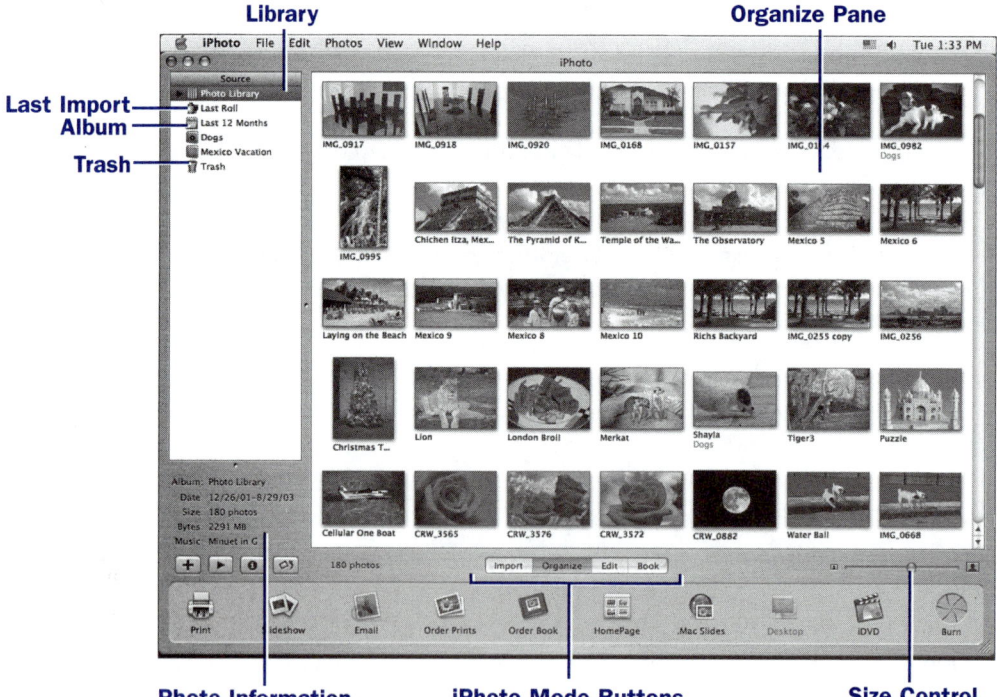

*The iPhoto window provides easy access to all functions for organizing, editing, and sharing photos.*

- **Edit mode**—Provides options to change the appearance of the selected photo. You can adjust the brightness and contrast, eliminate red-eye, enhance, retouch, convert to black and white, and resize from **Edit** mode.

- **Book mode**—With a connection to the Internet and an Apple account, you can create and order a custom photo book for the selected album. The book is printed and mailed to the address you specify. The **Book** button can be selected only if you have an album selected in the list on the left side of the iPhoto window.

As you change modes within iPhoto, the left pane of the iPhoto window remains unchanged. The left pane of the iPhoto window shows the Library list, which provides links to the iPhoto **Library** and corresponding albums. If you want to see the photos that were most recently imported into iPhoto, you can select the **Last Import** option. You can click the **Trash** option to see the list of photos that have been deleted. Photos remain in the trash until you select the **Empty Trash** option.

## Setting Thumbnail Size

When you are in **Organize** mode, iPhoto displays *thumbnail* images of the photos within the selected album (or the entire library if **Library** is selected). The thumbnail images are sized to a default size, but you can adjust the size of the thumbnails using the **Size Control** slider in the bottom-right corner of the iPhoto window. By default, the **Size Control** slider is in the center to produce an average size thumbnail image. You can drag the slider to the left to reduce the size of the thumbnails so that more thumbnail images are visible within the window. If you want to see more detail of the thumbnail images, drag the slider to the right to increase the size of the thumbnails.

**KEY TERM**

*Thumbnail*—A small version of a photo that allows you to identify the desired photo from a group of other photos.

 **TIP**

Drag the **Size Control** slider all the way to the right to see one photo at a time in the **Organize** pane. iPhoto sizes the photos to fit within the pane.

Depending on the screen resolution you have selected for your monitor, you might want to adjust the thumbnail size. The higher the screen resolution, the smaller the images, text, and so on will display on the monitor. With a higher screen resolution, you might want to use larger thumbnail images. If you prefer a lower screen resolution setting (to make text appear large), you can make the thumbnail images a little smaller so that you can see more of the images without scrolling through the album.

✔ **Start Here**

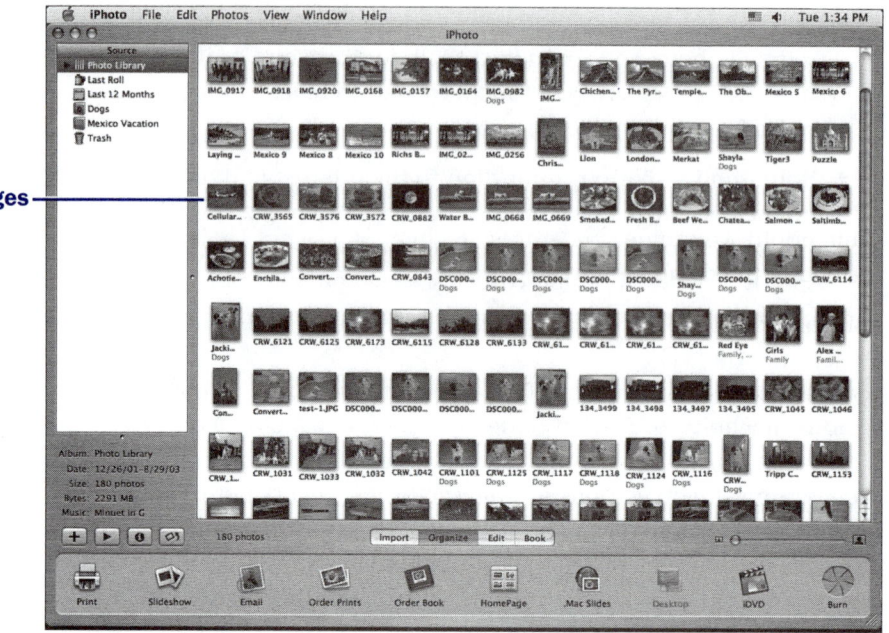

Small Thumbnail Images

Large Thumbnail Image        Size Control Slider

*Adjust the size of the thumbnail images using the **Size Control** slider.*

## Customize Photo Appearance

By default, when iPhoto displays your photo **Library** or a selected album, the background of the **Organize** pane is white, and each photo thumbnail has a drop shadow. Depending on the photos in your album, you might want to change the background and border settings to make your images stand out more. For example, if most of your photos are quite bright, you might prefer to view them on a black background instead of the default white background.

You can adjust the background and border settings on the **iPhoto Preferences** dialog box. You display the **Preferences** dialog box by choosing **iPhoto, Preferences**. On the **Preferences** dialog box, click the **Appearance** button to view options for changing the appearance of iPhoto.

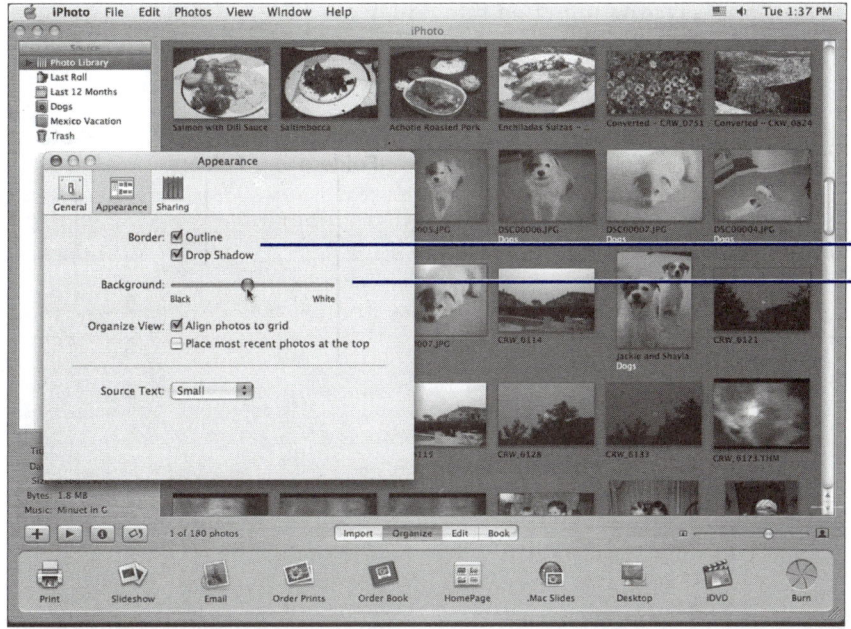

*Select the desired background shade and border style from the Preferences dialog box.*

You can select from two different border settings: **Outline** and **Drop Shadow**.

To change the background shade, drag the **Background** slider. You can select only shades of gray (a shade between black and white) for the background.

**The Drop Shadow** is visible only on a white or light gray background. On a dark gray or black background, you cannot see the drop shadowing.

If the background is black, the **Outline** option displays a white border around each photo. If the background is white, the border is black.

 **Start Here**

## iPhoto Storage Locations

When you import photos into iPhoto, either from a camera or another location, iPhoto stores all the photos in your **Pictures** folder. You can access the **Pictures** folder in **Finder** by clicking the **Home** button at the top of the **Finder** window. The **Pictures** folder is one of your default **Home** folders.

When you open the **Pictures** folder, you will find that iPhoto creates a folder called **iPhoto Library**. Within this folder, iPhoto stores all the photos you import into iPhoto, organized by import dates. For example, all photos that were taken during 2002 are placed within the **2002** folder. Within the year folder, iPhoto creates a separate month folder and names them with numbers. For example, the October folder has the label **10**. Finally, a day folder is created for each day within the month. This means a picture imported into iPhoto on 8/21/03 would be placed in the **21** folder inside the **08** month folder, which is inside the **2003** folder.

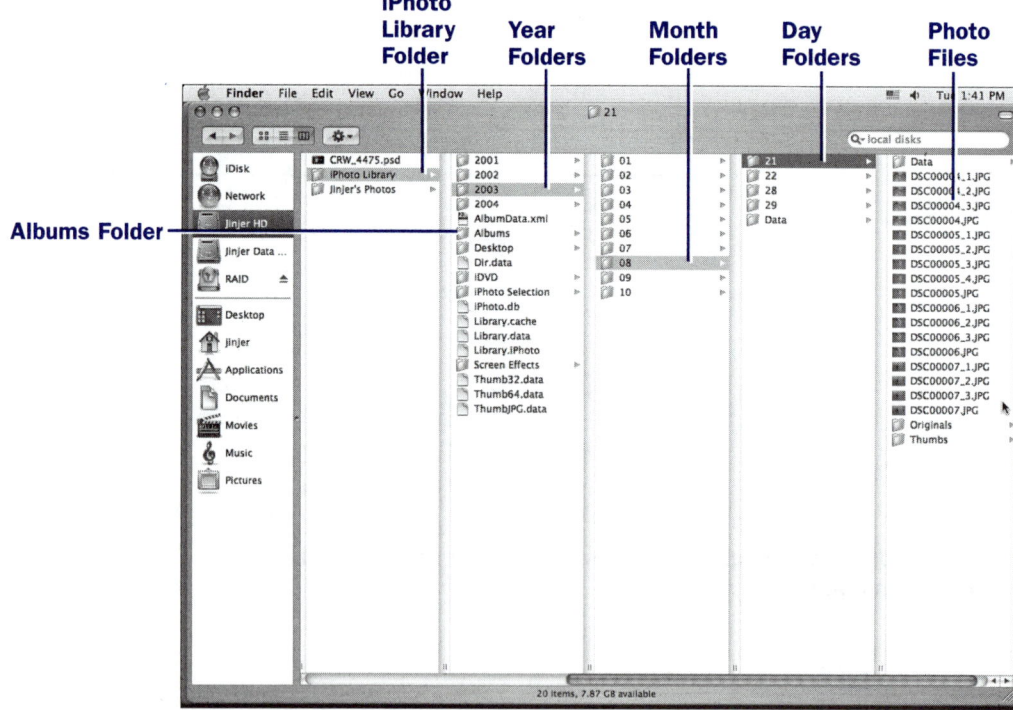

*You can find all the photos from your iPhoto Library organized by date within your **Pictures** folder.*

Start Here

Because of this system of organizing photos by date, it can get difficult to locate a photo you have stored within iPhoto. If you have to locate a photo, locate the photo first in iPhoto and check the date assigned to the photo. You can use that information to locate the photo in the appropriate folders in Finder.

If you view the **iPhoto Library** folder, you will see that iPhoto creates separate album folders for each album you create. iPhoto creates these album folders to keep track of the photos you assign to each album.

When you view these folders, it will appear that they contain copies of the photos assigned to that album. In reality, the each album contains a *link* to the actual photo file stored by the **iPhoto Library**.

## iPhoto File Types

iPhoto can import any photo that is saved in a format QuickTime recognizes. The following table lists the file types that can currently be imported into iPhoto.

| File Type | Description |
|---|---|
| BMP (Bitmap) | An uncompressed graphics file format developed by Microsoft. Graphics created with Microsoft Paintbrush have a **.bmp** extension. |
| GIF (Graphics Interchange Format) | Originally developed by CompuServe as a method for compressing files so that they could be transferred effectively. Still a common format on the Internet. |
| JPEG/JPG (Joint Photographic Experts Group) | A graphics file format standard for creating a compressed image. Uses a lossy compression format that shrinks the file size by eliminating nonessential elements of the picture. |
| MacPaint | Graphic images created using Apple's MacPaint program. |
| PICT (Picture File Format) | A graphics format developed by Apple. PICT uses a lossless compression format that maintains the quality of the original photo. |
| PNG (Portable Network Graphics) | A graphics file format standard that compresses the photo without losing the quality of the image. |
| PSD (Photoshop) | A graphics file created in Adobe Photoshop. Photoshop files can be created with different layers that can be imported into iPhoto. |
| SGI (Silicon Graphics Image Format) | The native file format for graphics files from Silicon Graphics workstations. |

 **TIPS**

To view detailed information about a photo in iPhoto, click to select the photo and then choose **File, Show Photo Info**. The date that displays in the **Original Date** field is the date that iPhoto uses to store the photo.

Instead of trying to locate the original photo in Finder, you can export the photo to a specific folder using the **Export** option in iPhoto.

**See Also**

✔ ❶ Transfer Pictures from a Digital Camera

✔ ❷ Import Digital Pictures from Other Sources

✔ ❹❺ Export a Photo

11

 **Start Here**

| File Type | Description |
|---|---|
| TGA (Targa File Format) | The graphics file format developed for computers using TrueVision video boards. |
| FlashPix | A graphics format that stores an image in multiple resolutions so that the image can be resized without losing picture quality. |
| TIFF (Tag Image File Format) | A graphics file format that creates a compressed file using a lossless compression that maintains the quality of the original photo. |

Although iPhoto can import an assortment of different file types, it can export files only in JPEG, TIFF, or PNG format. You select an export format based on your intended use of the photo. See **45 Export a Photo** for more information on exporting photos from iPhoto.

### Importing Files from a Camera

You can import photos directly into iPhoto from several different digital cameras. Apple maintains a list of the digital cameras that are compatible with iPhoto on its Web site. Even if the digital camera is listed on the Web site, you can only import JPEG images from the camera. Most digital cameras have a native file format that can be used to create a higher-quality image. iPhoto does not recognize these native camera file formats.

 **WEB RESOURCE**

Find a list of digital cameras that are compatible with iPhoto.

http://www.apple.com/iphoto/compatibility/camera.html

If your pictures are in the native camera format, you will have to use the file-conversion software provided with your digital camera to convert the photos to JPEG or another graphic format that iPhoto can import. You will have to import the photos from your digital camera into the provided software to create compatible files. After the files are created, you can import them into iPhoto as graphics files.

# iTunes

iTunes is probably the most popular iLife program because of the popularity of MP3 files. iTunes lets you organize your audio files in one central location. Within iTunes, you can create different playlists of audio files (see **57 About Playlists**). You can use playlists to create audio CDs and copy audio files to your iPod.

**Start Here** ✓

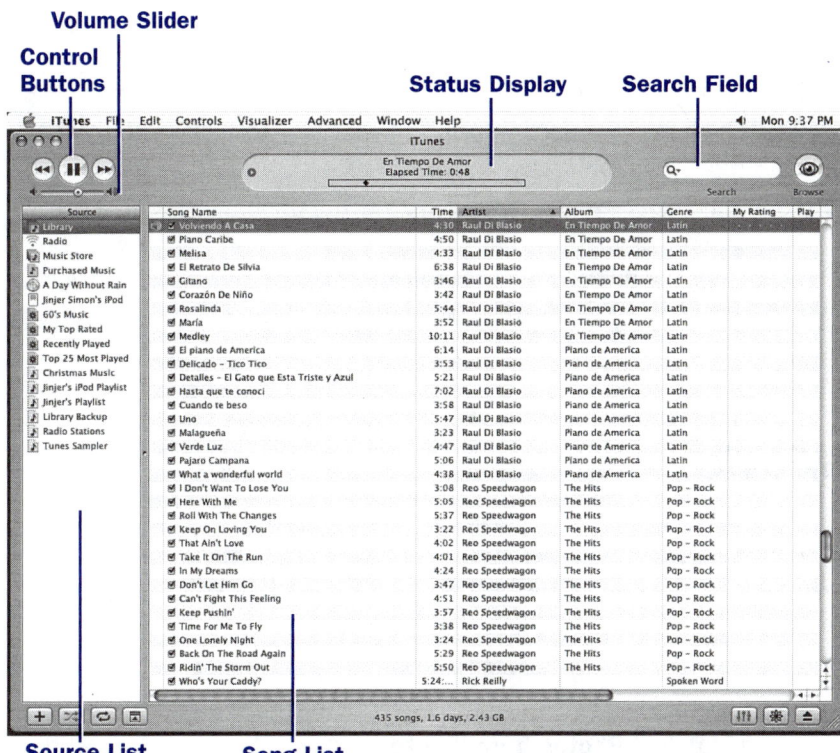

*Use iTunes to organize your audio files into different playlists.*

The iTunes interface is quite simple. It consists of two main elements: the **Source list** and the **Song list**. The **Source list**, on the left side of the window, lists all the sources available for listening, including available playlists, audio CDs, Music Store, Radio, and iPod.

On the right side of the window is the **Song list**. This list identifies the audio files within the selected source. For example, if the **Library** is selected, all the audio files display in the list. If you select a playlist, only the songs in the selected playlist display in the **Song list**.

At the top of the iTunes window is the **Status Display**. The display changes based on your selection. For example, when you are playing an audio file, iTunes displays the name of the audio file in the **Status Display** along with the amount of time the audio file selection has played. You can switch between the audio file information and an electronic spectrum display by clicking the arrow button on the left side of the **Status Display**.

✓ **Start Here**

> **NOTE**
>
> The **Volume Slider** controls the volume of all audio that plays within iTunes; it does not affect audio from other programs. Use the volume keys on your keyboard to adjust the volume level for your computer.

When the audio file information appears in the **Status Display**, you can click it to view additional information about the audio file that is playing. For example, if you click **Elapsed Time**, iTunes displays the **Remaining Time** for the audio file. Click **Remaining Time**, and iTunes displays the **Total Time**.

In the top-left corner of the iTunes window are the buttons for controlling the audio that plays within iTunes. The top center **Play** button plays or stops the selected audio file. Click the buttons on either side to play the **Previous** or **Next** audio file in the selected list. Use the **Volume Slider** under the control buttons to adjust the volume of the audio that plays within iTunes.

## iMovie

You can create your own personal movies using iMovie. You can import video from a digital video camera or use video created by other sources. When you import video, iMovie creates clips that can be added to your movie.

You can also add to your movie photos from your iPhoto Library and audio from iTunes. iMovie provides the capability to animate your photos. See **105** **Add Photos from iPhoto** for more information on working with photos in iMovie.

### iMovie Interface

**See Also**

✓ **95** About the Monitor

✓ **101** About the Timeline Elements

There are three main sections to the iMovie window: the **Monitor**, the iMovie panes, and the **Clips/Timeline Viewer**.

The **Monitor** displays any video that you play within iMovie, whether it is a video clip from the **Clips** pane, your movie from the **Timeline**, or a photo from the **Photos** pane. Directly underneath the **Monitor** is the **Scrubber bar**, which allows you to make edits to a clip by removing unwanted footage. For example, you can indicate the starting and ending points, and iMovie will remove any extra footage from the selected video clip. See **98** **Crop a Clip** for more information on eliminating unwanted footage from a video clip.

Start Here

*Use your media files to create a movie within iMovie.*

You control the playing of the selected video clip or movie using the control buttons under the **Scrubber bar**. There are three different control buttons: When you click the center **Play** button, iMovie plays the current selection in the **Monitor**. For example, if you select a clip in the **Clips** pane and click **Play**, that clip plays in the **Monitor**. If you select the movie in the **Clips/Timeline Viewer** at the bottom of the iMovie window and click **Play**, the entire movie plays.

To start from the beginning of the movie or the selected clip, click the **Go To Beginning** button to the left of the **Play** button. When you click this button, the **Playhead** moves to the beginning of the clip or movie, but the play does not start until you click the **Play** button.

### Clips Viewer or Timeline Viewer?
The **Clips/Timeline Viewer** has two different display modes. You can either view the individual video clips or you can view the entire timeline. You switch between the two display modes by clicking either the **Clip Viewer** button or the **Timeline Viewer** button.

**NOTE**

If you have a clip selected in the **Timeline Viewer** for your movie, only that clip plays when you click the **Play** button. To play the entire movie, make sure that none of the clips are selected.

 **Start Here**

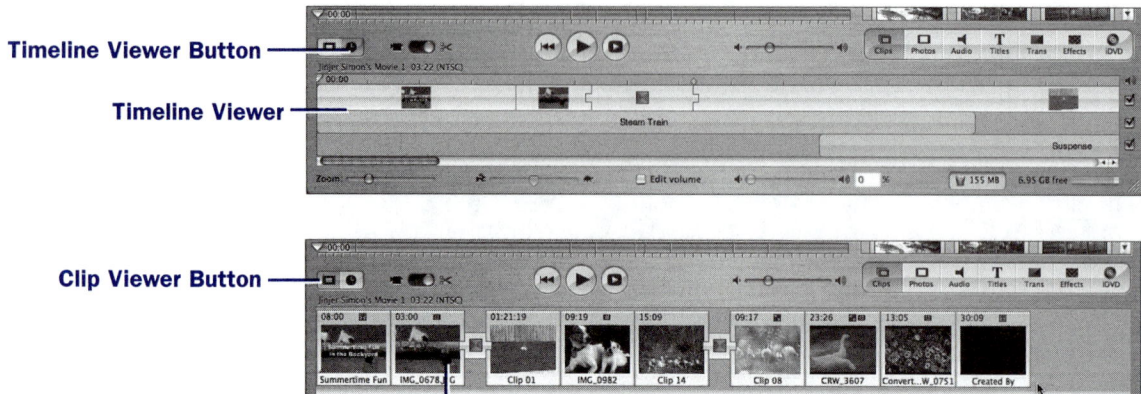

*You can switch between the **Clip Viewer** and the **Timeline Viewer** while creating your movie.*

**See Also**

- ✓ 118 Incorporate Sound Effects into a Movie
- ✓ 119 Add Music from iTunes
- ✓ 124 Adjust the Volume of a Clip

The **Clip Viewer** shows each video clip in the movie as a thumbnail image. The first frame of the video clip displays on each thumbnail. The **Clip Viewer** works well for putting the video clips in the desired order. You can click a clip and drag it to a different location in the timeline.

Probably the biggest disadvantage with the **Clip Viewer** is that you cannot see any of the audio tracks in your movie. None of the audio control tools are available when the **Clip Viewer** is displayed.

The **Timeline Viewer** allows you to see not only the video clips on the timeline but also the corresponding audio tracks. The **Timeline Viewer** provides two different audio tracks you can use to add audio files and sounds to your movie. You can adjust the sound levels for audio in your timeline using the **Edit Volume** slider under the timeline.

Unlike the **Clip Viewer**, you cannot move a clip on the **Timeline Viewer** by dragging it to another location. If you want to move a clip on the **Timeline Viewer**, you must remove the clip from the current location and paste it in the new location using the **Cut** and **Paste** options on the **Edit** menu.

# iDVD

If you want to create DVD movies complete with menus, you can accomplish that very easily using iDVD. To use iDVD, you must have an Apple SuperDrive in your computer.

Start Here

You make modifications to the DVD menu using the options available in the **Customize** drawer. When you click the **Customize** button, the **Customize** drawer slides open on the left side of the iDVD window. At the top of the **Customize** drawer are the **Customize Drawer Panel Buttons**. As you click each button, the **Customize** drawer changes to contain the options for the selected pane. For example, click the **Movies** button to display the movies that can be added to your DVD menu.

If you have an animated DVD menu or music added to the menu, make sure that the **Motion** button is turned on, or iDVD will not display any motion or audio. When the **Motion** button is selected, the button is colored green.

Not only can you add movies and photos to your DVD menu, you can also add folders so that you can create a submenu. To create a new folder, click the **Folder** button. See  **Use Movie Folders** for more information on creating folders for submenus in iDVD.

### TIP

One of the key factors to laying out a DVD menu is the selection of the theme for your menu. iDVD remembers the last theme you applied, but you can apply any of the available themes on the **Themes** pane. After selecting a theme, you can customize the look of the theme by changing the title and menu button styles on the **Settings** pane in the **Customize** drawer.

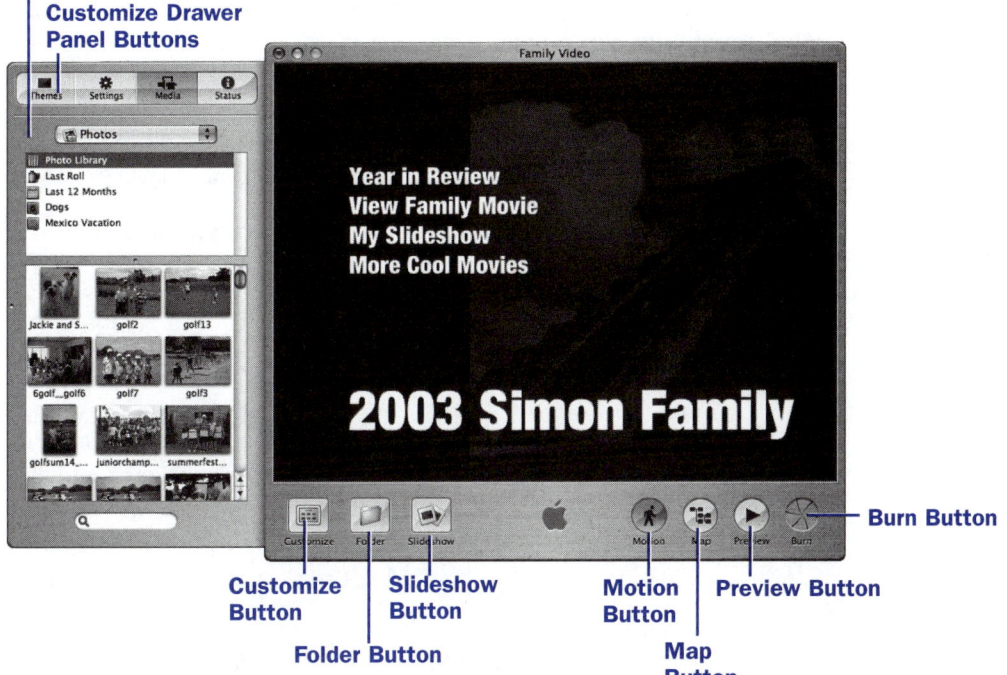

*Use iDVD to design a custom DVD, complete with menus.*

 **Start Here**

You can create slideshows in iDVD using photos from iPhoto. To add a slideshow to your DVD menu, click the **Slideshow** button at the bottom of the iDVD window. See **157 Manually Create a Slideshow Using the Media Pane** for more information on creating a slideshow using photos from your iPhoto library.

## Dealing with Copyrights

**Avoid downloading audio from audio-sharing sites. It is not legal to download music that you have not purchased.**

Unlike most things you do on your computer, you are probably more apt to run into copyright issues when working with the iLife programs than with any other programs you might use. Because most music, video, and photos that you import from audio CDs, DVDs, or the Internet have been copyrighted by the original authors, you must be careful not to break a copyright law when distributing media by creating DVDs and CDs, adding photos to a Web site, or creating slideshows.

Typically, when you purchase audio files, such as those on an audio CD or by downloading purchased music from the Internet, you can use that audio for your own purposes. For example, importing audio from a CD into iTunes to listen to on your computer is legal because you own the CD. You can also create MP3 files from the purchased audio and put them on your MP3 player. However, you cannot share those files with other people. You should use the same discretion with audio you purchase and with audio files you download from the Internet.

To help ensure that copyright laws are not broken, anything you download from the Apple Music Store can be listened to on only three different computers.

## GarageBand

GarageBand is the newest part of iLife, added to the application suite in 2004. Its purpose is to let you create original music of your own, either from your own performances on keyboard, guitar, voice, or any other instrument, or by using the application's built-in loops to build a great-sounding piece of music—even if you don't have a musical bone in your body.

Using GarageBand is a matter of blending three different forms of creative input. Depending on your musical ability, you can use any or all of these methods to create original songs:

- Assemble loops to create a background atmosphere for your song, or to develop an entire musical piece from existing building blocks.
- Play *synthesized* music using a USB or MIDI keyboard or the built-in virtual keyboard to develop an original musical track.
- Play a real instrument (or sing a vocal track) and record it digitally over the top of the synthesized music, creating a merging of *digitized* and computer-generated music.

**Start Here** ✓

### KEY TERMS

*Synthesized*—Music created from software algorithms to generate sound that resembles a real instrument and can be played at any pitch. Apple's **Software Instruments** are synthesized.

*Digitized*—Music directly recorded from a real performance, using a microphone or line-in jack. Digitized music is simply a series of sound samples taken at a certain frequency.

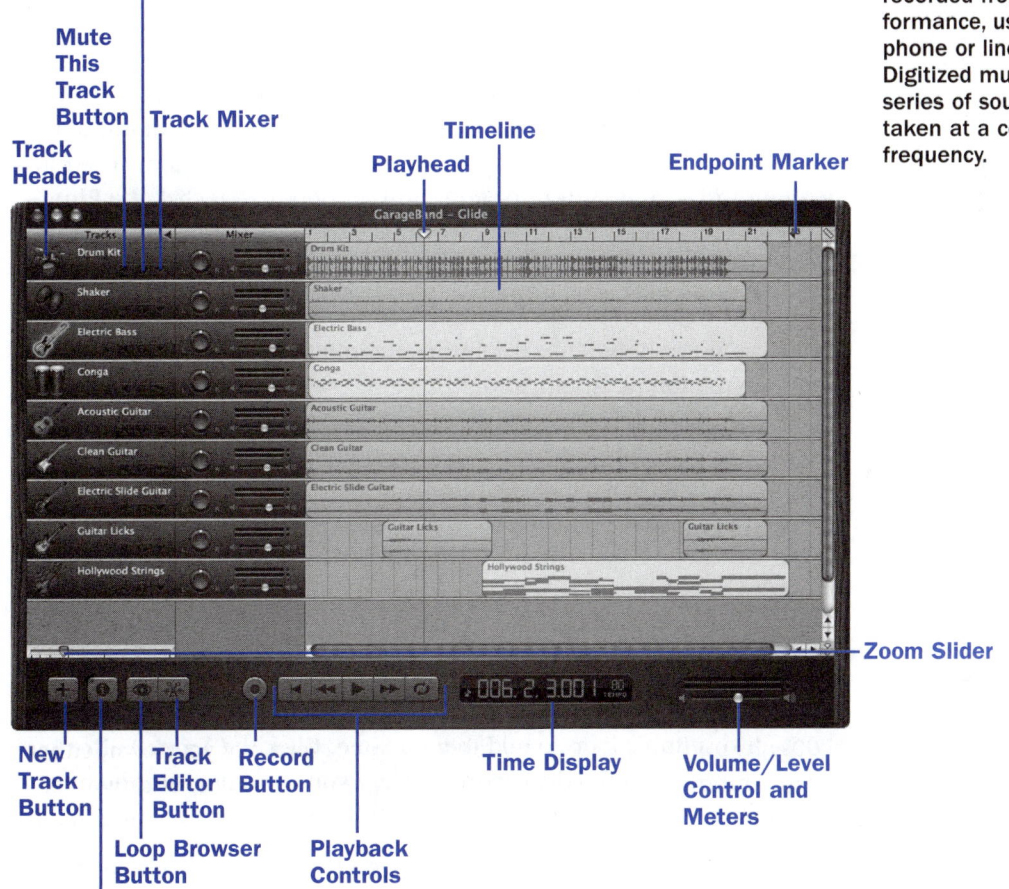

Mute All Other Tracks Button · Mute This Track Button · Track Mixer · Track Headers · Timeline · Playhead · Endpoint Marker · Zoom Slider · New Track Button · Track Editor Button · Record Button · Time Display · Volume/Level Control and Meters · Loop Browser Button · Playback Controls · Track Info Button

*With GarageBand, you can record digitized or synthesized music, use built-in loops, and play around with effects to create a unique sound.*

## ✓ Start Here

Each track in your song is a separate musical line, assigned to a certain instrument (either a **Software Instrument** or a **Real Instrument**). The **track header** for each track shows the icon for the chosen instrument, its name, and controls for listening to it on its own or in ensemble with the rest of the tracks.

The **Mixer** allows you to adjust the relative volume and balance (left or right) of each track. Click the **Mute This Track** button on any track to mute that one track and listen to the rest of the tracks. You can activate this button for multiple tracks to mute several tracks at once. Click the **Mute All Other Tracks** button to listen to only a single track—and any other tracks with this button activated.

The **timeline** area is what shows you the actual music in each of your tracks. For **Software Instruments**, you can see the individual notes in the track; for **Real Instruments**, you see a digitized waveform. The **playhead** indicates your current position in the song. If you click the **Play** button to start the song playing, the music begins where ever the playhead is.

After constructing your song, drag the **endpoint marker** to the position where the song should end. This stops the playhead and keeps the song from playing longer than it should.

Use the **zoom slider** to adjust how much of the song you can see in the timeline, or how closely you want to see the timing detail.

**NOTE**
Because the **Loop Browser** and the **Track Editor** panels occupy the same space at the bottom of the GarageBand window, you can show one or the other, but not both at once.

The **New Track** button creates a new track, to which you can then assign a **Software Instrument** or **Real Instrument**. Click the **Track Info** button to bring up the **Track Info** window, which lets you adjust the settings for the track's instrument or assign it to a different instrument.

Click the **Loop Browser** button to summon the **Loop Browser**, a panel along the bottom of the window which lets you browse through musical styles for a suitable loop to add to your song. Click the **Track Editor** button to open the **Track Editor** panel, where you can fine-tune your adjustments to the notes or sounds in a track.

Click the **Record** button to record music on the currently selected track. Click the **Play** button (one of the playback control buttons) to stop recording and playing. The rest of the playback control buttons control how the playhead moves, letting you play, stop, fast-forward, rewind, and jump to the beginning of the song. You can also repeat any section of the song endlessly as you work.

Start Here

The **Time display** indicates your position in the song, in either musical time (measures, beats, and ticks) or absolute time (hours, minutes, sections, and fractions). Click the left side of the display to switch between time-display modes.

The **Volume/Level control and meters** allow you to control the master output volume of the song and determine whether the volume is "clipping" (hitting the maximum recordable level). This is a flat, general volume adjustment; **see** **179** **Mix Your Song's Tracks** to adjust the volume of the song's tracks or to add fades or crescendos.

# PART I

## iPhoto

**IN THIS PART**

| | | |
|---|---|---|
| **CHAPTER 2** | Loading and Organizing Photos | 25 |
| **CHAPTER 3** | Editing Photos | 41 |
| **CHAPTER 4** | Creating Photo Books | 69 |
| **CHAPTER 5** | Creating a Slideshow in iPhoto | 89 |
| **CHAPTER 6** | Sharing Photos | 103 |

# 2

# Loading and Organizing Photos

## IN THIS CHAPTER:

1. Transfer Pictures from a Digital Camera
2. Import Digital Pictures from Other Sources
3. About Photo Libraries and Albums
4. Create New Albums
5. Create a Smart Album
6. Organize Photos in an Album
7. Remove Photos from an Album or the Library

### ① Transfer Pictures from a Digital Camera

You can use iPhoto to organize all your photographs. iPhoto allows you to use not only photos you've taken with your digital camera, but also photos you have acquired from other sources, such as a Photo CD or the Internet.

After you have imported the desired photos into iPhoto, you can create separate albums that contain related photos. For example, you can place all photos from your vacation in one album. Each photo album is part of your iPhoto library. Even though you can move photos to different albums, they still remain part of the entire library.

## ① Transfer Pictures from a Digital Camera

**See Also**

→ ② Import Digital Pictures from Other Sources

→ ⑥ Organize Photos in an Album

→ ⑦ Remove Photos from an Album or the Library

**🔍 KEY TERM**

**USB (Universal Serial Bus)**—A computer connection method for connecting external devices, such as digital cameras, to a computer. USB provides a connection speed of 1.5 megabytes per second.

You can transfer pictures directly from most digital cameras into iPhoto. To transfer pictures from a camera, you must connect the camera to the computer using a *USB* cable. You should have multiple USB ports on your computer. Most Mac machines also have a USB port on the keyboard.

After connecting the camera to the computer, you select the iPhoto **Import** option to copy all the pictures from the camera to iPhoto. As pictures are copied into iPhoto, they are automatically placed in the **Photo Library**. You can move them to separate albums to organize them. See ⑥ **Organize Photos in an Album** for more information on using photo albums.

Be aware that iPhoto only imports JPG images from cameras. If you are importing from a digital camera that provides a custom or raw format, you must use the custom import software provided with the camera to import your photos to your computer's hard disk (see ② **Import Digital Pictures from Other Sources**).

When you import images using iPhoto, *all the images* on the camera are imported. If you know that you want to import only a couple of images, you can use another program included with the Mac OS X operating system called Image Capture to select the photos to import. When you run this program, you import only the photos you select from the camera onto your computer. After you have imported the photos to your computer using Image Capture, you can use the **Import** option in iPhoto to bring those photos into iPhoto. See ② **Import Digital Pictures from Other Sources** for more information on importing photos.

# Transfer Pictures from a Digital Camera

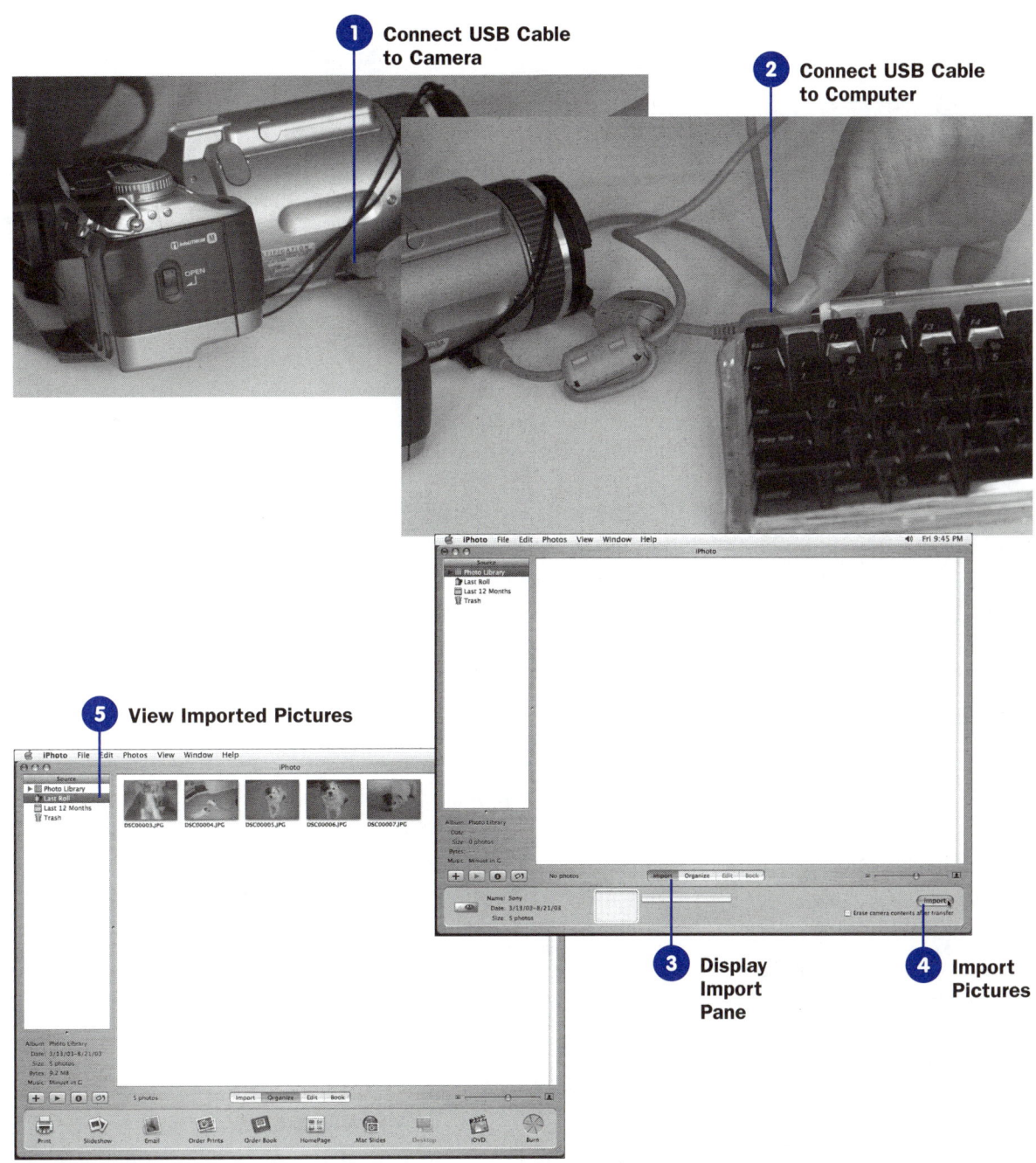

1. Connect USB Cable to Camera
2. Connect USB Cable to Computer
3. Display Import Pane
4. Import Pictures
5. View Imported Pictures

CHAPTER 2: Loading and Organizing Photos 27

**Transfer Pictures from a Digital Camera**

 **WEB RESOURCE**

Visit this Web site to find out whether your digital camera is supported by iPhoto.

http://www.apple.com/iphoto/compatibility/camera.html

### ❶ Connect USB Cable to Camera

Connect the USB cable to the USB port on your digital camera. Most digital cameras require a specific USB cable that has the proper connector for the camera. These cables are typically provided with your digital camera. For more information, refer to your digital camera documentation.

If you have several USB devices, you might have to purchase a USB hub that allows you to share the same USB port with several devices. USB hubs can be found at most stores that sell computer equipment.

### ❷ Connect USB Cable to Computer

Connect the USB cable to a USB port on the computer. Most Apple computers provide USB ports on the keyboard, but you can also find USB ports on the back of the computer.

### ❸ Display Import Pane

With iPhoto open on the desktop, click the **Import** button at the bottom of the window to display the **Import** pane. (iPhoto automatically displays the **Import** pane when it detects a digital camera connection.) iPhoto displays information about the camera that is connected and the number of pictures available for import from the camera in the bottom-left corner of the window.

**NOTE**

If iPhoto does not display camera information in the lower-left corner of the window, the camera is not turned on or properly connected.

### ❹ Import Pictures

Click the **Import** button in the lower-right corner of the window to import the pictures from the camera. iPhoto imports all pictures from the camera's memory. Each imported picture is added to the **Photo Library**. When the import is complete, iPhoto switches to **Organize** mode.

To cancel the import process, click the **Stop** button that displays in the lower-right corner of the window as the pictures are imported to iPhoto.

 **TIP**

Enable the **Erase camera contents after transfer** check box to remove the images from the camera's memory after they are transferred to the computer using iPhoto.

### ❺ View Imported Pictures

You can view the pictures you just imported by clicking the **Last Roll** option on the **Organize** pane. iPhoto displays a thumbnail image of each photo in the right pane.

PART I:   iPhoto

## ② Import Digital Pictures from Other Sources

You can import, or load, pictures from your computer or another computer you are connected to using the **Import** option in iPhoto. You can also use this option to import images from a CD or DVD. When you select the **Import** option, iPhoto displays the **Import Photos** dialog box, which you use to select the pictures you want to import.

You can import a single picture, multiple pictures, or an entire folder of images. As you import, iPhoto displays status information at the bottom of the **Import** pane.

**Before You Begin**

✔ ① Transfer Pictures from a Digital Camera

**See Also**

→ ⑤ Create New Albums
→ ⑥ Organize Photos in an Album

### ① Select File, Import

Choose **File, Import** to import pictures from other locations. You can import pictures from any location your computer can access. For example, if you are connected to a network, you can import pictures from the network.

### ② Locate Pictures to Import

In the **Import Photos** dialog box, navigate to the hard drive, CD-ROM drive, or network computer that contains the photos you want to import. Click to select the pictures you want to import. To select multiple pictures, press and hold the ⌘ key as you click each picture you want to import.

**TIP**

To import an entire folder, click the folder and then click the **Import** button. iPhoto imports all the pictures in the selected folder.

### ③ Import Pictures

Click the **Import** button on the **Import Photos** dialog box. iPhoto automatically switches to the **Import** pane and displays a status bar. A *thumbnail* of the picture being imported displays next to the status bar.

### ④ View Imported Pictures

On the **Organize** pane, view the **Photo Library** to see that your imported photo has been added to the list. You can now add the photo to an album. See ⑤ **Create New Albums** for more information on adding photos to albums.

**KEY TERM**

*Thumbnail*—A small version of a photo. When you are in iPhoto's **Organize** mode, iPhoto displays thumbnail versions of all the photos in the library.

CHAPTER 2:   Loading and Organizing Photos

## 2  Import Digital Pictures from Other Sources

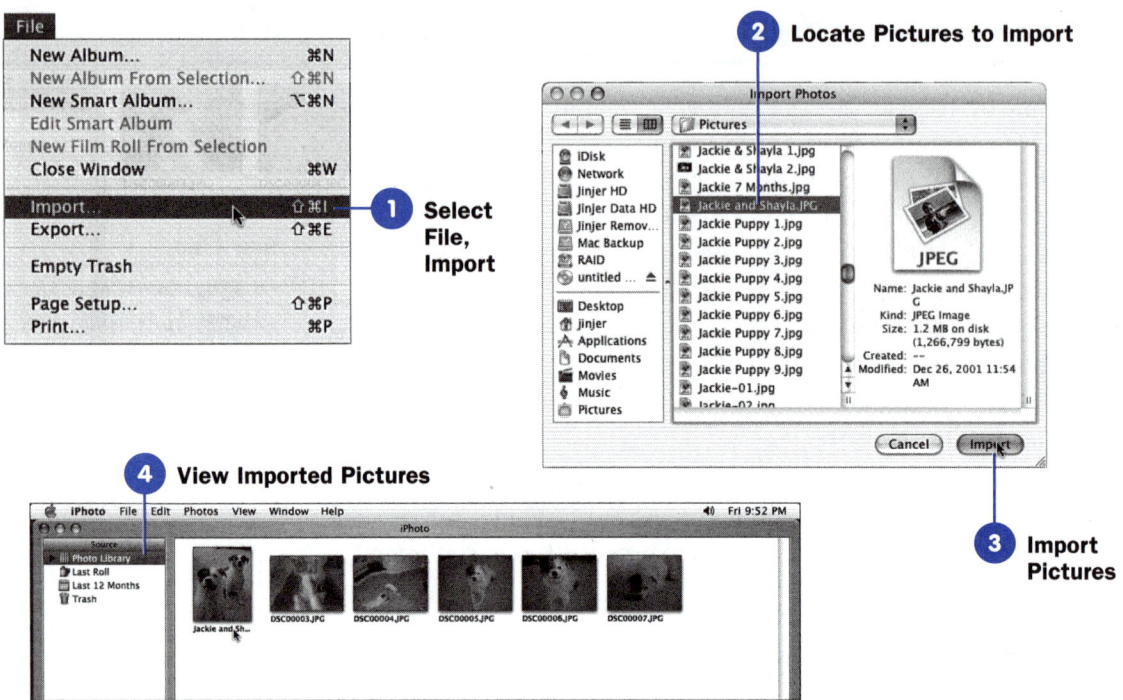

## 3  About Photo Libraries and Albums

**Before You Begin**

✔ ① Transfer Pictures from a Digital Camera

✔ ② Import Digital Pictures from Other Sources

**See Also**

→ ④ Create New Albums

→ ⑤ Create a Smart Album

→ ⑥ Organize Photos in an Album

→ ⑦ Remove Photos from an Album or the Library

iPhoto makes an excellent resource for capturing and organizing all your pictures in a central location. By using iPhoto, you can take all the pictures in the **Photo Library** and quickly organize them by placing them in specific albums. Even as you move pictures between different albums, all the images remain part of the main library.

You organize the photos within each album by moving the photos. Although you can have only one library, iPhoto allows you to create as many albums as necessary to organize your photos.

- **Where does iPhoto store the Photo Library?** iPhoto places the **Photo Library** in the **Pictures** folder. The **Pictures** folder is located in your **Home** folder. If you have multiple users on your computer, a different **Pictures** folder is created for each user.

About Photo Libraries and Albums

- **Can I place a copy of a photo in multiple albums?** Yes, iPhoto allows you to place a single photo in as many albums as you want. When you place the photo in an album, iPhoto does not actually copy the photo into the album. iPhoto just places a reference to the photo in the specified album. The actual photo remains in the **Photo Library**.

- **How are photos arranged in an album?** iPhoto organizes the photos in each album based on the date the photo was created. You can change the order of the photos. See **6 Organize Photos in an Album** for more information on organizing your photos in the album.

- **How does iPhoto name the photos I import?** When you import photos from any source (including a digital camera), iPhoto maintains the original filename and uses that as the photo name. All cameras assign filenames to each photo, and those filenames are imported into iPhoto. You can change the information that iPhoto displays about the photo, including the image title. See **9 Set Photo Information** for information on changing a photo name.

- **What is the difference between a standard album and a smart album?** Although both types of albums serve the same purpose of specifying a collection of photos, the difference is how the photos are placed in the album. With a standard album, you add photos manually by dragging them from the **Photo Library**. See **4 Create New Albums** for more information on creating a standard album.

  With a *smart album*, the photos are added to the album based on criteria you specify about the album. For example, you can specify that you want to add all photos with a specific *keyword*. See **19 Assign Keywords to Photos to Facilitate Searches** for more information on specifying keywords for a photo. See **5 Create a Smart Album** for more information on creating a smart album.

**TIP**

As with other important documents on your computer, consider making a backup of your **Pictures** folder to ensure that you don't lose your pictures if you have computer problems. You can back up photos to a CD-ROM as explained in **44 Create a Photo CD**.

**NOTE**

When you change the image title, iPhoto does not actually change the filename of the photo file on your hard disk, it just changes the name that displays for the file within iPhoto.

**KEY TERM**

*Smart album*—An album that contains only the photos that meet the criteria you specify. The contents of the album are updated automatically when you add or remove photos from your **Photo Library**.

**CHAPTER 2:** Loading and Organizing Photos

## 4 Create New Albums

### Before You Begin

✓ ③ About Photo Libraries and Albums

### See Also

→ ⑤ Create a Smart Album

→ ⑥ Organize Photos in an Album

→ ⑦ Remove Photos from an Album or the Library

**TIPS**

You can specify an album name of up to 265 characters.

You also can create a new album by clicking the + button in the bottom-left corner of the **Organize** window.

**NOTE**

When you add photos to an album, the photos remain in the **Photo Library** so that you can copy them to another album.

You can create different photo albums within iPhoto to organize the photos within the **Photo Library**. You can place any photos from the library in an album you create. After the photos have been added to an album, you can organize the photos based on the way you want to view them, similar to the way you organize photos in an old-fashioned photo album. See ⑥ **Organize Photos in an Album** for more information on organizing photos.

iPhoto allows you to create as many different albums as you want. iPhoto uses a default naming scheme for the albums you create; it names the first album **Album-1** and appends a different number to each new album. You should create a unique album name that identifies the photos contained in the album.

After you have created an album, you add the desired photos to it. There is no limit to the number of photos you can place in an album. Keep in mind that the more photos contained in the album, the more difficult it can be to locate a specific photo.

### ① Select File, New Album

Choose **File**, **New Album** to display the **New Album** dialog box.

### ② Specify Album Name

Type the desired name for the photo album. Assign a name that describes the pictures you plan to add to the album. Also remember that each album name should be unique.

When you have typed the desired album name, click the **OK** button to create the new album.

### ③ Add Photos to the Album

In the **Organize** window, click each photo you want to add to the new album and drag the photo's thumbnail image to the new album folder. You can select a range of photos by holding down the **Shift** key as you click the first and last picture in the range. When you drag the pictures, iPhoto displays a number to indicate the number of images being copied to the album.

## Create New Albums  4

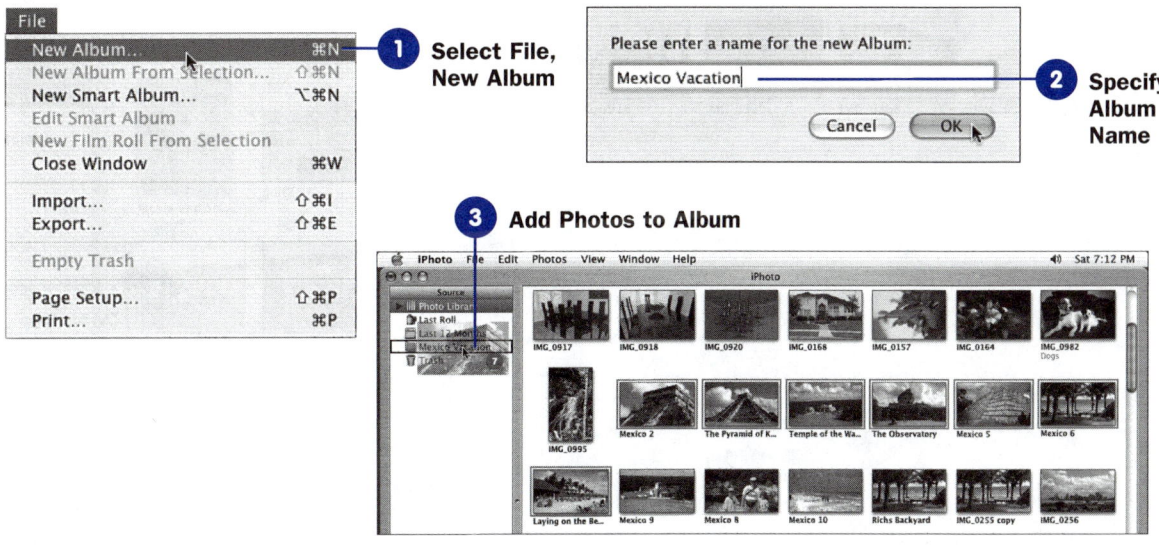

1. Select File, New Album
2. Specify Album Name
3. Add Photos to Album

---

### 5  Create a Smart Album

If you want your photo album to include only the photos that match a specific criteria—such as all photos with a certain *keyword* assigned or all photos from a specific date—instead of manually locating those photos and adding them to an album, you can create a *smart album* and let iPhoto automatically add those photos to the album. For example, you can specify that you want to have all photos with the **Family** keyword assigned to be placed in a **Family Photos** smart album. When you specify that condition, iPhoto searches through your entire **Photo Library** and locates all photos with that criteria. Only the photos that match the criteria you specify are added to the smart album.

Another cool thing about the smart album is that iPhoto continues to monitor your **Photo Library** looking for other photos with that criteria. If you add new photos with that criteria, iPhoto adds those photos to your smart album. If you remove a photo with that criteria from the **Photo Library**, the photo is also removed from your smart album.

**You Should Know**

✔  3  About Photo Libraries and Albums

**See Also**

→  4  Create New Albums
→  6  Organize Photos in an Album
→  7  Remove Photos from an Album or the Library

---

CHAPTER 2:  Loading and Organizing Photos          33

### 5  Create a Smart Album

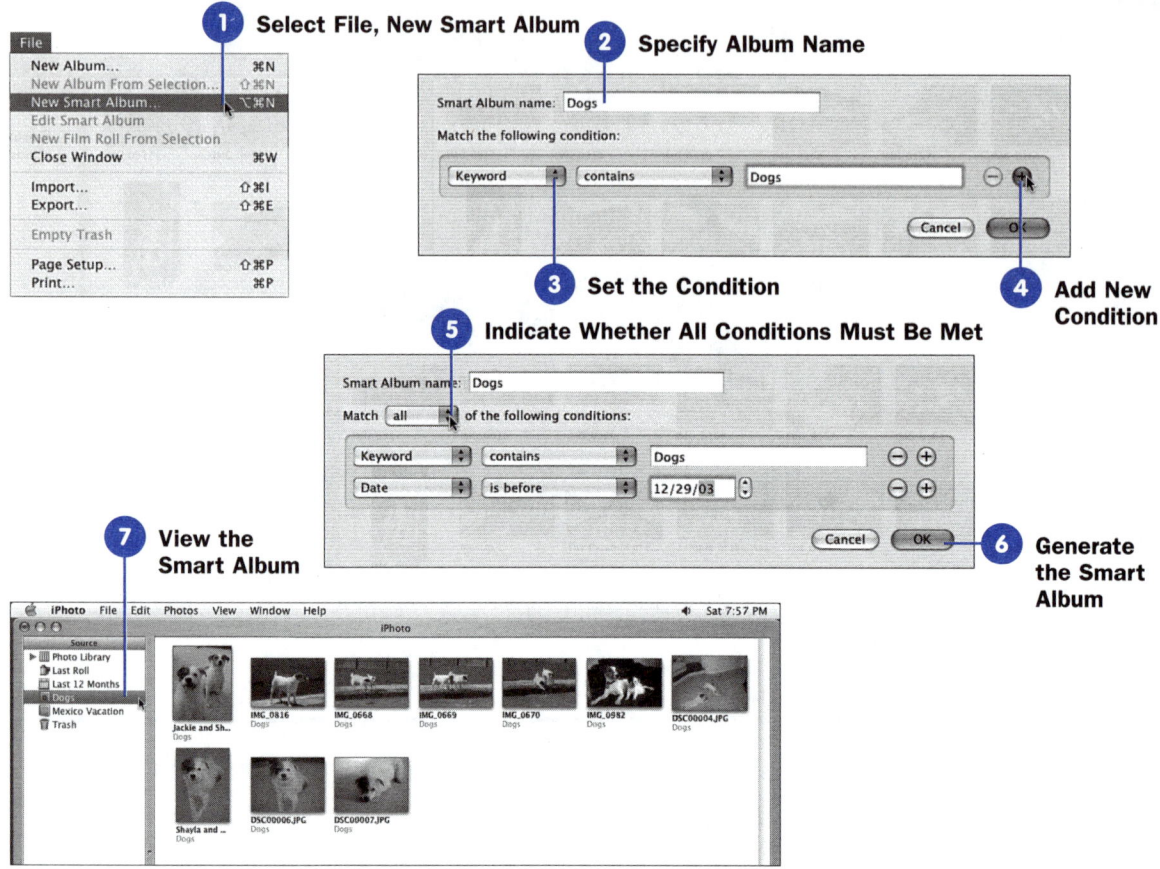

You can specify multiple conditions for your smart album criteria. For example, you can indicate that you want all photos with a specific keyword *and* a specific date range. If you specify multiple conditions, you must decide whether all the conditions (or just some of the conditions) must be met before a photo is added to the smart album. For example, if you want pictures with a **Family** keyword that also have a date between **1/1/2003** and **12/31/2003**, iTunes first finds the photos with the specified keyword and then checks to see whether the date is within the specified range. If the photo meets both conditions, it is added to the photo album.

If you indicate that you want to meet *any* of the specified conditions, iPhoto adds photos that meet at least one of the specified conditions (but

# Create a Smart Album

not necessarily both conditions). For example, a photo without the **Family** keyword but with a date of **3/1/2003** would be added because it meets the date condition.

Another point to keep in mind is that you cannot manually add or remove photos from a smart album. If you want to eliminate photos from a smart album, you must alter the criteria used to add photos.

### ① Select File, New Smart Album

Choose **File, New Smart Album** to display the **Smart Album** dialog box.

### ② Specify Smart Album Name

Type the desired name for the smart album. Assign a name that describes the pictures you plan to add to the album. Also remember that each album name should be unique.

**You can specify a smart album name of up to 255 characters. iPhoto allows you to have multiple smart albums active at one time. If a photo meets the criteria of multiple albums, it is added to each album.**

### ③ Set the Condition

From the first drop-down list under **Match the following condition**, select the criteria you want to apply to the search. For example, select **Keyword** to create a condition based on the photo's keyword. You can select from nine different criteria.

From the second drop-down list, select the comparison operator you want to use. For example, select **contains** if you want to find the photos with the **Family** keyword. The list displays different comparison operators based on the criteria you selected in the first field. For example, if the criteria value selected in the first field is **Date**, the condition operators in the second field deal with comparing dates.

In the third field, type the values you want to compare for the condition. If the conditional operator allows you to compare two values (as is true with the **is in the range** operator), two fields display.

### ④ Add a New Condition

If you want to insert an additional condition to the criteria statement for creating the smart album, click the + button next to the first condition. iPhoto adds a new condition line. Specify the new condition statement as specified in step 3.

**If you want to eliminate a condition, click the − button next to the corresponding condition.**

CHAPTER 2: Loading and Organizing Photos

### 6  Organize Photos in an Album

You can click the + button multiple times to add as many new conditions to the criteria as necessary.

#### 5  Indicate Whether All Conditions Must Be Met

If you have multiple conditions, you must specify whether a photo must meet all specified conditions before it is added to the smart album. From the **Match** drop-down list, select **all** to have the photo meet all the conditions you've specified. If you want the photo to meet only one of the conditions, select **any**.

#### 6  Generate the Smart Album

Click the **OK** button to create the smart album based on the specified conditions.

#### 7  View the Smart Album

Click the smart album in the **Source** list to view the current contents of the smart album.

**NOTE**
iPhoto identifies the smart albums in your **Source** list by placing a purple gear icon next to each smart album.

---

### 6  Organize Photos in an Album

**Before You Begin**

✔ **1** Transfer Pictures from a Digital Camera

✔ **2** Import Digital Pictures from Other Sources

**See Also**

→ **3** Create New Albums

→ **5** Create a Smart Album

→ **7** Remove Photos from an Album or the Library

You can customize the order of the photos within your album. When you initially add photos to an album, iPhoto orders the photos based on the date of each photo. This means that a photo taken on June 3 appears before a photo taken on June 6. This default order might not be what you want. For example, if you create a slideshow using the images in an album, iPhoto displays the photos in the order they are listed in the album. See **30** **Create a Slideshow** for more information on creating slideshows in iPhoto.

#### 1  Select Photos

Click to select the thumbnail of the photo you want to move. To select multiple photos, hold down the **Shift** key while you click each photo thumbnail.

PART I:  iPhoto

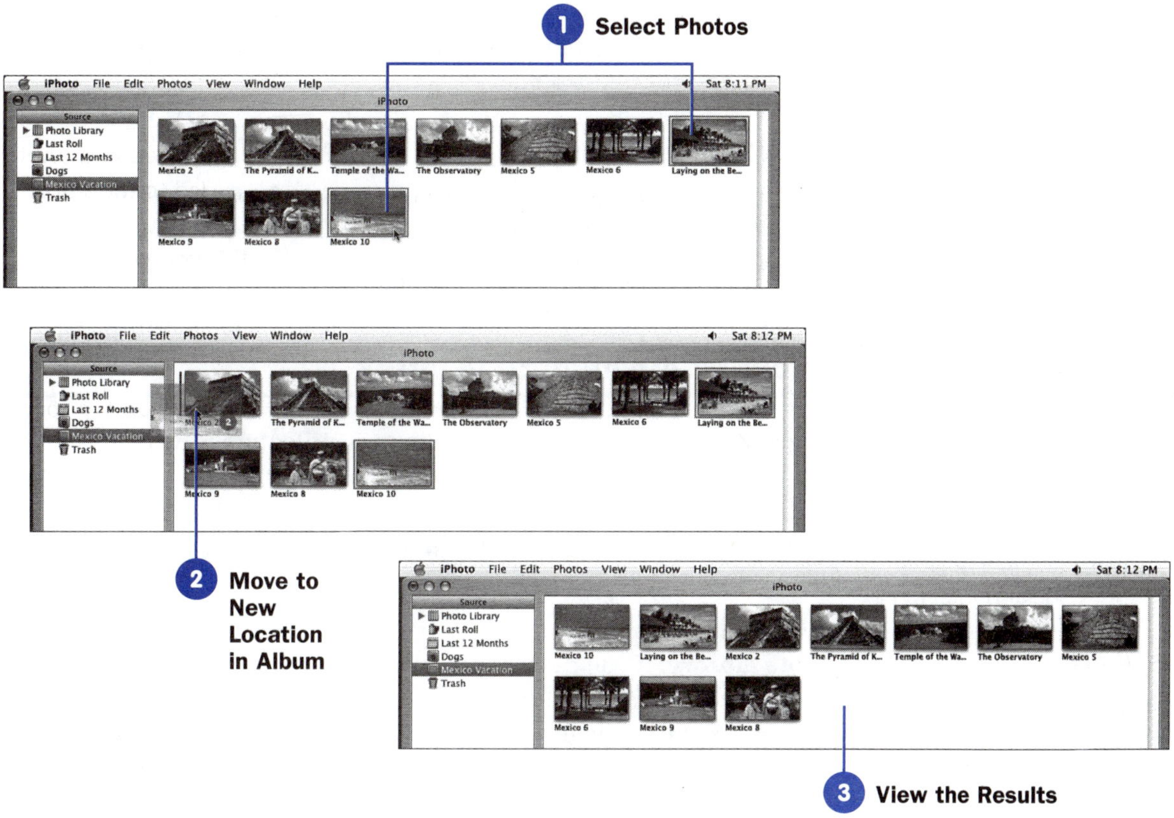

## Organize Photos in an Album

**① Select Photos**

**② Move to New Location in Album**

**③ View the Results**

### ② Move to New Location in Album

Hold down the mouse button and drag the selected photo thumbnails to the desired location within the album. As you drag the thumbnails, if you have selected more than one photo, a number displays indicating the number of photos that will be moved. A black horizontal bar indicates the location where the photos will be moved in the album.

**TIP**

You can manually change the order of the images in an album by clicking the thumbnail of the photo and dragging it to the desired location in the list.

**CHAPTER 2:    Loading and Organizing Photos**

## ⑦ Remove Photos from an Album or the Library

**TIP**

You can customize the name of the photo by typing a new name in the **Title** field. See ⑨ **Set Photo Information** for more on setting photo information.

When you release the mouse button, the photos are moved to the specified location in the album. Repeat these steps to move more photos within the album.

### ③ View the Results

In the **Organize** window, view the results of your organizational efforts to make sure that the photos were placed in the correct order.

## ⑦ Remove Photos from an Album or the Library

**Before You Begin**

✔ ① Transfer Pictures from a Digital Camera

✔ ② Import Digital Pictures from Other Sources

**See Also**

→ ④ Create New Albums
→ ⑤ Create a Smart Album
→ ⑥ Organize Photos in an Album

**NOTE**

When you delete a photo from an album, iPhoto removes the selected photo from the album, but the photo remains in the **Photo Library** and in any other albums that contain it. If you drag a photo from an album to the **Trash** icon, iPhoto does not actually place the image in the **Trash**, it just removes the image from the album.

You can remove photos from any album. This feature is helpful when you decide you no longer want a particular photo to be part of a particular album. When you remove the photos from an album, note that they remain in the **Photo Library** and in any other albums that contain them.

Removing a photo from an album is different than deleting it from the **Photo Library**. If you delete a photo from the **Photo Library**, the image file is placed in the **Trash** and is totally removed from the **Photo Library** and from any albums that contain the photo. When you choose the **File, Empty Trash** command, iPhoto deletes the photo in the **Trash** from your computer's hard disk, and the photo is gone forever.

### ① Select Photo to Remove

Click to select the photo that you want to remove from the current album. To remove multiple photos, hold down the ⌘ key while you click each photo you want to remove.

### ② Remove Photo from Album

iPhoto provides three different methods you can use to remove a photo from an album: You can click the photo in the album and drag it to the **Trash** icon on the left side of the window, you can select the image in the album and choose **Photos, Remove from Album**, or you can select the image and press the **Delete** key.

# Remove Photos from an Album or the Library

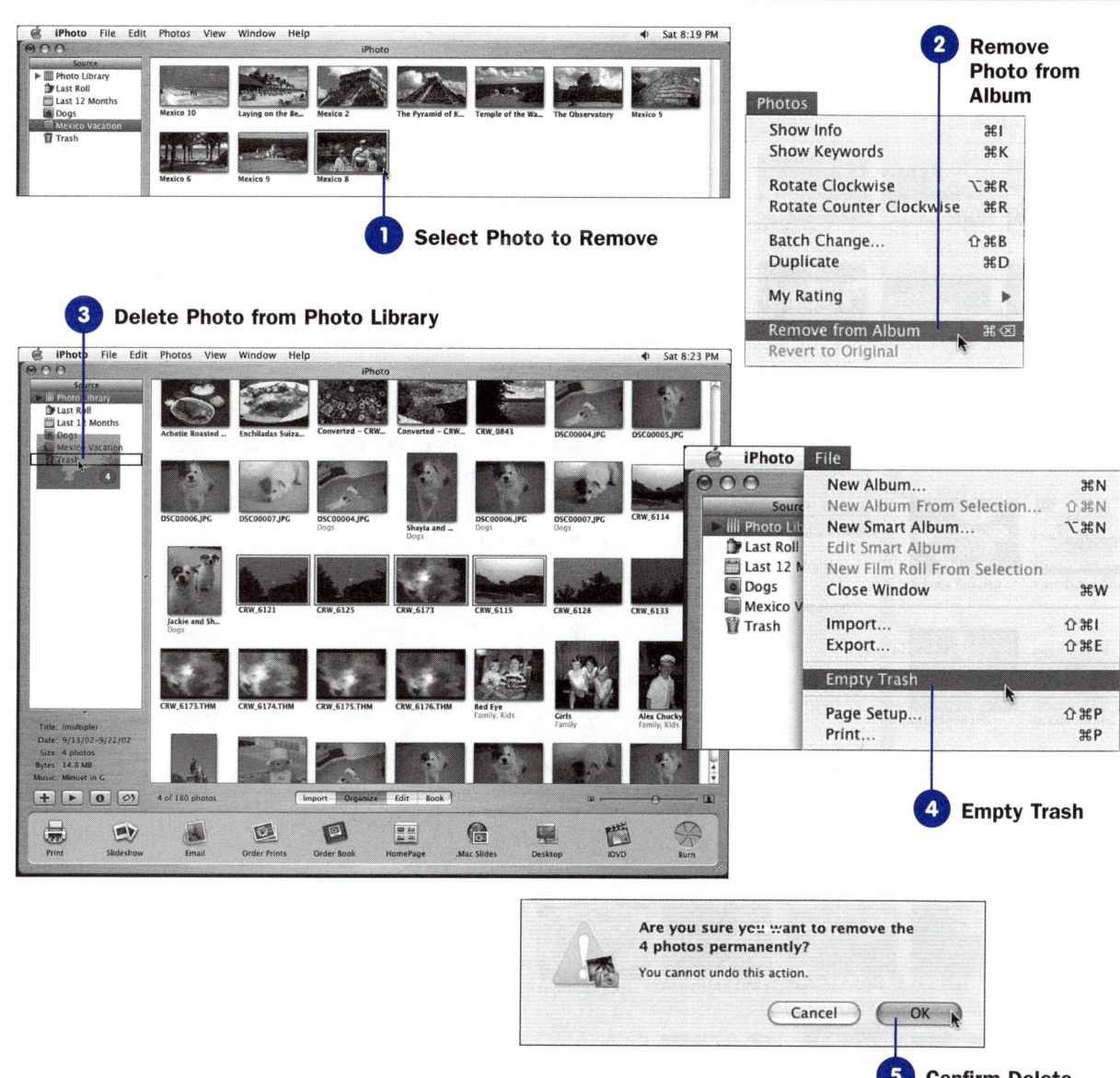

## CHAPTER 2: Loading and Organizing Photos

## 7 Remove Photos from an Album or the Library

 **TIP**

Undo the removal of photos (that is, return them to the album after you remove them) by choosing **Edit, Undo Remove Photos from Album**. You can also click and drag them back to the album from the **Photo Library**.

 **NOTE**

When you delete the photos in your **Trash**, they are permanently removed from your computer. You will have to re-import the photos to restore them.

### 3 Delete Photo from Photo Library

If you no longer want a photo to exist in iPhoto, you can delete it from the **Photo Library**—and consequently from any other albums that might contain the image. Click to display the **Photo Library** in the **Organize** window. Click the photo you want to delete and drag it to the **Trash** icon. You can also delete the photo by pressing the **Delete** key. To remove multiple photos, hold down the ⌘ key as you click each photo you want to remove.

### 4 Empty Trash

To empty the trash and completely remove the photo from your computer's hard disk, click the **Trash** icon on the left side of the window to display the contents of the **Trash**. Choose **File, Empty Trash** to delete all the photos that are in the **Trash**. iPhoto displays a dialog box to verify that you really want to delete these images from the hard disk.

### 5 Confirm Delete

Click the **OK** button on the confirmation dialog box to remove the displayed photos from iPhoto. The photos are permanently deleted and cannot be restored using the **Undo** command.

# 3

# Editing Photos

**IN THIS CHAPTER:**

- **8** About the Edit Pane
- **9** Set Photo Information
- **10** About Photo Resolution
- **11** Rotate Photos
- **12** Crop Photos
- **13** Change Brightness/Contrast of Photos
- **14** Eliminate Red Eye
- **15** Enhance Colors in a Photo
- **16** Retouch a Photo
- **17** Convert a Color Photo to Black and White
- **18** Switch to Original Version of a Photo
- **19** Assign Keywords to Photos to Facilitate Searches
- **20** Search for Photos

### 8  About the Edit Pane

iPhoto is not only a great tool for organizing photos, it also allows you to edit the photos in your library. For example, you can use iPhoto to remove a portion of a picture or increase the brightness of a dark picture. iPhoto even provides an option for converting a color photo to an artsy black-and-white version.

You make the desired modifications to a photo using the **Edit** pane. When you select the **Edit** option, the available editing options display at the bottom of the pane.

### 8  About the Edit Pane

**Before You Begin**

✔ **1** Transfer Pictures from a Digital Camera

✔ **2** Import Digital Pictures from Other Sources

**See Also**

→ **9** Set Photo Information

→ **11** Rotate Photos

→ **14** Eliminate Red Eye

→ **16** Retouch a Photo

The **Edit** pane in iPhoto provides several options for changing the appearance of a photo. Buttons for features such as changing the brightness, cropping the photo, or converting to black and white are available across the bottom of the **Edit** pane. The tools available on the **Edit** pane provide the basic editing features needed to quickly customize a photo.

For example, you can correct an overly dark photo by using the **Brightness** and **Contrast** sliders. If you want to eliminate a portion of the photo, you can remove the unwanted portion by using the **Crop** button. You can correct problems with the photo by clicking the **Retouch** button. If the subject of the photo has red eyes caused by a camera flash, you can remove them using the **Red Eye** button.

- **What happens to the original photo when I edit?** iPhoto creates a new version of the photo when you make edits. For example, if the original photo is **DSC00005.JPG**, iPhoto places an original copy of the photo in a folder called **Originals** before applying any edits. Every time you edit the photo, iPhoto makes sure that an original version of the photo exists and then applies the changes. This backup system allows you to revert back to the original version of the photo at any time.

## About the Edit Pane

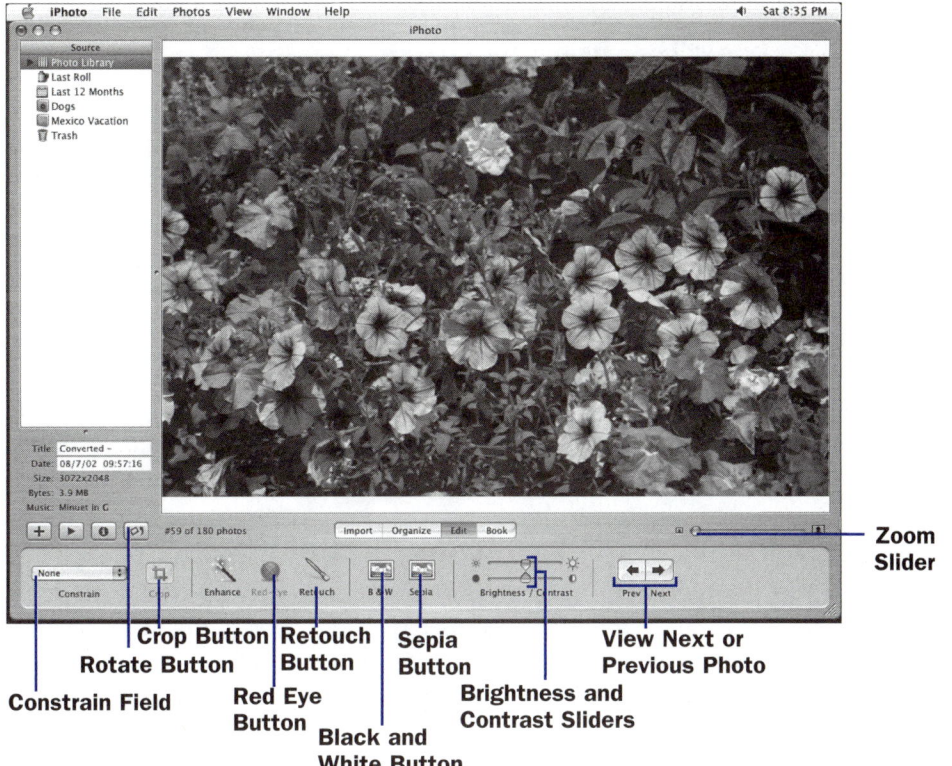

*Options in the Edit pane.*

- **Can I use another photo editor?** Yes. Although iPhoto provides some good photo editing capabilities, it does not provide the photo editing capabilities found in third-party products such as Adobe Photoshop. If you want to automatically edit with another photo editing package, choose **iPhoto**, **Preferences** to display the **Preferences** dialog box. Select the **Opens in Other** radio button and click the **Select** button to display the **Open** dialog box. Then select the photo editing software you want to use each time you double-click a photo thumbnail in iPhoto.

- **Can I return to the original version of the photo?** Yes. iPhoto allows you to switch back to the original version of the photo you're editing by choosing **File**, **Revert to Original**. See  **Switch to Original Version of Photo** for more information. When you select this option, iPhoto switches back to the original photo you loaded into iPhoto by copying the original photo into the

> **TIP**
>
> When you have set up iPhoto to use a third-party photo editing package, each time you double-click a photo, iPhoto opens the picture in the specified photo editing software. If you select the thumbnail and then click the **Edit** button, however, the photo opens in the **Edit** pane in iPhoto.

revision copy. All edits you have made to the photo using the **Edit** pane will be removed.

## 9 Set Photo Information

### Before You Begin

✔ **8** About the Edit Pane

### See Also

→ **11** Rotate Photos
→ **12** Crop Photos
→ **14** Eliminate Red Eye
→ **16** Retouch a Photo
→ **19** Assign Keywords to Photos to Facilitate Searches

**NOTE**

Any changes made to the photo information are applied to all locations in the photo library of that photo. For example, if you change the title of **CRW_6173.JPG** to **Shayla and Jackie,** every location of the photo (in the main **Photo Library** and in every album) will have the new title.

You can customize the information that iPhoto maintains for each photo. This information includes not only the title of the photo and the date the photo was created, but comments about each picture.

### 1 Select Desired Photo

Click to select the desired photo in the **Organize** pane. If necessary, display the **Organize** pane by clicking the **Organize** button at the bottom of the main iPhoto pane.

### 2 Display Photo Information

Click the **Photo Information** button in the lower-left of the iPhoto pane to display text fields where you can change the information for the photo. You can specify a new title, date, or comments. Keep in mind that this information displays for all instances of the photo.

### 3 Edit Photo Information

Type the desired changes in the text fields. Note that the name of the actual file does not change. If you alter the **Title** field, you are changing the title iPhoto displays for the selected photo, not the electronic filename.

If you want to know what the actual filename is for a picture in your iMovie **Photo Library**, select the photo and choose **File, Show Photo Info**. The **Photo Info** dialog box displays information about the actual photo file, including the filename and size.

If you want to change photo information for multiple photos so that they have the same title, date, or comments, you can use the **Batch Change** option. First, select the photos you want to change and then select **Photos, Batch Change**, and make the desired changes.

## Set Photo Information 9

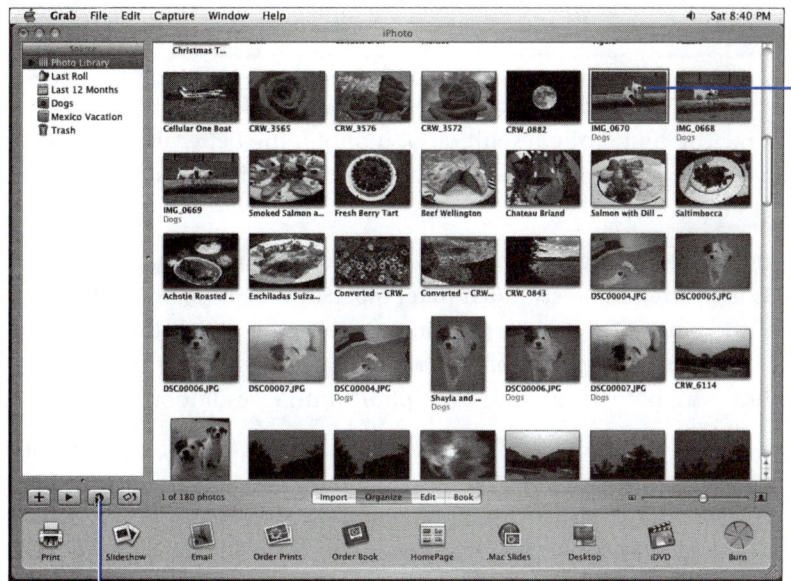

**1** Select Desired Photo

**2** Display Photo Information

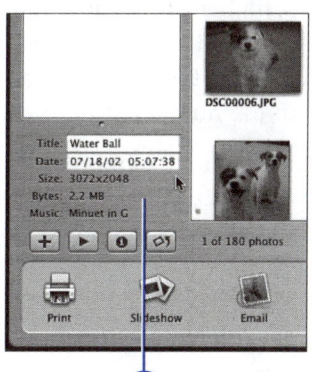

**3** Edit Photo Information

**CHAPTER 3: Editing Photos** 45

## 10 About Photo Resolution

**Before You Begin**

✔ 1 Transfer Pictures from a Digital Camera

✔ 2 Import Digital Pictures from Other Sources

**See Also**

→ 9 Set Photo Information

Probably the biggest factor that affects the quality of your photo is the resolution. The higher the resolution of a photo, the better the photo will look on your monitor or when printed—especially when you print larger-sized photos.

Resolution is determined when a photo is created. The resolution of a photo is measured in *pixels*. Each pixel represents a small dot or element of the photo. The more pixels in a picture, the higher the resolution of the photo. For example, a photo with a resolution of 1600×1280 pixels has a higher resolution than a photo with a resolution of 640×480 pixels.

If your photo was captured by a digital camera, the camera determines the photo resolution. Nearly all digital cameras have settings that allow you to select the resolution you want to use for your pictures. Obviously, you want your camera to capture the highest resolution possible. The higher the resolution, the more pixels of data are captured for each photo. But the higher the resolution of the photos, the fewer photos the camera can store on its memory device (the higher the resolution of a photo, the larger the file size). You must balance the resolution setting you select with the number of photos you can store on your camera.

### KEY TERMS

*Pixel*—A unit of measurement for specifying the resolution of a photo. For example, a photo with a resolution of 640×480 is 640 pixels wide by 480 pixels high.

*CCD (Charge-Coupled Device)*—A device in a digital camera that captures the light from an image and converts it into a digital image.

*Megapixel*—One million pixels. A measurement used to determine the maximum resolution of a digital camera.

All digital cameras have maximum resolutions based on the camera's *charge-coupled device (CCD)*. The larger the CCD of the camera, the higher the maximum resolution for photos created by the camera. CCDs contain light sensors that capture the image you are photographing. The measurement of the CCD size is done in *megapixels*. Therefore, a 1-megapixel digital camera can produce a photo with a maximum resolution of one million pixels. When shopping for a digital camera, the maximum resolution should be a key factor in your decision.

- **Aren't one million pixels enough?** It all depends on your intended use of the photos. If you create a photo with a resolution of 640×480 pixels, it has 307,200 total pixels. (That number is determined by multiplying the width by the height.) To maintain the full resolution of the photo, you would not want to print a photo with that resolution any bigger than 4"×6". If you printed it any larger, the image would have to be expanded and might seem grainy.

By purchasing a digital camera with a higher resolution, you ensure that you can take pictures with a resolution high enough that you will not have to expand the photo when you enlarge it.

- **How do I know what the resolution is when I load a picture from the Internet or another source?** iPhoto provides the capability to find information about a photo. Choose **File, Show Photo Information**. On the **Photo Info** dialog box, you can see the actual size of the photo in pixels.

- **How do I know what photo sizes I can order for my photo?** When you use the online photo option for ordering prints of your photos from Kodak, iPhoto checks the resolution of each photo. If a photo does not have the correct resolution for a specific print size, a yellow warning icon displays next to that size. See **37 Order Prints from an Online Photo Printer** for more information.

- **Can I change the resolution of a photo in iPhoto?** No. iPhoto does not offer the capability to change a photo's resolution when you're editing a photo. You can, however, export a photo at a lower resolution. See **45 Export a Photo** for information on exporting photos from iPhoto.

## 11 Rotate Photos

You can change the orientation of a photo by rotating it. For example, you might want to rotate a picture that was shot using a vertical orientation. As you have probably noticed, by default, iPhoto displays all photos using a horizontal orientation, with the long edge of the photo running horizontally. If you have a picture that you shot by turning the camera on its side so that the picture is taller than it is wide, you can rotate the photo by clicking the **Rotate** button. You can rotate the picture multiple times until it displays using the desired orientation. You can rotate a photo from either the **Organize** or **Edit** pane.

When you rotate a photo in iPhoto, you are simply changing the orientation of the photo as it displays within iPhoto or anything you create from iPhoto (such as a slideshow or photo book). The photo rotation process in iPhoto does not alter the actual photo file.

**Before You Begin**

✔ **8** About the Edit Pane

**See Also**

→ **12** Crop Photos

→ **13** Change Brightness/Contrast of Photos

→ **14** Eliminate Red Eye

→ **16** Retouch a Photo

→ **19** Assign Keywords to Photos to Facilitate Searches

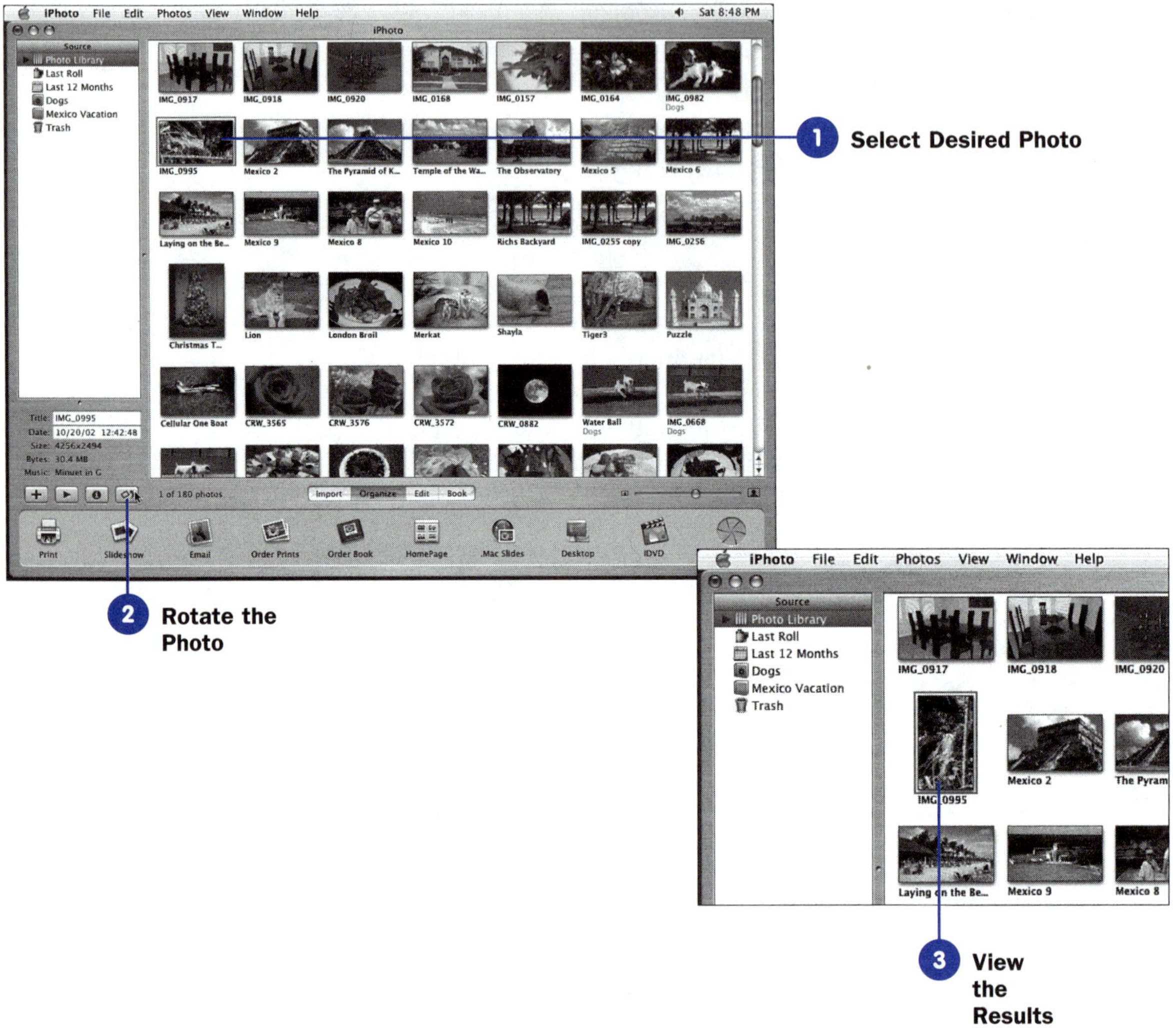

## 11  Rotate Photos

**1** Select Desired Photo

**2** Rotate the Photo

**3** View the Results

**TIP**
You can also rotate the photo that is currently displayed on the **Edit** pane.

Keep in mind that any changes you make to the orientation of a photo affect the orientation of that photo in every album. If you want to alter only one version of the photo, make a copy of the photo before altering it by selecting **File, Duplicate**. By doing this, the original version of the photo remains intact in your library, and you can make changes as needed to your copy.

PART I:    iPhoto

**Crop Photos** 12

### 1 Select Desired Photo

Click to select the desired photo on the **Organize** pane. If necessary, display the **Organize** pane by clicking the **Organize** button at the bottom of the main iPhoto pane.

### 2 Rotate the Photo

Click the **Rotate** button in the lower-left of the iPhoto pane to rotate the picture counterclockwise. Continue clicking the button until the picture displays in the desired orientation.

### 3 View the Result

Notice that the photo was rotated counter-clockwise so that the portion of the photo that was on the bottom is now the right side of the photo. If you click the **Rotate** button a second time, the photo will display upside-down in relation to the original orientation of the photo.

## TIPS

If you want to undo the rotation, choose **Edit, Undo Rotate Photo**. You can also return to the original orientation of the photo by continuing to click the **Rotate** button.

To reverse the rotation direction, press the **Option** key on the keyboard while you click the **Rotate** button.

You can also use the options on the menu to rotate a photo. Choose **Photo, Rotate, Clockwise** or **Photo, Rotate, Counter Clockwise**.

## 12 Crop Photos

You can use the **Crop** tool in iPhoto to remove parts of a photo. When you *crop* the photo, only the specified portion of the photo remains. The portion of the photo that is not selected is removed. For example, you might want to crop a photo to remove a building in the background. After you select all but the unwanted building, iPhoto crops the photo to remove the unwanted data from the file.

When you crop the image, you can specify the size you want iPhoto to make the remaining photo. For example, if you intend to create an 8×10 portrait, you should select that as the constraint size. When you specify the crop area, iPhoto ensures that the proper proportions are maintained for the photo.

Keep in mind that any changes you make by cropping a photo affect each instance of that photo in every album.

**Before You Begin**

✔ 8 About the Edit Pane

**See Also**

→ 11 Rotate Photos
→ 13 Change Brightness/Contrast of Photos
→ 14 Eliminate Red Eye
→ 16 Retouch a Photo
→ 17 Convert a Color Photo to Black and White
→ 18 Switch to Original Version of a Photo

CHAPTER 3: Editing Photos   49

## 12 Crop Photos

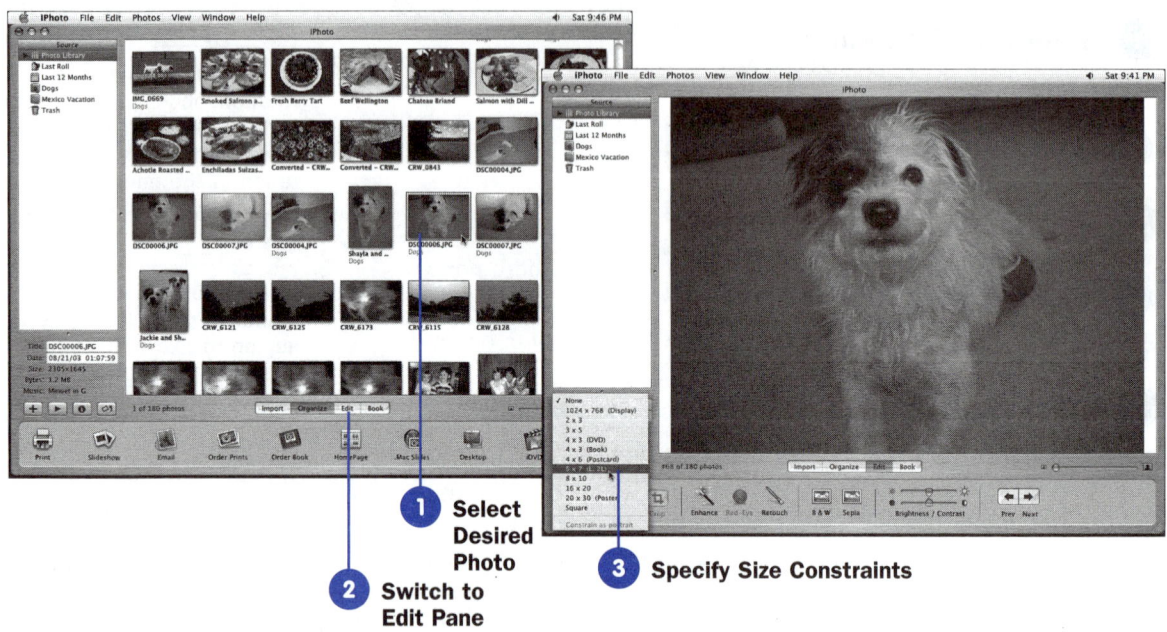

1. Select Desired Photo
2. Switch to Edit Pane
3. Specify Size Constraints

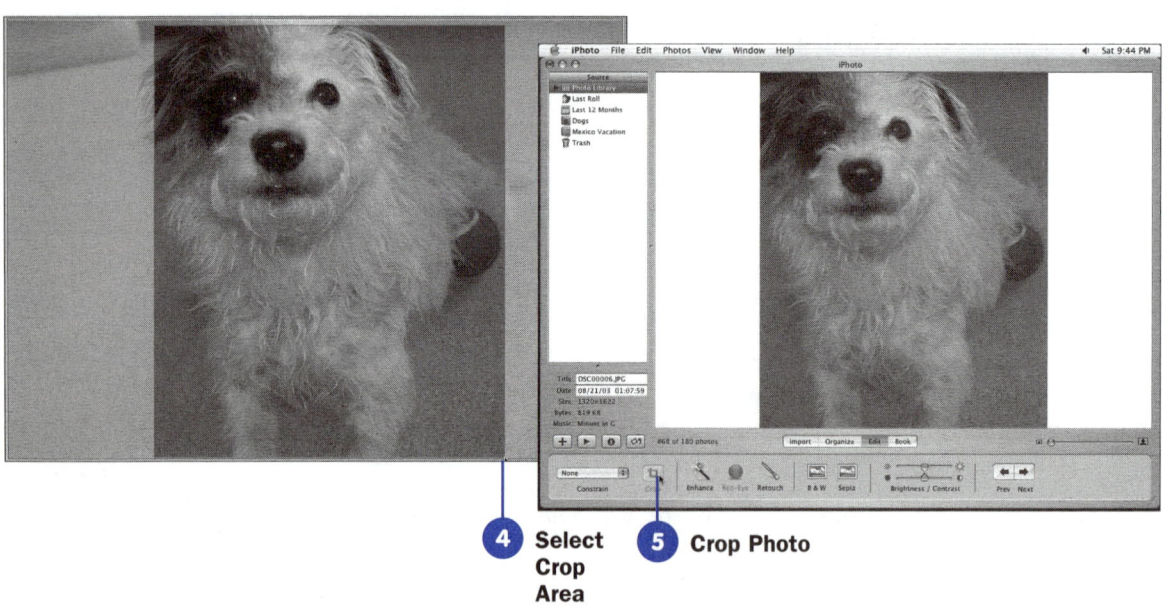

4. Select Crop Area
5. Crop Photo

PART I: iPhoto

## Crop Photos  12

### 1 Select Desired Photo

Click to select the desired photo on the **Organize** pane.

### 2 Switch to Edit Pane

Click the **Edit** button at the bottom of the iPhoto pane. The selected photo displays on the **Edit** pane.

### 3 Specify Size Constraints

Click the arrow button for the **Constrain** drop-down list in the lower-left corner of the pane and select the desired size for the photo. Select the size that matches the desired size of the finished photo. For example, if you plan to print a 5×7 photo, select that size to have iPhoto maintain those proportions when you crop.

### 4 Select Crop Area

Click a spot on the photo where you want to start cropping and drag to create the desired selection. When you click, the photo grays out; as you drag, the rectangular area you define regains its color and definition. Drag until the defined rectangular area encompasses the portion of the photo you want to retain. When you crop the photo, iPhoto will delete the grayed-out portion of the photo.

### 5 Crop Photo

Click the **Crop** button. iPhoto crops the photo by removing the unwanted (the grayed-out) portion. The new photo maintains the size proportions specified by the **Constrain** field.

**KEY TERM**

*Crop*—The process of removing unwanted portions of a photo. Only the selected portion of the photo remains.

**TIP**

You can double-click a photo thumbnail on the **Organize** pane to display the photo in the **Edit** pane.

**TIPS**

To move the selection, click inside the selected area and drag it on the photo.

To change the size of the selection, click a corner of the defined rectangle and drag in the desired direction.

**NOTE**

Press the **Control** key to compare the cropped photo to the original photo.

CHAPTER 3:  Editing Photos

## 13 Change Brightness/Contrast of Photos

**Before You Begin**

✓ ⑧ About the Edit Pane
✓ ⑨ Set Photo Information

**See Also**

→ ⑭ Eliminate Red Eye
→ ⑮ Enhance Colors in a Photo
→ ⑯ Retouch a Photo
→ ⑰ Convert a Color Photo to Black and White
→ ⑱ Switch to Original Version of a Photo

**KEY TERM**

*Contrast*—The amount of variation between the lightest and darkest areas of the picture.

You can adjust the brightness and *contrast* of each photo in your photo library. To adjust the brightness and contrast settings, you select the desired photo and then use the sliders on the **Edit** pane to make the adjustments.

Keep in mind that any changes you make to the brightness and contrast settings of a photo affect each occurrence of that photo in every album.

### ❶ Select Desired Photo

Click to select the desired photo on the **Organize** pane.

### ❷ Switch to Edit Pane

Click the **Edit** button at the bottom of the iPhoto pane. The selected photo displays on the **Edit** pane. Alternatively, double-click the desired image in the **Organize** pane to open it in the **Edit** pane.

### ❸ Make Brightness and Contrast Adjustments

Drag the **Brightness/Contrast** sliders at the bottom of the **Edit** pane to adjust the settings. Use the top slider to adjust the brightness of the photo. Drag the slider to the right to make the photo brighter; drag it to the left to make the photo darker.

Drag the bottom slider to adjust the contrast of the photo. Drag the slider to the right to add more contrast; drag it to the left to reduce the contrast.

### ❹ View the Result

Check the results of adjusting the contrast and brightness of the photo. In the sample photo, the brightness was increased, but the contrast was reduced in an effort to make the dark side of the dog's face more visible.

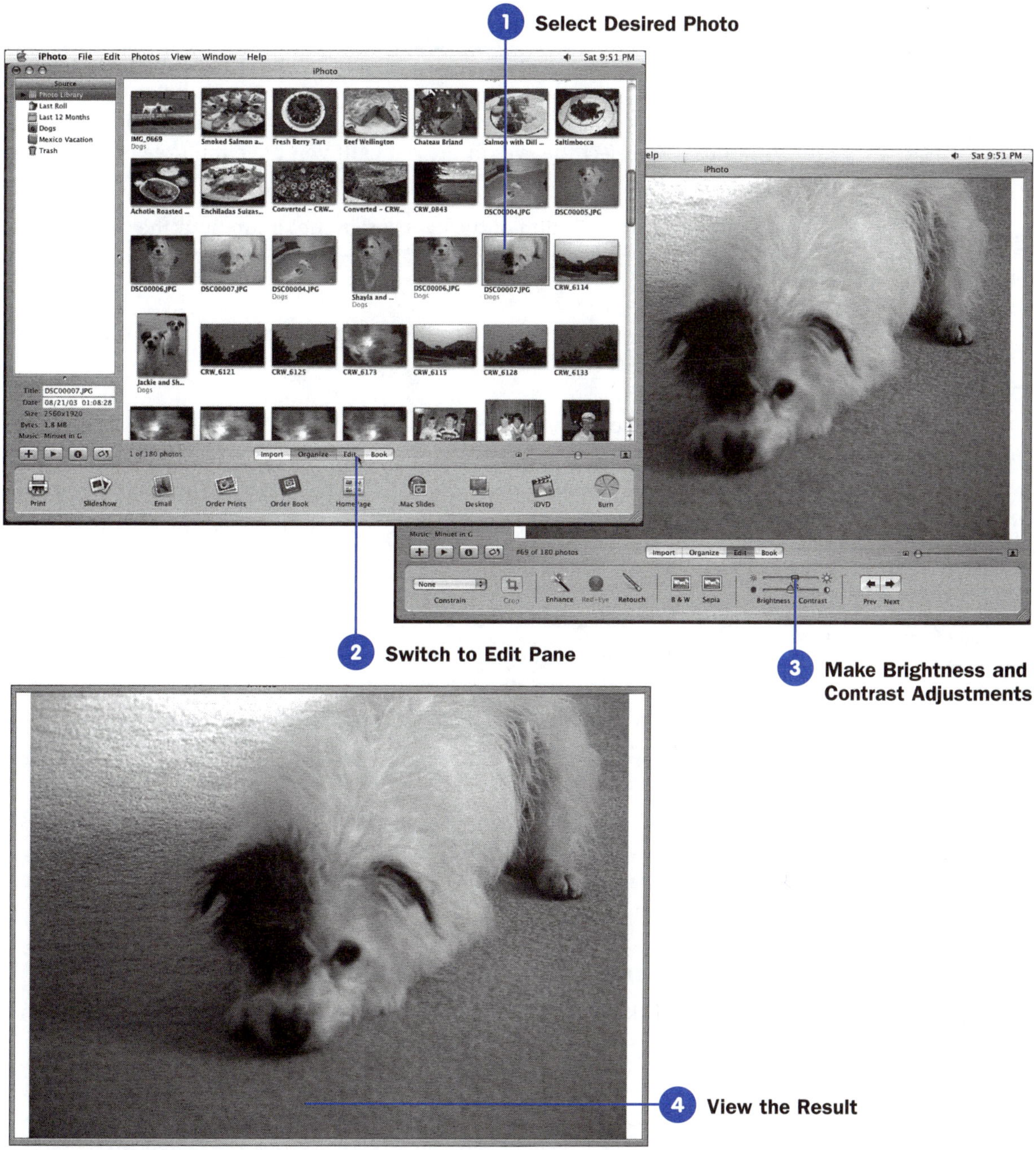

## Change Brightness/Contrast of Photos

**1** Select Desired Photo

**2** Switch to Edit Pane

**3** Make Brightness and Contrast Adjustments

**4** View the Result

**CHAPTER 3:** Editing Photos

## 14 Eliminate Red Eye

**Before You Begin**

✔ **8** About the Edit Pane
✔ **9** Set Photo Information

**See Also**

→ **16** Retouch a Photo
→ **17** Convert a Color Photo to Black and White
→ **18** Switch to Original Version of a Photo

### KEY TERM

*Red eye*—A common photo problem that occurs when a flash is used to take a picture of people. The bright flash reflects on the retinas of the eyes, causing the eyes to look red.

### TIP

When you select the area for the red-eye correction, make sure that you limit the area so that it is large enough to include only the red eyes. iPhoto will attempt to remove the red from whatever is selected.

You can remove the *red-eye* effect of subjects in your photos using the **Red-Eye** option in iPhoto. Before you apply the **Red-Eye** option, you must first select the eyes in the photo. If you have multiple people in the photo, select each person's eyes individually.

To make the selection of the eyes easier, make sure that the **Constrain** field is set to none, which will enable you to select a small portion of the photo.

Keep in mind that any changes you make to a photo using the **Red-Eye** option affect each occurrence of that photo in every album.

#### ❶ Select Desired Photo

Click to select the desired photo on the **Organize** pane and then click the **Edit** button. The selected photo displays on the **Edit** pane. Alternatively, double-click the desired image in the **Organize** pane to open it in the **Edit** pane.

#### ❷ Remove Size Constraints

Click the arrow button next to the **Constrain** field in the lower-left corner of the **Edit** pane and select **None** from the drop-down list. Now you can select a small area of the image.

#### ❸ Select Eye Area

Click the photo and drag to select the eyes of one of the subjects in the photo. When you click, the photo grays out. As you drag, the rectangular selection shows an area with color and definition; this is the area you will affect with the next command.

#### ❹ Remove Red Eye

Click the **Red-Eye** button. iPhoto corrects the red-eye condition in the selected area.

PART I: iPhoto

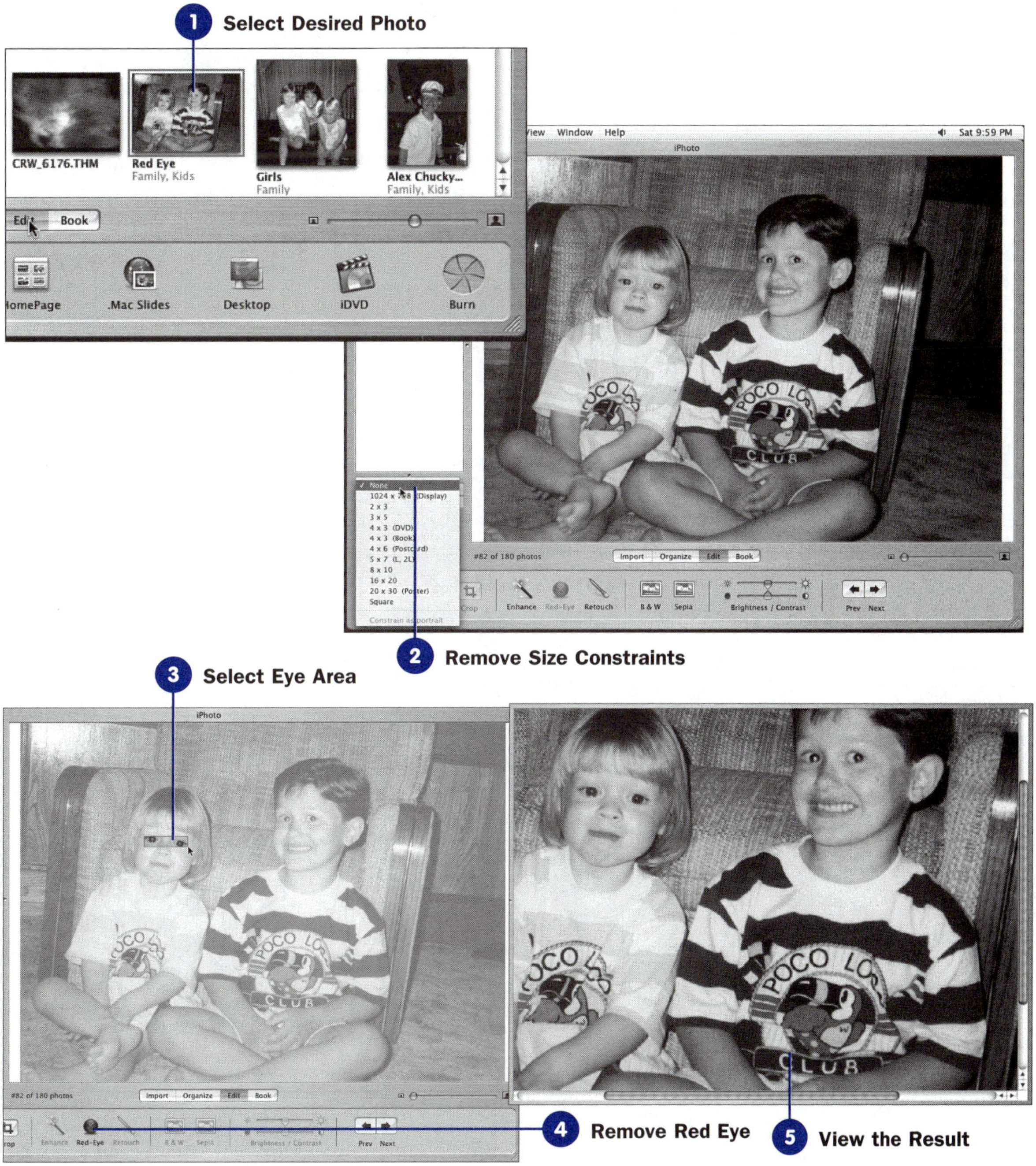

# Eliminate Red Eye 14

1. Select Desired Photo
2. Remove Size Constraints
3. Select Eye Area
4. Remove Red Eye
5. View the Result

CHAPTER 3: Editing Photos

## 15  Enhance Colors in a Photo

### ⑤ View the Result

After clicking the **Red-Eye** button, review the photo to make sure that you are happy with the correction. If the correction caused alterations to the person's face, you might want to undo the correction by choosing **Edit, Undo Reduce Red-Eye** and correcting a single eye at a time.

You can use the **Zoom** slider to zoom in on the photo and ensure that the correction was satisfactory. Zoom in to the photo by dragging the **Zoom** slider to the right.

If you want to correct additional eyes in the photo, repeat steps 3 and 4.

## 15  Enhance Colors in a Photo

**Before You Begin**

✓ ⑧ About the Edit Pane
✓ ⑨ Set Photo Information

**See Also**

→ ⑭ Eliminate Red Eye
→ ⑯ Retouch a Photo
→ ⑰ Convert a Color Photo to Black and White
→ ⑱ Switch to Original Version of a Photo

You can improve the overall look of a photo by applying the **Enhance** option. This tool works well for photos that look too dark or overexposed. The **Enhance** tool is a good tool to use to save a photo you might be tempted to delete.

When you select the **Enhance** option, iPhoto adjusts the brightness, contrast, and color of the image all at once. If you do not get the desired results the first time, you can apply the **Enhance** option again to continue to improve the look of the picture.

Keep in mind that any changes you make to a photo using the **Enhance** option affect each occurrence of that photo in every album.

### ① Select Desired Photo

Click to select the desired photo on the **Organize** pane and then click the **Edit** button. The selected photo displays on the **Edit** pane. Alternatively, double-click the desired image in the **Organize** pane to open it in the **Edit** pane.

### ② Enhance the Photo

Click the **Enhance** button at the bottom of the **Edit** pane. iPhoto adjusts the brightness, contrast, and color of the picture. If you like the improvements this tool makes to the image, click the **Enhance** button again to reapply the option.

Enhance Colors in a Photo  15

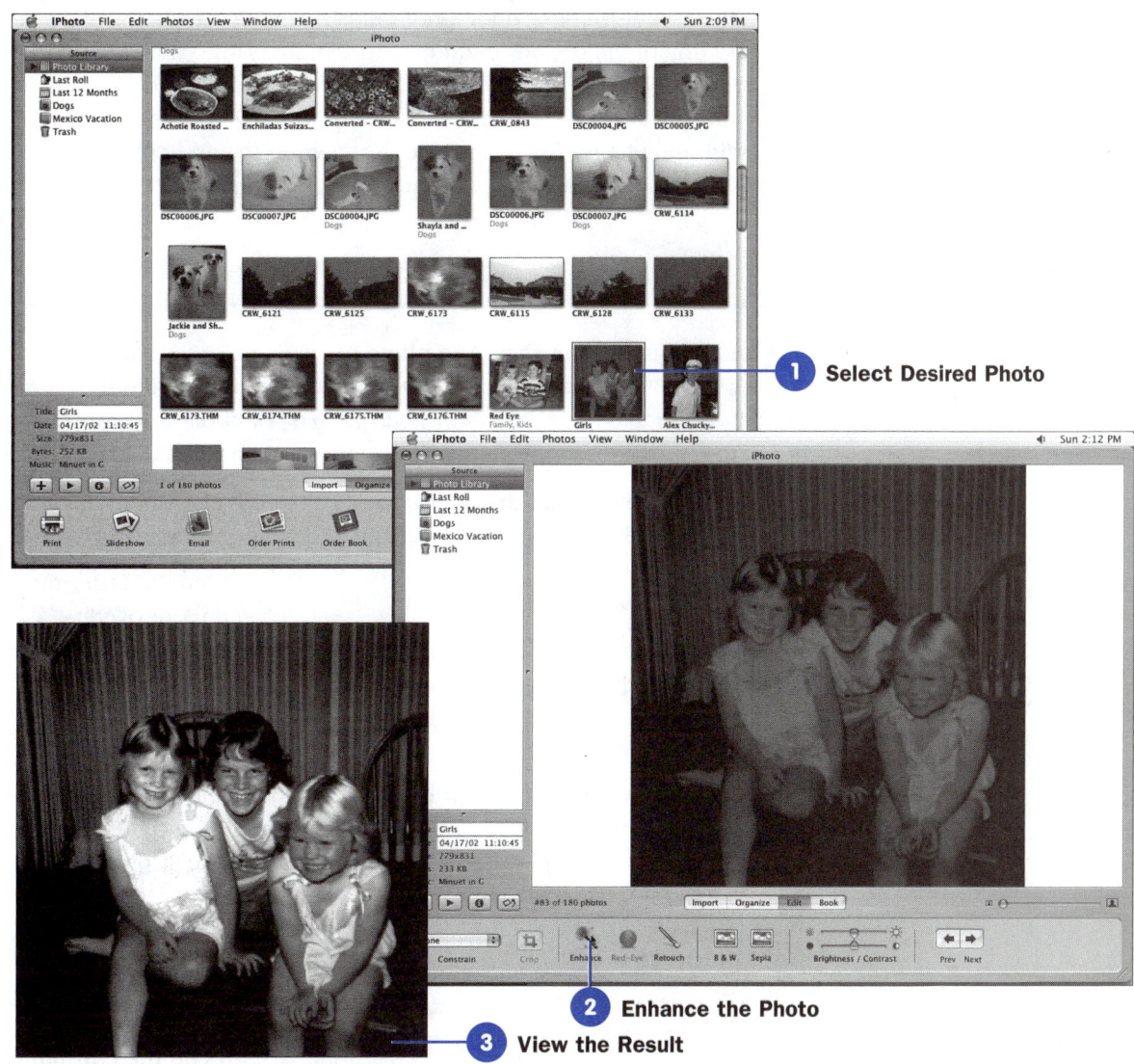

**Select Desired Photo**

**2** Enhance the Photo

**3** View the Result

**3** **View the Result**

Press the **Ctrl** key on the keyboard to compare the enhanced photo with the original version.

CHAPTER 3: Editing Photos

## 16  Retouch a Photo

**TIP**

If the photo appears grainy, choose **Edit, Undo Enhance Photo** to undo the last enhancement.

If you want to make additional adjustments to the photo, you can use any of the options available on the **Edit** pane. You can also click the **Enhance** button again to have iPhoto apply additional adjustments to the brightness, contrast, and color of the photo. With old pictures, such as the one shown in the example, you might have to click the **Enhance** button multiple times.

## 16  Retouch a Photo

**Before You Begin**

✔ **8** About the Edit Pane
✔ **9** Set Photo Information

**See Also**

→ **14** Eliminate Red Eye
→ **15** Enhance Colors in a Photo
→ **17** Convert a Color Photo to Black and White
→ **18** Switch to Original Version of a Photo

You can eliminate blemishes on a photo by using the **Retouch** tool in iPhoto. When you retouch a photo, you use the area around the blemished location to correct the blemished spot. For example, you can use the **Retouch** tool to remove a food stain or a scratch from an image.

When you are retouching the photo, click on the blemish and drag away from it a short distance. Repeat this process until the photo has the desired appearance. To make it easier to correct the photo, you should zoom in on the problem area.

Keep in mind that any changes you make to a photo using the **Retouch** option affect each occurrence of that photo in every album.

### ❶ Select Desired Photo

Click to select the desired photo on the **Organize** pane and then click the **Edit** button. The selected photo displays on the **Edit** pane. Alternatively, double-click the desired image in the **Organize** pane to open it in the **Edit** pane.

### ❷ Zoom In

Drag the **Size** slider at the bottom-right of the image pane to the right to zoom in on the photo. As the photo becomes too large for the pane, iPhoto adds scrollbars you can use to view the entire photo.

### ❸ Retouch Photo

Click the **Retouch** tool to change the cursor to a crosshair pointer. Click on the blemish in the image and drag away from that point with a short stroke. Repeat the process until the blemish is removed.

**TIP**

Click the **Retouch** tool again to deactivate the tool.

PART I:  iPhoto

Retouch a Photo   16

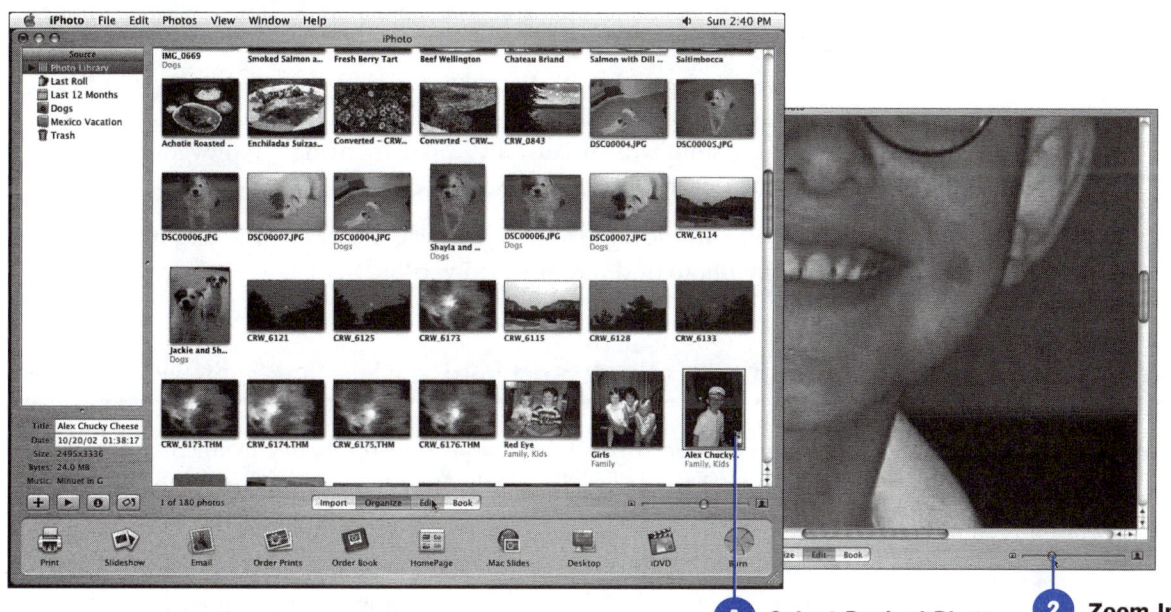

1  Select Desired Photo
2  Zoom In

3  Retouch Photo
4  View the Result

CHAPTER 3:   Editing Photos

## 17  Convert a Color Photo to Black and White

### ④ View the Result

Check the end result to make sure that you are happy with the corrections made using the **Retouch** tool. In the sample photo, the food stain was successfully and convincingly removed from the boy's cheek.

You can press the **Ctrl** key to switch between the original version of the photo and the corrected version.

## 17  Convert a Color Photo to Black and White

**Before You Begin**

- ✔ ⑧ About the Edit Pane
- ✔ ⑨ Set Photo Information
- ✔ ⑬ Change Brightness/Contrast of Photos

**See Also**

- → ⑭ Eliminate Red Eye
- → ⑮ Enhance Colors in a Photo
- → ⑯ Retouch a Photo
- → ⑱ Switch to Original Version of a Photo

You can convert any photo in your **Photo Library** from color to black and white. This feature is useful when you want to create the appearance of an older picture.

Keep in mind that any changes you make to a photo using the **B & W** option affect each occurrence of that photo in every album.

### ① Select Desired Photo

Click to select the desired photo on the **Organize** pane and then click the **Edit** button. The selected photo displays on the **Edit** pane. Alternatively, double-click the desired image in the **Organize** pane to open it in the **Edit** pane.

### ② Convert to Black and White

Click the **B & W** tool on the bottom of the **Edit** pane to convert the selected photo to black and white. iPhoto converts the entire photo. During the conversion process, a dialog box appears to show the progress.

### ③ Adjust the Brightness/Contrast

After converting the photo to black and white, check to make sure that the brightness and contrast are acceptable for the photo. You can adjust these settings using the **Brightness/Contrast** sliders on the bottom of the **Edit** pane. In the sample photo, the brightness was increased to make the background of the flowers more visible.

**TIPS**

To undo the conversion, choose **Edit, Undo Convert to B & W**.

You can also convert a photo to sepia tone by clicking the **Sepia** button.

PART I:   iPhoto

## Convert a Color Photo to Black and White 17

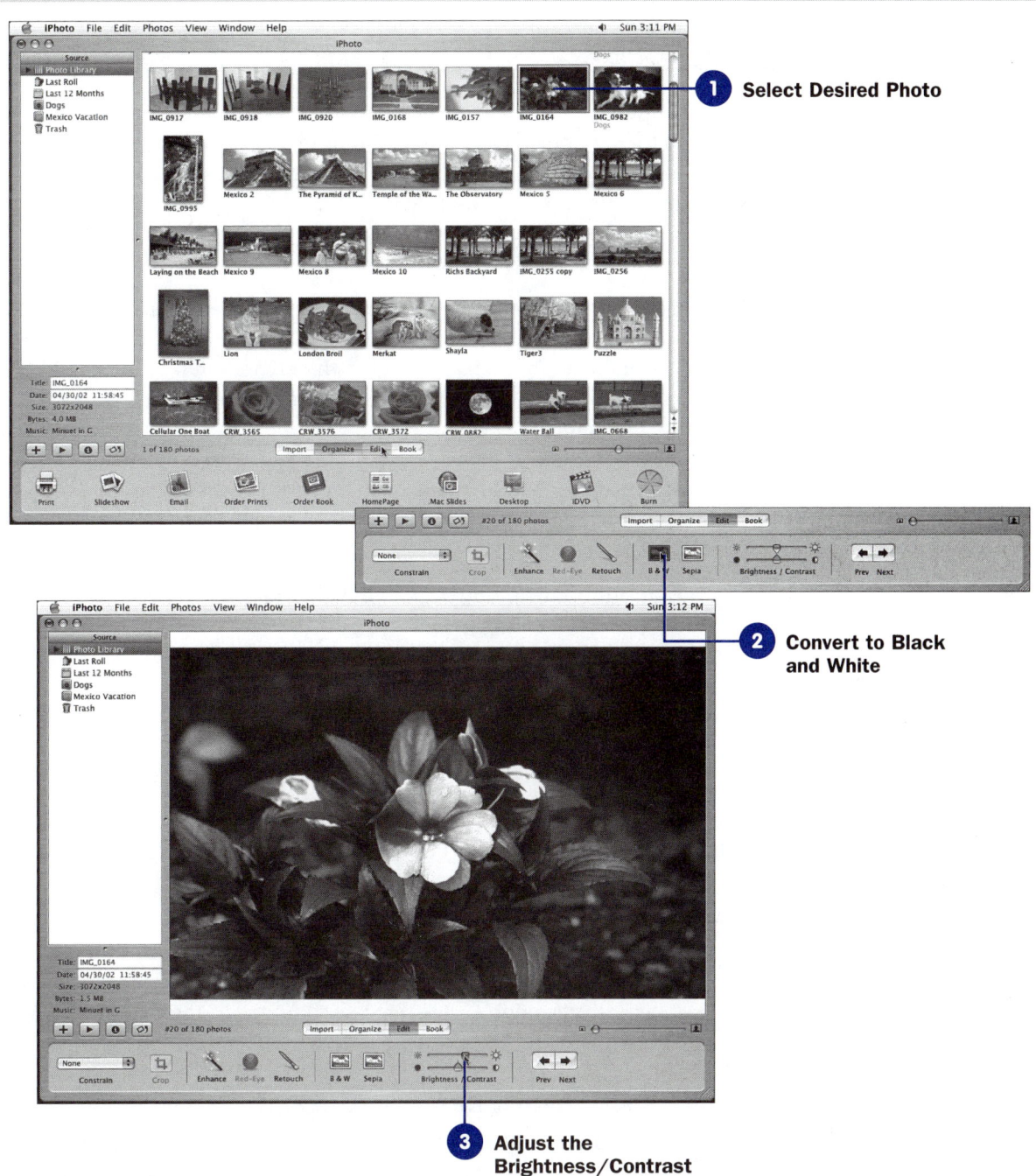

1. Select Desired Photo
2. Convert to Black and White
3. Adjust the Brightness/Contrast

**CHAPTER 3: Editing Photos**

## 18  Switch to Original Version of a Photo

### Before You Begin

✔ **8** About the Edit Pane
✔ **9** Set Photo Information

### See Also

→ **14** Eliminate Red Eye
→ **16** Retouch a Photo
→ **17** Convert a Color Photo to Black and White

You can remove all the edits you have made to a photo by reverting back to the original version of the photo. When you convert to the original, iPhoto deletes all the changes that have been made to the photo using the tools on the **Edit** pane. That means that any cropping, rotating, enhancing, retouching, red-eye reduction, brightness, contrast, and black-and-white conversion will be undone.

iPhoto can accomplish this reversal because it creates a separate version of the photo when you make the first edit. The copy of the original remains unaltered in a separate folder while iPhoto makes the modifications in the other version of the photo. When you revert back to the original, iPhoto actually copies the original file into the file containing the conversions, effectively reversing all the edits you have made since you first imported the file into iPhoto. It doesn't matter when the changes were made; iPhoto undoes *all* changes and reverts back to the original version.

In most instances, reverting back to the original version of the photo provides an adequate safety net, especially if you decide you don't like the effect of the modifications that have been made. In some cases, it can be aggravating to lose all the changes you've made and start over. Suppose that you crop a photo and then start adjusting the brightness and contrast settings. If you decide you don't like those adjustments, reversing all changes also loses the cropping you had done.

Keep in mind that if you convert a photo back to its original version, all occurrences of the photo within the album will be converted.

**TIP**

You might want to consider creating a different version of a photo each time you make a change you like by choosing **Photos, Duplicate** to copy the picture. Then make your new modifications in the copied version. This way, if you have to reverse the changes, the reversal only happens back to what the photo looked like when the copy was created.

### ① Select Desired Photo

Click to select the desired photo on the **Organize** pane and then click the **Edit** button. The selected photo displays on the **Edit** pane. Alternatively, double-click the desired image in the **Organize** pane to open it in the **Edit** pane.

### ② Select Photos, Revert to Original

Choose **Photos, Revert to Original** to convert the selected photo back to its original image. iPhoto displays a dialog box asking whether you're sure you want to revert.

PART I:  iPhoto

# Switch to Original Version of a Photo  18

**1** Select Desired Photo

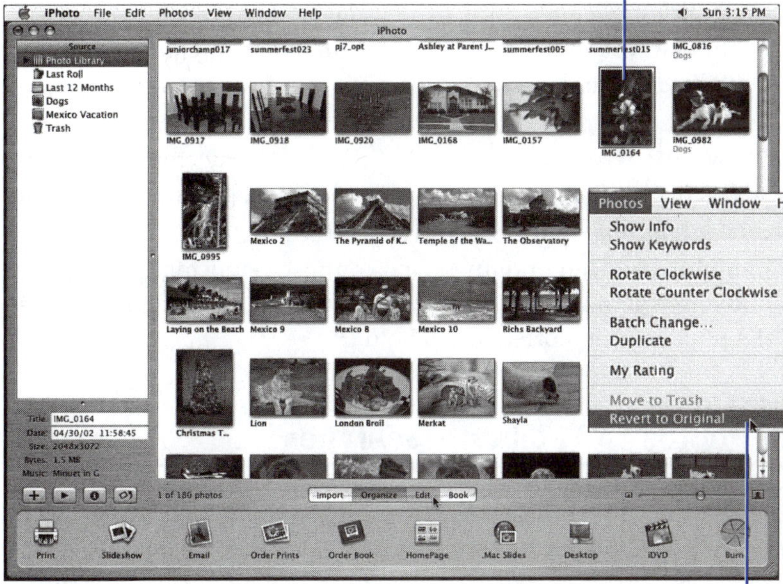

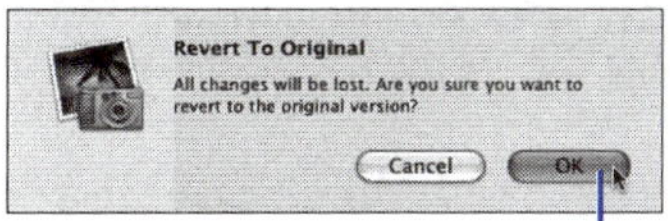

**2** Select Photos, Revert to Original

**3** Switch to Original

**4** View the Result

**CHAPTER 3:   Editing Photos**

## 19  Assign Keywords to Photos to Facilitate Searches

**NOTES**

You cannot undo a conversion back to the original photo.

If you have not made any changes to a photo, the **Revert to Original** command is grayed out on the **File** menu.

### ③ Switch to Original

Click **OK** on the dialog box to continue and convert the specified photo to its original version. iPhoto eliminates *all* changes you have made to the photo.

### ④ View the Result

Notice that all edits you have made to the photo using the options on the **Edit** pane have been reversed. These edits include cropping, rotating, adjusting brightness and contrast, retouching, enhancing, and removal of red eye. The reversal occurs back to the point when the photo was imported into iPhoto.

## 19  Assign Keywords to Photos to Facilitate Searches

**Before You Begin**

✔ ⑧ About the Edit Pane
✔ ⑨ Set Photo Information

**See Also**

→ ⑯ Retouch a Photo
→ ⑰ Convert a Color Photo to Black and White
→ ⑱ Switch to Original Version of a Photo
→ ⑳ Search for Photos

You use keywords to label pictures. By using keywords, you can locate all the pictures in the library that match that specific category. For example, if you assign the keyword **Vacation** to your vacation pictures, you can then search for photos with that keyword. iPhoto will locate all the photos that match that keyword. See ⑳ **Search for Photos** for more information on searching for photos using keywords.

iPhoto provides five default keywords you can assign to your photos. You can also create custom keywords for your photos. When you assign a keyword to a photo, the assigned keyword displays on the right side of the photo.

### ① Select Desired Photo

Click to select the desired photo on the **Organize** pane. To apply keywords to multiple images, press **Shift** or ⌘ and click multiple images.

### ② Display Keywords Dialog Box

Choose **Photos, Show Keywords** to display the **Keywords** dialog box.

### ③ Create New Keyword

Click the down arrow next to the **Keywords** field at the top of the dialog box and select **New**. iPhoto creates a new keyword called **untitled** in the list.

PART I:   iPhoto

## Assign Keywords to Photos to Facilitate Searches  19

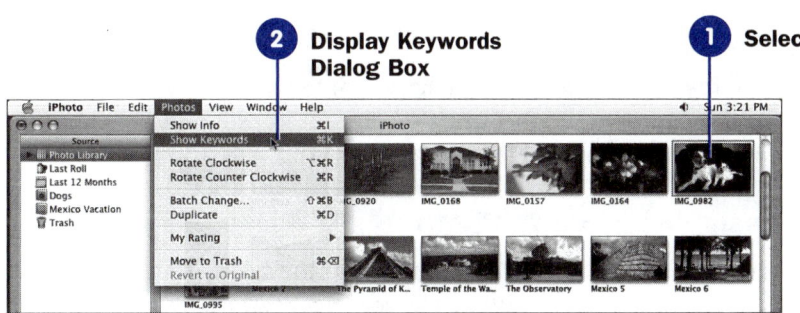

**2** Display Keywords Dialog Box

**1** Select Desired Photo

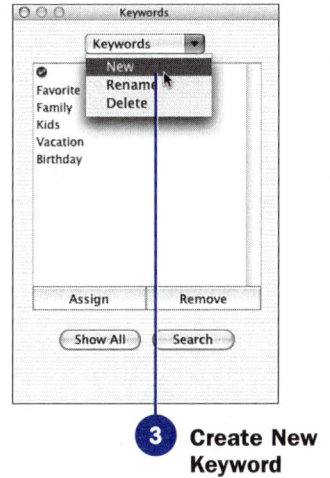

**3** Create New Keyword

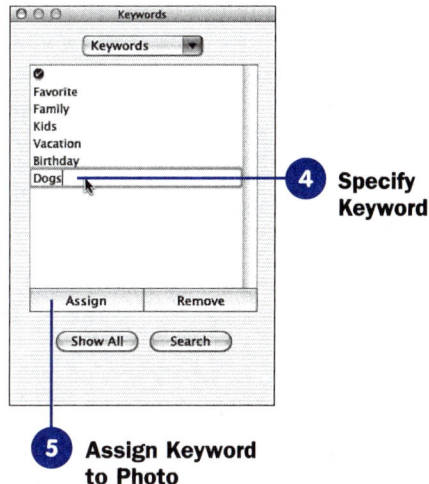

**4** Specify Keyword

**5** Assign Keyword to Photo

**6** View Result

**CHAPTER 3:** Editing Photos

## 20 Search for Photos

### ④ Specify Keyword

Type the desired name for the keyword; the keyword you type replaces the default label **untitled**. Repeat steps 3 and 4 to add additional keywords to the list.

### ⑤ Assign Keyword to Photo

Click the keyword you want to assign to the selected photo and then click the **Assign** button. The selected keyword is assigned to the photo you selected in step 1 and displays on the right side of the photo. You can assign multiple keywords to the same photo: Just select from the list the next keyword you want to apply to the selected photo and click **Assign** again.

### ⑥ View the Result

Close the **Keywords** dialog box to view the keywords you specified on the **Organize** pane. All the keywords you added display to the right of the corresponding photo thumbnail.

If you want to add additional keywords to the photos in your **Photo Library**, repeat steps 1 through 5.

**TIP**

By default, iPhoto disables the viewing of keywords. To show the keywords in the **Organize** pane, choose **View, Keywords** (so that the option has a check mark next to it).

**TIP**

To remove unwanted keywords from the list in the **Keywords** dialog box, highlight the keyword and click the down arrow next to the **Keywords** field at the top of the dialog box. From the drop-down list of options, select **Delete**.

## 20 Search for Photos

**Before You Begin**

✔ ⑨ Set Photo Information

✔ ⑲ Assign Keywords to Photos to Facilitate Searches

**See Also**

→ ⑱ Switch to Original Version of Photo

→ ㉔ Reorder Pages in a Book

You can use the keywords assigned to photos to locate a specific group of photos. For example, you might want to locate all photos that you have designated as **Family** photos by assigning that keyword. See ⑲ **Assign Keywords to Photos to Facilitate Searches** for more information on creating and assigning keywords to photos. The search option works only with keywords; it does not search the comments or titles of the photos.

To ensure that iPhoto looks in all albums in the **Photo Library**, make sure that the **Photo Library** (and not a specific album) is selected before displaying the **Keywords** dialog box. If you have a specific album selected, iPhoto looks for photos with the specified keywords only in that album.

PART I:   iPhoto

# Search for Photos 20

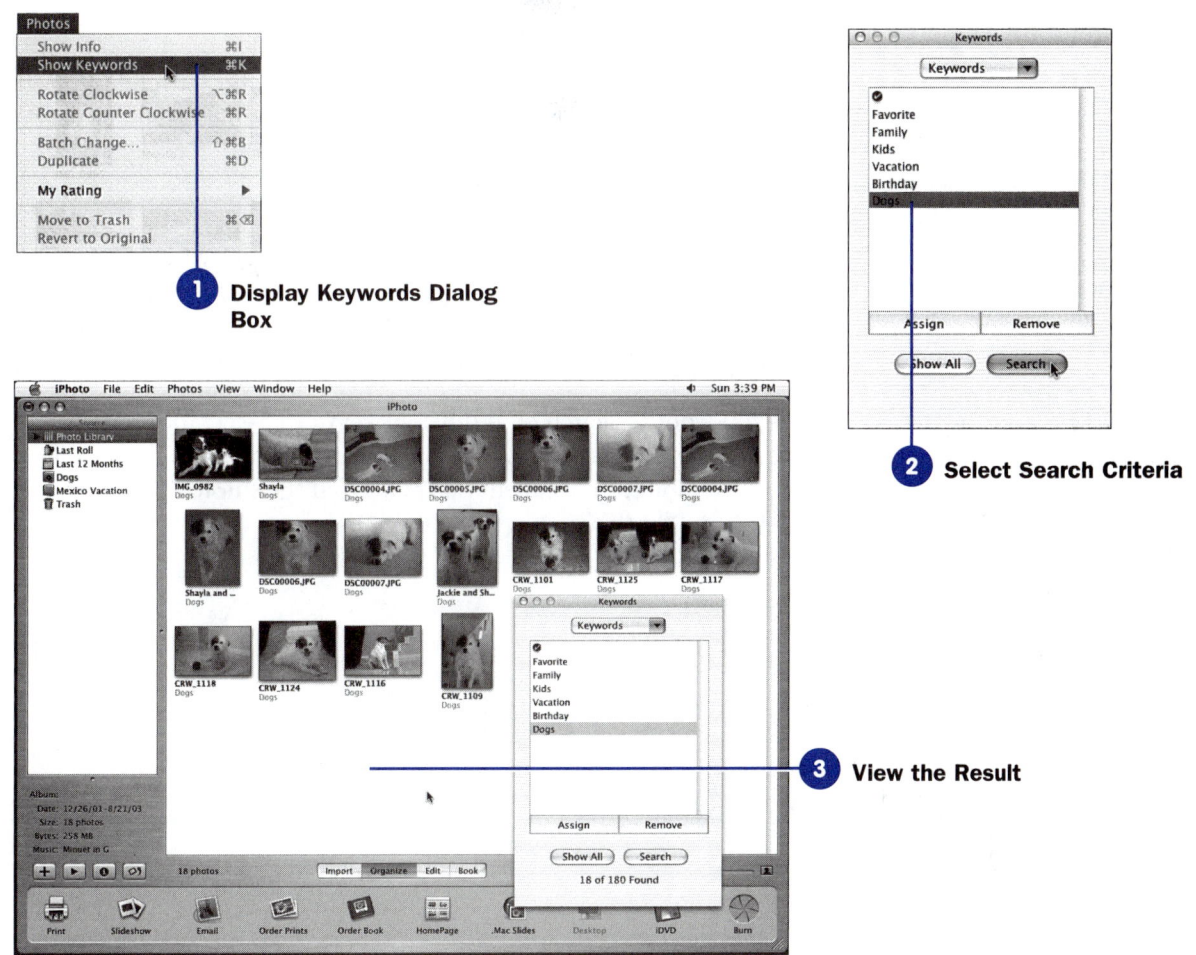

You can search using any of the keywords listed in the **Keywords** dialog box. If iPhoto finds photos that have the specified keywords, the **Organize** pane displays only the thumbnails for those matching photos.

### ① Display the Keywords Dialog Box

Switch to the **Organize** pane and select the **Photo Library**. If you select a specific album instead of the **Photo Library**, iPhoto will not look for photos outside that album.

Choose **Photos, Show Keywords** to display the **Keywords** dialog box.

CHAPTER 3:   Editing Photos    67

## 20 Search for Photos

**TIP**

You can select multiple keywords for your search by holding down the ⌘ key as you click each keyword. iPhoto finds only those photos that have *all* the selected keywords.

**TIP**

After you have completed a search, only the matching photos display on the **Organize** pane. Click the **Show All** button to show all photos in the library or album. You can also close the **Keywords/Search** dialog box to show all photos.

### ② Select Search Criteria

Select the desired keyword in the list and click the **Search** button. iPhoto searches through the library or selected album and displays all the photos with the specified keyword.

### ③ View the Result

Look at the list of photos displayed on the **Organize** pane. All photos will have the keywords selected on the **Keywords** pane. You can edit any of these photos by selecting the photo and then clicking the **Edit** button.

If you want to search on a different keyword, select the keyword and click **Search**. Again, iPhoto will search for photos within the current album that match the keyword. If the **Photo Library** is selected, iPhoto searches the entire library.

# 4

# Creating Photo Books

**IN THIS CHAPTER:**

- **21** About Photo Books
- **22** Select a Book Theme
- **23** Design Book Pages
- **24** Reorder Pages in a Book
- **25** Add Comments to the Photo Book
- **26** Print a Photo Book
- **27** Save a Photo Book as a PDF
- **28** Order a Photo Book Online

## 21 About Photo Books

You can turn the photos in an album in your **Photo Library** into a photo book. iPhoto allows you to create photo books that you can print yourself or that you can send to Apple to be printed as a hard-bound book. See **26 Print a Photo Book** for information on printing a photo book and **28 Order a Photo Book Online** for information on ordering one.

When you create an album, iPhoto automatically assigns a default photo book theme to the album. When you click the **Book** button, you can see the default book selections. You can customize the layout of each photo book using the options on the **Book** pane. For example, you can select one of six default themes, or you can customize each page of the book. You customize each page by selecting the number of photos to appear on the page, specifying the page style, and adding text as comments or titles.

## 21 About Photo Books

**Before You Begin**

✔ **4** Create New Albums
✔ **5** Create a Smart Album
✔ **6** Organize Photos in an Album

**See Also**

→ **20** Search for Photos
→ **22** Select a Book Theme
→ **23** Design Book Pages

The **Book** pane provides the tools needed to customize the look of your photo book. When you click the **Book** button, iPhoto creates a photo book using all the photos in the selected album or library. Therefore, before creating a book, you should create an album that contains the photos you want in your book. See **4 Create New Albums** for information on creating a photo album in iPhoto. See **5 Create a Smart Album** for information on creating a smart photo album in iPhoto.

iPhoto adds the photos to the photo book in the same order the photos are listed in the album. You can change the order either by reordering the album, as explained in **6 Organize Photos in an Album**, or by moving pages on the **Book** pane, as explained in **24 Reorder Pages in a Book**. Because iPhoto uses the order of the images in the photo album, the first photo in the album becomes the cover photo for your book.

- **Why can't I create a photo book for the Photo Library?** iPhoto is designed to use albums, not the main **Photo Library**, when creating photo books. If you click the **Book** button with the **Photo Library** selected, iPhoto displays a dialog box indicating that you must select an album. If you want to create a photo book containing all the pictures in your photo library, create an album and copy all the photos from the library to the new album.

PART I:   iPhoto

- **Do the blue lines around the title and comments print on the page?** No. iPhoto provides those blue lines as guides for laying out the photo book. If you don't care for the guides, disable the **Show Guides** check box to prevent the guidelines from appearing on the screen.

- **Why doesn't my photo look centered on the page?** Unfortunately, iPhoto does not allow you to manually position photos on the page. When you select the desired number of photos, iPhoto centers the pictures on the page using a 4×3 size ratio. Photos that do not have a 4×3 ratio might not appear properly centered on the page. You can adjust this by setting the **Constrain** option for the photo to 4×3 and cropping it on the **Edit** pane. See **11 Crop Photos** for more information on setting the Constrain size.

## 22 Select a Book Theme

When you click the **Book** button near the bottom of the iPhoto window, iPhoto automatically lays out the photo book using the current theme. When you create an album, iPhoto automatically assigns the default theme to the album, but you can select any of the six themes for your book. The theme represents the layout of the photos on the pages in the book. The default theme for books you create is the **Picture Book** option, which displays only photos on the pages. If you want to add text to the book, you must select a different theme.

When you select a theme, iPhoto automatically changes the pages in the book to reflect the selected theme. After selecting the theme, you can customize each page by changing the number of photos on the page, adding text, and inserting additional comments. See **23 Design Book Pages** for more information on customizing the pages in the book.

After you select the theme, you can specify any of three page options for the book: Titles, Comments, and Page Numbers. The **Titles** option displays the title you have assigned to the photo in iPhoto; the **Comments** option displays any comments you type about the picture; and the **Page Numbers** option displays page numbers on each page of the photo book. See **9 Set Photo Information** for more information on setting a photo title. Keep in mind that selecting any of these options affects the display on all pages in the photo book.

**Before You Begin**
✔ **21** About Photo Books

**See Also**
→ **23** Design Book Pages
→ **24** Reorder Pages in a Book
→ **25** Add Comments to the Photo Book

### NOTE
Make sure that you select your theme before making a lot of modifications to the layout of the pages. If you apply a new theme, you will lose all the page formatting you've already done for your book.

## 22  Select a Book Theme

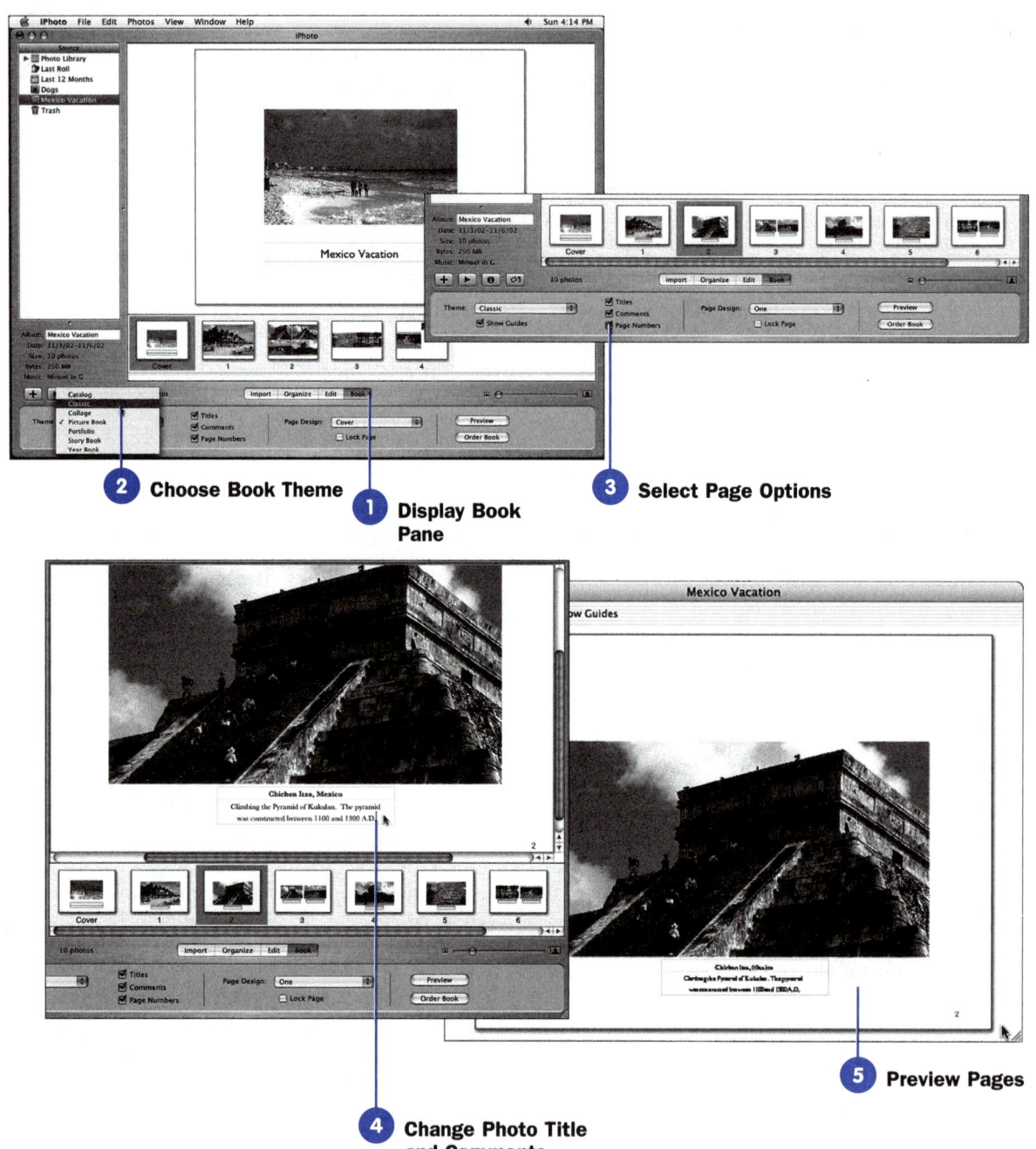

1. Display Book Pane
2. Choose Book Theme
3. Select Page Options
4. Change Photo Title and Comments
5. Preview Pages

PART I:  iPhoto

Select a Book Theme

### ① Display Book Pane

In the left pane of any iPhoto window, click to select the album you want to use to create a photo book and then click the **Book** button near the bottom of the window to display the **Book** pane.

### ② Choose Book Theme

Click the arrow button next to the **Theme** field to display a list of available themes. iPhoto displays a check mark next to the currently selected theme. Select the desired theme from the list. When you select a theme, iPhoto automatically updates the book pages to reflect the selected theme.

**TIP**

If you are not sure which theme to select, test different themes by applying them and seeing the results in the thumbnail images of the book pages.

### ③ Select Page Options

Click the check box next to each option you want to select for the photo book. You can add **Titles** and **Comments** to the images in your photo book and **Page Numbers** to each page in the photo book. iPhoto applies the options you select to all the pages in the photo book with exception of the first page (the cover of the photo book).

**NOTE**

Some book themes do not use all the page options. For example, the **Picture Book** theme does not display **Comments** and **Titles**.

### ④ Change Photo Title and Comments

If you have enabled the **Titles** check box at the bottom of the **Book** pane, you can customize the title for each photo in your book. By default, iPhoto places the title of the photo under or next to the photo. Of course, this might not be the title you want to display in the printed book. To change the title, click to select the title text and type the desired title for the text.

Under each title field, iPhoto provides a blank box in which you can type additional comments or descriptions about the photo. Type comments for the picture by clicking the box to select it and then typing the desired comments.

If you do not want a title or comments for the picture, make sure that the corresponding check boxes at the bottom of the **Book** pane are disabled. When the book is printed, the blue boxes are not printed.

**TIP**

You can customize the text on your photo pages by changing the font style, size, and typeface. See  **Add Comments to the Photo Book** for more information.

CHAPTER 4: Creating Photo Books 73

# 23 Design Book Pages

## 5 Preview Pages

After adding text to the pages in the book, click the **Preview** button in the bottom-right corner of the **Book** pane to see what the pages will look like when they are printed.

On the **Preview** window, disable the **Show Guides** check box to see the pages without the blue boxes around the text.

## 23 Design Book Pages

**Before You Begin**

✔ 21 About Photo Books
✔ 22 Select a Book Theme

**See Also**

→ 24 Reorder Pages in a Book
→ 25 Add Comments to the Photo Book

**NOTE**

You can customize every page in the photo book but the cover page. The cover page uses a default setup designed to fit the cover when you order your photo book online.

You can customize the pages in your photo book by specifying the number of photos you want on each specific page. You specify the page design by selecting one of the **Page Design** options associated with the selected book theme.

When you change the number of photos on a particular page, iPhoto makes adjustments to the remaining pages based on the specified number of photos. For example, if you increase the number of photos on a page, iPhoto pulls the additional photos from the next pages.

After you have customized a page design, you can keep it from being altered by locking it. If you lock a page, the graphics remain on that same page even if you alter the preceding page design.

### 1 Select a Page

Click the thumbnail of the page you want to modify. The selected page displays in the main viewing area so that you can modify the design or add comment text. See 25 **Add Comments to the Photo Book** for more information on adding text to a photo page.

74     PART I:    iPhoto

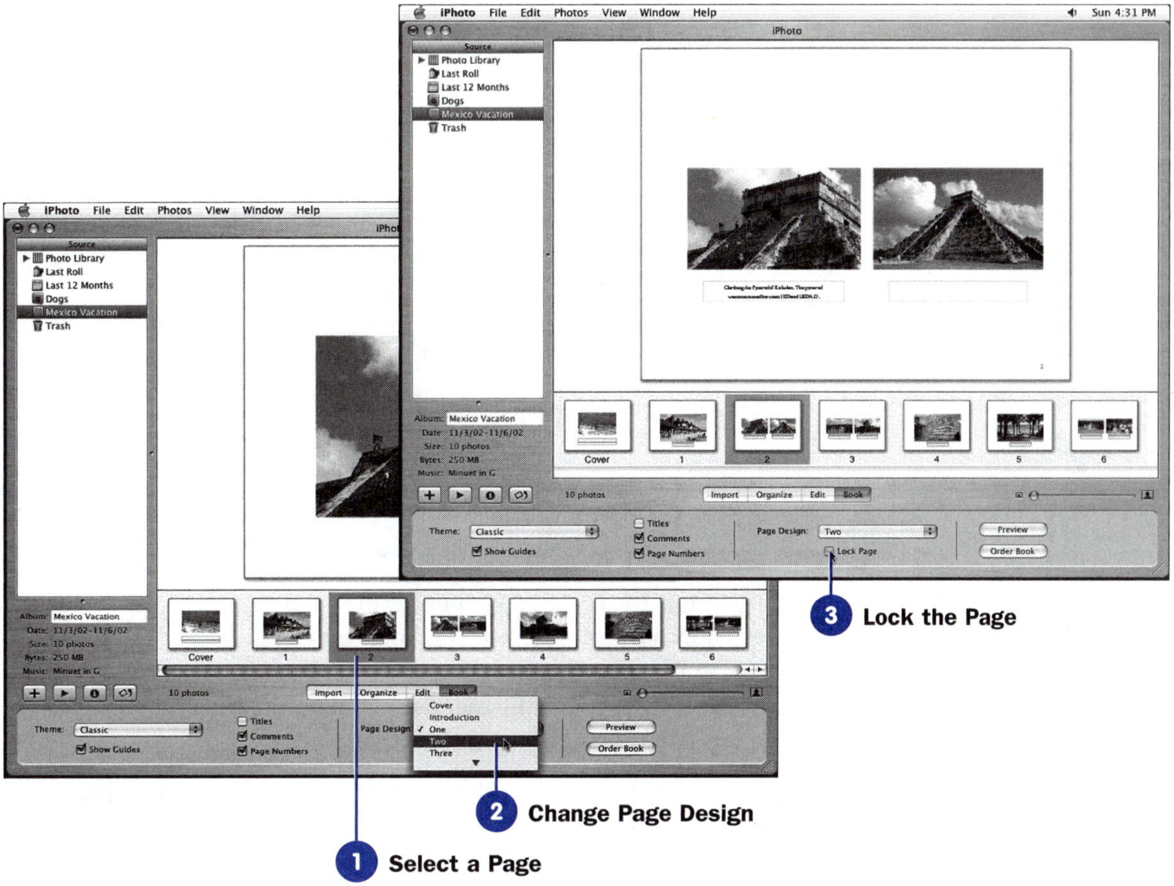

**Design Book Pages**

**Lock the Page**

**Change Page Design**

**Select a Page**

## Change Page Design

Click the arrow button next to the **Page Design** field and select the desired page design. The **Page Design** options vary based on the **Theme** selected for the photo book. Each design is named according to the number of photos that are placed on the page. For example, if you want your page to contain two photos, select the **Two Page Design**. There are two additional page designs, the **Cover** page and an **Introduction** page. The **Cover** page contains a photo and a title for the book. The **Introduction** page contains only a title field and a comments field (no photos appear on this page). Add an **Introduction** page if you want to provide a page of text.

**NOTE**

You cannot change the design of the **Cover** page. In fact, iPhoto uses the same page design for the **Cover** page of all six themes.

**CHAPTER 4:** Creating Photo Books    75

## 24 Reorder Pages in a Book

### ③ Lock the Page

Enable the check box next to the **Lock Page** option to lock the current photos on the page. Any changes you make to the surrounding pages will not affect a locked page.

Here you can see that I increased the number of photos on the second page of my photo book from one to two. The "new" photo on page 2 came from the left side of page 3, and the photos on all the remaining pages in the book scooted up to fill in the blanks. Because I've locked page 2, if I now increase the number of photos on page 1, nothing will happen to page 2. The new photos on page 1 come from the first non-locked page. In this case, the photo would come from the left side of page 3.

## 24 Reorder Pages in a Book

**Before You Begin**

✔ 21 About Photo Books
✔ 22 Select a Book Theme
✔ 23 Design Book Pages

**See Also**

→ 25 Add Comments to the Photo Book
→ 26 Print a Photo Book
→ 27 Save a Photo Book as a PDF

You can change the order of the photos in a book either in the **Book** pane or the **Organize** pane. On the **Book** pane, you can reorder photos by changing the order of the photo pages. You can change the order of the photos on an individual page, but you cannot reorder photos by moving a photo from one page to another.

If you have several photos to move, it is typically easier to reorganize the photos in the **Organize** pane. See ⑥ **Organize Photos in an Album** for more information on reordering photos in the **Organize** pane.

You reorder pages in the **Book** pane by dragging them to the desired location. As you drag the page thumbnail, iPhoto renumbers the pages in the book accordingly. When you move the page, iPhoto moves all the photos on that page to the new location in the book.

If the page contains multiple photos, you can move the photos around on that page. For example, if after moving a page that contains two photos, you want to change the order of those photos, you can click one photo and drag it behind the other photo.

### ① Select a Page

Click the thumbnail of the page containing the photos you want to move. The selected page appears in the main display area so that it can be modified.

PART I:  iPhoto

Reorder Pages in a Book  **24**

① Select a Page

② Move the Page

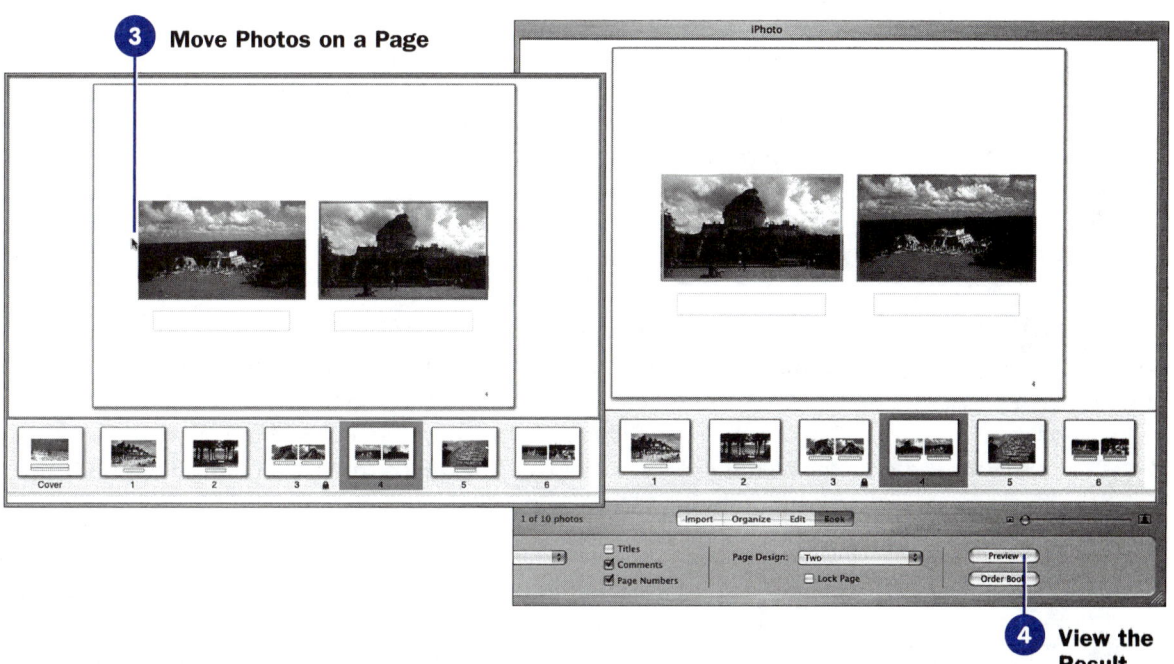

③ Move Photos on a Page

④ View the Result

**CHAPTER 4:** Creating Photo Books

## 25  Add Comments to the Photo Book

**NOTE**

iPhoto does not allow you to move another page in front of the **Cover** page. To change the cover page, switch to the **Organize** pane and select a different photo as the first photo in the album.

### 2  Move the Page

Drag the thumbnail image of the page either left or right to the desired location. As you drag the page, iPhoto reorders the pages accordingly. The photos are also reordered in the corresponding album.

### 3  Move Photos on a Page

Click to select a page that contains multiple photos. Click one of the photos on the page and drag it to the other side of another photo on that same page. iPhoto moves the selected photo on the page.

iPhoto displays a light gray box to show the photo being dragged on the page. When you release the mouse, the selected photo is automatically dropped in the selected location and the other photos on the page are moved.

### 4  View Result

Click the **Preview** button to view the photo book with the rearranged pages and photos. In this example, the beach photo was moved from the first page to the fourth page. The pyramid photos were swapped on the third page so that the observatory picture displays first on the page.

## 25  Add Comments to the Photo Book

**Before You Begin**

✔ **21** About Photo Books
✔ **22** Select a Book Theme
✔ **23** Design Book Pages

**See Also**

→ **26** Print a Photo Book
→ **27** Save a Photo Book as a PDF
→ **28** Order a Photo Book Online

You can add captions to photos in a book as long as you have the **Comments** option selected for the photo book. You can specify text in the blue comments box associated with each photo. Because the comments boxes have predefined sizes, you must make sure that your text fits within the box. If your text is too long, it will be truncated on the page. Only the text that displays in the box will be printed in the photo book.

You can adjust the font settings for the text using the **Fonts** dialog box. iPhoto assigns a default font to each photo, but you can change the font style, size, and typeface. Any font changes you make affect all the text in the comments box for the photo; the font style, size, and typeface for any other comments box in the photo book are unaffected by the changes you make to the current comments box.

## Add Comments to the Photo Book  25

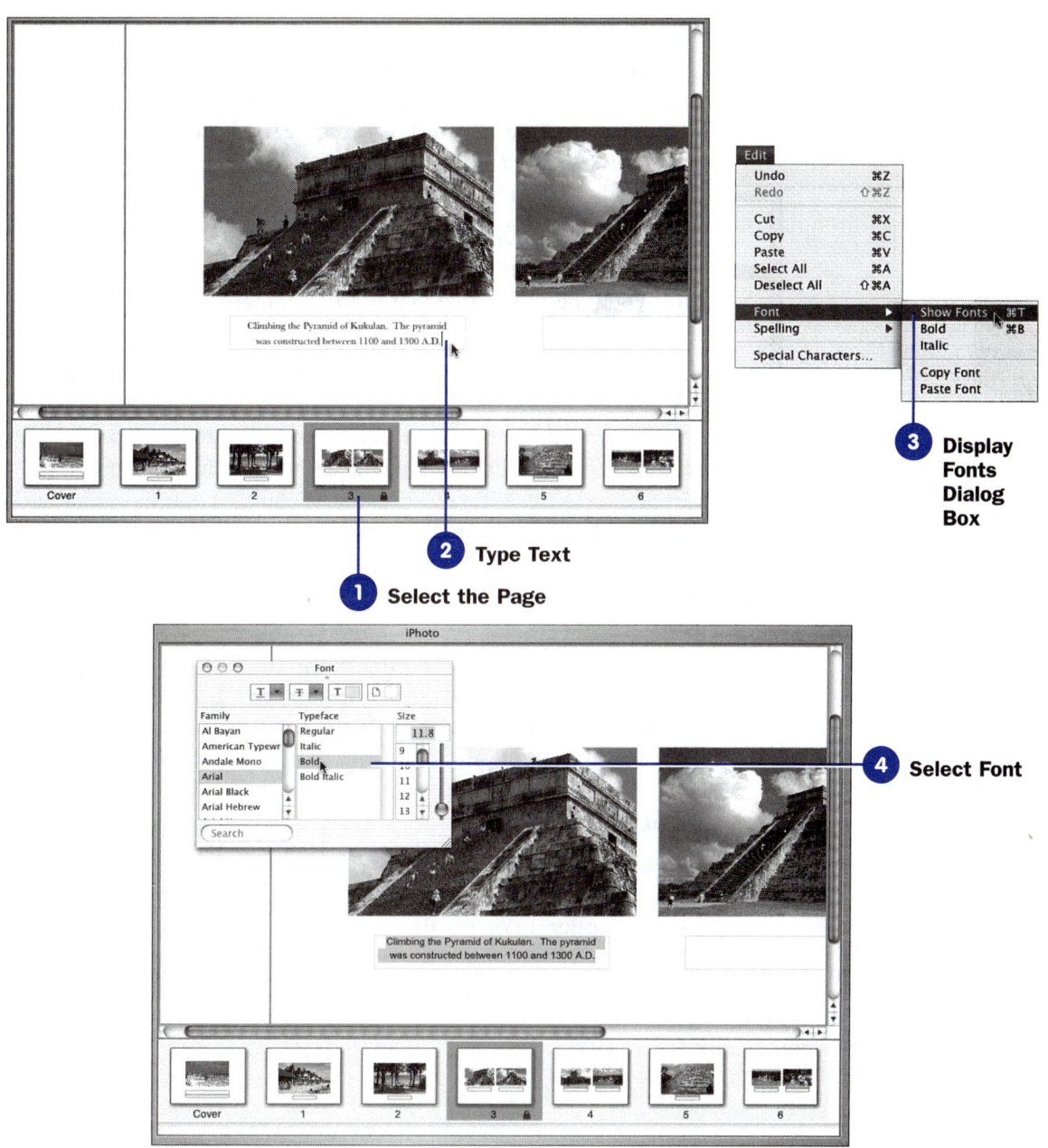

**CHAPTER 4:** Creating Photo Books

## 25  Add Comments to the Photo Book

### NOTE
Recall that the **Photo Book** theme does not allow you to add comments to the images in the book.

### TIP
If the blue boxes are not visible, make sure that the **Show Guides** check box at the bottom of the **Book** pane is enabled.

### TIP
Choose **Edit, Font, Bold** to display the text in the current comments box in bold; choose **Edit, Font, Italic** to display the text in the current comments box in italics.

### NOTE
If you want to add a bunch of text, create an **Introduction** page. To insert an **Introduction** page, select the thumbnail of the page you want to turn into an Introduction page and select **Introduction** from the **Page Design** menu at the bottom of the **Book** pane. The unlocked photos scoot backward down the pages in the photo book to make room for the new text page. Now you can add as much text to your photo book as will fit on the **Introduction** page.

### ① Select the Page

Click the thumbnail image of the page you want to modify. iPhoto displays the selected page with blue boxes around the location where you can type text. In this example, because there are two images on the selected page, there are two blue comments boxes, one directly under each image.

The text on the **Cover** page of most photo book themes is simply the title of the photo album. To change the text on the **Cover** page, you type the desired text in the comments field on the **Cover** page.

### ② Type Text

Click to place the cursor in the blue box associated with the photo you want to annotate and type the desired text for the caption for that photo. To have iPhoto check the spelling as you type, choose **Edit, Spelling, Check Spelling As You Type**.

### ③ Display Fonts Dialog Box

If you want to change the typeface, the font size, or the font style (bold, italic, or bold italic) for the text in the current comments box, choose **Edit, Font, Show Fonts** to display the **Fonts** dialog box. You might want to reduce the font size, for example, if you have a lengthy caption that doesn't fit in the comments box.

### ④ Select Font

The **Fonts** dialog box has three different columns. You can select the font **Family**, **Typeface** (or font style), and **Size**. If you don't select an option in one of the columns, iPhoto maintains the current setting. As you make selections in the **Fonts** dialog box, the results of those selections display on the photo page.

## 26 Print a Photo Book

Although the **Book** pane is designed to allow you to create a photo book that you can order online from Apple, you can also print the book on your own printer. When you print the book on your printer, iPhoto prints the book in *landscape* mode using the default margin settings for the printer. The book prints using all the settings specified on the **Book** pane.

When you select the **Print** command, iPhoto sends each page of the photo book to the printer. A dialog box displays on the screen indicating the progress.

### 1 Select the Photo Book

From the left side of the **iPhoto** window, select the album for the photo book you want to print. The **Cover** page of the selected photo book displays in the main viewing area.

If the **Book** pane is not displayed, click the **Book** button on the bottom of the window.

### 2 Display the Print Dialog Box

Choose **File**, **Print** to display the **Print** dialog box.

### 3 Select Advanced Options

When the **Print** dialog box displays, it provides the standard options, which include the selection of **Printer** and the number of **Copies**. To see more printing options, click the **Advanced Options** button.

The **Advanced Options** allow you to select a range of pages to print, to change the number of pages that print on a sheet of paper, to change the print quality, and to select two-sided printing.

### 4 Select an Advanced Print Option

Select the desired print option from the drop-down list of choices. In this case, the **Layout** option is selected. The options on the **Print** dialog box change to reflect the selection you make here. There are seven different advanced options to select:

**Before You Begin**
- ✔ 21 About Photo Books
- ✔ 22 Select a Book Theme
- ✔ 23 Design Book Pages

**See Also**
- → 27 Save a Photo Book as a PDF
- → 28 Order a Photo Book Online

**KEY TERM**

*Landscape*—A print mode that specifies the orientation of the paper. When printing in landscape mode, the long sides of the paper become the top and bottom. Therefore, the page is wider than it is tall.

CHAPTER 4:   Creating Photo Books

## 26 Print a Photo Book

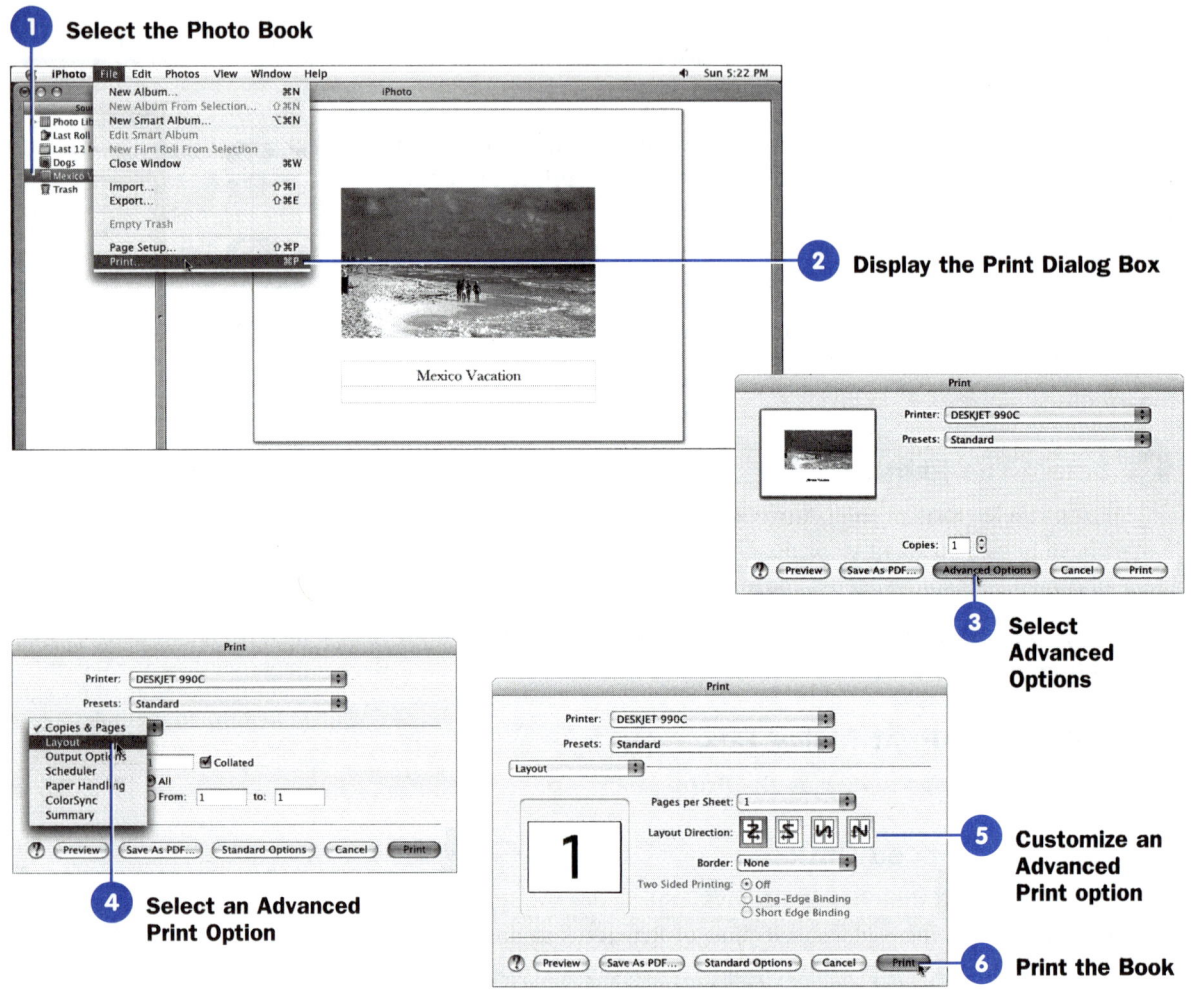

- **Copies & Pages.** Allows you to specify the range of pages you want to print from the book. You can also specify the desired number of copies.

- **Layout.** Allows you to specify the number of pages that print on each sheet of paper. You can also select a border to print on each page. If duplex (two-sided) printing is available on your printer,

## Print a Photo Book — 26

you can select this option. If you select duplex printing, you need to specify how the book will be bound. You can select from binding on the top or on the side.

- **Output Options**. Allows you to save the document as a PDF file. This is the same as clicking the **Save As PDF** button. See **27** **Save a Photo Book as a PDF** for more information on creating a PDF file.

- **Scheduler**. Allows you to specify when you want to print. For example, if you are printing something large, you might want to delay printing until a later time.

- **Paper Handling**. Allows you to print only even or odd pages. You can also print pages in reverse order, printing the last page first.

- **ColorSync**. Allows you to customize how colors are filtered during printing. You can select filters to modify the colors of your photos or to add special effects.

- **Summary**. This option simply summarizes all the print settings for your print job. If you see any settings that are not correct, select the corresponding **Advanced Option** and make the desired modifications.

### 5 Customize an Advanced Print Option

Make the desired adjustments to each **Advanced Option**. This example shows the **Paper Type/Quality** option, which provides three tabs for customizing the **Paper**, **Color Options**, and **Ink**. The **Best** radio button has been selected to have the book printed at the highest quality. (The quality settings are all printer specific, but if you select **Best**, you get the best printout for your printer.)

### 6 Print the Book

Click the **Print** button to print the book to the printer specified in the **Printer** field. If you have multiple printers available, select the desired printer from the **Printer** drop-down list. A progress dialog box appears as the photo book spools to the printer and prints.

If you want to cancel the print job, click the **Cancel** button that appears on the dialog box as iPhoto creates each page of the book.

**TIPS**

If you want to print only a range of pages from the currently selected photo book, click the **Advanced Options** button on the **Print** dialog box and then select the **From** radio button. Type the page numbers for the start and end pages.

To print multiple copies, type the desired number of copies in the **Copies** field or click the spin buttons to change the number.

## 27  Save a Photo Book as a PDF

**Before You Begin**

✔ **21** About Photo Books
✔ **22** Select a Book Theme
✔ **23** Design Book Pages

**See Also**

➔ **26** Print a Photo Book
➔ **28** Order a Photo Book Online

**KEY TERM**

*PDF (Portable Document Format)*—An electronic file format developed by Adobe for distributing electronic documents in a standardized format.

If you want to distribute your photo book digitally, a good method is to create a *PDF* version of it. By creating a PDF, you can distribute the completed photo book electronically so that others can view it using Adobe Acrobat Reader. By creating a PDF of your photo book, you can distribute a single file to others, instead of individual photo files.

When you save a photo book as a PDF file, iPhoto creates the PDF file using basically the same process you use to print the photo book. You must specify a name for the PDF file and the location where you want to store the file. As a default, iPhoto stores the file in your personal **Documents** folder, but you can store it in any other location.

### 1 Select the Photo Book

From the left side of the iPhoto window, select the album for the photo book you want to print. The **Cover** page of the selected photo book displays in the main viewing area.

### 2 Display the Print Dialog Box

Choose **File**, **Print** to display the **Print** dialog box.

### 3 Click Save As PDF

Click the **Save As PDF** button to display the **Save to File** dialog box.

### 4 Specify PDF Filename and Click Save

Type a name for the PDF file in the **Save As** field. iPhoto creates the PDF file using the specified filename and a **.PDF** file extension. To store the file in a different location than your personal **Documents** folder, select the desired location from the **Where** drop-down list.

Click the **Save** button to create the PDF file. Just like printing a document, iPhoto creates each page of the book and displays a dialog box to show the progress of the operation.

PART I:   iPhoto

## Save a Photo Book as a PDF

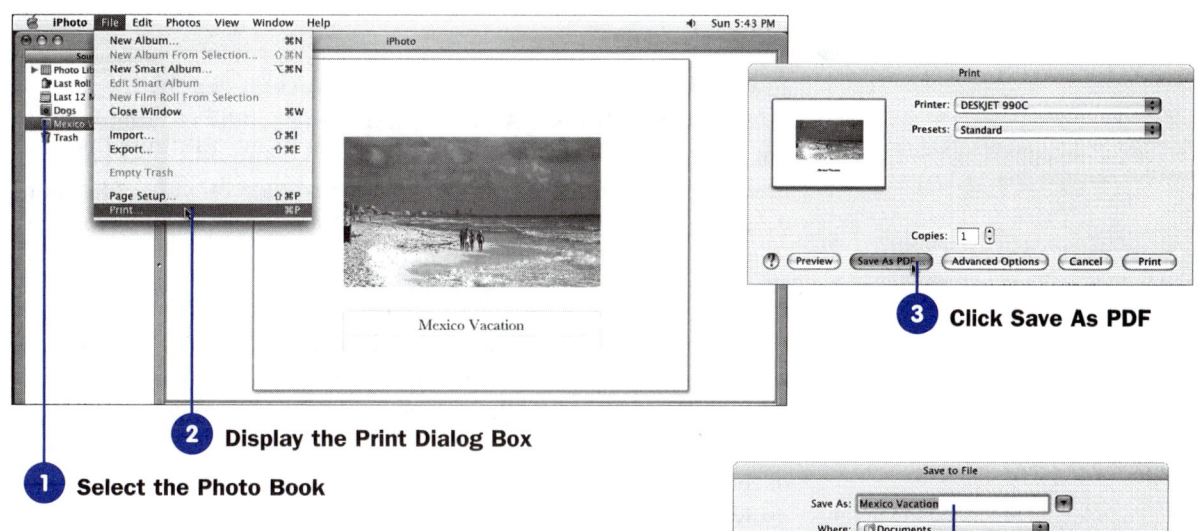

① **Select the Photo Book**

② **Display the Print Dialog Box**

③ **Click Save As PDF**

④ **Specify PDF Filename and Click Save**

⑤ **View the PDF**

**CHAPTER 4:** Creating Photo Books

## Order a Photo Book Online

**⑤ View the PDF**

To view the PDF file, you or any other user can open the file in Adobe Acrobat Reader. A free version of this reader is available, but for a small charge, you can buy a fully featured version of this product. After Adobe Acrobat Reader is installed on your computer, double-click the PDF filename in your **Documents** folder to launch the reader and display the photo book.

If you don't want to use Adobe Acrobat Reader, Mac OS X offers Preview, a program that can be used to view PDF files. To view the PDF file with Preview, open Preview and then select **File, Open** to display the **Open** dialog box. Select the PDF file you want to view from your **Documents** folder; the file opens in Preview. Each page of the PDF displays as a thumbnail image in the **Thumbnails** drawer. You can switch between pages by clicking different thumbnails.

## WEB RESOURCE

Download the free Adobe Acrobat Reader from the Adobe Web site.

http://www.adobe.com

## Order a Photo Book Online

**Before You Begin**

✔ ㉑ About Photo Books
✔ ㉒ Select a Book Theme
✔ ㉓ Design Book Pages

**See Also**

→ ㉖ Print a Photo Book
→ ㉗ Save a Photo Book as a PDF

The pricing of the books is based on the number of pages. This pricing is subject to change without notice.

You can order a hard-bound version of your photo book from Apple. When you select this option, you receive a book that is professionally bound and printed. The books all come in a 9×11.25 size with the photo you selected for your **Cover** page printed on the hard cover of the book.

Before you can order your first book, you must create a 1-Click account. This is an Apple account containing personal information such as your name, address, and credit card number. Apple uses this information when you order photo books. If you do not have an account created when you try to order for the first time, the **Set Up Account** button displays in the bottom-right corner of the **Order Book** dialog box. Follow the steps on the screens to create your 1-Click account. After your account is created, you can order a photo book by simply filling out the **Order Book** form and clicking the **Buy Now** button.

PART I:   iPhoto

## Order a Photo Book Online  28

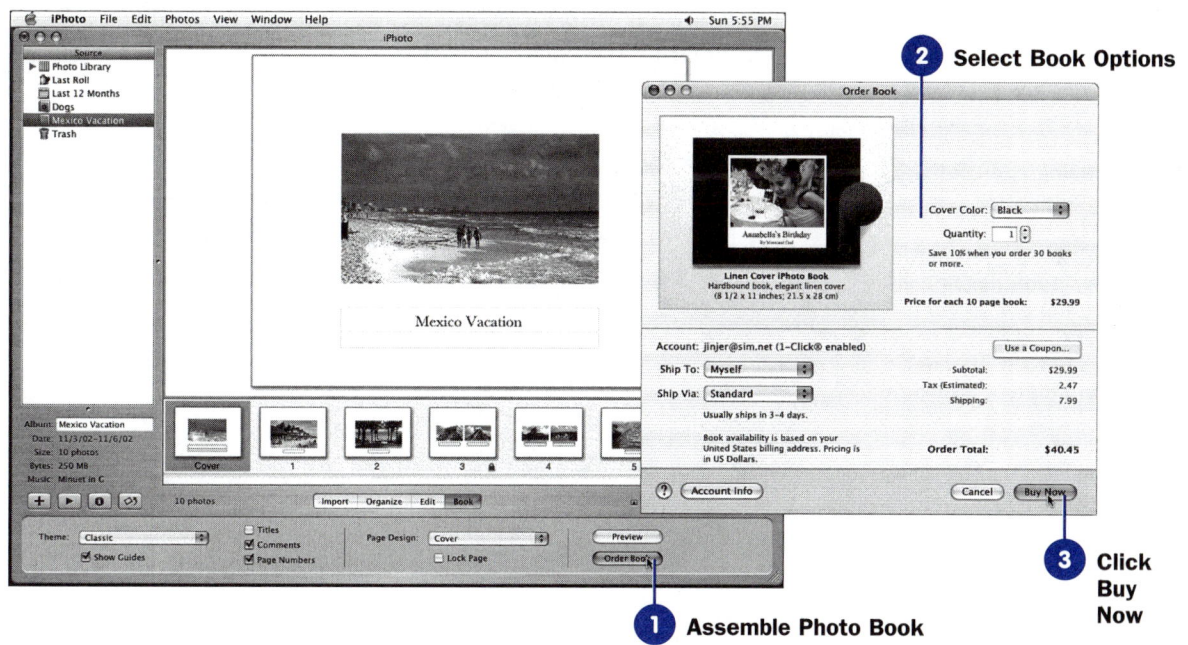

 Select Book Options

 Click Buy Now

① Assemble Photo Book

### ① Assemble Photo Book

Select the photo book you want to order online from the left side of the **iPhoto** window. Click the **Order Book** button at the bottom of the window. iPhoto creates the file it needs to upload so that you can order the hard-bound photo book. As the book file is being created, a dialog box displays the status information.

### ② Select Book Options

The **Order Book** dialog box displays the options for ordering your book. Select the color of the book cover from the **Cover Color** drop-down menu. Type the number of copies of the selected photo book you want to order in the **Quantity** field.

You must specify the shipping information. Your default address is automatically selected as the **Ship To** address. To specify another address, select the appropriate address from the **Ship To** drop-down menu. Indicate whether you want **Standard** or **Express** shipping in the **Ship Via** field. The **Shipping** cost adjusts automatically

**TIP**

Click the **Preview** button to check the book before ordering. Make any necessary corrections to the photo book and then click **Order Book** again.

**NOTE**

All books are printed with at least 10 pages. If you have less than 10 pages in your book, blank pages will be added.

**CHAPTER 4:** Creating Photo Books  87

## Order a Photo Book Online

 **TIPS**

To add a new **Ship To** address, choose **Add New Address** from the **Ship To** drop-down list. Type the new shipping address for your account.

If options are grayed out in the **Order Book** dialog box, you have not yet set up a 1-Click account with Apple. Click the **Set Up Account** button to create a 1-Click account.

based on your **Ship Via** selection. The shipping method you select does not alter the book's creation time. It takes 3 to 4 days for Apple to create the book before shipping.

**③ Click Buy Now**

Click the **Buy Now** button to send your photo book order to Apple. The book will be printed using the specified options.

# 5

# Creating a Slideshow in iPhoto

**IN THIS CHAPTER:**

- **29** Play a Slideshow
- **30** Adjust Slideshow Display Settings
- **31** Customize Music for a Slideshow
- **32** Export a Slideshow to QuickTime
- **33** Export a Slideshow to iDVD

## 29  Play a Slideshow

One cool feature of iPhoto is its built-in slideshow capability. You can quickly display the photos in your library or an individual album by playing the slideshow. When you play the slideshow for an album, iPhoto displays each photo so that it fills your entire screen.

iPhoto also allows you to customize the slideshow by controlling the display length of the photos and randomizing the order in which the photos are displayed. You can also customize the music that plays with the slideshow.

Not only can you view the slideshow within iPhoto, but you can also export it as a QuickTime movie or place it on a DVD in iDVD.

## 29  Play a Slideshow

**Before You Begin**

✔ **4** Create New Albums
✔ **5** Create a Smart Album

**See Also**

→ **30** Adjust Slideshow Display Settings
→ **31** Customize Music for a Slideshow
→ **32** Export a Slideshow to QuickTime
→ **33** Export a Slideshow to iDVD

Because slideshows are one of the most basic features of iPhoto, it is fairly simple to play one. In fact, you can play a slideshow for your entire **Photo Library** or for an individual photo album by simply selecting the library or album and clicking the **Play** button at the bottom of the left side of the iPhoto window.

You play a slideshow from the **Organize** pane in iPhoto. Before clicking the **Play** button, make sure that the appropriate photo album is selected. iPhoto plays all photos in the selected album. If you want to create a custom album for your slideshow, you can do so and then add the appropriate photos. See **4** **Create New Albums** for information on creating photo albums. See **5** **Create a Smart Album** for information on creating photo albums.

When iPhoto plays the slideshow, it uses default settings—each photo displays for about two seconds, and the photos appear in the order they are listed in the album. You can customize the slideshow display settings by using the **Slideshow Settings** dialog box. See **30** **Adjust Slideshow Display Settings** for more information on customizing the slideshow display. iPhoto also assigns a default song that plays when you view the slideshow. The default song, **Minuet in G**, is assigned to all photo albums, but you can change it to any other song in your iTunes library. See **31** **Customize Music for a Slideshow** for information on customizing the music for each slideshow.

Play a Slideshow 29

① **Select Photo Album**

② **Play Slideshow**

③ **View the Slideshow**

① **Select Photo Album**

On the **Organize** pane, click the name of the photo album for which you want to view a slideshow. If you select the main **Photo Library**, the slideshow will show every photo in your library.

 **TIP**

Click the **Organize** button to view the **Organize** pane.

② **Play Slideshow**

Click the **Play** button on the bottom-left of the window.

③ **View the Slideshow**

iPhoto plays the slideshow and displays each photo in the order in which it appears in the photo album. The photos are displayed full-screen on a black background on the screen.

**CHAPTER 5:** Creating a Slideshow in iPhoto

## 30  Adjust Slideshow Display Settings

**TIPS**

You can change the speed of the slideshow by pressing the **Up** arrow key to increase it or the **Down** arrow key to decrease it.

Use the **Right** and **Left** arrow keys to move through the slides manually.

As the slideshow plays, the music assigned to the album also plays. iPhoto assigns the default song, **Minuet in G**, to each album, but you can change that music. See **31 Customize Music for a Slideshow** for information on customizing the music for each slideshow. Use the volume buttons on the keyboard to adjust the volume of the music.

To stop the slideshow, click anywhere on the screen with the mouse. You can also stop the slideshow by pressing **Esc**. To pause the slideshow on a particular image, press the space bar; press the space bar again to resume the automatic play of the slideshow.

## 30  Adjust Slideshow Display Settings

**Before You Begin**

✔ **4** Create New Albums

✔ **5** Create a Smart Album

✔ **29** Play a Slideshow

**See Also**

→ **31** Customize Music for a Slideshow

→ **32** Export a Slideshow to QuickTime

→ **33** Export a Slideshow to iDVD

When you view a slideshow in iPhoto, it applies the default settings to the slideshow. The iPhoto defaults are to display each photo in the order it is listed in the photo album, with each photo displaying for two seconds on the screen. The slideshow will play once through and then stop, returning to the iPhoto **Organize** pane when play is finished. A default song plays during the slideshow, looping around to play continuously as long as the slides are being displayed. You can customize those settings using the **Slideshow** dialog box.

iPhoto allows you to specify the amount of time, in seconds, that you want each photo to display. This value applies to *all* photos in the slideshow, not to individual photos. You can also have the photos display in random order, instead of the order in which they are listed in the photo album.

If you enable the **Repeat slideshow** option, the slideshow plays continuously until you stop it. Otherwise, iPhoto displays all the slides once and then returns to the **Organize** pane.

**1 Display Slideshow Dialog Box**

Click the **Slideshow** button at the bottom of the left side of the **Organize** pane to display the **Slideshow** dialog box.

**2 Select Transition**

Click the arrow button next to the **Transition** field and select the transition. When you select a transition, a sample of the transition displays in the **Preview** window. If your transition has a direction, select the transition direction from the **Direction** field. You can also specify the speed of the transition by dragging the **Speed** slider.

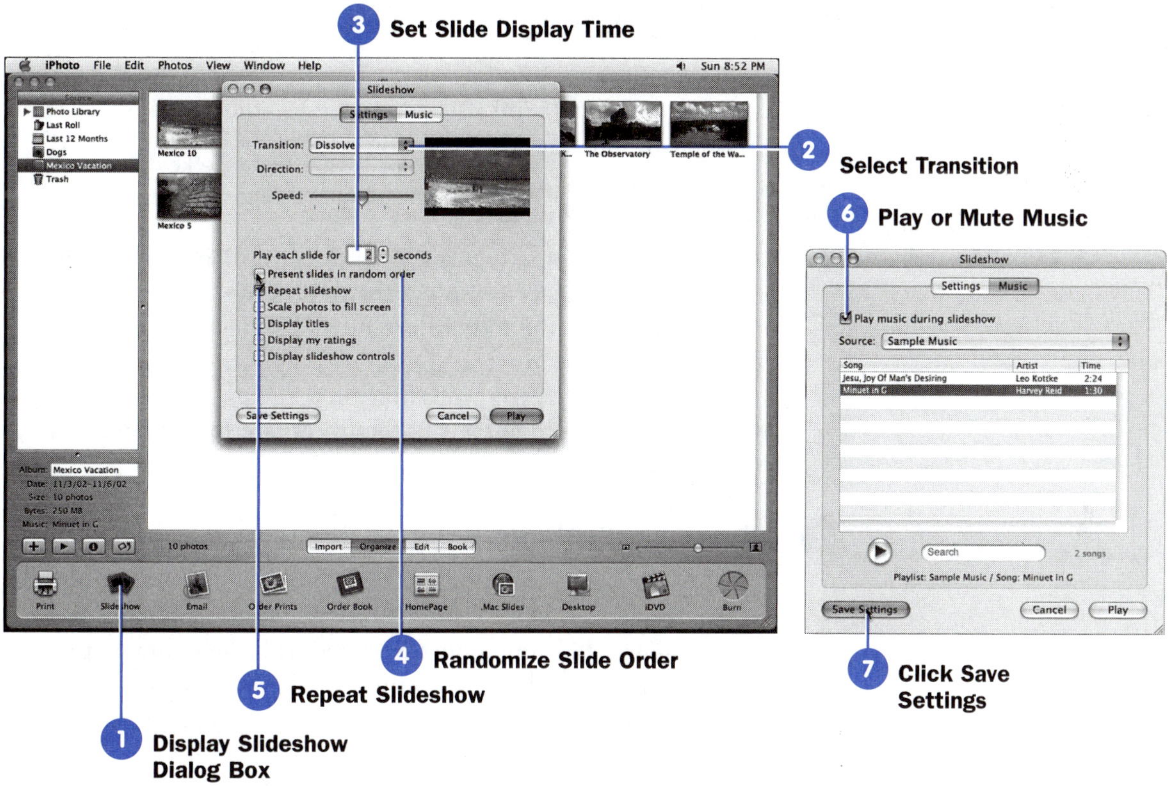

# Adjust Slideshow Display Settings  29

**3 Set Slide Display Time**

**2 Select Transition**

**6 Play or Mute Music**

**4 Randomize Slide Order**

**5 Repeat Slideshow**

**7 Click Save Settings**

**1 Display Slideshow Dialog Box**

## 3 Set Slide Display Time

Click the **Up Arrow** button next to the **Play each slide for** box to increase the display time of each slide; click the **Down Arrow** button to decrease the display time. You can also type a number in the field, if desired.

**TIP**

You can type a value between 1 and 30 in the **Play each slide for** box.

## 4 Randomize Slide Order

Enable the **Present photos in random order** check box if you want iPhoto to randomly display photos from the photo album. This option is nice if you intend to leave the slideshow running continuously. If you leave this option disabled, iPhoto displays the photos in the same order in which they are listed in the photo album.

**NOTE**

Enabling the **Present photos in random order** option automatically enables the **Repeat slideshow** option.

**CHAPTER 5:** Creating a Slideshow in iPhoto

**NOTE**

You can specify whether you want to display your photo titles and ratings with the slideshow by clicking the **Display titles** and **Display my ratings** check boxes.

## 5 Repeat Slideshow

Enable the **Repeat slideshow** check box if you want the slideshow to continue playing until you stop it. To stop the slideshow, click anywhere on the screen or press **Esc**.

## 6 Play or Mute Music

Click the **Music** button to display the music options. By default, iPhoto plays a song as it displays the photos. You can mute the music by disabling the **Play music during slideshow** check box. The default song, **Minuet in G**, is one of the sample songs that comes with iPhoto. If you want to change the music that plays for the slideshow, refer to 31 **Customize Music for a Slideshow** for more information.

## 7 Click Save Settings

Click the **Save Settings** button at the bottom of the **Slideshow** dialog box to save the new settings for your slideshow. iPhoto saves the slideshow settings in a file associated with the photo album. The settings are referenced each time you view the slideshow. iPhoto also saves the settings if you click the **Play Slideshow** button on the **Slideshow** dialog box.

# 31 Customize Music for a Slideshow

### Before You Begin

✓ 29 Play a Slideshow

### See Also

→ 30 Adjust Slideshow Display Settings

→ 32 Export a Slideshow to QuickTime

→ 33 Export a Slideshow to iDVD

→ (59) Create a Smart Playlist

You can customize the music that plays when you view a slideshow by assigning a specific song to the photo album or **Photo Library**. When you create a photo album, iPhoto automatically assigns a song to the album. The default song is called **Minuet in G**. You can see the music assigned to the photo album by clicking the **Information** button (the *i* in a circle) at the bottom of the left pane in the **Organize** pane. See 9 **Set Photo Information** for more information about the **Information** button.

You can customize the music for each photo album by selecting one of your iTunes songs from the **Slideshow** dialog box. When you assign a song to the slideshow, that same song is assigned to the photo album.

## Customize Music for a Slideshow

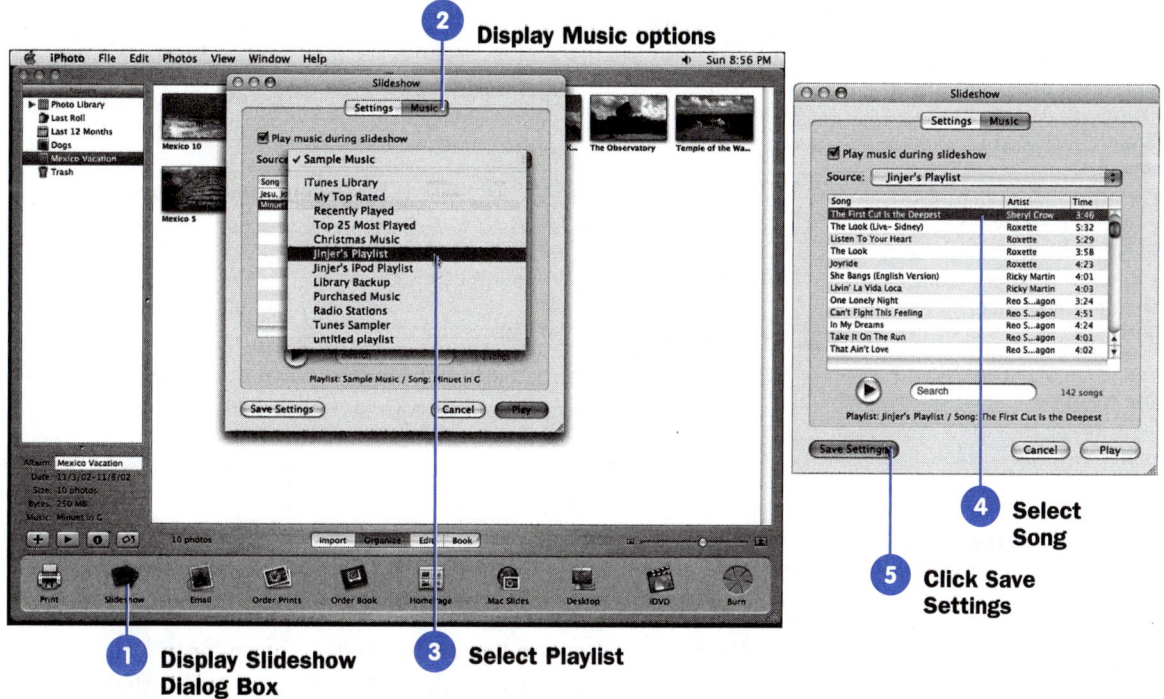

① **Display Slideshow Dialog Box**

Click the **Slideshow** button at the bottom of the **Organize** pane to display the **Slideshow** dialog box.

② **Display the Music Options**

Click the **Music** button to display the options for setting the music for your slideshow.

③ **Select Playlist**

Make sure that the **Music** check box is enabled. From the drop-down menu of playlists, select the desired *playlist*. You can select any of your iTunes playlists or select the iTunes library to view a list of all the music you have in iTunes.

### KEY TERM

*Playlist*—A collection of songs organized by theme, album, singer, composer, or some other category of your choice. See  **About Playlists** for information on playlists.

### NOTE

iPhoto provides some sample music that can be used with your slideshow. Select the **Sample Music** playlist to see the available songs.

**CHAPTER 5:** Creating a Slideshow in iPhoto

 **Export a Slideshow to QuickTime**

## TIPS

If you don't want any music to play while the slideshow is running, disable the **Music** check box.

Click the **Play** button (the black right arrowhead) in the **Slideshow** dialog box to preview a song before assigning it to your slideshow.

### ④ Select Song

Select the song in the list that you want to assign to the slideshow. You can use the scrollbar to scroll through the list of songs in the selected playlist.

You can also search for a song in the selected playlist by typing text in the **Search** field. As you type, the list scrolls to match the search string.

### ⑤ Click Save Settings

Click the **Save Settings** button at the bottom of the **Slideshow** dialog box to save the new settings for your slideshow. iPhoto also saves the settings if you click the **Play Slideshow** button.

---

 **Export a Slideshow to QuickTime**

### Before You Begin

✔ ㉙ Play a Slideshow

### See Also

→ ㉚ Adjust Slideshow Display Settings

→ ㉛ Customize Music for a Slideshow

→ ㉝ Export a Slideshow to iDVD

If you want to share your slideshow with other users, you can save it as a *QuickTime* movie that can be viewed on any computer by simply loading the QuickTime viewer available from Apple. By creating a QuickTime movie, you don't have to worry about whether the person who will view your slideshow has iPhoto on their machine. In fact, QuickTime movies can be played on machines running Microsoft Windows.

### WEB RESOURCE

Visit this site for information about the QuickTime movie player and to download a free copy of the player for use on computers running Mac OS or Microsoft Windows.

http://www.apple.com/quicktime/download

To create a QuickTime movie, you must export the photos in a photo album as a QuickTime file. When you select a photo album for export, iPhoto exports all the photos in the order in which they are listed in the album. If you want the exported slideshow to play the photos in a different order, you must reorder the photos in the photo album before exporting it. See ⑥ **Organize Photos in an Album** for more information on ordering photos.

### KEY TERM

*QuickTime*—A multiplatform software program developed by Apple to handle multimedia files such as video, audio, and animation.

**Export a Slideshow to QuickTime** 32

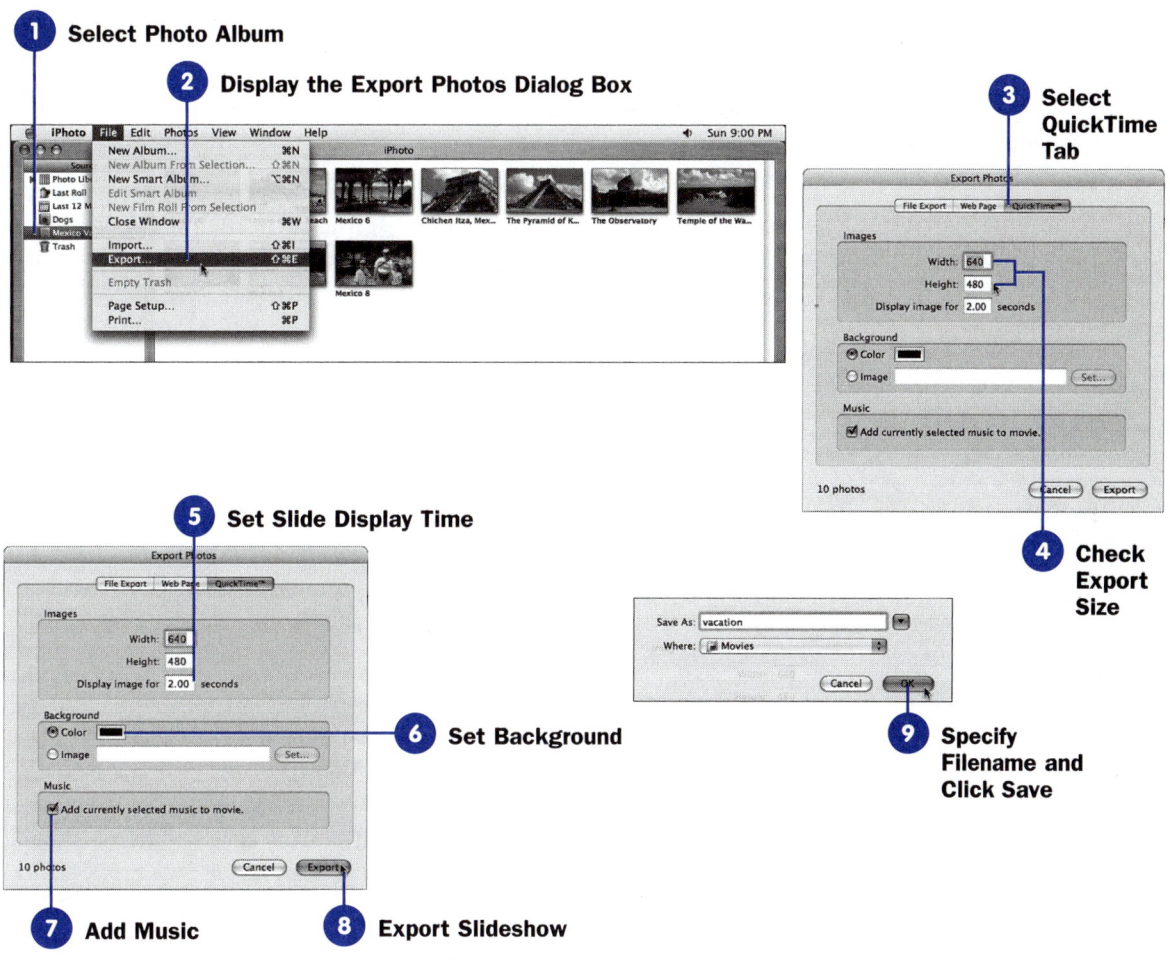

### ① Select Photo Album

From the **Organize** pane, select the album of photos you want to export. Make sure that none of the photos in the album are selected so that iPhoto will export the entire album.

### ② Display the Export Photos Dialog Box

Choose **File**, **Export** to display the **Export Photos** dialog box.

CHAPTER 5:  Creating a Slideshow in iPhoto     97

**32** Export a Slideshow to QuickTime

### TIP
To export only a portion of the album, hold down the ⌘ key and click to select the individual photos you want to export.

### KEY TERM
*Pixel*—A unit used to measure the size of an image or the supported resolution of a monitor.

### ③ Select QuickTime Tab

If it is not already not selected, click the **QuickTime** tab on the **Export Photos** dialog box to display the options for QuickTime movies.

The options on the **QuickTime** tab allow you to customize the slideshow creation. Keep in mind that none of the photos settings you might have specified in the **Slideshow Settings** dialog box affect the export of the QuickTime movie.

### ④ Check Export Size

By default, iPhoto exports the QuickTime movie to a size of 640×480 *pixels* (these values are in the **Width** and **Height** fields). This is a common size for viewing photos and ensures that all monitors can display the photos in the movie. You can adjust this size if desired. Make sure that you keep the resolution small enough to be viewed on the monitor.

### ⑤ Set Slide Display Time

You can change the display time of each photo in the movie by typing a different value in the **Display image for** field. The value you type is the length of time each photo is displayed. The total length of the QuickTime movie can be determined by multiplying the number of photos by the amount of time specified here.

### ⑥ Set Background

By default, QuickTime displays your images against a black background. To use a different background color, click the color square to display the **Colors** dialog box. Select the desired color for your background and click the red **Close** button on the top-left corner of the dialog box to close the **Colors** dialog box. Your selection displays in the color square in the **Export Photos** dialog box.

If you want your photos to display against a background image, enable the **Image** radio button and then click the **Set** button. In the **Open** dialog box that appears, select the image you want to use as the background and click **OK**. The image filename appears in the **Export Photos** dialog box.

PART I:   iPhoto

# Export a Slideshow to iDVD 33

**7  Add Music**

Enable the **Add currently selected music to movie** check box to add the music associated with the photo album to the QuickTime movie.

**8  Export Slideshow**

Click the **Export** button at the bottom of the **Export Photos** dialog box to create the QuickTime movie using the specified settings.

**9  Specify Filename and Click Save**

Type a filename for the QuickTime movie in the **Save as** field. iPhoto automatically appends the **.MOV** file extension. To store the file in a different location than your **Movies** folder, select that location from the **Where** drop-down list.

Click the **Save** button to create the movie file. iPhoto creates each slide of the movie file and displays a dialog box to show the progress.

> **NOTE**
>
> When you use the iPhoto **Slideshow** dialog box to select a song for your slideshow, as described in **31 Customize Music for a Slideshow**, iPhoto also assigns that song to the photo album. QuickTime uses the song assigned to the photo album when it creates the movie. To change the song associated with the photo album, open the **Slideshow** dialog box.

## 33  Export a Slideshow to iDVD

You can place your slideshow on a DVD using iDVD. When you transfer your slideshow to iDVD, iPhoto transfers all the photos in the selected photo album along with the associated music file.

After iPhoto has transferred the slideshow to iDVD, iDVD opens so that you can customize the look of the DVD. You can customize the DVD in several ways, including customizing the background and changing the menu. See **144 Create a Custom Background** and **146 Change Menu Title** for information on customizing the DVD. See **156 Create a Slideshow Using an iPhoto Album** for information on working with the slideshow within iDVD.

**1  Select Photo Album**

In the **Organize** pane, select the album of photos you want to export as a slideshow to iDVD. Make sure that none of the photos in the album are selected so that iPhoto will export the entire album. If any of the photos are selected, only those photos are exported to iDVD.

**Before You Begin**

✔ **29** Play a Slideshow
✔ **30** Adjust Slideshow Display Settings
✔ **31** Customize Music for a Slideshow

**See Also**

→ **32** Export a Slideshow to QuickTime
→ **139** Create a Menu for a Movie with Chapter Markers
→ **156** Create a Slideshow Using an iPhoto Album

CHAPTER 5:   Creating a Slideshow in iPhoto          99

## 33  Export a Slideshow to iDVD

**1** Select Photo Album

**2** Transfer Slideshow to iDVD

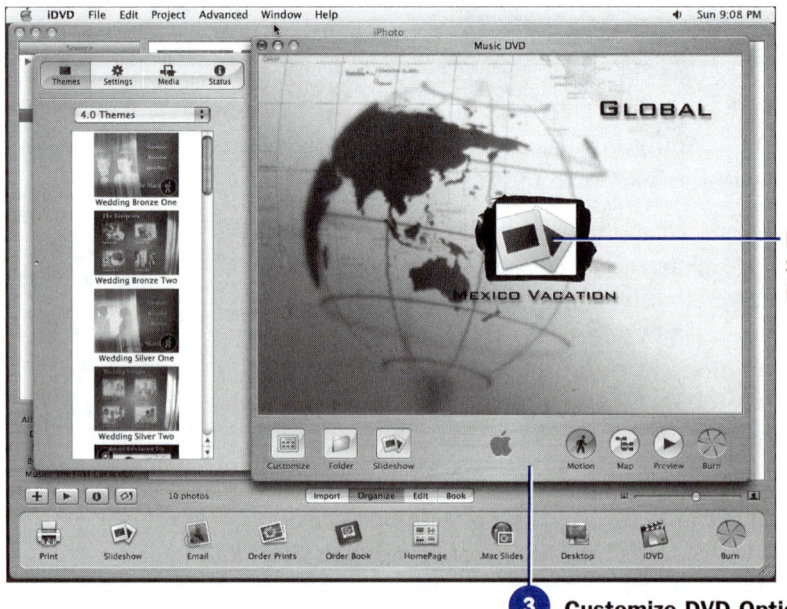

**DVD Menu Displays Slideshow from iPhoto**

**3** Customize DVD Options

PART I:  iPhoto

## ② Transfer Slideshow to iDVD

Click the iDVD button at the bottom of the **Organize** pane to transfer the album photos to iDVD. iDVD adds the photos as a slideshow with the same name as the selected iPhoto album.

## ③ Customize DVD Options

The iPhoto slideshow displays on the menu for the DVD. The iPhoto album name becomes the name of the slideshow on the menu. You can change the name of the slideshow within iDVD. See **147 Change Text of Buttons/Titles** for more information on changing text in iDVD.

Click the **Customize** button on the **iDVD** window to display the **Customize** drawer. The **Customize** drawer provides options for selecting a new theme to change the background of the DVD, setting the text options, selecting the audio for the DVD menu, and adding photos and other movies to the menu.

You can also customize the slideshow layout from within iDVD by double-clicking the menu option. See **156 Create a Slideshow Using an iPhoto Album** for information on customizing the slideshow within iDVD.

# 6

# Sharing Photos

**IN THIS CHAPTER:**

- **34** Print Photos from iPhoto
- **35** Create a Greeting Card
- **36** Print a Contact Sheet
- **37** Order Prints from an Online Photo Printer
- **38** Email Photos
- **39** Publish Photos to View on the Internet
- **40** Share a Slideshow over the Internet
- **41** Set iDisk Slideshow as Screensaver
- **42** Create a Photo Screensaver
- **43** Add a Photo to the Desktop
- **44** Create a Photo CD
- **45** Export a Photo

## 34  Print Photos from iPhoto

Not only does iPhoto make a good photo management solution, it also provides different methods for you to share your photos with other people. If you have a photo printer, you can print your own photos from iPhoto. Not only can you print portraits, you can also create greeting cards and contact sheets using iPhoto. If you don't want to print the photos yourself, you can order photos printed on high-quality photo paper online from photo-processing sources.

You can share photos electronically by emailing them to other people or by placing them on a Web site. Photos can also be used as a screensaver on your own computer. If you have a CD burner, you should consider creating a photo CD. Photo CDs are good not only as a method of sharing photos with others, but also for archiving photos.

## 34  Print Photos from iPhoto

**Before You Begin**

✔ **3** About the Photo Library and Albums

✔ **6** Organize Photos in an Album

**See Also**

→ **35** Create a Greeting Card

→ **36** Print a Contact Sheet

→ **37** Order Photos from an Online Photo Printer

You can print photos directly from iPhoto. Not only can you print a full-size photo, you can have iPhoto size the photo to a common print size, such as 5×7. This feature works very well if you want to print your photos on your own color photo printer instead of paying for them to be printed commercially.

When you print your photos, you first select the photos you want printed. iPhoto allows you to select one or multiple photos. If you are printing smaller photos (at sizes such as 5×7, 4×6, or 2×3), you can either print multiple photos on one page or print each photo on a separate page.

iPhoto comes with preset printing options for some printers. These presets are designed to work with specific types of paper. If iPhoto provides these preset printing options, they are listed in the **Presets** field on the **Print** dialog box. If the presets are available, you select the style that matches the type of paper you are printing on to achieve the best results. If you don't select a preset option, iPhoto uses the standard printer settings to print the photos.

**TIP**

If you want to print all the photos in an album, make sure that *none* of the photos are selected on the **Organize** pane. Instead, select just the album in the left column.

### ❶ Select Photos

On the **Organize** pane, select the photos you want to print. To select multiple photos, hold down the ⌘ key while you click each photo thumbnail. You can select photos from the main **Photo Library** or from an individual album.

PART I:   iPhoto

Print Photos from iPhoto 34

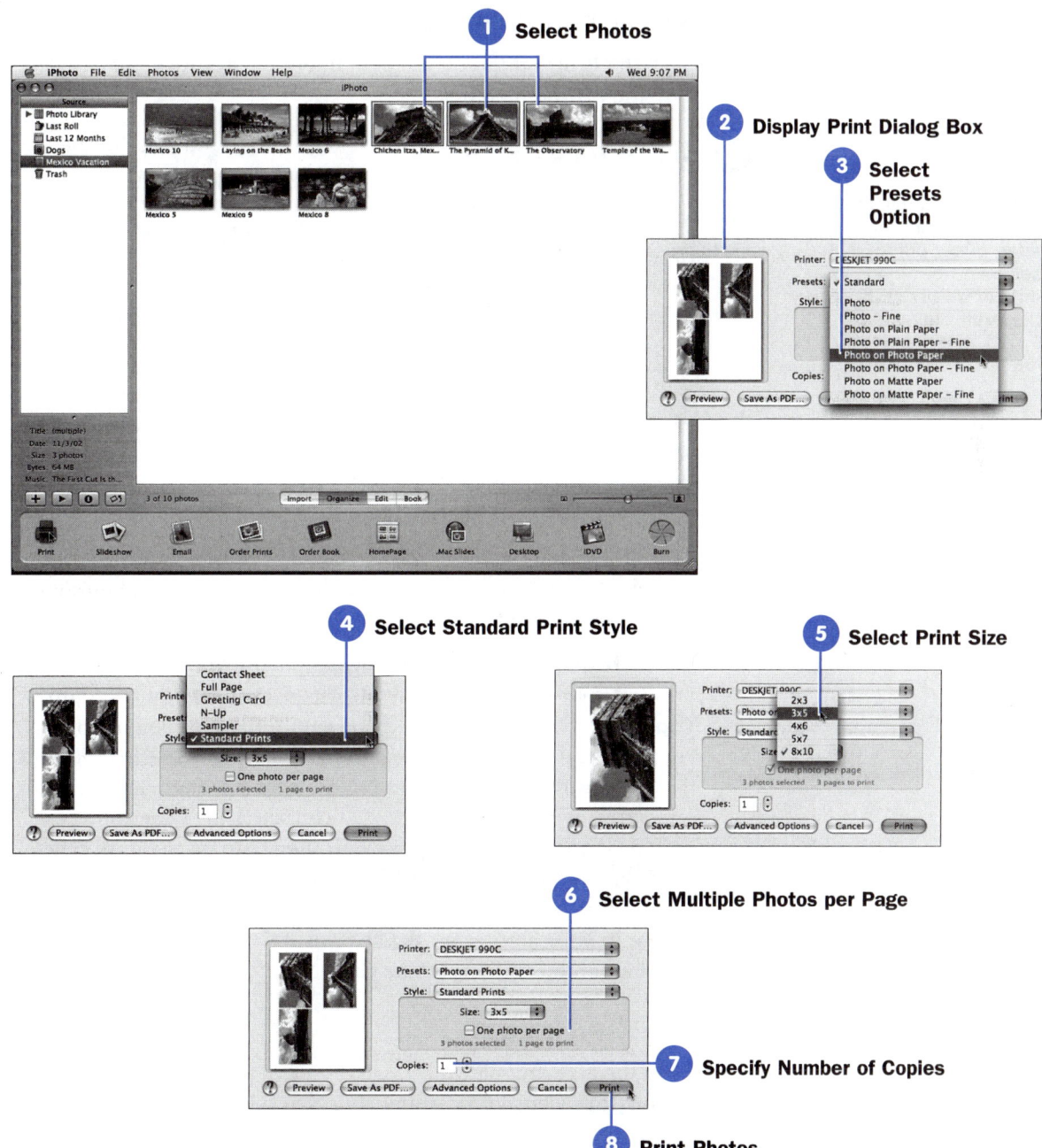

CHAPTER 6: Sharing Photos

## 34 Print Photos from iPhoto

**TIPS**

You can also display the **Print** dialog box by choosing **File, Print**.

If you have multiple printers, make sure that the appropriate printer is selected from the **Printer** drop-down list at the top of the **Print** dialog box.

### 2 Display Print Dialog Box

Click the **Print** button on the bottom of the **Organize** pane to display the **Print** dialog box.

### 3 Select Presets Option

From the **Presets** drop-down menu, select the option that matches the type of paper you are printing on. For example, the **HP DeskJet 990C** provides **Preset** options for printing photos on plain paper, matte paper, and photo paper. If you have photo paper in your printer, you can select the **Print on Photo Paper—Fine** option to get the highest quality photo from this printer.

The available **Preset** options vary for each printer. Select the **Preset** option that most closely matches your individual setup to achieve the best results.

### 4 Select Standard Print Style

From the **Style** drop-down menu, select the **Standard Prints** option. The options on the **Print** dialog change to include options for the desired print size of the photos.

The **Style** drop-down list also provides other layout options for printing your photos. For example, the default style option, **Full Page**, prints the photo on the page within the specified margins. You can print a specific number of photos on the page by selecting the **N-Up** option. The **Sampler** option creates a photo layout using one of the available templates. You can select the **Greeting Card** option to create a greeting card with the photo on the front cover. See **35 Create a Greeting Card** for more information on creating greeting cards. You can provide contact sheets showing the photos in your library. See **36 Print a Contact Sheet** for more information on creating contact sheets.

### 5 Select Print Size

From the **Size** drop-down list, select desired print size. The **Size** options vary depending on the **Style** you selected.

106    PART I:    iPhoto

## (6) Select Multiple Photos per Page

Make sure that the **One photo per page** check box is not selected if you want iPhoto to print two photos on the same page. iPhoto can print two photos on the page only if you select the 5×7, 4×6, 3×5, or 2×3 size. If you select the 8×10 size, only one photo prints on the page, regardless of whether the check box is selected.

If the **One photo per page** check box is enabled, iPhoto prints only one photo on each page, even if there is room for two photos.

## (7) Specify Number of Copies

By default, iPhoto prints one copy of the selected photo(s). You can print multiple copies by typing the desired number in the **Copies** field. You can also use the spin buttons to specify the desired number of copies.

**NOTE**

iPhoto indicates the number of photos that were selected for print and the number of pages that will be printed under the **One photo per page** check box.

## (8) Print Photos

Click the **Print** button at the bottom of the **Print** dialog box to send the selected photos to the printer.

## (35) Create a Greeting Card

Not only can you use iPhoto to print photos, you can also use it to create greeting cards. When you print a greeting card, iPhoto prints the selected photo as the cover for the card.

You have two options when you print a photo greeting card: You can create a single-fold or a double-fold card. With both card types, the photo appears on the cover of the card—the difference is how the card is folded. If you create a single-fold card, the card is printed so that you can fold the page in half with the photo displaying on the front of the card. If you select the double-fold option, you must fold the paper twice so that the photo appears on the cover of the card. You need to fold the paper in half vertically and then again horizontally. The double-fold option produces a smaller card.

### Before You Begin

✔ (3) About the Photo Library and Albums

✔ (6) Organize Photos in an Album

### See Also

→ (34) Print Photos from iPhoto

→ (36) Print a Contact Sheet

→ (37) Order Photos from an Online Photo Printer

**CHAPTER 6:** Sharing Photos

**Create a Greeting Card**

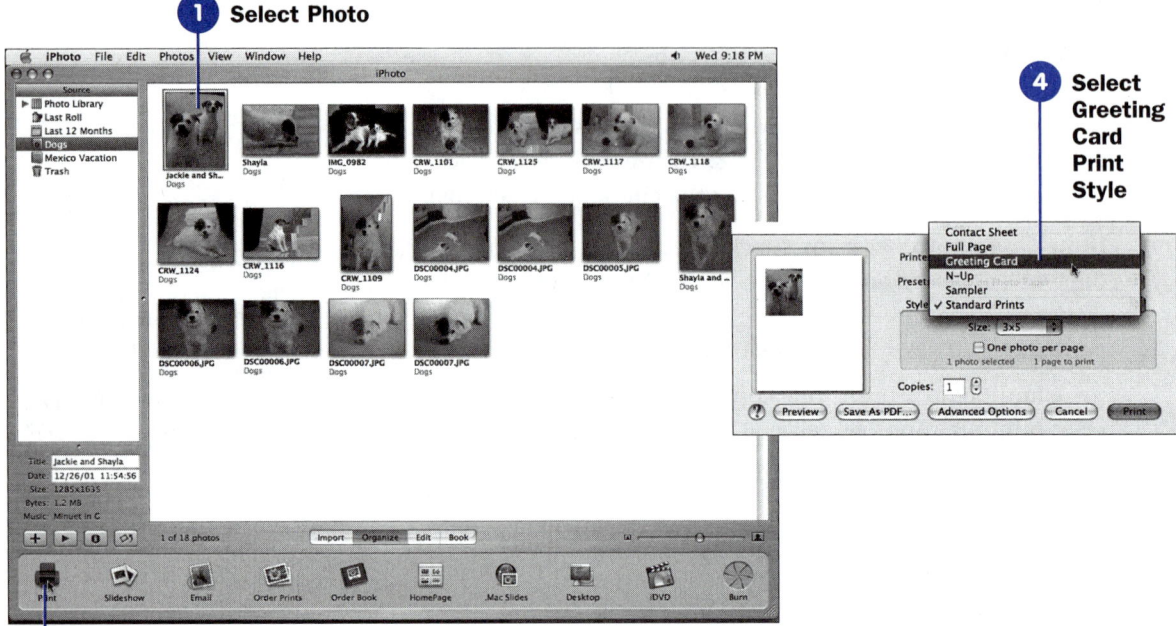

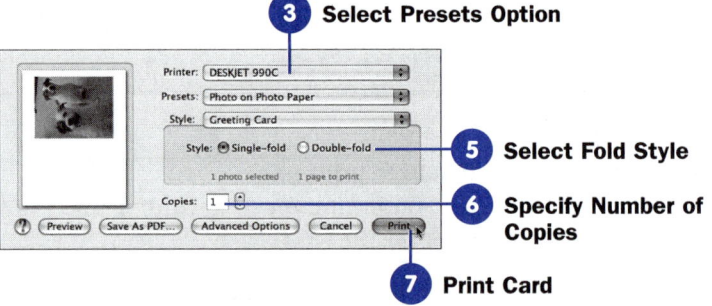

### ① Select Photo

On the **Organize** pane, select the photo you want to print on the greeting card. You can select photos from the main **Photo Library** or from an individual album.

To select multiple photos, hold down the ⌘ key while you click on each photo thumbnail. If you select multiple photos, iPhoto prints each photo on a separate greeting card.

## Create a Greeting Card    35

**② Display Print Dialog Box**

Click the **Print** button at the bottom of the **Organize** pane to display the **Print** dialog box. You can also choose **File**, **Print** to display the **Print** dialog box.

**③ Select Presets Option**

From the **Presets** drop-down menu, select the option that matches the type of paper you are printing on. For example, the **HP DeskJet 990C** printer provides **Preset** options for printing photos on plain paper, matte paper, and photo paper. If you have photo paper in your printer, you can select the **Print on Photo Paper—Fine** option to get the highest quality photo from this printer.

The available **Preset** options vary for each printer. Select the **Preset** option that most closely matches your individual setup to achieve the best results.

**④ Select Greeting Card Print Style**

From the **Style** drop-down list, select the **Greeting Card** option.

The **Style** drop-down list also provides other layout options for printing your photos. For example, the default style option, **Full Page**, prints the photo on the page within the specified margins. You can print a specific number of photos on the page by selecting the **N-Up** option. The **Sampler** option creates a photo layout using one of the available templates. You can select the **Standard Prints** option to create photos at standard print sizes, such as 4×6. See **34 Print Photos from iPhoto** for more information on printing standard photos. You can provide contact sheets showing the photos in your library. See **36 Print a Contact Sheet** for more information on creating contact sheets.

**⑤ Select Fold Style**

Enable the **Single-fold** option if you want to create a card by folding the paper in half. Enable the **Double-fold** option to create a card by folding the paper into fourths.

**⑥ Specify Number of Copies**

By default, iPhoto prints one copy of the greeting card with the selected photo. If you selected multiple photos, iPhoto prints one

**TIP**

The preview area on the **Print** dialog box shows how the printed page will look with the current selections.

CHAPTER 6:   Sharing Photos

## 36 Print a Contact Sheet

### TIP

You can get a full-sized preview of what will be printed by clicking the **Preview** button at the bottom of the **Print** dialog box. The print preview opens up in Adobe Acrobat Reader.

card for each photo. You can print multiple copies of the card by typing the desired number in the **Copies** field or by using the spin buttons to specify the desired number of copies.

### 7 Print Card

Click the **Print** button at the bottom of the **Print** dialog box to send the greeting card to the selected printer.

## 36 Print a Contact Sheet

### Before You Begin

✔ **4** Create New Albums
✔ **5** Create a Smart Album

### See Also

→ **30** Adjust Slideshow Display Settings
→ **31** Customize Music for a Slideshow
→ **32** Export a Slideshow to QuickTime
→ **33** Export a Slideshow to iDVD

### KEY TERM

*Contact sheet*—A sheet typically printed for a roll of film to allow the photographer to select the photos she wants to develop. The sheet contains thumbnail images of all the photos.

### TIPS

To deselect any selected photos, click in the white space between the photo thumbnails on the **Organize** pane.

To deselect a photo from a group, press and hold the ⌘ key and click the photo.

You can print *contact sheets* in iPhoto to create an index sheet containing small versions of multiple photos. You can create contact sheets for an entire album or for just a selection of photos. You can use the contact sheet to determine which photos of a large selection of photos you want to print in full size.

When you print a contact sheet, you decide the number of photos you want displayed on each row of the page. The more photos you specify, the more are printed on the page and the smaller the individual images. As you adjust the sizing, iPhoto indicates the number of pages that will print.

iPhoto automatically adjusts the pictures so that they are all sized and positioned equally. Typically, a vertical photo is rotated to print horizontally on the contact sheet. If you don't want iPhoto to conserve paper by adjusting the orientation of the photos, make sure that the **Save paper** option is disabled.

### 1 Select Album

On the **Organize** pane, select the album that contains the photos you want to print on the contact sheets. If you want photos from multiple albums, select the main **Photo Library**. To print all photos in the selected album, do not select any individual photos. To print only specific photos, hold down the ⌘ key as you click each photo you want to print.

### 2 Display Print Dialog Box

Click the **Print** button at the bottom of the **Organize** pane to display the **Print** dialog box.

---

110    PART I:    iPhoto

Print a Contact Sheet **36**

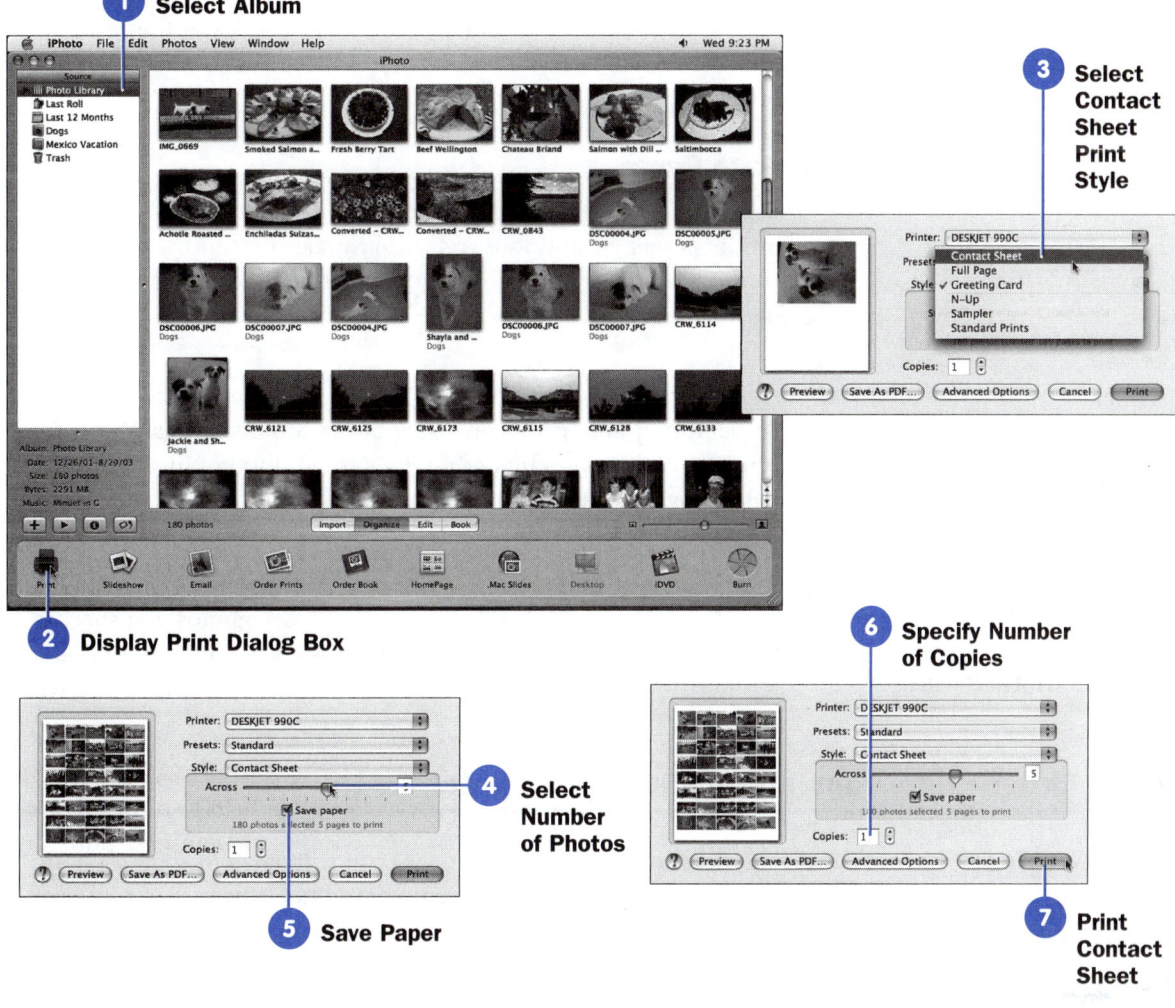

### Select Contact Sheet Print Style

From the **Style** drop-down list, select the **Contact Sheet** option.

### Select Number of Photos

Drag the **Across** slider to the right to increase the number of photos that print in each row of the contact sheet. Drag the slider to

CHAPTER 6: Sharing Photos

## 37  Order Prints from an Online Photo Printer

the left to decrease the number of photos in each row. You can also type a number in the field next to the slider. Look at the preview area on the left side of the dialog box to see how your selections affect the look of the printed page.

### 5  Save Paper

Enable the **Save paper** check box to have iPhoto fit more photos on the page by rotating the vertical images so that they print horizontally on the contact sheet. Rotating the images in this fashion allows more photos to be printed on each page.

### 6  Specify Number of Copies

By default, iPhoto prints one copy of the contact sheets. You can print multiple copies by typing the desired number in the **Copies** field or by using the spin buttons to specify the desired number of copies.

### 7  Print Contact Sheets

Click the **Print** button at the bottom of the **Print** dialog box to send the contact sheets to the printer.

> **TIP**
> You can preview the contact sheets by clicking the **Preview** button at the bottom of the **Print** dialog box. The print preview opens up in Adobe Acrobat Reader.

## 37  Order Prints from an Online Photo Printer

**Before You Begin**
- ✔ 4  Create New Albums
- ✔ 5  Create a Smart Album
- ✔ 6  Organize Photos in Albums

**See Also**
- → 19  Search for Photos
- → 26  Print a Photo Book
- → 34  Print Photos from iPhoto
- → 44  Create a Photo CD

If you do not have a photo printer, you can still get your digital photos printed on photo paper by ordering them online. When you order prints online, you select the prints you want printed and the size you want each print to be. The photos are printed and mailed to you or to any other address you specify.

To order prints online, you must have a 1-Click account established with Apple. This account contains your personal contact information, including your name, address, and a credit card number for ordering purposes. If you select the **Order Prints** option and do not have a 1-Click account active, the **Set Up Account** button displays in the bottom-right corner of the **Order Prints** dialog box. Click the button and follow the screen options to create your 1-Click account. When your 1-Click account is active, you can order the desired photos by selecting them and clicking the **Buy Now** button.

PART I:  iPhoto

## Order Prints from an Online Photo Printer  37

When you display the **Order Prints** dialog box, you have the option of ordering photos of all the same size or of different sizes. If you want to order 4×6 prints for all the selected photos, you can use the **Quick Order** option at the top of the dialog box to select that print size for all photos. Each time you click the **Up Arrow** button, one 4×6 print is ordered for each selected photo.

In addition to the iPhoto service described here, there are other online photo-printing services you can use. To work with these Web sites, you need to upload a JPEG image that you export from iPhoto. See  **Export a Photo for Use in Another Application** for more information on exporting photos from iPhoto.

> **TIP**
> You must have a shipping address in the United States or Canada to use the **Order Prints** option in iPhoto.

http://www.shutterfly.com

http://www.snapfish.com

http://www.dotphoto.com

**WEB RESOURCE**

These Web sites are just a few of the other locations on the Internet where you can order prints from your digital photos.

CHAPTER 6:   Sharing Photos                                                           113

# 37 Order Prints from an Online Photo Printer

**TIP**

Leave all the thumbnail images deselected in an album if you want to order prints for the entire album.

**TIP**

If the options are grayed out on the **Order Prints** dialog box, click the **Set Up Account** button to create or activate your 1-Click account.

### ① Select Photos

On the **Organize** pane, select the album that contains the photos you want to order. Select each photo in the album that you want to print. If you want to print photos from multiple albums, select the main **Photo Library**.

To select multiple photos, hold down the ⌘ key while clicking the thumbnail images of the desired photos.

### ② Display Order Prints Dialog Box

Click the **Order Prints** button at the bottom of the **Organize** pane to display the **Order Prints** dialog box. iPhoto passes the photos you selected in the **Organize** pane to the dialog box so that you can select the size and number of each photo you want to order.

### ③ Select Print Sizes

Type the number of each print size in the box corresponding to the selected print. The price for each print is listed in the column on the left. As you select your prints, the **Subtotal** amount automatically updates.

When the **Order Prints** dialog box displays, iPhoto checks the *resolution* of each of the selected photos. If the resolution is not high enough to produce a good quality photograph at a certain size, a yellow warning triangle appears next to those sizes for the photo. You can still order that size print, but the print might be a little grainy. The following table indicates the minimum resolutions your photos must have to produce the highest quality prints.

| Print Size | Minimum Resolution |
|---|---|
| Wallet | 320×240 |
| 4×6 | 640×480 |
| 5×7 | 1024×768 |
| 8×10 | 1536×1024 |
| 16×20 | 1600×1200 |
| 20×30 | 1600×1200 |

**KEY TERM**

*Resolution*—Indicates the size of the photo based on a measurement of the total pixels in the image. Each pixel is essentially one small dot on the image. A photo with a resolution of 640×480 is 640 pixels wide and 480 pixels high.

You can check the resolution of a photo on the **Organize** pane by viewing the photo information. See ⑨ **Set Photo Information** for more information on viewing the photo information.

## (4) Specify Shipping Information

By default, iPhoto assumes that you want to ship the photos you are ordering to yourself at the address you provided when you set up your 1-Click account. If this is indeed true, leave the **Ship To** field set to **Myself**.

To change the shipping information, select a different shipping location from the **Ship To** drop-down list. If you want to specify a new location, select the **Add New Address** option. Your 1-Click Account will open, allowing you to create an additional shipping address.

From the **Ship Via** drop-down list, select the type of shipping you want for the selected photos. Shipping options are **Standard** (ships in 1 to 2 business days) and **Overnight**. The shipping cost displays in the **Shipping** field on the right side of the dialog box, and the estimated shipping time displays under the **Ship Via** field.

## (5) Order Prints

Click the **Buy Now** button to send the order directly to Kodak to be printed.

## 38  Email Photos

You can select photos that you want to email to others, and iPhoto will create a mail message containing the photos. When you select the **Email** option, iPhoto prompts you for a size and then passes the photos to the email program you have specified as your default.

To use the **Email** option, you must have an email program specified in your **Preferences** for iPhoto. iPhoto allows you to use Mac OS X Mail, Microsoft Entourage, Eudora, or America Online as your email program. Whichever program you have specified opens when you select the **Email** option. If you don't specify an email program, iPhoto defaults to Mac OS X Mail.

**Before You Begin**

✔ **4** Create New Albums
✔ **5** Create a Smart Album
✔ **6** Organize Photos in Albums

**See Also**

→ **34** Print Photos from iPhoto
→ **39** Publish Photos to View on the Internet
→ **44** Create a Photo CD

## 38 Email Photos

**1** Set Email Preferences

**2** Select Photos

**3** Display Mail Photo Dialog Box

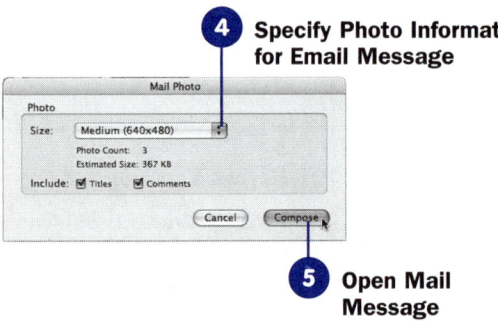

**4** Specify Photo Information for Email Message

**5** Open Mail Message

**6** Send Message

116     **PART I:**   iPhoto

Email Photos  38

### 1. Set Email Preferences

From the main menu, choose **iPhoto, Preferences** to open the **Preferences** dialog box. The **Mail** field indicates the name of the email program that will be launched when you select the **Email** option in iPhoto. To change the mail program, select the desired email program from the **Mail** drop-down list.

### 2. Select Photos

On the **Organize** pane, click to select the photos you want to email. To select multiple photos, hold down the ⌘ key while clicking on each photo.

### 3. Display Mail Photo Dialog Box

Click the **Mail** button at the bottom of the **Organize** pane to open the **Mail Photo** dialog box. All the photos you selected in the **Organize** pane will be passed to the default email program.

### 4. Specify Photo Information for Email Message

On the **Mail Photo** dialog box, select the desired size for the photos from the **Size** drop-down list. You can choose **Small**, **Medium**, **Large**, and **Full Size**. Keep in mind that the smaller the photo size you select here, the smaller the file size of the email message. iPhoto reduces the size of the photo by reducing the photo resolution. For example, if you select the **Medium** size option, all photos you are emailing are reduced to a resolution size of 640×480. On the other hand, if you want the person receiving the message to have the highest quality image, send the **Full Size** version of all photos.

You can include the title and comments information specified in iPhoto about each photo by enabling the **Titles** and **Comments** check boxes on the **Mail Photo** dialog box.

### 5. Open Mail Message

Click the **Compose** button in the **Mail Photo** dialog box to launch the default email program so that you can compose the email message and specify the recipient.

**NOTE**
To send email messages, you must have access to the Internet through an ISP (Internet service provider). Although America Online is one of the most popular ISPs, you can find several other local providers in your area.

**TIPS**
Make sure that the selected email program is set up to send and receive email messages from your Internet account.

To close the **Preferences** dialog box, click the red button in the upper-left corner of the dialog box.

**NOTE**
Changing the size of the photo for email purposes does not affect the version of the photo stored by iPhoto. iPhoto maintains the highest resolution version of the photo.

CHAPTER 6: Sharing Photos    117

### 39  Publish Photos to View on the Internet

**TIP**

To send an email message, you must have the email program set up to properly send and receive email messages from your Internet account.

**6  Send Message**

A new email message opens in the preferred email program with the selected pictures attached. Specify the email address for the recipient in the **To** field, type a **Subject** line, and add any text to the main body of the message. When you're ready to send the photos, click the **Send** button to send the message.

For more specific information about sending email messages, refer to the online help available for your email program.

### 39  Publish Photos to View on the Internet

**Before You Begin**

✔ **4** Create New Albums
✔ **5** Create a Smart Album
✔ **6** Organize Photos in Albums

**See Also**

→ **34** Print Photos from iPhoto
→ **38** Email Photos
→ **40** Share a Slideshow Over the Internet
→ **44** Create a Photo CD

If you want to allow people to access your photos from the Internet, you can place them on a Web site using Apple's **HomePage** option. With this option, you can place your photos on a personal Web site hosted by Apple. The cool thing about this feature is that by simply selecting the photos you want to place on your Web site, iPhoto will copy them to the site without any other work on your part.

To create an Apple HomePage, you must have a .Mac account. When you select the HomePage option, iPhoto prompts you to create a .Mac account if you do not have one already. When you create a .Mac account, you get personal storage space called *iDisk* (which includes the HomePage space) where you can store files you want to share with others.

**WEB RESOURCE**

Create a .Mac account and reserve your iDisk Web space by going to this site. You pay a small monthly fee to maintain your .Mac account.

http://www.mac.com

When you create your HomePage, you select the photos in iPhoto that you want to place on the page. You can add custom text to the top of the page describing the pictures. For example, if you place pictures of your vacation on your HomePage, you might want to add text describing the vacation. You can also customize the look of the page by adding borders to the photos or by inserting a counter on the page to show the number of visitors the page has received. This method allows you to create an online photo album that anyone can view with just a few simple steps.

**KEY TERM**

*iDisk*—100 megabytes of personal storage on Apple's online servers. You can access your iDisk Web space from any location with Internet access. Other people can view files stored in your **Public** folders.

PART I:  iPhoto

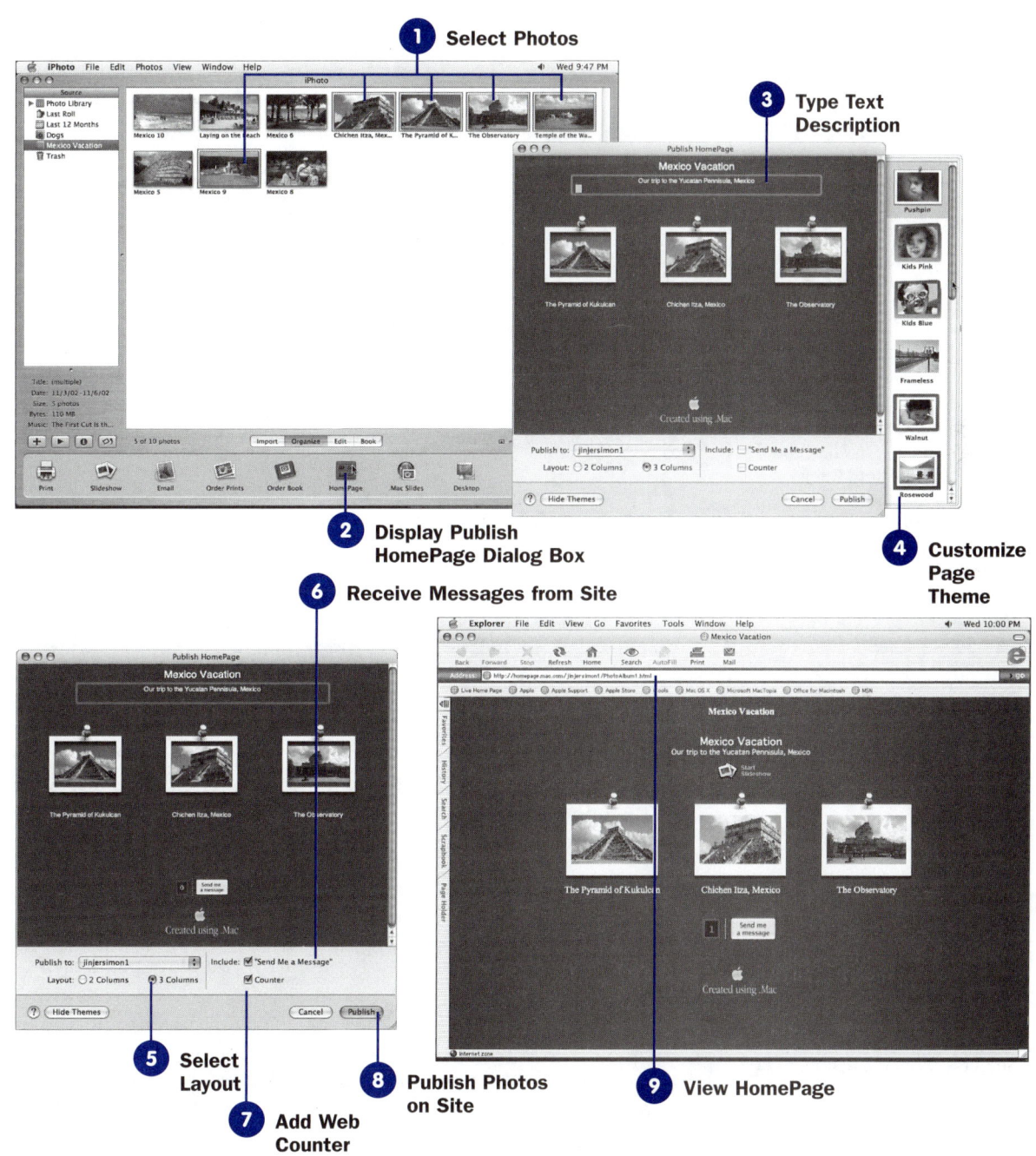

## 39  Publish Photos to View on the Internet

### ① Select Photos

On the **Organize** pane, click to select the photos you want to place on the Web site. To select multiple photos, hold down the ⌘ key while clicking each photo.

You can select photos from an individual album by selecting the desired album from the left side of the Organize pane. If you want to select photos from multiple albums, select the main **Photo Library**.

### ② Display Publish HomePage Dialog Box

Click the **HomePage** button at the bottom of the **Organize** pane to open the **Publish HomePage** dialog box. iPhoto passes the photos you selected on the **Organize** pane to the **Publish HomePage** dialog box.

### ③ Type Text Description

You can modify any of the text on the Web page you are creating. To change the text, click it; a box appears around the text, and you can type to add or edit the text. If you don't want text at a specific location, delete the text from the box so that the field is blank.

iPhoto automatically passes the name of the photo album you selected in step 1 as the title for the Web page. You can alter the title by selecting the text and typing the desired text. If you selected the photos from the **Photo Library**, that is the default name assigned to the page.

iPhoto also passes the photo titles for each of the photos. You can modify the title of each photo by clicking on the text under the photo and typing the desired photo title.

### ④ Customize Page Theme

Click the desired theme for all the photos on the page. You can select any of the themes displayed. The theme you select is applied to all the photos on your HomePage. For example, if you select the **Pushpin** theme, the photos appear to be attached to the page with push pins. If the **Themes** drawer does not display on the right, click the **Show Themes** button. Click **Hide Themes** to close the **Themes** drawer.

### TIPS

If you don't have a .Mac membership, a dialog box displays when you click the **HomePage** button. Click **Join Now** to create a .Mac membership account.

To specify your .Mac account settings, click **Open Internet Prefs** and type the account name and password for your .Mac account.

You must be connected to the Internet before you can create a photo HomePage.

### TIP

The name of the .Mac account that will be used to publish the Web page is displayed in the **Publish to** field. If you have multiple .Mac accounts, you can select a different account from the **Publish to** drop-down list.

## Publish Photos to View on the Internet

### ⑤ Select Layout

You can display your photos in either two or three columns on your Web page. Click the appropriate radio button for the layout. If you select the **2 Columns** option, the pictures will be larger on the page.

### ⑥ Receive Messages from Site

If you want to allow visitors to send you a message when they visit your site, enable the **Send Me a Message** check box. When you do this, a button is added to the Web page that visitors can click if they want to send you an email message. iPhoto and your .Mac account use the email address you provided when you set up your .Mac account as the email address used to send you email messages.

### ⑦ Add Web Counter

If you want to show the number of visitors to your site, you can add a counter by enabling the **Counter** check box. The counter updates on the Web page each time the site is visited.

**NOTE**
The counter doesn't know whether the same person is revisiting the site or if a new visitor is coming to the site. It just keeps track of the number of times the Web site is visited.

### ⑧ Publish Photos on Site

Click the **Publish** button to publish your HomePage for your .Mac account. After the page has been published, others can view your pictures by visiting your site.

### ⑨ View HomePage

When the process of publishing your homepage is complete, a dialog box displays. Click the **Visit Page Now** button to see your HomePage.

You can view your HomePage at any time. In your Web browser, type the URL for your HomePage. The URL is **http://homepage.mac.com/accountname**, where **accountname** is your .Mac account name. You do not have to type the page name. Your HomePage automatically loads when you type the URL. If you have multiple pages, the first page you created displays with links to the other pages.

**TIP**
Visitors can also see a slideshow of the images you placed on your HomePage by clicking the **Start Slideshow** button at the top of the page.

## 40  Share a Slideshow over the Internet

**Before You Begin**

✔ **4** Create New Albums
✔ **5** Create a Smart Album
✔ **6** Organize Photos in Albums

**See Also**

→ **29** Play a Slideshow
→ **32** Export a Slideshow to QuickTime
→ **39** Publish Photos to View on the Internet
→ **41** Set iDisk Slideshow as Screensaver
→ **44** Create a Photo CD

You can publish a slideshow on the Internet so that others can view it directly from their computers. To accomplish this, you create a slideshow that is shared from your Apple .Mac account. After you have created the slideshow, other Mac OS X users can view your slideshow as their screensaver.

To create a slideshow, you select the photos you want to publish and then use the **.Mac Slides** option. If you have a .Mac account, the slideshow is placed on your account so that other users can access it. If you do not have a .Mac account established, you are prompted to create one when you click the **.Mac Slides** button. The slideshow is actually stored in a **Public** folder in your *iDisk* Web space. Because it is in a **Public** folder, anyone who knows your .Mac member name can access your slideshow.

### WEB RESOURCE

Create a .Mac account and reserve your iDisk Web space by going to this site.

http://www.mac.com

**TIP**

If you do not have a .Mac account, iPhoto prompts you to create the account. Follow the onscreen instructions to create the .Mac account and get your iDisk Web storage space.

#### 1 Select Photos

On the **Organize** pane, click to select the photos you want to turn into a slideshow. To select multiple photos, hold down the ⌘ key while clicking each photo.

You can select photos from an individual album by selecting the desired album from the left side of the **Organize** pane. If you want to select photos from multiple albums, select the main **Photo Library**.

#### 2 Select the .Mac Slides Button

Click the **.Mac Slides** button at the bottom of the **Organize** pane to send the selected photos to your iDisk Web space as a slideshow.

PART I:   iPhoto

## Share a Slideshow over the Internet  40

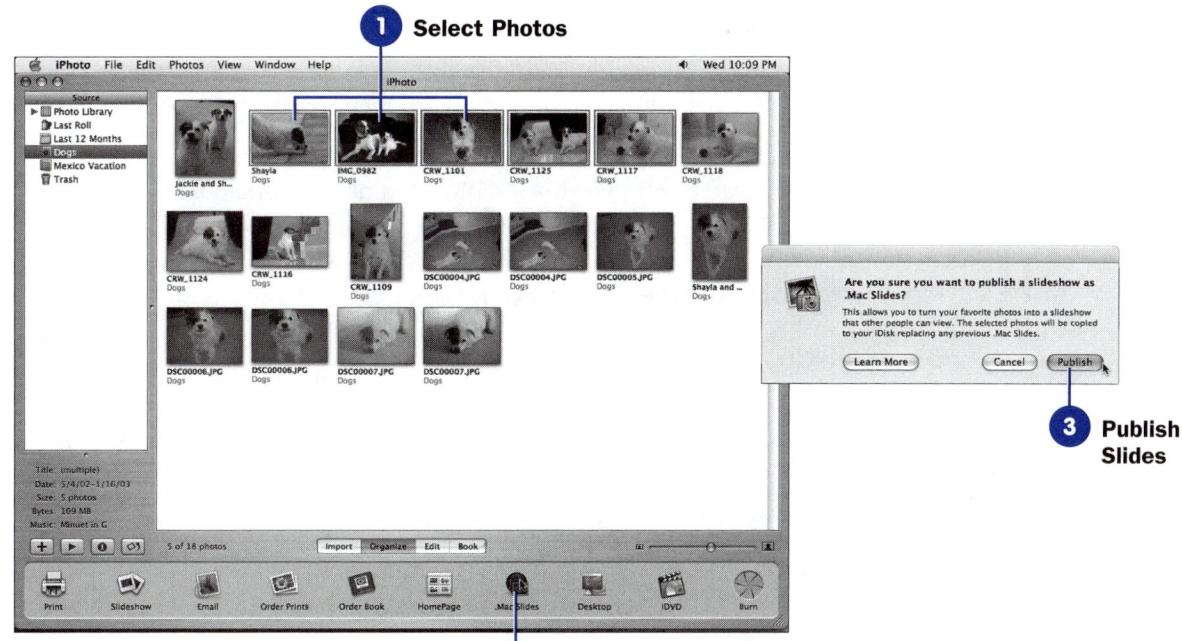

**1** Select Photos

**2** Select .Mac Slides button

**3** Publish Slides

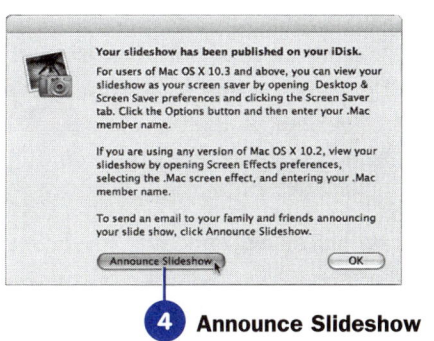

**4** Announce Slideshow

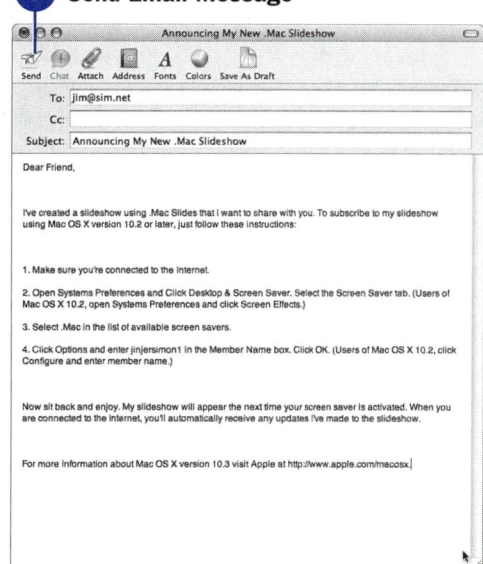

**5** Send Email Message

**CHAPTER 6:   Sharing Photos**

### ③ Publish Slides

On the dialog box that displays, click the **Publish** button to place the selected photos on your iDisk Web space as a slideshow that other people can access.

iPhoto displays a status dialog box as each photo is copied to the iDisk storage space associated with your .Mac account.

### ④ Announce Slideshow

After the photos for the slideshow are copied to your iDisk Web space, iPhoto displays a dialog box showing the completion of the process. You can send an email message about your slideshow to other users by clicking the **Announce Slideshow** button. When you click the button, iPhoto launches your default email program and creates a message announcing your slideshow.

### ⑤ Send Email Message

If you clicked the **Announce Slideshow** button, an email message is created to announce your slideshow and describe how to set up your slideshow to run as a screensaver. Type the email address of each individual you want to notify about the slideshow in the **To** field; separate multiple email addresses by inserting a semicolon after each address.

After specifying the desired email address(es), click the **Send** button. iPhoto uses the email program set up as your default email program on the iPhoto **Preferences** dialog box. See ③⑧ **Email Photos** for more information on setting the default email program.

See ④① **Set iDisk Slideshow as Screensaver** for information on setting up the slideshow as a screensaver on your machine.

**TIP**

If you want to change your slideshow, repeat these steps and upload the photos you want in your new slideshow. The new photos replace the original slides.

## 41  Set iDisk Slideshow as Screensaver

You can launch a slideshow from anyone's .Mac account by changing the settings on the **Screen Effects** panel. The **Screen Effects** panel is one of the options available on the **System Preferences** panel.

After you load the slideshow, the slideshow runs whenever your screensaver is activated. This option is available for all individuals running Mac OS X version 10.2 or later.

The cool thing about using this feature is that you can load slideshows from multiple .Mac accounts. For example, if you have a .Mac account and your brother has an account, you can load slideshows from both accounts and view the photos in both slideshows as your screensaver. When your brother updates his slideshow, you automatically see the new pictures the next time your screensaver is activated on your machine.

### ❶ Open Desktop & Screen Saver

Choose **Apple, System Preferences** from the menu at the top of the screen to open the **System Preferences** panel. Click the **Desktop & Screen Saver** icon.

### ❷ Select .Mac Option

Click the **.Mac** option in the **Screen Savers** list box on the left side of the **Screen Saver** panel. The **Preview** window changes to display the current settings for the **.Mac** option.

### ❸ Configure Settings

Click the **Options** button to display a dialog box in which you can specify the .Mac slideshows you want to view as your screensaver.

### ❹ Specify Slideshow

Type the .Mac account name for the first slideshow you want to use as your screensaver in the **.Mac Membership Name** field. Do not add @mac.com to the end of the .Mac account name in the **.Mac Membership Name** field. Select the desired display options for the slides by enabling the corresponding check boxes. When you have the desired selections, click the **OK** button. The dialog box closes and the selected slideshow plays in the **Preview** window on the **Screen Effects** panel.

**Before You Begin**

✔ **40** Share a Slideshow over the Internet

**See Also**

→ **39** Publish Photos to View on the Internet

→ **42** Create a Photo Screensaver

**NOTE**

You can also find the **System Preferences** icon on your Dock at the bottom of the screen.

**TIPS**

To add an additional slideshow from a different .Mac account, repeat steps 3 and 4 and specify the next .Mac account name.

If you specify multiple slideshows, you can specify which slideshows display by clicking the check box in the **Selected** column.

**NOTE**

To have the slideshow play whenever you move the mouse to a corner of the screen, click the **Hot Corners** tab on the **Screen Effects** dialog box and select the desired screen corners.

CHAPTER 6:  Sharing Photos

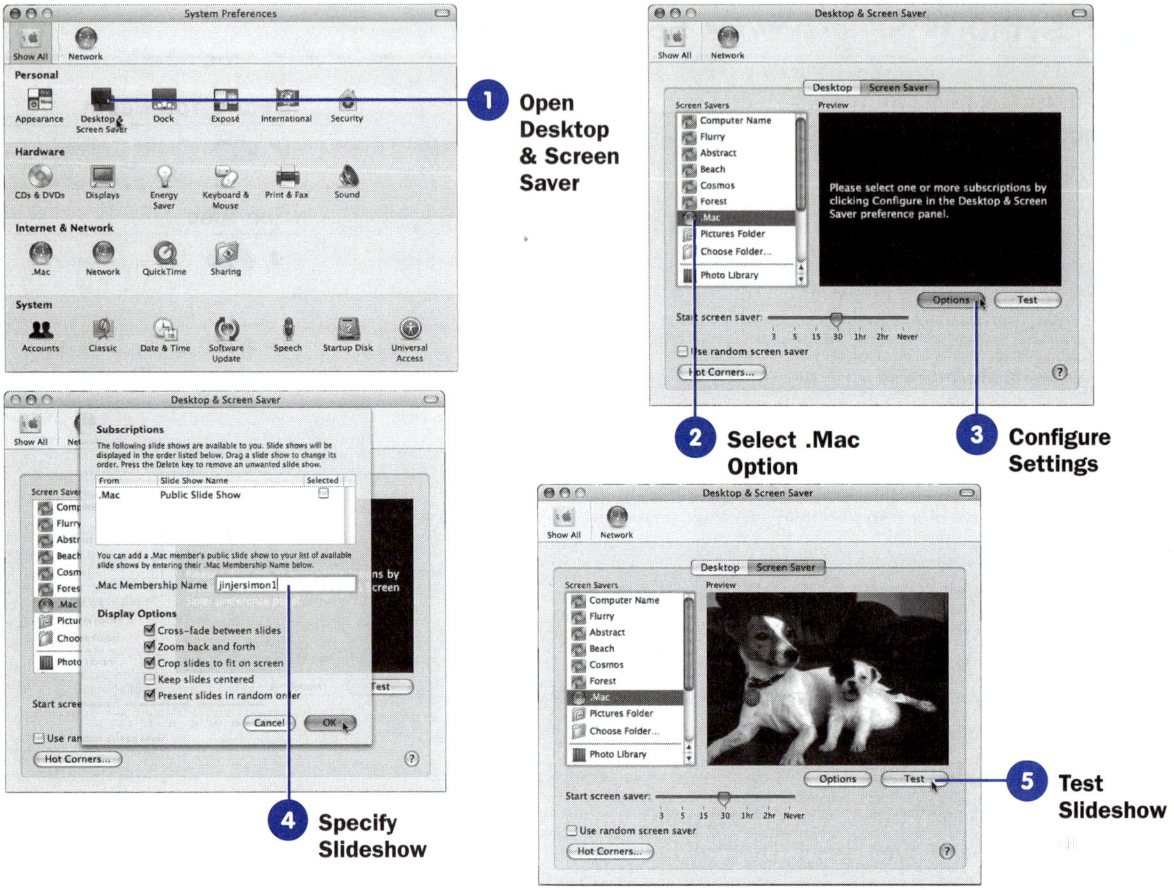

## 41 Set iDisk Slideshow as Screensaver

**1** Open Desktop & Screen Saver

**2** Select .Mac Option

**3** Configure Settings

**4** Specify Slideshow

**5** Test Slideshow

---

**TIPS**

If the slideshow does not load, you might not be connected to the Internet. Check your Internet connection.

Choose **System Preferences, Quit System Preferences** to close the dialog box and close **System Preferences**.

### 5 Test Slideshow

Click the **Test** button on the **Desktop & Screen Saver** panel to see the slideshow in full screen. The slideshow plays until you move your mouse or press a button on the keyboard.

126    PART I:   iPhoto

## 42  Create a Photo Screensaver

You can use the pictures in your iPhoto albums on your computer as slideshows that run as your screensaver. You specify the photo album that you want to load on the **Desktop & Screen Saver** panel. The **Desktop & Screen Saver** panel is one of the options available on the **System Preferences** panel.

After you specify the **Screen Effects** settings, the photos from your iPhoto album display whenever your screensaver is activated.

When you create a slideshow using photos from your iPhoto albums, you do not have to be connected to the Internet to view the slideshow. The slideshow is created from photos you have stored on your machine. When you use a slideshow from a .Mac account, as described in **41 Set iDisk Slideshow as Screensaver**, the slideshow displays only if you are connected to the Internet.

**Before You Begin**

✔ **4** Create New Albums
✔ **5** Create a Smart Album
✔ **6** Organize Photos in an Album

**See Also**

→ **29** Play a Slideshow
→ **40** Share a Slideshow over the Internet
→ **41** Set iDisk Slideshow as Screensaver
→ **43** Add a Photo to the Desktop

### 1  Open Desktop & Screen Saver Panel

Select **Apple, System Preferences** from the menu at the top of the screen to open the **System Preferences** panel and then click the **Desktop & Screen Saver** icon.

### 2  Select a Photo Album

Select the desired album option from the **Screen Savers** list on the left side of the **Screen Saver** panel. The **Preview** window changes to display the current photos in the selected album. To view all photos in your library, select **Photo Library**.

### 3  Configure Settings

Click the **Options** button to display a dialog box in which you can specify the settings for the photos that display as your screensaver.

## 42 Create a Photo Screensaver

**1** Open Desktop & Screen Saver Panel

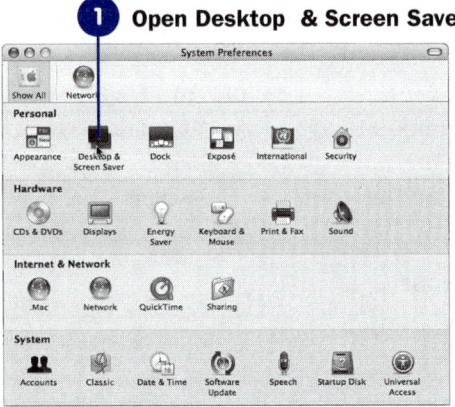

**2** Select a Photo Albumm

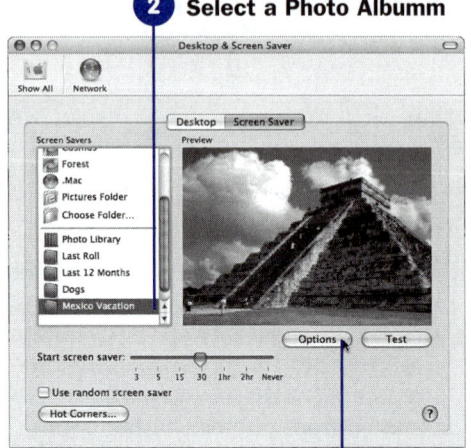

**3** Configure Settings

**4** Adjust Settings

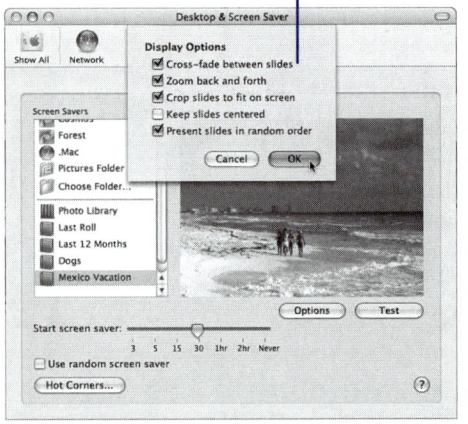

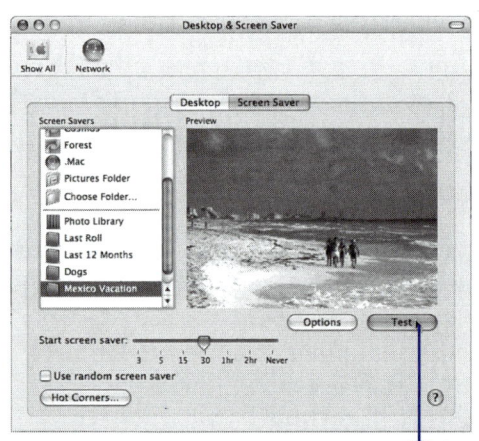

**5** Test Screensaver

PART I:   iPhoto

Add a Photo to the Desktop

**④ Adjust Settings**

Select the desired display options for the screensaver photos by enabling the corresponding check boxes. For example, if you want to display the photos from the album in random order, enable the **Present slides in random order** check box. When you have made the desired selections, click the **OK** button. The dialog box closes, and the screensaver plays in the **Preview** window on the **Screen Effects** panel.

💡 **TIP**

You can also select a photo album folder by dragging the folder from the **Finder** window onto the **Slide Folder** icon on the configuration dialog box.

**⑤ Test Screensaver**

Click the **Test** button to see the photo screensaver in full screen. The screensaver plays until you move your mouse or press a button on the keyboard.

## ㊸ Add a Photo to the Desktop

You can add your favorite photo to your desktop as the background image. When you place a photo on your desktop, it becomes the background that displays whenever you do not have the desktop filled with windows from other programs.

**① Select Photo**

On the **Organize** pane, select the photo you want to place on the desktop. You can select the photo from the main **Photo Library** or from an individual photo album.

If you select multiple photos, Mac OS X assigns one photo to the desktop and then adds the other selected photos to the screensaver slideshow. See ㊷ **Create a Photo Screensaver** for more information.

**② Place Photo on Desktop**

Click the **Desktop** button at the bottom of the **Organize** pane to add the photo to the desktop.

**Before You Begin**

✔ ① Transfer Pictures from a Digital Camera

✔ ② Import Digital Pictures from Other Sources

✔ ④ Create New Albums

✔ ⑤ Create a Smart Album

**See Also**

→ ㉞ Print Photos from iPhoto

→ ㊷ Create a Photo Screensaver

→ ㊺ Export a Photo

**CHAPTER 6:** Sharing Photos

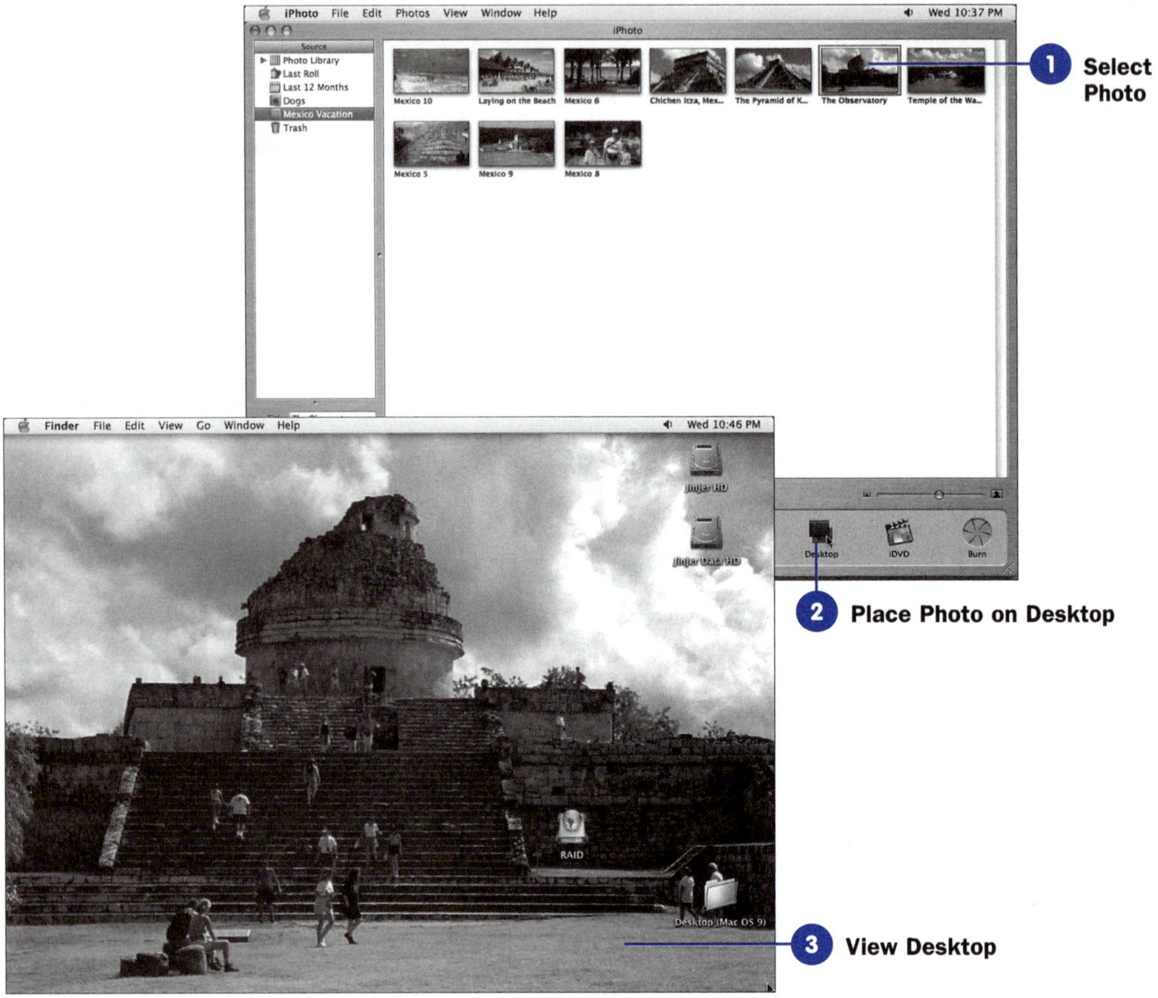

**43** Add a Photo to the Desktop

**1** Select Photo

**2** Place Photo on Desktop

**3** View Desktop

**TIP**
If you want to change the desktop background, select a different photo and repeat steps 1 and 2.

**3** **View Desktop**

Click the **Minimize** button on the upper-left corner of the iPhoto window to minimize iPhoto so that you can see the desktop.

PART I:   iPhoto

## 44 Create a Photo CD

You can create a CD that contains selected photos from your iPhoto library using the **Burn** option. You can place your entire **Photo Library** or just select photos on the CD. The **Burn** option is good for creating a backup copy of your photos for storage purposes. The CD that contains your photos is typically referred to as a *Photo CD*.

When you *burn* images onto a Photo CD, iPhoto creates an album containing all the photo titles, comments, and keywords you have specified for each photo. With this information stored on the CD, anyone can view the photos using iPhoto on their machine. In fact, when you insert a Photo CD in your machine, iPhoto automatically displays it as one of the available photo albums on the left side of the **Organize** pane.

You can also burn the photos onto a DVD from iPhoto if you are running Mac OS X version 10.2 or higher. If you have this version, insert a DVD in your drive instead of a CD and follow the steps outlined in this task.

### 1 Select Photos

On the **Organize** pane, select the photos you want to place on the CD. To select multiple photos, press the ⌘ key while you click the desired photos.

To copy the entire **Photo Library** to the CD, select the **Photo Library** from the list on the left side of the pane. Make sure that none of the individual photos are selected. If you select the **Photo Library**, all library information—including the albums—will be copied to the CD.

### 2 Click Burn Button

Click the **Burn** button at the bottom of the **Organize** pane. iPhoto displays the **Insert Disc** dialog box.

### Before You Begin
- ✓ **4** Create New Albums
- ✓ **5** Create a Smart Album
- ✓ **6** Organize Photos in Albums

### See Also
- → **27** Save a Photo Book as a PDF
- → **32** Export a Slideshow to QuickTime
- → **33** Export a Slideshow to iDVD
- → **45** Export a Photo

### KEY TERM
*Burn*—The process of saving files on a CD or DVD using a CD or DVD burner.

### TIPS
To select multiple albums, press the ⌘ key and click each album name.

A CD can store about 700 megabytes. The number of photos you can store is based on the size of each photo. For example, if each photo averages four megabytes, you can store approximately 175 photos on a CD.

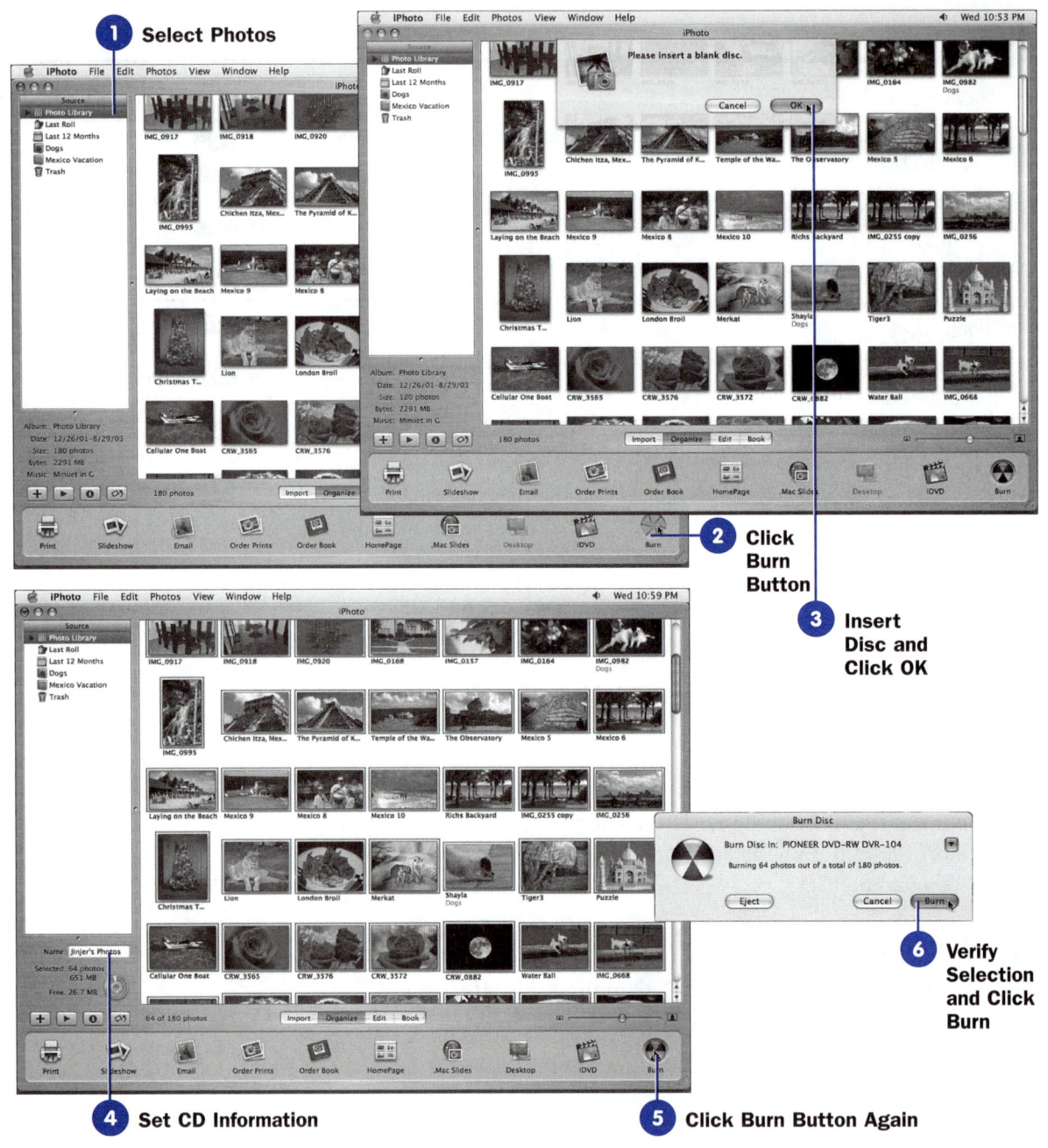

## Create a Photo CD  44

### ③ Insert Disc

Insert the CD or DVD disc in the drive of your burner and click the **OK** button.

### ④ Set Disc Information

In the **Disc Name** field in the bottom-left corner of the **Organize** pane, type a descriptive name for the CD. This is the name you will see when the disc is inserted into a computer.

iPhoto displays additional information about the CD that will be created. The information includes the number of photos that will be added and the amount of space required for that number of photos. The amount of available space displays next to the **Free** field. If the text **Disc Full** displays, you'll have to eliminate some of the selected photos before clicking the **Burn** button.

### ⑤ Click Burn Button Again

Click the **Burn** button on the **Organize** pane again to start the process of creating the Photo CD.

iPhoto verifies that there is enough room on the CD to store all the photos. If there is not enough room, a dialog box displays. You will have to deselect some of the photos and then click the **Burn** button again.

### ⑥ Verify Selection and Click Burn

iPhoto displays a dialog box to verify the selection before starting to creating the Photo CD. To continue the process and create the CD, click the **Burn** button.

iPhoto creates the Photo CD. Depending on the number of photos selected, this process might take a while. During the process, a dialog box displays the status of the burn process.

# 45 Export a Photo

**Before You Begin**

✔ **4** Create New Albums

**See Also**

→ **32** Export a Slideshow to QuickTime

→ **34** Print Photos from iPhoto

→ **38** Email Photos

### KEY TERM

**JPEG (Joint Photographic Experts Group)**—A graphics file format standard for creating a compressed image. JPEG uses a lossy compression format that shrinks the file size by eliminating nonessential elements of the picture.

**TIFF (Tag Image File Format)**—A graphics file format that creates a compressed file format using a lossless compression that maintains the quality of the original photo.

**PNG (Portable Network Graphics)**—A graphics file format standard that compresses the photo without losing the quality of the image.

### TIP

You can export multiple photos by pressing the ⌘ key as you click each photo. You must export all the selected photos with the same settings and in the same folder.

If you want to use a photo you have stored in iPhoto in another application, such as inserting it in a printed brochure you are creating in a page layout software package, you can export it. When you export a photo from iPhoto, you have the option of specifying the desired file format and photo resolution. This allows you to customize the photo based on your intended use.

When you export the photo, you can export it in its original format or in **JPEG**, **TIFF**, or **PNG** format. You can also indicate the desired size for the photo. As a default, iPhoto exports using the default image size, but you can also customize the photo size by specifying a width and height in pixels.

You indicate the name of the exported photo by selecting the current filename, the iPhoto title, or the album name.

### ❶ Select Photo

On the **Organize** pane, select the photo you want to export. You can select a photo from any album or from the main **Photo Library**.

### ❷ Display Export Photos Dialog Box

Choose **File**, **Export** to display the **Export Photos** dialog box.

### ❸ Select File Export Tab

In the **Export Photos** dialog box, click the **File Export** tab (if it is not already selected) to display the **File Export** options.

### ❹ Select File Format

From the **Format** drop-down list, select the desired file format for the exported photo. Typically, you select a file format based on the desired use of the photo. For example, not all applications can open a PNG file.

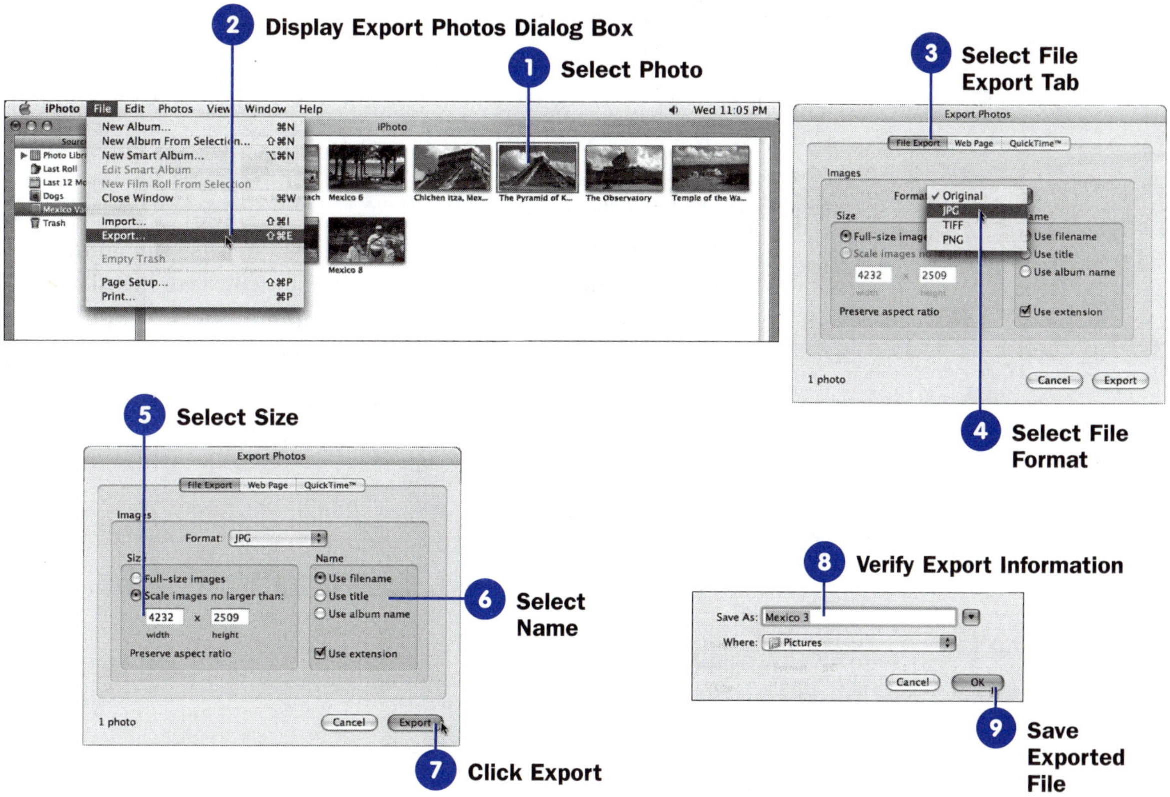

Export a Photo

**Display Export Photos Dialog Box** — 2
**Select Photo** — 1
**Select File Export Tab** — 3
**Select File Format** — 4
**Select Size** — 5
**Select Name** — 6
**Click Export** — 7
**Verify Export Information** — 8
**Save Exported File** — 9

### 5 Select Size

To export the photo using the current resolution, click the **Full-size images** option. If you want to set a custom size, click the **Scale images no larger than** option and type the desired width or height in pixels. iPhoto adjusts the photo sizing to maintain the original aspect ratio. For example, if you type a value in the **width** field, iPhoto creates the corresponding **height** value.

### 6 Select Name

Click the radio button corresponding to the name you want to assign to the photo file. If you select **Use filename**, iPhoto assigns the current photo filename to the image file. If you select **Use title**, iPhoto assigns the current title you gave the photo in iPhoto.

**TIP**

Make sure that the **Use extension** check box is enabled to ensure that the appropriate file extension is assigned to the file. The file extension is necessary for Microsoft Windows machines.

**CHAPTER 6:** Sharing Photos      135

## Export a Photo

### (7) Click Export

Click the **Export** button at the bottom of the **Export Photos** dialog box to export the selected photo using the settings specified on the **Export Photos** dialog box.

### (8) Verify Export Information

A dialog box displays the filename that will be assigned to the exported file and the location where iPhoto will store the file. To change the filename, type the desired name in the **Save as** field. Make sure that you don't alter the file extension.

By default, iPhoto stores the exported photos in your **Pictures** folder. To store the file in another location, select the desired folder from the **Where** drop-down list.

### (9) Save Exported File

Click the **Save** button to export the selected photo and save it in the specified location.

# PART II

## iTunes

**IN THIS PART**

| | | |
|---|---|---|
| **CHAPTER 7** | Loading Sound Files | 139 |
| **CHAPTER 8** | Organizing Sound Files | 173 |
| **CHAPTER 9** | Listening to Sound Files | 209 |
| **CHAPTER 10** | Creating Music CDs | 237 |

# 7

# Loading Sound Files

### IN THIS CHAPTER:

- **46** About Audio Formats
- **47** Capture Audio Files from CDs
- **48** Import Internet Music
- **49** Purchase Audio from the Music Store
- **50** Link to Audio Files in Other Locations
- **51** Get CD Information from the Internet
- **52** Change Song Information
- **53** Download Audio Book Files from the Internet
- **54** Set the Import Format for Audio Files
- **55** Set Custom MP3 Quality Options
- **56** Set Music File Storage Location

## 46 About Audio Formats

**KEY TERMS**

**MP3 (Moving Picture Experts Group Audio Layer III)**—A standardized format for compressing audio to produce nearly CD-quality sound. You can use iTunes to create MP3 audio files.

**iPod**—A portable MP3 player developed by Apple. iPod players are popular because they have large storage spaces and can interface directly with iTunes.

 **TIP**

Downloading copyrighted material without permission is against the law. To avoid legal issues, make sure that you get music only from reputable sites.

Copying music onto your computer from your personal music CDs or the Internet has become one of the latest crazes. After the music is available on your computer, you can listen to it using your computer speakers, burn the music to CDs, or save it on handheld MP3 players, such as the Apple iPod. iTunes provides a great central location for organizing your sound files. You can sort the files into different playlists based on your own interests. See **57 Create Smart Playlists** for more information on creating playlists in iTunes. You can burn customized CDs that contain your favorite songs, regardless of who sings the songs or what styles of music the songs represent. See **86 Burn an Audio CD** and **87 Burn an MP3 CD** for more information on creating music CDs from iTunes.

You can download audio files from different locations on the Internet. The most common format available on the Internet is MP3. Although downloading MP3 files has become the latest craze, you must be mindful of copyright laws that exist to protect the artists and record companies. To aid you in avoiding illegal activities, Apple provides its own Music Store that is available from within iTunes. If you are connected to the Internet, you can purchase and download music from a multitude of different artists directly to your computer. After the songs are downloaded, the music is yours to play from the computer that you downloaded them to. Although you can create a CD containing music you purchase from the Music Store, you cannot create more than 10 copies of the CD.

When you download from the Apple Music Store, you can download all the music in AAC format (if you have that set as your default download encoder). See **54 Set the Import Format for Audio Files** for more information on setting the format iTunes uses to import music.

When you import audio files into iTunes, you can select the format you want the files saved in. For example, although you might be importing a MP3 file, you can have iTunes convert all imported audio into another format, such as WAV or AIFF. Even after selecting the import format, you can customize the settings for that specific format. Especially with MP3 files, you'll want to specify the quality for each audio file. See **55 Set Custom MP3 Quality Options** for more information on the MP3 settings.

## 46 About Audio Formats

You can import different types of audio files into your iTunes library. The files can contain music, sounds, or even spoken dialog. You can import these audio files from a CD or DVD, your hard drive, or the Internet. iTunes also can import music from commercial audio CDs.

Although MP3 is the most popular audio format (because of its ability to compress the audio file and still maintain a very acceptable result), it is not the only format you can import into iTunes. iTunes can import most other common audio file formats, including *WAV*, *AIFF*, *AAC*, *MOV*, and *AU*.

When you import an audio file into iTunes, iTunes creates a new audio file using the specified file format. You can import the file as an AAC, AIFF, MP3, or WAV file. By default, iTunes creates MP3 files, but you can select any of the four file formats. See **54 Set the Import Format for Audio Files** for more information on selecting the import format.

- **Why can't I select AAC as my import option?** To create an AAC audio file, you must have the AAC encoder loaded on your computer. This audio encoder does not come with iTunes. It loads onto your machine when you load QuickTime 6.2 or later. If you have not loaded QuickTime 6.2 or later, you will not be able to select the AAC encoder import option. iTunes supports only the MPEG-4 AAC format files. It does not support older versions of AAC.

  However, if you have the **Software Update** option turned on in Mac OS X, the most current version of QuickTime should load when you connect to the Internet. The **Software Update** option is available as part of the **System Preferences**. Select the **Automatically check for updates when you have a network connection** option and then specify the time frame. For example, if you click **Daily**, the **Software Update** option will check daily for updates from Apple's Web site, as long as you are connected to the Internet.

- **What file format is used to create the Music CDs I purchase?** The standard audio format for music CDs is AIFF. AIFF is a high-quality, uncompressed format. When you import an audio file using AIFF or WAV as the import encoder, iTunes creates an exact replica of the original audio file. If you plan to burn audio files to

### See Also

→ **47** Capture Audio Files from CDs

→ **48** Import Internet Music

→ **49** Purchase Audio from the Music Store

→ **53** Download Audio Book Files from the Internet

### KEY TERMS

*WAV (Windows Audio)*—An uncompressed audio format used to create CD-quality audio files in Microsoft Windows. The format was developed jointly by Microsoft and IBM as a sound standard.

*AIFF (Audio Interchange File Format)*—An uncompressed audio file format used by Macintosh computers to create CD-quality audio. AIFF files typically have either an .AIF or .IEF file extension.

*AAC (Advanced Audio Coding)*—A new standard in compressing audio while maintaining high sound quality. AAC files typically produce better sound quality than MP3 files.

*AU*—An audio format commonly used to create sound files you can download from the Internet. AU files play on most operating systems, including Microsoft Windows and Mac OS X.

## 46 About Audio Formats

**MOV**—QuickTime Movie format. When you import .MOV files into iMovie, only the audio portion of the movie is imported.

Do not distribute copyrighted music to other people without obtaining proper permissions.

a CD, you should import using the AIFF encoder to produce the highest quality sound. However, the higher-quality AIFF file requires more disk space to store it. Be careful about importing too many AIFF files because they are substantially larger than the popular MP3 files. Figure that an uncompressed audio file requires about 10 megabytes of storage space for each minute. This means that a 4-minute, uncompressed AIFF song takes about 40 megabytes of hard disk space to store.

- **Isn't MP3 the best format for creating audio files?** Actually, MP3 is not the best format if you want the highest quality audio. MP3 files gained popularity because of their ability to highly compress an audio file and still sound almost as good as the original. An MP3 file is compressed to nearly one-tenth the size of the original audio file. For example, a 4-minute audio file that requires 40 megabytes to store as an AIFF file needs only about 4 megabytes of storage space as an MP3 file.

  An MP3 file is compressed by eliminating any portions of the audio that are difficult to hear. The compression technique, similar to the compression used to create JPEG images, is referred to as lossy because part of the information is lost.

  If you have adequate disk space, consider creating AIFF or WAV files to produce the highest quality sound. If hard disk space is at a premium, use the AAC format if it is available on your computer. Keep in mind that after the audio is available in iTunes, you can export it in any format. Note that you cannot improve the audio over the original. For example, converting an MP3 file to AIFF format will not improve the quality of the audio file.

- **Which uncompressed format is best, AIFF or WAV?** Both AIFF and WAV produce an uncompressed copy of the original audio file. Select the format based on your intended usage. AIFF is the standard format for uncompressed audio files on the Mac. WAV is the standard format for uncompressed audio files on Microsoft Windows. If you intend to share the audio files with a Microsoft Windows computer, consider creating WAV files to ensure compatibility. Otherwise, the choice is your own personal preference.

## 47  Capture Audio Files from CDs

If you want to create a collection of audio files in iTunes, one of the easiest methods is to import your favorite audio files—both music and spoken word—from CDs. By importing your audio files into iTunes, you can listen to them at any time right from your computer. After you have imported the audio into iTunes, you can combine the files with other audio and export them to your Apple iPod or create a personal favorites CD. See **67 Sync Playlists with iPod** for information on placing audio on an iPod or **86 Burn an Audio CD** for information on creating CDs from iTunes.

When you insert an audio CD in your computer, iTunes displays the contents of the CD. Each separate file on the CD is referred to as a *track*. If you are connected to the Internet, iTunes connects to the *CDDB* (CD Database) and downloads the title information for the CD and each track. If iTunes is unable to connect to the Internet or if it cannot find a match for the CD, then iTunes simply displays each track by number, such as **Track 1**, **Track 2**, and so on. If you are not connected to the Internet, you can import the songs from the CD and connect to the Internet later to retrieve the CD information. See **51 Get CD Information from the Internet** for more information on retrieving information about CDs.

You can import the entire contents of the CD into iTunes or select individual tracks. All the tracks you select are added to your iTunes library.

### 1 Insert the CD in the Drive

Insert in your computer's CD drive the audio CD containing the audio files you want to copy. iTunes adds the CD to the **Source** list on the left side of the iTunes window and displays the contents of the CD on the right side of the window.

If you are connected to the Internet, iTunes connects to the CDDB and downloads the track information, if it is available.

### 2 Select Files to Import

As a default, iTunes automatically selects for import all tracks on the CD by enabling the check box next to each track. If there are tracks you do not want to import, click the box next to the track to remove the check mark.

---

**Before You Begin**

✓ **46** About Audio Formats

**See Also**

→ **48** Import Internet Music

→ **49** Purchase Audio from the Music Store

→ **51** Get CD Information from the Internet

→ **53** Download Audio Book Files from the Internet

→ **59** Create Smart Playlists

### KEY TERMS

*Track*—A separate song or audio file stored on a CD or DVD.

*CDDB*—A database maintained by a company called Gracenote that contains track information about all commercial audio CDs. The information includes track name, artist, and album name.

### TIPS

If you are not sure which tracks you want to copy, click a track and then click the **Play** button at the top-left of the window to listen to the track.

To deselect the tracks, press ⌘ and click on any of the check boxes next to the tracks.

## 47 Capture Audio Files from CDs

**1** Insert the CD in the Drive

**2** Select Files to Import

**3** Import Audio Files from CD

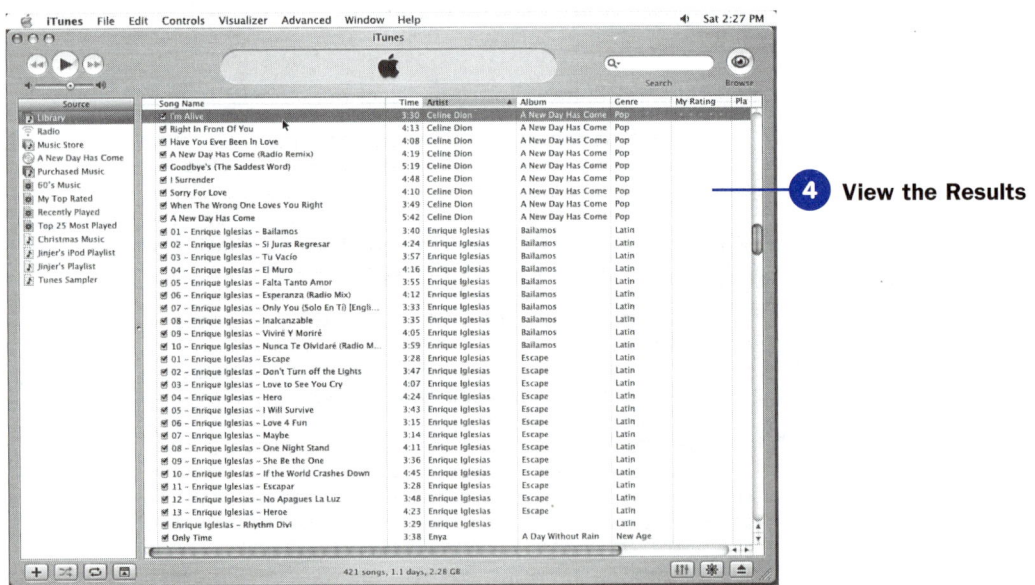

**4** View the Results

144   PART II:   iTunes

## ③ Import Audio Files from CD

Click the **Import** button to import the selected tracks from the audio CD. iTunes creates a copy of the specified tracks using the default import format. The default import format is MP3, which means that iTunes creates an MP3 file for every track you import.

As the tracks are copied onto your computer, iTunes shows the status of the import process. A green circle containing a check mark displays next to each track that has been successfully copied to your computer. iTunes displays an orange circle next to the track that is currently being copied.

**NOTE**

The process of importing audio files from a CD to a computer is commonly referred to as *ripping*.

## ④ View the Results

Click the **Library** in the **Source** pane to view a list of all the audio files currently available in your iTunes Library. Use the scrollbar on the right side of the screen to scroll through the list and locate the new audio tracks. Verify that you have copied all the desired tracks before removing the CD from the drive.

## 48  Import Internet Music

There are multitudes of different sites on the Internet where you can download music files. Because the only Web site that iTunes can connect to to download music is the Music Store, any other audio files you download must be downloaded to a folder on your computer and then added to your iTunes Library.

You must be mindful of the music copyright laws when downloading music from the Internet. Although many sites offer free music, if you download copyrighted music without paying the appropriate fees, you can face fines. Other sites allow you to purchase and download music, similar to the Apple Music Store. If you find sites offering free music, make sure that the music has not been copyrighted. Some sites offer royalty-free music you can download and distribute freely, but this music won't be anything you hear on the radio. These royalty-free music sites are great because they provide music you can add to your movies and audio CDs freely.

**Before You Begin**

✓ 46  About Audio Formats

**See Also**

→ 47  Capture Audio Files from CDs

→ 49  Purchase Audio from the Music Store

→ 53  Download Audio Book Files from the Internet

## 48 Import Internet Music

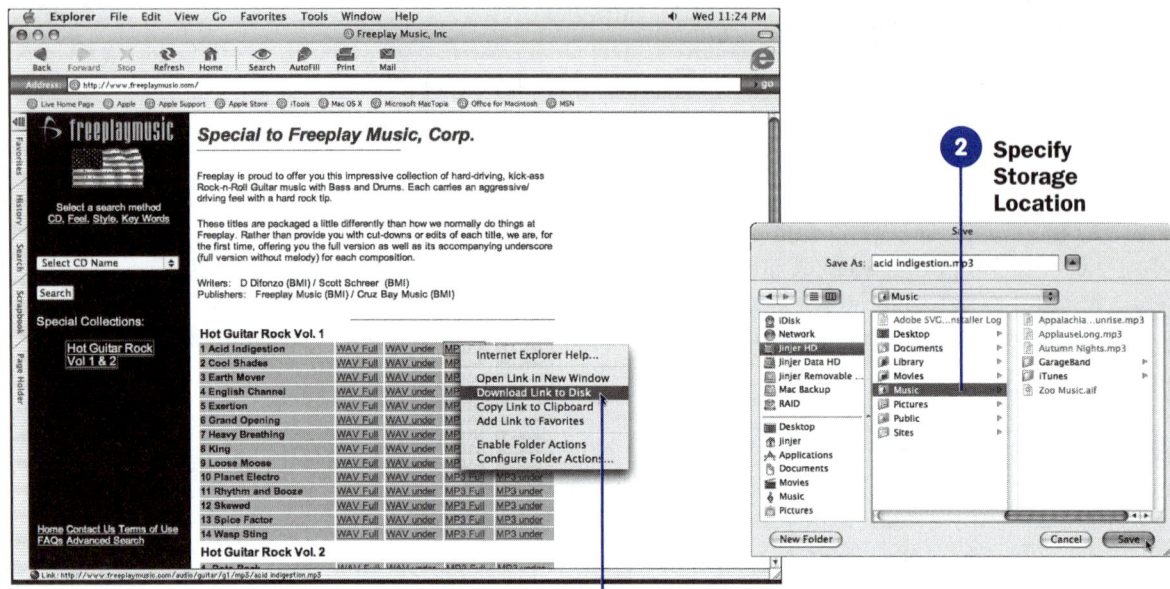

**1** Download Music File

**2** Specify Storage Location

**3** Add Downloaded Music to iTunes

**4** Find Imported Music in iTunes Library

146     **PART II:**    iTunes

After you have downloaded a song from the Internet, the audio file is stored in the folder you specified. To add the song to your iTunes Library, use the **Add to Library** option. When you add the song to your library, it is either copied to your **Library** folder, or iTunes creates a link to the location where it is stored. You use the **Preferences** dialog box to specify whether or not iTunes copies the music files to your iTunes **Music** folder. See  **Set the Import Format for Audio Files** for more information on specifying the import options.

When you download music from some Internet sites, a link to the actual URL of the music file on the Internet downloads, instead of the actual file. If this is the case when you add the song to your iTunes Library, iTunes places a broadcast symbol next to the song name. Songs with this symbol can be played in iTunes only when you are connected to the Internet. You cannot copy these songs to your iPod or burn them on an audio CD.

### WEB RESOURCE

http://www.mp3.com

Visit this site to download MP3 files from different artists. Similar to the Apple Music Store, MP3.com requires you to pay a subscription fee before you can download music.

### WEB RESOURCE

http://www.freeplaymusic.com

Provides royalty-free music you can download for free. This music can be freely distributed to other people.

 **Download Music File**

On the Web site containing the audio file you want to download, you might notice several download link options for each song. Press the **Control** key and click the download link for the format for which you want to display a menu of options.

Select the **Download Link to Disk** option to display the **Save** dialog box.

**❷ Specify Storage Location**

Select the location where you want to store the selected audio file. As a default, Mac OS X selects your **Music** folder as the storage

## 49 Purchase Audio from the Music Store

location for the downloaded audio file. To store the file in a different location, select the appropriate folder.

The name of the file you are downloading displays in the **Save As** field. If you want to store the audio file with a different name, type that name in the **Save As** field.

When you have made the desired selections, click the **Save** button to download the file from the Internet and save it in the specified folder.

### 3 Add Downloaded Music to iTunes

In iTunes, choose **File, Add to Library** to display the **Add to Library** dialog box.

By default, iTunes opens your **Music** folder as the place from which it will load audio files. If the downloaded music is stored in another location, locate that folder. Select the audio file you want to import to iTunes and click the **Choose** button. iTunes adds the selected file to your library.

### 4 Find Imported Music in iTunes Library

In the **Source** list on the left side of the iTunes window, click the **Library** option to view all the audio files in your iTunes Library. Use the scrollbars on the right side of the window to scroll through the list and locate the file you added.

To listen to the audio file, click to select it and then click the **Play** button.

## 49 Purchase Audio from the Music Store

**Before You Begin**

✓ **46** About Audio Formats

**See Also**

→ **47** Capture Audio Files from CDs

→ **48** Import Internet Music

→ **53** Download Audio Book Files from the Internet

If you want to download music from the Internet, the best place to get it is from Apple's *Music Store*. This download option works best with iTunes because anything you choose to download is loaded directly into your iTunes Library. Also, you don't have to worry about breaking any laws when you download music from this site, as long as you follow the rules specified on the site. The Music Store allows you to play the music you purchase on three different computers. To get the music, you pay a small fee to download a single song or a separate fee for the entire album. In most cases, you pay just 99 cents for a single song or $9.99 for an entire album.

PART II: iTunes

Purchase Audio from the Music Store **49**

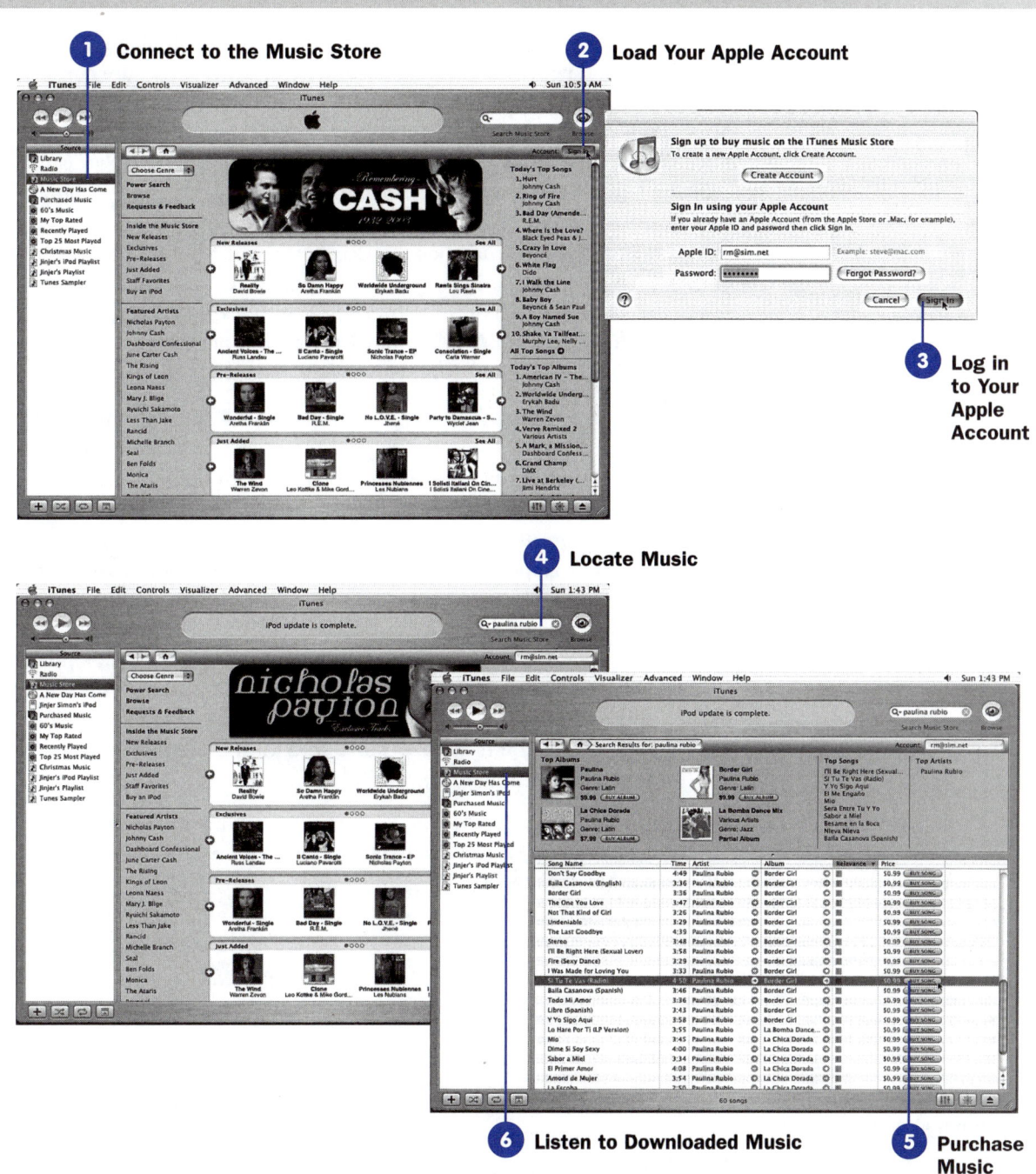

1. Connect to the Music Store
2. Load Your Apple Account
3. Log in to Your Apple Account
4. Locate Music
5. Purchase Music
6. Listen to Downloaded Music

**CHAPTER 7:** Loading Sound Files   149

## 49  Purchase Audio from the Music Store

**KEY TERM**

*Music Store*—A Web site created by Apple that you can access from iTunes to purchase music.

**NOTE**

You must have a billing address in the United States to purchase music from the iTunes Music Store. The Apple account you use to purchase music is different than the .Mac account you use to publish photos and movies to the Web.

**TIPS**

If you have version 4.2 or later of iTunes you can also download audiobook files from iTunes. Click the **Choose Genre** drop-down list at the top left of the Music Store and select the Audiobooks option. Select the books you want to download using the steps outlined for purchasing music from the Music Store.

You can also download audiobooks for **Audible.com**. See **53** **Download Audio Book files from the Internet** for more information.

The **Music Store** option appears in your **Source** list on the left side of the iTunes window when you load iTunes 4.0 or later. If you are connected to the Internet, click the **Music Store** option to open the store within iTunes. You can browse the store to find the songs you want to download. If you decide to download a song, you can purchase it using your Apple account. You connect to your account by clicking the **Sign In** button in the top-right corner of the iTunes window. If you don't have an Apple account, you can click the **Create Account** button on the **Sign In** dialog box to create an account. This Apple account is the same one you use to purchase Photo Books and prints in iPhoto. See **28** **Order Photo Book Online** and **37** **Order Prints from an Online Photo-Printer** for information on using your Apple account with iPhoto.

Even after you download the music from the Music Store, you must continue to authorize your computer to play the music. The authorization is created when you initially download the songs from the Music Store, and it is maintained on your computer as long as you don't select the **Deauthorize Computer** option. Because you can share the songs purchased with your Apple account on three different computers, you can also play music purchased with your Apple account from a different computer. All music that has been purchased by your account from the current computer displays when you select the **Purchased Music** option from the **Source** list. To play music you purchased from other computers, you must share the purchased music playlists from those machines. See **60** **Share Playlists with Other Users** for more information on sharing playlists with other computers.

After you purchase music, you can play it at any time from iTunes. You can also copy the music to your iPod or create an audio CD containing the downloaded music. Note that you can burn only 10 CDs from a playlist (without modifying the playlist contents) containing music purchased from the Music Store. See **67** **Sync Playlists with iPod** for information on copying audio to your iPod. See **86** **Burn an Audio CD** for information on creating CDs from iTunes.

**1** **Connect to the Music Store**

Click the **Music Store** option in the **Source** list on the left side of your iTunes window. If you are connected to the Internet, the Apple Music Store opens.

## Purchase Audio from the Music Store

You must be running iTunes 4.0 or later to use the Music Store. If you don't have the latest version of iTunes, you can download it free from Apple's Web site.

### WEB RESOURCE

http://www.apple.com/itunes/download/

Download the latest version of iTunes free from Apple's Web site.

### ② Load Your Apple Account

Click the **Sign In** button on the upper-right corner of the **Music Store** to sign in to your Apple account.

If you have already set up iTunes to use an Apple account, iTunes connects to that account and your account name will display in place of the **Sign In** button.

### ③ Log in to Your Apple Account

In the **Apple ID** field of the **Sign In** dialog box, type your Apple account ID and type your password in the **Password** field. Click the **Sign In** button to connect to your account.

If you don't have an Apple account, click the **Create Account** button to create one. You will be asked to provide contact information and a credit card number that can be used to pay for any purchases. When the account is created, you can also use it to purchase Photo Books and prints from iPhoto.

After you have connected to your account, the Apple Account ID displays in the upper-right corner of the Music Store.

### ④ Locate Music

Locate the music you want to download from the Music Store. To search for a specific artist or song, type the desired search string in the **Search Music Store** field in the top right corner and press **Enter**. A list of matching songs and albums displays. Use the scroll bar on the right to scroll through the list and find the desired song.

### ⑤ Purchase Music

Click the **Buy Song** button next to the song to purchase the selected song. Click the **Buy Album** button to purchase an entire album.

### TIP

If **Music Store** is not listed on the **Source** list, choose **iTunes, Preferences** from the menu bar to display the **Preferences** dialog box. Click the **Store** icon and then select the **Show iTunes Music Store** option.

### NOTE

It is not necessary to sign in to an Apple account until you have found a song or album that you want to download to your computer.

### TIPS

If you are not sure which song you want to download, you can double-click the song to hear a preview of the song.

You can also search for music by genre. Display the **Choose Genre** drop-down list at the top-left of the Music Store to view a list of available genres.

You can click the **Browse** button to locate a song by selecting genre, artist, and then album name. The Music Store displays a list of songs that match the specified criteria.

**CHAPTER 7:** Loading Sound Files

### 49  Purchase Audio from the Music Store

Before purchasing, iTunes requires you to enter the password for your Apple account to ensure that you are the person purchasing the music for download. The price of the song or album always displays on the screen. Typically, a song costs $0.99, and an album costs $9.99.

If you want to download a bunch of music from the Music Store, use the **Shopping Cart** option. With this option, iTunes places all the music you select in your shopping cart and then downloads it all at once when you click the **Buy Now** button. To switch to the Shopping Cart feature, choose **iTunes, Preferences** and then click the **Store** button on the dialog box. Select the **Buy Using a Shopping Cart** option. When this option is enabled, an **Add Song** button displays next to each song instead of a **Buy Song** button. When you click the **Add Song** buttons, the selected songs are placed in the shopping cart. They are not downloaded until you click the **Buy Now** button.

### 6  Listen to Downloaded Music

**NOTE**
Any songs you download from the Music Store are also added to your playlist.

Click **Purchased Music** option in the **Source** list on the left side of the iTunes window to see the songs you have downloaded from the Music Store. A green icon displays next to the **Purchased Music** option. To listen to a downloaded song, click the song to select it and then click the **Play** button.

If you are sharing your Apple account with another computer and songs are purchased using that computer, you can share the songs over a network. Shared music displays with a blue icon next to it. See **60 Share Playlists with Other Users** for more information on sharing music with other computers. Although you can listen to music you purchased on a different computer, you cannot create audio CDs or copy those songs to your iPod. This is another copyright feature built into the Apple Music Store.

## 50 Link to Audio Files in Other Locations

You do not have to add audio files you have stored on your computer or a network computer to your iTunes library. You can have iTunes create a link to those audio files. For example, if you have a central audio library that you share between multiple computers, you can link to that library so that the audio files remain in the central location and are not copied into your **Music** folder. This not only conserves disk storage space, but reduces the redundancy of having multiple copies of the same audio file.

To create only links to audio files you add to your library, you must deselect the **Copy files to iTunes Music folder when adding to library** option on the **Preferences** dialog box. When this option is deselected, all audio you add to iTunes using the **Add to Library** option will be added by creating a link to the original file. If you later decide you want the audio files copied into your **Music** folder, you can do so by enabling the **Consolidate Library** option. See **64 Copy Audio Files to a Central Location** for more information on consolidating audio files.

### Before You Begin
✓ **46** About Audio Formats

### See Also
→ **47** Capture Audio Files from CDs
→ **48** Import Internet Music
→ **49** Purchase Audio from the Music Store
→ **53** Download Audio Book Files from the Internet

### ❶ Display Preferences Dialog Box

Choose **iTunes**, **Preferences** to display the **Preferences** dialog box.

### ❷ View Advanced Options

If it is not already selected, click the **Advanced** option at the top of the dialog box. The name of the **Preferences** dialog box changes based on the selected option. When you select the **Advanced** option, the title of the dialog box is **Advanced**.

### ❸ Deselect the Copy Files Option

Make sure that the **Copy files to iTunes Music folder when adding to library** option is not selected. When this option is disabled, any audio files you add to your library are linked to the original files, instead of copying the files into your **Music** folder.

Click the **OK** button to close the **Preferences** dialog box and save the settings.

## Link to Audio Files in Other Locations

**1** Display Preferences Dialog Box

**2** View Advanced Options

**3** Deselect the Copy Files Option

**4** Display Add To Library Dialog Box

**5** Select Audio Files

**6** View Results

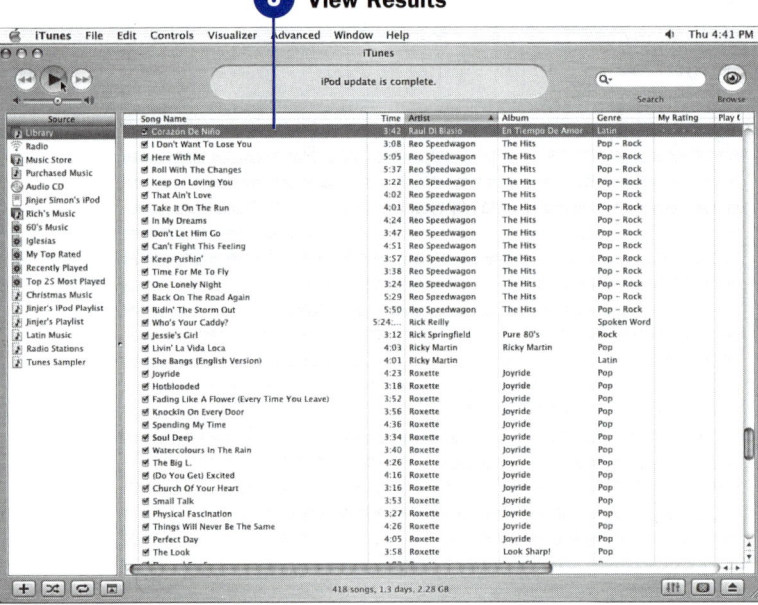

### TIP

If you want to add multiple audio files to your library, hold down the ⌘ key while you click each audio file you want to add.

### **4** Display Add To Library Dialog Box

Choose **File**, **Add to Library** to display the **Add To Library** dialog box.

# Get CD Information from the Internet

**⑤ Select Audio Files**

Locate the folder containing the audio file you want to add to your library. Click to select the audio file you want to add and then click the **Choose** button. iTunes adds a link to that audio file to your Library and closes the dialog box.

**⑥ View Results**

Locate the new audio in the song list of your Library. You can add the audio to a playlist, add it to your iPod, or even place it on an audio CD. All iTunes functionality is available for the linked audio file, even though it is not stored in your **Music** folder.

To play the file, click the file in the song list to select it and then click the **Play** button.

> **TIP**
> To view the storage location of a specific audio file, select the song in the song list and then choose **File**, **Get Info** to display a dialog box with information about the selected song. The **Where** field on the **Summary** tab indicates the storage location of the selected audio file.

## 51 Get CD Information from the Internet

If you imported audio files from a CD when your computer was not connected to the Internet, the track and album information would not have been downloaded from the Internet. You can get that information for CD files you have imported when you are connected to the Internet.

The option to add the CD information later makes it possible to load all your CD information into your computer and then have iTunes determine the CD information for each track.

When you request the CD track name information, iTunes connects to the *CDDB* (CD Database) maintained by Gracenote and retrieves the information. The database contains track and album information on almost every commercial audio CD. When you connect to the database, iTunes looks for an exact match in the database. The CD database is set up on the premise that there are no two CDs of the same length. Every CD is laid out differently with tracks of different lengths. This track information is how iTunes locates a match for your CD in the database.

**Before You Begin**

✔ **47** Capture Audio Files from CDs

**See Also**

→ **48** Import Internet Music

→ **49** Purchase Audio from the Music Store

→ **52** Change Song Information

CHAPTER 7: Loading Sound Files    155

**Get CD Information from the Internet**

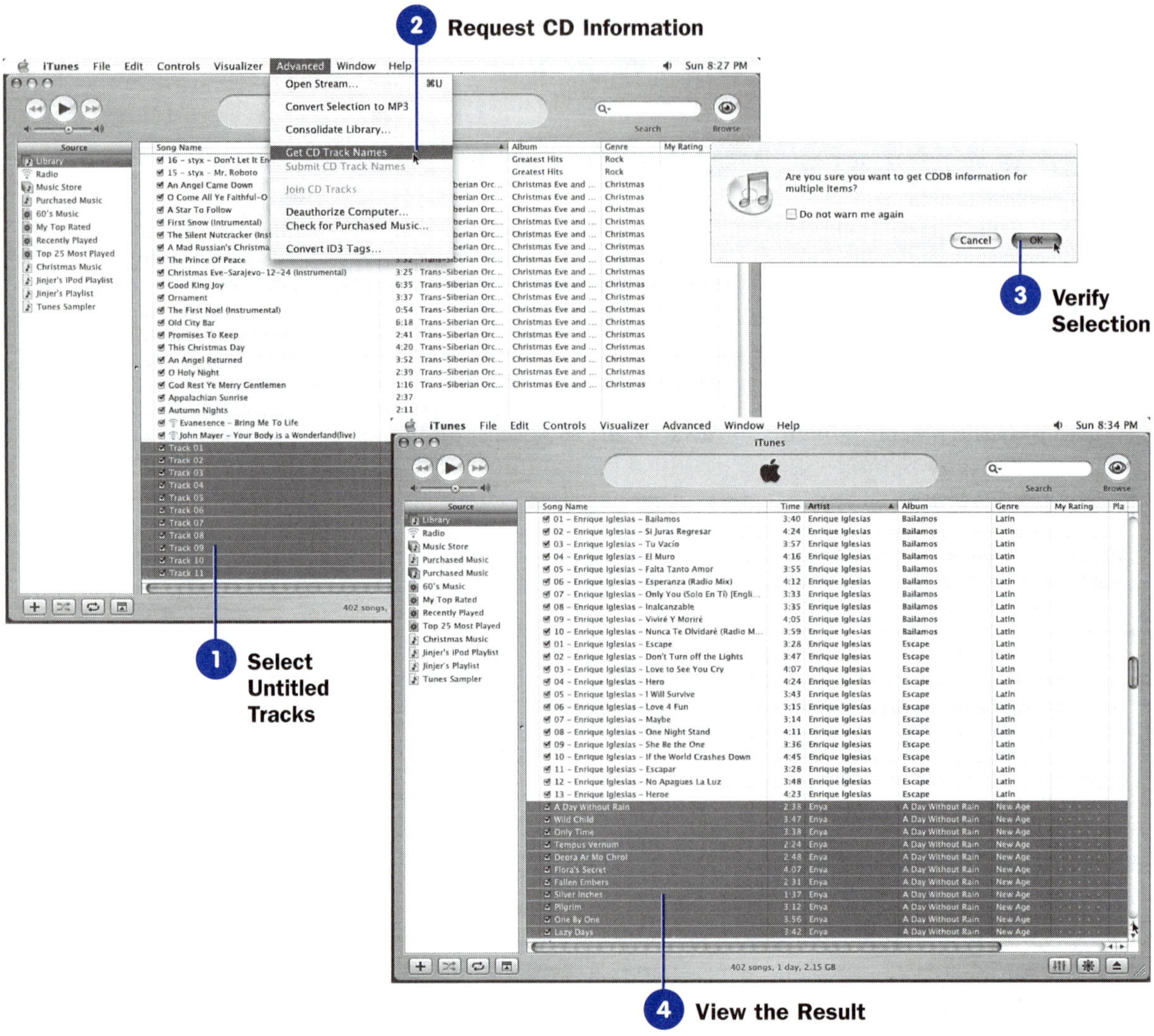

**② Request CD Information**

**③ Verify Selection**

**① Select Untitled Tracks**

**④ View the Result**

### ① Select Untitled Tracks

Connect your computer to the Internet. In the iTunes Library, select the tracks for which you want to get the CD information. Remember, if the CD information was not available when you imported music from a CD, iTunes imports the tracks by naming them numerically based on the order they were listed on the track.

**PART II:** iTunes

For example, the first track is **Track 01**. You might want to select all the numbered tracks from an import operation to retrieve title information for all the tracks at once.

**② Request CD Information**

Choose **Advanced, Get CD Track Names** to display a dialog box that verifies your selection.

**③ Verify Selection**

Click the **OK** button in the confirmation dialog box to have iTunes connect to the CDDB and get the track and album information for the selected songs.

As the information is being downloaded from the CDDB, iTunes displays a status box. When the process is complete, the selected tracks are automatically renamed within your Library.

**④ View the Result**

When the song information has been downloaded, the information is automatically updated in the iTunes Library. You can see the renamed songs by clicking the scrollbar on the right side of the window and scrolling to find the songs. The songs you selected in step 1 are still selected in the Library window.

### TIP
To select a range of songs, click the first song and then hold down the **Shift** key until you click the last song in the range.

### NOTE
If iTunes is unable to find a match for any of the selected songs in the CDDB, a message to that effect appears.

## 52 Change Song Information

When you view the list of songs available in your iTunes Library, iTunes displays the description information available for the song in the audio file. This information typically consists of the song name, artist name, album name, length, and genre. If you would prefer to see different title information, iTunes provides the ability to modify the information for each song.

If you imported the song from a CD, iTunes would have retrieved the CD information from the CDDB maintained by Gracenote. However, because the information about CDs is added to the database by different individuals, it does not look the same for all CDs. For example, the information for one CD might have the song names in all capital letters, while other song titles might be in initial caps.

**Before You Begin**

✔ **46** About Audio Formats

✔ **47** Capture Audio Files from CDs

**See Also**

→ **48** Import Internet Music

→ **49** Purchase Audio from the Music Store

→ **54** Set the Import Format for Audio Files

## 52  Change Song Information

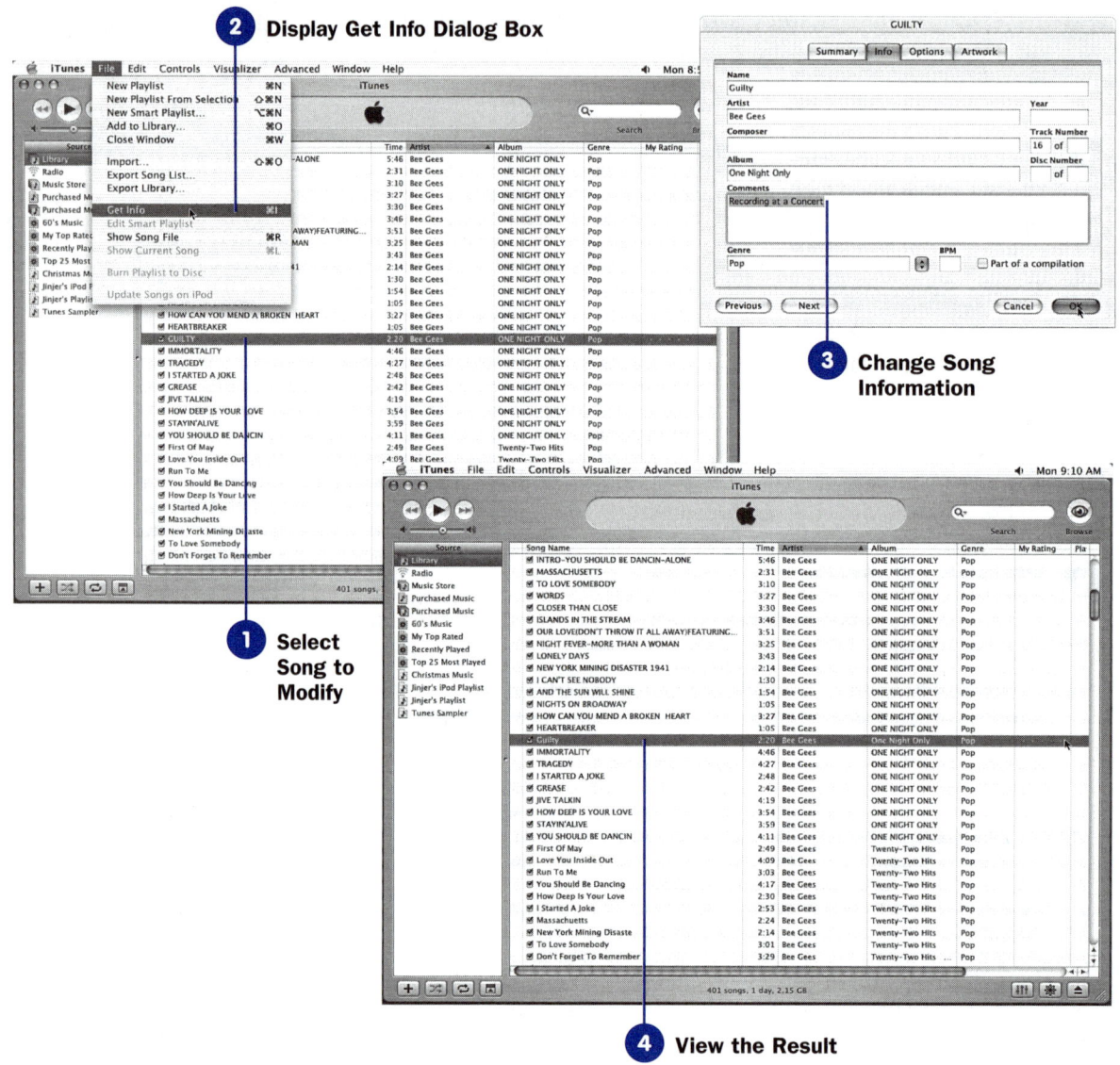

You can modify the song information for all songs using the **Get Info** dialog box. Any changes you make are saved in the associated audio file. For example, if you change the name of the song, the name of the audio file is modified on your computer. Note that if you added the song

## Change Song Information

to your iTunes library by creating a link to another storage location, you cannot change the song's filename. See **56 Set Music File Storage Location** for more information on setting the storage location of audio files.

### ① Select Song to Modify

In your iTunes Library, select the song whose information you want to modify. If you want to modify the song name, select only one song in the list.

### ② Display Get Info Dialog Box

Choose **File, Get Info** to display the **Get Info** dialog box.

### ③ Change Song Information

The **Get Info** dialog box opens to the **Info** tab, where you can change the information that appears in the iTunes Library window.

The text in the **Name** field displays in the **Song Name** column. Make the desired modifications to the **Name, Artist, Composer, Album, Year, Track Number, Disc Number,** and **Comments** fields. You can also select a different genre for the song by clicking the arrow button next to the **Genre** field and selecting a genre from the list.

Click the **OK** button to save the changes to the selected song and close the dialog box.

### ④ View the Result

View the modified songs in the iTunes Library to ensure that the changes are correct. Here, you can see that I've started my crusade to change the song titles in my iTunes Library so that they all appear in uppercase and lowercase letters, instead of in all caps.

### TIP

When you create an MP3 file, the information about the MP3 file (including song name, artist name, album, release date, track number, genre, comments, and lyrics) is stored in ID3 tags in the file. This information is exported with the MP3 file so that MP3 players can display the song information.

### NOTE

If you want to change the artist or album information for multiple songs, hold down the ⌘ button and click to select several songs. Any changes made affect all the selected songs.

### TIP

Click the **Previous** and **Next** buttons to alter the information for the previous and next songs in the iTunes Library list.

### TIP

To display additional information in the Library list, choose **Edit, View Options** to display the **View Options** dialog box. Enable the options you want to view as columns in the iTunes Library list. For example, enable the **Composer** option to view the names of the composers of your classical music collection.

**CHAPTER 7:** Loading Sound Files

## 53 Download Audio Book Files from the Internet

**Before You Begin**

✓ **46** About Audio Formats

**See Also**

→ **47** Capture Audio Files from CDs
→ **48** Import Internet Music
→ **49** Purchase Audio from the Music Store

 **KEY TERM**

**Audible.com**—A Web site that provides audio versions of books, magazines, newspapers, and even radio shows you can download for a fee.

If you love to read but don't have the time to sit down with a book, you can download your favorite books as audio files that you can listen to in iTunes. You can purchase and download audio book files from *Audible.com*. After the audio files have been downloaded to your computer, you can add them to your iTunes library.

To download audio book files from Audible.com, you must create an account with Audible.com. The company offers different account types based on your interests. When you have created your account, you can download a file and add it to iTunes.

When you download an audio book from Audible.com, you must specify the format for the file that you want to download. You select a format based on the type of Internet connection you have and the amount of time you are willing to wait for a download. For example, if have a 56k modem and select Format 2, you get AM radio quality audio that takes about 12 minutes to download 1 hour's worth of audio. The best format is Format 4, which produces MP3 quality audio. However, if you select Format 4, audio files will take the most time to download. You can find out more about the different format levels available on the Audible.com site.

 **WEB RESOURCE**

This Web site offers audio books, magazines, newspapers, and radio shows you can download for a fee.

http://www.audible.com

Similar to the way the Apple Music Store works, Audible.com allows you to use the same audio book files on up to three different computers. You set up the account information for your Audible.com account the first time you add an audio book file to iTunes. iTunes requires you to enter your Audible.com user name and password so that it can verify your account with Audible.com.

**TIP**

If you want to put the audio book you are downloading from Audible.com on your iPod, download the file in Format 2, 3, or 4. See **67** Sync Playlists with iPod for more information on adding audio to your iPod.

 **Download Audio Book File**

On the Audible.com site, select the audio book file you want to download and follow the steps to purchase it. After you have purchased the audio file, it is placed in your Library to be downloaded and the **My Library** page displays. On the **My Library** page of the Audible.com Web site, select the desired download format by selecting the corresponding number. The file size of the file that will be downloaded is listed under each format.

## Download Audio Book Files from the Internet 53

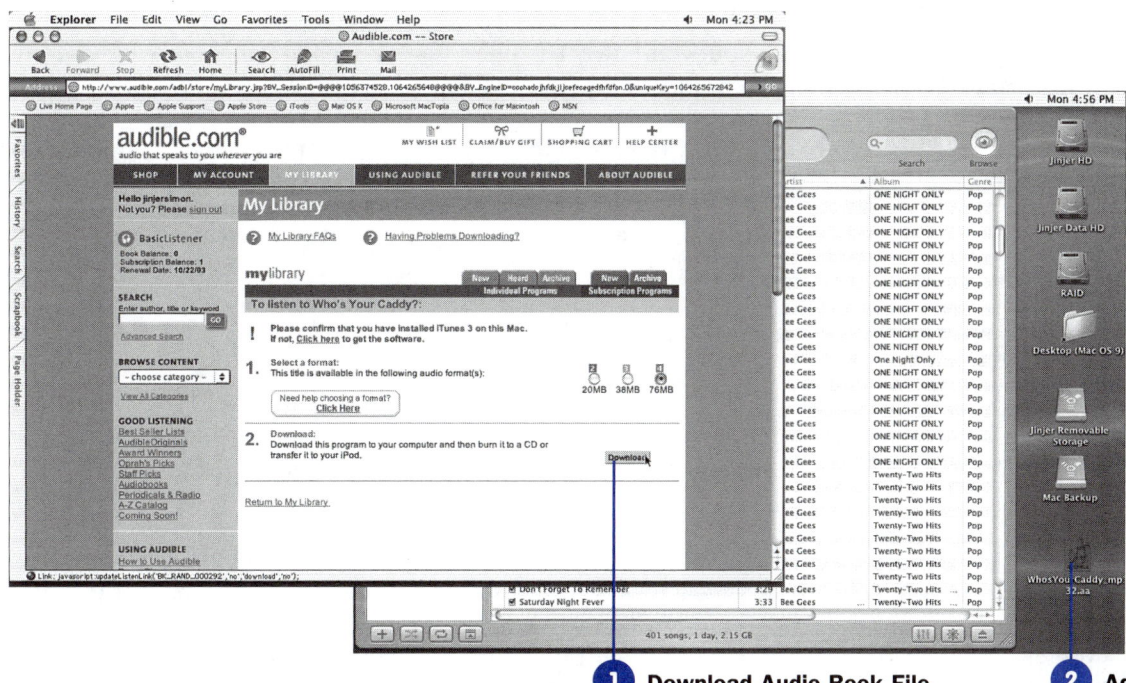

1. Download Audio Book File
2. Add Audio Book File to iTunes

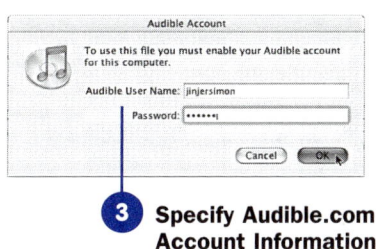

3. Specify Audible.com Account Information

4. Listen to File

CHAPTER 7: Loading Sound Files    161

## 53 Download Audio Book Files from the Internet

### TIPS

Before you can download files from Audible.com, you must create an account on the Web site. You will need this account information to listen to the first audio book file in iTunes.

The files you download are placed in the download location of your Web browser. If you want to change that location, you must change the download folder of your Web browser.

### TIP

You can deauthorize a computer from an Audible.com account so that you can set up the account on another computer. To deauthorize a computer, choose **Advanced, Deauthorize Computer** from the iTunes menu bar and then select the **Deauthorize Computer for Audible Account** option.

Click the **Download** button to download the selected audio book to your computer. The file is downloaded to your computer and an icon is placed on your desktop.

### ② Add Audio Book File to iTunes

Click the audio book icon on your desktop and drag it onto the iTunes window. All audio book files that you download from Audible.com have the file extension **.AA**.

iTunes copies the selected audio book file into your iTunes Library.

### ③ Specify Audible.com Account Information

If this is the first audio book you have added to iTunes, the **Audible Account** dialog box displays requesting your Audible.com account information.

Type your username in the **Audible User Name** field. Type the password for your account in the **Password** field. iTunes transmits this information to Audible.com to verify your account and make sure that your computer can access the file. Keep in mind that Audible.com allows you to download an audio file to only three computers. If you have already placed this audio file on three other computers, you will not be able to open it in iTunes on this computer.

### ④ Listen to File

Locate the audio book file in your iTunes Library and click the **Play** button to listen to it.

You can move your audio books into a separate playlist in iTunes. See **57 About Playlists** for more information about playlists in iTunes. You can also put the audio book file on your iPod. See **67 Sync Playlists with iPod** for more information on placing files on your iPod.

PART II:   iTunes

## 54 Set the Import Format for Audio Files

When you import audio into iTunes, the file is saved using the format specified for importing. For example, the default format in iTunes is to import audio files as MP3 audio files. However, iTunes can also create AIFF, WAV, and AAC files. You can select the desired import from the **Preferences** dialog box.

When selecting the desired format for importing audio files into iTunes, be mindful of the intended use for the audio files and your available disk space. Although WAV and AIFF provide an uncompressed, CD-quality sound, they both require a lot of storage space. When selecting these formats, expect that every minute of your audio file will use about 10 megabytes of storage space on your hard drive. With that in mind, consider saving audio files as MP3 files, which require about a tenth of the storage of the AIFF and WAV formats (MP3 files compress the audio data by eliminating some of the subtle sounds from the audio, thus reducing the size of the audio file). In fact, MP3 has become a standard for compressed audio files. Several Web sites offer MP3 versions of audio files that you can download. You can also purchase portable devices that play MP3 files, such as the Apple iPod.

When you select the MP3 format, you can also customize the import by selecting the quality level for the file. iTunes provides three different quality levels for MP3 files: **Good Quality** (128 kilobits per second, or Kbps), **High Quality** (160Kbps), and **Higher Quality** (192Kbps). If those three settings are not what you are looking for, you can also customize the quality level by selecting the **Custom** option. The quality level is actually an indication of the compression used on the file. The compression is expressed as the *bit rate*. The higher the bit rate number, the larger the file that is created because of the reduced compression. Because there is less compression, the MP3 file has a higher sound quality. Typically, the acceptable bit rate for music files is between 128 and 192Kbps, with 128Kbps being closer to FM radio quality. The default iTunes settings create 128Kbps formatted files, which is adequate in most cases (although higher bit rate formats produce better quality sound).

### Before You Begin

✓ 46 About Audio Formats

### See Also

→ 47 Capture Audio Files from CDs
→ 48 Import Internet Music
→ 49 Purchase Audio from the Music Store
→ 53 Download Audio Book Files from the Internet
→ 56 Set Music File Storage Location

### KEY TERM

*Bit rate*—A compression measurement indicating the average number of bits required for one second of sound. The higher the bit rate, the higher the quality of the sound.

### TIP

Consider using the **High Quality** (**160Kbps**) setting for improved sound quality, although you also get larger files (about 1 megabyte for each minute of music). For example, a 3-minute song takes about 3 megabytes of disk space to store if it is in **160Kbps** format.

## 54 Set the Import Format for Audio Files

① **Display Preferences Dialog Box**

② **Display Importing Options**

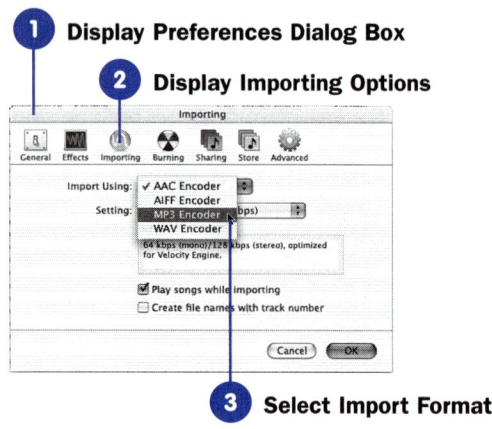

③ **Select Import Format**

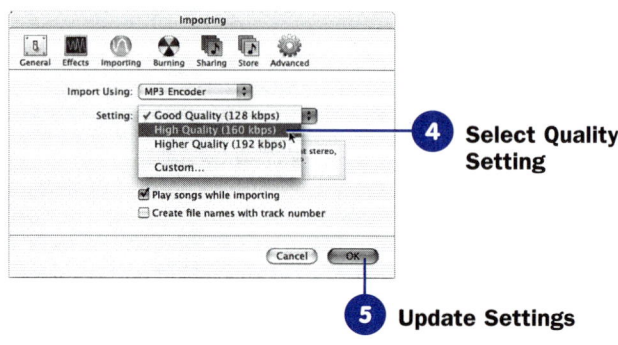

④ **Select Quality Setting**

⑤ **Update Settings**

If you have loaded QuickTime 6.2 or later on your computer, you have the option of using a fourth compressed audio format, **AAC (Advanced Audio Coding)**. AAC is a new audio format developed to compress audio files more than MP3 with higher quality sound. AAC files compressed at 128Kbps produce near CD-quality sound. The sound quality of an AAC file at 128Kbps is much better than that of an MP3 file at 128Kbps. As with the MP3 format, you can select custom configurations to increase or decrease the bit rate of ACC files. If ACC is available on your computer, consider using this format as the default in iTunes. Note that AAC is not supported by MP3 players, with the exception of the Apple iPod. Your iPod supports AAC files, as long as you are using version 1.3 or higher of the iPod software.

### ① Display Preferences Dialog Box

Choose **iTunes**, **Preferences** to display the **Preferences** dialog box.

### ② Display Importing Options

If the **Importing** tab is not displayed, click the **Importing** button to display these options on the **Preferences** dialog box. The **Preferences** dialog box displays the last set of options that were used.

The **Preferences** dialog box lets you set seven different types of options: General, Effects, Importing, Burning, Sharing, Store, and Advanced. When you select one of the options on the top of the dialog box, the options change on the dialog box to reflect that selection.

164  PART II: iTunes

## Set Custom MP3 Quality Options

### ③ Select Import Format

Select the desired import format from the **Import Using** drop-down list. If you want to ensure that your imported music will play on most devices, select the **MP3 Encoder** option.

### ④ Select Quality Setting

Some import formats, such as MP3 and ACC, allow you to select a quality option. From the **Settings** drop-down list, select the bit rate setting you want to use for importing audio files. Select **High Quality (160Kbps)** or higher to produce an MP3 file that sounds close to CD quality.

### ⑤ Update Settings

Click the **OK** button to update the import settings for all future audio files imported into iTunes. Note that the selections you make in this dialog box do not affect any audio files you have already downloaded or imported into iTunes.

**TIPS**

Enable the **Play songs while importing** check box if you want iTunes to play the files while they are importing. When this option is enabled, iTunes starts playing the first song in the import list as it begins importing the songs.

If you want to see the track number as part of the song name, enable the **Create file names with track number** check box. This option works for MP3 files only.

## 55 Set Custom MP3 Quality Options

When you import files into iTunes as MP3 files, you can use one of the three **Quality** settings or you can create your own custom MP3 settings. For example, although iTunes provides the capability to select a 192Kbps setting, you might want to create even higher quality MP3 files.

You create a custom MP3 import format with the **MP3 Encoder** dialog box. This dialog box gives you the capability to select from 16 different bit rates (between 16Kbps and 320Kbps). You can also have iTunes use *variable bit rate* encoding to automatically reduce the bit rate of MP3 files based on the complexity of the audio.

You can also customize the sample rate used to create each MP3 file. Typically, you want to use the default **Auto** setting to allow iTunes to automatically set the sample rate based on the audio file you are downloading. However, if you are going to import a voice recording with no music, you can lower the sample rate to 22.050KHz to reduce the disk space used to store the MP3 file.

**Before You Begin**

✔ 46 About Audio Formats

**See Also**

→ 47 Capture Audio Files from CDs
→ 48 Import Internet Music
→ 54 Set Import Format for Audio Files
→ 56 Set Music File Storage Location

CHAPTER 7: Loading Sound Files 165

## 55 Set Custom MP3 Quality Options

**KEY TERMS**

*Variable bit rate (VBR)*—A compression method that reduces the bit rate of the song according to the complexity. For example, a quiet section requires a much lower bit rate than another portion with complex sounds.

*Joint Stereo* —The process of combining high frequency stereo sounds into a single channel to make them easier to detect.

By default, iTunes automatically determines whether the imported audio is stereo or mono. If you want to record everything in stereo—even if it is a mono audio file—you can set the **Channels** field to **Stereo**. You can also set it to **Mono** to record everything as mono. If you have the **Auto** or **Stereo** option selected for the **Channels** field, you can select between recording high frequencies as normal or *Joint Stereo*.

When you have specified the custom settings, import an audio file using the new settings and then listen to it to make sure that you are happy with the results. If you did not achieve the desired results, modify the settings and reimport the sample audio file.

### ❶ Display Preferences Dialog Box

Choose **iTunes**, **Preferences** to display the **Preferences** dialog box.

### ❷ Display Importing Options

The **Preferences** dialog box lets you set seven different types of options: **General, Effects, Importing, Burning, Sharing, Store**, and **Advanced**. The **Preferences** dialog box displays the last set of options that were used. When you click one of the icons at the top of the dialog box, the options change on the dialog box to reflect that selection.

If the **Importing** tab is not displayed, click the **Importing** icon at the top of the dialog box to display these options.

### ❸ Select MP3 Encoder

From the **Import Using** drop-down list, select the **MP3 Encoder** option. This option allows you to create audio files you can play on most devices.

**TIP**

You can also select one of the default bit rate settings in the **Settings** drop-down list. Select the **High Quality (160Kbps)** option to create MP3 files that are close to CD-quality audio.

### ❹ Select Custom Setting

From the **Setting** drop-down list, select the **Custom** option to display the **MP3 Encoder** dialog box.

166   PART II:   iTunes

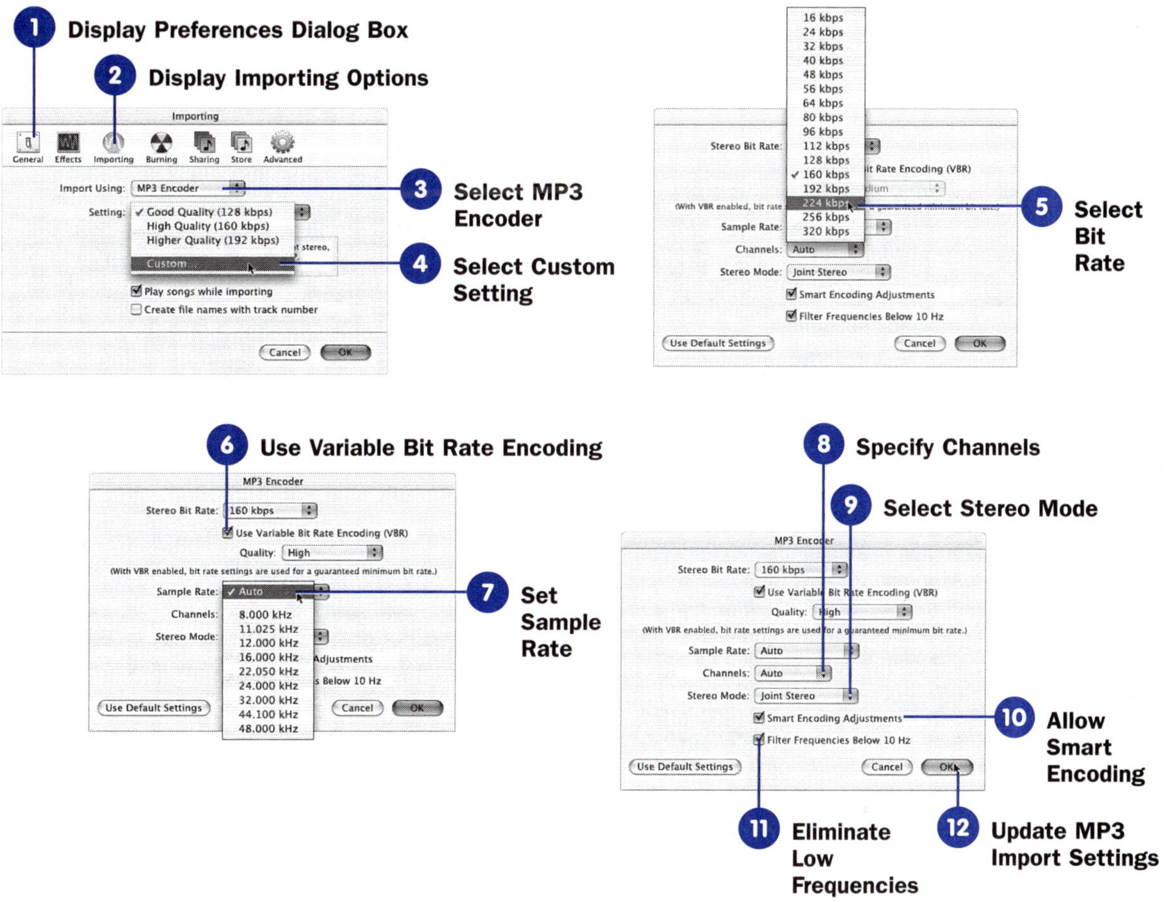

# Set Custom MP3 Quality Options

**1** Display Preferences Dialog Box

**2** Display Importing Options

**3** Select MP3 Encoder

**4** Select Custom Setting

**5** Select Bit Rate

**6** Use Variable Bit Rate Encoding

**7** Set Sample Rate

**8** Specify Channels

**9** Select Stereo Mode

**10** Allow Smart Encoding

**11** Eliminate Low Frequencies

**12** Update MP3 Import Settings

## **5** Select Bit Rate

From the **Stereo Bit Rate** drop-down list in the **MP3 Encoder** dialog box, select the desired bit rate for MP3 files. For music files, you should set the bit rate at 128Kbps or higher to achieve the best results. A bit rate of 128Kbps is similar to listening to an FM radio. Bit rates of 160 to 192Kbps are considered to be nearly CD-quality audio. Anything higher produces much higher quality audio sound, but the compression is reduced, creating a much larger MP3 file.

 **TIP**

If you are importing audio files from voice recordings, you can use a bit rate less than **128Kbps** to produce a more compressed file.

**CHAPTER 7:** Loading Sound Files

## 55 Set Custom MP3 Quality Options

### 6 Use Variable Bit Rate Encoding

Enable the **Use Variable Bit Rate Encoding** option to have iTunes reduce the bit rate of portions of the audio file that are less complex. The maximum bit rate of the audio file will not exceed the rate selected in the **Stereo Bit Rate** field.

If you select the **Use Variable Bit Rate Encoding** option, choose the quality you want to use for the variable bit rate encoding option by making a selection from the **Quality** drop-down list.

### 7 Set Sample Rate

If you plan to import voice recordings, select **22.050 kHz** from the **Sample Rate** drop-down list to compress the audio file. Otherwise, set the **Sample Rate** to **Auto** to have iTunes determine the appropriate sample rate.

### 8 Specify Channels

Set the **Channels** field to have iTunes automatically determine whether to record in **Mono** or **Stereo** based on the imported audio file. If you want to force all audio files to be saved as mono to help reduce disk space, select the **Mono** option.

### 9 Select Stereo Mode

If you selected **Auto** or **Stereo** in the **Channels** field, select either **Normal** or **Joint Stereo** from the **Stereo Mode** drop-down list to specify how you want to deal with high frequencies in audio files. To have iTunes combine high frequencies into one channel, select the **Joint Stereo** option.

### 10 Allow Smart Encoding

Enable the **Smart Encoding Adjustments** check box to have iTunes adjust your encoding settings based on the specified bit rate. iTunes tweaks the settings to achieve the maximum results for the bit rate setting.

**PART II:** iTunes

## Set Music File Storage Location ⑤⑥

### ⑪ Eliminate Low Frequencies

Enable the **Filter Frequencies Below 10 Hz** check box to have iTunes filter out inaudible low-frequency sounds. This reduces the size of the MP3 file by eliminating sounds that you will not hear.

### ⑫ Update MP3 Import Settings

Click the **OK** button to close the **MP3 Encoder** dialog box and save the custom MP3 settings.

**TIP**

If you are not happy with settings you created for importing MP3 files, open the **MP3 Encoder** dialog box and click the **Use Default Settings** button. Then, iTunes changes all the settings back to the default settings for importing MP3 files.

## ⑤⑥ Set Music File Storage Location

By default, iTunes stores your music library in an iTunes folder in the **Music** folder in your **Home** folder. In fact, you can find your iTunes music library using the **Finder** by clicking the **Home** button and then clicking the **Music** folder. In most cases, there is no reason to alter that storage location. However, if you want to move your music library to another location, iTunes provides that option.

One good reason for moving your library is a shortage of hard disk space. If you find that your hard disk is getting full, you can have iTunes move your music storage location to another hard disk. When you do this, all future audio files that you import are stored in the new storage location.

When you alter the storage location for your iTunes Library, the original library remains intact. iTunes updates the library to create links back to the audio files stored in the old iTunes library.

If you want to move all audio files into the new music folder location, you can use the **Consolidate Library** option. When you select this option, iTunes copies all of the audio files in your library into the current music folder. See ⑥④ **Copy Audio Files to a Central Location** for more information on consolidating audio files. After you consolidate the library, you will have to use **Finder** to delete the audio files from the original music library folder.

**Before You Begin**

✔ ㊻ About Audio Formats

**See Also**

→ ㊼ Capture Audio Files from CDs

→ ㊽ Import Internet Music

→ ㊾ Purchase Audio from the Music Store

### ① Display Preferences Dialog Box

Choose **iTunes, Preferences** to display the **Preferences** dialog box.

**CHAPTER 7:** Loading Sound Files

## 56  Set Music File Storage Location

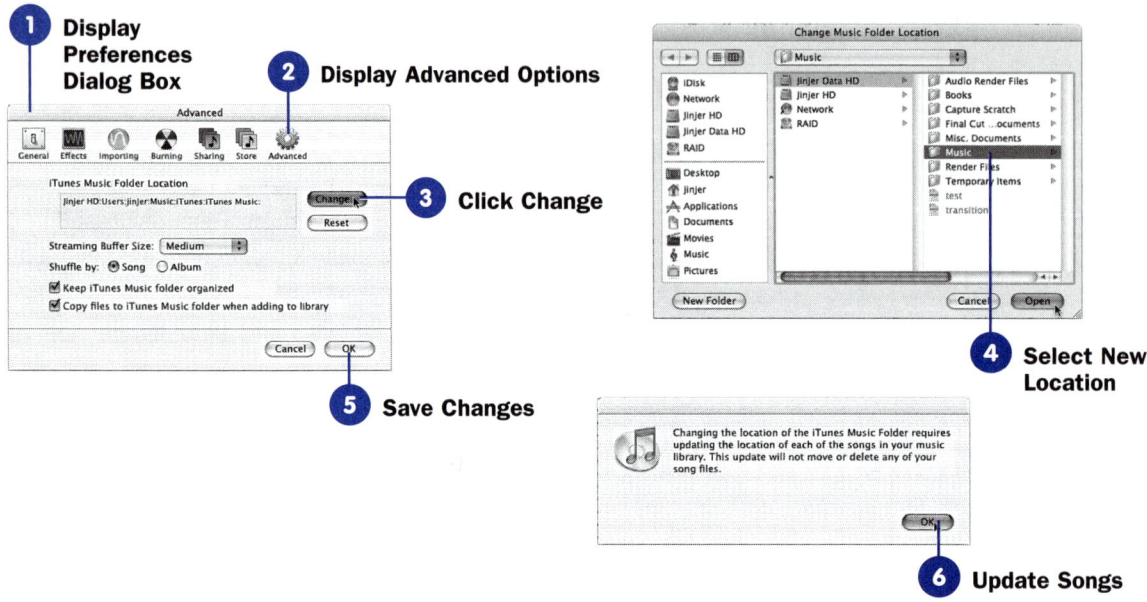

### 2  Display Advanced Options

The **Preferences** dialog box lets you set seven different types of options: General, Effects, Importing, Burning, Sharing, Store, and Advanced. The **Preferences** dialog box displays the last set of options that were used. When you click one of the icons at the top of the dialog box, the options change on the dialog box to reflect this selection.

If the **Advanced** tab is not already displayed, click the **Advanced** button to display these options on the **Preferences** dialog box.

### 3  Click Change

Click the **Change** button to display the **Change Music Folder Location** dialog box.

### 4  Select New Location

On the **Change Music Folder Location** dialog box, select the folder where you want to store all new audio files that you import into iTunes.

Click the **Choose** button to select the new folder and close the dialog box. The iTunes **Music Folder Location** field on the **Preferences** dialog box is updated to show the new storage location.

**TIP**

If you want to switch back to the default import location, click the **Reset** button on the **Preferences** dialog box.

**⑤ Save Changes**

On the **Preferences** dialog box, click the **OK** button to save the changes and update the audio file storage location.

**⑥ Update Songs**

When you change the audio file storage location, a dialog box displays to indicate that iTunes is updating the links to the music in your iTunes library. Click the **OK** button to continue. iTunes does not physically move any audio files during this process (the old iTunes files remain in their original storage location), but it does create links to the files in the original Library folder.

# 8

# Organizing Sound Files

**IN THIS CHAPTER:**

- **57** About Playlists
- **58** Customize a Playlist
- **59** Create a Smart Playlist
- **60** Share Playlists with Other Users
- **61** Rate Music Tracks
- **62** Remove Audio from the Library
- **63** Search for Songs
- **64** Copy Audio Files to a Central Location
- **65** About iPod
- **66** Set iPod Preferences
- **67** Sync Playlists with iPod
- **68** Manually Update iPod
- **69** Customize View of Song List

## 57 About Playlists

**KEY TERM**

*Playlist*—A list of songs created in iTunes for a specific purpose. For example, if you have music you like to listen to at Christmas, you can place those audio files on your Christmas playlist.

When you add audio files to iTunes, they are all placed in the Library. iTunes provides several tools to organize and locate audio files within your Library. You can create a *playlist* containing related audio files, search for specific audio files, rank audio files, and manage files on your iPod.

After the audio files are added, you can organize collections of the audio files related to your interests. These collections of audio files are called playlists. You can create playlists not only for the purpose of listening to music in iTunes, but for burning to a CD or copying to your iPod. See **86 Burn an Audio CD** for more information on burning audio CDs from iTunes.

iTunes interfaces directly with your iPod to control the audio files that are added. You can create a custom playlist containing the specific audio files you want to copy to your iPod, or you can copy the entire library to your iPod. You specify the audio files to be copied to the iPod using the **iPod Preferences** dialog box. You can have iTunes automatically copy audio files from specific playlists, or you can specify that you want to manually update the iPod.

You can use the search options to locate specific audio files within your Library. You search using the selected information on the song list. iTunes provides options for rating your audio files and then using those rankings to sort your list of audio files.

## 57 About Playlists

**See Also**

→ **58** Customize a Playlist
→ **59** Create a Smart Playlist
→ **60** Share Playlists with Other Users
→ **67** Sync Playlists with iPod

The iTunes Library provides an excellent storage location for all your audio files, but with all the audio files accessible from the Library, it can be a little overwhelming to find the files you want to listen to. Playlists allow you to simplify your library by creating collections of songs that you want to listen to together. For example, you can create a playlist that contains all your Christmas holiday music. By adding your Christmas music to the Christmas playlist, you can listen to only the music on that playlist. You can also create a playlist that contains only the music that you want copied onto your iPod.

## About Playlists  57

When you create a regular playlist, you manually add the desired songs to the playlist from the Library. iTunes also allows you to create *smart playlists*. With smart playlists, iTunes monitors your Library looking for audio files that meet the conditions of each list. When you add an audio file to the Library that matches the criteria for a particular smart playlist, iTunes adds the song to the list. iTunes comes with four default smart playlists, but you can create several more.

A playlist is simply a list of audio files from the Library. The playlist does not contain the actual song files, just a list of the songs. Therefore, you can use the same song on several different playlists.

| Default Smart Playlist | Conditions |
|---|---|
| 60's Music | Finds the songs with a year between 1960 and 1969. |
| My Top Rated | Finds all the audio files with a rating greater than three stars. |
| Recently Played | Finds the specific songs you have played within the last two weeks. |
| Top 25 Most Played | Finds the 25 songs that you play most frequently. |

When you use smart playlists in iTunes, only the audio files that match the criteria are added to the list. You cannot manually add an audio file to a smart playlist.

iTunes uses different icons for the playlists and smart playlists in your **Source** list. These icons also differentiate the playlists from the audio CD, Music Store, Internet Radio, and Library options in the Source list. See **47 Capture Audio Files from CDs** for information on working with audio CDs. See **49 Purchase Audio from the Music Store** for information on purchasing music from the Apple Music Store. See **71 Listen to Internet Radio** to learn more about listening to Internet radio stations in iTunes.

> **KEY TERM**
>
> *Smart playlist*—A playlist set up to find all the audio files that meet specific criteria. For example, you might want to load all the Enya songs in your Library to one of your smart playlists.

**CHAPTER 8:** Organizing Sound Files

### 57  About Playlists

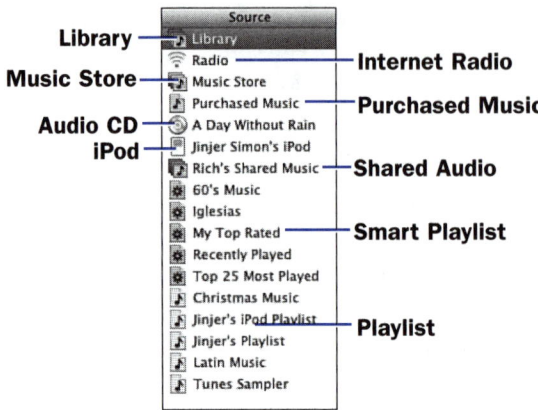

*The iTunes **Source** list uses icons to differentiate the various kinds of music.*

- **Can I add a song to multiple playlists?** Yes. You can place any audio files in your iTunes Library in as many different playlists as you want. When you add a song (or other type of audio file) to a playlist, iTunes just adds a link to the location where the song is stored. The selected song remains in the Library at all times. If the Library contains a link to an audio file in another location, iTunes just copies that link and adds it to the playlist.

- **What is the difference between a playlist and a smart playlist?** The big difference between a playlist and a smart playlist is the method used to add audio files to the list. When you create a playlist, you add audio files to it by dragging them from the Library to the playlist. With a smart playlist, you create conditions that must be met in order to add the songs to the playlist. Conditions can be "all songs by the artist Enya," or "all songs released in the 90s." You can create one or multiple conditions for your smart playlist, but only the songs that meet the conditions are added to the list. You cannot manually add songs to a smart playlist.

- **What happens if I delete a song from a playlist?** When you delete a song from a playlist, iTunes just removes that link from the playlist. The song remains part of your iTunes Library. Also, any other playlists that contain the song are unaffected by the deletion.

If you delete an audio file from the Library, iTunes also removes the file from all playlists.

- **Do I have to keep the default smart playlists included with iTunes?** No. You can delete those playlists at any time. You can also delete the **Tunes Sampler** playlist. If you delete a playlist that is empty, iTunes removes the playlist as soon as you click the **Clear** option. If you remove a playlist containing items, iTunes displays a confirmation prompt before deleting.

## 58 Customize a Playlist

You can create playlists within iTunes to specify a collection of audio files. For example, you might want to create a playlist for a specific artist, such as Enrique Iglesias, or for a specific type of music, such as Rock Music. You can also create playlists for the music you want to place on a CD or on your iPod.

When you create a playlist, iTunes adds a new playlist with the name **untitled playlist 1** to the list. Each time you create a new playlist, the number at the end of the name increases. Because the default playlist name does not indicate what is on the playlist, you should give the playlist a more meaningful name. iTunes allows you to assign the same name to multiple playlists, but you should use unique names for your playlists so that you can differentiate between the lists. After you have created the list, you add songs to the list by dragging them from the Library.

iTunes plays the songs in the order they are listed on the playlist by default. Therefore, you should put the songs in the desired play order. This same order is used if the playlist is used to create an audio CD. As an option, you can have iTunes randomize the order of the songs when they play. See **74 Randomize Songs Being Played Back** for information on randomizing the play order in iTunes.

### 1 Create Playlist

Choose **File, New Playlist** to create a new empty playlist in the **Source** list.

**Before You Begin**
✓ **57** About Playlists

**See Also**
→ **59** Create a Smart Playlist
→ **60** Share Playlists with Other Users
→ **61** Rate Music Tracks
→ **67** Sync Playlists with iPod
→ **69** Customize View of Song List

**TIP**

Even though you select songs from the Library to add to your playlist, iTunes only creates a link to the song on the playlist; the original song remains in the Library.

CHAPTER 8: Organizing Sound Files

## Customize a Playlist

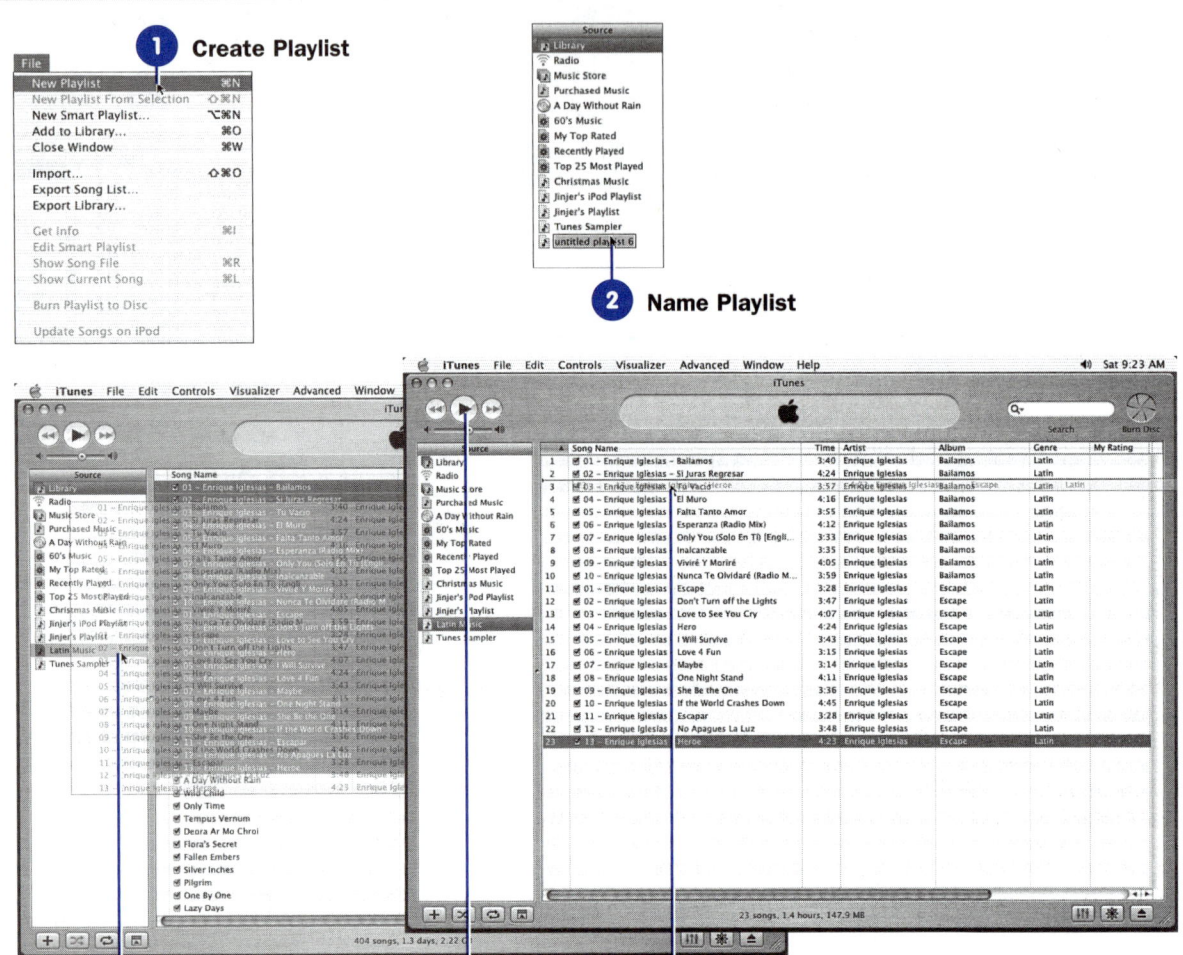

iTunes creates a playlist using the naming convention of **untitled playlist #**, where # indicates a number added to the end of the default name. For example, the first time you create a new playlist, the playlist is named **untitled playlist 1**. Each successive playlist is given a number, so the second playlist is **untitled playlist 2**.

Customize a Playlist

**② Name Playlist**

Select the new playlist name in the **Source** list and type the desired name for the playlist. You should type a name that provides a good description of the playlist.

**③ Add Songs**

In the **Library**, click to select the songs you want to add to the new playlist. To select a range of songs adjacent to each other in the **Library**, click the first song in the range and hold the **Shift** key as you click the last song. iTunes selects the entire range of songs. To select songs that are not adjacent in the list, hold down the ⌘ key when you click each song.

When you have selected the desired songs, click the selection and drag it to the new playlist in the **Source** list.

**④ Specify Song Order**

When you add a playlist to an audio CD or listen to the playlist in iTunes, iTunes plays the songs in the order they appear in the playlist. To change the order of the songs in the list, click to select a song from the list and drag it to the desired location in the list. Repeat this step to move each song within the new playlist. As you drag selections in the song list, a horizontal line displays the location where the selected song will be placed.

You can also sort the song list using the columns at the top. See **69 Customize View of Song List** for information on customizing and sorting the song list columns.

**⑤ Listen to Playlist**

Click the **Play** button to listen to the new playlist. By default, iTunes plays the songs in the order they appear in the list. See **74 Randomize Songs Being Played Back** for information on randomizing the playback of songs in the playlist.

### TIPS

If the name of the playlist is not selected in the **Source** list, you can select it by slowly clicking on playlist name twice.

Your playlist names can be 255 characters in length, but the width of the playlist column dictates the number of characters that are visible.

To remove an unwanted playlist, click the playlist name in the **Source** list and then choose **Edit, Clear**. You can also delete a playlist by selecting it and then pressing the **Delete** key.

### NOTE

You can also create a playlist from a selection of audio files. Select the audio files and then choose **File, New Playlist From Selection** to create a playlist containing the selected files.

CHAPTER 8: Organizing Sound Files

## 59  Create a Smart Playlist

**Before You Begin**

✓ **57** About Playlists

**See Also**

→ **60** Share Playlists with Other Users

→ **61** Rate Music Tracks

→ **67** Sync Playlists with iPod

→ **69** Customize View of Song List

 **TIP**

You can have multiple smart playlists active at once. For example, the four default playlists (**60's Music**, **My Top Rated**, **Recently Played**, and **Top 25 Most Played**) are all active. You can delete or modify the default smart playlists.

If you want your playlist to include only those songs that match a specific criteria, such as all songs from a particular artist or a specific genre, instead of manually adding the songs to a playlist, you can let iTunes add them by creating a smart playlist. When you create a smart playlist, you specify the criteria the songs must meet before they are added to the playlist. For example, you can indicate that you want all songs with an **Artist** name that contains the word *Iglesias*. When you specify this condition, iTunes searches through your entire Library and finds all matching artists. Songs by the artists Julio Iglesias and Enrique Iglesias are added to the playlist.

You can specify multiple conditions for the songs you add to your playlist. For example, you might want songs by a particular artist that were recorded in the 1990s. If so, you create two condition statements: The first condition looks for the artists whose name contains *Iglesias*, and the second condition looks for years in the range 1990 to 1999. When iTunes creates the smart playlist, it first finds the songs by the specified artists; then from that list, it locates the songs released within the specified years.

You can also set limits on the smart playlist to limit the number of songs added, the size of the playlist, and so on. For example, if you want to create a playlist that contains your top 25 rated songs, you set the limit to 25 songs with the highest rating.

If you want to have iTunes continue to update the playlist as additional audio files are added, enable the **Live Updating** option. If you don't enable this option, iTunes adds songs to the playlist only when the playlist is created.

**1 Create a Smart Playlist**

Choose **File**, **New Smart Playlist** to display the **Smart Playlist** dialog box where you can specify the conditions for your new smart playlist.

Create a Smart Playlist **59**

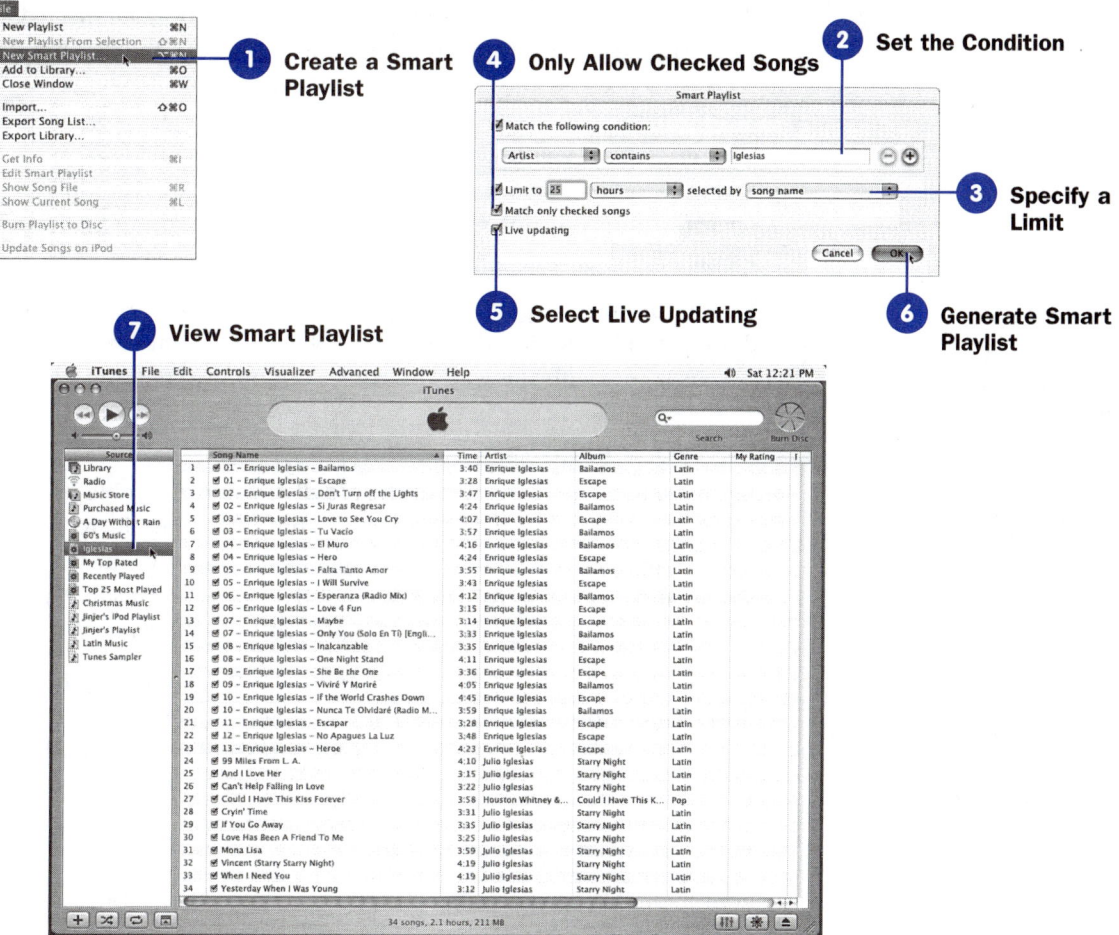

## ② Set the Condition

Under the **Match the following condition** option, select the first criteria you want to apply to the search from the first drop-down list. For example, select **Artist** to create a condition based on the artist's name. There are 20 different criteria you can select from.

From the second drop-down list, select the comparison operator you want to use. For example, select **Contains** if you want to find the artist names that contain the word *Iglesias*. This list displays

CHAPTER 8: Organizing Sound Files            181

## 59  Create a Smart Playlist

different comparison operators based on the criteria you selected in the first field. For example, if the criteria selected in the first field represents a string value, the comparison operators deal with strings. If the criteria you select is a numeric value, the comparison operators allow you to compare different numeric values. For example, if you selected **Year** from the first field, the comparison operators are **is**, **is not**, **is greater than**, **is less than**, and **is in the range**.

In the third field, type the values you want to compare for the condition. If the conditional operator allows you to compare two values, as is true with the **is in the range** option, two fields display.

**Click the + button to add a second condition line and repeat step 2 to add a second condition to the search for songs. Remember, the songs added to the smart playlist must meet all the specified conditions.**

**If you want to eliminate a condition, click the – button.**

**If you plan to burn the playlist to a CD, verify the available storage space on the CD before creating the playlist. Although most CDs hold 700MB of data, some hold only 650MB.**

### 3  Specify a Limit

If you want to limit the size of the playlist, you can enable the **Limit** check box and then specify the limit. For example, to limit the playlist to the 25 most recently played songs that match the specified condition, type **25** in the first field, select **songs** in the second field, and select **most recently played** in the third field.

You can limit a playlist by specifying not only a song limit, but also an allowable time or size. For example, if you are creating a playlist to burn on a CD, you can specify a size limit of 700MB, or you can specify a time limit of no more than 74 minutes for a CD.

### 4  Only Allow Checked Songs

Enable the **Match only checked songs** option if you want to add songs to the playlist only if they are checked in your Library. By selecting this option, you can eliminate any songs you don't want in your playlist by removing the check mark next to those songs in the Library.

### 5  Select Live Updating

Enable the **Live updating** option to have iTunes continue to add and remove songs from the playlist as music is added to and removed from your Library.

If this option is not enabled, the playlist does not change after it is created.

**⑥ Generate Smart Playlist**

Click the **OK** button to create the smart playlist based on the specified conditions.

iTunes creates the playlist and assigns a name based on the specified conditions. You can modify the name by clicking the smart playlist name in the **Source** list and typing the desired name.

**⑦ View Smart Playlist**

Click the smart playlist in the **Source** list to view the current contents of the smart playlist.

## 60 Share Playlists with Other Users

If are connected to other computers using a local network, you can share your playlists with up to five other computers. To share your playlists, the other computers must be running Mac OS X version 10.2.4 or later. You can share all audio files with the extensions MP3, AIFF, WAV, and AAC. You can also share radio station links, but you cannot share audio book files downloaded from Audible.com.

When you share your playlists, you select the specific playlists you want to share. You specify the name you want to use to identify your shared music on other computers. You can also password-protect the shared music files to ensure that only users who have the correct password can share your playlists.

When you share selected playlists, they all show up on one playlist on the other computers. For example, if you share your **Purchased Music** playlist and **Christmas Music** playlist under the shared name of **Jinjer's Playlists**, **Jinjer's Playlists** displays as a shared source on all computers on the network that are set up to look for shared music.

The shared playlists are available only if both computers are turned on. When your computer is turned off or is not connected to the network, your shared playlists are not available to other users. Note that the audio files remain in their original location (on your hard disk) and are streamed over the network to the computer viewing the shared playlist. The other users can listen to all the songs in the shared playlist, but they cannot copy them to their Library lists, add them to an iPod, or transfer them to a CD.

**Before You Begin**

✔ **57** About Playlists

**See Also**

→ **61** Rate Music Tracks
→ **67** Sync Playlists with iPod
→ **69** Customize View of Song List

**NOTE**

Only computers on your local network can access your iTunes playlists. Users connected to your network through the Internet do not have access to your playlists.

CHAPTER 8: Organizing Sound Files

## 60 Share Playlists with Other Users

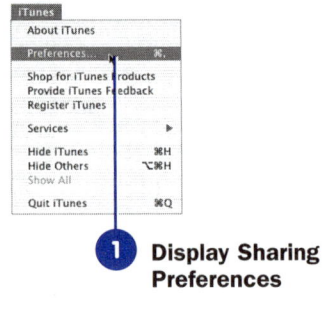

**1** Display Sharing Preferences

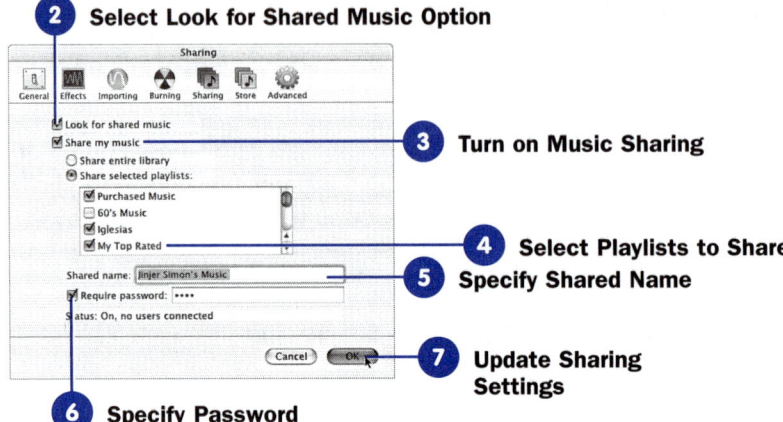

**2** Select Look for Shared Music Option
**3** Turn on Music Sharing
**4** Select Playlists to Share
**5** Specify Shared Name
**6** Specify Password
**7** Update Sharing Settings

**8** View Shared Music Files

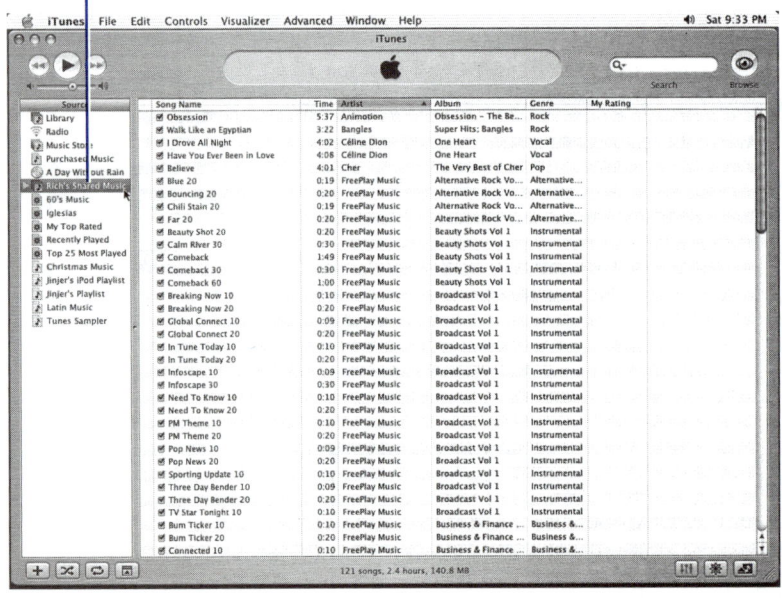

### **1** Display Sharing Preferences

Choose **iTunes**, **Preferences** to display the **Preferences** dialog box.

If the **Sharing** page of the **Preferences** dialog box is not displayed, click the **Sharing** icon to display the music sharing options. You

## Share Playlists with Other Users

use the **Preferences** dialog box to specify all setting in iTunes. The dialog box always displays the last options you modified.

### ② Select Look for Shared Music Option

Enable the **Look for shared music** option to display all music that is available for sharing on your network. When this option is selected, iTunes adds a separate shared option to your **Source** list for each computer that has shared music.

> **NOTE**
> iTunes displays shared music from other computers on your network that have the **Share my music** option selected.

### ③ Turn on Music Sharing

Enable the **Share my music** option to share music from your iTunes playlists with other users on the network. Now, you must specify whether you want to share your entire Library or just the music in specific playlists.

To share everything in your iTunes Library, enable the **Share entire library** option. When you select this option, other computers can access your entire iTunes Library.

To share only the songs on selected playlists, enable the **Share selected playlists** option.

### ④ Select Playlists to Share

If you enabled the **Share selected playlists** option, you must select the specific playlists you want to share from the list box. iTunes lists all your playlists, including your **Purchased Music** playlist and smart playlists. Click to place a check mark in the box next to each playlist you want to select.

> **TIP**
> You can create one playlist that contains all the music you want to share. See ⑤⑧ **Customize a Playlist** for more information on creating playlists.

### ⑤ Specify Shared Name

In the **Shared name** field, type the name you want to display on other computers. This name is what appears on the other computers as another playlist in the **Source** list.

### ⑥ Specify Password

Enable the **Require password** option if you want to have users on other computers type a password before accessing your shared songs. If you require a password, a dialog box requesting the password appears when other users click your shared playlist option in their **Source** list.

> **NOTE**
> You will not see your shared music as a separate playlist on your own computer.

**CHAPTER 8:** Organizing Sound Files    185

## 61 Rate Music Tracks

### 7 Update Sharing Settings

Click the **OK** button to close the **Preferences** dialog box and save settings for sharing music on your computer. The settings take effect immediately.

### 8 View Shared Music Files

Click a shared link in your **Source** list to see the shared playlist for another computer. Shared playlists display in blue on your **Source** list.

## 61 Rate Music Tracks

**Before You Begin**

✔ **57** About Playlists

**See Also**

→ **58** Customize a Playlist

→ **59** Create a Smart Playlist

→ **60** Share Playlists with Other Users

→ **67** Sync Playlists with iPod

→ **69** Customize View of Song List

 TIP

If the **My Rating** column is not visible, choose **Edit, View Options**. On the **View Options** dialog box, select the **My Ratings** option. See **69** **Customize View of Song List** for more information on customizing the columns.

iTunes provides the ability to rate songs within your Library to show which ones you prefer the most. You can rate the songs in your Library by assigning zero to five stars to each song.

After you have rated the songs in your Library, you can use the ratings to sort the Library or a specific playlist, create a smart playlist, or just browse the Library.

You assign the ratings based on your own preferences. When you use the rating stars to create a smart playlist or to sort the list, iTunes considers five stars to be the highest rating.

### 1 Select Song

In the song list, click the song you want to rate.

### 2 Specify Rating

In the **My Rating** column, iTunes displays five dots to indicate the available rating levels for the selected song. Click the dot that represents the rating you want to assign to the selected song. For example, click the fourth dot to assign a four-star rating to the song. iTunes inserts the specified number of stars.

You can change the rating by clicking a different dot to increase the rating or clicking a star to decrease the rating.

## Rate Music Tracks 61

1. **Select Song**

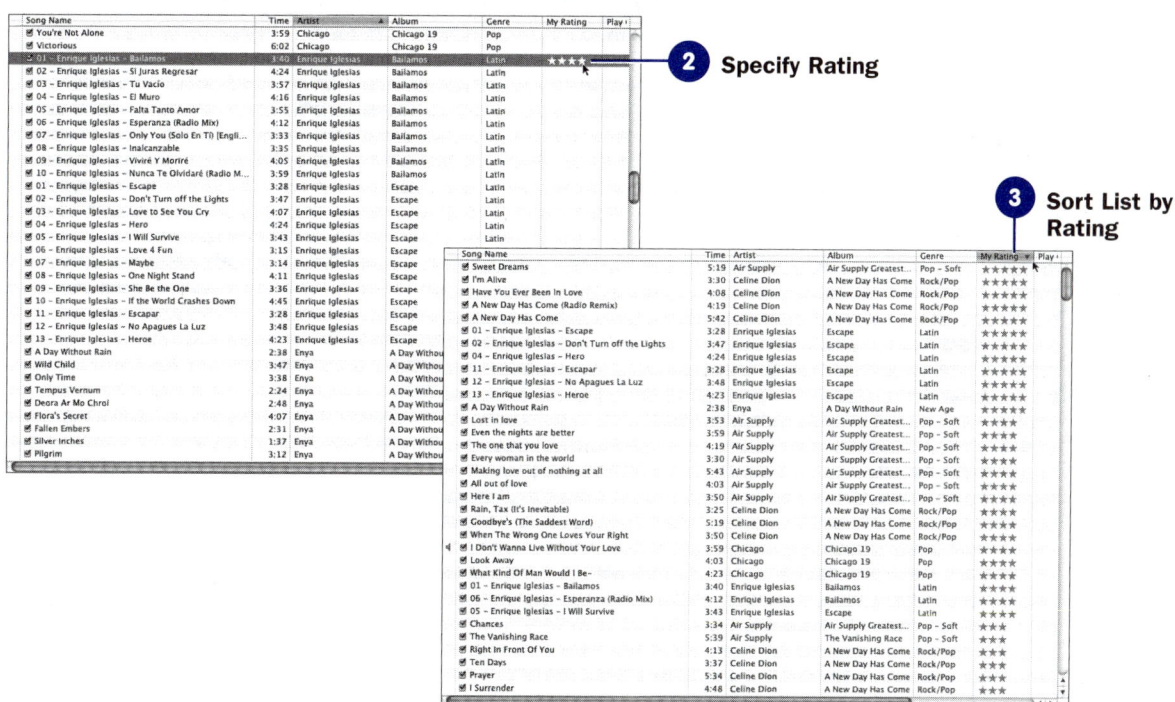

2. **Specify Rating**

3. **Sort List by Rating**

**CHAPTER 8: Organizing Sound Files**

## 62 Remove Audio from the Library

### TIPS

Repeat steps 1 and 2 for each song you want to rate in your Library.

To remove the entire rating for a song, click to the left of the first star. The stars are replaced by the dots.

### 3 Sort List by Rating

Click the **My Rating** column heading to sort the entire Library or the current playlist by the song ratings.

When you click the column the first time, iTunes sorts the song list in ascending order based on the values in the **My Rating** column. This means that the songs with no rating appear at the top of the list, followed by the songs with one star. Click the column again to sort in descending order, with the highest-rated songs at the top of the list.

## 62 Remove Audio from the Library

### Before You Begin

✓ **57** About Playlists

### See Also

→ **47** Capture Audio Files from CDs

→ **48** Import Internet Music

→ **58** Customize a Playlist

### NOTE

The **Music** folder is the storage location on your hard disk where iTunes stores all the audio files you import. See **56** Set Music File Storage Location to specify the location of the **Music** folder on your computer.

If you decide you no longer want to listen to a particular audio file, you can remove it from your iTunes Library. If the audio file you select to delete in iTunes is located in your iTunes **Music** folder, not only can you remove the file from iTunes, you can also remove the file from your hard disk.

When you specify that you want to delete a song from your Library, iTunes verifies the location of the actual audio file for the song. If the audio file is located in your iTunes **Music** folder, iTunes displays a dialog box to determine whether you want to remove the actual audio file from your hard disk. If you indicate that you want to remove the audio file from your computer, you will have to import the audio file again from the original location if you decide you want to listen to it again. If you do not delete it from your computer, you can add the file to the Library again using the **File, Add To Library** command.

You can remove audio from iTunes only from within the Library. If you delete a song from a playlist, the song is removed from that playlist, but remains in the Library and on other playlists.

If the audio you select to delete is not located in your iTunes **Music** folder, iTunes does not delete the actual audio files. If you want to remove those files from your computer, you must manually locate them using the **Finder**. You can verify the location of the audio files on your hard disk by selecting the song and choosing **File, Show Song File** to view the folder containing the selected file in a **Finder** window.

# Remove Audio from the Library  62

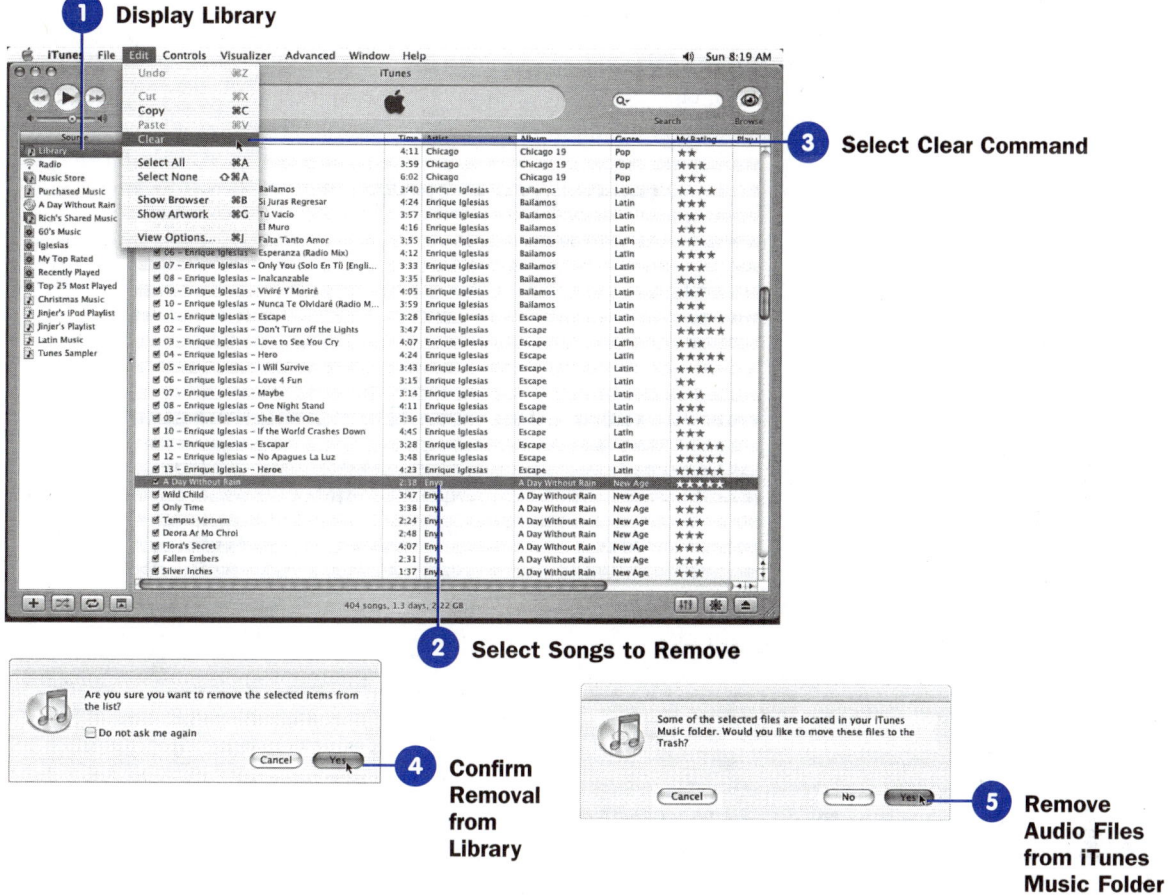

## 1 Display Library

If the Library is not currently selected, choose the **Library** option in the **Source** list to view the entire list of audio files in your Library.

## 2 Select Songs to Remove

Click to select the song you want to remove from the iTunes **Library**. To select a consecutive range of songs, click the first song and hold the **Shift** key while you click the second song. If the songs you want to remove are not consecutive in the list, hold down the ⌘ key while you click each song.

CHAPTER 8: Organizing Sound Files

## 63 Search for Songs

**NOTE**

You can also press the **Delete** key to remove the selected audio files from iTunes.

**TIPS**

To view the contents of your Trash, double-click the **Trash** icon on the OS X Dock.

If you change your mind and want to cancel the entire process and keep the audio files in iTunes, click the **Cancel** button in either of the confirmation dialog boxes.

### ③ Select Clear Command

Choose **Edit, Clear** to remove the selected audio files from the iTunes Library. iTunes displays a dialog box to verify the selection.

### ④ Confirm Removal from Library

On the confirmation dialog box that displays, click the **Yes** button to remove the selected audio from your iTunes Library. The selected audio files will be removed from the entire Library, including all playlists.

### ⑤ Remove Audio Files from iTunes Music Folder

If the audio file is located in your iTunes Music folder, a second dialog box displays to determine whether you want to remove the actual audio file from your computer's hard disk. If you click the **Yes** button, iTunes deletes the audio file and places it in the Trash.

## 63 Search for Songs

**Before You Begin**

✔ **47** Capture Audio Files from CDs
✔ **49** Purchase Audio from the Music Store
✔ **57** About Playlists

**See Also**

→ **58** Customize a Playlist
→ **59** Create a Smart Playlist
→ **60** Share Playlists with Other Users
→ **61** Rate Music Tracks
→ **67** Sync Playlists with iPod
→ **69** Customize View of Song List

If your iTunes Library contains many songs, it can become difficult to locate the desired song within the list simply by scrolling. To simplify the search process, iTunes provides a **Search** field in the top-right corner of the window.

To use the **Search** feature in iTunes, you must first decide which column of information you want to search. For example, if you want to search the song list to find a specific song title, click the **Song Name** column heading.

After you have selected the appropriate column heading, type the text you are looking for in the **Search** field. As you type, iTunes displays only the songs that include the text you are typing. For example, if the first letter you type is Z, iTunes removes all songs from the song list that do not have a Z as the first character in the title. The more letters you type, the more the list is narrowed.

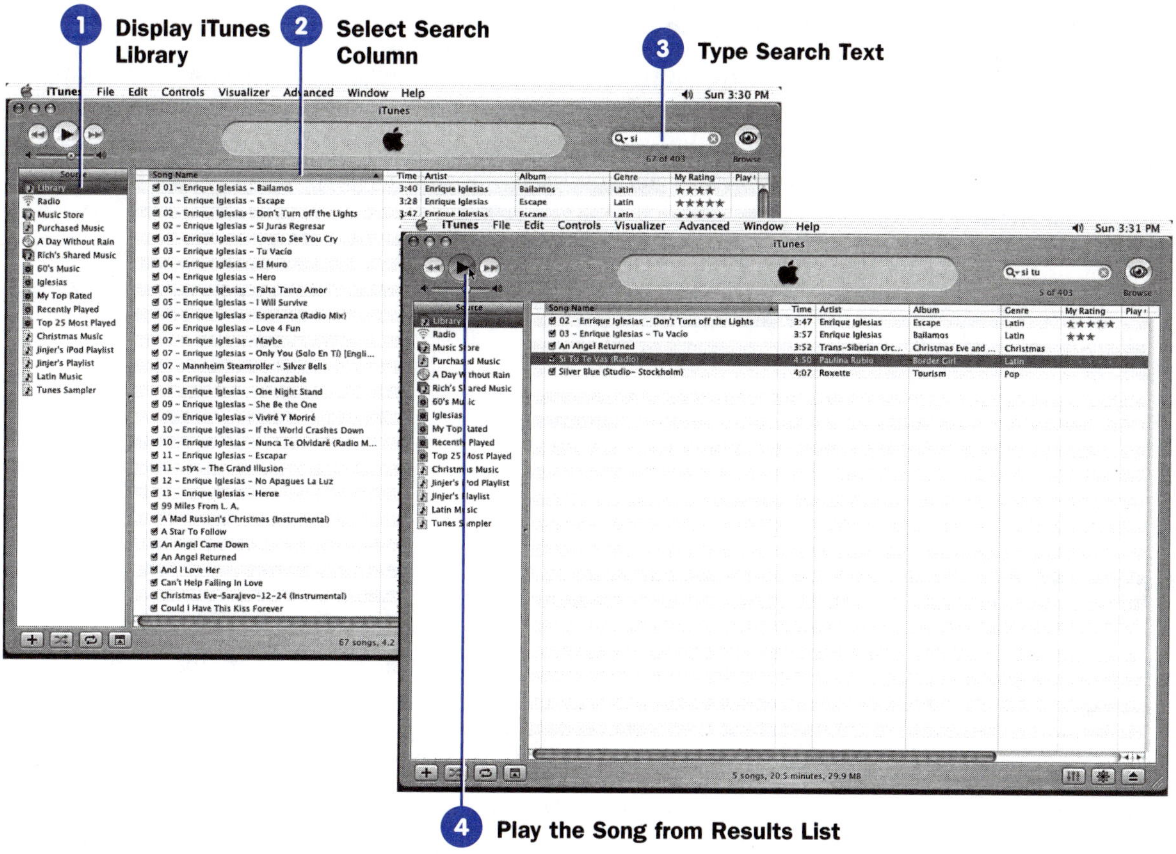

Search for Songs

**① Display iTunes Library**   **② Select Search Column**   **③ Type Search Text**

**④ Play the Song from Results List**

**① Display iTunes Library**

If the Library is not currently selected, click the **Library** option in the **Source** list to view the entire list of audio files in your Library.

**② Select Search Column**

Click the desired column heading in the song list. The heading for the column you select is highlighted in blue, and the song list is sorted in ascending order based on the selection. For example, if you click the **Song Name** column heading, iTunes sorts all the songs based on the song names.

 **TIP**

When you click a column heading, iTunes sorts the song list based on the column you have selected. You might find that by simply sorting based on a specific column, you can quickly spot the song you are looking for.

**CHAPTER 8:** Organizing Sound Files 191

## 64  Copy Audio Files to a Central Location

**TIP**

To change the sort order, click the arrow button on the right side of the column name. If the arrow points up, the list is sorted in ascending order (from A to Z). If the arrow points down, the list is sorted in descending order (from Z to A).

To restart the search, clear the text from the **Search** field to redisplay the entire list.

### 3  Type Search Text

In the **Search** field, type the text for the song you want to locate. As you type each letter, the list is updated to display only those songs that match the search string you are typing. Continue typing text until you locate the desired song in the list.

### 4  Play the Song from the Results List

Click the song you were looking for from the song list and click the **Play** button.

---

## 64  Copy Audio Files to a Central Location

**Before You Begin**

✔ **56** Set Music File Storage Location
✔ **57** About Playlists

**See Also**

→ **60** Share Playlists with Other Users
→ **62** Remove Audio from the Library
→ **67** Sync Playlists with iPod
→ **69** Customize View of Song List

You can have iTunes move all the music files in your Library into one central location by consolidating the Library. When you perform a consolidation, iTunes copies all the audio files into the current iTunes **Music** folder. You might want to use this option when some of the songs in your Library are located outside of the iTunes **Music** folder. For example, you might have linked to songs on another machine. When you consolidate the Library, the songs you linked to are copied to the current **Music** folder. See **50** **Link to Audio Files in Other Locations** for more information on linking to audio files.

When you select the consolidation command, iTunes copies all the songs in your Library to the current **Music** folder. The original audio files remain in their original locations, but instead of pointing to those locations, iTunes is updated to point to the copies of the audio files in the **Music** folder.

The consolidation option allows you to share your playlists with other users on your network and ensure that they have access to all your songs. When you consolidate your library, iTunes copies the songs in your library into your iTunes **Music** Folder. This can make shared playlists easier to access, especially if you have links to music stored in locations that other users cannot access. Consolidating also provides the ability to back up all your music from one central location.

192   PART II:   iTunes

**Copy Audio Files to a Central Location** 64

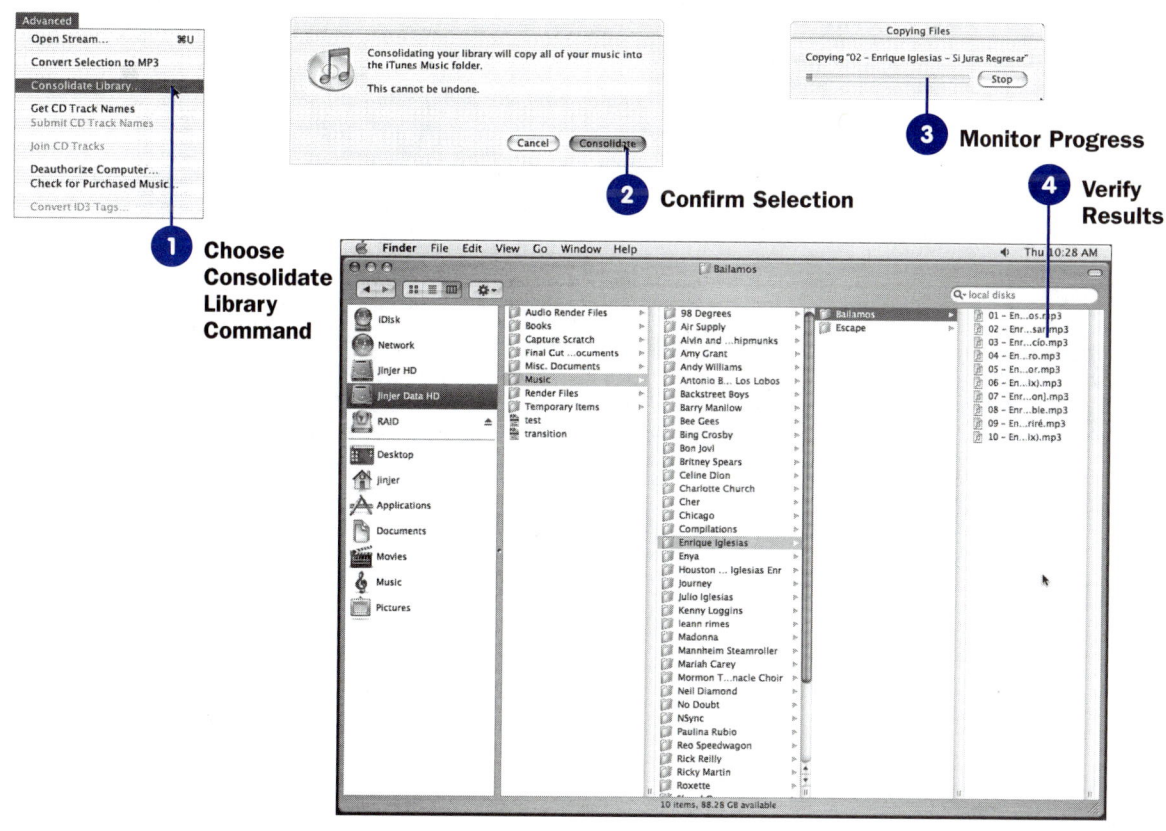

① **Choose Consolidate Library Command**

② **Confirm Selection**

③ **Monitor Progress**

④ **Verify Results**

After you consolidate your Library, you cannot undo the process. If you decide you don't want specific audio files in the centralized location, you must delete the files from the iTunes **Music** folder on your computer's hard disk and reimport them into iTunes. See 48 **Import Internet Music** for information on importing music from another location and 62 **Remove Audio from the Library** for information on deleting audio files.

Be aware that when you consolidate your Library, you will not see any noticeable differences in your playlists. The files are simply moved into your default iTunes **Music** folder and the links are updated to point to the files in the new locations. The main advantage to consolidating is that all your audio files are placed in one central location. You also

CHAPTER 8: Organizing Sound Files 193

## 65 About iPod

increase reliability if you were playing music links to other drives on your network.

### ① Choose Consolidate Library Command

Choose **Advanced, Consolidate Library** to copy all audio files in your Library list into your current iTunes **Music** folder. If you have not modified your default settings, iTunes places your library in the **Music** folder of your **Home** folder.

### ② Confirm Selection

On the confirmation dialog box that displays, click the **Consolidate** button to move all audio files into the current iTunes **Music** folder.

### ③ Monitor Progress

A progress dialog box displays on the screen as the audio files are copied to the current **Music** folder.

If you want to cancel the process, click the **Stop** button. Note that canceling the operation after it has begun does not remove the audio files that have already been copied.

### ④ Verify Results

Locate the **Music** folder in **Finder** to see whether the audio files have been copied.

> **TIP**
> Before consolidating your music files, you can change the storage location on the **Preferences** dialog box: Choose **iTunes, Preferences** and then click the **Advanced** option. See **56 Set Music File Storage Location**.

## 65 About iPod

**Before You Begin**
✔ **57** About Playlists

**See Also**
→ **66** Set iPod Preferences
→ **67** Sync Playlists with iPod
→ **68** Manually Update iPod

As you are probably aware, Apple has developed a portable music player called the iPod. Unlike other portable MP3 players on the market, iPod was designed by Apple to interface directly with iTunes. This relationship allows you to quickly transfer your favorite songs from your iTunes Library to your iPod by selecting the desired playlists.

One thing that has made the iPod so popular is its large storage capacity. Apple iPods provide more storage space than any other portable player on the market. In fact, you can store nearly your entire iTunes Library on your iPod. iPods come in several different storage sizes. The current iPods have 10GB, 20GB, and 40GB of storage space.

About iPod  65

After you have specified what playlists you want to copy to your iPod, each time you connect your iPod to your computer, iTunes automatically connects and updates your iPod. In fact, you can specify the songs you want transferred to your iPod while it is not connected to your computer; then, as soon as you connect, the songs are transferred.

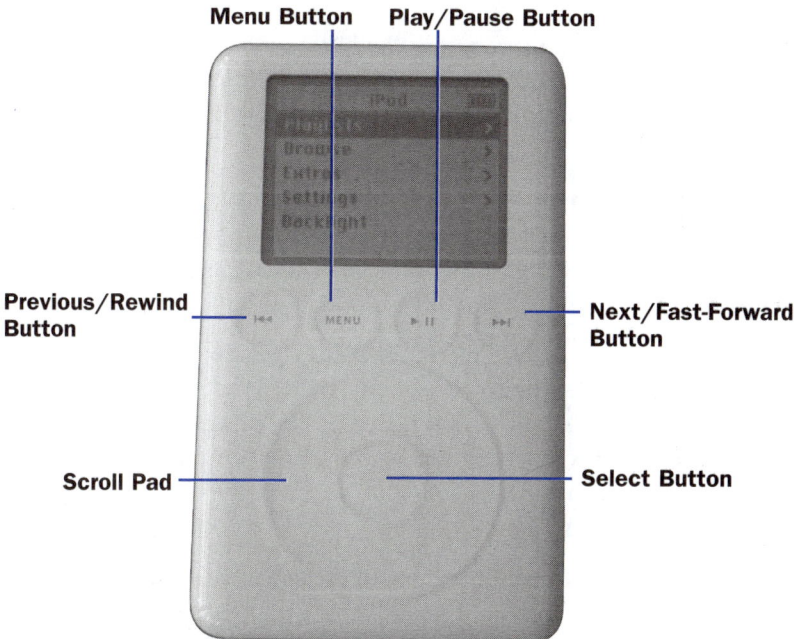

*The iPod is fully compatible with iTunes; its simple buttons make using it intuitive.*

The control buttons on the iPod are fairly simple. When you press the **Menu** button, your iPod turns on and displays a menu of options. You make selections from the menu by pressing the **Select** button in the center of the iPod. The **Scroll Pad** allows you to scroll through the options displayed on the menu.

**NOTE**
The layout of the buttons on older iPods is slightly different than what is shown here.

- **Why can't I add a song directly to the iPod?** Actually, you can, but it you must first select the manual update option. By default, iTunes automatically updates your iPod whenever it is connected to your computer; the iPod song list appears grayed out because iTunes is responsible for automatically updating it based on the settings you specify on the **iPod Preferences** dialog box. See  **Set iPod Preferences** for information on setting the preferences

**CHAPTER 8:** Organizing Sound Files  195

**66  Set iPod Preferences**

for adding songs to your iPod. See **68  Manually Update iPod** for information on manually adding and removing songs from your iPod.

- **How do I turn off my iPod?** With all the cool buttons on the iPod, there is no Off or On button. Although the screen automatically goes blank after a short time, the iPod does not turn off automatically. If you do not turn off your iPod, the battery will run down much faster than expected. To turn off the iPod, hold down the **Play/Pause** button until the screen goes blank (about two seconds).

- **How do I know how much available space is left on my iPod?** When you view your iPod song list in iTunes, the used and available disk space displays at the bottom of the window. iTunes also indicates the number of songs on the iPod and the amount of time it will take to listen to the entire list.

- **How long does it take to charge my iPod?** The amount of time required to charge your iPod is based on the amount of charge the device has when you plug it in. To completely charge the iPod requires about 4 hours. You can charge the battery to about 80 percent capacity in about an hour.

- **Why can't I copy audio from my iPod to my computer?** In an effort to deal with copyright issues, Apple added an anti-piracy system to the iPod to prevent copying of audio files from the iPod to your computer. Although you can add and delete audio files on the iPod, you cannot copy from the iPod to the computer.

**NOTE**

Your iPod is bound to one particular computer; your iPod can transfer music from only that computer. If you plug your iPod into a different computer, you will be prompted to wipe out everything currently on the iPod and sync it to the contents of the new computer.

## 66  Set iPod Preferences

**Before You Begin**

✓ **65** About iPod

**See Also**

→ **60** Share Playlists with Other Users

→ **67** Sync Playlists with iPod

→ **68** Manually Update iPod

You can control how your iPod is updated on the **iPod Preferences** dialog box. To display the **iPod Preferences** dialog box, your iPod must be connected to your computer. You connect your iPod by placing it on the dock or by connecting the iPod cable to the dock connector port on the bottom of the iPod. Plug the other end of the iPod cable into the *FireWire* port on your computer.

196     PART II:     iTunes

## Set iPod Preferences

When your iPod is connected, an iPod option displays in the **Source** list in iTunes. When you click the iPod option, you see the audio files on the iPod and also the **iPod Preferences** button at the bottom of the iTunes window.

On the **iPod Preferences** dialog box, you specify how you want to update the audio files on your iPod device. You can either have iTunes automatically update your audio files or you can do it manually. If you want iTunes to automatically update your iPod, indicate whether you want your entire Library copied to your iPod or just individual playlists. If you decide to just add playlists, you must select the specific playlists from the list box. Consider creating a separate playlist for your iPod so that you can add to the list only the audio you want on your iPod. See **58 Customize a Playlist** to create a playlist or **59 Create a Smart Playlist** to create a *smart playlist* for your iPod.

> **KEY TERM**
>
> *FireWire*—A small six-pin cable that connects a computer and an external device, such as an Apple iPod. FireWire, also referred to as IEEE 1394, provides a high-speed connection for transferring data. The connection speed can be up to 400 megabits per second.

You have the option of using your iPod as a separate storage location for non-audio files from your computer. This works well if you want to transfer files from one location to another, such as from the office to home. You can use your iPod as the storage location for the files. To use the iPod to store other files, select the **Enable FireWire disk use** option on the **iPod Preferences** dialog box.

### 1 Connect the iPod FireWire Cable to Computer

Connect the end of the iPod FireWire cable to a FireWire port on your computer. On most Apple computers, the FireWire port is located on the back of the computer.

After you have connected the FireWire cable to the back of your computer, you can keep it there at all times so that you can easily reconnect your iPod.

### 2 Connect iPod to the FireWire Cable

Connect the iPod to the FireWire cable. If you have an iPod dock, place the iPod in the dock. If you do not have the dock, connect the FireWire cable to the dock connector port on the bottom of the iPod unit.

Some older iPods have a port for the FireWire cable on the *top* of the iPod. These iPods do not work with the iPod dock.

> **NOTE**
>
> If your iPod did not come with a dock, you can purchase one for it as long as your iPod has a dock connector port on the bottom.

**CHAPTER 8:** Organizing Sound Files

## 66 Set iPod Preferences

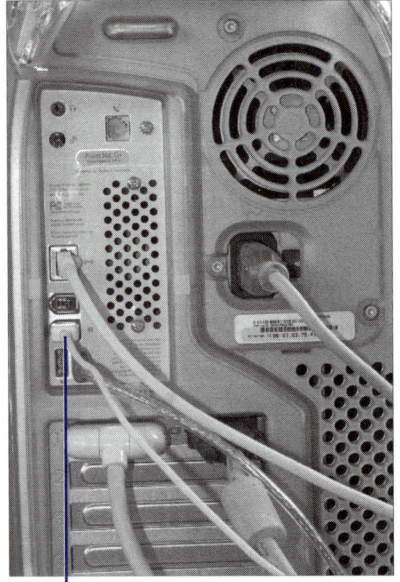

**1** Connect the iPod FireWire Cable to Computer

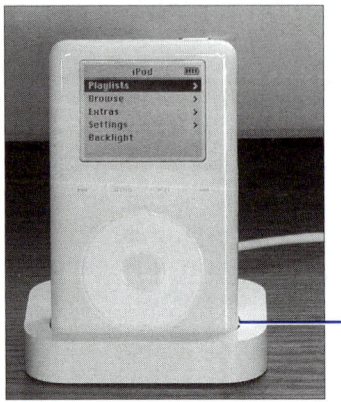

**2** Connect iPod to the FireWire Cable

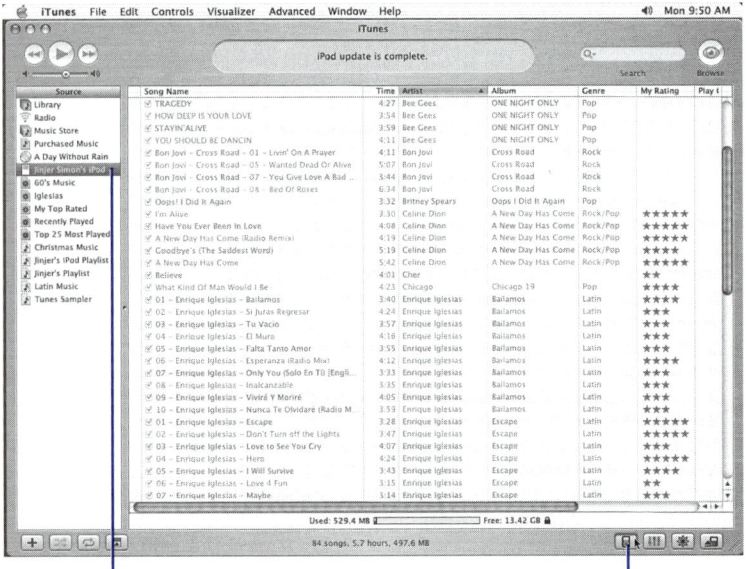

**3** Select the iPod Option in the Source List

**4** Display iPod Preferences Dialog Box

**5** Select Update Option

**6** Have iTunes Open Automatically

**7** Enable FireWire Disk Usage

**8** Only Update Selected Songs

**9** Update iPod Preferences

PART II:   iTunes

## Set iPod Preferences

### ③ Select the iPod Option in the Source List

Click the **iPod** option in the **Source** list to view the contents of the iPod.

### ④ Display iPod Preferences Dialog Box

Click the **iPod Preferences** button on the bottom of the iTunes window to display the **iPod Preferences** dialog box. The **iPod Preferences** button displays only when the **iPod** option is selected in the **Source** list.

### ⑤ Select Update Option

Click the option that indicates how you want to update the iPod. By default, iTunes selects the **Automatically update all songs and playlists** option. This means that your entire iTunes Library will be copied onto your iPod. To copy only specific playlists, click the **Automatically update selected playlists only** option. If you select this option, you must select the playlists you want to add to your iPod.

You can also manually add and remove songs from your iPod by clicking the **Manually manage songs and playlists** option. If you select this option, iTunes will not automatically add any audio to your iPod.

### ⑥ Have iTunes Open Automatically

Enable the **Open iTunes when attached** option to have iTunes automatically launch whenever you connect your iPod to the computer.

If this option is not selected, you must manually launch iTunes to access the audio files on your iPod from your computer.

### ⑦ Enable FireWire Disk Usage

If you want to be able to copy files to your iPod from **Finder**, select the **Enable FireWire disk use** option.

When this option is selected, your iPod displays as another disk in **Finder**. You can copy files to your iPod by clicking and dragging them onto the "disk."

**TIPS**

You can rename the iPod option in the **Source** list by clicking the name to select it and then typing the new name. The name you specify appears on the **Source** list and in the **Finder** when you view the FireWire disk.

You can create a smart playlist that adds audio files based on specific criteria. For example, you might want to copy only those songs with a specific rating.

CHAPTER 8: Organizing Sound Files

### 8  Only Update Selected Songs

If you want to add only the selected songs (the ones with a check mark in the Library list) to your iPod, enable the **Only update checked songs** option. When this option is selected, iTunes does not copy songs that are not selected to your iPod, even if they are on the playlist.

### 9  Update iPod Preferences

Click the **OK** button to update iTunes to use the specified settings when connecting to your iPod. If you have one of the automatic update options selected, iTunes automatically updates the iPod to match the selected folders.

## 67  Sync Playlists with iPod

**Before You Begin**

✔ 57  About Playlists
✔ 65  About iPod

**See Also**

→ 58  Customize a Playlist
→ 59  Create a Smart Playlist
→ 66  Set iPod Preferences
→ 68  Manually Update iPod

**TIP**

If you want to create a playlist for your iPod that will display at the top of the list, you can add a hyphen (-) to the beginning of the name. For example, **-Tom's Favorites** displays before **All My Favorites** because iPod sorts punctuation characters to the top of the list.

If you only want to add to your iPod the audio files that are in your playlists, you can specify that only those playlists are loaded onto your iPod when you connect it to your computer. By doing this, you can ensure that only the music you want to listen to on your iPod is transferred there and not your entire Library.

When you add playlists to your iPod, they are listed on the iPod in alphabetical order. In other words, the playlist **All My Favorites** appears before **Christmas Music**.

After you have selected the playlists you want to add to your iPod, each time you connect your iPod to your computer, iTunes will update the iPod based on the current playlist settings. This means that not only will new songs be added to your iPod, but if you remove songs from a playlist, they are removed from your iPod, too.

### 1  Connect the iPod to the Computer

Connect the end of the iPod FireWire cable to a FireWire port on your computer. On most Apple computers, the FireWire port is located on the back of the computer.

After you have connected the FireWire cable to the back of the computer, you can keep it there at all times so that you can easily reconnect your iPod.

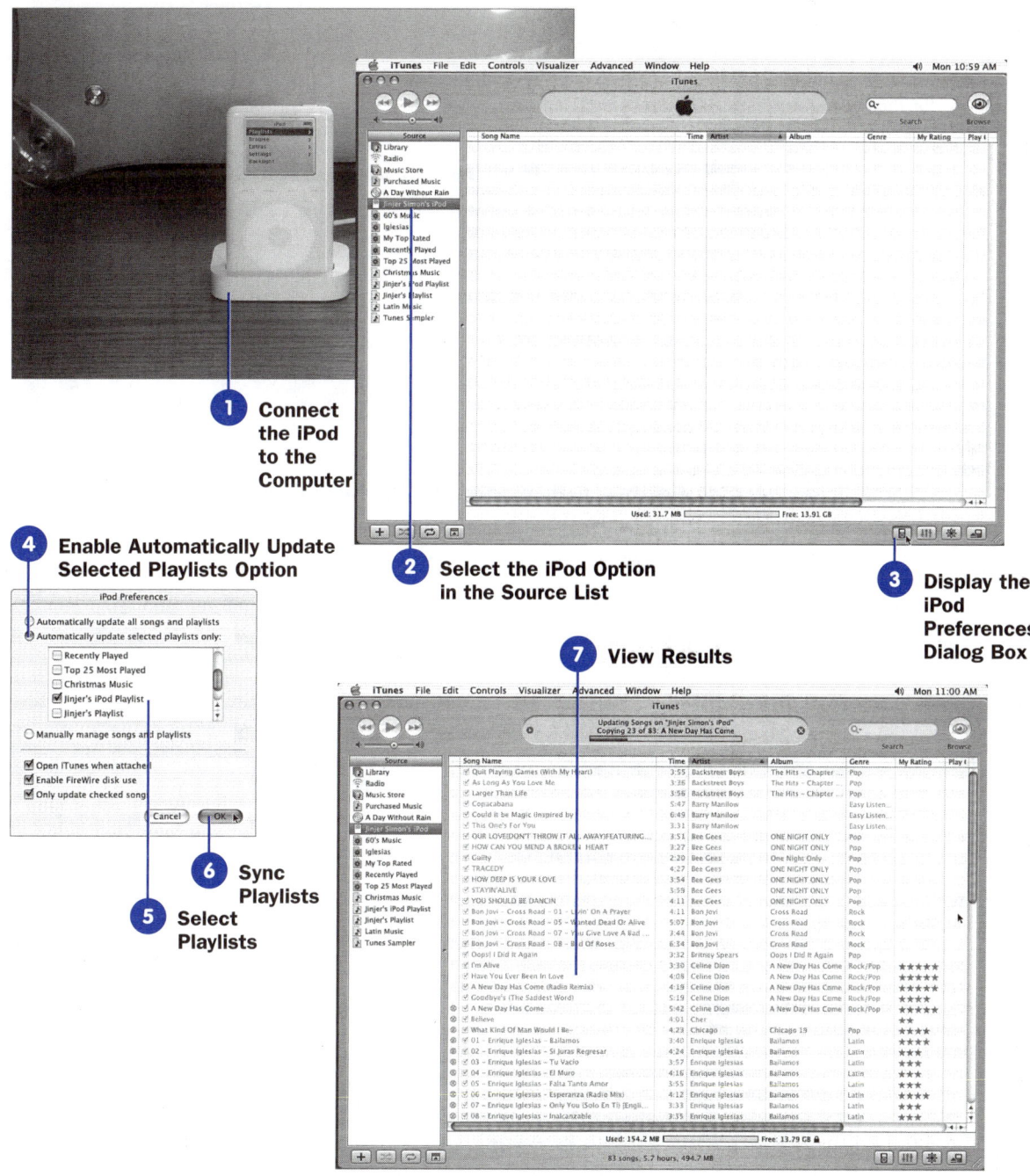

## Sync Playlists with iPod

1. Connect the iPod to the Computer
2. Select the iPod Option in the Source List
3. Display the iPod Preferences Dialog Box
4. Enable Automatically Update Selected Playlists Option
5. Select Playlists
6. Sync Playlists
7. View Results

**CHAPTER 8: Organizing Sound Files** 201

## 67 Sync Playlists with iPod

**Some older iPods have a port for the FireWire cable on the *top* of the iPod. These iPods do not work with the iPod dock.**

Connect the iPod to the FireWire cable. If you have an iPod dock, place the iPod in the dock. If you do not have a dock, connect the FireWire cable to the dock connector port on the bottom of the iPod.

### ② Select the iPod Option in the Source List

Click the **iPod** option in the **Source** list to view the contents of the iPod.

### ③ Display the iPod Preferences Dialog Box

Click the **iPod Preferences** button on the bottom of the iTunes window to display the **iPod Preferences** dialog box. The **iPod Preferences** button displays only when you select the **iPod** option in the **Source** list.

### ④ Enable Automatically Update Selected Playlists Option

Enable the **Automatically update selected playlists only** option to add to your iPod only the music from the playlists you select.

### ⑤ Select Playlists

In the list box, click the check box next to each of the playlists that you want to add to your iPod. If you have more than five playlists, a scrollbar displays on the right side of the list box. Use the scrollbar to scroll through the list.

### ⑥ Sync Playlists

Click the **OK** button. iTunes immediately begins to update the iPod so that it contains only the audio files listed in the selected playlists.

**If the iPod contains audio files that are not on the selected playlists, those files are removed from the iPod during the update process.**

### ⑦ View Results

View the iPod song list in iTunes. iTunes immediately displays the entire list of audio files for the iPod. An icon displays next to each audio file on the song list until it has been copied to your iPod. As the audio files are transferred to your iPod, a status message displays at the top of the window.

Do not disconnect your iPod from the computer while it is being updated.

**TIP**
Choose **Controls, Eject iPod** to disconnect the iPod from your computer.

## 68 Manually Update iPod

If you want to be able to manually add and remove audio files from your iPod, you use the manual update option on the **iPod Preferences** dialog box. When you enable this option, you have complete control over *what* is added to your iPod and *when* it is added.

You add songs to your iPod manually by dragging a song from the Library onto the iPod option in the **Source** list. You can also create playlists on the iPod, just as you can in iTunes. After you create a playlist on the iPod, you drag the desired songs to the playlist from the iTunes Library.

**Before You Begin**
✓ 65 About iPod

**See Also**
→ 66 Set iPod Preferences
→ 67 Sync Playlists with iPod

### ❶ Select the iPod Option in the Source List

Click the **iPod** option in the **Source** list to view the contents of the iPod.

### ❷ Display the iPod Preferences Dialog Box

Click the **iPod Preferences** button on the bottom of the iTunes window to display the **iPod Preferences** dialog box. The **iPod Preferences** button displays only when the **iPod** option is selected in the **Source** list.

**TIP**
If the iPod option is not listed on the **Source** list, your iPod is not properly connected to your computer. Make sure that the FireWire cable is connected to the computer and to the iPod.

### ❸ Enable the Manually Manage Songs and Playlists Option

On the **iPod Preferences** dialog box, enable the **Manually manage songs and playlists** option so that iTunes will allow you to add and delete songs and playlists manually on your iPod.

If you don't select this option, the only way to modify the content of your iPod is by specifying a different playlist. You cannot manually add and delete songs from the iPod when one of the automatic update options is selected.

**CHAPTER 8:** Organizing Sound Files

## Manually Update iPod

**1** Select iPod Option in the Source List

**3** Enable the Manually Manage Songs and Playlists Option

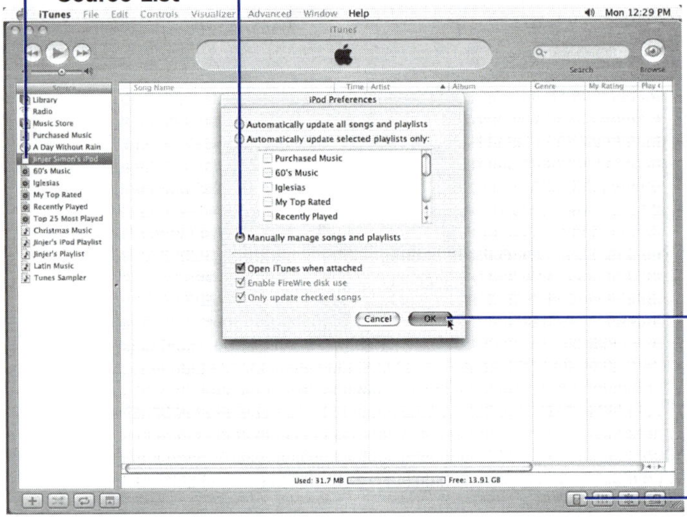

**5** Create a Playlist

**4** Close Dialog Box

**2** Display the iPod Preferences Dialog Box

**6** Display the iTunes Library

**7** Add Audio Files to iPod

**8** View Results

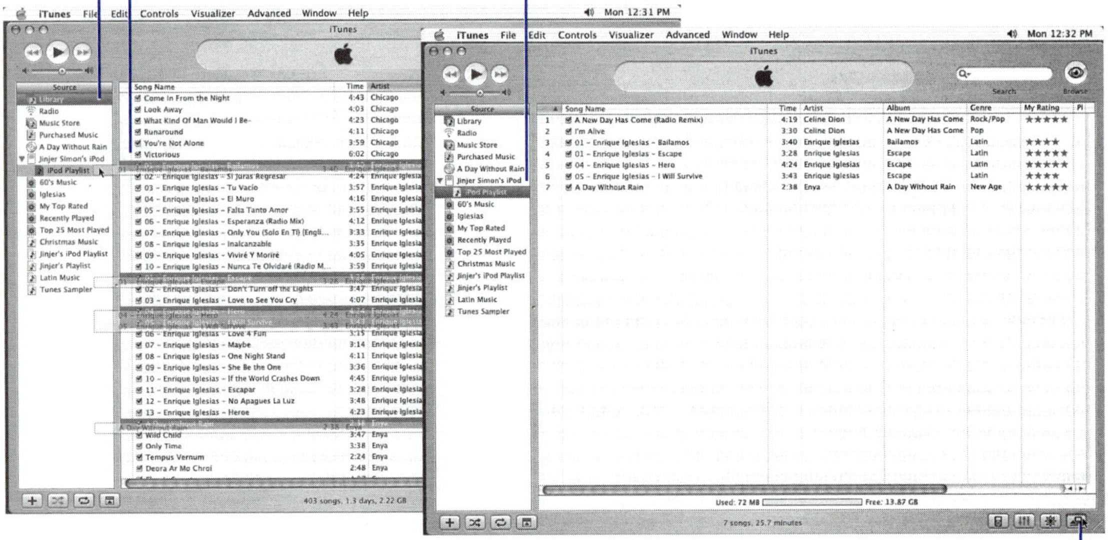

**9** Eject iPod

204   PART II:   iTunes

## Manually Update iPod 68

### 4 Close Dialog Box

Click the **OK** button to update the iPod settings to allow manual updating of the iPod.

### 5 Create a Playlist

Make sure that the iPod option is still selected in the **Source** list and choose **File, New Playlist** to create a new playlist on your iPod. Just as in iTunes, the new playlist is named **untitled playlist 1** with the number at the end incremented each time you create a new playlist.

If desired, you can rename the playlist by clicking it and typing the desired name. See 58 **Customize a Playlist** for more information on creating playlists.

**NOTE**

iTunes lists the playlists on your iPod in an indented arrangement under the **iPod** option. By displaying the names of all your iPod playlists this way, it is easy for you to access the playlists you want to modify.

### 6 Display the iTunes Library

Click the **Library** option in the **Source** list to view the complete song list for your iTunes Library.

### 7 Add Audio Files to iPod

Select the songs you want to add to your iPod and drag them to the iPod playlist you created in step 5. You can select multiple songs by holding down the ⌘ key while you click on each song.

### 8 View Results

Click the iPod playlist in the **Source** list to see the list of songs you just added to the playlist.

### 9 Eject iPod

When you have finished updating your iPod, click the **Eject iPod** button in the bottom-right corner of the iTunes window.

CHAPTER 8: Organizing Sound Files

## 69 Customize View of Song List

### TIPS

Avoid disconnecting your iPod when the message **Do not disconnect** displays. You can damage the files on your iPod if you disobey the message.

To delete songs from your iPod, select the song in the iPod song list and press the **Delete** key.

When you are manually updating the iPod, iTunes remains connected to your iPod and the **Do not disconnect** message displays on the iPod. When you are finished working in manual mode, click the **Eject iPod** button so that iTunes will release control of the iPod.

When you select the **Eject iPod** button, your iPod will no longer display on the **Source** list, even if it is still connected to your computer. You can disconnect your iPod from the dock or the FireWire cable as soon as the message clears from the iPod's display.

## 69 Customize View of Song List

**Before You Begin**

✓ **57** About Playlists

**See Also**

→ **58** Customize a Playlist
→ **61** Rate Music Tracks
→ **63** Search for Songs

### NOTE

Even if you want to apply all your playlist view options to all your playlists, you must select the playlists one at a time and change the view options for each one separately.

When you view the Library or a specific playlist, information about each song in the list displays on the song list. Each column displays different information. For example, when you view a playlist, the first column always displays a number identifying the song location in the list and the second column contains the song name. The remaining columns on the list are customizable.

When you create a playlist, iTunes assigns default columns to the song list display. You can add or remove columns from the display and change the order in which the columns display. You can make these changes for every playlist, including the Library. Remember, you cannot move or alter the first and second columns.

### 1 Select Playlist

In the **Source** list, select the playlist for which you want to change the view options.

### 2 Display the View Options Dialog Box

Choose **Edit, View Options** to display the **View Options** dialog box.

### 3 Select Columns for the Song List

Click the check box next to the names of the columns of information you want to view for the selected playlist.

You can deselect a column by clicking the check box to remove the check mark.

206      PART II:   iTunes

# Customize View of Song List

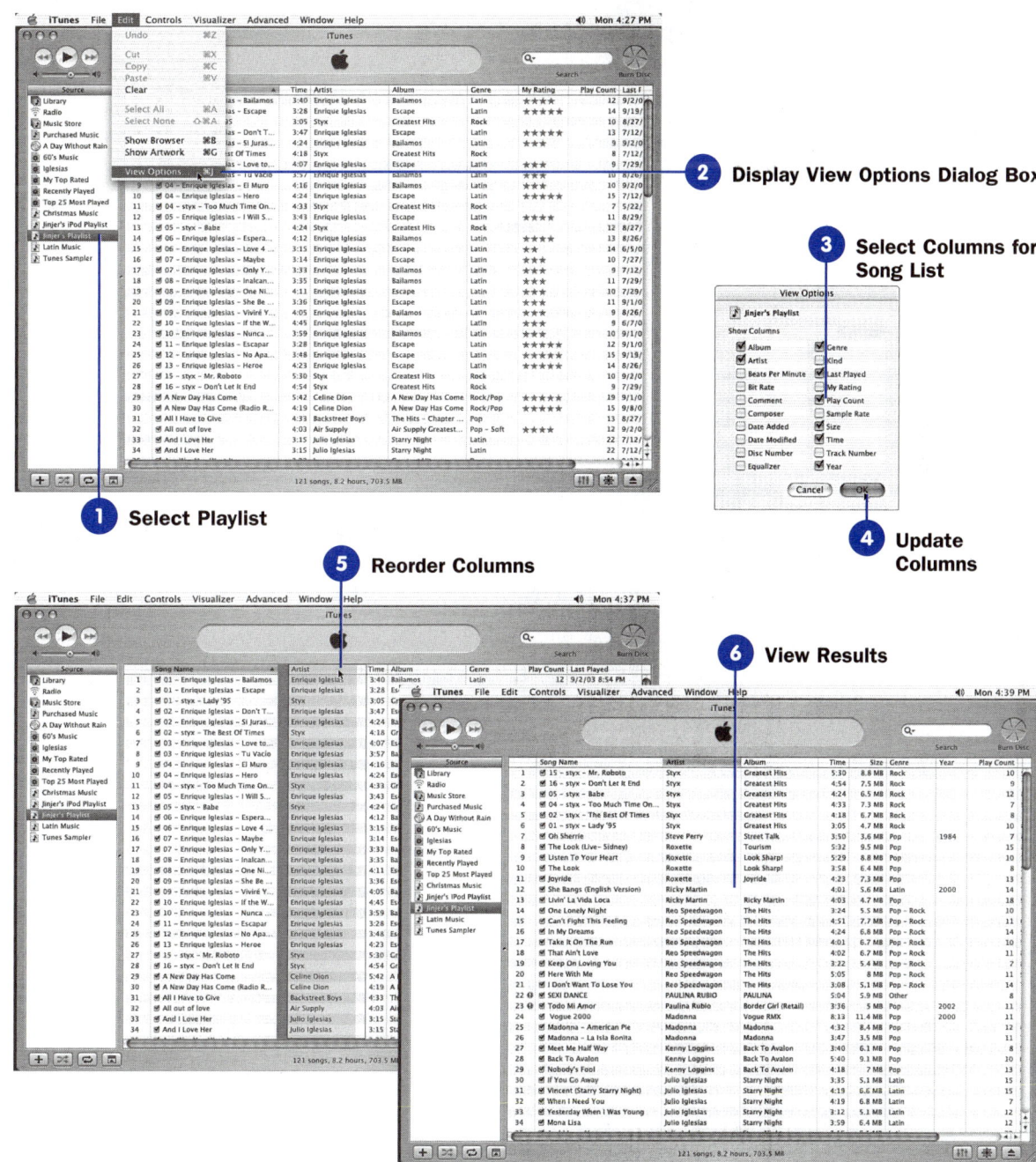

1. Select Playlist
2. Display View Options Dialog Box
3. Select Columns for Song List
4. Update Columns
5. Reorder Columns
6. View Results

**CHAPTER 8: Organizing Sound Files**

## Customize View of Song List

### ④ Update Columns

Click the **OK** button to update the columns that appear in the song list. iTunes inserts the new columns you select at the right end of the screen. If you cannot see the columns you just added, use the scrollbar at the bottom of the window to scroll to the right.

### ⑤ Reorder Columns

Click a column heading and drag it to move it to another location in the window. For example, you might want to have the **Artist** column follow the **Song Name** column. To do so, click the **Artist** column heading and drag it in front of the **Time** column.

Repeat the process until you have moved all the columns into the preferred order.

### ⑥ View Results

Verify that you have the desired layout for the selected playlist. You can repeat these steps to modify the layout of another playlist or of the main Library itself.

# 9

# Listening to Sound Files

## IN THIS CHAPTER:

- **70** About Internet Radio
- **71** Listen to Internet Radio
- **72** Load New Internet Streaming Audio Sites
- **73** Store Favorite Internet Radio Sites
- **74** Randomize Songs Being Played Back
- **75** Adjust Sound Level of Music Library
- **76** About Equalizers
- **77** Equalize the Sound
- **78** Save Equalizer Settings
- **79** Apply an Equalizer Preset to an Individual Song
- **80** Create Fades Between Audio Files
- **81** Use Visual Effects with Audio Files
- **82** Shuffle Songs by Album

## 70 About Internet Radio

> **KEY TERM**
>
> **Streaming audio**—Audio played from a specific Web site. The audio is downloaded in small chunks of data that can be played immediately. Playback occurs during the download process. Your computer downloads each chunk of data and buffers it until you listen to it. After playing the audio in the buffer, iTunes replaces that data with the next chunk of data. Because the audio is buffered, nothing is stored on your hard drive.

With iTunes, you can listen not only to audio you import from CDs or download from the Internet, but also to audio broadcast over the Internet from various locations around the world. Several sites on the Internet broadcast radio stations to which you can listen at any time. You can also connect to special live broadcasts, such as a company's earnings report. These live broadcasts are commonly referred to as *streaming audio*.

When working with audio you have imported, you can customize your playback options. For example, instead of listening to a playlist in order, you can have iTunes randomly play the songs on the playlist. If you want to hear an entire album played randomly, you can use the album **Shuffle** option.

You can adjust the sound of the audio played from your Library. You can also liven up your screen during audio playback by having iTunes display visual effects as the audio plays.

## 70 About Internet Radio

**See Also**

→ **71** Listen to Internet Radio

→ **72** Load New Internet Streaming Audio Sites

→ **73** Store Favorite Internet Radio Sites

> **KEY TERM**
>
> **Buffer**—A temporary storage location for data during a transfer process between computers.

iTunes is not limited to just the audio you import from CDs or download from the Internet. You can also use it to listen to live radio station broadcasts over the Internet. Just like an AM or FM radio station, Internet radio stations broadcast audio you can listen to live. When you listen to Internet radio, you cannot select or record the audio; you simply listen to whatever is currently being broadcast on the selected radio site.

So that you can listen to the broadcast live, Internet radio sites provide *streaming audio*. The cool thing about streaming audio is that you hear the audio within a few seconds of clicking the link. The audio is transmitted in small chunks that are *buffered* on your computer. As soon as the buffer is full, the audio begins playing on your computer. At the same time audio is playing, the download continues by placing additional audio in the buffer. As long as the download process is faster than the playback, you get a smooth audio feed on your computer. If the download process is delayed at all, you might hear breaks in the audio.

**About Internet Radio** 70

Although audio can be streamed in different formats, iTunes can receive only MP3 or AAC streaming audio. iTunes provides a list of several radio stations to which you can listen by clicking their links. If you don't find the desired station on the list, you can load other radio stations by specifying the corresponding URLs.

When you view the list of available radio stations in iTunes, you will see that some radio stations offer audio streams at different *bit rates*. The bit rate information not only tells you how compressed the audio is, but also gives an indication of how fast your Internet connection should be to listen to the audio stream. For example, if you are connecting to the Internet using a 56KBps modem, you should select streams with a 56KBps bit rate or lower. If you select a higher bit rate, you will not be able to listen to the selected station very well.

**KEY TERM**

**Bit rate**—A measurement of the compression for a file or streaming media. The bit rate is expressed in kilobytes per second (KBps).

- **Why can't iTunes play the Internet radio site I specified?** iTunes can play only MP3 or AAC streaming audio files. Not all streaming audio is in MP3 or AAC format. Some sites provide streaming audio using other formats, such as WAV, RealAudio, and QuickTime. If you are unable to listen to a site within iTunes, try using the Apple QuickTime player.

**WEB RESOURCE**

Download the Apple QuickTime media player from this site.

- **What bit rate should I select with my DSL connection?** If you have a DSL connection, you should be able to listen to streaming media sites at rates of 128KBps or lower.

- **Does it matter which bit rate I select?** The higher the bit rate of a streaming media site, the less compression that is used on the audio. Because compression reduces the size by eliminating portions of the audio, the less compressed the file is, the better quality the sound. Select the bit rate that most closely matches your connection speed.

**TIP**

For example, if you are connecting with a dial-up modem, your connection speed is probably 56KBps, so you should select a streaming media site with a bit rate of 56KBps or slower. Cable modems, DSL, and T1 lines are all considered high-speed connections. If you have one of these types of connections, you should be able to select 128KBps sites.

- **How do I add my favorite radio sites?** You cannot add new radio sites to those available when you select the **Radio** option from the Library source list. You can, however, create your own playlist that contains the sites you like to listen to. See  **Store Favorite Internet Radio Sites** for more information on storing a list of favorite radio sites.

CHAPTER 9: Listening to Sound Files   211

# 71 Listen to Internet Radio

**Before You Begin**

✔  About Internet Radio

**See Also**

→  Load New Internet Streaming Audio Sites

→ **73** Store Favorite Internet Radio Sites

**NOTE**

You must be connected to the Internet before you can see the list of Internet radio stations.

**NOTE**

When you select a genre, the number of stations for that genre displays next to the selected genre name.

iTunes provides several different Internet radio stations, identified as *streams*, to which you can connect. The streams are sorted into different genres to make it easier to locate the radio station to which you want to listen.

When you select a radio station, make sure that you select one with a bit rate that matches your Internet connection. You do not want to select a site with a bit rate that exceeds your connection speed. For example, if you are connected to the Internet using a 56KBps modem, you should not select a site with a bit rate that exceeds 56KBps.

### 1 Select the Radio Option

Select the **Radio** option from the **Source** list to view the genres of the available radio station streams.

### 2 Display Radio Stations for a Genre

Double-click the genre name to display the list of available radio stations for that genre. You can also display the list by clicking the triangle next to the genre name.

When you click a genre, iTunes connects to the tuning service and downloads the current list of available radio stations within that genre. This process might take a few seconds, depending on the speed of your Internet connection. The list of stations iTunes displays contains only those stations in the streaming format supported by iTunes. You can select any of these stations without worrying whether iTunes can play the station.

### 3 Select a Radio Station

Click to select the radio station in the list to which you want to listen. If the radio station provides multiple streams, select the stream with a bit rate that most closely matches your Internet connection speed.

**Listen to Internet Radio**

① **Select the Radio Option**

② **Display Radio Stations for a Genre**

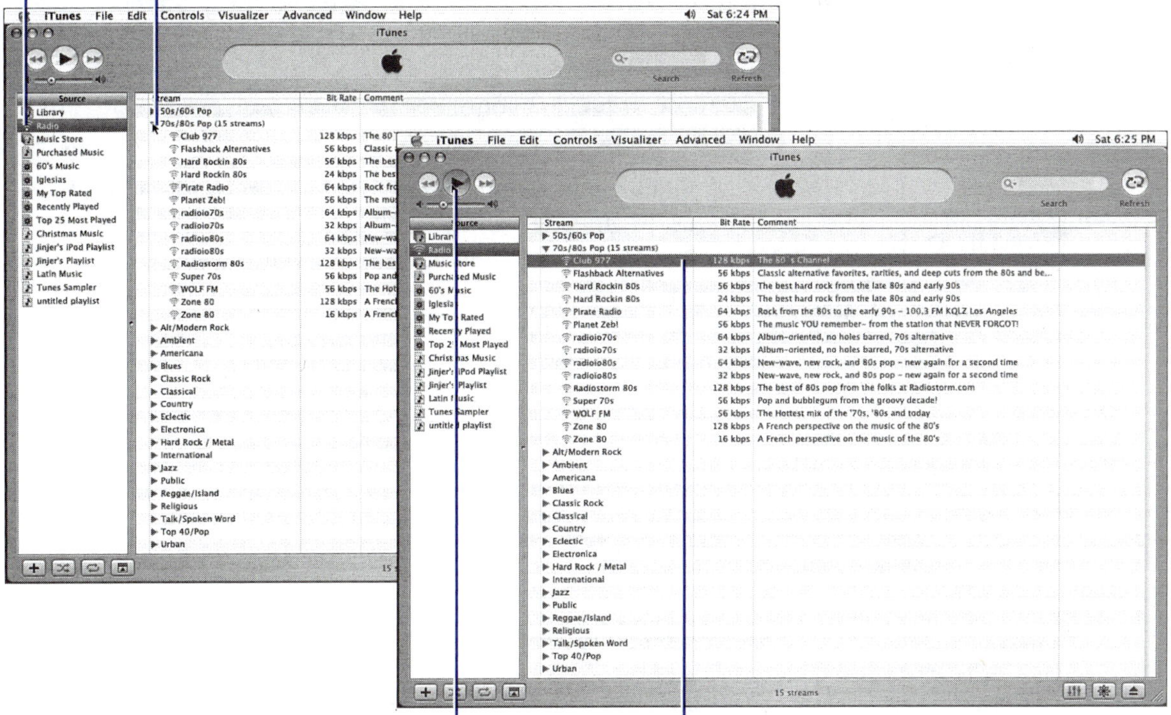

③ **Select a Radio Station**

④ **Play the Selected Radio Station**

④ **Play the Selected Radio Station**

Click the **Play** button to listen to the selected radio station. iTunes connects to the Internet site, and the station should start playing within a few seconds. The **Play** icon displays in the first column of the **Stream** list to show the radio station that is playing.

If you click the **Forward** button, iTunes plays the next radio station on the list. Click the **Back** button to play the previously listed radio station.

**TIP**

You can also play a radio station by double-clicking it with the mouse.

CHAPTER 9: Listening to Sound Files   213

## 72 Load New Internet Streaming Audio Sites

**Before You Begin**

✔ **70** About Internet Radio

**See Also**

→ **71** Listen to Internet Radio

→ **73** Store Favorite Internet Radio Sites

When you click the **Radio** option in the **Source** list, you are not limited to the streaming radio stations listed by iTunes. You can also connect to other audio streams on the Internet. For example, you can connect not only to continuous radio streams, you can also connect to special broadcasts, such as a company stock report.

The only stipulation when connecting to a streaming audio site is that the audio must be streamed as MP3 or AAC audio. iTunes can process only MP3 and AAC streaming audio; it does not work with other formats of streaming audio. Most Web sites indicate the format in which their audio is streamed. For example, if the audio is streamed as MP3 streaming audio, typically, that information is mentioned on the Web page.

If you locate a radio station to which you want to listen again, you can add it to a playlist. See **73** **Store Favorite Internet Radio Sites** for more information on adding radio streams to an iTunes playlist.

### NOTE

If you select an MP3 streaming audio site from your Web browser, the audio automatically opens and starts playing in iTunes.

**① Display Open Stream Dialog Box**

Choose **Advanced, Open Stream** from the iTunes menu bar to display the **Open Stream** dialog box.

**② Specify URL for Audio Stream**

Type the URL of the streaming audio to which you want to connect.

### WEB RESOURCE

These are just a few of the Internet sites that provide links to MP3 radio stations to which you can listen in iTunes.

http://www.shoutcast.com

http://www.somafm.com

http://www.flashbackradio.com

**③ Close Open Stream Dialog Box**

Click the **OK** button on the **Open Stream** dialog box. iTunes connects to the specified URL and plays the audio stream.

Load New Internet Streaming Audio Sites 72

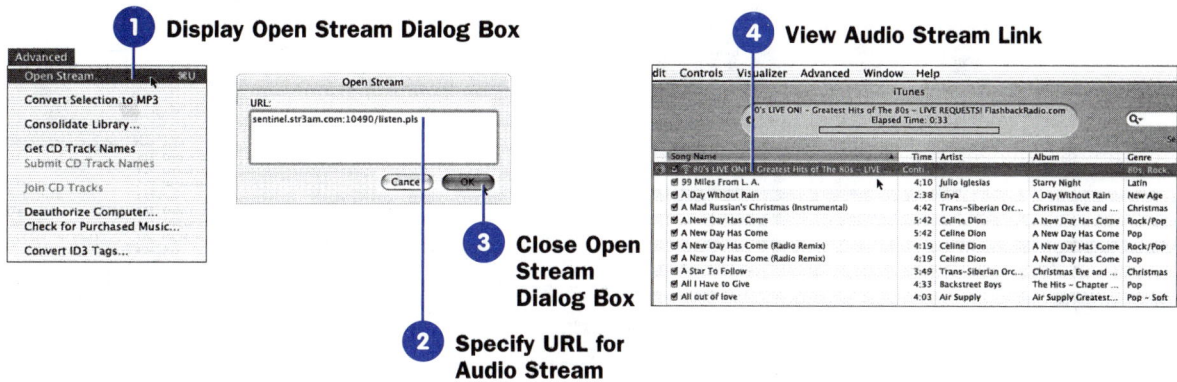

## ④ View Audio Stream Link

iTunes places an audio link to the specified URL in your Library song list. An icon displays next to the radio station link indicating that it is a link to an Internet site.

The radio site is added to the song list for your Library based on the selected sort order of the list. For example, if your Library playlist is sorted by song name, the radio station name becomes the song name and is inserted in the list at that location. See **69 Customize View of Song List** for more information on sorting the song list in iTunes.

### 💡 TIPS

To pause the radio station, click the **Pause** button. When you click the **Play** button again, iTunes reconnects to the radio station.

Information about the selected radio station displays in the time display at the top of the iTunes window. It also displays the amount of time you have been listening to the station as the Elapsed Time.

## 73 Store Favorite Internet Radio Sites

If you have specific radio stations to which you like to listen, you can create a *playlist* that contains those stations. A radio station playlist works well with both the radio stations available when you click the **Radio** option in the **Source** list and for radio stations that you specify with the **Open Stream** dialog box. The nice thing about having a radio station playlist is that you have all your favorite stations in one location without having to search for the station under a specific genre.

### Before You Begin

✔ **70** About Internet Radio

### See Also

→ **72** Load New Internet Streaming Audio Sites

CHAPTER 9: Listening to Sound Files        215

**Store Favorite Internet Radio Sites**

1. Create a New Playlist
2. Name the Playlist
3. Add Radio Station to Playlist

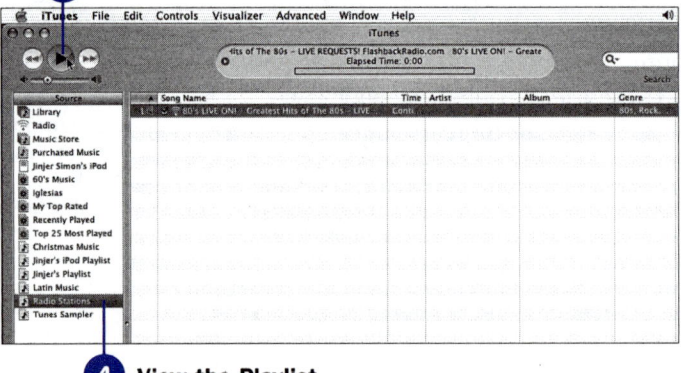

4. View the Playlist
5. Play a Favorite Station

When you add radio stations to a playlist, iTunes simply remembers the link to the selected station. Each time you click the link, iTunes connects to that radio station. Unlike other playlists, a playlist containing radio stations does not automatically switch between radio stations in the list.

216　　**PART II:** iTunes

Store Favorite Internet Radio Sites

Only the station you select plays. If you want to hear another station in the list, select it manually.

**① Create a New Playlist**

Choose **File, New Playlist** to create a new untitled playlist in the **Source** list. iTunes creates a playlist with the name **untitled playlist**. See  **Customize a Playlist** for more information on creating playlists in iTunes.

> **TIP**
> If you have the radio station link selected in the iTunes radio list, choose **File, New Playlist From Selection** to create a new playlist that contains the selected radio station.

**② Name the Playlist**

When you create a new playlist, the playlist name is automatically selected in the **Source** list. To rename the playlist, type the desired playlist name.

If the playlist name is not selected, click to select it.

**③ Add Radio Station to Playlist**

Select the radio station you want to add to the playlist from your Library or the radio list and drag it into the new playlist.

The radio stations you add to your playlist remain in your Library or in the radio list. iTunes just creates a copy of the link in your new playlist.

**④ View the Playlist**

In the **Source** list, click the new playlist to view your list of radio stations.

> **TIPS**
> Repeat step 3 for each radio station you want to add to the new playlist.
>
> If you click on the **Next** and **Previous** buttons, iTunes plays the next or previous radio station in your playlist.

**⑤ Play a Favorite Station**

Double-click the radio station to play it. You can also play a radio station by selecting it and then clicking the **Play** button.

CHAPTER 9: Listening to Sound Files  217

## 74  Randomize Songs Being Played Back

**Before You Begin**

✓ **57** About Playlists

**See Also**

→ **58** Customize a Playlist

→ **59** Create a Smart Playlist

→ **69** Customize View of Song List

→ **82** Shuffle Songs by Album

You don't have to listen to the songs on a playlist in the order they are listed. iTunes can randomize the playback of songs using the **Shuffle** option. When you click the **Shuffle** button, iTunes plays back the songs in the selected playlist in random order. If the first column is selected in the song list when you click the **Shuffle** button, the entire playlist is shuffled into the order that will be used when you click the **Play** button. If another column is selected (such as the **Song Name** column), iTunes shuffles the list by randomly playing different songs in the list.

If you want to make the replay of the music continuous, you can select the **Repeat** option to have iTunes start over when all the songs on the playlist have been played. The **Repeat** button allows you to listen to continuous music without restarting the playlist.

### ❶ Select a Playlist

Select the desired playlist from the **Source** list. If you want to listen to the entire Library, you can click the **Library** option.

### ❷ Select the First Column

Click to select the first column on the song list. By selecting this column, iTunes sorts the songs into random order within the playlist. You will be able to see the new sort order after you click the **Shuffle** button.

**TIP**
You can also shuffle the songs in a playlist by choosing **Controls, Shuffle**.

**NOTE**
When you shuffle a song list, it is no longer listed in any specific order. Click the **Shuffle** button again to return it to its previously sorted order.

### ❸ Click Shuffle Button

Click the **Shuffle** button at the bottom-left corner of the iTunes window. When the **Shuffle** option is selected, the lines on the **Shuffle** button display in blue.

### ❹ Select Repeat Option

To have the songs on the playlist repeat when iTunes reaches the end of the playlist, click the **Repeat** button on the bottom-left corner of the iTunes window. (The **Repeat** button has two arrows on it forming a circle.) The music plays continuously until you click the **Pause** button. Note that the playlist is shuffled only when you click the **Shuffle** button. iTunes does not reshuffle the list when it repeats.

PART II:   iTunes

## Randomize Songs Being Played Back  74

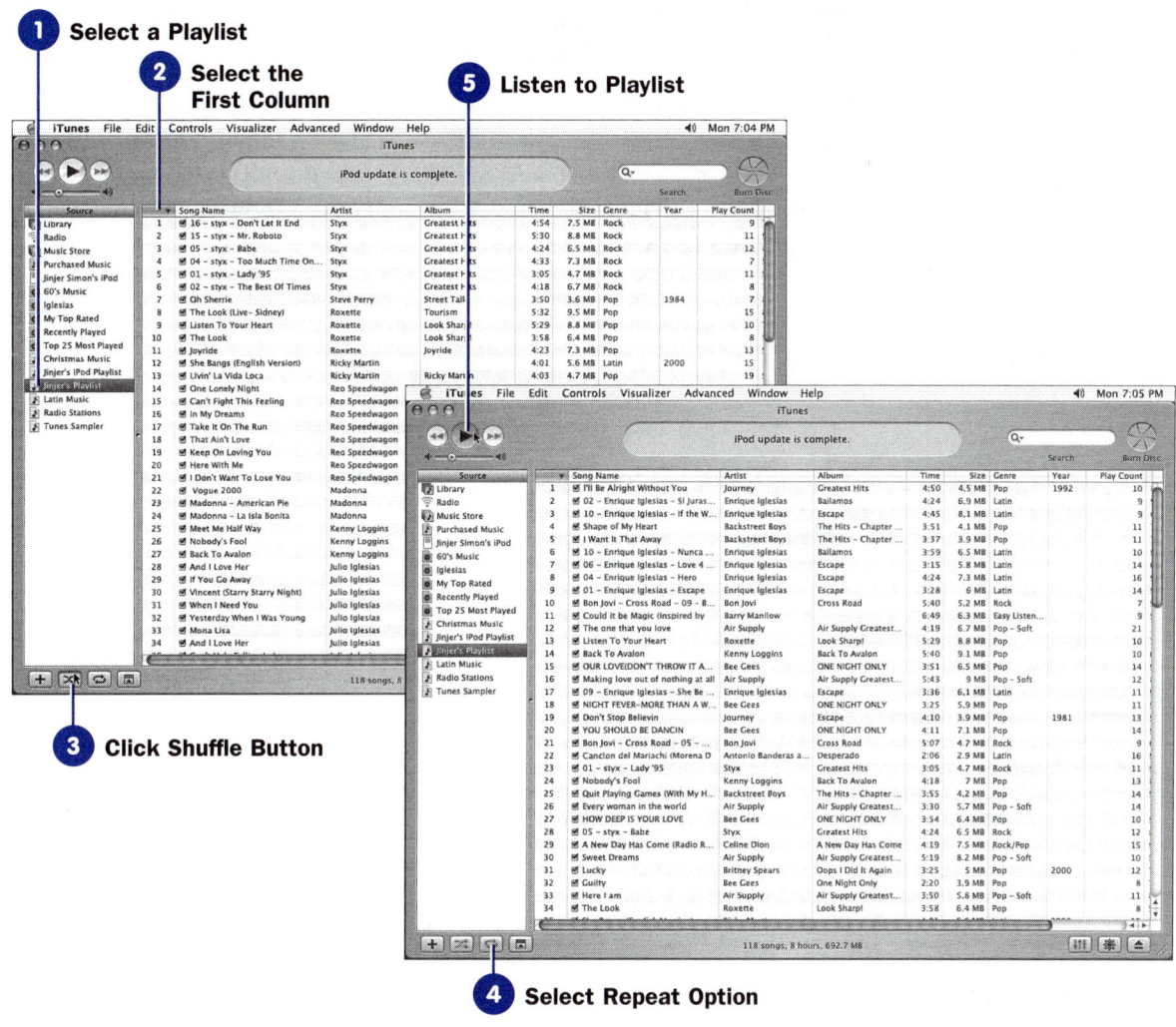

① Select a Playlist
② Select the First Column
③ Click Shuffle Button
④ Select Repeat Option
⑤ Listen to Playlist

### ⑤ Listen to Playlist

Click the **Play** button to listen to the shuffled playlist. If you've clicked the **Repeat** button, iTunes plays all the songs in the playlist before repeating any of them.

**CHAPTER 9: Listening to Sound Files** 219

## 75 Adjust Sound Level of Music Library

**Before You Begin**

✔ **57** About Playlists

**See Also**

→ **74** Randomize Songs Being Played Back
→ **76** About Equalizers
→ **77** Equalize the Sound
→ **80** Create Fades Between Audio Files

When you load songs from different albums or those that you purchase over the Internet, you might find that each song plays at a different volume level. To correct this, you can have iTunes adjust the playback volume so that every song in a playlist plays at the same level by selecting the **Sound Check** option.

When you select this option, the song files themselves are not modified, iTunes just controls the volume level when the songs play. This setting affects all audio within your iTunes Library.

### 1 Display the Preferences Dialog Box

Choose **iTunes**, **Preferences** to display the **Preferences** dialog box.

### 2 Display Effects Options

If the **Effects** options are not displayed, click the **Effects** icon at the top of the dialog box.

**NOTE**

You can use the **Crossfade playback** option in the **Preferences** dialog box to create fades between audio files. See **80** Create Fades Between Audio Files for more information.

### 3 Enable Sound Check Option

Enable the check box next to the **Sound Check** option. This option forces iTunes to optimize the playback volume of all audio so that it plays at a consistent volume level based on the volume you specify with the **Sound** slider.

### 4 Close Preferences Dialog Box

Click the **OK** button to close the **Preferences** dialog box.

### 5 Listen to Music

Click the **Play** button to listen to the songs in the current playlist or the iTunes Library.

### 6 Adjust Volume for Playback

Adjust the **Sound** slider under the **Play** button to the desired level. iTunes will maintain that same volume level for all songs. The **Sound Check** option ensures that all audio played in iTunes matches the volume specified by the **Sound** slider.

# Adjust Sound Level of Music Library

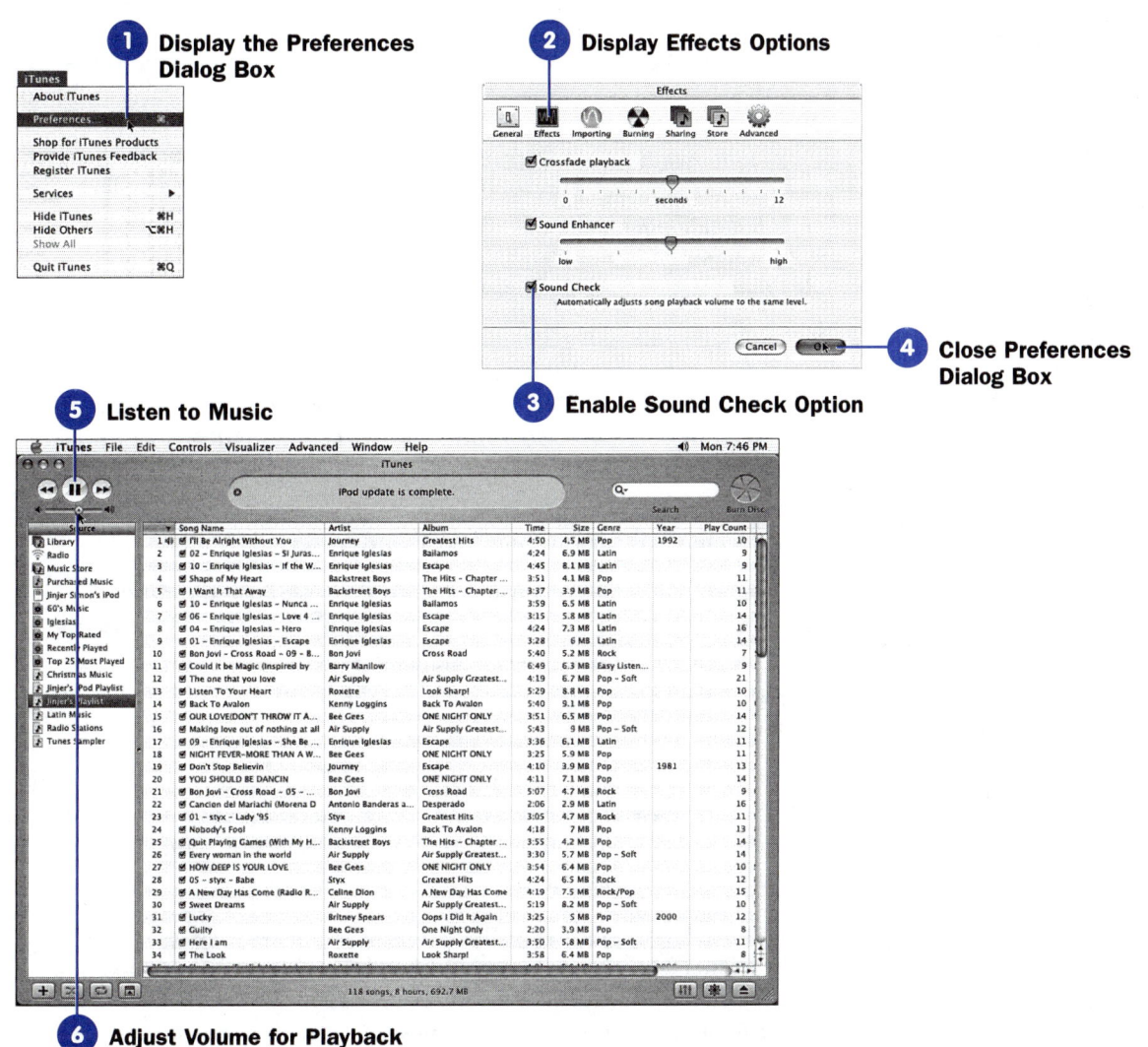

The **Sound** slider adjusts the volume for all the songs in the iTunes Library. The volume keys on your keyboard control the sound level for *everything* on your computer, including audio from iTunes.

**CHAPTER 9:** Listening to Sound Files   221

## 76 About Equalizers

### Before You Begin
✔ **57** About Playlists
✔ **71** Listen to Internet Radio

### See Also
→ **77** Equalize the Sound
→ **78** Save Equalizer Settings
→ **79** Apply an Equalizer Preset to an Individual Song

### KEY TERMS

*Equalizer*—A hardware or software device that allows you to adjust the frequency ranges of the audio stream. For example, you can boost the high-level frequencies to make them easier to hear.

*Hertz (Hz)*—A measurement used to represent a sound frequency.

*Decibel (dB)*—A unit of measurement to determine the intensity of each sound frequency.

### NOTE

The **Sound Check** option you can enable in the **iTunes Preferences** dialog box balances the sound levels of all the songs you play so that all songs sound like they are playing at the same volume level. The Equalizer adjusts the settings for individual frequencies in the audio.

iTunes enables you to do more than just adjust the volume of your audio; you can also use the *Equalizer* to adjust the sound quality. Using the Equalizer, you can control the audio levels for 10 frequency levels on the sound spectrum. Using the iTunes Equalizer is similar to adjusting the bass and treble settings on your stereo, except that the Equalizer provides more frequencies to adjust.

The frequency levels are based on the spectrum of human hearing. The levels are measured in *hertz (Hz)*. The lowest or deepest frequency is 32Hz. This frequency is deeper than most of us can hear. The mid-range frequencies are between 250Hz and 500Hz. The highest frequency, 16 kilohertz (KHz), is nearly as high as the human ears can hear. In fact, 16KHz sounds are hard for most humans to detect, although they are still not as high as the high-pitched sounds detected by dogs.

Each sound frequency is measured in *decibels* (dB) using a range of –12 dB to 12 dB. When working with the iTunes Equalizer, you use the sliders on each frequency level to adjust the decibel settings. As you increase the slider position, you increase the intensity of the sound at that level.

On the left side of the Equalizer window is a **Preamp** control. Adjust this control to increase or decrease the volume of *all* frequency levels. This control is useful when you have audio that was recorded under very loud or very quiet conditions.

On the top of the Equalizer window is a **Preset** field. This option allows you to select from one of the preset Equalizer settings. For example, if you are listening to classical music, you can select the **Classical** preset to load frequency settings that are preset for listening to that type of music. iTunes provides 12 different preset Equalizer settings from which you can select. You can also create your own preset settings.

- **Are the Equalizer settings applied to one song or to the entire Library?** When you specify the settings on the Equalizer window, those settings apply to all audio played in iTunes. The settings remain in effect until you apply new settings.

**About Equalizers** **76**

**Preset List**

**Preamp Slider**   **Frequency Sliders**

*The iTunes Equalizer lets you control 10 frequency levels for the songs in your Library.*

You can, however, apply an Equalizer preset to an individual song. For example, if you have an audio book that you downloaded from Audible.com, you might want to apply the **Spoken Word** preset to that specific audio file (but not to the rest of the files in your iTunes Library). You apply the preset from the song list by selecting the desired preset in the **Equalizer** column.

- **Do the Equalizer settings affect the way music is exported from iTunes?** No. The settings on the Equalizer window control the way audio plays within iTunes. The settings do not alter the actual audio files. When the audio files are exported by burning an audio CD, iTunes exports the actual audio files and ignores the Equalizer settings. See  **Burn an Audio CD** for more information on creating audio CDs in iTunes.

- **How do I know which frequencies to adjust?** The process of adjusting the frequencies is really based on your personal preferences. The frequencies that typically require the most adjustment are the low and high ones because human ears are more sensitive to lower and higher frequencies.

**TIP**

See **79** **Apply an Equalizer Preset to an Individual Song** for more information. See **53** **Download Audio Book Files from the Internet** for more information on loading audio books purchased from Audible.com.

**TIP**

The only time Equalizer settings are exported is when you transfer audio files to your iPod.

**CHAPTER 9: Listening to Sound Files**      223

## 77 Equalize the Sound

**Before You Begin**

✔ 76 About Equalizers

**See Also**

→ 78 Save Equalizer Settings

→ 79 Apply an Equalizer Preset to an Individual Song

You can specify the frequency settings for the audio you listen to in iTunes using the Equalizer window. On the Equalizer window, you can use the sliders to adjust the settings for each of the 10 different frequencies. If you move the slider up, the frequency is boosted for all iTunes audio files.

Before you can apply the Equalizer settings, you must turn on the Equalizer by enabling the **On** check box. If the Equalizer is on, the lines on the Equalizer button at the bottom-right corner of the iTunes window display in blue.

The Equalizer settings are applied to all audio that you listen to in iTunes. If you want to adjust the settings for one song, you must create a specific preset that you can apply to the selected audio file in the song list. See 78 **Save Equalizer Settings** for information on creating a preset and 79 **Apply an Equalizer Preset to an Individual Song** for information on applying the custom Equalizer settings to an individual song.

### ① Open the Equalizer Window

Click the **Equalizer** button at the bottom-right corner of the iTunes window to open the **Equalizer** window.

### ② Turn on the Equalizer

Click the check box next to the **On** button to turn on the Equalizer settings. While the Equalizer is turned on, iTunes adjusts the playback of all audio to match the specified settings for each frequency.

### ③ Adjust the Frequency Settings

Adjust the frequency settings by dragging the sliders up to boost the volume of each frequency or down to decrease it.

### ④ Close the Equalizer Window

Click the red **Close** button in the left corner of the Equalizer window to close it.

**TIP**

You can select one of the preset frequency options from the drop-down list at the top of the Equalizer window. The default presets have names that match popular types of music.

# Equalize the Sound 77

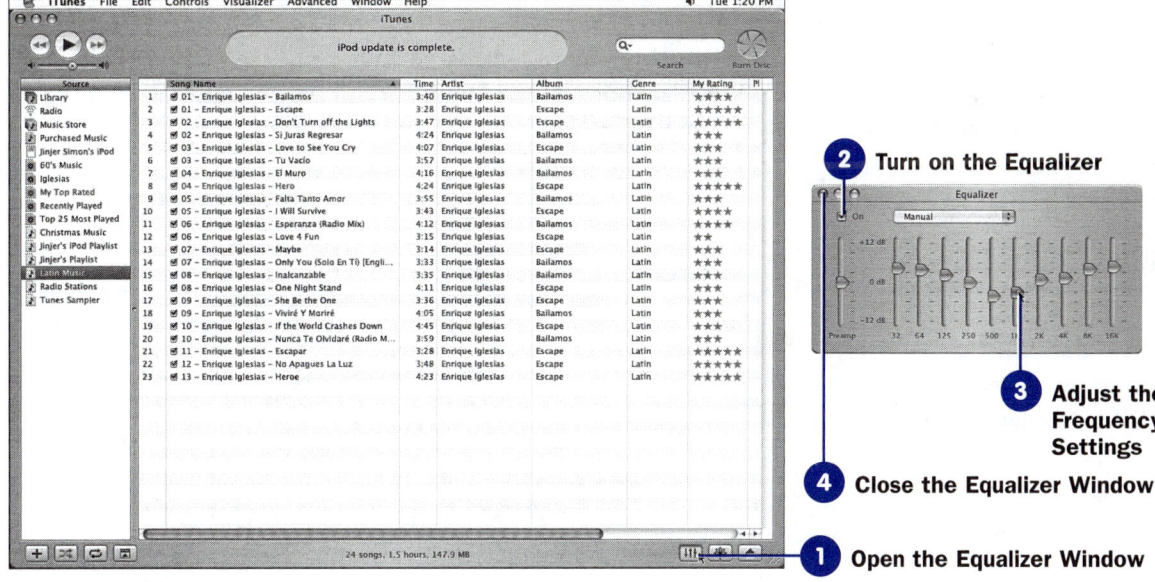

**2** Turn on the Equalizer

**3** Adjust the Frequency Settings

**4** Close the Equalizer Window

**1** Open the Equalizer Window

**5** Listen to Audio

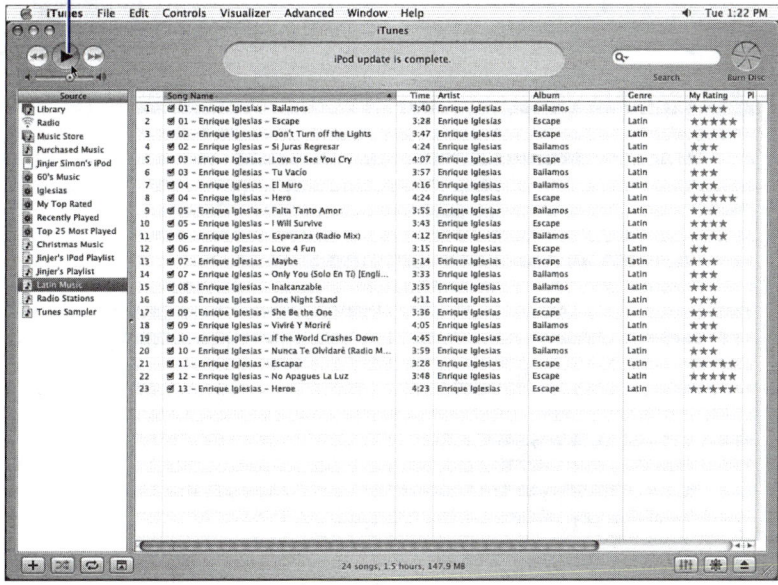

**CHAPTER 9: Listening to Sound Files** 225

## 78 Save Equalizer Settings

**TIP**

Repeat steps 1 through 4 to modify the equalizer settings as needed.

**5 Listen to Audio**

Click the **Play** button to listen to your audio using the Equalizer settings. The lines on the **Equalizer** button in the lower-right corner of the iTunes window are blue, indicating that the Equalizer settings are being applied.

## 78 Save Equalizer Settings

**Before You Begin**

✔ **76** About Equalizers
✔ **77** Equalize the Sound

**See Also**

→ **79** Apply an Equalizer Preset to an Individual Song

You can create your own custom presets that contain the Equalizer settings you prefer. To create a custom preset, you must first determine the appropriate frequency settings on the Equalizer window and then save the settings as a new preset. When you save the preset, iTunes requests a name to identify the preset in the list. The unique name you specify allows you to identify the present in the list that displays on the Equalizer window.

After you have saved the Equalizer settings, you can apply them to any other song in iTunes by simply selecting the preset from the Equalizer window. See **79** Apply an Equalizer Preset to an Individual Song for more information on applying presets to songs in the song list.

**1 Display Equalizer Window**

Click the **Equalizer** button in the bottom-right corner of the iTunes window to display the Equalizer window.

**2 Adjust Frequency Settings**

Adjust the settings for the desired frequency by dragging the appropriate sliders up to increase the volume of the selected frequency or down to decrease it.

**3 Display Preset List**

Click the arrow button in the top center of the Equalizer window to display a list of available presets.

**4 Select Make Preset Option**

Select the **Make Preset** option to display the **Make Preset** dialog box.

PART II: iTunes

# Save Equalizer Settings 78

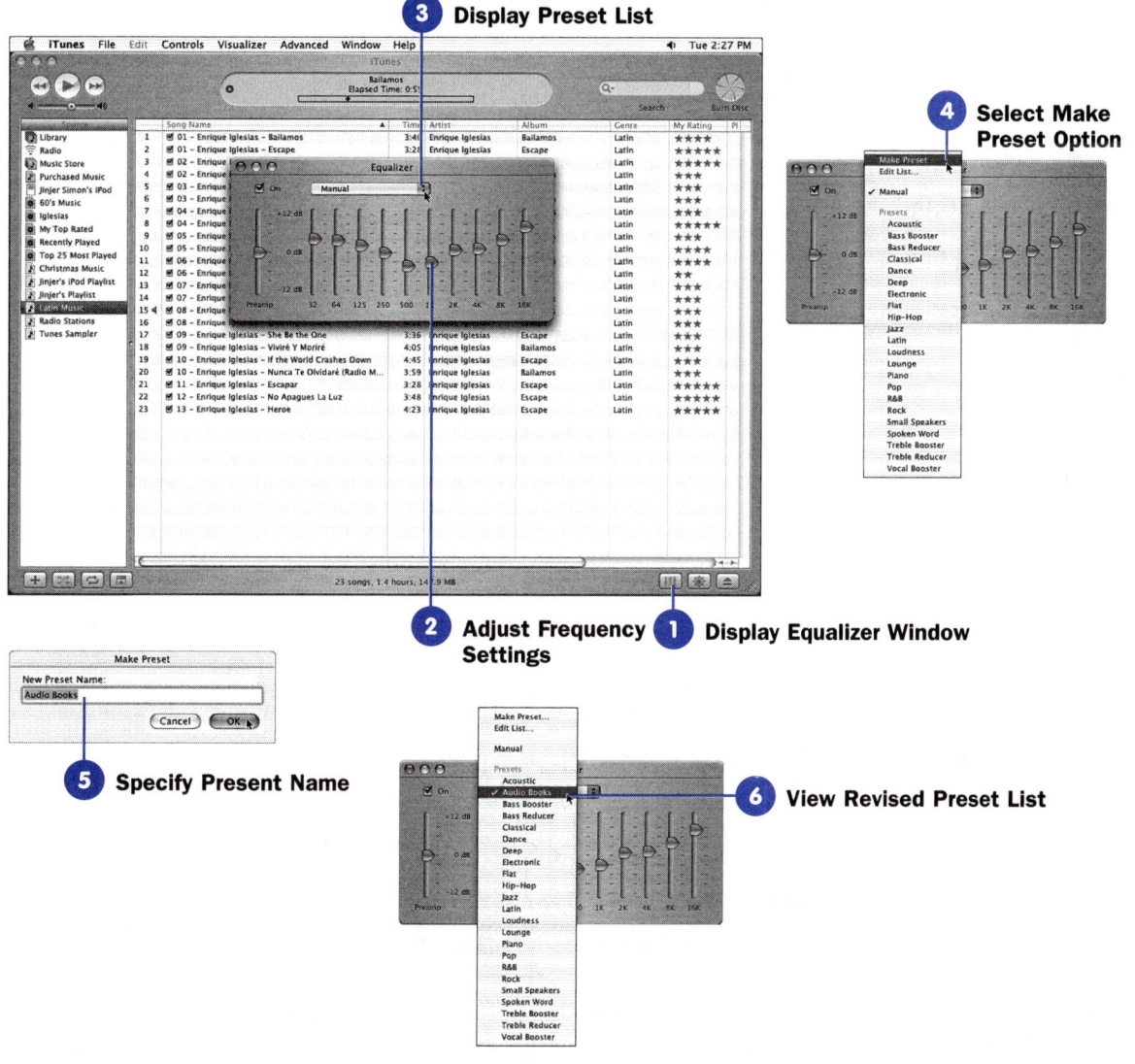

## 5 Specify Preset Name

Type the name for the preset you are creating and click the **OK** button. iTunes creates a preset that records the frequency settings you specified in step 2, saves it with the name you specify here, and closes the **Make Preset** dialog box.

**CHAPTER 9:** Listening to Sound Files

## 79 Apply an Equalizer Preset to an Individual Song

**6 View Revised Preset List**

On the Equalizer window, click the arrow button to display the **Preset** list again. The newly created preset is displayed in the list.

## 79 Apply an Equalizer Preset to an Individual Song

**Before You Begin**

✔ **76** About Equalizers

**See Also**

→ **77** Equalize the Sound

→ **78** Save Equalizer Settings

If your iTunes Library contains a variety of different audio files, applying one Equalizer setting for all of your files might not be appropriate. You might want to apply different settings to individual files. For example, you probably want different settings for your rock music and your classical music.

You can select from any of the default presets that come with iTunes, or you can apply any custom presets you have created. See **78** **Save Equalizer Settings** for more information on creating a custom preset.

**1 Select Playlist**

In the iTunes **Source** list, select the playlist containing the song to which you want to assign a preset. iTunes displays the songs on the song list for the selected playlist.

**2 Display the View Options Dialog Box**

Choose **Edit**, **View Options** to display the **View Options** dialog box.

**3 Enable Equalizer Option**

The View Options dialog box lists all the column names you can display for the songs in your song list. Enable the check box next to the **Equalizer** option to make the **Equalizer** column display in the song list for the selected playlist. Then click the **OK** button to close the **View Options** dialog box and update the columns for the selected playlist.

**TIP**

You can reorder the columns in the song list to make it easier to see the **Equalizer** column by dragging the column titles. See **69** **Customize View of Song List** for more information on reorganizing columns.

**4 Locate Song**

In the song list, locate the song you want to customize by assigning it an Equalizer preset. To assign the same preset to multiple songs, hold down the ⌘ key and click the desired songs in the song list. Choose **File**, **Get Info** and select the preset from the **Equalizer Preset** drop-down list.

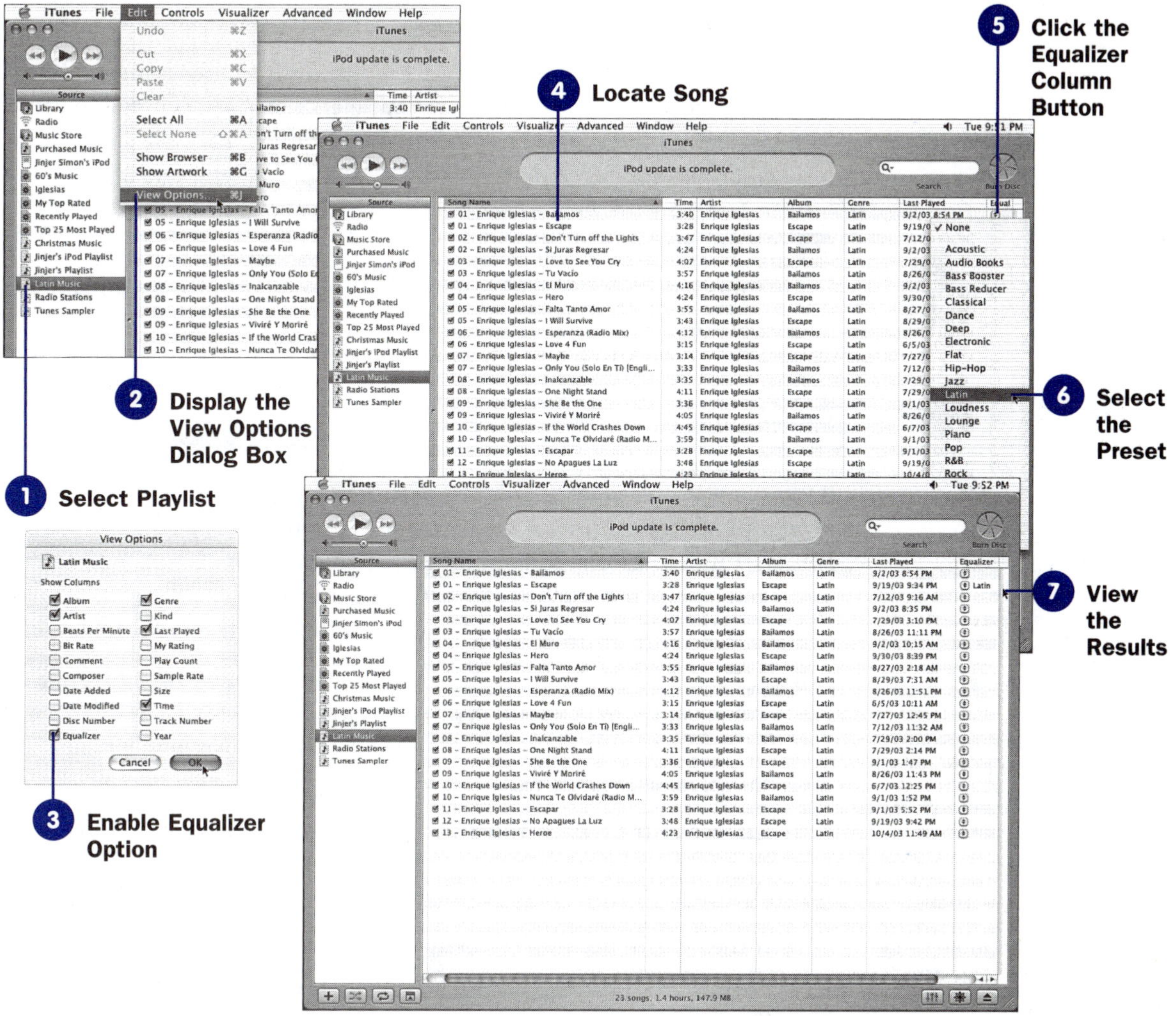

## Apply an Equalizer Preset to an Individual Song

① Select Playlist
② Display the View Options Dialog Box
③ Enable Equalizer Option
④ Locate Song
⑤ Click the Equalizer Column Button
⑥ Select the Preset
⑦ View the Results

### ⑤ Click the Equalizer Column Button

Click the button in the **Equalizer** column for the desired song to display a list of available presets. The preset list is identical to the one you can view from the Equalizer window; but, whereas selecting a preset from the Equalizer window affects all the audio files you play in iTunes, selecting a preset from the **Equalizer** column affects only the selected song.

**TIP**

When you transfer songs to your iPod, iTunes transfers the selected presets with the songs.

CHAPTER 9: Listening to Sound Files          229

# 80 Create Fades Between Audio Files

## 6 Select the Preset

Click the desired preset in the list to assign it to the corresponding song when it plays. The preset you select here affects how the song plays only in iTunes. The preset does not affect how the song plays when the song is exported to a CD.

**TIP**

To remove a preset from an individual song, repeat steps 4 through 6 and select **None** from the preset list.

## 7 View the Results

iTunes displays the name of the selected preset in the **Equalizer** column.

# 80 Create Fades Between Audio Files

**Before You Begin**

✓ **57** About Playlists

**See Also**

→ **58** Customize a Playlist

→ **59** Create a Smart Playlist

→ **74** Randomize Songs Being Played Back

→ **81** Use Visual Effects with Audio Files

**KEY TERM**

*Crossfade*—The process of fading out one song as another song fades in, eliminating breaks in the audio caused by one song stopping and another starting.

If you want to eliminate the gaps of silence between songs when listening to your playlist, you can use the **Crossfade** option. When you select this option, iTunes fades one song in as the previous song fades out. For example, if you specify a *crossfade* of six seconds, six seconds before a song ends iTunes starts to fade that song out and begins to fade the next song in.

iTunes allows you to specify a crossfade time between 0 and 12 seconds. You set the time frame on the **Preferences** dialog box.

## 1 Display Preferences Dialog Box

Choose **iTunes**, **Preferences** to display the **Preferences** dialog box.

## 2 Display Effects Options

If they are not already displayed, click the **Effects** icon at the top of the dialog box to display the options for adjusting the sound effects in iTunes.

## 3 Enable Crossfade Playback Option

Enable the check box next to the **Crossfade playback** option to turn the option on.

## 4 Set Length of Crossfade

Drag the **Crossfade playback** slider to set the length of time for the crossfade. The average time for a crossfade is 6 seconds, but you can create a crossfade between 0 and 12 seconds. This same amount of time will be used to create crossfades for all music in your Library.

230     PART II:   iTunes

# Create Fades Between Audio Files  80

**① Display Preferences Dialog Box**

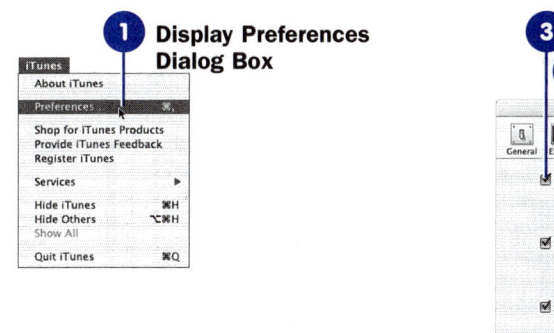

**③ Enable Crossfade Playback Option**

**② Display Effects Options**

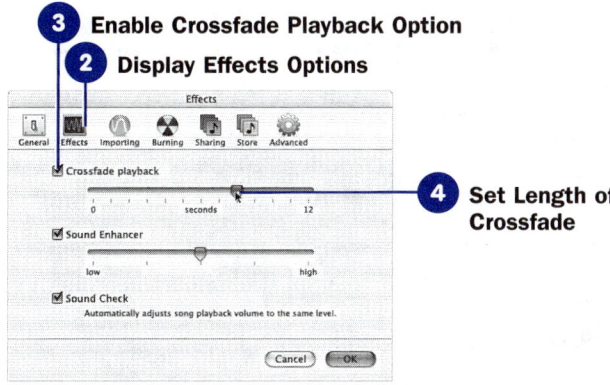

**④ Set Length of Crossfade**

**⑤ Listen to Audio**

Click the **OK** button to close the **Preferences** dialog box and save the crossfade settings.

**⑤ Listen to Audio**

Select a playlist from the **Source** list and click the **Play** button to listen to the playlist with the specified crossfade settings.

 **TIP**

Select the **Sound Enhancer** option to add depth to your music. Drag the slider to the right to create brighter, higher sounds. Drag the slider to the left to create deeper, richer sounds.

**CHAPTER 9:** Listening to Sound Files    231

## 81 Use Visual Effects with Audio Files

**Before You Begin**

✔ **57** About Playlists

**See Also**

→ **58** Customize a Playlist

→ **59** Create a Smart Playlist

→ **71** Listen to Internet Radio

You can liven up your listening experience in iTunes by adding visual effects to the screen. When you turn on visual effects, iTunes displays random effects on the screen instead of the song list. The visual effects "pulse" with the rise and fall of the frequencies in the audio file.

You can have the visual effects display within the iTunes window, or you can fill the entire screen with the visual effects. You can also customize the options used to create the visual effects from the **Visualizer Options** dialog box. On this dialog box, you can select any of the options described in the following table:

| Option | Description |
| --- | --- |
| **Display frame rate** | Displays the frame rate of the visual effects displayed on the screen. The frame rate displays in the upper-left corner of the window. |
| **Cap frame rate at 30 fps** | Maintains the speed of the visual effects at 30 frames per second or slower. |
| **Always display song info** | Constantly displays the current song information in the lower-left corner of the window. If this option is not selected, the information displays for only the first 10 seconds when the song starts playing. |
| **Use OpenGL** | Uses OpenGL to create the visual effects. OpenGL is a graphics service used by Mac OS X to improve the look of graphic images and 3D rendering. |
| **Faster but rougher display** | Speeds up the visual effects, but the effects are not as smooth. If the **Cap frame rate at 30 fps** option is selected, the visual effects will not exceed 30 frames per second, even if you enable the **Faster but rougher display** option. |

### 1 Select Playlist

In the **Source** list, select the playlist to which you want to listen and to which you want to apply visual effects. Click the **Play** button to listen to the songs in the selected playlist.

# Use Visual Effects with Audio Files 81

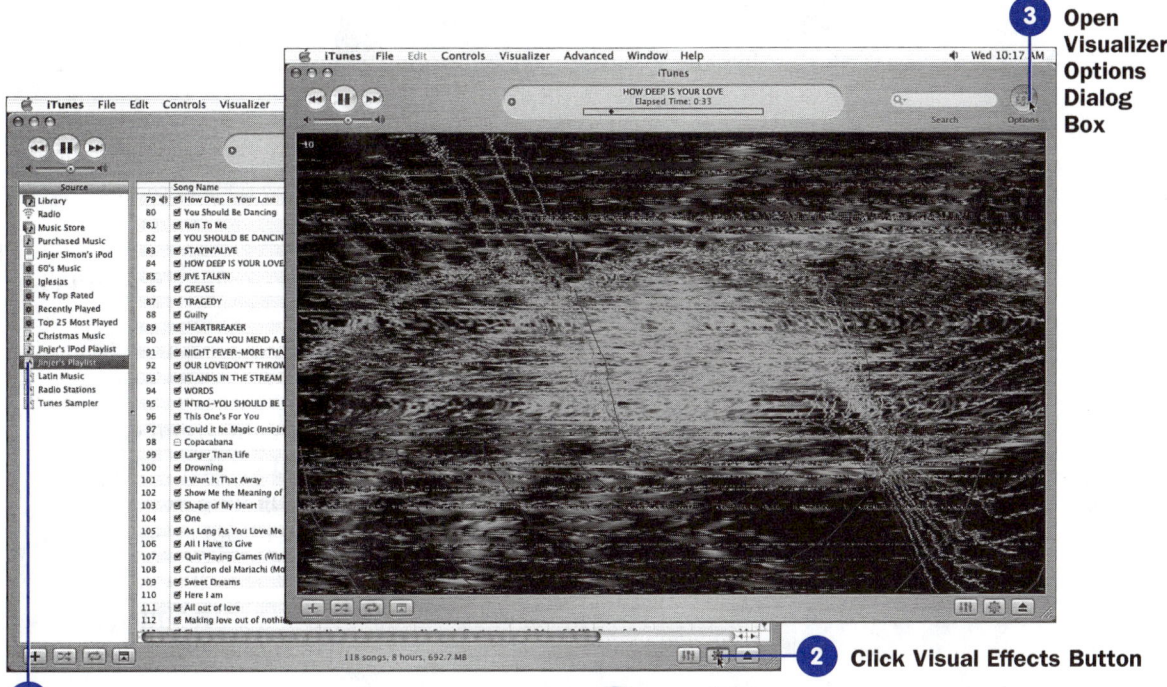

**3** Open Visualizer Options Dialog Box

**2** Click Visual Effects Button

**1** Select Playlist

**5** Change the Visual Effects Display Size

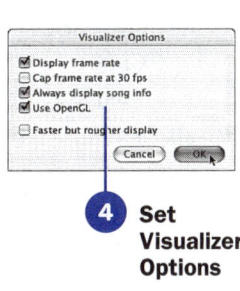

**4** Set Visualizer Options

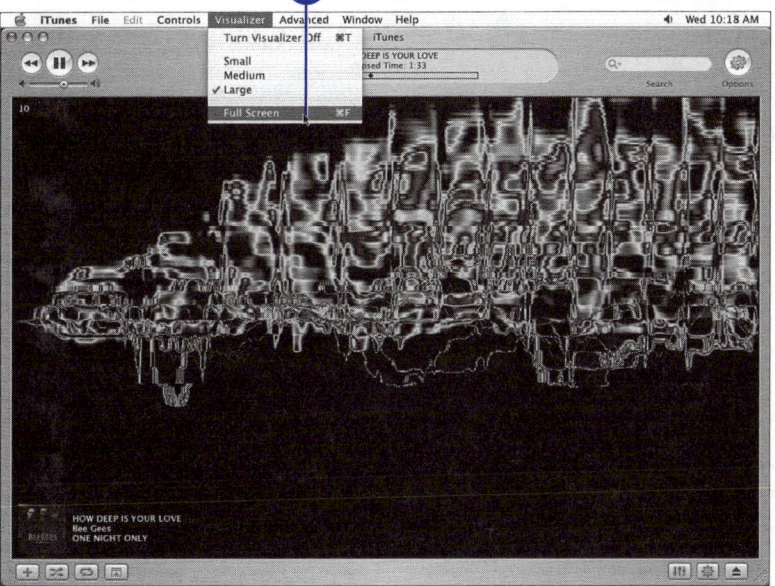

**CHAPTER 9: Listening to Sound Files** 233

## 82 Shuffle Songs by Album

 **TIP**
You can also turn on visual effects by choosing **Visualizer, Turn Visualizer On** from the menu bar.

**② Click Visual Effects Button**

Click the **Visual Effects** button in the bottom-right corner of the iTunes window to display visual effects for the selected audio. iTunes immediately replaces the **Source** list and song list with the Visualizer screen—a pulsing, colorful graphics display.

**③ Open Visualizer Options Dialog Box**

Click the **Options** button in the upper-right corner of the Visualizer screen to display the **Visualizer Options** dialog box.

**④ Set Visualizer Options**

Select the options you want to use to display the visual effects as you listen to music. For example, you might want to enable the **Always display song info** option to have the song name, artist, and album information display in the bottom-right corner of the window.

When you have made your selections, click the **OK** button to close the **Visualizer Options** dialog box and update the Visualizer screen.

 **TIP**
Click the **Visual Effects** button to switch back to the song list view of your Library or selected playlist. You can also turn off the Visualizer by choosing **Visualizer, Turn Visualizer Off**. If the Visualizer is in Full Screen mode, press the **Esc** key to return to the song list view.

**⑤ Change the Visual Effects Display Size**

By default, iTunes displays the visual effects in the entire window. You can change the size of the visual effects display: Choose **Visualizer** from the menu bar and then select the desired size for the graphic display. You can select **Small**, **Medium**, **Large**, or **Full Screen**.

If you select the **Large** option, the visual effects fill the iTunes window. With the **Medium** and **Small** options, the effects fill only a portion of the window.

## 82 Shuffle Songs by Album

**Before You Begin**

✔  About Playlists

By default, when you shuffle the songs in your playlist, iTunes plays each song in the playlist in random order. It doesn't matter whether the songs are from the same album or different albums. If your playlist contains songs from multiple albums, you might want to hear all the songs from one album before jumping to the next album. To do this, you want

## Shuffle Songs by Album  82

iTunes to shuffle the songs based on the albums. When you turn the **Shuffle by Album** option on, it affects all audio that you listen to in iTunes.

### 1 Select Playlist

In the **Source** list, select the desired playlist. Although the **Shuffle by Album** option affects *all* playlists in the Library, you typically first select the particular playlist you want to shuffle.

### 2 Click Shuffle Button

Click the **Shuffle** button in the bottom-left corner of the iTunes window. The lines on the button display in blue to indicate that the shuffle option is selected.

### 3 Display Preferences Dialog Box

Choose **iTunes**, **Preferences** to display the **Preferences** dialog box.

### 4 Display Advanced Options

If they are not already displayed, click the **Advanced** icon at the top of the **Preferences** dialog box to display the **Advanced** options. The name of the **Preferences** dialog box changes to reflect the selected option. For example, when the **Advanced** option is selected, the dialog box name changes to **Advanced**, and the corresponding options display on the dialog box.

### 5 Enable Shuffle by Album Option

Enable the **Album** radio button next to the **Shuffle by** field to have iTunes shuffle the music in the selected playlist by album name when the **Shuffle** option is selected.

Click **OK** to save the changes and close the **Preferences** dialog box.

### 6 Listen to Playlist

Click the **Play** button to listen to the playlist using the new shuffle settings.

### See Also

→ 58 Customize a Playlist
→ 59 Create a Smart Playlist
→ 69 Customize View of Song List
→ 74 Randomize Songs Being Played Back

### TIP

You can also enable the shuffle option by choosing **Controls, Shuffle** from the menu bar. A check mark next to the **Shuffle** option on the **Controls** menu indicates that the option is selected.

### TIP

Unless you have turned on the Shuffle option by clicking the **Shuffle** button or by choosing **Controls, Shuffle**, iTunes will not shuffle songs by album, even if you have enabled the **Shuffle by Album** option in the **Preferences** dialog box.

**CHAPTER 9:** Listening to Sound Files

**Shuffle Songs by Album**

① Select Playlist

③ Display Preferences Dialog Box

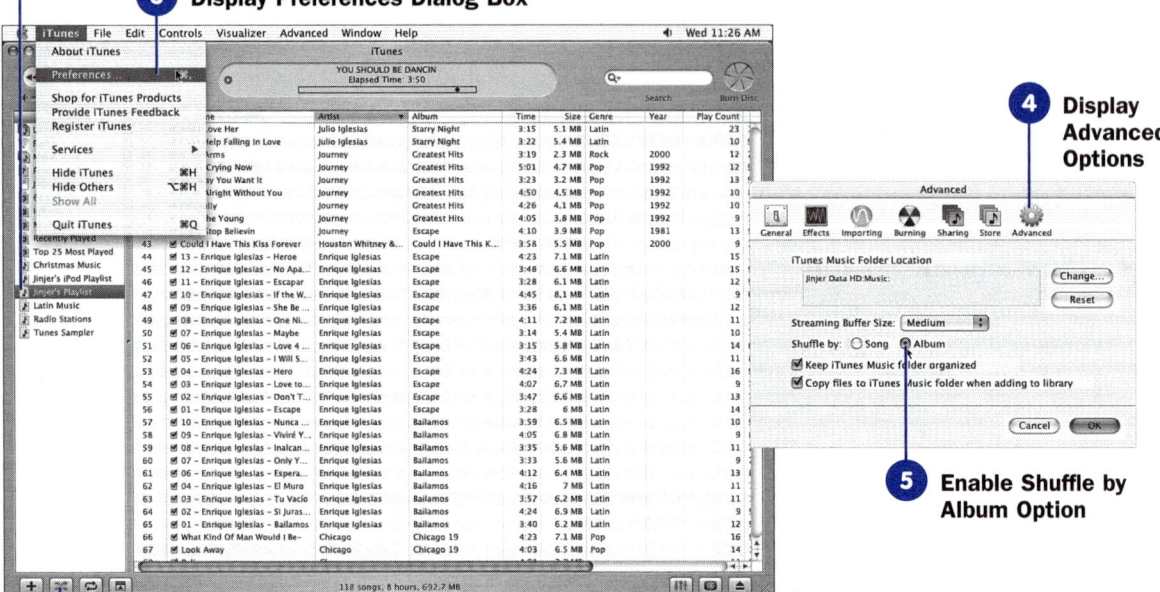

④ Display Advanced Options

② Click Shuffle Button

⑥ Listen to Playlist

⑤ Enable Shuffle by Album Option

PART II: iTunes

# 10

# Creating Music CDs

**IN THIS CHAPTER:**

- **83** About CD Burners
- **84** Adjust CD Burning Speed
- **85** Set Pauses Between Audio Files on CD
- **86** Burn an Audio CD
- **87** Burn an MP3 CD
- **88** Burn a CD with Segmented Audio Files
- **89** Create a Backup of Your Music Library

## 83 About CD Burners

iTunes provides the capability to create a CD from any of your playlists. You can create three different types of CDs in iTunes: an audio CD, an MP3 CD, or a data CD. Make sure that you select the correct type of CD before clicking the **Burn Disc** button.

When you create an audio CD, you create a CD you can play in nearly all CD players. When you create the CD, iTunes makes sure that the audio placed on the CD matches the format used by CD players.

**NOTE**
Because many external CD players cannot read MP3 files, make sure that your CD player can read MP3 CDs before you burn the disc. Because of the popularity of MP3 files, it's likely that newer CD players can read MP3 discs.

If your CD player can read MP3 files, you can create an MP3 CD. When you choose this format, iTunes can compress the audio files, allowing the placement of more audio files on the CD.

If you want to make a backup of a music Library, you can create a data CD. When you use this option, you create a CD that contains the audio files from your Library in the same format as they appear in the Library. If you have a DVD burner on your computer, you can create your backup on a DVD so that you can store additional audio files on the same disk.

## 83 About CD Burners

**See Also**

→ **84** Adjust CD Burning Speed
→ **85** Set Pauses Between Audio Files on CD
→ **86** Burn an Audio CD
→ **87** Burn an MP3 CD
→ **88** Burn a CD with Segmented Audio Files
→ **89** Create a Backup of your Music Library

To *burn* a CD from iTunes, you must have a CD burner connected to your computer. All new Apple computers are sold with either a *CD-RW drive* or a *SuperDrive* capable of burning CDs from iTunes or any other Mac OS X application. From iTunes, you can burn audio files onto any of the disc formats supported by the available drive. For example, if your computer has a CD-RW drive, you can burn audio CDs on *CD-R* and *CD-RW* discs. With a SuperDrive, you can burn audio files on *DVD-R* and *DVD-RW* discs. Even if you have a SuperDrive in your computer, you can burn DVDs from iTunes only if you are running Mac OS X version 2.4 or later. Unlike a CD, which can hold only about 650 megabytes of data, a DVD can hold 4.7 gigabytes. See **135** *About DVDs* for more information on working with DVDs on your computer.

Typically, you will create audio CDs from iTunes so that you can listen to your music in other locations, such as the car or your home stereo. When burning CDs from iTunes, keep two things in mind. First off, you have to know what format the CD player supports. If the CD player supports MP3 files, you can create a CD containing more audio files by burning an MP3 CD. A typical audio CD can hold about 20 songs, but an MP3 CD can hold as many as 150 songs, depending on the size of each MP3 file.

The other thing you need to be aware of is whether your CD player can read a CD-RW disc. Although these discs are great because you can re-burn the CD if you want to change its contents, they are not supported by many older audio CD players. Most newer audio CD players can read CD-RW discs, so check your player. Typically, the CD players are marked on the front to indicate what formats they can read. If you use a CD-RW disc, you must delete the entire contents before you can re-burn audio on the disc in iTunes.

Another thing to keep in mind is the speed of your burner. All CD and DVD burners have a maximum speed at which they can burn a disc. For example, the SuperDrive that currently ships with Apple computers can burn a CD-R disc at 16× speed, a CD-RW disc at 10× speed, and a DVD-R disc at 4× speed. You should keep these speeds in mind when buying discs to burn. You don't have to purchase CD-Rs or DVD-Rs that are capable of a faster speed than your burner. For example, even if you purchase 32× speed CD-R discs, a SuperDrive can burn the discs at only 16× speed.

- **What if my computer does not have a CD burner?** If you have an older computer, you might not have a CD burner. If so, you can purchase one for your computer. Depending on your computer, you might be able to have the drive installed in your Mac, or you can purchase an external drive. You can purchase an external CD burner that connects to the FireWire port on your computer.

- **Why don't I get 150 songs on my MP3 CDs?** The actual number of songs you can store on a CD is based on several factors, but the key factor is the actual size of each audio file. The size of each MP3 file is based on the settings you used to create the MP3 files when you added them to your computer. For example, if you created MP3 files with a bit rate of 128KBps, the files will be smaller than those created with a bit rate of 190KBps. See **54 Set Import Format for Audio Files** for more information on specifying how MP3 files are created when you import them into iTunes.

## KEY TERMS

*Burn*—A term used to identify the process of copying computer files to a CD or DVD disc. The hardware used to create CDs is typically called a CD burner, while a DVD burner refers to the hardware capable of burning DVDs.

*CD-RW drive*—A CD drive capable of both reading and burning CDs. These drives can burn both CD-R and CD-RW discs.

*SuperDrive*—The DVD burner drive that comes in many of the new Apple computers. This drive is capable of reading and burning both CDs and DVDs.

*CD-R*—A CD that you can use to copy files from your computer. You can only copy files to a CD-R disc once, even if you do not fill the disc.

*CD-RW*—A CD that is rewritable. With this type of disc, you can erase the disc and reuse it as many times as you want.

*DVD-R*—A DVD that you can copy files to once. You cannot erase or add more files after the initial burn.

*DVD-RW*—A DVD that is rewritable. You can erase the disc or add additional files at any time, if the disc is not full.

# 84 Adjust CD Burning Speed

## WEB RESOURCE

Visit the Apple Web site to learn more about the CD drives you can purchase for your computer.

**http://www.apple.com**

- **Why can't I add more audio files to the CD-RW disc?** When you use CD-RW discs to create audio or MP3 CDs, iTunes treats them the same as CD-R discs. If the CD-RW disc is not empty (brand new), iTunes will not allow you to burn additional audio to the disc, even if there is still available space. You must clear all the files off the CD-RW disc, and then you can burn the contents of a new playlist onto the disc.

- **How do I get the files off my CD-RW disc?** You cannot delete files from a CD-RW from within iTunes or even from Finder. Although a CD-RW is rewritable, iTunes sees it as a read-only disc if it contains audio. To erase the contents of a CD-RW disc, use the **Disk Utility** program that comes with Mac OS X. You can find the program from Finder by clicking the **Applications** folder and then opening the **Utilities** subfolder.

  When running the **Disk Utility** program, make sure that you select your CD-RW disc as the disk you want to erase.

# 84 Adjust CD Burning Speed

**Before You Begin**

✔ **83** About CD Burners

**See Also**

→ **86** Burn an Audio CD
→ **87** Burn an MP3 CD
→ **88** Burn a CD with Segmented Audio Files
→ **89** Create a Backup of your Music Library

When you burn a playlist to a CD, iTunes automatically examines the blank CD and determines the best speed for burning based on the rating of the CD. There might be times when you feel you need to manually specify the CD burning speed. For example, if you are using CDs that are rated at a much slower speed than the maximum speed of your CD burner, you might want to set the burning speed to match the CDs to ensure that there are no errors during the burning process.

You change the speed the burner uses to burn the CD on the **Preferences** dialog box. You can select any speed up to the maximum speed of the burner.

After you have changed the speed for burning CDs, iTunes continues to use that speed until you change it again. In most cases, you should be able to select the **Maximum Possible** speed option, and iTunes will adjust the speed based on the disc in the drive.

# Adjust CD Burning Speed  84

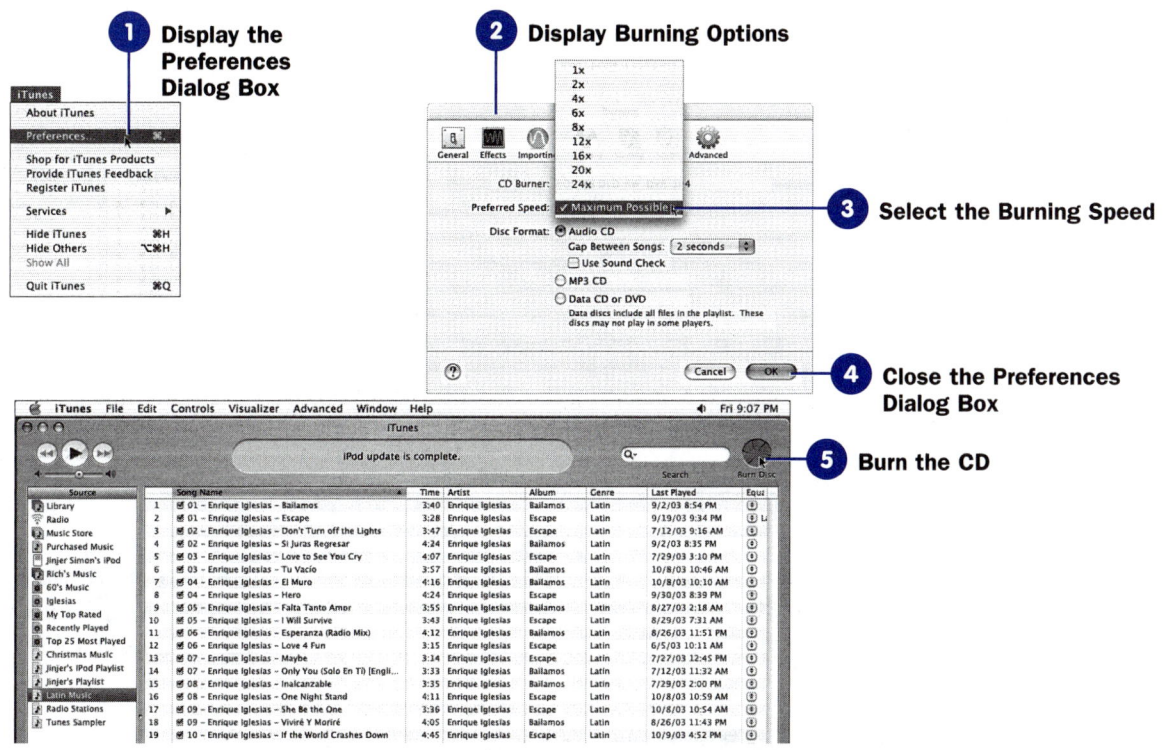

### ① Display the Preferences Dialog Box

Choose **iTunes, Preferences** to display the **Preferences** dialog box.

### ② Display Burning Options

The name of the selected option on the **Preferences** dialog box displays as the title of the dialog box. You use the **Preferences** dialog box to specify all the settings in iTunes. The dialog box always opens to display the last options you modified.

If the **Burning** page of the **Preferences** dialog box is not displayed, click the **Burning** icon to display the CD burning options.

### ③ Select the Burning Speed

From the **Preferred Speed** pop-up list, select the desired burning speed for the CDs you burn using iTunes.

**CHAPTER 10:** Creating Music CDs            241

## 85  Set Pauses Between Audio Files on CD

If you are not having any problems burning CDs, select the **Maximum Possible** option. When you select this option, iTunes adjusts the burn speed based on the maximum speed rating of the CD-R or CD-RW in the drive.

If you want to ensure that the CD-R will not have problems burning, set the speed to match the speed rating of the CD-R or CD-RW you are burning. The speed rating of the disc is generally given on the disc's jewel box cover sheet.

### 4  Close the Preferences Dialog Box

Click the **OK** button to close the **Preferences** dialog box and save the specified settings.

### 5  Burn the CD

Click the **Burn Disc** button to burn the contents of the selected playlist to a CD or DVD in your burner. See **86 Burn an Audio CD** for more information on creating an audio CD. See **87 Burn an MP3 CD** for more information on burning an MP3 music CD.

## 85  Set Pauses Between Audio Files on CD

**Before You Begin**

✓ **83** About CD Burners

**See Also**

→ **86** Burn an Audio CD
→ **87** Burn an MP3 CD
→ **88** Burn a CD with Segmented Audio Files
→ **89** Create a Backup of your Music Library

When burning an audio CD, you can customize the length of time iTunes places between each audio file on the CD. By default, iTunes places a two-second gap between each audio file on the disc, but you can increase that gap to up to five seconds in length. You can also decrease the gap to one second or remove the gap altogether. For example, some songs are designed to flow into the next song with no gap; if that is the case with the songs you are burning, you can remove the gap before burning the CD by selecting the **none** option. The pause length you specify affects *all* audio placed on the audio CD. You cannot specify different pause lengths between audio files.

You specify the size of the gap between audio files on the **Preferences** dialog box. You can specify the size of the gap between songs only when you are creating an audio CD. If you burn an MP3 CD, you cannot alter the gap length between the MP3 files on the CD.

PART II:   iTunes

### Set Pauses Between Audio Files on CD

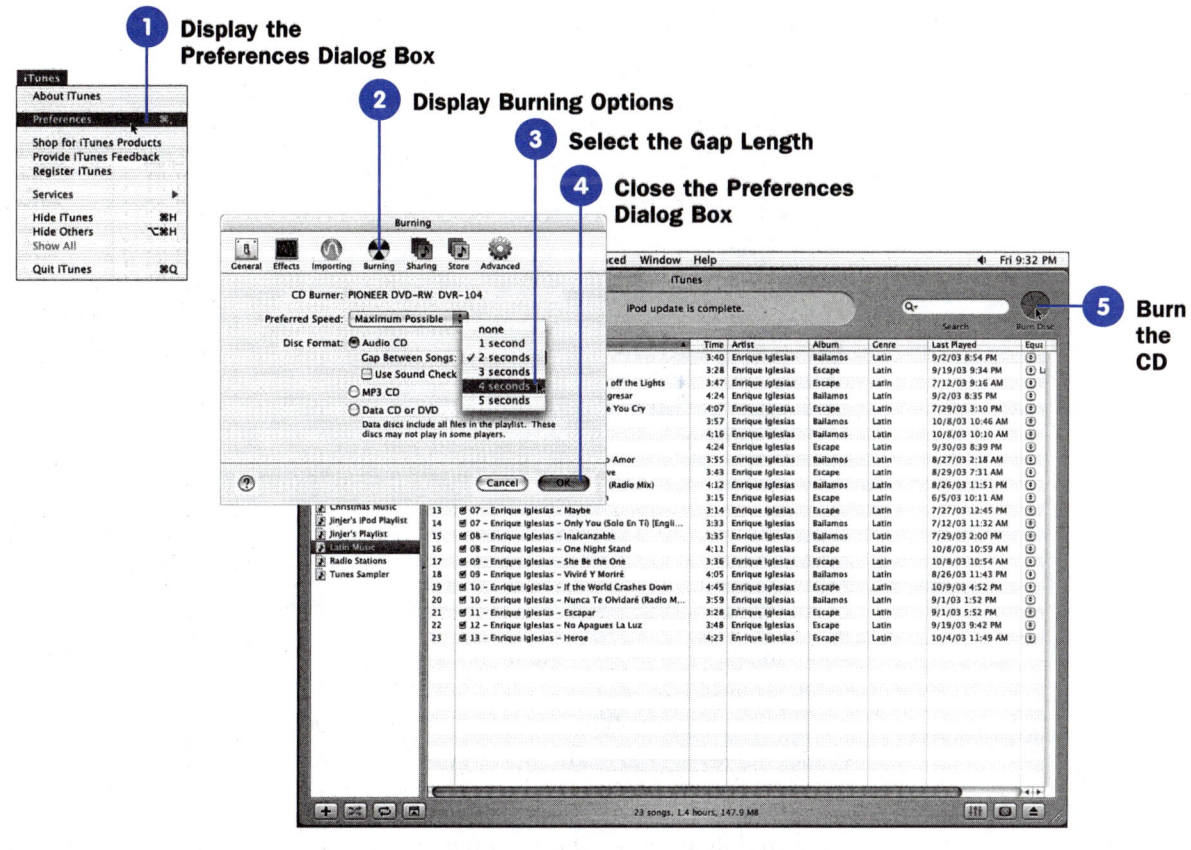

### ① Display the Preferences Dialog Box

Choose **iTunes**, **Preferences** to display the **Preferences** dialog box.

### ② Display Burning Options

The name of the selected option on the **Preferences** dialog box displays as the title of the dialog box. You use the **Preferences** dialog box to specify all the settings in iTunes. The dialog box always opens to display the last options you modified.

If the **Burning** page of the **Preferences** dialog box is not displayed, click the **Burning** icon to display the CD burning options.

**CHAPTER 10:** Creating Music CDs

## 86  Burn an Audio CD

### ③ Select the Gap Length

Click the arrow button next to the **Gap Between Songs** field to display a list of available gap lengths. Select a gap length between 1 and 5 seconds, or select the **none** option to eliminate all gaps.

### ④ Close the Preferences Dialog Box

Click the **OK** button to close the **Preferences** dialog box and save the specified settings.

### ⑤ Burn the CD

Click the **Burn Disc** button to burn the contents of the selected playlist to the CD or DVD in your burner. See **86 Burn an Audio CD** for more information on creating an audio CD.

## 86  Burn an Audio CD

**Before You Begin**
- ✔ **57** About Playlists
- ✔ **83** About CD Burners

**See Also**
- → **84** Adjust CD Burning Speed
- → **85** Set Pauses Between Audio Files on CD
- → **87** Burn an MP3 CD

You can use iTunes to create audio CDs that you can play in any of your external audio CD players, such as CD players that are part of a home stereo or an automobile sound system. When you create an audio CD, iTunes copies all the audio files to the CD to create an audio CD you can play in external CD players.

You can only burn a CD from a playlist. You should create a separate playlist that contains the audio files you want to place on the CD. Make sure that the length of the playlist does not exceed the maximum capacity of the CD. CDs come in two sizes: 650MB CDs allow you to create an audio CD that holds 74 minutes of audio, and 700MB CDs allow you to create an audio CD that holds 80 minutes of audio. You can determine the length of the selected playlist by looking at the bottom of the iTunes window. If the playlist exceeds the capacity of the disc, iTunes places audio files on the CD until the disc is full, in the order the files are listed on the playlist. See **58 Customize a Playlist** for more information on creating a playlist.

### ① Display the Preferences Dialog Box

Choose **iTunes**, **Preferences** to display the **Preferences** dialog box.

# Burn an Audio CD    86

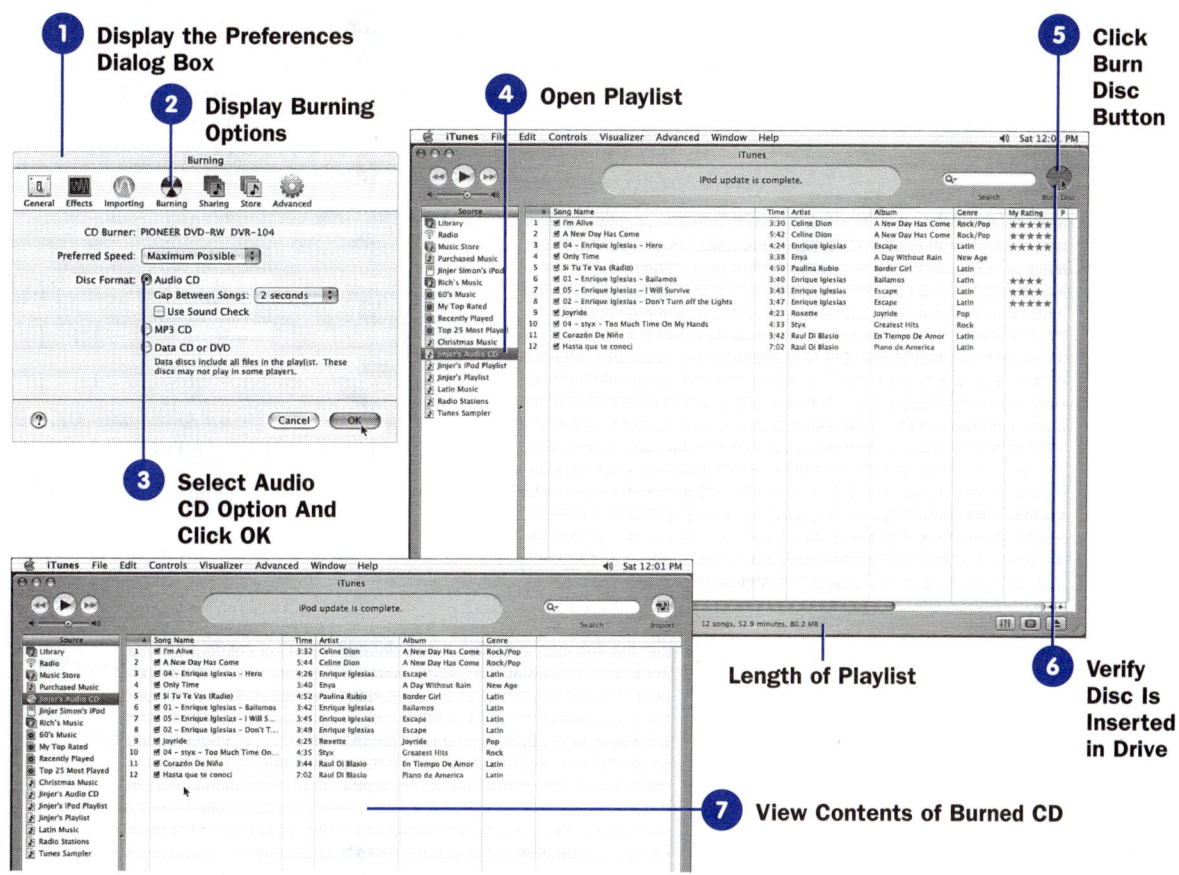

## ② Display Burning Options

The name of the selected option on the **Preferences** dialog box displays as the title of the dialog box. You use the **Preferences** dialog box to specify all the settings in iTunes. The dialog box always opens to display the last options you modified.

If the **Burning** page of the **Preferences** dialog box is not displayed, click the **Burning** icon to display the CD burning options.

## ③ Select Audio CD Option and Click OK

Click the **Audio CD** option to record an audio CD that you can play in any audio CD player. You can adjust the gap between

CHAPTER 10:  Creating Music CDs    245

  **Burn an Audio CD**

songs on an audio CD by selecting a different value from the **Gap Between Songs** drop-down list. See **85 Set Pauses Between Audio Files on CD** for more information on adjusting the gap.

Click the **OK** button to save the CD burning settings and close the **Preferences** dialog box.

### TIP
If you have the **Use Sound Check** option selected on the **Effects** page of the iTunes **Preferences** dialog box, you can apply that same effect setting to the audio files you burn to the CD by enabling the **Use Sound Check** option on the **Burning** page of the **Preferences** dialog box. When this option is enabled, iTunes adjusts the volume to the same level for all audio files you burn to the disc.

### NOTE
Most audio CDs can hold a maximum of 80 minutes of audio, although some CDs can hold only 74 minutes. The maximum capacity is normally printed on the front of the CD.

### NOTE
Review the contents of the CD to make sure that all the desired audio files were copied to the disc. You can even listen to the audio from the CD by clicking a track to select it and then clicking the **Play** button.

 **Open Playlist**

In the **Source** list in the iTunes window, click the playlist you want to burn to the CD. iTunes can only burn CDs from a playlist; you cannot burn a CD directly from the Library.

Make sure that the length of the playlist does not exceed the maximum capacity of the CD media to which you are burning. If it does, you can still burn the CD, but iTunes places on the CD only the audio files that fit.

**5 Click Burn Disc Button**

With the desired playlist selected, click the **Burn Disc** button in the upper-right corner of the iTunes window. iTunes checks to make sure that the CD burner contains a blank disc. If the disc is not blank, or if the drive is empty, a message box displays on the screen.

 **Verify Disc Is Inserted in Drive**

Make sure that you have a disc inserted in the burner and click the **Burn Disc** button again. iTunes creates the CD by copying each of the songs in the playlist to the CD.

**7 View Contents of Burned CD**

When the CD is created, iTunes adds the CD to the **Source** list and displays the contents of the CD you just burned in the song list. The name of the CD is the name of the playlist used to create the CD.

## 87 Burn an MP3 CD

iTunes allows you to create MP3 CDs you can play in any audio CD player that can read MP3 files. MP3 has become the biggest buzzword when dealing with audio files, specifically music. The format is popular because it compresses the audio files, allowing you to store more audio in the same amount of space. For example, on a 650MB CD, you can store 74 minutes of audio, which equates to about 20 songs, depending on the length of each song. With an MP3 CD, you can store over 12 hours of audio files or about 150 songs. This capability to store substantially more audio makes the MP3 format appealing to many users.

To burn an MP3 CD, you must change the **Disc Format** option on the **Preferences** dialog box. After you change this format option, all CDs you burn will result in MP3 audio until you change the **Disc Format** option again.

To burn a CD from iTunes, you must first create a playlist that contains all the audio files you want to place on the CD. See **58 Customize a Playlist** for more information on creating a playlist. If your iTunes Library contains MP3 files, you can use the size of the playlist to determine the number of songs you can burn on the CD. You cannot place more than 650MB or 700MB of audio on a CD, depending on the maximum capacity of the CD. If you have audio files in other formats, you will have to use the time measurement to determine the number of audio files that will fit. When you click the **Burn Disc** button, iTunes compares the length of the playlist with the available disc space and notifies you if the selected songs will not fit on the disc.

### 1 Display the Preferences Dialog Box

Choose **iTunes, Preferences** to display the **Preferences** dialog box.

### 2 Display Burning Options

The name of the selected option on the **Preferences** dialog box displays as the title of the dialog box. You use the **Preferences** dialog box to specify all the settings in iTunes. The dialog box always opens to display the last options you modified.

If the **Burning** page of the **Preferences** dialog box is not displayed, click the **Burning** icon to display the CD burning options.

### Before You Begin

✔ **83** About CD Burners

### See Also

→ **84** Adjust CD Burning Speed

→ **85** Set Pauses Between Audio Files on CD

→ **86** Burn an Audio CD

→ **88** Burn a CD with Segmented Audio Files

**NOTE**

You can put only MP3 files on an MP3 CD. You cannot put files of other formats on MP3 CDs. Before you start burning MP3 CDs, make sure that your audio CD player can read MP3 files.

## 87  Burn an MP3 CD

### ③ Select MP3 CD Option and Click OK

Enable the **MP3 CD** check box to record an MP3 CD that you can play in any audio CD player capable of reading MP3 files.

Click the **OK** button to save the CD burning settings and close the **Preferences** dialog box.

### ④ Open Playlist

In the **Source** list in the iTunes window, click the playlist you want to burn to the CD. iTunes can only burn CDs from a playlist; you cannot burn a CD directly from the Library.

Make sure that the length of the playlist does not exceed the capacity of the CD media to which you are burning. If it does, you can still burn the CD, but iTunes places on the CD only the MP3 files that fit.

### ⑤ Click Burn Disc Button

Click the **Burn Disc** button in the upper-right corner of the iTunes window. iTunes checks to make sure that the CD burner contains a blank disc. If the disc is not blank, or if the drive is empty, a message box displays on the screen.

### ⑥ Verify Disc Is Inserted in Drive

Make sure that you have a disc inserted in the burner and click the **Burn Disc** button again. iTunes creates the CD by copying each of the songs in the playlist to the CD.

### ⑦ View Contents of Burned CD

When the CD is created, iTunes adds the MP3 CD to the **Source** list and displays the contents of the CD you just burned in the song list. The name of the CD is the name of the playlist used to create the CD.

**NOTE**

You can only burn an MP3 CD in iTunes from a playlist. If you are viewing the Library, the **Burn Disc** button is not available.

**NOTE**

Review the contents of the CD to make sure that all the desired audio files were burned to the CD. You can even listen to the MP3 files from the CD by clicking an MP3 file in the song list to select it and then clicking the **Play** button.

Burn an MP3 CD **87**

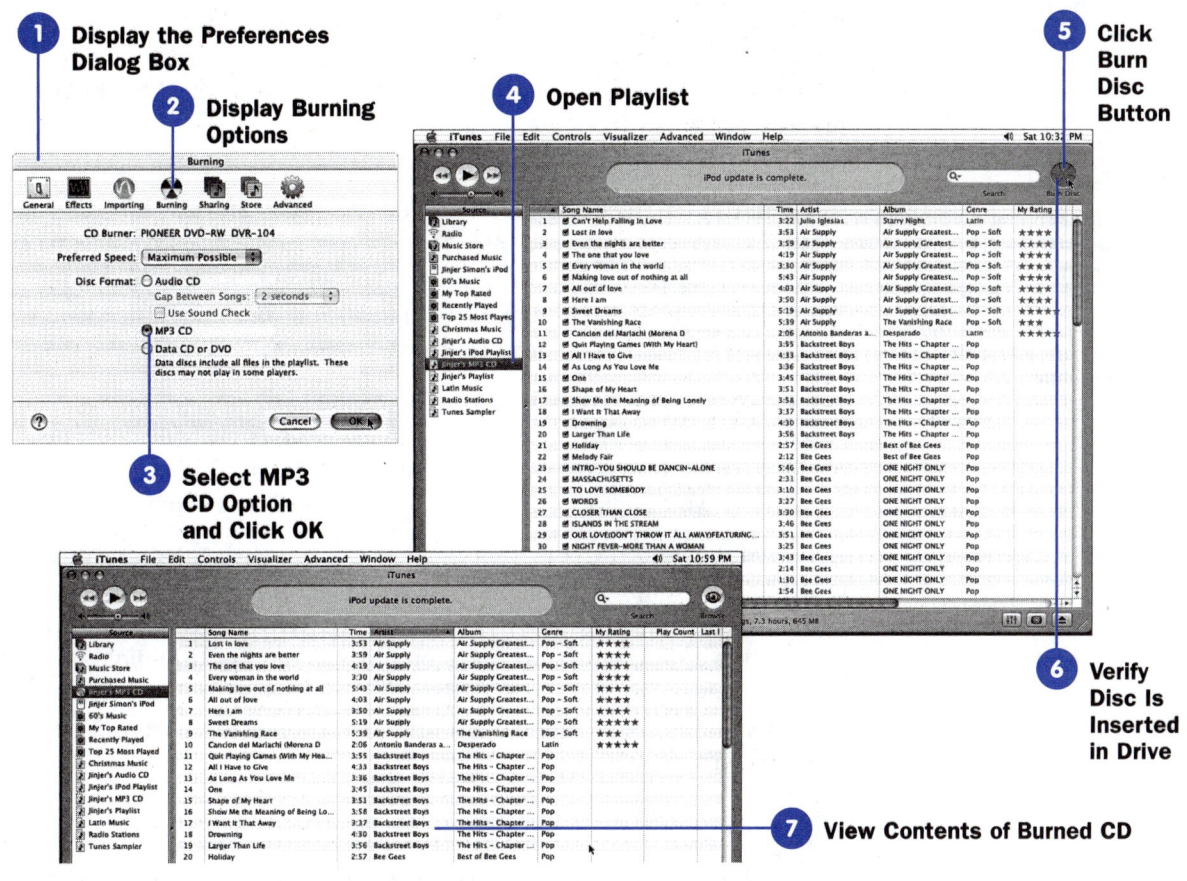

## **88** Burn a CD with Segmented Audio Files

If you have a large audio file, such as an audio book you downloaded from Audible.com, you probably won't be able to fit the entire file on one audio CD. If the length of the audio file is too long for the capacity of the CD, you must break the audio file into smaller files that will fit on CDs. For example, if you are burning an audio book to a 74-minute CD, you must break the file into 74-minute chunks that can be placed on separate discs.

**Before You Begin**

✔ **83** About CD Burners

**See Also**

→ **85** Set Pauses Between Audio Files on CD

→ **86** Burn an Audio CD

→ **87** Burn an MP3 CD

CHAPTER 10: Creating Music CDs

## 88  Burn a CD with Segmented Audio Files

If you are running iTunes 4.1 or later, iTunes automatically breaks the audio file into separate chunks, but the breaks occur at the point when the CD is filled. You have no control over the location where the breaks are inserted.

**NOTE**

If you are running a version of iTunes before 4.1, you must break a large audio file into smaller chunks because iTunes does not segment the audio file automatically.

To break a file into chunks that can fit on a CD, you specify a start and stop point in the file using the **Get Info** dialog box. The first time you create the CD, you specify a **Start Time** of 0:00 and a **Stop Time** of 1:14 (1 hour and 14 minutes or 74 minutes). The second disc should have a **Start Time** of 1:14 and a **Stop Time** of 2:28. You continue this process to create new CDs until you have copied the entire audio book to the CDs.

You can specify any **Stop Time**, as long as the total length does not exceed 74 minutes. Listen to the audio file and determine the appropriate **Stop Time**. For example, in an audio book file, if a chapter ends at 70 minutes, you might want to specify **1:10** as the **Stop Time**.

If you want, you can create a separate playlist for each CD that will be created. For example, the first playlist could be Audio Book 1, followed by Audio Book 2. Copy the complete audio book file to each playlist and then set the appropriate start and stop times in the **Get Info** dialog box for each copy of the file. If you don't want to hassle with that many playlists, simply create one playlist and then change the start and stop times for each CD you need to burn.

### 1  Select Playlist

In the **Source** list in the iTunes window, select the playlist containing the large audio file you want to segment.

**NOTE**

You can burn audio files from Audible.com only to audio CDs. You cannot place these audio book files on MP3 CDs. Make sure that you are burning audio CDs by selecting the **Audio CD** option on the **Preferences** dialog box. See **86** **Burn an Audio CD** for more information on creating audio CDs.

If the audio file is not in a playlist, you must create a playlist and copy the file to that playlist. See **58** **Customize a Playlist** for more information on creating playlists in iTunes.

### 2  Select the Audio File to Segment

Click to select the audio file you want to segment into smaller chunks that will fit on the CD.

### 3  Open the Get Info Dialog Box

Choose **File, Get Info** to display the **Get Info** dialog box, where you can view and modify information about the selected audio file.

## Burn a CD with Segmented Audio Files

### ④ Display the Options Tab

Click the **Options** tab in the **Get Info** dialog box to display the options for setting the start and stop times for the audio file.

The **Options** tab also displays options for adjusting the volume of the audio file, selecting the **Equalizer Preset**, and setting the rating of the audio file. See **61 Rate Music Tracks** for more information on rating your audio files. See **79 Apply an Equalizer Preset to an Individual Song** for more information on selecting an equalizer preset for an individual audio file.

### ⑤ Specify the Start and Stop Times

Enable the **Start Time** check box and type the start time for the block of the audio file you want to place on the CD. For example, if you want to start at the beginning of the audio file, type **0:00** in the **Start Time** field.

Enable the **Stop Time** check box and type the stop time for the block of the audio file you want to place on the CD. For example, for the first CD, if the **Start Time** is 0:00, you must specify a stop time of around 1:14 for a 74-minute CD.

Click the **OK** button to save the settings and close the **Get Info** dialog box.

### ⑥ Click Burn Disc Button

Click the **Burn Disc** button in the upper-right corner of the iTunes window. iTunes checks to make sure that the CD burner contains a blank disc. If the disc is not blank, or if the drive is empty, a message box displays on the screen.

### ⑦ Verify Disc is Inserted in Drive

Make sure that you have a disc inserted in the burner and click the **Burn Disc** button again. iTunes creates the CD by copying the first part of the audio file to the CD.

### ⑧ View Contents of Burned CD

When the CD is created, iTunes adds the audio CD to the **Source** list and displays the contents of the CD you just burned in the song list. The name of the CD is the name of the playlist used to create the CD.

> **TIP**
>
> Before starting the burning process, you can listen to the audio book file and find the exact spots where you want to segment the audio. You can determine the **Stop Time** locations by viewing the **Elapsed Time** in the time display at the top-center of the iTunes window. The time displays in the format **hh:mm:ss**. For example, 1:45 is 1 minute and 45 seconds.

> **TIP**
>
> Repeat steps 2 through 7 for each segment of the audio file, changing the **Start Time** and **Stop Time** for each disc you burn. Make sure that you number each disc as you burn it so that you don't inadvertently get the discs out of sequence.

**CHAPTER 10: Creating Music CDs**

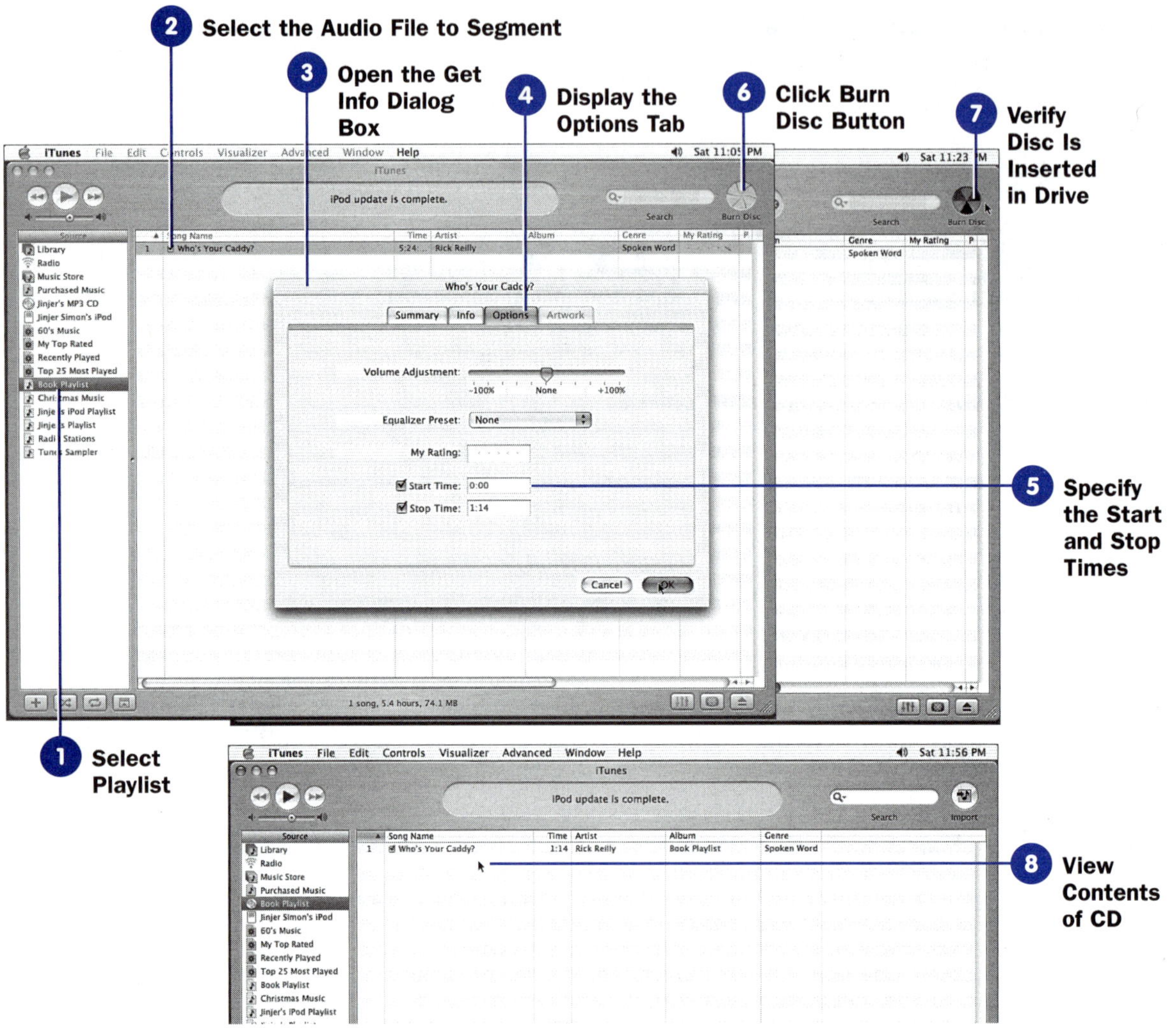

## 88 Burn a CD with Segmented Audio Files

① Select Playlist
② Select the Audio File to Segment
③ Open the Get Info Dialog Box
④ Display the Options Tab
⑤ Specify the Start and Stop Times
⑥ Click Burn Disc Button
⑦ Verify Disc Is Inserted in Drive
⑧ View Contents of CD

**TIP**

If desired, you can copy one chunk of a segmented audio file to your iPod so that you have room for other audio files. When you have listened to that portion, you can replace it with another segment.

Review the contents of the CD to make sure that it contains your segmented audio file. You can even listen to the segmented audio file from the CD by clicking the audio file to select it and then clicking the **Play** button.

252  PART II: iTunes

## 89 Create a Backup of your Music Library

You can use iTunes to create a backup copy of the audio files in your iTunes Library. You do this by creating a data CD. iTunes calls it a *data CD* because it contains a copy of the actual audio file used by iTunes in the same format. For example, if you have a WAV file that you are listening to in iTunes, a copy of the WAV file is placed on the CD without altering the file format. A data CD that you use to back up your Library files can contain AIFF, WAV, AAC, and MP3 files, depending on the makeup of your Library.

Before you can create a backup of your music Library, you must first set **Data CD or DVD** as the default format for burning CDs. If you have a SuperDrive, you can burn a DVD, which can hold more audio on one disc than a CD can hold.

You must also create a playlist that contains all the audio files within your music Library. To accomplish this, create a new playlist and then copy all the contents of the Library to the playlist. Note that any streaming audio files from the Internet (such as radio station links) are not backed up onto the CD.

When you click the **Burn Disc** button, iTunes checks to make sure that the entire playlist can be copied onto the disc. If all the audio files will not fit on the disc, a message displays indicating that only the files that fit will be copied. If you have a SuperDrive, you can use a DVD to back up more, if not all, of your Library files to a single disc. Otherwise, you will have to create multiple CDs to back up the entire Library. If you have to create multiple CDs, create a separate playlist for each CD. You can determine the size of the playlist by looking at the bottom of the iTunes window. If the size of the playlist exceeds the maximum capacity of the disc, reduce the songs in the playlist before burning the CD. iTunes copies to the CD only the portion of the playlist that fits on the disc.

### Before You Begin
✔ **83** About CD Burners

### See Also
→ **84** Adjust CD Burning Speed
→ **85** Set Pauses Between Audio Files on CD
→ **86** Burn an Audio CD
→ **87** Burn an MP3 CD
→ **88** Burn a CD with Segmented Audio Files

**NOTE**

When you create a data CD, you are creating a copy of the actual audio files, but the data disc you end up with cannot be played by most audio CD players. The data CD is primarily for archiving purposes. You can import files into iTunes from the data CD if you accidentally delete them from your iTunes library.

**❶ Display the Preferences Dialog Box**

Choose **iTunes, Preferences** to display the **Preferences** dialog box.

CHAPTER 10: Creating Music CDs

**Create a Backup of your Music Library**

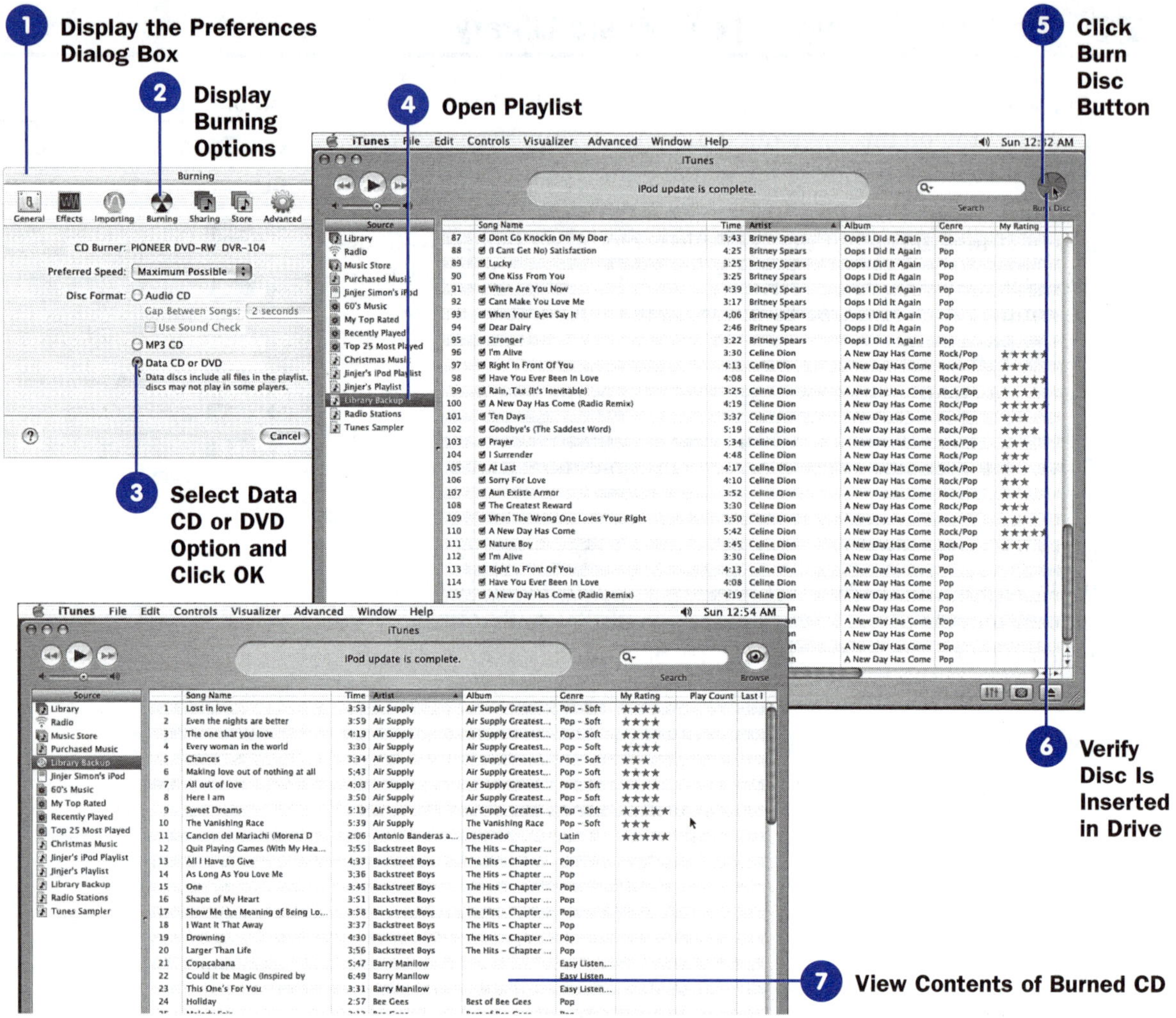

**1** Display the Preferences Dialog Box

**2** Display Burning Options

**3** Select Data CD or DVD Option and Click OK

**4** Open Playlist

**5** Click Burn Disc Button

**6** Verify Disc Is Inserted in Drive

**7** View Contents of Burned CD

**2** **Display Burning Options**

The name of the selected option on the **Preferences** dialog box displays as the title of the dialog box. You use the **Preferences** dialog box to specify all the settings in iTunes. The dialog box always opens to display the last options you modified.

254     **PART II:**    iTunes

Create a Backup of your Music Library

If the **Burning** page of the **Preferences** dialog box is not displayed, click the **Burning** icon to display the CD burning options.

**③ Select Data CD or DVD Option and Click OK**

Enable the **Data CD or DVD** option to back up the audio files specified in the selected playlist.

Click the **OK** button to save the CD burning settings and close the **Preferences** dialog box.

**④ Open Playlist**

In the **Source** list in the iTunes window, click the playlist you want to use to back up the library. iTunes can only burn CDs from a playlist; you cannot burn a CD directly from the Library.

Make sure that the length of the playlist does not exceed the capacity of the CD media you are burning. If it does, you can still burn the CD, but iTunes will give you the option to back up the playlist on multiple CDs. If you select this option, you will need multiple CDs to back up the playlist.

**⑤ Click Burn Disc Button**

Click the **Burn Disc** button in the upper-right corner of the iTunes window. iTunes checks to make sure that the CD burner contains a blank disc. If the disc is not blank, or if the drive is empty, a message box displays on the screen.

**⑥ Verify Disc Is Inserted in Drive**

Make sure that you have a disc inserted in the burner and click the **Burn Disc** button again. iTunes creates the CD by copying each of the songs in the playlist to the CD.

**⑦ View Contents of Burned CD**

When the CD is created, iTunes adds the data CD to the **Source** list in the iTunes window and displays the contents of the CD in the song list. The name of the CD is the name of the playlist used to create the CD.

**NOTE**

If you have a SuperDrive or other DVD burner, you can back up your audio files to a DVD so that more audio files can be saved on one disc.

**TIP**

You must have iTunes 4.1 or later to back up the audio files in the playlist onto multiple CDs. If you have an earlier version of iTunes, you can only back up the files that fit on one CD.

**NOTE**

Review the contents of the CD to make sure that all the desired audio files were burned to the disc. You can even listen to the audio files from the CD by clicking a song to select it and then clicking the **Play** button.

**CHAPTER 10:** Creating Music CDs

# PART III

# iMovie

## IN THIS PART

| | | |
|---|---|---|
| **CHAPTER 11** | Importing Video Clips | 259 |
| **CHAPTER 12** | Working with Video Clips | 271 |
| **CHAPTER 13** | Creating Movies | 285 |
| **CHAPTER 14** | Adding Visual Effects to a Movie | 307 |
| **CHAPTER 15** | Adding Sound to a Movie | 325 |
| **CHAPTER 16** | Sharing a Movie | 349 |

# 11

# Importing Video Clips

**IN THIS CHAPTER:**

- **90** About Connecting a Digital Video Camera
- **91** Capture Digital Video
- **92** Import Video Files from Other Sources
- **93** About Importing Nondigital Video
- **94** Set Clip Breaks for Importing

### 90 About Connecting a Digital Video Camera

To create a movie, you must transfer the desired video footage into iMovie. Although video footage typically comes from a digital video camera, you can also import video footage from other locations, such as video from the Internet or from a non-commercial DVD.

When you connect a digital video camera to your Apple computer, iMovie controls the video camera by identifying the individual clips and placing them either in the **Clips** panel or in the movie **Timeline**. You can use the controls in iMovie to control the video camera by performing actions such as playing the video and rewinding the tape.

Although iMovie is designed to work with digital video cameras, you can also use it to capture video recorded using a nondigital (analog) video source. To capture this kind of footage, you typically need to use a separate capture card within your computer or first transfer the analog footage to a digital video source. This approach makes it possible to use footage from older sources, such as 8mm video cameras.

### 90 About Connecting a Digital Video Camera

**See Also**

→ **91** Capture Digital Video

→ **92** Import Video Files from Other Sources

→ **93** About Importing Nondigital Video

→ **94** Set Clip Breaks for Importing

**KEY TERM**

*FireWire*—A small six-pin cable that connects a computer and an external device, such as a digital video camera. FireWire, also referred to as IEEE 1394, provides a high-speed connection for transferring data (up to 400 megabits per second).

You capture video clips from your digital video camera by connecting the camera to your computer. Typically, you use a *FireWire* cable to make the connection between the computer and the video camera. You connect the FireWire cable to the FireWire port on your computer. After you have made the FireWire connection, you turn on your video camera to playback mode and let iMovie control the video transfer.

iMovie can control only those video cameras that are connected to your computer using a FireWire connection. If your digital video camera requires a different type of connection, you must manually start and stop the video camera.

- **Do you have a FireWire port?** All new Apple computers come with a FireWire port you can use to transfer video, audio, and photos onto your computer. Typically the port is located on the back of your machine. Simply connect the FireWire cable from the video camera to this port.

PART III: iMovie

## About Connecting a Digital Video Camera  90

If your computer does not have a FireWire port, you can have a FireWire card installed. If you have to purchase a FireWire card, consider one that allows you to input both *analog* and *digital video*. With this flexibility, you can transfer footage not only from a digital video camera, but also from an analog video camera, such as a Hi-8 video recorder. See  93  **About Importing Nondigital Video**.

- **Aren't there multiple types of FireWire cables?** Yes, the ends of cables come in different sizes. Check the size of the connection on your video camera before purchasing a cable. The connector for the computer is the same size on all FireWire cables.

- **How do I locate a digital video camera?** Digital video cameras are widely sold in all shapes and sizes. Digital video cameras are available in multiple formats, the most common being miniDV (DV that records all audio and video on a small cassette), although there are also digital video cameras that record on rewritable compact discs, CD-RWs, and DVD-RAM discs.

Keep not only size, but quality in mind when selecting a digital video camera. For example, a camera with a larger lens can capture more light and therefore should create a better-quality video, but those cameras are also larger and more cumbersome to carry. Also consider the number of *CCDs*, or charge-coupled devices, in the camera. Video cameras with three CCDs produce better color clarity than video cameras that have only one CCD. Information about the number of CCDs in a video camera is typically listed on the outside of the box when you purchase the camera.

### KEY TERMS

**Digital video**—A format that stores all video elements, including sound, using a binary format of ones and zeros. A digital video camera records an exact replica of the sound and video received and stores it in each frame.

**Analog video**—A format that stores a recording of the sound and light fluctuations that occur. Each fluctuation in sound and light is recorded on the video, similar to the process used by your eyes to view an image and by your ears to hear a sound. This format loses quality each time the video tape is copied or viewed.

**CCD**—A semiconductor chip with light sensors for capturing the images from the camera lens. If the camera has three chips, it uses one chip to capture each of three colors: red, green, and blue. If the camera has only one chip, that single chip captures all three colors. CCDs vary in size. The larger the chip, the more light sensors it contains.

## 91 Capture Digital Video

**Before You Begin**

✔ **90** About Connecting a Digital Video Camera

**See Also**

→ **92** Import Video from Other Sources

→ **93** About Importing Nondigital Video

→ **94** Set Clip Breaks for Importing

### KEY TERM

*Project*—A folder created by iMovie to store the elements used to create your movie. Movie elements include the video clips along with any other titling, transition, and effects files created for the project.

### TIP

If you plan to use the same computer for all video transfers, leave the FireWire cable attached to the computer. Each time you want to transfer digital video footage, simply reconnect the cable to your video camera.

You capture digital video from a digital video camera by connecting the camera to your computer through the FireWire port. Although each digital video camera provides different options, each provides a FireWire port to allow the video to be transferred directly from the camera to your computer. See **90** About Connecting a Digital Video Camera for more information about FireWire.

When you use iMovie to capture the video from the camera, you can control the digital video camera directly within iMovie. This allows you to capture only specific clips or the entire video. iMovie provides controls for playing, importing, fast-forwarding, and rewinding the footage on the video tape in the camera.

When you open iMovie, it opens the last *project* that you worked on. The project specifies the location where the imported video will be placed. All work done in iMovie requires a project. If you want to import a video clip in a different video project, you can open another existing project or create a new project. Although video clips are placed in the folder of a specific video project, you can import those same clips into other projects. See **92** Import Video from Other Sources for more information on importing video clips.

### ❶ Connect FireWire Cable to Computer

Connect the FireWire cable to the FireWire port on your computer. On most Apple computers, the FireWire port is located on the back of the computer.

### ❷ Connect FireWire Cable to Camera

Connect the FireWire cable to the FireWire port on your camera. On many digital video cameras, the FireWire port is labeled DV. Be aware that if you have multiple FireWire devices, they might not all share the same size FireWire cable. Check the connector size carefully before inserting it into your camera to avoid damaging either the cable or the camera.

### ❸ Set Video Camera Mode

Turn the video camera on and put it in playback mode. Digital video cameras typically label this mode **VCR** or **VTR**.

**Capture Digital Video** 91

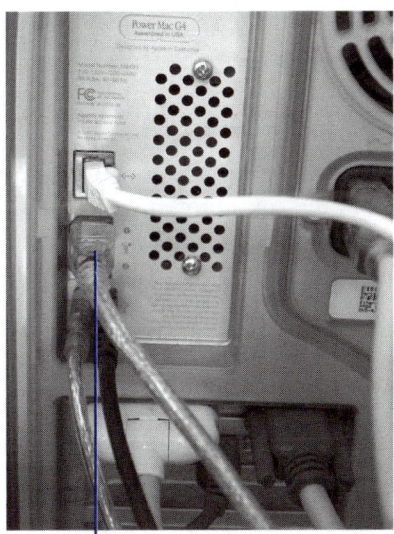

① Connect FireWire Cable to Computer

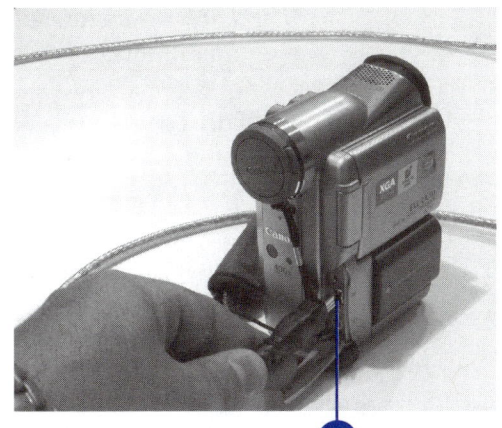

② Connect FireWire Cable to Camera

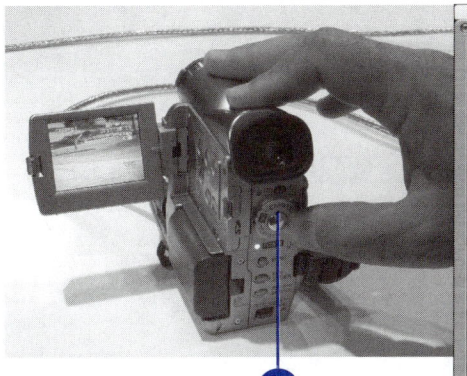

③ Set Video Camera Mode

④ Switch to Import Video Mode in iMovie

⑥ Import Video Footage

⑤ Locate Desired Video Footage

⑦ Stop Import

Available Disk Space

**CHAPTER 11:** Importing Video Clips 263

## 91  Capture Digital Video

If you are unsure about the appropriate setting, consult the documentation that came with the video camera.

### 4  Switch to Import Video Mode in iMovie

Launch iMovie and click the **Camera** icon under the **Monitor** window. If a video camera is connected to the computer, the **Import** and **Playback** buttons will be available (that is, they will not be grayed out) under the **Monitor** window.

The **Monitor** window displays a blue screen with the text **Camera Connected**. The numbers in the upper-right corner of the **Monitor** are the tape counter. The counter indicates the current position on the digital video camera tape.

### 5  Locate Desired Video Footage

Use the playback buttons under the **Monitor** to locate the desired footage on the video camera. You can rewind and fast-forward the footage as needed using these buttons. If you click the **Play** button, you can view the footage at the current location on the video tape.

### 6  Import Video Footage

When you locate the desired video footage, click the **Record with Camera** button. iMovie copies the video into the **Clips** pane based on the current import settings. See **94 Set Clip Breaks for Importing** for information on setting the import settings.

If you want to import all the footage from the video tape, rewind the tape and click the **Record with Camera** button. iMovie will import all existing footage. If the tape is not full, iMovie stops importing when it locates the empty portion of the tape.

iMovie imports video using the import settings. If you selected the option to break the video when there is a scene break, iMovie creates separate clips each time the scene changes on the video. If this option is not selected, iMovie creates one continuous clip until it reaches the end of the recorded footage or until you stop the import. See **94 Set Clip Breaks for Importing** for more information on controlling the clip breaks during the import process.

**TIP**

If you want to import the video into a different, existing project, choose **File, Open Project** and select the project. Choose **File, New Project** to create a new project for the imported video.

**NOTE**

If the text **No Camera Attached** displays on the **Monitor**, the digital video camera is either not properly connected through the FireWire cable to the computer or the video camera is not turned on in VCR playback mode. The buttons under the **Monitor** window remain grayed out until iMovie is able to connect to the video camera.

**NOTE**

Each time you stop and start the import process, iMovie creates a new video clip. You can manually create individual video clips simply by clicking the **Stop Camera** button and then clicking the **Import** button to start the process again.

Import Video Files from Other Sources

### 7  Stop Import

When you locate the last frame of video you want to import, click the **Stop Camera** button. Any remaining video on the camera is not imported. If you want to import additional video from the same video source, repeat steps 5 through 7.

iMovie monitors the disk space left on your computer's hard drive and displays this information in the bottom-right corner of the screen, using different colors based on the amount of space left:

- **Green**: More than 400MB of disk space
- **Yellow**: 200–400MB
- **Red**: 100–200MB

You cannot import additional video if the available disk space is less than 50MB.

**NOTE**

When importing video from your video camera to your computer, be mindful of available disk space. It requires approximately 1 gigabyte of hard disk space for every five minutes of video you import. Monitor your available disk space by looking at the bottom-right corner of the Monitor window.

##  Import Video Files from Other Sources

You can import video files into iMovie to add to your movie. For example, you might want to add a video that another person has created or video that you've downloaded from the Internet.

To bring in video from sources other than a video camera, you use the **Import** option. You can import any files located on your computer or on another machine you can access through a network connection.

You can also use the **Import** option to import video clips from another iMovie project. If you want to use video you have already imported for another project, you can import that video into your current project. To import video from another project, locate the original project folder and follow these steps.

**Before You Begin**

✔ 91 Capture Digital Video

**See Also**

→ 93 About Importing Nondigital Video

**TIP**

When importing video from a video camera or other source, make sure that the screensaver and sleep options are turned off. If the screensaver comes on, iMovie might not properly import the desired video. To turn off the sleep option, click **Apple, System Preferences, Energy Saver** and drag the slider to **Never**. To turn off the screensaver, click **Apple, System Preferences, Screen Effects, Activation** and drag the slider to **Never**.

CHAPTER 11: Importing Video Clips     265

## 92 Import Video Files from Other Sources

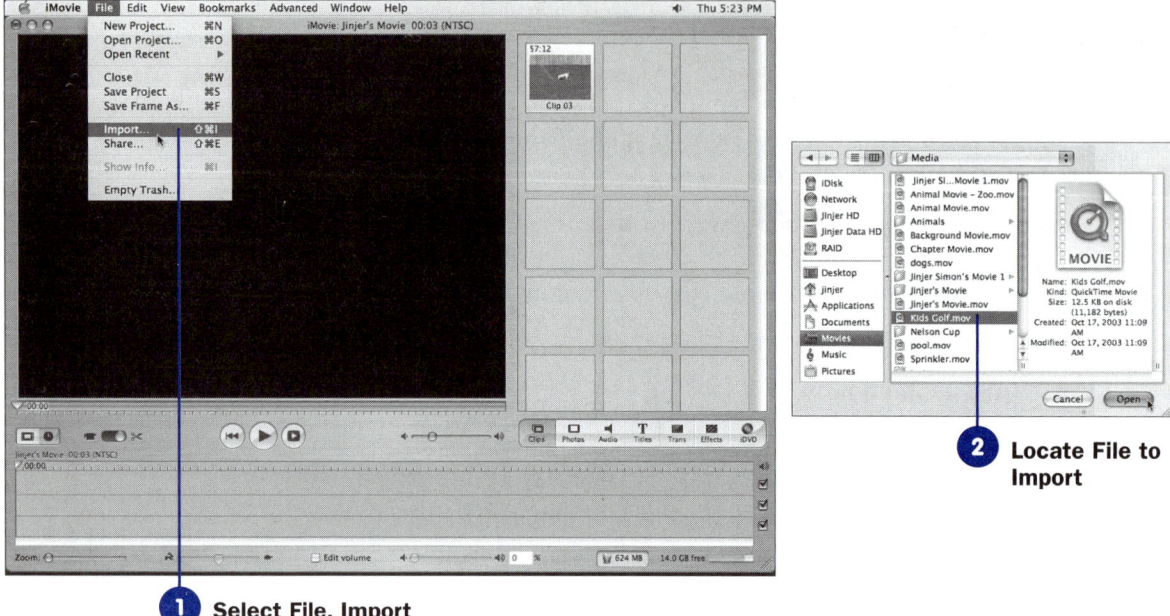

① Select File, Import

② Locate File to Import

### ① Select File, Import

Choose **File**, **Import** to display a list of available files. iMovie grays out the names of files that cannot be imported. For example, you can import movie files with an *.avi* or a *.mov* file extension, but iMovie prevents you from selecting word processing files. iMovie also allows you to import photo files (with **.jpg**, **.png**, and **.tiff** extensions) and sound files (with **.wav**, **mp3**, or **.aiff** extensions).

### ② Locate the File to Import

Highlight the file you want to import and click **Open**. The **Open** button is available only after you select a valid file to import. Keep in mind that you can browse any available folders to find the files you want to open.

### KEY TERMS

*.avi*—Audio Video Interleave. A multimedia format common to Microsoft Windows programs. You can import any *.avi* file into iMovie.

*.mov*—File extension used for QuickTime multimedia files. iMovie stores all movies in *.mov* format. You can also export movies with this format that can be streamed from a Web site.

## About Importing Nondigital Video

As iMovie imports the selected files, an **Import Files** dialog box displays to show the import progress by indicating the amount of time left to import the selected files. After a file is imported, it is placed in the **Clips** panel so that you can add it to your movie. See **103 Add Clips to the Timeline**.

> **TIP**
> You can select multiple files to import simultaneously. To select multiple files, hold down the **Shift** key while you click each file you want to import. When you click **Open**, iMovie imports each file individually as separate clips.

### 93  About Importing Nondigital Video

If you have video footage that was created on a nondigital (analog) video camera, such as Hi-8 or VHS, you can transfer that footage to your computer so that you can use it in iMovie. After the footage has been transferred, it becomes digital footage you can edit.

To transfer analog video, you need equipment designed to capture analog video. You can either install a capture card in your computer that accepts analog input, or you can record the analog video onto a digital video source. Analog video cameras do not use FireWire cable. You connect the analog camera using either a composite video cable or an S-Video cable. Refer to the analog camera's documentation for more information.

Some digital video cameras allow you to connect an analog video source so that you can record the analog video to the media on your digital video camera. If your video camera has a *pass-through* option, you can connect the analog source to the digital video camera and record directly on the computer ("through the digital camera," so to speak). If you do not have that option, you can connect your analog source to a digital video recorder (either a digital video camera or a digital video recording deck) and record the analog video as digital video and then transfer that digital video to your computer. After the video is recorded, transfer the footage to iMovie as digital video. See **91 Capture Digital Video**. You can also install an analog video capture card in your computer. This card allows you to plug your analog video source directly into your computer.

**Before You Begin**

✔ **90** About Connecting a Digital Video Camera

**See Also**

→ **91** Capture Digital Video

→ **92** Import Video Files from Other Sources

> **KEY TERM**
> *Pass-through*—The process of using the digital video camera or recorder to send the analog video to a computer. To accomplish this, the analog video camera is connected through the digital video camera to the computer. When you play the video on the analog video camera, it is captured in iMovie as digital video.

**CHAPTER 11:** Importing Video Clips

## 94 Set Clip Breaks for Importing

- **How do I use the pass-through option to record analog video?** If your digital video camera allows you to perform a pass-through, you must first connect the digital video camera to the computer using the FireWire cable. See **91 Capture Digital Video** for more information on capturing video. Connect the analog source to the digital video camera using either the composite video or S-Video cable. Set the digital video camera to the **A/V—DV Out** option (or similar) and select the **Play** option on the analog source. If you click **Import** in iMovie, you can record the analog video.

- **What if my digital video camera cannot perform a pass-through?** You can record directly from an analog video source to a digital video camera. After the video has been recorded onto your digital video camera, you can capture the video in iMovie. See **91 Capture Digital Video** for more information on capturing video. You must connect the two video cameras together using the composite video cables. Keep in mind that not all digital video cameras have a composite video connection. If your camera does not have this option, you must connect to your computer using a separate video capture card or a digital video recording deck.

- **Will my analog video footage look any different when I transfer it to digital?** Footage recorded with a digital video camera typically looks crisper because of the recording process. Analog video typically loses quality each time it is played. When you transfer video from analog to digital, you get a copy of the existing analog video with only a slight loss of quality during the transfer. After the transfer is complete, the quality of the new digital video footage does not change.

## 94 Set Clip Breaks for Importing

### Before You Begin

✔ **90** About Connecting a Digital Video Camera

### See Also

→ **91** Capture Digital Video

You can specify whether you want iMovie to detect breaks in your video footage during the import process. By default, iMovie detects these breaks, causing separate video clips to be created for each break in the footage. You can select whether or not this detection option is in operation based on the video footage you intend to import.

PART III: iMovie

## Set Clip Breaks for Importing

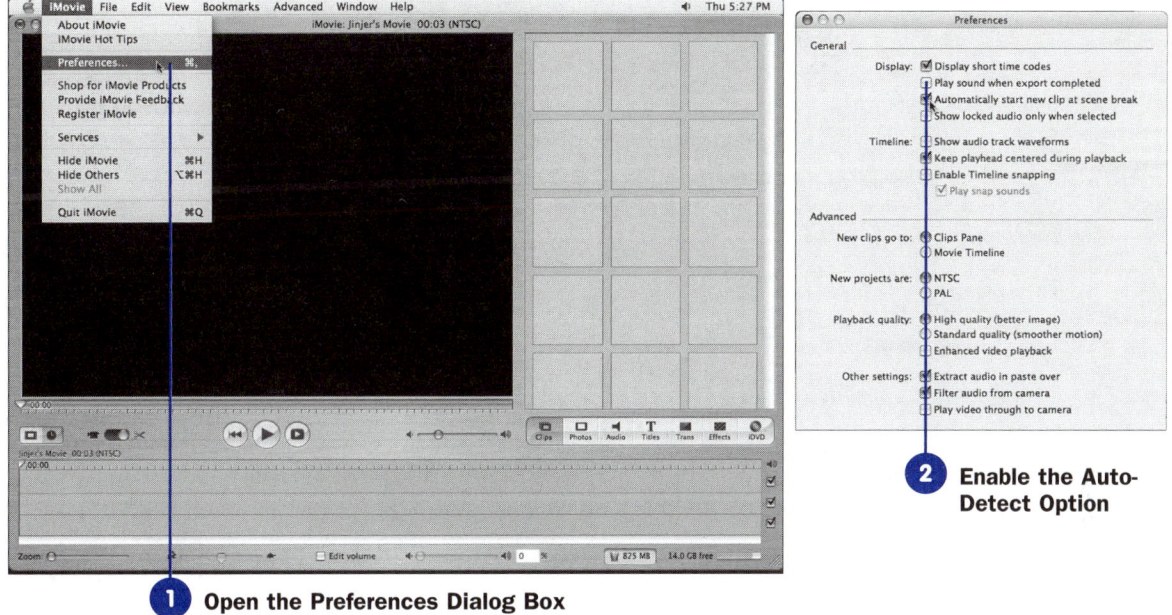

 Enable the Auto-Detect Option

① Open the Preferences Dialog Box

If you don't have iMovie detect the scene breaks when you import video from a video camera or other digital video source, iMovie creates a clip containing the video imported from the point when you click the **Import** button until you click the **Stop Camera** button. In this way, you can import an entire video tape, but it can be tedious to break the large clip into smaller clips.

Typically, a video tape contains breaks created by stopping and starting the recording process. For example, if you are taping your child's soccer game, you might only record the moments when your child is actually on the field playing. iMovie can detect those breaks in the recording and create separate video clips that start and stop at those break points. To have iMovie detect breaks, you must select the appropriate option.

① **Open the Preferences Dialog Box**

Choose **File, Preferences** to display the **Preferences** dialog box, where you set the options for working with iMovie.

### TIPS

You can press the **Spacebar** during an import process to start or stop the import.

By default, iMovie imports all clips to the **Clips** pane. You can add the clips to the **Timeline** instead by enabling the **Movie Timeline** option in the **Preferences** dialog box.

**CHAPTER 11:** Importing Video Clips          269

### Set Clip Breaks for Importing

**② Enable the Auto-Detect Option**

Enable the **Automatically start new clip at scene break** check box. Close the **Preferences** dialog box. The next time you import video from your digital video camera, iMovie will create individual clips based on the breaks in the recorded footage.

# 12

# Working with Video Clips

**IN THIS CHAPTER:**

- **95** About the Monitor
- **96** Name a Clip
- **97** Split a Clip
- **98** Crop a Clip
- **99** Set the Direction of a Clip
- **100** Create a Freeze Frame Image

## (95) About the Monitor

Every movie you create in iMovie is composed of one or more video clips or photos that you customize within iMovie. You customize video clips by removing unwanted footage, modifying play speed, adding effects, or even changing the play direction of the clip by reversing it. In iMovie, your clips can appear in three locations: the **Clips** pane, the **Photos** pane, and the **Monitor**. You view and modify clips using the **Monitor**. The **Clips** pane houses all the video clips available for your movie. Any modifications made to the clips in the Monitor are updated in the **Clips** pane. For example, if you split a clip, the **Clips** pane is updated to contain both of the smaller clips. The **Photos** pane shows your iPhoto library. You can add any of the photos on the pane to your movie. See (105) **Add Photos from iPhoto** for more information on using the **Photos** pane.

Not only can you use video footage in your movie, you can also use the footage to create still images. You can use the still images within your movie or save them to a file for other uses, such as placing an image on a Web page.

## (95) About the Monitor

### Before You Begin

✔ (91) Capture Digital Video
✔ (94) Set Clip Breaks for Importing

### See Also

→ (96) Name a Clip
→ (97) Split a Clip
→ (98) Crop a Clip
→ (107) Add Motion to a Photo

The Monitor displays each *clip* you select in the **Clips** pane. You use the controls under the **Monitor** to control the playback of a movie clip. The **Scrubber bar**, which displays directly under the Monitor, provides a timeline for the video clip. As you play a video clip, the **Playhead** moves along the Scrubber bar to show the position of the current *frame* within the video. A number also appears next to the *Playhead* to specify the position. For example, **01:14** identifies the frame that is one second and 14 frames into the clip. You can click the mouse on any location along the Scrubber bar, and the Playhead will jump to that location as the Monitor displays the corresponding frame.

## About the Monitor 95

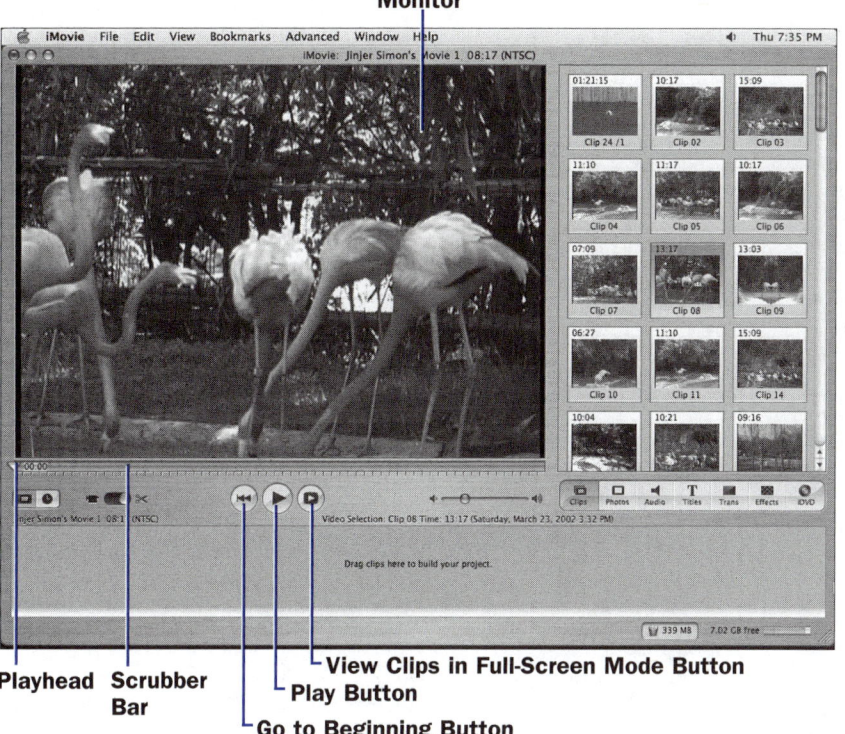

**Monitor**

**Playhead** · **Scrubber Bar** · **View Clips in Full-Screen Mode Button** · **Play Button** · **Go to Beginning Button**

*Elements of the Monitor.*

- **Do you want to eliminate part of the video clip?** You can use the crop markers that display under the Scrubber bar to identify a series of frames that you want to remove from a video clip. See **98 Crop a Clip** for more information.

- **Do you want to view the video clip in full-screen mode?** You can display the video so that it covers the entire Monitor screen by clicking the **View clips in full-screen mode** button. When you click this button, the clip begins playing on the full screen. Click the screen with the mouse to return to the normal mode within iMovie.

### KEY TERMS

*Clip*—A piece of video footage or a still photo. Clips often contain a specific scene of video footage. A movie typically contains multiple clips.

*Frame*—A single image or picture within a video clip or movie. The number of frames that display on the screen within a second is called *frames per second* or *frame rate*. Within the United States, iMovie uses the NTSC rate of 29.97 frames per second. Another common frame rate, PAL, used in some European countries, provides a frame rate of 25 frames per second. iMovie automatically makes this adjustment based on the attached video camera format.

*Playhead*—A triangular icon that moves along the Scrubber bar to indicate the position of the frame within the current video clip. You can drag the Playhead along the Scrubber bar or click the **Play** button to advance the video.

**CHAPTER 12: Working with Video Clips** 273

## 96 Name a Clip

**Before You Begin**

✔ **95** About the Monitor

**See Also**

→ **97** Split a Clip
→ **98** Crop a Clip
→ **99** Set the Direction of a Clip

💡 **TIPS**

Create a unique, descriptive name for each clip. However, iMovie can display only the first 15 characters of the clip name in the **Clips** pane. To view any undisplayed characters, click the video clip name and scroll with the arrow keys on the keyboard.

Avoid changing the filenames of movie clips outside of iMovie (for example, with Mac OS). If the filename changes, iMovie will no longer be able to locate the video clip.

You can change the name of any clip that appears in the **Clips** pane. As you import clips into iMovie from your video camera, each clip is named sequentially starting with **01**. The only significance of the clip naming is that the clips are named in the order in which they appeared on the original video tape. If you split a clip, iMovie maintains the original clip name and adds a **/1** to the end of the second part of the clip. See **97 Split a Clip** for more information.

You can change the names of clips to make the names more descriptive. By doing this, it is easier to identify the clips you want to add to your movie.

**① Select Image**

Click to select the desired clip in the **Clips** pane. iMovie highlights the selection in blue.

**② Open Clip Info**

Choose **File, Show Info** from the menu bar.

**③ Specify Clip Name**

In the **Clip Info** dialog box for the selected clip, type a descriptive name for the clip in the **Name** field and click **OK**.

When you change the name of the video clip, you are only changing the name assigned to the clip when it displays in the **Clips** pane. You are not altering the actual clip filename. Notice that the **Clip Info** dialog box displays the **Media File** name. This is the name of the actual file containing the clip on your computer's hard disk. When you change the clip name, iMovie maintains the reference between your clip name and the actual filename.

Name a Clip  96

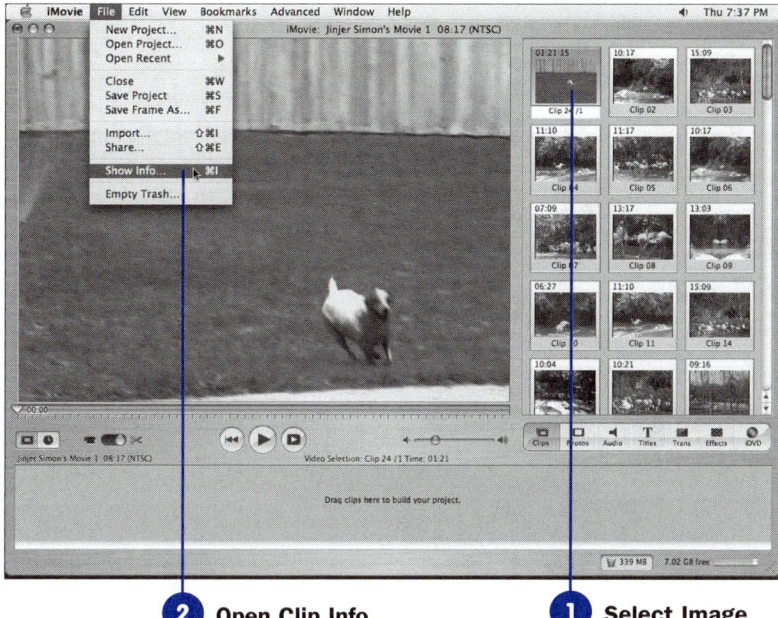
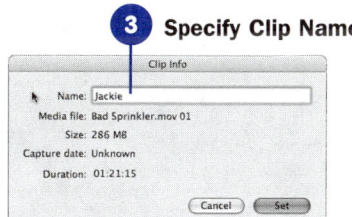

③ Specify Clip Name

② Open Clip Info

① Select Image

## 97  Split a Clip

You can split a video clip into two or more smaller clips. There are multiple reasons for splitting a clip. For example, you might want to put only a portion of a video clip in your movie, or you might want to use the last part of the video clip first in your movie.

To split a clip, you must view the desired clip in the **Monitor** and then use the **Playhead** to locate the specific frame location in the clip where you want to split the video clip. The frame where you initiate the split becomes the first frame of the new clip.

When you split a clip, iMovie names the new clip with the name of the original clip followed by /**1**. For example, if the original clip is named **Clip 10**, the split clip is named **Clip 10/1**. You can rename a clip in the **Clips** pane. See  96  **Name a Clip** for more information.

**Before You Begin**

✔ 95  About the Monitor
✔ 96  Name a Clip

**See Also**

→ 98  Crop a Clip
→ 99  Set the Direction of a Clip

 **TIP**

You can also split a video clip that has been added to the **Timeline**. See  103  **Add Clips to the Timeline** for more information.

CHAPTER 12:   Working with Video Clips       275

## 97 Split a Clip

1 Select the Video Clip

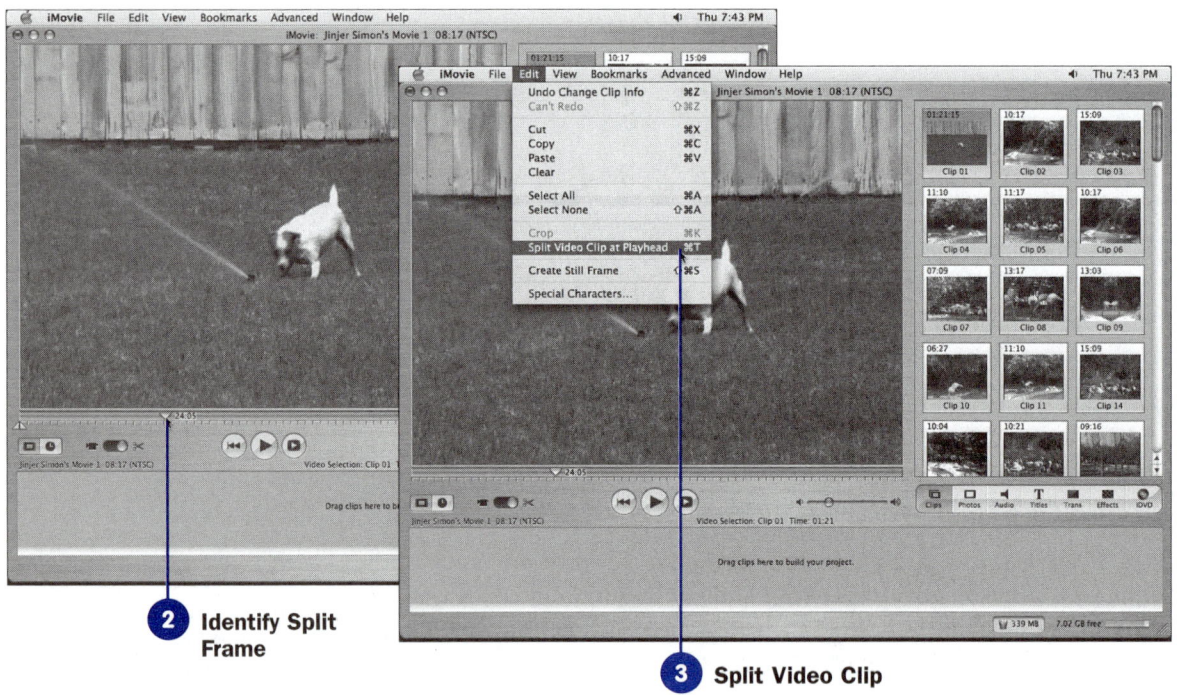

2 Identify Split Frame

3 Split Video Clip

Crop a Clip

### 1 Select the Video Clip

Select the desired clip in the **Clips** pane. The first frame of the selected clip displays in the **Monitor**.

### 2 Identify Split Frame

Drag the **Playhead** along the **Scrubber bar** to locate the frame where you want to split the video clip. As you drag the **Playhead**, the **Monitor** displays the frame at the current location within the clip.

Make sure that you position the **Playhead** so that the frame that displays in the **Monitor** is the first frame you want in the new clip. The frame that precedes the selected frame becomes the last frame in the original video clip.

### 3 Split Video Clip

Choose **Edit, Split Video Clip at Playhead** to split the clip. iMovie splits the video clip, and the new clip remains selected.

### TIPS

If you split the clip at the wrong location, you can recover the original clip: Select the split clip and choose **Advanced, Restore Clip** from the menu bar. When you select this option, all frames that were removed from the video clip are restored. Any new clips you created by splitting the original clip remain in the **Clips** pane.

When you split a clip, iMovie doesn't remove any frames from the original video clip file. It just keeps track of the frame where the split occurs.

## Crop a Clip

If you have imported a clip that has unneeded footage at the beginning or end, you can remove the unwanted footage from the clip by cropping it. When you crop a video clip, you mark the part of the clip that you want to keep by indicating the start and end points. Any footage outside the marks is deleted.

When iMovie deletes excess video footage, the deleted frames are placed in the **Trash**. The clips remain in the **Trash** until you empty the Trash. After you empty the **Trash**, however, you cannot restore the original video clip. Therefore, before emptying the **Trash**, make sure that you are happy with any clips you have cropped.

### Before You Begin

✔ 95 About the Monitor
✔ 96 Name a Clip

### See Also

→ 97 Split a Clip
→ 99 Set the Direction of a Clip
→ 103 Add Clips to the Timeline

### TIP

Because the items in the **Trash** use hard disk space, you should delete the **Trash** as needed. iMovie displays the amount of available disk space next to the **Trash**. Choose **File, Empty Trash** to clear the iMovie **Trash** and free up disk space.

## 98 Crop a Clip

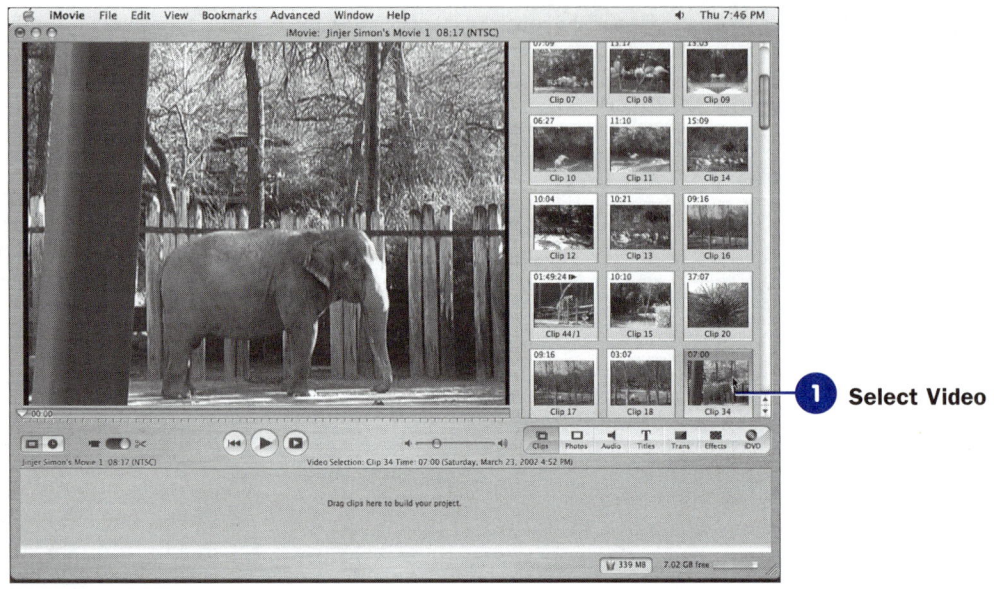

1 Select Video Clip
2 Mark Crop Points
3 Crop Clip

PART III: iMovie

## Set the Direction of a Clip · 99

### ① Select Video Clip

Select the desired clip in the **Clips** pane. The first frame of the selected clip displays in the **Monitor**.

### ② Mark Crop Points

Click each *crop mark* under the **Scrubber bar** and drag the marks to identify the crop area for the selected video clip. The right crop mark indicates the desired end point for the video clip, and the left crop mark indicates the desired start point. iMovie marks the crop area (the area to keep) in yellow. The frames that are blue will be discarded when you select the **Crop** command.

Before performing the crop, you can review the selected frames by dragging the **Playhead** across the marked section.

### ③ Crop Clip

Choose **Edit**, **Crop** to remove the excess frames from the video clip. iMovie updates the clip in the **Clips** pane to contain only the specified frames (those in the yellow area in step 2). Click **Play** to run the clip to ensure that your cropping is correct.

If you decide you did not crop the video clip correctly, undo the most recent crop by choosing **Edit**, **Undo Crop**. You cannot undo a crop if you have already emptied the Trash.

> **KEY TERM**
>
> *Crop marks*—Triangular marks that display on the ruler under the **Scrubber bar** below the **Monitor**. Use the crop marks to indicate the frames to remove from a video clip. iMovie removes the frames that appear before the left crop mark and after the right crop mark.

> **TIP**
>
> If you want to know how long the cropped clip will be, click the right crop mark. When you do so, iMovie indicates the length of the clip in the format hh:mm:ss:ff, where 02:12:14 means 2 minutes, 12 seconds, and 14 frames in length.

## 99 Set the Direction of a Clip

If you want to change the order in which actions occur in your video, you can reverse the clip direction. When you reverse the clip, iMovie totally reorders all frames in the clip so that the clip plays in reverse order, starting with the last frame in the clip. When you watch a reversed clip, it might appear that all actions are being performed backwards.

**Before You Begin**

✔ 95 About the Monitor

**See Also**

→ 97 Split a Clip
→ 98 Crop a Clip
→ 100 Create a Freeze Frame Image
→ 104 Set the Speed of a Clip

**CHAPTER 12:** Working with Video Clips

## 99  Set the Direction of a Clip

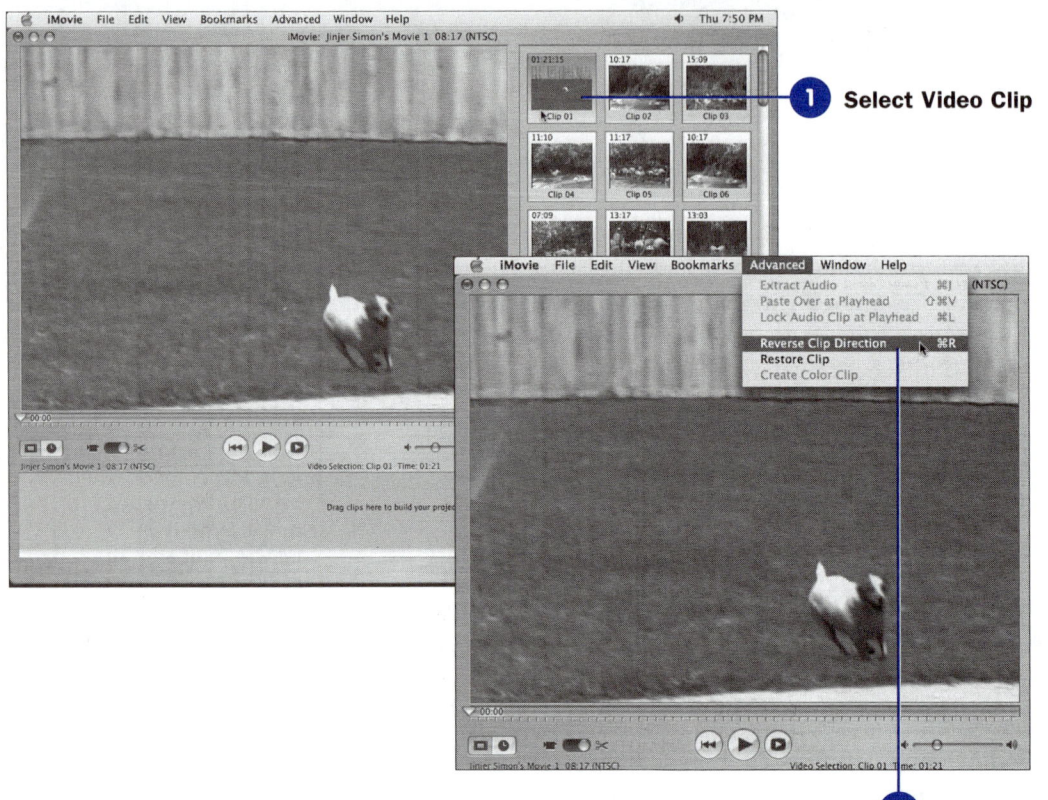

① Select Video Clip

② Reverse Clip Direction

To identify a reversed clip, iMovie places an arrow icon in the top-right corner of the clip on the **Clips** pane. Also, the last frame in the original clip is used as the thumbnail image for the reversed clip in the **Clips** pane.

### ① Select Video Clip

Select the desired clip in the **Clips** pane. The first frame of the selected clip displays in the **Monitor**.

## Create a Freeze Frame Image 100

You can also select a clip from the **Timeline** viewer. See 103 **Add Clips to the Timeline** for more information.

**② Reverse Clip Direction**

Choose **Advanced, Reverse Clip Direction** from the menu bar. iMovie reverses the entire clip by reversing the play order of the frames within the clip.

**TIP**

You can undo a reversed clip by performing the same steps to reverse the clip. When you do this, you are telling iMovie to reverse the clip again, which returns the clip to its original play order. iMovie also removes the **Reversed** icon from the thumbnail image in the **Clips** pane.

### 100 Create a Freeze Frame Image

You might want to create a still image, or photo, out of a frame in a video clip. For example, you might want to make your movie more dramatic by creating the appearance of the movie stopping on a particular frame. You can also save a frame as a still image for use with other software programs, such as iPhoto, to place on a Web site or to send through email.

When you save a frame from your video clip, you have the option of selecting the format used to save the image. Select the format based on how you want to use the image. You can select one of the following formats:

- **PICT.** A format developed to provide a high-quality, uncompressed image. Images created with this format maintain the same quality level as the original image. Because PICT images do not use *compression*, they are said to have a "lossless" format. Select this format if you want to import the image back into iMovie for use in your movie.

- **JPEG.** If you plan on emailing the image or placing it on a Web site, save it as a JPEG. JPEG is a standard format for compressing images so that files are smaller. JPEG images are created using lossy compression. The file size is reduced by eliminating some of the data. For example, portions of the image with similar shades are blended together.

**Before You Begin**

✔ 95 About the Monitor

**See Also**

→ 97 Split a Clip
→ 98 Crop a Clip

**KEY TERM**

*Compression*—The process of reducing the size of a graphic image so that it requires less disk space to store. Compression occurs by removing information from the graphic that is typically not obvious. Images stored with compression are said to have a "lossy" format. A highly compressed image will not have the same crisp appearance as an uncompressed image. The most commonly used format for compressed images is JPEG.

**CHAPTER 12: Working with Video Clips**

## 100 Create a Freeze Frame Image

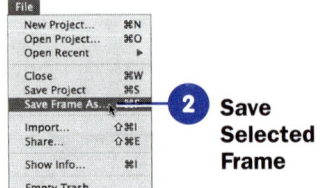

**2** Save Selected Frame

**1** Locate Frame in Video Clip

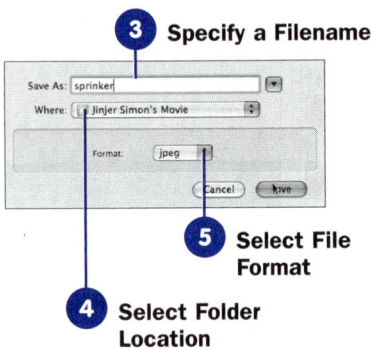

**3** Specify a Filename

**5** Select File Format

**4** Select Folder Location

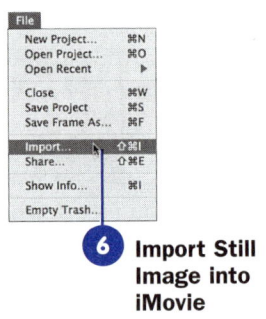

**6** Import Still Image into iMovie

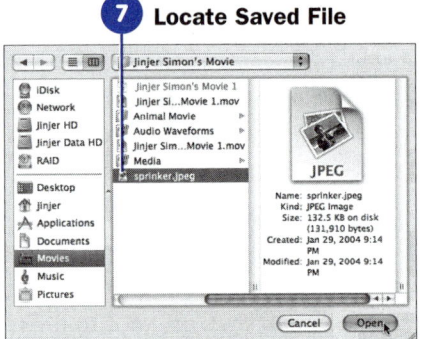

**7** Locate Saved File

### ① Locate Frame in Video Clip

Select the desired clip in the **Clips** pane or from the **Timeline** viewer. The selected clip displays in the **Monitor**. Click and drag the **Playhead** along the **Scrubber bar** to locate the clip you want to save as a still image.

## Create a Freeze Frame Image

### ② Save Selected Frame

Choose **File, Save Frame As** from the menu bar to display the **Save As** dialog box.

### ③ Specify a Filename

On the **Save As** dialog box, type a unique name for the frame image in the **Save As** field.

### ④ Select Folder Location

By default, iMovie saves the image in the **Media** folder located in the current iMovie project folder. Remember, iMovie creates separate folders for each project in your **Movies** folder.

If you plan to import the image back into the same project, consider saving it in the same folder. If you are saving the image for other uses, you can select the desired folder location. Click the down arrow next to the **Where** field and navigate to the folder in which you want to save the image.

### ⑤ Select File Format

From the **Format** list, select the appropriate file format for the image depending on whether or not you want a compressed image. Click **Save** to create the image file in the specified folder location.

### ⑥ Import Still Image into iMovie

If you want to use the still image you just created in your iMovie video, you can import the image back into your project as a separate clip. To do so, choose **File, Import** from the menu bar to display the **Import** dialog box.

### ⑦ Locate Saved File

iMovie automatically opens the **Media** folder associated with the current movie project. Locate the still image file you want to import and click **Open**. iMovie adds the selected image clip to the **Clips** pane.

---

**NOTE**

When you save a frame as a still image, the original frame remains in the video clip. iMovie simply saves a copy of the selected frame without altering the video clip.

**TIPS**

When you import a still image, iMovie automatically applies the **Ken Burns** effect to the image to make the image appear animated. See **107 Add Motion to a Photo** for more information on working with the **Ken Burns** effect.

If you are creating a still frame image for the sole purpose of adding it to your movie, locate the image in the video clip (step 1) and choose **Edit, Create Still Frame** to create the image and add it to the **Clips** pane in a single step.

---

**CHAPTER 12:    Working with Video Clips**                                283

# 13

# Creating Movies

**IN THIS CHAPTER:**

- **101** About the Timeline Elements
- **102** About Rendering
- **103** Add Clips to the Timeline
- **104** Set the Speed of a Clip
- **105** Add Photos from iPhoto
- **106** Adjust Display Time of a Photo
- **107** Add Motion to a Photo
- **108** Add a Still Image from Another Application
- **109** Trim Clips in the Timeline
- **110** Add Bookmarks to Your Movie

### 101 About the Timeline Elements

After you have video footage imported into iMovie, the next step in creating a movie is to select the desired clips and place them in the appropriate order. You lay out your movie by adding clips to the **Timeline**. You add clips to the **Timeline** by dragging them from the **Clips** pane. You can also create clips from photos (still images) and add them to the **Timeline** as part of the movie.

> **KEY TERM**
>
> *Timeline*—Displays the audio and video clips in the order they will play in the movie. You can switch between the **Timeline viewer** (which indicates the amount of time required for each clip) and the **Clip viewer** (which just shows the order of the clips).

When you add clips to the **Timeline**, the clips play at standard speed. If want a clip to last longer, you can slow down the speed of the clip. You change the clip speed from the Timeline.

iMovie provides the **Ken Burns effect** for creating motion effects for a photo. The motion is created by giving the appearance of zooming in or out on the photo. iMovie allows you to customize the zooming effects and the amount of time the photo clip displays on the screen.

### 101 About the Timeline Elements

**Before You Begin**

✓ 91 Capture Digital Video
✓ 95 About the Monitor

**See Also**

→ 96 Name a Clip
→ 97 Split a Clip
→ 98 Crop a Clip
→ 103 Add Clips to the Timeline
→ 104 Set the Speed of a Clip
→ 105 Add Photos from iPhoto
→ 109 Trim Clips in the Timeline

You use the **Timeline viewer**, located at the bottom of the iMovie window, to lay out your movie by adding the desired video clips, sounds, audio clips, and special effects. The **Timeline viewer** contains three separate tracks: The first track is the **video track**. All video clips you add to your movie are placed on this track, along with any **Titles** and **Transitions** you create. See 111 **Insert a Transition Between Video Clips** for more information on adding transitions and 112 **Create a Movie Title** for more information on adding titles.

The other two tracks on the **Timeline** are the **audio tracks**. iMovie provides two audio tracks to make it easier to mix your audio for the movie. You can use audio clips from iTunes or any of the sound clips provided with iMovie. See Chapter 15, "Adding Sound to a Movie," for more information on adding and modifying sounds clips.

The **Timeline viewer** provides a **ruler** across the top to help you gauge the length of the entire movie and of each individual clip. As the **Playhead** moves across the **Timeline**, the ruler indicates the position of the current frame within the movie. As the Playhead moves across the Timeline, the corresponding frame displays on the Monitor.

**About the Timeline Elements** 101

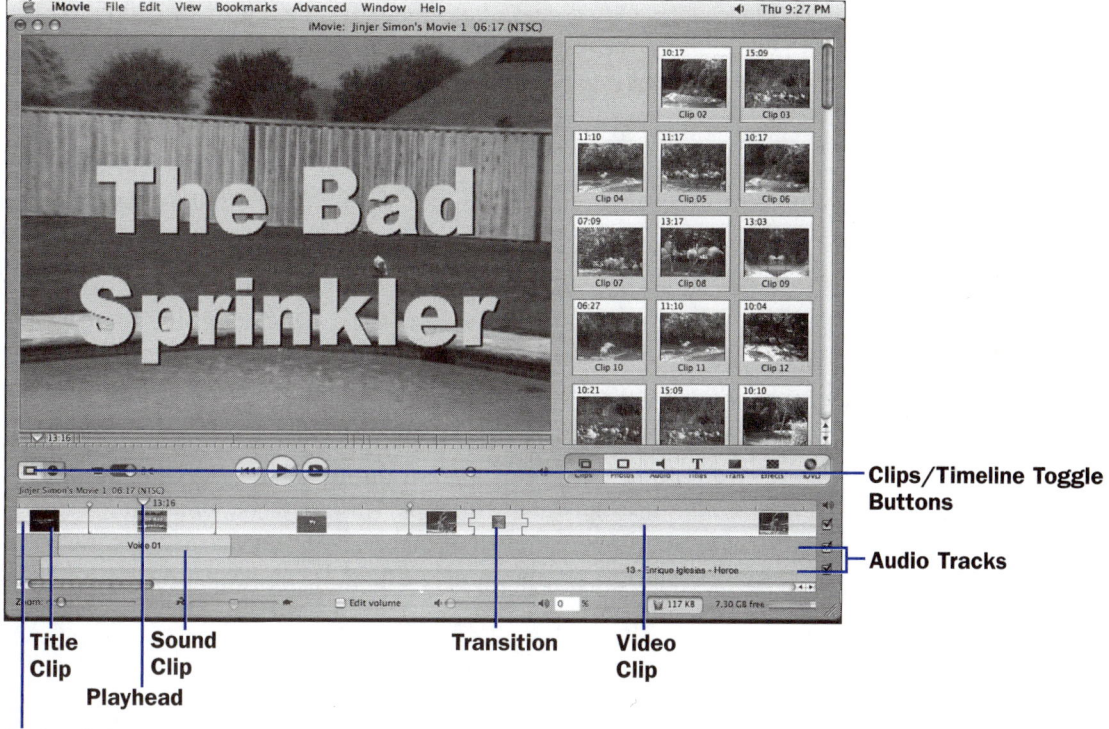

The elements of the *Timeline viewer* make it easier for you to assemble the pieces of your movie into a cohesive whole.

- **What is the difference between the Timeline viewer and the Clips viewer?** iMovie allows you to quickly switch between the **Clips viewer** and the **Timeline viewer** by clicking the corresponding icon below the Monitor. The **Clips viewer** displays when you click the button with the film clip on it. The **Timeline viewer** button has a clock on it.

  The **Clips viewer** displays the individual video clips along with any *transitions*. If you have assigned audio clips to your movie, they are not visible from the **Clips viewer**. Use the **Clips viewer** to pull together a quick movie using clips from the **Clips** pane.

- **What if I don't want to hear an audio track?** iMovie provides a check box next to each track in the **Timeline viewer**. If you remove the check mark from a track, that track is ignored (muted) when you play the movie. Because video clips typically contain

**CHAPTER 13:** Creating Movies 287

## 102 About Rendering

their own audio, a check box also exists next to the video track. If you remove the check mark from the video track, the video will still play, but iMovie will ignore all the audio in the video clips.

This "mute" feature is especially helpful when you want to check the audio in one track only. See Chapter 15, "Adding Sound to a Movie," for more information on working with audio clips.

- **Can I change the size of the Timeline?** The **Timeline** can be adjusted to show the amount of detail you want to see by using the **Zoom** slider in the lower-left corner. The higher the *zoom* level, the more detail you can see about a specific clip in the **Timeline**. By reducing the zoom level, you can view more clips, but it might be more difficult to determine the clip size.

- **Can I change the volume of an audio track?** With iMovie, you can not only adjust the volume of an audio clip, you can also have the volume change at specific points within the clips. See **124 Adjust the Volume of a Clip** for information on changing the volume of a clip.

### KEY TERM

*Zoom*—The process of magnifying the displayed image to make it easier to view the details. When you zoom out, you reduce the magnification to get a broader vision of the entire image.

## 102 About Rendering

**Before You Begin**

✓ **101** About the Timeline Elements

**See Also**

→ **103** Add Clips to the Timeline

→ **107** Add Motion to a Photo

→ **111** Insert a Transition Between Video Clips

### KEY TERM

*Rendering*—The process of applying the selected transition, effect, or title to each of the appropriate frames within a clip.

When you apply specific effects to a clip, iMovie goes through the process of *rendering* to create the effect. For example, if you apply the **Sepia Tone** effect to a video clip, iMovie must apply that same effect to every frame within the video clip. Depending on the length of the selected video clip, it might take a few minutes to render a transition.

By default, iMovie immediately renders each visual effect you add to your movie. For example, if you add a new transition, iMovie begins rendering the transition as soon as you add it to the **Timeline**. iMovie displays a status bar under the associated clip or transition so that you know rendering is in progress. You can continue working on your movie as iMovie renders the transition, but your computer might not respond as quickly because of the amount of system resources required for rendering.

## About Rendering 102

Rendering an Effect

*Whenever you add a visual effect to your movie, iMovie renders all the frames affected by the effect.*

- **Why does iMovie render a photo I add to the Movie?** If you apply the **Ken Burns** effect to a photo, iMovie must create the individual frames to show the zoom motion. The amount of time required to render the motion photo is based on the specified duration. See **107 Add Motion to a Photo** for more information.

- **Can I manually render the entire movie after adding effects and transitions?** No. iMovie automatically detects when a clip or transition must be rendered and immediately performs the rendering. This is different than high-end video editing packages, such as Final Cut Pro, which allow you to manually perform the rendering of the entire project. The nice part of the automatic rendering feature in iMovie is that when you complete the assembly of your movie, it is immediately ready to be shown to others.

- **Do I have to wait for rendering to finish before making changes?** It is not necessary to wait for the rendering process to finish before making changes to or previewing your movie. However, iMovie might run more slowly while it is rendering clips (the rendering process is pretty system-intensive), but you can continue the process of creating your movie.

**CHAPTER 13:** Creating Movies

## 103 Add Clips to the Timeline

**Before You Begin**

✓ **95** About the Monitor
✓ **101** About the Timeline Elements

**See Also**

→ **104** Set the Speed of a Clip
→ **105** Add Photos from iPhoto
→ **111** Insert a Transition Between Video Clips
→ **113** Add an Effect

You can use any of the clips that exist on the **Clips** pane in your movie. Clips are added to the **Clips** pane when you capture or import video. See **91** **Capture Digital Video** for information on capturing video from a digital video camera. See **92** **Import Video from Other Sources** for information on importing other video.

To add a clip to the movie, you select it and drag it from the **Clips** pane to the **Timeline** viewer. As you add the clip to the **Timeline**, iMovie sizes the clip on the **Timeline** based on the play length of the clip. iMovie removes the clip from the **Clips** pane and adds it to the **Timeline**.

### ① Display Clips Pane

Click the **Clips** button to display the **Clips** pane. All the clips that you have imported into the current movie project display on the **Clips** pane.

### ② Select Desired Clip

Click the desired clip on the **Clips** pane to select it. When you select the clip, it displays in the Monitor, where you can preview it, if desired.

If you do not want to use the entire clip, you can crop the clip to remove unwanted footage. See **98** **Crop a Clip** for information on cropping. You can also split a clip into multiple clips, as explained in **97** **Split a Clip**.

### ③ Drag Clip to Timeline

Drag the selected clip from the **Clips** pane onto the **Timeline** viewer. The selected clip appears grayed out in the **Clips** pane until you release the mouse button. After you release the mouse button, iMovie adds the clip to the movie at the selected location in the **Timeline** and removes it from the **Clips** pane.

**TIP**

Use the scrollbar on the right side of the **Clips** pane to help locate the desired clips.

**TIP**

If the **Timeline** contains multiple video clips, you must decide where to insert the new clip. For example, you can add a new clip between two existing clips by dropping the new clip between the existing clips.

290  PART III:  iMovie

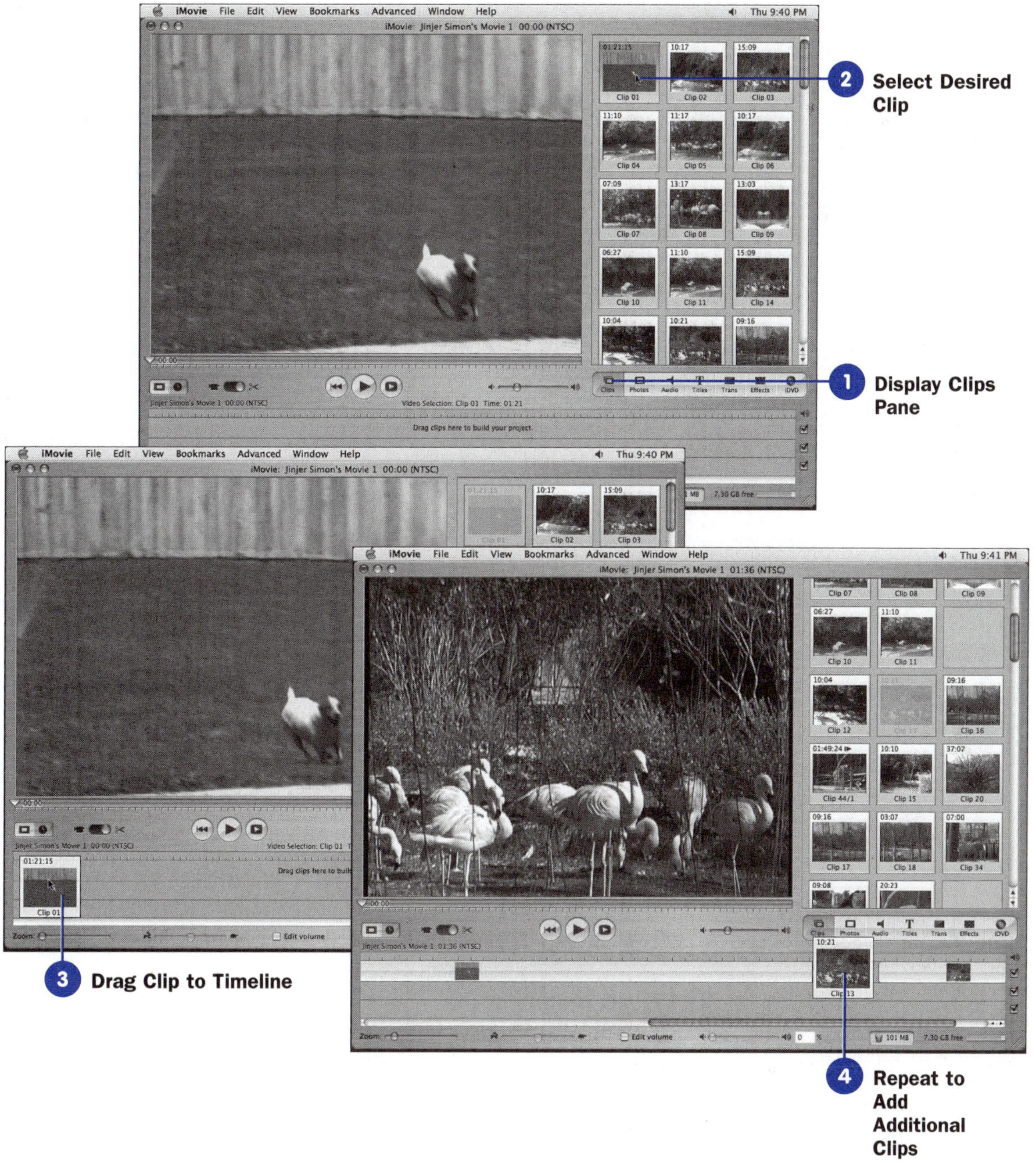

## Add Clips to the Timeline

**2** Select Desired Clip

**1** Display Clips Pane

**3** Drag Clip to Timeline

**4** Repeat to Add Additional Clips

**CHAPTER 13: Creating Movies**

**104** Set the Speed of a Clip

### TIP

If you want to reuse a clip that has already been added to the **Timeline**, select the clip in the **Timeline** and choose **Edit, Copy**. Move the **Playhead** to the desired location for the copy and choose **Edit, Paste** to insert a copy of the selected clip.

**4 Repeat to Add Additional Clips**

Continue adding clips to the **Timeline** by repeating steps 2 and 3. As you add clips, you can drop them anywhere on the **Timeline**.

Keep in mind, however, that iMovie does not allow you to add a clip in the middle of another video clip. If you want to insert a clip in the middle of another clip, you must split the first clip. See **97 Split a Clip** for information on splitting clips.

## 104 Set the Speed of a Clip

### Before You Begin

✔ **101** About the Timeline Elements
✔ **103** Add Clips to the Timeline

### See Also

→ **109** Trim a Clip in the Timeline
→ **111** Insert a Transition Between Video Clips
→ **113** Add an Effect

### TIP

When you slow down a video clip, you also slow down the audio in the clip. You might want to mute the audio of the video track. You can also extract the audio from the video before changing the speed. See **122 Extract Audio from Video** for more information.

You can adjust the speed of a clip to create an interesting effect in your movie. For example, if you want to make sure that the viewer sees each detail of an event, you might want to slow the clip down to create a slow-motion effect. You can also increase the speed of a clip.

When you change the speed of a clip, the speed changes for the *entire video clip*. If you do not want to change the speed of the entire clip, you must split the clip so that you have a clip that contains only the video you want to slow down or speed up. See **97 Split a Clip** for information on splitting a video clip.

You change the speed of the clip on the **Timeline** using the **Speed** slider under the **Timeline**. When the slider is at the center location, the clip plays at normal speed. Moving the slider to the left, toward the rabbit, speeds up the clip. Moving the slider to the right, toward the turtle, slows down the clip and makes it last longer.

You do not have to make drastic changes in the speed of the clip. If you have footage that was shot on a windy day where the camera moved a lot, you can slow down the footage a little to remove the camera movement.

**1 Select Clip in the Timeline**

On the **Timeline**, click the clip you want to change. iMovie highlights the selected clip in blue and displays the selection in the **Monitor**.

PART III: iMovie

**Set the Speed of a Clip** 104

① Select Clip in the Timeline

② Change the Speed

## ② Change the Speed

Drag the slider to the right to slow down the clip and make it take longer. iMovie reduces the clip speed by one half for each mark on the slider. So, if you move the slider all the way to the right, the clip will take about four times as long to play.

Drag the slider to the left to speed up the clip. iMovie plays the clip twice as fast for each mark on the slider. So, if you move the slider all the way to the left, the clip will play about six times faster than normal speed.

CHAPTER 13: Creating Movies

## 105 Add Photos from iPhoto

**Before You Begin**

✓ **1** Transfer Pictures from a Digital Camera

✓ **4** Create New Albums

✓ **5** Create a Smart Album

✓ **101** About the Timeline Elements

✓ **103** Add Clips to the Timeline

**See Also**

→ **106** Adjust Display Time of a Photo

→ **107** Add Motion to a Photo

→ **108** Add a Still Image from Another Application

### TIP

If you have a lot of photos in iPhoto, you might want to use your photo albums to locate the desired photo. You can display a specific photo album by choosing one from the **Photo Library** drop-down menu. Only the photos from that album display on the **Photos** pane.

You can use photos within your movie to create different effects. For example, photos are frequently added to documentary types of movies. By displaying a photo in your movie, you can create emphasis on a particular image. iMovie provides a simple method for incorporating any of the photos you have added to iPhoto. Without opening iPhoto, iMovie can quickly display on the **Photos** pane all the photos you have set up in iPhoto. You can even select from the different albums you have created. See **6 Organizing Photos in an Album** for more information on organizing photos in iPhoto.

When you add a photo to a movie, iMovie sets a default display time for the photo. You can change the amount of time the photo displays. See **106 Adjust Display Time of a Photo** for more information. You can also make the photo appear to have motion. See **107 Add Motion to a Photo** for more information.

#### 1 Open the Photos Pane

Click the **Photos** button to display the **Photos** pane. By default, iMovie displays all the clips available in your iPhoto Photo Library.

#### 2 Locate the Desired Photo

Click the desired photo on the **Photos** pane to select it. When you select the photo, it displays in the preview window at the top of the **Photos** pane. You can use the scrollbar on the right side of the **Photos** pane to scroll through the list of available photos.

You can select multiple photos to add to the **Timeline** at once. To do so, hold down the **Shift** key while you click each photo. iMovie adds the photos to the **Timeline** in the same order you clicked them.

#### 3 Add Photo to the Timeline

Drag the selected photo from the **Photos** pane to the **Timeline** viewer. A copy of the selected photo is added to the movie at the specified location on the **Timeline**.

PART III: iMovie

## Add Photos from iPhoto  105

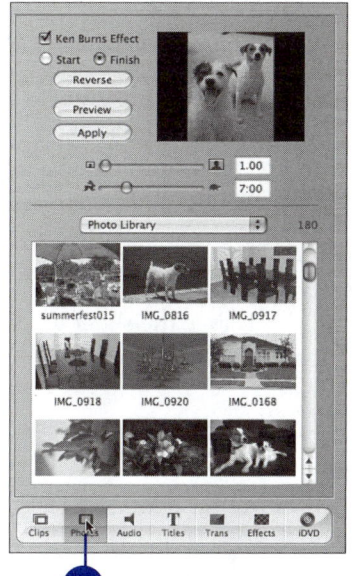

**1** Open the Photos Pane

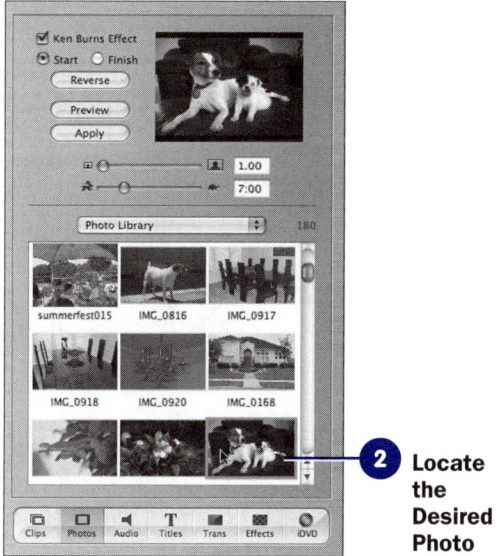

**2** Locate the Desired Photo

**3** Add Photo to the Timeline

**CHAPTER 13:** Creating Movies    295

## 106 Adjust Display Time of a Photo

**Before You Begin**

✔ **1** Transfer Pictures from a Digital Camera

✔ **101** About the Timeline Elements

✔ **105** Add Photos from iPhoto

**See Also**

→ **107** Add Motion to a Photo

→ **108** Add a Still Image from Another Application

**TIP**

You can specify a display time using only seconds and frames. The largest display time you can specify is **59:29**. If you want to display a photo for more than one minute, you must add the photo to the **Timeline** a second time.

When you add a picture from the **Photos** pane to the **Timeline**, iMovie assigns a default display time of approximately five seconds to each photo. The display time for a photo appears in the **Duration** field when you select a photo either in the **Photos** pane or in the **Timeline** viewer.

If you want the photo to display longer, you can change the display time using the **Duration** slider. If you move the slider to the left, you decrease the amount of time the photo will display. Move the slider to the right to increase the display time. The **Duration** field updates to show the new display time.

### ❶ Select the Photo

Locate the desired photo in the **Timeline** viewer and highlight it. The selected photo displays on the **Monitor**.

### ❷ Change the Duration

Drag the **Duration** slider at the top of the **Photos** pane to set the desired duration for the photo. If you drag the slider to the left, you reduce the amount of time the photo will display. If you drag the slider to the right, you increase the amount of time the clip displays. You can also type a specific amount of time for the clip in the **Duration** field using ss:ff format. Movies display at the rate of 30 frames per second; to have a photo display for four and a half seconds, you would type **4:15**. iMovie interprets this value as 4 seconds and 15 frames.

### ❸ Update the Photo

Click the **Update** button to update the photo within the **Timeline** so that it uses the new display time. It might take a few seconds for iMovie to create the additional frames needed to display the selected photo for the specified amount of time. iMovie creates 30 frames for each second of time you specified.

PART III:   iMovie

## Adjust Display Time of a Photo 106

2 Change the Duration

1 Select the Photo

3 Update the Photo

**CHAPTER 13: Creating Movies** 297

## 107 Add Motion to a Photo

**Before You Begin**

✔ ❶ Transfer Pictures from a Digital Camera

✔ ❷ Import Digital Pictures from Other Sources

✔ 101 About the Timeline Elements

✔ 105 Add Photos from iPhoto

**See Also**

→ 106 Adjust Display Time of a Photo

→ 108 Add a Still Image from Another Application

**KEY TERMS**

*Ken Burns effect*—A method created by film documentary specialist Ken Burns for adding motion to a photograph by panning across the image or by zooming in and out on the image.

*Panning*—A process of moving across an image from one side to another.

**NOTE**

You can also apply a **Ken Burns** effect to a photo that is already on the **Timeline** viewer. To do so, simply click the desired photo on the **Timeline** and apply steps 2 through 5, creating the motion effects. When you have specified the motion, click the **Update** button.

You can create more interest in photos you insert into your movies by adding motion. iMovie provides a tool called the *Ken Burns effect* for creating motion with photos. With the **Ken Burns** effect, you can create the appearance of movement in the photo by *panning* from side to side or by zooming in or out.

When you apply the **Ken Burns** effect, you must specify the start and end position for the photo. For example, if you want to start the photo at its normal size, you should specify a **Zoom** value of **1** for the **Start**. To zoom in on the photo, set the **Finish** position at the desired zoom level.

If you want to add panning to your photo, click the image in the preview window and drag it in the desired direction to create the panning effect. Make sure that you set the **Start** and **Finish** positions.

iMovie automatically generates the frames necessary to join the **Start** and **Finish** frames for your photo. The longer the duration of the photo, the slower the panning or zooming motion will occur for the photo. See 106 **Adjust Display Time of a Photo** for more information on setting the duration of the photo.

### ❶ Select the Photo

Click the desired photo on the **Photos** pane to select it. When you select the photo, it displays in the preview window at the top of the **Photos** pane. You can use the scrollbar on the right side of the **Photos** pane to scroll through the list of available photos.

### ❷ Turn on Motion

Enable the **Ken Burns Effect** check box at the top of the **Photos** pane to enable the motion options for the photo. When you enable this option, iMovie makes the **Start** and **Finish** radio buttons available for specifying the motion.

### ❸ Set the Start Frame

Click the **Start** radio button and specify the settings for the first frame of the photo. For example, to pan the photo, click on the photo in the preview window and drag it to the location where you want it to appear when the effect starts.

## Add Motion to a Photo

**2** Turn on Motion

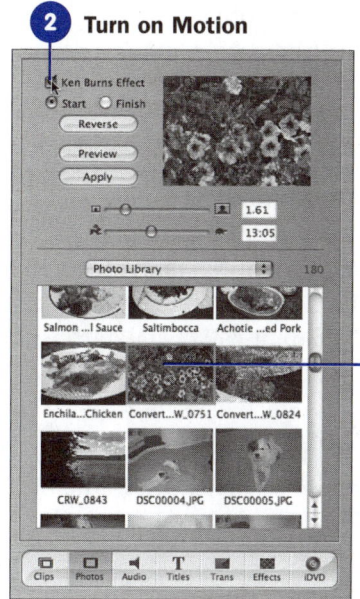

**1** Select the Photo

**3** Set the Start Frame

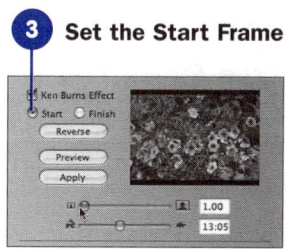

**4** Set the Finish Frame

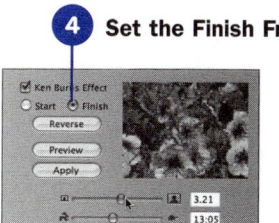

**6** Add the Photo

**5** Select Location for the Photo

**CHAPTER 13:** Creating Movies   299

**Add a Still Image from Another Application**

 **TIPS**

The minimum **Zoom** amount of 1.00 is the complete photo. You can specify a maximum zoom amount of 5.00.

Not all photos zoom well. If you are using a low-resolution photo, it might appear pixelated if you zoom in too closely.

You can also change the zoom of the initial frame by dragging the **Zoom** slider or by typing a value in the **Zoom** field.

### ❹ Set the Finish Frame

Click the **Finish** radio button and specify the settings for the last frame of the photo. You can click the photo in the **Preview** window and drag it to the location where you want it to display in the last frame of the clip. For example, if you want the photo to scroll off the screen, drag the photo out of the **Preview** window so that it is not visible. When iMovie renders the clip, it will create a transition that appears to be scrolling the picture off the screen.

### ❺ Select the Location for the Photo

Drag the playhead in the **Timeline** viewer to the location where you want to insert the photo.

### ❻ Add the Photo

Click the **Apply** button to add the photo to the **Timeline** at the location of the playhead. When you add the photo to the **Timeline**, iMovie renders the photo clip to create the frames to show the motion. See ⓘ02 **About Rendering** for more information about the rendering process.

## ⓘ08 Add a Still Image from Another Application

**Before You Begin**

✔ ⓘ01 About the Timeline Elements
✔ ⓘ05 Add Photos from iPhoto

**See Also**

→ ⓘ11 Insert a Transition Between Video Clips
→ ⓘ13 Add an Effect

You can add graphic images to your movie that are not part of your iMovie or iPhoto photo collections. iMovie can import standard graphic image file types, including **.jpg** and **.tif** images. When you import a graphic image from another graphic application into iMovie, it is added to the **Clips** pane.

iMovie also applies the most recent **Ken Burns Effect** settings to the imported graphic. For example, if the last time you applied the **Ken Burns** effect to a photo you specified a duration of 15 seconds with a zoom effect, those same settings are applied to the imported graphic. If you want, you can set the **Ken Burns Effect** photo motion options before importing the graphic so that the settings are applied as the graphic is imported. See ⓘ07 **Add Motion to a Photo** for more information.

PART III: iMovie

## Add a Still Image from Another Application 108

Select the Import Option

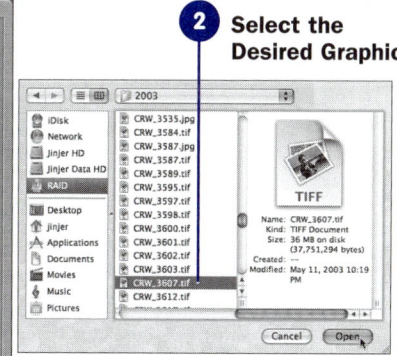
Select the Desired Graphic

Add the Graphic to the Movie

CHAPTER 13: Creating Movies 301

### 108  Add a Still Image from Another Application

After the graphic image has been imported into the **Clips** pane, you can add it to the **Timeline** viewer just as you can a video clip. You can also modify the **Ken Burns Effect** motion settings after the clip has been added to the **Timeline**.

#### ① Select the Import Option

Choose **File**, **Import** to display the **File** dialog box. In the list of available files, iMovie grays out the names of files that cannot be imported. For example, because iMovie cannot open word processing files, a Microsoft Word document with a **.DOC** file extension would appear grayed out. Note that iMovie allows you to import movie and sound files. See **92 Import Video from Other Sources** for more information on importing video files.

#### ② Select the Desired Graphic

Highlight the file you want to import and click **Open**. You can click the **Open** button only after you select a valid file to import. You can browse any available folders on your hard drive or network to find the files you want to open.

As iMovie imports the selected graphic, the graphic is rendered using the current **Ken Burns Effect** motion settings on the **Photos** pane. See **107 Add Motion to a Photo** for more information on motion settings.

#### ③ Add the Graphic to the Movie

Drag the imported photo clip from the **Clips** pane onto the **Timeline** viewer. The selected clip appears grayed out in the **Clips** pane until you release the mouse button. After you release the mouse button, iMovie adds the clip to the movie at the selected location and removes the clip from the **Clips** pane.

### TIP
You can select multiple graphic files to import simultaneously. To select multiple files, hold down the **Shift** key while you click each file you want to import. When you click **Open**, iMovie imports each graphic file individually and places it in the **Clips** pane.

**PART III:** *iMovie*

## 109 Trim Clips in the Timeline

If you are using iMovie 4.0 or later, you can trim a clip after you have placed it on the **Timeline**. This editing approach can be useful if you want to eliminate a few seconds of footage from a clip to make your entire movie shorter.

When you trim a clip in the **Timeline**, you are simply dragging the ends of the clip toward the center of the clip to eliminate any unwanted frames from the video. The nice thing about using this method to trim your clips is that the trimmed video footage remains part of the clip; iMovie just hides the frames you trimmed. You can drag the ends of the clip in and out until you locate the exact spots where you want the clip to start and stop. The clipped frames remain a part of the video clip until you empty the iMovie **Trash**. Therefore, make sure that you have the movie exactly as you want it before emptying the trash.

### 1 Click Edge of Clip

In the **Timeline**, locate the clip you want to trim. Click at the beginning or end of the clip, depending on which "end" of the video you want to trim off.

### 2 Drag Toward Center of Clip

Drag the edge of the clip toward the center of that clip to trim it. As you drag the edge, the current frame of the clip displays in the **Monitor**.

Drag the opposite direction, away from the center of the clip, to restore trimmed frames to the clip. Continue dragging the edge of the clip in and out until you locate the frame where you want the clip to start or stop.

As you trim a clip on the **Timeline**, iMovie moves the remaining clips on the **Timeline** to fill the trimmed space.

**You Should Know**

✔ 101 About the Timeline Elements
✔ 103 Add Clips to the Timeline

**See Also**

→ 96 Split a Clip
→ 97 Crop a Clip

### 💡 TIPS

To restore the clip to its original size, select the clip on the **Timeline** and choose **Advanced, Restore Clip** from the menu bar.

Avoid emptying the iMovie **Trash** until you are sure that you do not want to restore the frames for the clips you have trimmed.

Use these same steps to trim audio clips on the **Timeline**. See 117 **About Audio Tracks and Audio Formats** for more information about audio tracks in iMovie.

## 109  Trim Clips in the Timeline

1 Click Edge of Clip

2 Drag Toward Center of Clip

PART III:   iMovie

## 110  Add Bookmarks to Your Movie

If you are using iMovie 4.0 or later, you can use *bookmarks* in your movie to mark specific frames. When you insert a bookmark, iMovie places a small green diamond marker on the **Timeline** ruler at the selected frame on the timeline. After you have inserted bookmarks in your movie, you can use them to quickly locate specific frames.

You can use bookmarks for any purpose. For example, you might want to insert bookmarks at locations where you might want to trim footage, or where you want to add a transition.

When you insert a bookmark, it actually marks a specific spot *in time* on the movie **Timeline** and not a specific frame. Therefore, if you trim a clip on the **Timeline** or move a clip, the bookmark remains in the same location on the timeline; the bookmark is not associated with a frame and so does not move with the rearranged clips.

### You Should Know
- ✔ **101** About the Timeline Elements
- ✔ **103** Add Clips to the Timeline

### See Also
- → **111** Insert a Transition Between Video Clips
- → **113** Add an Effect
- → **132** Add Chapter Markers

### 1  Position Playhead

Drag the playhead to the location on the **Timeline** where you want to insert a bookmark.

### 2  Insert Bookmark

Choose **Bookmarks, Add Bookmark** to insert a bookmark at the specified location.

### 3  Repeat to Add Additional Bookmarks

Repeat steps 1 and 2 to add additional bookmarks to your movie timeline.

### 4  Jump to a Bookmark

Choose **Bookmarks, Next Bookmark** to jump to the next bookmark in your **Timeline**. Choose **Bookmarks, Previous Bookmark** to view a previous bookmark. When you jump to a bookmark, the playhead jumps to that location and the current frame of the movie (the frame that is located at the bookmark's position) displays on the **Monitor**.

**TIP**

To remove all bookmarks from your movie, choose **Bookmarks, Delete All Bookmarks**. To remove the currently selected bookmark, choose **Bookmarks, Delete Bookmark**.

CHAPTER 13:   Creating Movies

**Add Bookmarks to Your Movie**

**2** Insert Bookmark

**1** Position Playhead

**3** Repeat to Add Additional Bookmarks

**4** Jump to a Bookmark

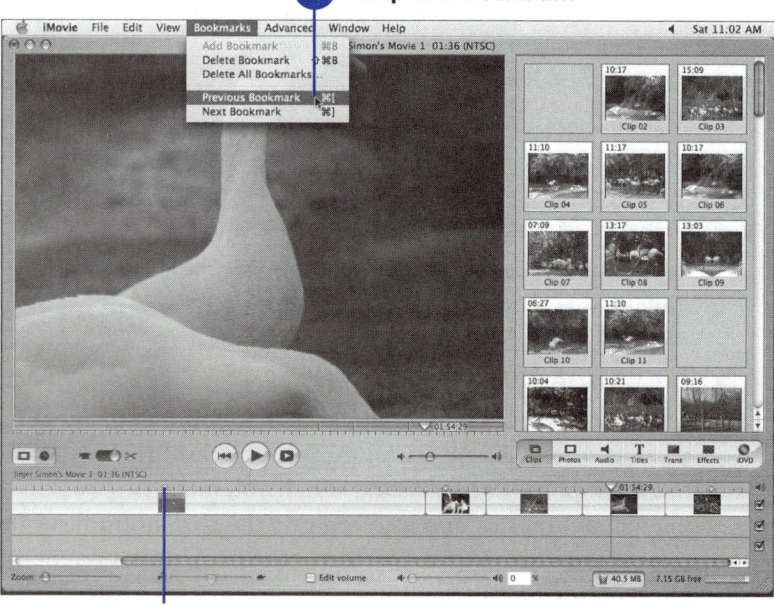

Bookmark Icon

306   PART III:   iMovie

# 14

# Adding Visual Effects to a Movie

## IN THIS CHAPTER:

- **111** Insert a Transition Between Video Clips
- **112** Create a Movie Title
- **113** Add an Effect
- **114** Apply an Effect Over Time
- **115** Modify Applied Transitions
- **116** Add Movie Credits

## 111  Insert a Transition Between Video Clips

Creating an appealing movie involves more than just adding video and photo clips to the **Timeline**. Most movies also include other visual effects, such as transitions between different clips, titling, or other effects such as adding the appearance of rain.

iMovie provides three different panes you can use to add visual effects to your movie. Most movies include a combination of effects from each of the three panes. The **Titles** pane provides different types of titling that can be added on top of a clip or as a separate clip with a black background.

The **Transitions** pane contains different transitions you can use to make the movement from one video clip to the next smoother. The **Effects** pane contains effects you can apply directly to the selected clip on the **Timeline**. For example, if you select the **Sepia Tone** effect, the clip is converted so that it uses only sepia tones instead of a rainbow of colors.

## 111  Insert a Transition Between Video Clips

**Before You Begin**

- ✔ **101** About Timeline Elements
- ✔ **103** Add Clips to the Timeline
- ✔ **105** Add Photos from iPhoto

**See Also**

- → **113** Add an Effect
- → **115** Modify Applied Transitions

### KEY TERM

*Transition*—A special effect available in iMovie to smooth out the change between two separate clips. The transition typically uses frames at the end of the first clip and the beginning of the second clip. The longer the transition, the more clips are used.

You can add *transitions* between each of your clips in a movie. The transition creates a smooth change between two clips. iMovie provides 12 different transitions you can select for your movie. You can customize the length of each transition by adjusting the transition **Speed** slider.

If you choose the **Push** transition, you can also specify the direction for the motion. For example, if you want the new clip to push the existing clip off the screen from the bottom, you must select the up arrow button. The arrow buttons are not used for any of the other default iMovie transitions.

**① Display the Transitions Pane**

Click the **Trans** button to display the **Transitions** pane. On the **Transitions** pane, iMovie displays the last transition you used, along with its settings.

**② Select the Transition**

Click to select the desired transition from the **Transitions** pane.

PART III:   iMovie

## Insert a Transition Between Video Clips

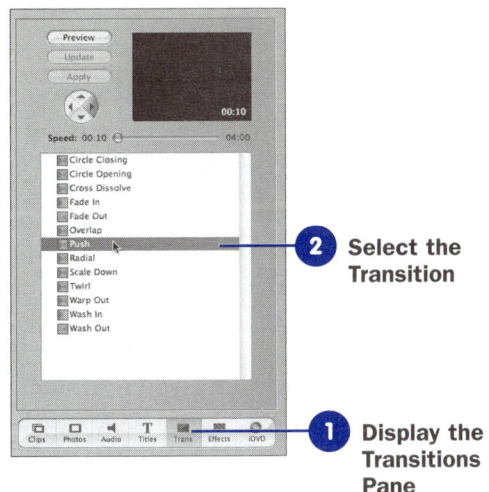

**1** Display the Transitions Pane

**2** Select the Transition

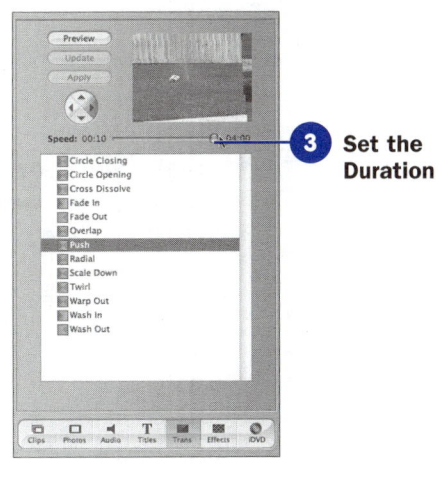

**3** Set the Duration

**4** Add Transition to the Timeline

**5** View the Transition

**CHAPTER 14:** Adding Visual Effects to a Movie

**111** Insert a Transition Between Video Clips

## WEB RESOURCE

Apple lists some of the available third-party transition packages at this Web site.

http://www.apple.com/imovie/visual_effects.html

Although iMovie provides several different transitions, third-party developers have created additional transitions. When you download additional transitions, the installation packages add the transitions to iMovie so that they are available on the **Transitions** pane.

### ③ Set the Duration

Drag the **Speed** slider to specify the amount of time you want the transition to last. You can select a duration time between 10 frames and 4 seconds.

The transition time displays in the bottom-right corner of the preview window in the format ss:ff, where 03:08 is 3 seconds and 8 frames. (Remember, there are 30 frames per second.)

If you select the **Push** transition, click the arrow that corresponds to the direction you want the transition to occur. For example, if you want the new clip to push the old clip off the right edge of the viewing area (that is, the new clip moves into the viewing area from the left edge of the screen, pushing the old clip off the right edge), click the right arrow.

Each time you modify the transition, the transition replays in the preview window. You can also view the transition by clicking the **Preview** button.

## TIP

iMovie uses the clips located at the Playhead as the clips used for previewing the transition. Move the Playhead on the **Timeline** to preview the current transition at a different location.

### ④ Add the Transition to the Timeline

After you have specified the transition settings, drag the transition from the **Transitions** pane to the desired location on the **Timeline**. As you drag the transition, iMovie separates the closest clips to show the location where the transition will be inserted.

When you release the mouse button, iMovie inserts the transition and renders the appropriate frames in the clips on either side of the transition to incorporate the new transition.

PART III: iMovie

Create a Movie Title

### ⑤ View the Transition

After adding the transition to the **Timeline**, drag the **Playhead** in front of the new transition and click the **Play** button. iMovie plays the video with the added transition in the **Monitor**.

If necessary, you can modify the transition. See **115 Modify Applied Transitions** for more information on altering a transition on the **Timeline**.

> **TIP**
> You cannot insert a new clip between a transition and an existing clip on the Timeline. If you want to add a clip at that location, delete the transition and then add the new clip. After the clip is added, you can reinsert the transition to use the new clip.

## 112 Create a Movie Title

You can create text titles that display as part of your movie. You create titles using the **Titles** pane in iMovie. iMovie provides several different titling styles. The title styles vary by the methods used to display the text. For example, if you select the **Centered Title** style, the specified text displays in the center of the clip and then fades back out. Other styles, such as the **Cartwheel** style, animate each letter of the words in the text. Make sure that you pick a style that matches the movie you are creating.

After selecting a style, you specify not only the text to display, but also the font style, size, and attributes (bold, italic, and underline) of the text. For example, the default text color is white, but you can select any other color from the **Color** dialog box. Make sure that the color you select stands out well against the selected clip. For example, if you have video of the kids playing in the snow, you should use a font color other than white so that the title will stand out.

### ① Display the Titles Pane

Click the **Titles** button to display the **Titles** pane. On the **Titles** pane, iMovie displays the last title style you used along with its settings.

### ② Select Title Style

Click to select the desired title style. Drag the **Speed** slider to specify the amount of time you want the title to display on the clip. The actual display time you can select varies based on the title style selected. For example, if you select the **Rolling Credits** style, you can select a display time between 3 and 45 seconds.

**Before You Begin**
- ✔ **101** About the Timeline Elements
- ✔ **103** Add Clips to the Timeline

**See Also**
- → **111** Insert a Transition Between Video Clips
- → **113** Add an Effect
- → **116** Add Movie Credits

> **NOTE**
> You can also place the text on a black background. See **116 Add Movie Credits** for more information on placing text titles on a black background.

**CHAPTER 14:** Adding Visual Effects to a Movie

### 112  Create a Movie Title

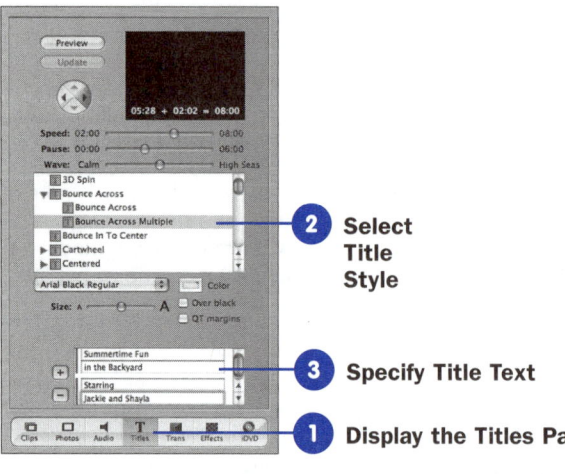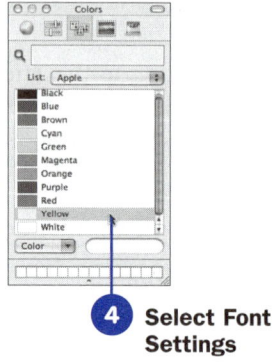

- **2** Select Title Style
- **3** Specify Title Text
- **4** Select Font Settings
- **1** Display the Titles Pane
- **5** Add Title to Clip
- **6** View the Title

**312**  PART III:  iMovie

Create a Movie Title

The display time for the title appears in the bottom-right corner of the preview window in the format ss:ff, where 05:08 is 5 seconds and 8 frames. Remember that there are 30 frames per second.

For some title styles, you also specify the pause time, or the amount of time the text pauses in the center of the screen before scrolling or fading back off. You can specify a pause time of up to six seconds. The **Bounce Across** and **Bounce Across Multiple** title styles also use a **Wave** slider to indicate how wavy the text appears as it scrolls across the screen.

Each time you modify the title, the title replays in the preview window. You can also view the title by clicking the **Preview** button.

### 3 Specify Title Text

Type the text for the title. All title styles use at least two lines of text. Some styles allow you to specify additional lines of text. If you select a title style that allows multiple lines of text, iMovie displays the text two lines at a time. The more text you type on the line, the smaller the text will be when displayed so that it can all fit on the screen.

A couple of title styles, such as the **Music Video** style, allow you to specify a block of text instead of individual lines.

### 4 Select Font Settings

You can specify the font used for the title text by clicking the arrow button next to the **Font** field. A list of available fonts displays for selection. Although you can select from any of the fonts available on your computer, you should avoid fonts with fine lines because these can be hard to read on a television screen.

Drag the **Text Size** slider to change the size of the text for the title. The text gets smaller when you drag the slider to the left and larger when you drag it to the right.

Change the font color by clicking the **Color** button to display the **Colors** dialog box. Select the desired color for the text, keeping in mind the dominant colors in the clip against which the title will display.

**TIP**

Use the arrows to specify the start direction for the selected title style. If arrows are grayed out, text cannot scroll in those directions for the selected title style.

**NOTE**

You can add additional lines of text by clicking the **Plus** button. If you click the **Minus** button, iMovie removes lines. iMovie adds and removes lines in sets of two, but it always retains at least four lines.

**TIPS**

If you are creating a movie for a Web site, click the **QT Margins** button to spread out the text on the screen. Do not use this option if the movie will be viewed on a television screen.

To preview the title text with the appropriate clip, click the clip on the **Timeline** and then click the **Preview** button at the top of the **Titles** pane. The preview displays on the **Monitor**.

**CHAPTER 14:** Adding Visual Effects to a Movie

### 113  Add an Effect

#### 5  Add Title to Clip

After you have created the desired title, drag the title from the **Titles** pane to the left of the desired clip on the **Timeline**. iMovie adds the title and renders a text clip containing the specified title and the portion of the video clip needed to match the specified duration of the title clip. For example, if the total length of the title is 10 seconds, iMovie removes the first 10 seconds from the video clip and combines it with the title to create a new clip.

#### 6  View the Title

After the title clip has been created, it displays on the **Timeline** as a new clip. Drag the **Playhead** to the beginning of the title clip and click the **Play** button to view the clip.

Make sure that the text is visible on top of the video. You want the text to display in a color that provides the most contrast with the video clip. For example, if you have video taken at night, you should use a brighter color such as white or yellow for the text.

If you decide you want to update the settings for the title clip, select the clip and make modifications to the title settings on the **Titles** pane. When you click **Update**, iMovie rerenders the title clip with the new settings. For example, you might decide that the text color does not stand out well enough on your video clip, so you can modify the clip to use a different text color.

> **TIP**
>
> If you decide you no longer want the title text, you can delete it by selecting the title clip on the **Timeline** and pressing the **Delete** key. When you delete the title clip, iMovie maintains the video and places it back in the original video clip. For example, if 10 seconds of the video clip were part of the title clip, those 10 seconds are added back to the original video clip—without the title text.

---

### 113  Add an Effect

**Before You Begin**

✔ **101** About the Timeline Elements
✔ **103** Add Clips to the Timeline

**See Also**

→ **111** Insert a Transition Between Video Clips
→ **114** Apply an Effect Over Time
→ **115** Modify Applied Transitions

You can apply the special effects available in iMovie to change the appearance of a video clip. For example, you might want to create the appearance of an old movie by applying the **Aged Film** effect. iMovie provides 18 different special effects you can apply to your video clips. Each of the effects on the **Effects** pane has settings you can adjust to customize the specific effect. For example, on the **Adjust Colors** effect, you can use the **Lightness** slider to adjust the brightness of the clip.

When you apply an effect to your clip, iMovie applies the effect to the entire clip. You can also have the effect added or removed gradually. See **114 Apply an Effect Over Time** for more information.

### Add an Effect 113

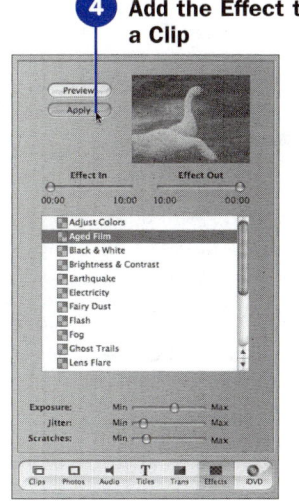

**4** Add the Effect to a Clip

**2** Display the Effects Pane

**3** Select the Effect

**1** Select a Video Clip

**5** View the Effect

**CHAPTER 14:** Adding Visual Effects to a Movie      315

**Add an Effect**

### ① Select a Video Clip

On the **Timeline**, click to select the video clip where you want to apply the effect.

### ② Display the Effects Pane

Click the **Effects** button to display the **Effects** pane. On the **Effects** pane, iMovie displays the last effect you used along with its settings.

 TIP

You can apply the effect to adjacent clips by clicking the first clip and then pressing the ⌘ key while you click the last clip. You cannot apply an effect to a transition.

 **WEB RESOURCE**

Apple lists some of the available third-party packages at this Web site.

http://www.apple.com/imovie/visual_effects.html

Although iMovie provides only several default effects, you can load additional effects that have been created by third-party developers. When you run the installation programs for the effects packages, the new effects are automatically loaded so that they display on the **Effects** pane.

### ③ Select the Effect

Click to select the desired effect from the **Effects** pane. Drag the corresponding sliders under the list of effects to customize the settings for the effect. As you make changes to the settings, the preview window shows the changes.

TIP

You can preview the effect on the selected clip on the **Timeline** in the **Monitor** by clicking the **Preview** button.

### ④ Add the Effect to a Clip

After you have specified the settings for the effect, click the **Apply** button to add the effect to the selected clip on the **Timeline**. iMovie renders the selected video clip to add the effect.

### ⑤ View the Effect

After the effect is rendered, the clip images are updated on the **Timeline** to show the applied effects. Move the **Playhead** in front of the clip and click the **Play** button to preview the clip with the applied effect.

If you are not happy with the effect, you can use the options on the **Effects** pane to modify it. To do so, select the clip on the **Timeline** and make the desired modifications. Click the **Apply** button to update the effect for the clip.

## 114  Apply an Effect Over Time

You can gradually add an effect at the beginning of a clip and/or gradually remove an effect from the end of the clip. This fade-in/out feature allows you to avoid the instant appearance of the effect when the clip starts and the sudden cessation of the effect when the clip ends. Adding the effect over time is often more appealing because the effect gradually appears after the clip starts.

iMovie allows you to specify up to 10 seconds of time to elapse before the effect is totally visible on the clip. You set the fade-in time using the **Effect In** slider. You can also set the amount of time before the end of the clip, when the effect will start to fade out, using the **Effect Out** slider. The time specified with **Effect Out** is measured from the end of the clip.

### ① Select the Video Clip

On the **Timeline**, click to select the video clip where you want to apply the effect.

### ② Select the Effect and Adjust Settings

Click to select the desired effect from the **Effects** pane. Drag the corresponding sliders to customize the settings for the effect as you want it to appear when it is at full intensity. As you make changes to the settings, the preview window shows the changes.

### ③ Set the Start Point

Drag the **Effect In** slider to indicate the amount of time you want to elapse from the start of the clip until the effect is fully visible. You can specify a fade-in time between 0 and 10 seconds. The amount of time specified displays in the bottom-left corner of the preview window in the format ss:ff. For example, 08:10 would be 8 seconds and 10 frames. Remember that there are 30 frames per second in the movies you create in iMovie.

### ④ Set the End Point

Drag the **Effect Out** slider to indicate the amount of time before the end of the clip to fade out the effect. You can specify a fade-out time between 0 and 10 seconds. The amount of time specified displays in the bottom-right corner of the preview window in the format ss:ff.

**Before You Begin**

- ✔ 101 About the Timeline Elements
- ✔ 103 Add Clips to the Timeline
- ✔ 113 Add an Effect

**See Also**

- → 115 Modify Applied Transitions

**TIP**

Make sure that the amount of time you specify for the **Effect In** and **Effect Out** sliders does not exceed the length of the clip. The length of the selected clip displays above the **Timeline**.

**CHAPTER 14:** Adding Visual Effects to a Movie

## 114  Apply an Effect Over Time

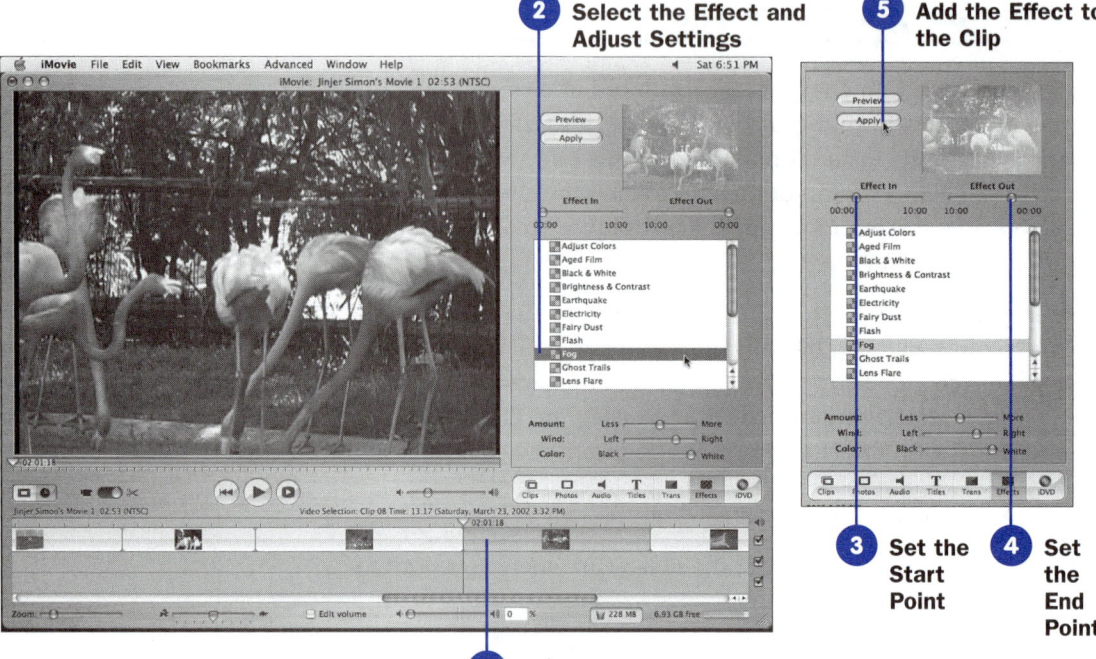

② Select the Effect and Adjust Settings

⑤ Add the Effect to the Clip

③ Set the Start Point

④ Set the End Point

① Select the Video Clip

⑥ View the Effect

PART III: iMovie

## 5 Add the Effect to the Clip

After you have specified the effect settings and the fade-in and fade-out times, click the **Apply** button to add the effect to the selected clip on the **Timeline**. iMovie renders the selected video clip to add the effect.

## 6 View the Effect

After the effect is rendered, the clip images are updated on the **Timeline** to show the applied effect. Move the **Playhead** in front of the clip and click the **Play** button to preview the clip with the applied effect.

When you apply an effect over time, be mindful of the amount of time you want the effect to display at full intensity. Make sure that amount of time is left when you subtract the **Effect In** and **Effect Out** times from the total length of the clip. If you take too long to fade in an effect on a short clip, the clip might appear to suddenly disappear.

If you are not happy with the timing of the effect, you can use the options on the **Effects** pane to modify it. To do so, select the clip on the **Timeline** and make the desired modifications to the **Effect In** and **Effect Out** sliders. Click the **Apply** button to update the effect for the clip.

### TIPS

You can apply multiple effects to the same video clip. To do so, apply the first effect to the selected clip by clicking the **Apply** button. Apply additional effects using the same steps.

When you apply an effect to a clip with a transition, the effect invalidates the transition. iMovie prompts you to rerender the clip as the effect is applied and the transition is being deleted. Click the **OK** button on the dialog box that displays.

## 115 Modify Applied Transitions

After a transition has been created and added to the **Timeline**, you can modify the transition at any time, even after the movie has been saved. To modify a transition, you select the transition from the **Timeline** and then make the appropriate selections on the **Transitions** pane.

You can change not only the settings for the current transition, you can also switch to a different transition. For example, you might decide that the current transition does not properly convey the desired look for your movie, so you switch to a completely different transition.

**Before You Begin**

✔ 101 About the Timeline Elements

✔ 111 Insert a Transition Between Video Clips

✔ 113 Add an Effect

**See Also**

→ 114 Apply an Effect Over Time

**CHAPTER 14:** Adding Visual Effects to a Movie

## 115 Modify Applied Transitions

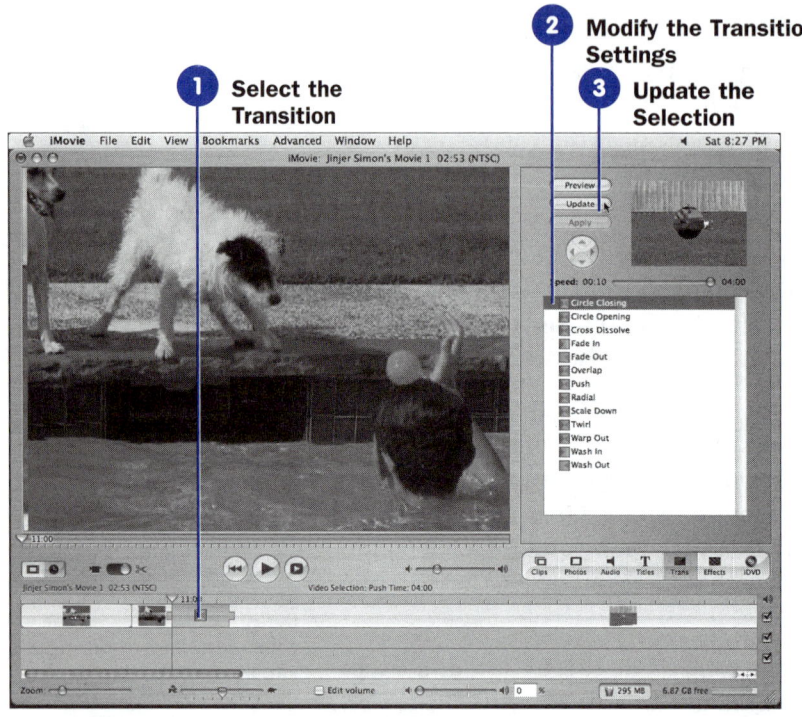

1. Select the Transition
2. Modify the Transition Settings
3. Update the Selection

4. View the Transition

## Add Movie Credits — 116

### 1  Select the Transition

Choose the desired transition on the **Timeline**. iMovie highlights the selected transition in blue and displays the first frame of the transition on the **Monitor**. The current settings for the selected transition display on the **Transitions** pane.

### 2  Modify the Transition Settings

You can make any desired changes to the transition settings on the **Transitions** pane. You can change the speed or direction, and you can even select a different transition. See **111 Insert a Transition Between Video Clips** for more information about adding transitions.

As you make changes, the modifications display in the preview window.

### 3  Update the Selection

Click the **Update** button to update the selected transition on the **Timeline**. When you click the button, iMovie renders the transition.

### 4  View the Transition

After updating the transition on the **Timeline**, drag the **Playhead** in front of the transition and click the **Play** button. iMovie plays the video with the revised transition in the **Monitor**. For example, if you changed from a **Push** transition to a **Circle Closing** transition, you will see the new transition with any modified settings. You should also verify that the **Speed** of the new transition is correct.

**NOTE**

When you make any modifications to a transition on the **Timeline**, iMovie must rerender the entire transition.

**TIP**

When you switch transitions, iMovie maintains the same speed settings. With more dramatic transitions, such as **Circle Closing** or **Push,** you might want to keep the transition longer so that iMovie can show the full effect of the transition.

## 116  Add Movie Credits

You can create text titles that roll up off the screen resembling *movie credits*. To accomplish this effect, you create a separate title clip that you add to the **Timeline** for your movie. When you use this type of titling in iMovie, you can place the movie credit text on a black background. You specify the black background when you click the **Over Black** check box. Although iMovie provides two specific title styles for credits, **Rolling Credits** and **Rolling Centered Credits**, you can actually create movie credit clips using any of the title styles. For example, if you

**Before You Begin**

✔ **101** About the Timeline Elements
✔ **112** Create a Movie Title

**See Also**

→ **128** Preview the Completed Movie in iMovie

CHAPTER 14:  Adding Visual Effects to a Movie

## 116  Add Movie Credits

**KEY TERM**

**Movie credits**—Refers to text typically added to the end of a movie to credit those involved in the production. Text typically scrolls from the bottom to the top of the screen.

want the text to pause in the center of the screen, you can select the **Scroll with Pause** title style.

As with any title, after you select the style you want to use for the movie credits, you specify the text for the credits, the desired font, the font size, and the text color. Remember to select a color that will stand out well on a black background.

You can also place your movie credit text on top of a video clip. See **112 Create a Movie Title** for more information on adding a text title to a clip.

### 1 Select the Credits Style

Click to select the desired style for your movie credits from the **Titles** pane. Although you can select any style, the **Rolling Credits** and **Rolling Centered Credits** are designed specifically to look like typical movie credits. Both of these styles have the text scroll from the bottom of the screen off the top of the screen. You can also select other text styles for your movie credits. For example, you can select the **Gravity** style that has letters appear on the screen and then fall into place. Test the different text styles to find the effect you want for your credits clip.

Drag the **Speed** slider to specify the amount of time you want the credits clip to last. You can create a clip between 3 and 45 seconds in length. The selected display time appears in the bottom-right corner of the preview window. See **112 Create a Movie Title** for more information on creating a title.

### 2 Add the Credits Text

Type the text for the credits title clip. Each set of lines is a separate credit, with the first line being the text on the left and the second line being the text on the right of the two-column credit line. For example, if the first line is *Created By* and the second line is **Jinjer Simon**, the first credit line displays as *Created By…Jinjer Simon* (if you selected the **Rolling Credits** style).

As mentioned, you can use any of the other text styles for your movie credit text. Keep in mind that not all the styles allow you to add additional lines of text. iMovie identifies the multiple-line styles by adding the word "Multiple" to the names. With each of the multiple-line styles, the style displays two lines at a time.

**TIP**

Click the **Plus** button to add additional lines of text for the credits. iMovie adds lines in sets of two.

# Add Movie Credits

**1** Select the Credits Style

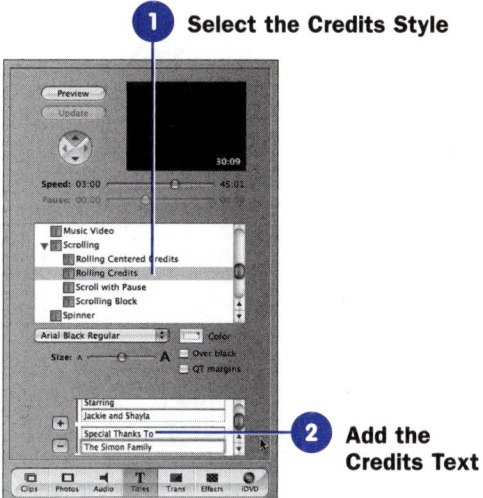

**2** Add the Credits Text

**3** Select Font Settings

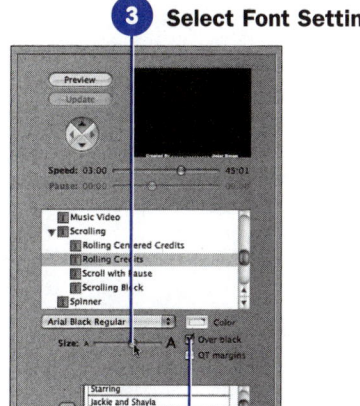

**4** Select Black Background

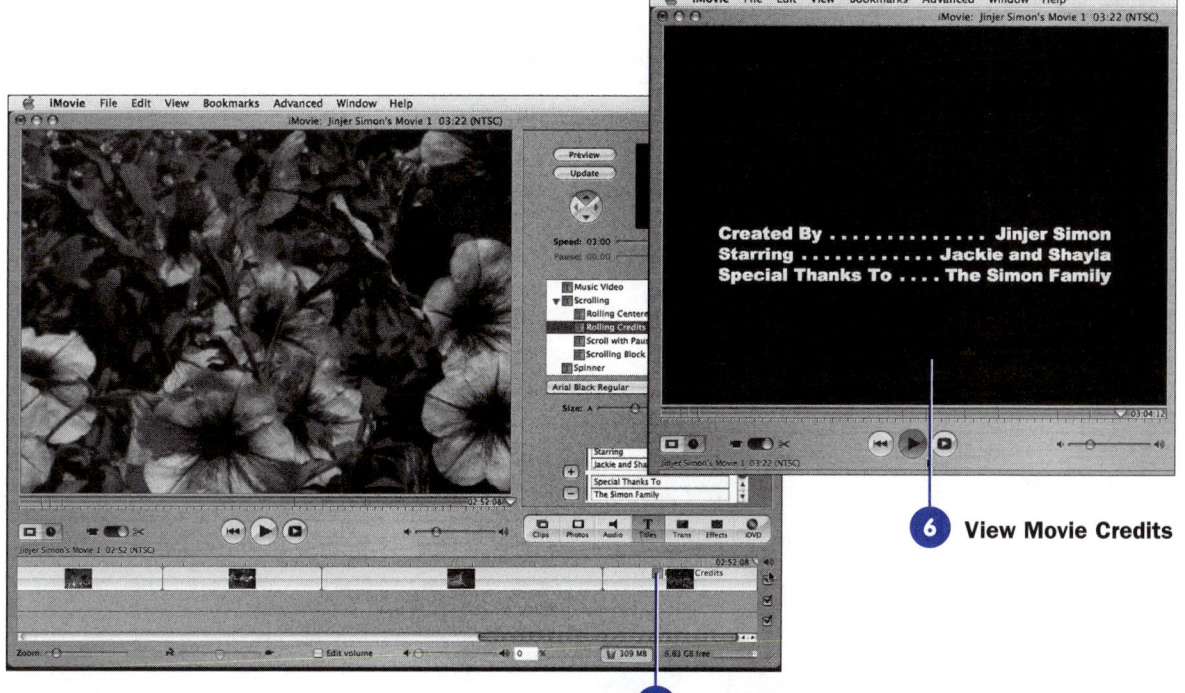

**5** Add Credits Clip to the Movie

**6** View Movie Credits

**CHAPTER 14:** Adding Visual Effects to a Movie

**TIP**

If you are creating a movie for a Web site, enable the **QT Margins** check box to spread out the text on the screen. Do not use this option if the movie will be viewed on a television screen.

**TIP**

If you deselect the **Over Black** check box, you can add movie credits to any video clip. See 112 **Create a Movie Title** for more information on adding text to a clip.

### 3 Select Font Settings

You can specify the font used for the credit text by clicking the arrow button next to the **Font** field. A list of available fonts displays for selection. Although you can select from any of the fonts available on your computer, you should avoid fonts with fine lines because these can be hard to read on a television screen.

Drag the **Text Size** slider to change the size of the text used for the credits. The text gets smaller when you drag the slider to the left and larger when you drag it to the right. You can change the font color by clicking the **Color** button to display the **Colors** dialog box. Select the desired color for the text, keeping in mind the dominant background color against which you plan to display the credits.

### 4 Select Black Background

Enable the **Over Black** check box if you want to create a separate credits clip that you can add to the **Timeline**. If you select either the **Rolling Credits** or the **Rolling Centered Credits** title style, this option is selected automatically.

### 5 Add Credits Clip to the Movie

After you have created the desired title, make sure that the Playhead is located where you want to insert the credit clip on the **Timeline**. Drag the credit from the **Titles** pane to end of the **Timeline**. iMovie adds the clip and renders a text clip containing only the specified title with a black background.

### 6 View Movie Credits

After the movie credits clip has been created, it displays on the **Timeline** as a new clip. Drag the **Playhead** to the beginning of the clip and click the **Play** button to view the clip.

If you decide you want to update the settings for the movie credits clip, select the clip and make modifications to the settings on the **Titles** pane. When you click **Update**, iMovie rerenders the movie credits clip with the new settings. For example, you might decide to modify the text color.

# 15

# Adding Sound to a Movie

## IN THIS CHAPTER:

- **117** About Audio Tracks and Audio Formats
- **118** Incorporate Sound Effects into a Movie
- **119** Add Music from iTunes
- **120** Add Music from a CD
- **121** Create Voiceover Effects
- **122** Extract Audio from Video
- **123** Split an Audio Clip
- **124** Adjust the Volume of a Clip
- **125** Mix Audio Track Levels
- **126** Fade Audio
- **127** Lock Audio Clip to Video Clip

**About Audio Tracks and Audio Formats**

Sound plays an important part in any movie. Although most video you import includes an audio track, you might also want to add additional audio to your movie, such as music or narration. You can record narration for your movie directly into iMovie using a microphone. The type of sound you include in your movie determines the mood of the movie. For example, narration makes the movie feel like a documentary, whereas lively music can create a more fun and relaxed movie experience for your viewers.

**NOTE**

**Although iMovie allows you to add any audio to your movie, you must be mindful of copyrights. Avoid distributing movies containing copyrighted music without first obtaining proper permission.**

Because iMovie is part of iLife, it interfaces directly with iTunes. You can add any of your iTunes songs directly to your movie by selecting them from the **Audio** pane. You can also access audio on a CD from the **Audio** pane.

The **Audio** pane also provides access to several sounds that come with iMovie. For example, if you want to add the sound of a horse running, you can select the **Gallop** sound effect.

Not only can you add audio to your movie, you can modify the audio clips to achieve the effect you want. For example, at a specific point you might want to fade out one audio track and fade in the audio on another track.

To make it easier to work with different audio clips, iMovie provides two separate audio tracks. Audio can also be part of the video track if the video clip contains audio. You can have up to three different audio clips playing simultaneously. You can use the iMovie features to balance the audio on these tracks for professional results.

 **About Audio Tracks and Audio Formats**

**Before You Begin**

✔  About Timeline Elements

✔ 103 Add Clips to the Timeline

You use the audio tracks within iMovie to create the sounds you want for your movie. For example, if you have video clips that show a wedding, you might want to add some romantic music to set the mood. Music that you add to your movie is placed on one of the two audio tracks in the **Timeline**.

When you work with audio in iMovie, keep in mind that not only are there two separate audio tracks, but your video track might also contain audio. So, you must balance the audio between the three tracks.

## About Audio Tracks and Audio Formats

iMovie can open all audio files that you use in iTunes along with all audio formats supported by QuickTime. The most common audio file formats are **MP3**, **WAV**, and **AIFF**. To ensure the highest quality sound for your movie, you should consider using an uncompressed audio file format, if possible. WAV and AIFF formats both provide an uncompressed format for audio files.

You can view the waveforms of your audio tracks by choosing **iMovie**, **Preferences** and then selecting **Show audio track waveforms** on the **Preferences** dialog box. This allows you to see a graphic representation of the audio intensity.

Audio can also be part of other file types, such as MOV and DV video formats. When you import these types of files into iMovie, they become part of the video clip list available on the **Clips** pane. You can separate the audio from the video clips as described in **122 Extract Audio from Video**.

- **Can I use audio from any audio CD?** iMovie allows you to import audio from any audio CD, as long as it is in a format supported by QuickTime (which includes nearly all the common audio file formats). If you can import audio from a particular CD, the available audio tracks will be visible on the **Audio** pane. See **120 Add Music from a CD** for more information. Do not use copyrighted music in a movie you plan to distribute to other people without obtaining proper permissions.

- **What is the best format for audio in a movie?** If possible, select an uncompressed audio format for the highest quality audio. The best formats for uncompressed audio are the WAV and AIFF audio formats.

- **Why is the audio so bad from my digital video?** A lot of factors affect the quality of sound when it's recorded with a digital video recorder: background noise, wind, and distance from the subject. One of the biggest causes of poor audio in a video clip is the quality of the built-in microphone. If the sound is important when you are recording video, you should consider using an *external microphone*. Many digital video cameras provide a jack for attaching an external microphone, which you can place closer to the subject to capture better quality sound. You can also add voiceover effects after recording the video, as explained in **121 Create Voiceover Effects**.

### See Also
→ **118** Incorporate Sound Effects into a Movie
→ **119** Add Music from iTunes
→ **120** Add Music from a CD

### KEY TERMS

*MP3 (Moving Picture Experts Group Audio Layer III)*—A standardized format for compressing audio to produce nearly CD-quality sound.

*WAV (Windows Audio)*—An uncompressed audio format used to create CD-quality audio files in Microsoft Windows. The format was developed jointly by Microsoft and IBM as a sound standard.

*AIFF (Audio Interchange File Format)*—An uncompressed audio file format used by Macintosh computers to create CD-quality audio. AIFF files typically have either an **.AIF** or an **.IEF** file extension.

*External microphone*—A microphone attached to a video camera through a special jack. You can purchase both wired and wireless microphones to capture the audio portion of a video.

**CHAPTER 15:** Adding Sound to a Movie

## 118  Incorporate Sound Effects into a Movie

### Before You Begin
✓ **117** About Audio Tracks and Audio Formats

### See Also
→ **119** Add Music from iTunes
→ **120** Add Music from a CD
→ **121** Create Voiceover Effects

### KEY TERM

**Skywalker Sound Effects**—A collection of sound effects created by Skywalker Sound. The company creates sound effects for a good deal of the blockbuster movies produced today.

You can add different sound effects to your movie using the available sound effects in iMovie. iMovie provides several built-in sound effects. For example, if you want to add the sound of laughter, you can select the **Indoor Laugh** sound effect.

You can find the available sound effects on the **Audio** pane by selecting the **iMovie Sound Effects** option. When you select this option, you will notice that the sound effects are sorted into two different categories: the *Skywalker Sound Effects* and the **Standard Sound Effects**. Each sound effect can be added to your movie by dragging the effect onto the **Timeline**.

#### ❶ Display the Audio Pane

Click the **Audio** button to display the **Audio** pane. iMovie remembers the last sound effect you used and highlights it on the **Audio** pane.

#### ❷ Select the Sound Effects Option

Click the arrow next to the drop-down list at the top of the **Audio** pane to display a list of available audio types. Choose the **iMovie Sound Effects** option to display a list of available sound effects.

### WEB RESOURCE

You can lengthen the list of sound effects available on the **Audio** pane by downloading effects files from this Web site.

http://www.hollywoodedge.com

After you have downloaded any new sound effects, you can load the sound effects in an iTunes playlist that you can access from the **Audio** pane. See **59** Create a Smart Playlist for more information on creating a playlist.

#### ❸ Locate the Desired Effect

Click to select the desired sound effect. You can use the scrollbar on the left to scroll through the list and locate the desired sound.

All the available sound effects are fairly short. The length of each sound effect appears in the **Time** column next to the sound effect **Name** in the format ss:ff. For example, a sound effect with a time of 09:21 will play for 9 seconds and 21 frames.

### TIP

Preview a sound effect before adding it to your movie by clicking the **Play** button located under the list of sound effects.

PART III:   iMovie

**Incorporate Sound Effects into a Movie** 118

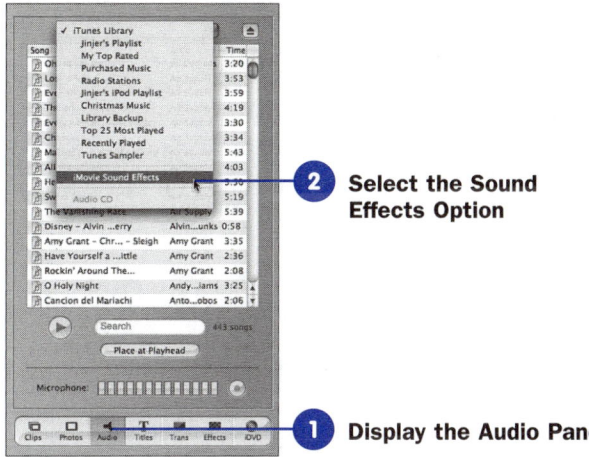

② Select the Sound Effects Option

① Display the Audio Pane

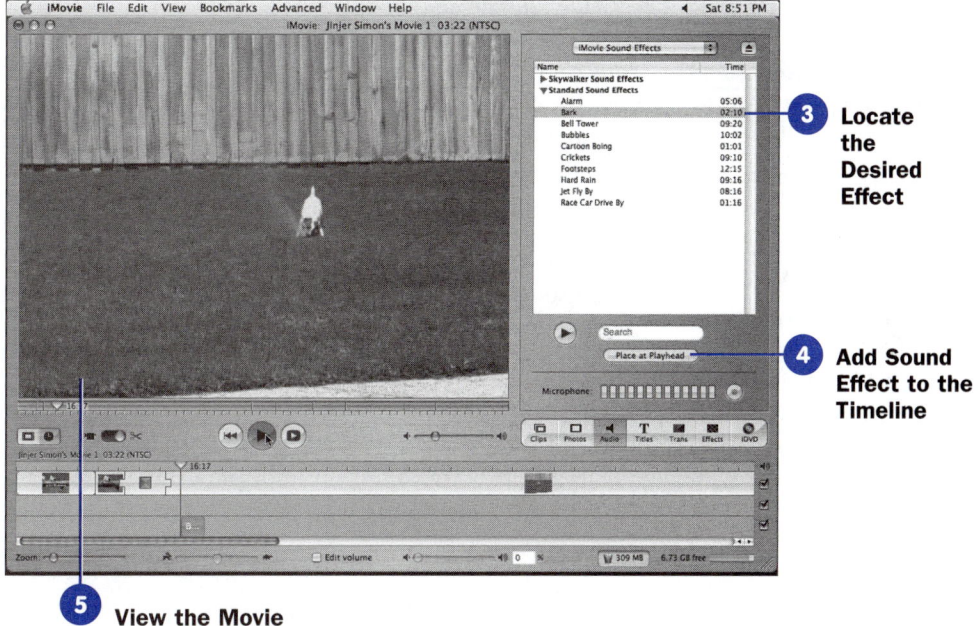

③ Locate the Desired Effect

④ Add Sound Effect to the Timeline

⑤ View the Movie

**CHAPTER 15:** Adding Sound to a Movie

**119  Add Music from iTunes**

**TIPS**

If you want the same sound to last longer, you must add the sound effect again to the **Timeline**. Continue to add the same sound effect until you reach the desired length.

You can reduce the length of a sound effect by splitting or cropping it. See **123 Split an Audio Clip** for information on splitting audio clips.

**4  Add Sound Effect to the Timeline**

Click the **Place at Playhead** button to add the selected sound effect to the movie at the Playhead position. You can also drag the selected sound effect from the **Audio** pane to an audio track on the **Timeline**. You can place the sound at any location on the **Timeline**. As you drag the sound along the **Timeline**, the Playhead moves with the sound.

**5  View the Movie**

After adding the new audio clip, click the **Play** button to view the movie with the new audio.

---

**119  Add Music from iTunes**

**Before You Begin**

✔ **57** About Playlists
✔ **117** About Audio Tracks and Audio Formats

**See Also**

→ **118** Incorporate Sound Effects into a Movie
→ **120** Add Music from a CD
→ **122** Extract Audio from Video
→ **125** Mix Audio Track Levels
→ **126** Fade Audio

**NOTE**

Audio clips that you place in the first audio track are colored purple. Audio clips in the second audio track are colored orange to help you identify the two tracks.

You can add music from your iTunes library to your movie. In iMovie, you can access your entire iTunes library from the **Audio** pane by selecting the **iTunes Library** option. You can also view any of your *playlists*. Playlists are a helpful organizational tool when you have an extensive list of music in your iTunes library.

When you add music from iTunes to your movie, iMovie inserts the entire song or audio clip. If you want only a portion of the song, you must split the clip after it appears on the **Timeline**. See **123 Split an Audio Clip** for more information.

**1  Display the Audio Pane**

Click the **Audio** button to display the **Audio** pane. iMovie remembers the last sound effect you used and highlights it on the **Audio** pane.

**2  Select the Desired Playlist**

Click the arrow button next to the drop-down list at the top of the **Audio** pane to display a list of available audio sources. Choose the desired playlist under the **iTunes Library** option. If you select the main **iTunes Library** option, you will see *every* audio file you have loaded in iTunes.

Add Music from iTunes **119**

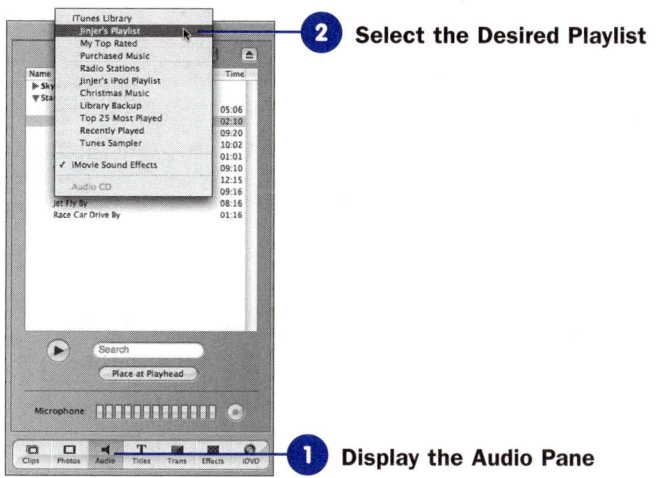

**2** Select the Desired Playlist

**1** Display the Audio Pane

**3** Locate the Desired Music

**4** Add Music to the Timeline

**CHAPTER 15:** Adding Sound to a Movie   331

### 120 Add Music from a CD

**TIP**

Use the **Search** field to locate the desired audio file. Click the desired column (song title, artist name, or length) to search and type the desired text. For example, to find songs by Air Supply, click the **Artist** column and type **Air Supply** in the **Search** field located under the list of songs. Only the songs that match that **Artist** name appear in the list. Delete text from the **Search** field to show the entire list once again.

**③ Locate the Desired Music**

Click to select the desired music in the selected playlist. You can use the scrollbar on the left to scroll through the list of the songs in the playlist. To help you locate the desired music for your video, iMovie provides three columns of information: the song title, the artist name, and the length of the clip.

**④ Add Music to the Timeline**

Move the Playhead to the desired location on the **Timeline** and click the **Place at Playhead** button. You can also click an audio clip and drag it to the desired location on one of the audio tracks in the **Timeline**.

### 120 Add Music from a CD

**Before You Begin**

✔ **117** About Audio Tracks and Audio Formats

**See Also**

→ **118** Incorporate Sound Effects into a Movie

→ **119** Add Music from iTunes

→ **121** Create Voiceover Effects

**NOTE**

Be mindful of copyrights when adding music to your movie. Although you can use music you have purchased within your personal movies, you must obtain permission to sell or distribute a movie containing copyrighted music. This includes a movie that you plan to show in a public setting, such as work or school.

You can add music to a movie from any audio CD. You access the tracks on audio CDs from the **Audio** pane by selecting the CD as the desired audio source.

When you add music from an audio CD, iMovie inserts the entire song at the specified location on the timeline. If you want only a portion of the song in the movie, you must split the audio clip on the **Timeline**. See **123** Split an Audio Clip for more information.

**① Display the Audio Pane**

Click the **Audio** button to display the **Audio** pane. iMovie remembers the last sound effect you used and highlights it on the **Audio** pane.

**② Select the Audio CD**

Click the arrow button next to the drop-down list at the top of the **Audio** pane to display a list of available audio types. Choose the audio CD under the **Audio CD** option. If your CD has been labeled with a name, the CD name displays under **Audio CD**. If there is no name, iMovie displays the text **Audio CD**.

PART III: iMovie

**Add Music from a CD** 120

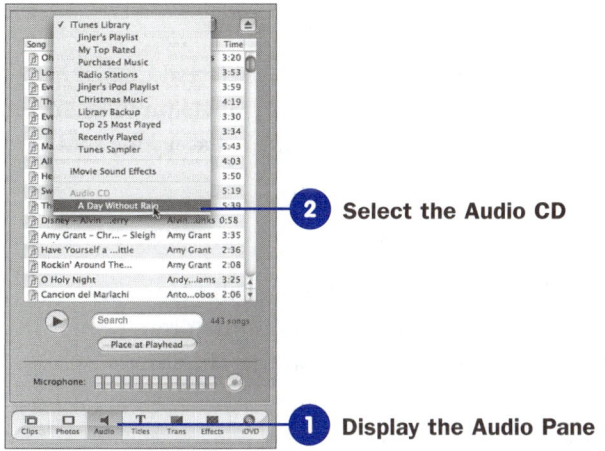

2. Select the Audio CD

1. Display the Audio Pane

3. Locate the Desired Music

4. Add Music to the Timeline

**CHAPTER 15:** Adding Sound to a Movie   333

## 121 Create Voiceover Effects

### TIP

By default, iMovie displays the columns of information about the audio CD in this order: Song, Artist, and Time. If you want to change the column order, click the column heading and drag it to the location you prefer. For example, drag the Artist column left to make it the first column.

### ③ Locate the Desired Music

Click to select the desired music track on the selected CD. To help you locate the desired music for your video, iMovie provides three columns of information: the song name, the artist name, and the length of the song.

### ④ Add Music to the Timeline

Move the playhead to the desired location on the **Timeline** and click the **Place at Playhead** button. You can also drag a song from the **Audio** pane to the desired location on the **Timeline**.

## 121 Create Voiceover Effects

**Before You Begin**

- ✔ 117 About Audio Tracks and Audio Formats
- ✔ 118 Incorporate Sound Effects into a Movie
- ✔ 119 Add Music from iTunes

**See Also**

- → 122 Extract Audio from Video
- → 125 Mix Audio Track Levels
- → 126 Fade Audio

### TIP

Make sure that the red **Record** button is available on the **Audio** pane. If it is grayed out, iMovie did not find a microphone connected to your computer. See your microphone documentation for more information on connecting it to an Apple computer.

You can record your own voiceover narration for a movie directly into iMovie. You record voiceover using the **Microphone** portion of the **Audio** pane.

To record a voiceover, you must have a microphone connected to your computer. The **Record** button is available only if you have a microphone connected. You can use any type of microphone as long as iMovie recognizes it.

### ① Determine Start Location for Voiceover

Drag the Playhead on the **Timeline** to locate the frame where you want to insert the first voiceover clip. As you drag the Playhead on the **Timeline**, the current frame displays on the **Monitor**.

### ② Record Voiceover

Click the red **Record** button and start talking into the microphone to add the voiceover. As you talk, iMovie creates an audio clip on the first audio track. The first voiceover clip you create is named **Voice 01**. Each additional clip is numbered sequentially.

## Create Voiceover Effects 121

**2** Record Voiceover

**1** Determine Start Location for Voiceover

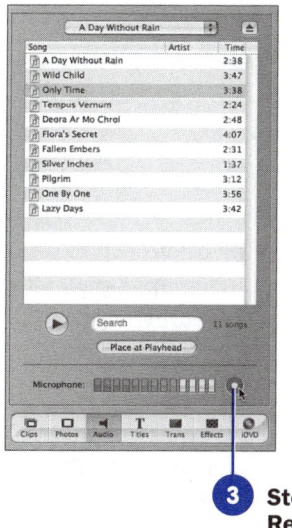

**3** Stop Recording

**4** Preview Audio Clip

**CHAPTER 15:** Adding Sound to a Movie 335

Monitor the sound level of the microphone as you record the voiceover. If your sound level displays in the red bars, the sound is too loud. Try to maintain a sound level within the green and yellow bars.

### ③ Stop Recording

When you have completed the voiceover, click the **Record** button again to stop the recording process. At this point, you have an audio clip you can modify as needed. For example, if you want to remove part of the clip, you can split it as described in **123 Split an Audio Clip** for information on splitting audio clips.

### ④ Preview Audio Clip

After you have created the voiceover, drag the **Playhead** back to the beginning of the audio clip and click the **Play** button. Listen to the audio clip and make sure that it syncs up correctly with the corresponding video clip.

## 122 Extract Audio from Video

**Before You Begin**

✔ **117** About Audio Tracks and Audio Formats

**See Also**

→ **124** Adjust the Volume of a Clip

→ **125** Mix Audio Track Levels

**NOTES**

You can extract audio from any video clip on the **Timeline**. If you want to exact audio from a clip in the **Clips** pane, you must first add it to the **Timeline**. After the audio is extracted, you can remove the video clip from the **Timeline**.

You can separate the audio from any video clip. This is useful when you no longer want to use the audio portion of a video clip, or if you want to use that audio with a different video clip in your movie.

When you extract audio from a video clip, iMovie creates a separate audio clip that contains the corresponding audio for the selected video clip. At that point, you have the option of moving the audio clip to another location in the **Timeline** or removing the audio clip completely. After the audio and video are separated, they become totally separate clips. Therefore, changes made to one clip do not affect the other clip.

### ① Select Video Clip in the Timeline

Click on the **Timeline** to select the video clip that contains the audio you want to extract. When you select a video clip, iMovie displays the selected clip in blue on the **Timeline**.

## Extract Audio from Video    122

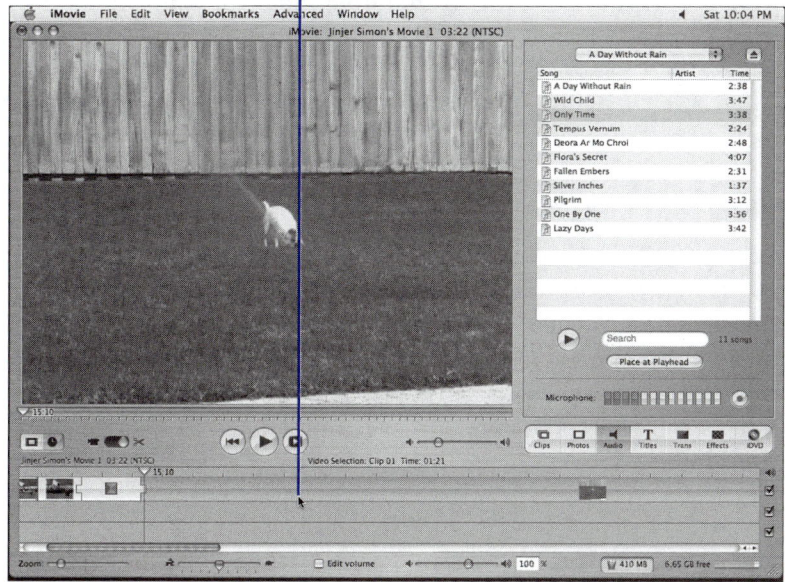

**1** Select Video Clip in the Timeline

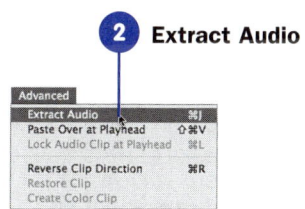

**2** Extract Audio

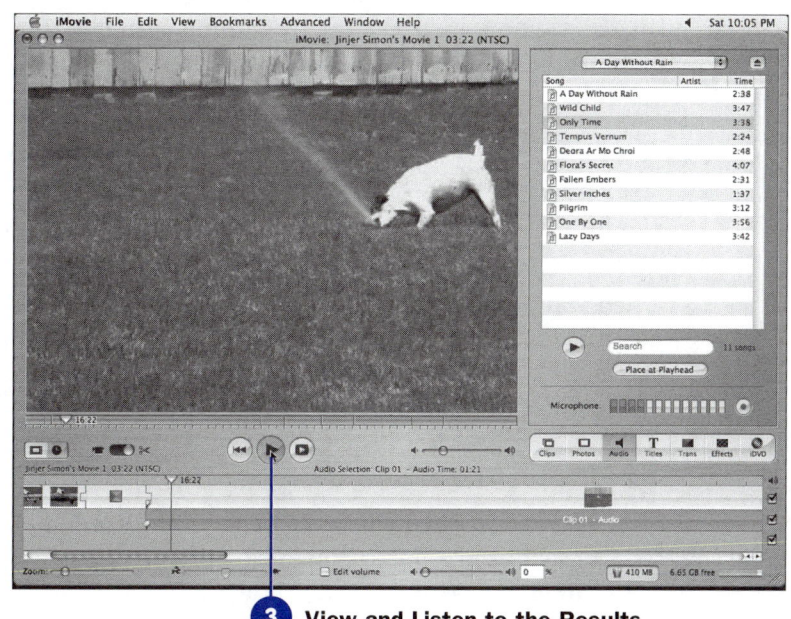

**3** View and Listen to the Results

**CHAPTER 15:** Adding Sound to a Movie    337

## 123 Split an Audio Clip

### 2 Extract Audio

Choose **Advanced, Extract Audio** from the menu bar. iMovie creates a new audio clip containing all the audio from the selected video clip. The new audio clip has the same name as the original video clip. For example, the audio from a video clip labeled **Clip 20** becomes **Clip 20-Audio**.

### 3 View and Listen to the Results

iMovie places the separated audio clip in the first audio track on the **Timeline**. If the audio track contains an audio clip, iMovie simply places the new clip on top of the existing clip. Moving the audio clips from the first audio track before separating the audio from the video clip ensures that you can still access all audio clips. iMovie still plays all audio, but you cannot access any audio clip that is under another audio clip.

**TIP**

If you want to remove the audio clip created from the extraction, select the audio clip in the audio track of the **Timeline** and press **Delete**. To delete the video clip and leave the audio clip, select the video clip in the **Timeline** and press **Delete**.

## 123 Split an Audio Clip

**Before You Begin**

- ✔ 117 About Audio Tracks and Audio Formats
- ✔ 118 Incorporate Sound Effects into a Movie
- ✔ 119 Add Music from iTunes

**See Also**

- → 120 Add Music from a CD
- → 124 Adjust the Volume of a Clip
- → 126 Fade Audio

You can split an audio clip into two or more smaller clips. There are multiple reasons for splitting an audio clip. You might want to split an audio clip so that you can remove a portion of the clip from your movie.

To split an audio clip, you select the desired audio clip on the **Timeline** and then position the Playhead in the location where you want to split the clip. To hear the audio clip, play it and stop the clip when you find the location where you want the split.

When you split an audio clip, iMovie names the new clip with the same name as the original audio clip followed by **/1**. For example, if the original clip is **Track 06**, the new clip is named **Track 06/1**. Subsequent clips made from the original clip are numbered sequentially.

### 1 Select the Audio Clip

Select the desired audio clip on the **Timeline**. If the clip you want to split is not on the **Timeline**, you must first add it to the **Timeline** before you can split it.

PART III:   iMovie

## Split an Audio Clip

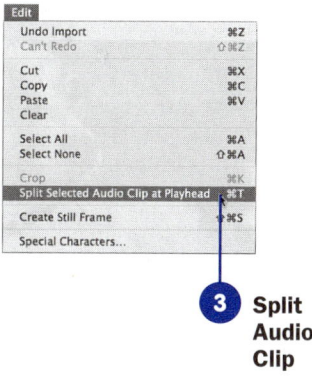

**1** Select the Audio Clip

**2** Identify Split Location

**3** Split Audio Clip

**4** View the Results

**CHAPTER 15:** Adding Sound to a Movie

## 124  Adjust the Volume of a Clip

### ② Identify Split Location

Click the **Play** button to play the movie until you locate the position where you want to split the audio clip. Click the **Play** button again to stop the playhead at the desired split position. As the movie plays, the Playhead moves along the **Timeline**.

If you don't stop the Playhead on the correct frame, you can drag the Playhead along the **Timeline** to locate the desired frame. As you drag the Playhead, the **Monitor** displays the current frame.

### ③ Split Audio Clip

Choose **Edit, Split Selected Audio Clip at Playhead** to split the clip. iMovie splits the audio clip, and both clips remain selected in the **Timeline**.

### ④ View the Results

If you look at the **Timeline**, you will find the two audio clips that were created by the split. After the audio clip is split, you can move the individual clips around on the **Timeline** by dragging them on the **Timeline**. If you want to eliminate an audio clip, click it and then press the **Delete** key. The modifications you make to an audio clip on the **Timeline** do not affect the original audio clip listed on the **Audio** pane.

> **TIP**
>
> You can undo the split by choosing **Edit, Undo Split**.

---

## 124  Adjust the Volume of a Clip

**Before You Begin**
- ✔ 117 About Audio Tracks and Audio Formats
- ✔ 119 Add Music from iTunes
- ✔ 120 Add Music from a CD

**See Also**
- → 121 Create Voiceover Effects
- → 126 Fade Audio

You can adjust the volume of individual audio clips to make them play either louder or softer. If you have a music clip in one audio track and a narration audio clip in another track, you can reduce the volume of the music to make it sound like background music for the narration.

By default, iMovie plays all audio clips at 100% of their original volume levels. You can change the audio level using the **Volume** slider or by typing the desired percentage. Keep in mind that the changes you specify affect only the selected audio clip.

Adjust the Volume of a Clip

① **Select the Audio Clip**

② **Adjust the Clip Volume**

## ① Select the Audio Clip

Click to select the desired audio clip on the **Timeline**. When an audio clip is selected, it displays in a darker color than the other clips on the **Timeline**.

## ② Adjust the Clip Volume

Drag the **Volume** slider to set the volume for the selected clip. As you drag the slider, the volume percentage changes in the volume text box. Alternatively, you can type the volume percentage in the text box if you know the desired percentage. You can specify a value between 0 and 150%.

**TIP**

Any adjustments you make to the audio level affect only the selected clip. If you want to change multiple clips, you must change each clip individually.

**CHAPTER 15:** Adding Sound to a Movie     341

##  Mix Audio Track Levels

**Before You Begin**

✔ 117 About Audio Tracks and Audio Formats

✔ 119 Add Music from iTunes

✔ 121 Create Voiceover Effects

**See Also**

→ 126 Fade Audio

### KEY TERMS

*Mixing*—A process of adjusting the volume levels of individual audio clips that overlap on the Timeline. Mixing can be used to increase or decrease the volume of clips over a period of time.

*Volume level bar*—A horizontal line that displays on an audio clip to indicate the volume level for the clip.

*Volume marker*—A small, round marker that appears when you click the volume level bar. Drag the marker to set the volume level for a specific frame location.

 TIP

If you insert a volume marker in the wrong location, you can remove it by selecting it and pressing Delete.

You can adjust the volume level of an audio clip so that it changes during the clip. For example, you might want one audio clip to be loud at first, but use the *mixing* capabilities of iMovie to have it get quieter when another audio clip starts. By adjusting the volume levels of each audio track, you can specify the dominate or loudest audio track.

To adjust the volume level of an audio clip, you use the *volume level bar* for the corresponding clip. By default, the volume level bar is located in the center of each audio clip, which means that the volume plays at the normal level of the clip. By dragging the *volume marker* up or down, you increase or decrease the volume setting starting at that location, or frame, in the clip. iMovie gradually adjusts the volume to the specified level. You can also use the volume marker to create a fade-in at the beginning of a clip or a fade-out at the end of an audio clip.

You can set multiple volume markers within a single audio clip to change the volume of that clip based on the other audio in the movie. For example, you can have music playing for your movie, but reduce the volume of the music for a voiceover clip that describes the current video clip.

### 1 Display Volume Level Bars

Enable the **Edit Volume** check box under the **Timeline** to display a volume level bar for each audio clip on the **Timeline**. Any video clips on the **Timeline** that contain audio also display a volume level bar. If the volume has not been altered for a clip, the volume level bar displays horizontally across the center of the clip to indicate that the clip volume is at its normal level.

### 2 Insert Volume Marker

In the clip where you want to change the volume, click the location where you want to change the volume. iMovie inserts a volume marker at that location in the clip. The volume change will occur between the volume marker you just placed and the next volume marker or the end of the audio clip.

If the volume marker is not in the right location, drag it along the volume level bar until it is in the desired frame.

Mix Audio Track Levels 125

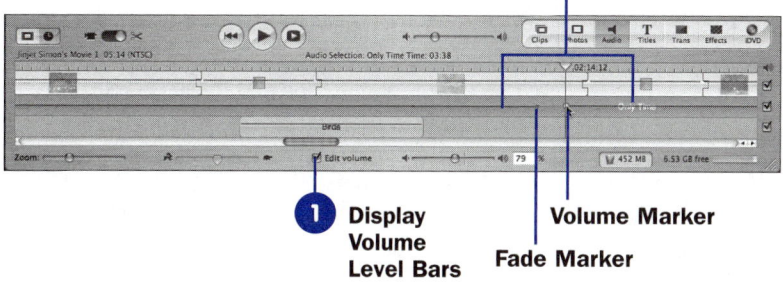

**① Display Volume Level Bars**  
**Volume Level Bars**  
**Volume Marker**  
**Fade Marker**

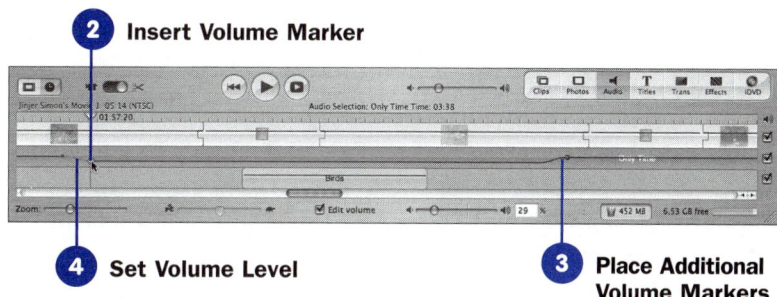

**② Insert Volume Marker**  
**④ Set Volume Level**  
**③ Place Additional Volume Markers**

 **Place Additional Volume Markers**

If desired, you can insert another volume marker within the same clip. To do so, click the location or frame where you want to end the volume adjustment. The volume change will occur between the two volume markers in the clip.

If you want the volume change to be in effect until the clip ends, you do not have to add a second volume marker.

**TIP**

Insert a new volume marker at each position in the audio clip where you want to change the volume level.

**CHAPTER 15: Adding Sound to a Movie** 343

### ④ Set Volume Level

Drag the volume marker up to increase the volume starting at that location; drag it down to decrease the volume. The volume adjustment remains in effect until iMovie encounters another volume marker or until the end of that audio clip.

When you insert a volume marker, iMovie inserts a smaller marker that indicates the location where the volume change starts by fading louder or softer. You can adjust the length of the fading. See **126 Fade Audio** for more information on fading audio.

## 126 Fade Audio

### Before You Begin

✔ **117** About Audio Tracks and Audio Formats

✔ **118** Incorporate Sound Effects into a Movie

✔ **119** Add Music from iTunes

✔ **120** Add Music from a CD

### See Also

→ **124** Adjust the Volume of the Clip

You can fade audio in at the beginning of an audio clip or out at the end of an audio clip to make the sound smoother within your movie. This avoids the abrupt start and stop of a sound as the audio transitions from one clip to the next.

If you have multiple audio clips within your movie, you can place the clips on the two audio tracks and have the new clip fade in as the other clip is fading out. You accomplish this by placing each clip on a separate audio track so that you can have one clip start before the next ends. By overlapping the clips so that one starts before the next ends, you can specify the fades in the areas where the clips overlap.

### ① Insert Audio Clips

Insert the desired audio clips on the **Timeline**. If you want to fade between two clips, place each clip on a separate audio track on the **Timeline**. You can use any of the audio sources available on the **Audio** pane.

# Fade Audio 126

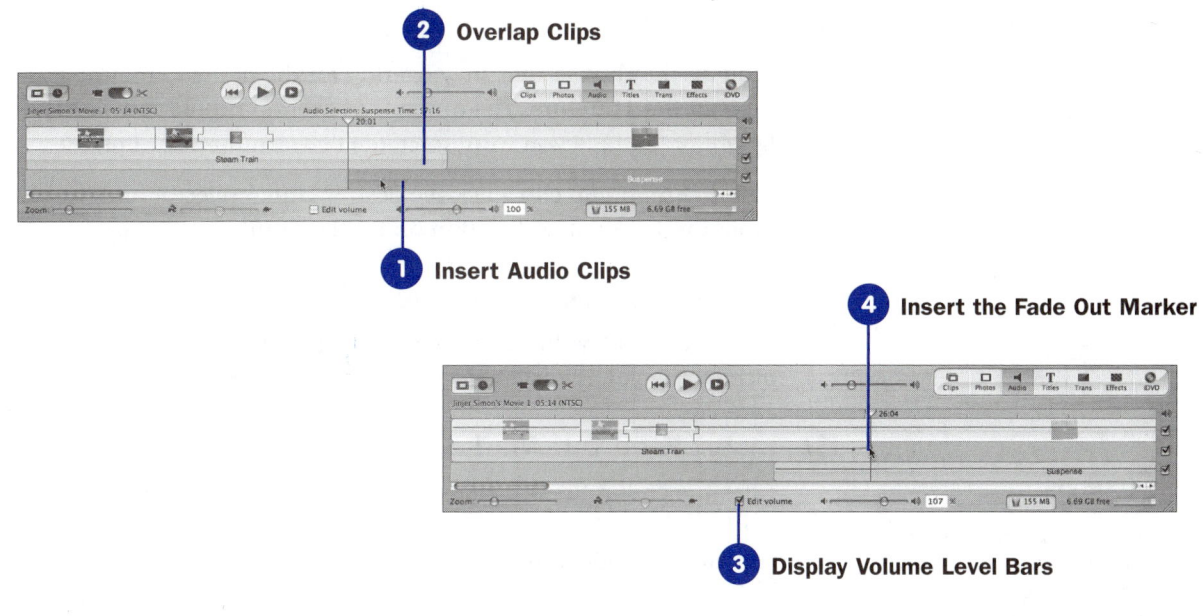

**2** Overlap Clips
**1** Insert Audio Clips
**4** Insert the Fade Out Marker
**3** Display Volume Level Bars

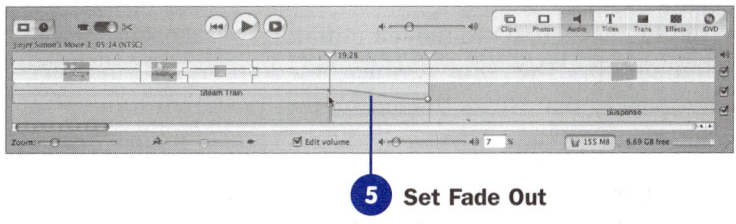

**5** Set Fade Out

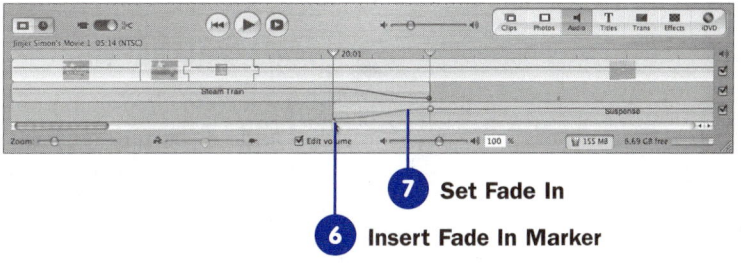

**7** Set Fade In
**6** Insert Fade In Marker

**CHAPTER 15:** Adding Sound to a Movie

## 126  Fade Audio

**② Overlap Clips**

Position the clips so that they overlap for the desired amount of time on the **Timeline**. The amount of overlap should match the length of the fade you want to create between the two clips.

To move an audio clip, click the desired clip to select it and then drag it in the desired direction on the **Timeline**.

**③ Display Volume Level Bars**

Enable the **Edit Volume** check box at the bottom of the screen to display the volume level bar for each audio clip on the **Timeline**.

**④ Insert Fade Out Marker**

Click the end of the first audio clip to insert a volume marker. You want to insert the marker at the end of the first clip so that you can create a fade to that location.

**TIP**

When you insert a volume marker, iMovie inserts a smaller marker, called a *fade marker*, to the right of the volume Marker. You specify the length of a fade based on the distance between the two markers.

**⑤ Set Fade Out**

Drag the smaller marker to the left until it is over the start of the second audio clip. The point at which you drop the fade marker specifies the location where the first audio clip will start to fade out.

Drag the volume marker at the end of the first audio clip to the bottom of the audio clip to indicate that the audio clip should completely fade out by the time the clip ends.

**⑥ Insert Fade In Marker**

In the second clip, click to insert a volume marker where you want the audio to be totally faded in. Typically, you mark the frame that matches the end of the first clip, but you can specify any location.

**⑦ Set Fade In**

Drag the smaller marker next to the volume marker to the left until it lines up with the bottom-left corner of the second clip. This indicates that you want to start fading the audio clip in at the beginning.

PART III:   iMovie

## 127 Lock Audio Clip to Video Clip

If you want to ensure that an audio clip always starts at a specific location in a video clip, you can lock the two clips together. When you lock an audio clip to a video clip, no matter where you move the video clip, the audio clip remains attached to it at that location. Locking clips is especially useful when you have added narration clips to your movie. By locking the video and narration clips together, you ensure that they will always play together.

### ① Specify Start Point

Drag the audio clip to the location on the **Timeline** where you want to lock it to the video clip. You do not have to lock the audio clip to the first frame of the video clip.

iMovie places the Playhead at the beginning of the audio clip and displays the current frame of the video clip on the **Monitor**.

### ② Lock Audio Clip

Choose **Advanced, Lock Audio Clip at Playhead** to lock the audio clip to the video clip at the position of the Playhead.

You can repeat these steps to lock other audio clips within the movie.

If you want to unlock an audio clip, select the audio clip on the **Timeline** and choose **Advanced, Unlock Audio Clip**.

**Before You Begin**

✔ 117 About Audio Tracks and Audio Formats

**See Also**

→ 119 Add Music from iTunes

→ 121 Create Voiceover Effects

→ 122 Extract Audio from Video

**TIP**

When you lock an audio clip, iMovie adds icons that resemble yellow push pins to show that the audio and video clips are locked.

CHAPTER 15: Adding Sound to a Movie

# 127 Lock Audio Clip to Video Clip

**1** Specify Start Point

**2** Lock Audio Clip

348  PART III:  iMovie

# 16

# Sharing a Movie

**IN THIS CHAPTER:**

- **128** Preview the Completed Movie in iMovie
- **129** About Movie Export Formats
- **130** Store the Movie on DV Tape
- **131** Create a QuickTime Movie from iMovie
- **132** Add Chapter Markers
- **133** Create an iDVD File
- **134** Put a Movie on the Web

## 128 Preview the Completed Movie in iMovie

After you create your video, you must decide how you want to share the movie with others. iMovie provides the capability to transfer your movie back to a digital video camera, to create a QuickTime movie, or to create a movie file that can be saved on a DVD using iDVD.

By transferring the movie back to your digital video camera, you can store the video on a digital video tape that can then be easily viewed on a television by connecting the camera to the TV. Because most people have DVD players, creating a DVD of your movie is a great way to share the movie—with the added convenience of adding menus to a DVD. See **137 Add a Movie to the DVD Menu** for more information about creating a custom DVD and adding movies to the menu.

*QuickTime* provides multiple formats you can use to distribute your video for viewing on other computers. If you are creating a video that you want to place on a Web site, you typically create a lower-quality version with a smaller file size, which allows people to download it more quickly.

### KEY TERM

*QuickTime*—A multiplatform software program developed by Apple to handle multimedia files such as video, audio, and animation.

---

## 128 Preview the Completed Movie in iMovie

**Before You Begin**

✓ **95** About the Monitor
✓ **103** Add Clips to the Timeline
✓ **111** Insert a Transition Between Video Clips

**See Also**

→ **130** Store the Movie on DV Tape
→ **131** Create a QuickTime Movie from iMovie
→ **133** Create an iDVD File

### KEY TERM

*Full-screen*—The process of filling the entire computer screen with video. No other menu options or content display on the screen as the video plays.

When you have finished creating your movie in iMovie by adding clips, transitions, and audio, you should preview the entire movie to ensure that you have the desired results before saving it in another format.

To preview a movie, you play the entire movie within iMovie. You can have iMovie display the movie using the *full-screen mode*. This mode shows the movie in its entirety displayed on your entire screen (not just on the Monitor).

### ① Position the Playhead

Drag the playhead to the beginning of the **Timeline**. The playhead should be positioned at 00:00, which is the start of the movie.

Whenever you load iMovie, it automatically loads the last movie you worked on. If the movie you want to preview is not loaded, choose **File**, **Open Project** and select the project that contains the movie you want to preview.

350     PART III:     iMovie

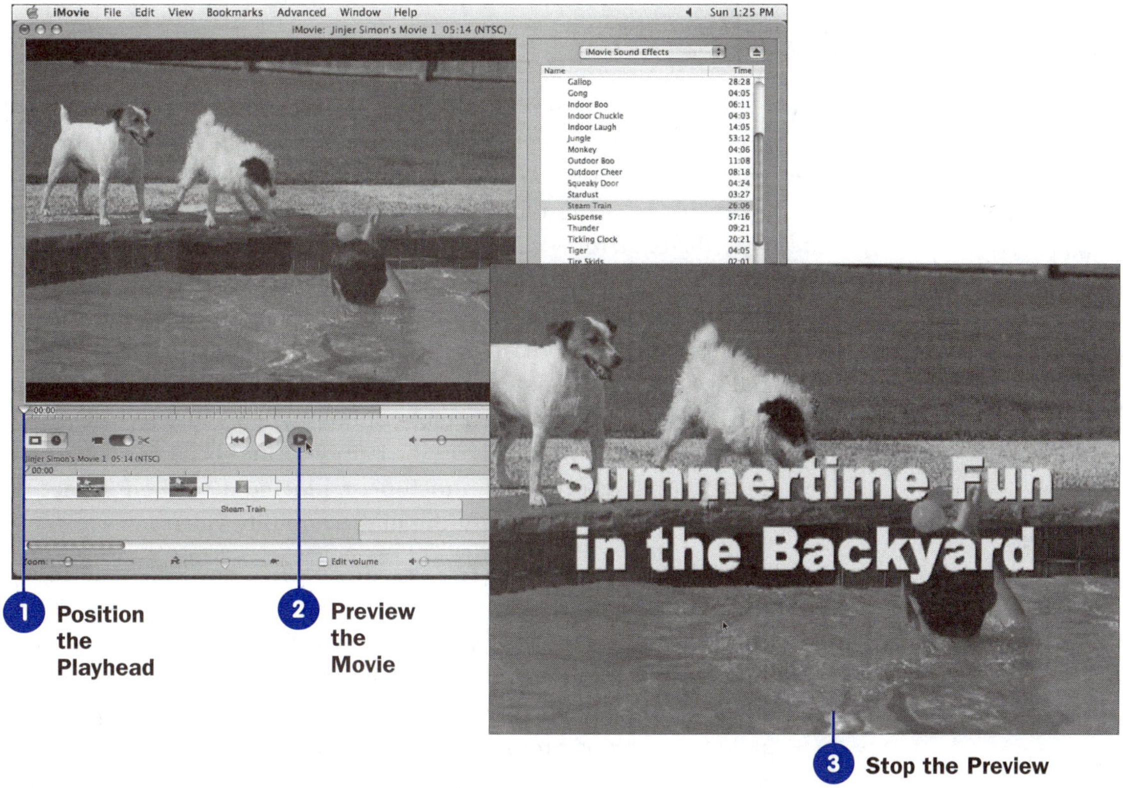

## Preview the Completed Movie in iMovie 128

① Position the Playhead

② Preview the Movie

③ Stop the Preview

### ② Preview the Movie

Click the **Full-Screen** mode button to preview the entire movie in full-screen mode. The movie immediately starts playing from the location of the playhead.

### ③ Stop the Preview

As the movie plays, it fills the entire screen. You can switch back to iMovie by clicking anywhere on the screen with the mouse. When you switch back to iMovie, the last framed played displays in the Monitor.

You can continue viewing the movie in the Monitor by clicking the **Play** button. To continue in full-screen mode, click the **Full-Screen Mode** button.

**TIP**

You can press the **Home** key to position the playhead at the beginning of the movie.

**NOTE**

If a video clip is selected when you click the **Full-Screen** or **Play** buttons, iMovie only plays the selected clip and not the entire movie.

CHAPTER 16: Sharing a Movie     351

## 129 About Movie Export Formats

**Before You Begin**

✔ **95** About the Monitor
✔ **101** About the Timeline Elements

**See Also**

→ **130** Store the Movie on DV Tape
→ **131** Create a QuickTime Movie from iMovie
→ **133** Create an iDVD File

When you export or share a movie from iMovie, you have to select the desired export format. The format you select should be based on the intended purpose of the exported movie. For example, if you want to save the movie back on a tape in the video camera, you can export directly to the camera by selecting the video camera option. iMovie keeps the export process fairly simply by making export locations available from the button bar at the top of the **Share** dialog box. You can email the movie, publish it on your .Mac HomePage, store it on a video tape, put it on a DVD, create a QuickTime file, or place it on a Bluetooth device. You have even more options when you select the QuickTime option: You can specify the actual format based on whether you are sending it as an email attachment, placing it on the Internet, creating a CD-ROM, or just want the highest quality video.

- **How do I select a QuickTime format?** When you select the **To QuickTime** option, iMovie displays a list of formats you can select from depending on your desired purpose for the movie. The different formats are designed to keep the file size as small as possible based on the intended purpose. For most formats, the file size is reduced by reducing the quality of the QuickTime movie. Because you want to avoid emailing an extremely large file, the Email format keeps the QuickTime movie as small as possible.

  iMovie uses built-in settings for customizing the movie export based on your selection. You cannot alter the settings for the selected format. You should select the format that matches your intended purpose for the movie. In other words, if you plan on emailing the movie, select the **Email** format and not the **CD-ROM** format.

- **What if I have multiple uses for the QuickTime Movie?** Ideally, when you export a movie, you select the format that matches the intended use. But if you have different purposes for the movie, you might want to export it multiple times. For example, you can export one version of the movie that you want to email out to certain people. Another version can be used to place on a Web site.

  As you export multiple versions of a movie, make sure that the filename identifies each version. When iMovie creates a QuickTime movie, every filename has a **.mov** extension. You must name the files appropriately so that you can quickly differentiate

- **Can't iDVD work with any QuickTime file?** Yes, the **To iDVD** option creates an initial iDVD project by inserting the movie on the menu. Each time you save your iMovie project, iMovie saves the project files in a format you can import into iDVD. You can add a movie from an iMovie project to your DVD by selecting it from the **Movies** pane. See **137 Add a Movie to the DVD Menu** for more information on adding movies from iMovie to your DVD.

- **What is the difference between a Web and a Web Streaming movie export?** You should consider the size of your movie when deciding whether to export using the **Web** or **Web Streaming** format. When you select the **Web** format, the movie downloads in its entirety to the visitor's machine before it start playing. With the **Web Streaming** format, the movie starts playing before it is completely downloaded. Although the **Web Streaming** method is appealing, especially for large movies, the movie might appear a little choppy if it has to stop and wait for more video to download.

- **Is a .Mac account the only Web site where I can place my movie?** No, you can create a file in QuickTime Web format and place that file on any Web site. If you have a .Mac account, iMovie automatically creates the QuickTime file and places it on your .Mac HomePage for you. See **134 Put a Movie on the Web** for more information on copying a movie to your .Mac HomePage.

- **Am I creating a PAL or NTSC Movie?** You must specify the video format for your iMovie project in the **Preferences** dialog box before you create the movie project. iMovie supports two video formats: *NTSC*, which stands for National Television Standards Committee, and *PAL*, or Phase Alternating Lines. Select the video format used in the country where your movie will be viewed. For example, for movies that will be viewed in the United States, select the default format **NTSC**. If you want to create a movie to send to a friend in England, select the PAL format before creating the movie project.

  To select the format, choose **iMovie, Preferences** to open the **Preferences** dialog box and select the appropriate video format. Select **NTSC** to create NTSC movies for the United States, Canada, Mexico, and Japan. Select **PAL** to create movies for most European countries and Latin America.

### KEY TERMS

***NTSC***—A television/video format standard used in the United States, Canada, Mexico, and Japan. Specifies that the video has 30 frames per second and 525 horizontal scan lines.

***PAL***—A television/video format standard used in most European and Latin American countries. There are 25 frames per second and 625 horizontal scan lines. Movies to be viewed in these countries must be created using the PAL format.

iMovie does not allow you to change the video format after the movie project is created. If you want to switch the format of a movie, you must create a new movie project with the appropriate format.

- **What is Bluetooth?** Bluetooth is a wireless technology that allows you to share files between your computer and other wireless Bluetooth devices, such as cellular phones, computers, personal digital assistants, and so on. If your computer has a Bluetooth controller, you can transfer movies to Bluetooth devices using the **Bluetooth** option in the **Share** dialog box.

## 130 Store the Movie on DV Tape

**Before You Begin**

✔ 128 Preview the Completed Movie in iMovie

**See Also**

→ 131 Create a QuickTime Movie from iMovie

→ 133 Create an iDVD File

**KEY TERM**

*Digital video recording deck*—A digital tape recorder that allows you to record and playback video on digital video tapes, normally MiniDV. This unit is similar to a video cassette recorder (VCR) used to record onto VHS tapes.

After creating a movie, you can store it on a digital video tape. By storing the movie on a digital video tape, you can easily view your movie on a television by connecting the digital video camera to the TV or by using a *digital video recording deck*.

To store your video on a digital video tape, you must connect your digital video camera or recording deck to the computer using the FireWire port. See 90 **About Connecting a Digital Video Camera** for more information on connecting a digital video camera using the FireWire port.

You can have iMovie add a separator to the front and back of the movie by specifying a number of seconds of black to add to the movie. A separator breaks up the video on the tape by leaving the tape blank before the start or after the end of the movie. These separators are useful later; if your tape contains other video, the separators allow you to quickly identify where your movie starts or stops.

### 1 Connect FireWire Cable to the Computer

Connect the FireWire cable to the FireWire port on your computer. On most Apple computers, the FireWire port is located on the back of the computer.

### 2 Connect FireWire Cable to the Camera

Connect the FireWire cable to the FireWire port on your camera. On many digital video cameras, the FireWire port is labeled **DV**. If you have multiple FireWire devices, be aware that they might not all share the same size FireWire cable.

## Store the Movie on DV Tape

**1** Connect FireWire Cable to the Computer

**2** Connect FireWire Cable to the Camera

**4** Select Share Option

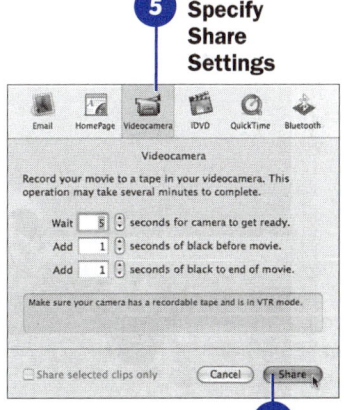

**5** Specify Share Settings

**6** Export Video

**3** Set Camera Mode

CHAPTER 16: Sharing a Movie    355

## 130  Store the Movie on DV Tape

 **TIP**

Make sure that the tape in your video camera is queued to the spot where you want to record the movie. When you export from iMovie, the movie is recorded to the current location on the tape. If there is other video footage, the movie will overwrite that footage.

**③ Set Camera Mode**

Turn the video camera on and put it in playback mode. Digital video cameras typically label this mode **VCR** or **VTR**.

If you are unsure about the appropriate setting for your camera, consult the documentation that came with the video camera.

**④ Select Share Option**

Make sure that the project containing the movie you want to export is open in iMovie and then choose **File**, **Share** to display the **Share** dialog box.

If you don't have the correct project open, you can open the project by choosing **File**, **Open Project** and then selecting the desired project.

**⑤ Specify Share Settings**

From the button bar at the top of the **Share** dialog box, click the **Video Camera** option. The **Share** dialog box options change based on the button you click.

In the **Wait** field, specify the amount of time for iMovie to wait before starting to transfer the movie to the digital video camera. The **Wait** time provides for the camera to actually start recording after the **Record** button is pressed. The default is five seconds, but you can adjust that value as needed. For most video cameras, the default time is adequate, but if your camera seems to start recording more slowly than this, increase the **Wait** time. If the video camera starts up before the specified **Wait** time has elapsed, additional seconds of blank tape are added to the front of the movie.

 **TIP**

Make sure that you specify enough time in the **Wait** field so that the camera has time to start recording. If the export process starts too quickly, the camera might not capture the entire movie.

You can add some blank footage to the beginning and end of the movie using the **Add** fields. The default time is one second, but consider increasing the amount of time to create a longer transition between other videos on the DV tape.

**⑥ Export Video**

Click the **Share** button. iMovie exports the current movie to the DV tape loaded in the camera. As the movie exports, a dialog box displays on the screen indicating the process. The entire movie plays on the **Monitor** as iMovie exports it to the DV tape.

## 131 Create a QuickTime Movie from iMovie

You use the *QuickTime* movie formats to export a movie so that it can be shared with others. The QuickTime format you select is based on your intended method for distributing the movie. For example, if you want to email the movie to another person, you should use the **Email** format option. With this option, iMovie exports the movie in a highly compressed QuickTime version to make it easier to email. With the **Email** format, you will probably not be content with the quality of the movie, but it will transfer much faster through email than any of the other QuickTime formats.

QuickTime is a multimedia program developed by Apple to play video files. Because it runs on different platforms, it has become a standard for distribution of movie files. All QuickTime movie files have the file extension .**mov**.

**Before You Begin**

✔ **128** Preview the Completed Movie in iMovie

**See Also**

→ **130** Store the Movie on DV Tape

→ **133** Create an iDVD File

→ **134** Put a Movie on the Web

### WEB RESOURCE

http://www.apple.com/quicktime/

The QuickTime viewer is a free program available for download from Apple's Web site. You can download the appropriate version for your operating system.

If you want the highest quality version of the movie, select the **Full Quality DV** option. This creates the highest quality QuickTime format movie, but it also creates the largest file.

There are two different formats available for placing movies on the Web, depending upon your intended usage. If you have a large movie, consider the *Web Streaming* option. With this QuickTime format, the movie starts playing before it has been totally downloaded to the visitor's browser. Although play starts more quickly, the movie might have to stop and wait for additional portions to be downloaded to the visitor's computer. If you select the **Web** format option, the movie will typically download in its entirety before it starts playing.

**KEY TERM**

**Web Streaming**—A QuickTime video format that allows a video to start playing before it is entirely downloaded.

**❶ Select the Share Option**

Make sure that the project containing the movie you want to export is open in iMovie and then choose **File**, **Share** to display the **Share** dialog box.

If you don't have the correct project open, you can open another project by choosing **File**, **Open Project** and then selecting the desired project.

CHAPTER 16: Sharing a Movie

## 131  Create a QuickTime Movie from iMovie

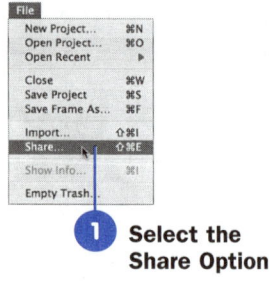
**1** Select the Share Option

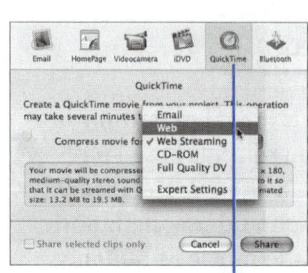
**2** Select QuickTime Format

**3** Specify File Location and Click Save

### ② Select QuickTime Format

Click the **QuickTime** button on the button bar at the top of the **Share** dialog box. The **Share** dialog box options change based upon the button you select.

Choose the desired QuickTime format in the **Compress movie for** drop-down field. Select a format that matches the method in which you intend to distribute the movie. For example, if you want to place the movie on a Web site, select either the **Web** or **Web Streaming** format. iMovie places a check mark next to the selected QuickTime format.

Click the **Share** button to start the export process.

### ③ Specify File Location and Click Save

You must specify the file location and name for the movie file you are creating. By default, iMovie names the QuickTime file to match the current movie file. You can type a different name in the **Save as** field. Do not alter the three-character file extension **MOV** that is added to all QuickTime movie files.

By default, iMovie stores the movie in your **Documents** folder. To change the folder, click the down-arrow button to display a list of folders and select the desired location.

When the **Where** field specifies the correct location, click the **Save** button. As the movie exports, a dialog box displays on the screen indicating the process.

**TIPS**

If you intend to distribute the movie using multiple methods, consider creating separate export files for each method.

If you want import your movie into another video editing package, choose the **Full Quality DV** option.

358    PART III:    iMovie

## 132  Add Chapter Markers

You can create *chapter markers* in your movie that are exported when you create an iDVD movie file. Note that chapter markers work only if you are going to use your movie in iDVD 3 or later. If you open an exported movie in iDVD 2, the chapter markers are ignored.

When you insert a chapter marker, iMovie marks the chapter marker location with a yellow diamond on the **Timeline**. Each chapter marker is listed on the iDVD pane. You can add as many chapter markers as you want to your movie.

### 1  Determine Chapter Marker Location

Make sure that the project containing the movie you want to export is open in iMovie. Drag the Playhead along the **Timeline** until you locate the frame you want to mark. The frame that displays on the Monitor is where iMovie will place the chapter marker.

If you don't have the correct project open, you can open another project by choosing **File**, **Open Project** and then selecting the desired project.

### 2  Add Chapter Marker

Click the **iDVD** button to display the **iDVD Chapter Markers** pane. Click the **Add Chapter** button. iMovie creates a chapter marker for the frame you selected in step 1 and inserts it in the list of markers on the **iDVD Chapter Markers** pane.

### 3  Set Chapter Title

Type the desired name for the chapter in the **Chapter Title** column. The chapter name should reflect the movie location. What you type is the chapter title that will be used by iDVD. See  **Create a Menu from a Movie with Chapter Markers** for more information on working with chapter markers.

### Before You Begin

✔ **128** Preview the Completed Movie in iMovie

### See Also

→ **133** Create an iDVD File

→ **139** Create a Menu from a Movie with Chapter Markers

### KEY TERM

*Chapter marker*—A marker inserted in a movie to indicate a specific point that can be indexed from a menu. Each marker becomes a button in an iDVD 3 menu.

### NOTE

You can remove a chapter marker by clicking the desired marker in the list on the **iDVD Chapter Markers** pane and then clicking the **Remove Chapter** button.

### TIPS

Repeat these steps for each chapter marker you want to create for the movie.

Chapters should reflect the arrangement of the movie. For example, create a new chapter for each day of a vacation video or for each event at a wedding.

**CHAPTER 16:** Sharing a Movie

### 132 Add Chapter Markers

1. Determine Chapter Marker Location

2. Add Chapter Marker

3. Set Chapter Title

### 133 Create an iDVD File

**Before You Begin**

✔ 128 Preview the Completed Movie in iMovie

If you want to place a movie on a DVD, you can transfer that movie directly from iMovie into a new iDVD project. By saving your movie as an iDVD project, you can open the iDVD project in iDVD and quickly create your DVD.

### Create an iDVD File

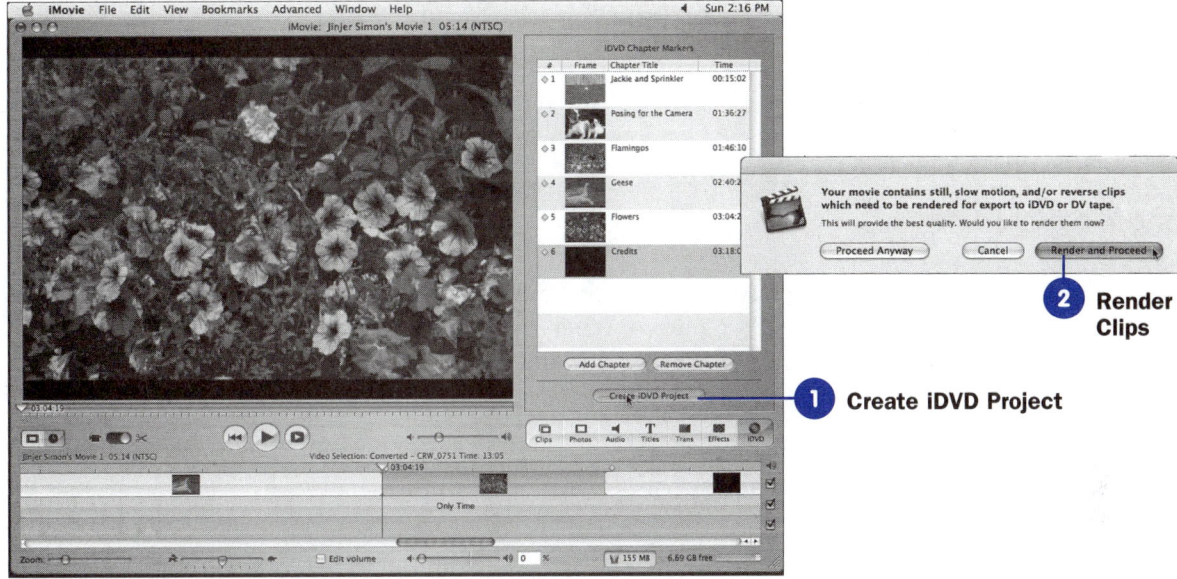

If you transfer to an iDVD project a movie that contains chapter markers, the markers are also exported for the movie—as long as you are using iDVD 3. If you have an earlier version of iDVD, the chapter markers are ignored.

After the movie has been exported, iDVD opens so that you can work with the exported iDVD project.

It is not necessary to export a movie from iDVD if you want to use it in your movie. When iMovie saves a project, the movie files are saved in the correct format for iDVD. You can quickly add movies to your iDVD project using the **Movies** pane. See **137 Add a Movie to the DVD Menu** for more information on adding movies to a DVD from within iDVD.

####  Create iDVD Project

Make sure that the project containing the movie you want to export is open in iMovie. Click the **iDVD** button to display the **iDVD Chapter Markers** pane. Click the **Create iDVD Project** button.

**See Also**

→ **130** Store the Movie on DV Tape
→ **131** Create a QuickTime Movie from iMovie
→ **165** Burn a DVD

**TIP**

If you don't have the correct project open, you can open another project by choosing **File, Open Project** and then selecting the desired project.

**CHAPTER 16:** Sharing a Movie         361

## 134  Put a Movie on the Web

### ② Render Clips

iMovie verifies that all transitions and effects you have in your movie are properly rendered. If portions of the movie must be rendered before the movie can be exported (for example, any edits you've made to the movie that have not been rendered), a dialog box displays. Click **Render and Proceed** to have the effects in the movie re-rendered.

iMovie renders the entire movie again to ensure that it is all properly rendered. When the process is complete, iDVD launches. See **136 Create a Menu from a Movie with Chapter Markers** for more information on working with chapter markers in iDVD.

## 134  Put a Movie on the Web

**You Should Know**

✔ **131** Create a QuickTime Movie from iMovie

**See Also**

→ **39** Publish Photos to View on the Internet

→ **40** Share a Slideshow over the Internet

### 💡 TIP

If you want to place your movie on a different Web site, use the **QuickTime** option on the **Share** dialog box and export the movie as either a **Web** or **Web Streaming** movie. After the movie is exported, you can place it on your Web site. See **131 Create a QuickTime Movie from iMovie** for more information on exporting movies using QuickTime.

You can place your movie on a Web site so that other people can easily view your movie by simply connecting to your site. If you have created a *.Mac account*, Apple provides a personal Web site with storage space called *iDisk*, where you can store movies and photos that you want to share with other people. You create your Web site options using the **HomePage** option on your .Mac account.

After you have set up your .Mac account, you can copy your movie to iDisk by clicking the **HomePage** button on the **Share** dialog box. When you select this option, iMovie connects to your .Mac account and copies your movie to your iDisk storage space.

After iMovie copies your movie to iDisk, you customize the page that will display the movie on your Web site. Using the **HomePage** application from your .Mac account (this application makes it easy to create and modify Web sites without having to know HTML), you can select a theme for the movie page and customize the text that displays on the page. When you have customized your movie page, publish it to your Web site so that other people can access it.

### ① Select the Share Option

Make sure that the movie project containing the movie you want to place on the Web site is open in iMovie. Choose **File**, **Share** to display the **Share** dialog box.

If you don't have the correct project open, open the project by choosing **File, Open Project** and then selecting the desired project.

## ② Select the HomePage Option

Click the **HomePage** button on the button bar at the top of the **Share** dialog box. The **Share** dialog box options change based on the button you click.

By default, iMovie creates a **.MOV** QuickTime file with the same name as the current project. This is the name of the file that will be placed on your .Mac Web site. If you want to give the file a different name, change the name in the **Name of saved movie** field.

Click the **Share** button to copy the movie to your iDisk space on your .Mac account. As the movie is exported to a **.MOV** file and copied to iDisk, a dialog box appears to indicate the progress. If you don't have enough space in your iDisk, iMovie will tell you so and won't be able to upload the movie file. To check how much space you have left in iDisk, check the **.Mac System Preferences**.

## ③ Select Movie Page Theme

After your movie has been copied to iDisk, you are connected to your .Mac account. From the **HomePage** application window that automatically opens, you can customize your movie page before it is copied to your Web site for others to view.

Click to select one of the themes that appears on the screen. The theme you select displays as a backdrop for the Web page that plays your movie.

## ④ Edit Page

After you click to select a theme, the page opens as it will appear on your site. Click the **Edit** button to modify the page by adding your movie and modifying the text on the page.

### TIPS

You can cancel the upload process at any time by clicking the **Cancel** button on the progress dialog box.

If you have Mac OS X Panther, you can view the contents of your iDisk at any time from a **Finder** window by clicking the **iDisk** icon on your desktop.

## 134 Put a Movie on the Web

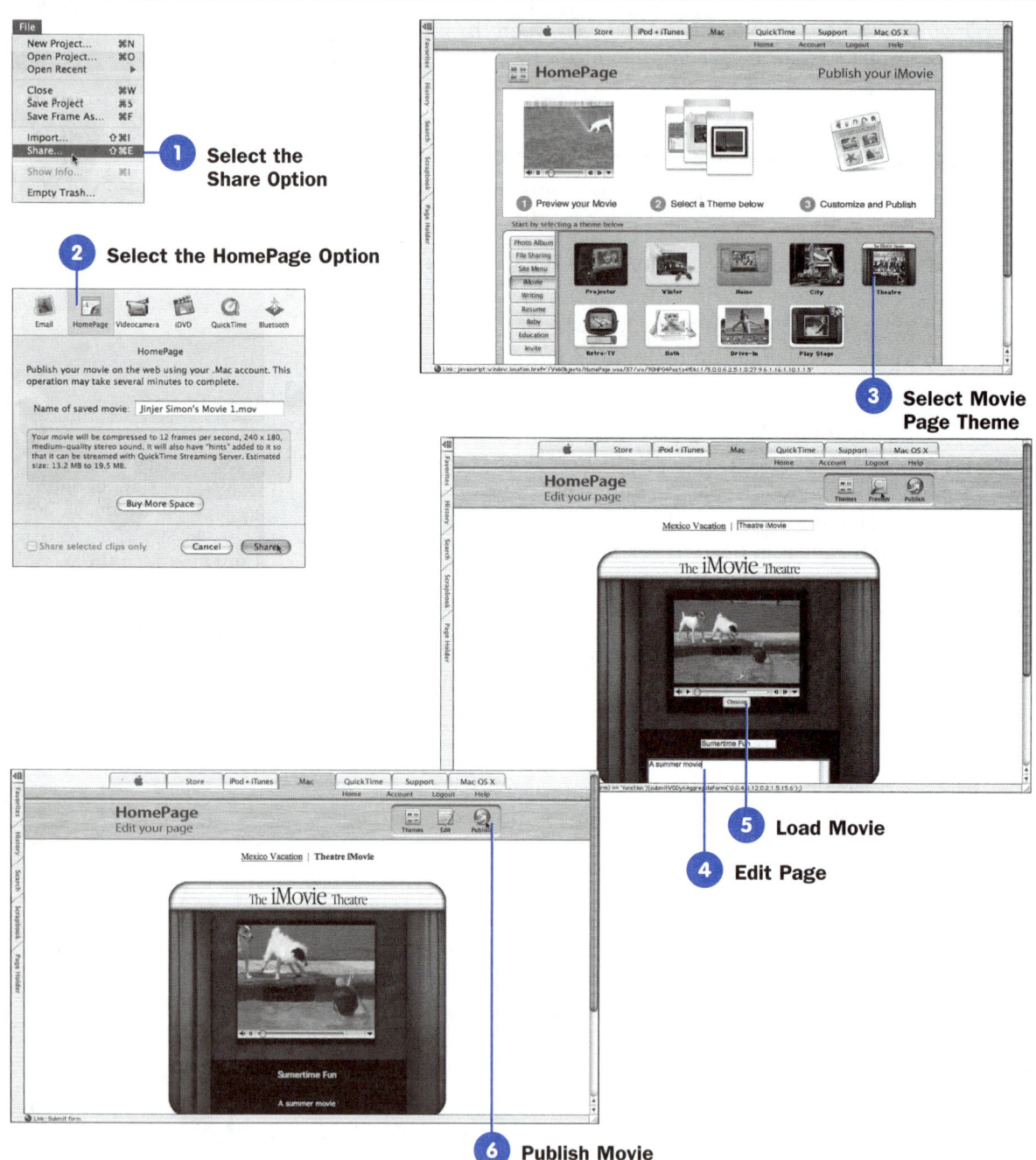

## Put a Movie on the Web

### 5. Load the Movie

If you have more than one movie on your iDisk, click the **Choose** button to select the movie to load on this movie page for your Web site. The **HomePage** application accesses the **Movies** folder on your iDisk and displays all the movies you have copied there. Select the movie you want to place on the Web page and then click the **Choose** button. (If you have uploaded only one movie to your iDisk, that movie is automatically selected and loaded.)

The selected movie displays in the frame on the **HomePage** creation page.

### 6. Publish the Movie

On the **HomePage** creation page, verify that the page is laid out as desired. When you have the page the way you want it to appear on your Web site, click the **Publish** button.

The page is uploaded to your Web site. After the page is published, other people can view the page containing the movie by visiting your site.

**TIP**

You can modify the text in any of the text boxes on the page. You can specify the movie title and a description of the movie by typing text in the appropriate text boxes.

**TIPS**

To preview your Web page before publishing it, click the **Preview** button at the top of the **HomePage** creation page.

The URL for your Web page is **http://homepage.mac.com/<accountname>**, where **<accountname>** is your .Mac member name.

CHAPTER 16: Sharing a Movie

# PART IV

## iDVD

**IN THIS PART**

**CHAPTER 17** Laying Out a DVD — 369

**CHAPTER 18** Customizing the DVD — 387

**CHAPTER 19** Adding a Slideshow to a DVD — 417

**CHAPTER 20** Creating a DVD — 435

# 17

# Laying Out a DVD

**IN THIS CHAPTER:**

- **135** About DVDs
- **136** Select a DVD Theme
- **137** Add a Movie to the DVD Menu
- **138** Use Movie Folders
- **139** Create a Menu from a Movie with Chapter Markers
- **140** About Drop Zones
- **141** Add Images to Drop Zones

## 135 About DVDs

If you have a *SuperDrive*, you can use iDVD to burn DVDs containing your movies and photos. iDVD can take movies created in iMovie, photos and slideshows from iPhoto, and music from iTunes and create a professional-looking DVD with menus and music similar to commercial DVDs.

> **KEY TERM**
>
> *Menu*—A page of clickable buttons that provides access to the contents of the DVD. Each menu can contain up to six buttons.

Before you can burn the DVD, you must lay out its contents in the iDVD application. iDVD comes with several default themes you can use to lay out your DVD. You lay out the contents of your DVD by adding buttons to the *menus* that provide the ability to select the contents of the DVD. Each DVD you create is saved as a separate project. This allows you to return and reload a previous DVD project at any time.

Because you can place a maximum of only six item buttons on each menu, you can create nested menus. When you click the item button in a top menu, a submenu opens from which you can select another item, which can lead to another submenu or to the item you want to view.

When you export movies from iMovie, you have the option of creating chapter markers for your movie. If the movie has chapter markers, iDVD uses those markers to create a scene menu for the DVD.

Not only can you add buttons to the DVD menu, but some themes provided with iDVD allow you to add photos or even a movie to the DVD in an area referred to as the *drop zone*. Movies and photos in the drop zone display when the DVD menu is viewed, but they cannot be selected.

## 135 About DVDs

**See Also**

→ 136 Select a DVD Theme
→ 137 Add a Movie to the DVD Menu
→ 138 Use Movie Folders
→ 139 Create a from a Movie with Chapter Markers
→ 145 Create a Custom Motion Menu

iDVD is designed to place movies and photos on a DVD that can be viewed by other people. DVDs have become the most popular media for the distribution of commercial movies, and they work equally well for the distribution of your even more precious personal movies.

To create a DVD, you must have access to a DVD drive capable of burning DVDs, commonly referred to as a *DVD burner*. Apple provides the *SuperDrive* option available for most computers. If your computer has a SuperDrive, you already have a DVD burner. If you do not have a DVD burner in your computer, you can have one installed, or you can purchase an external burner that you can attach to your computer.

## About DVDs

You must make sure that you have the proper DVD medium for working with iDVD. Apple states that you can use **DVD-R** discs with the Apple SuperDrive, but the drive is also capable of burning a **DVD-RW** disc. These RW discs are handy for making sure that you like the results of the movie before permanently burning the final version on a DVD-R. To use a DVD-RW disc to store a project in iDVD, you must outsmart iDVD during the burning process. See **164 Burn a Test Version on a DVD-RW** for more information on burning a movie on a DVD-RW in iDVD. You might not be able to play your DVD-RW disc in your standalone DVD player. Many DVD players do not support DVD-RW; you can, however, view the DVD-RW on the computer where you burn the disc.

When you create a DVD, iDVD uses **MPEG-2** to compress the video placed on the disc. MPEG-2 is an industry standard format for all video placed on DVDs. Therefore, all DVD players are capable of reading this format. The DVD-Rs and DVD-RWs that you use can hold 4.7 gigabytes of data, which typically translates to between 90 and 120 minutes of video.

- **Why are commercial DVDs longer than what I can create in iDVD?** iDVD can create a DVD with a maximum length of 90 minutes. Some commercial DVDs hold movies that are longer than two hours. Commercial DVD manufacturers can create two-layer DVDs, which can hold nearly twice as much as the standard DVD-R and DVD-RW discs on the market. This means that a two-layer DVD can hold about 7.95 gigabytes of data.

  Unfortunately, the process of creating a two-layer DVD is not readily available for the consumer. Therefore, you are limited to creating single-side DVDs containing your movies when working with iDVD.

- **What about other DVD formats available on the market?** If you read the literature from Apple, you will learn that your SuperDrive supports only DVD-R discs. However, as shown in **164 Burn a Test Version on a DVD-RW**, you can also burn to DVD-RW discs. In addition to DVD-R and DVD-RW discs, DVD+R and DVD+RW discs are available. However, do not purchase DVD+R and DVD+RW discs for your SuperDrive because they require a format your SuperDrive does not support.

  Some newer SuperDrives do support DVD+R and DVD+RW discs, as long as you have Mac OS X Panther (also known as Mac OS 10.3)

### KEY TERMS

**SuperDrive**—A drive included with many current Apple computers that can burn both DVDs and CDs.

**DVD-R**—A DVD to which you can copy files once. The disc cannot be erased and no more files can be added to it after the initial burn.

**DVD-RW**—A DVD that is rewritable. You can erase the disc at any time or add additional files, if the disc is not full. DVD-RW discs do not play in many standalone DVD players; they are most commonly used in computers.

**MPEG-2 (Motion Picture Experts Group-Version 2)**—The compression format used to place video on a DVD for higher quality video. QuickTime movies are exported from iDVD in MPEG-2 video format.

## 135 About DVDs

loaded on your computer. Refer to the documentation for your computer to determine whether your SuperDrive supports these disc formats.

- **Why can't I watch the DVD on my personal DVD player?** Not all DVD players, especially older models, can read a DVD-R created from your computer. If this happens, the only remedy is to purchase a DVD player with that capability. Fortunately, nearly 85% of the DVD players currently being manufactured can read DVD-R discs, so the odds are pretty good that yours will. The problem is typically found in older versions of DVD players that were manufactured before the availability of DVD burners and DVD-R discs.

- **How do I select a personal DVD player?** If you are going to purchase a new DVD player to watch the DVDs you create from your computer, make sure that the player is capable of reading DVD-R discs. To make the player even more versatile, look for a drive that can read DVD-RW, CD-R, and CD-RW discs so that you can play not only DVDs, but also music CDs.

### WEB RESOURCE

Apple's compatibility site lists DVD players by make and model and whether they can play DVD-R 4.7 gigabyte General Use media discs.

http://www.apple.com/dvd/compatibility/

- **Can I create DVDs that can play in other countries?** Yes, but you must make sure that your movies are saved using the correct video format in iMovie. The default video format for movies created in iMovie is NTSC, which stands for National Television Standards Committee. NTSC was developed in the United States in the 1940s as the method of displaying video on a television. This format specifies 30 frames per second and 525 horizontal scan lines. All televisions sold in the United States use NTSC. NTSC is also used in Mexico, Canada, and Japan.

If you are sending your DVD to most European and Latin American countries, you need to create movies with the PAL format, Phase Alternating Lines. This format has 25 frames per second and 625 horizontal scan lines.

A third format, known as SECAM, is used in France, Poland, Russia, and other Eastern European countries. iMovie does not support this format.

You must set these video formats in iMovie before you create a new movie project. The setting is specified on the **Preferences** dialog box by choosing **iMovie, Preferences** and then selecting **NTSC** to create NTSC movie projects or **PAL** to create PAL movie projects.

Because iDVD is simply creating the DVD, it does not matter which format your movies are in. You can create DVDs containing movies with either PAL or NTSC format—although you shouldn't place movies in both formats on the same DVD.

**NOTE**

You must specify the NTSC or PAL video format before creating your movie project. The selected video format remains in effect for all future movie projects until you change the setting in the **Preferences** dialog box.

## 136 Select a DVD Theme

When you use iDVD to create the layout for your DVD, you can select any of the available themes to design your DVD menu. When you first load iDVD, the first theme in the list is selected, but you can change to any of the available themes. You select the desired theme from the **Customize** drawer. After you have created a DVD, iDVD always loads the last project settings.

After you have selected a theme, you can customize it more by changing the background, menu title, button text, button images, and even by adding custom buttons.

Most of the themes provided by iDVD have a motion option that animates the theme on the screen. You can turn the motion off and on using the **Motion** button. If the motion is turned off, you won't see the animation or video shots or hear the music associated with the theme. You will still, of course, be able to view and hear the movie on the DVD.

**Before You Begin**

✔ 135 About DVDs

**See Also**

→ 137 Add a Movie to the DVD Menu
→ 138 Use Movie Folders
→ 142 Customize the Image or Movie in the Drop Zone
→ 144 Create a Custom Background
→ 146 Change Menu Title
→ 147 Change Text of Buttons/Titles
→ 149 Change Image Displayed on the Button

### 1 Open the Customize Drawer

Click the **Customize** button in the bottom-left corner of the iDVD window to display the **Customize** drawer.

**136** Select a DVD Theme

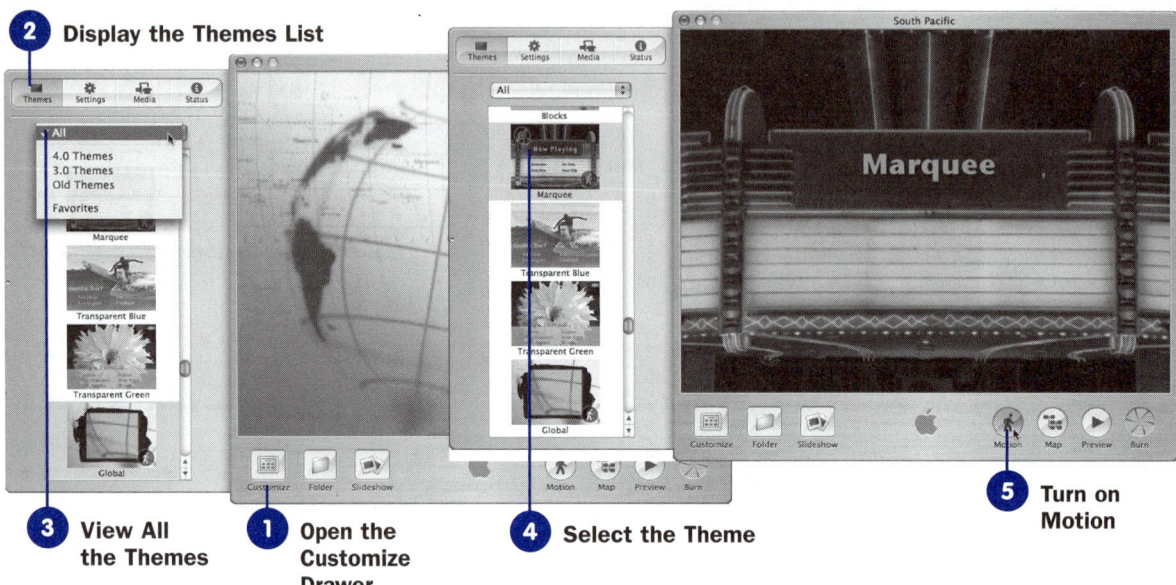

- ② Display the Themes List
- ③ View All the Themes
- ① Open the Customize Drawer
- ④ Select the Theme
- ⑤ Turn on Motion

 **TIP**

iDVD launches when you click the **iDVD** option on the Mac OS X Dock. You can also launch iDVD from the Finder. When iDVD launches, it opens the last DVD project you worked on. To load a different project, choose **File, Open Project** and select the desired iDVD project. To create a new DVD project, choose **File, New Project**. In the dialog box that appears, type the name of the new project and click the **Create** button.

The **Customize** drawer displays on the left side of the window. It contains options for customizing the layout of the DVD menu. The buttons across the top allow you to specify the type of customizations you want to make. From the **Customize** drawer you not only select the desired theme, you can also adjust the settings for the theme, select different audio, and select the photos and movies you want on the DVD. See **137** **Add a Movie to the DVD Menu** for information on adding movies. See **153** **Change the Audio that Plays for the DVD Menu** for information on customizing the audio for the selected theme. You add photos, music, and movies using the *Media pane* that allows you to view media files available in iPhoto, iTunes, and iMovie.

② **Display the Themes List**

If it's not selected already, click the **Themes** button at the top of the **Customize** drawer to display the available themes for your DVD. iDVD automatically selects the first theme in the list as the theme for your DVD.

PART IV: iDVD

## ③ View All the Themes

Click the arrow button next to the drop-down list at the top of the list of themes and select the **All** option to view all the available themes.

If you have previously saved custom themes, you can select the **Favorites** option from this drop-down list to view only those themes. See **154** **Save a Custom Theme** for more information on saving a custom theme in iDVD.

## ④ Select the Theme

Click to select the theme you want to apply to your DVD. The selected theme displays in the iDVD window. iDVD separates the available themes into two different categories: **New Themes** and **Old Themes**. The **New Themes** option displays all the themes added to the current version of iDVD. The **Old Themes** option displays only the themes available in previous versions of iDVD.

## ⑤ Turn on Motion

If it's not selected already, click the **Motion** button to view any motion that is part of the selected theme. In iDVD, "motion" includes the audio portion of the theme.

> **KEY TERM**
>
> **Media pane**—An option available on the **Customize** drawer that allows you to import files directly from iTunes, iMovie, and iPhoto. Click the **Media** button to view the **Media** pane where you can select media from iTunes, iMovie, and iPhoto.

> **TIP**
>
> The **Motion** button is selected by default when you first load iDVD. If you want to temporarily turn off the motion and sound while working on the DVD menu, click the **Motion** button to deselect this option. The **Motion** button is selected when it has a green background.

## 137 Add a Movie to the DVD Menu

To add content to the DVD, you must add the movies you want to place on the DVD to the DVD menu. The best method for adding movies to your DVD menu is to use the **iMovie** browser that displays on the **Customize** drawer. The **iMovie** browser displays all the movies with a .MOV extension contained in your **Movies** folder on your computer. The list includes not only movies created with iMovie, but also QuickTime movies created with other programs, such as Apple Final Cut Pro and Final Cut Pro Express.

When you add a movie to your DVD menu, iDVD creates a separate button for that movie. The appearance of the button is based on the default settings of the selected theme.

**Before You Begin**

✔ **135** About DVDs
✔ **136** Select a DVD Theme

**See Also**

→ **138** Use Movie Folders
→ **139** Create a Menu from a Movie with Chapter Markers
→ **145** Create a Custom Motion Menu

CHAPTER 17: Laying Out a DVD

### 137  Add a Movie to the DVD Menu

**① Open the Customize Drawer**

Click the **Customize** button in the bottom-left corner of the iDVD window to display the **Customize** drawer.

**② Display the Media Pane**

If it's not selected already, click the **Media** button at the top of the **Customize** drawer to display the **Media** pane.

**③ Selct the Movies Option**

If it is not already selected, choose **Movies** from the drop-down list at the top of the **Media** pane. When the **Movies** option is selected, the **Media** pane displays all movies currently in you **Movies** folder (the default location where iMovie places all the movies you create).

**④ Add a Movie to the DVD Menu**

Click the desired movie and drag it into the menu area for the DVD. iDVD creates a button for the selected movie using the default options for the selected theme. iDVD creates the button by assigning it the name of the movie. For example, if the movie you selected is **vacation.mov**, the button in the DVD menu has the label **Vacation**.

Repeat this step to add additional movies to the DVD menu.

If you add a movie that contains chapter markers, iDVD actually creates a folder with the name of that movie file. See  **Create a Menu from a Movie with Chapter Markers** for more information about working with movie files that contain chapter markers.

**⑤ View Menu**

View the menu of movies you have added to the DVD. If you add multiple movies, the movie buttons are placed in the menu in the order you add them.

You can customize the text and look of the menu items. See  **Change Text of Buttons/Titles** for information on changing the text. See 149 **Change Image Displayed on the Button** for information on changing the look of the buttons.

---

**TIP**

If you want to add a movie stored in another location on your computer, you must add that folder to the **Preferences** dialog box. Choose **iDVD, Preferences** and then click the **Movies** option. Click the **Add** button and select the folder containing the movies you want to access from the **Customize** drawer's **iMovie** browser.

**TIP**

When you drag the movie to the DVD menu, make sure that you do not drop it in the drop zone. See  **About Drop Zones** for more information on working with the drop zone.

**TIP**

To move a button, click the item in the DVD menu and drag it to the desired location in the list. To remove a button from the DVD menu, click the button and then press the **Delete** key.

Add a Movie to the DVD Menu 137

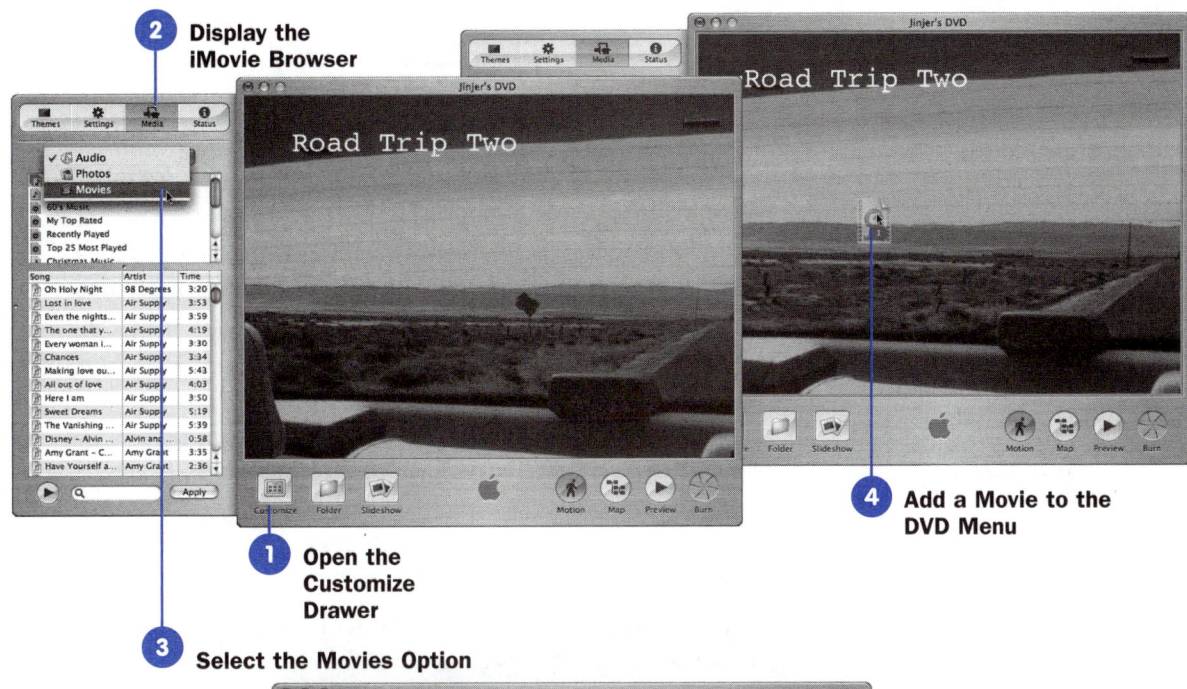

**2** Display the iMovie Browser

**1** Open the Customize Drawer

**3** Select the Movies Option

**4** Add a Movie to the DVD Menu

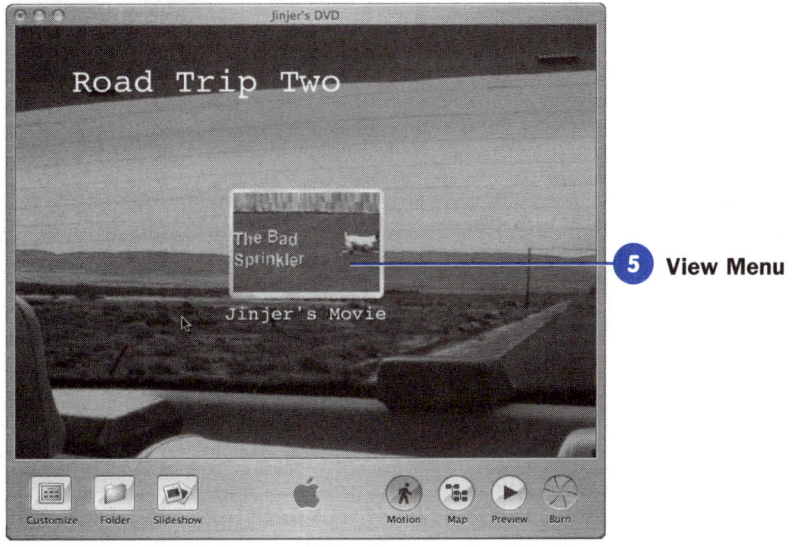

**5** View Menu

**CHAPTER 17:** Laying Out a DVD           377

## 138  Use Movie Folders

**Before You Begin**

✔ 135 About DVDs
✔ 136 Select a DVD Theme

**See Also**

→ 137 Add a Movie to the DVD Menu
→ 139 Create a Menu from a Movie with Chapter Markers
→ 145 Create a Custom Motion Menu

When you add movies to your DVD menu, iDVD allows you to add a maximum of 12 buttons to the menu. If you have several small movies that you want to put on your DVD, that limit of 12 buttons might not be enough to identify all your little movie shorts. Fortunately, iDVD provides a solution. You can add folders to your DVD menu. Each folder opens a new submenu to which you can add an additional 12 menu item buttons. Submenus can contain not only movies but also other folders for additional submenus. However, the combination of folder and movie buttons in a single menu cannot exceed 12.

You can add as many folders to your DVD menu as desired. For example, you might want to group all your movies into different folders so that the main menu contains only the submenu folders.

### NOTE

When you add a new folder button, iDVD uses the default folder name **My Folder**. You can customize the text and look of the menu items, as explained in 147 **Change Text of Buttons/Titles**. See 149 **Change Image Displayed on the Button** for information on changing the look of the button.

### TIPS

You can apply a different theme to each submenu folder using the **Themes** list on the **Customize** drawer. See 136 **Select a DVD Theme** for more information on applying themes.

Click the **Return** button (the left-pointing arrow) that displays on the submenu to return to the parent menu that contained this submenu folder.

### ❶ Select Folder Button

Click the **Folder** button at the bottom of the iDVD window to add a folder button to the DVD menu of the current iDVD project. The appearance of the folder button on the menu varies based on the selected theme. For some themes, the button might just appear as text.

### ❷ Open Folder

Double-click the **My Folder** button to open the new submenu folder. By default, the submenu folder uses the same theme as the main DVD menu.

### ❸ Display Media Pane

At the top of the **Customize** drawer, click the **Media** button to display the **Media** pane. From the drop-down list at the top of the **Media** pane, choose **Movies** to display all the movies currently in your **Movies** folder. The **Movies** folder is the default location where iMovie places all the movies you create.

### ❹ Add Movies to Folder

Click the desired movie and drag it to the displayed submenu. Remember that you can add 12 items to any DVD menu. See 137 **Add a Movie to the DVD Menu** for more information on adding movies to menus.

## Use Movie Folders 138

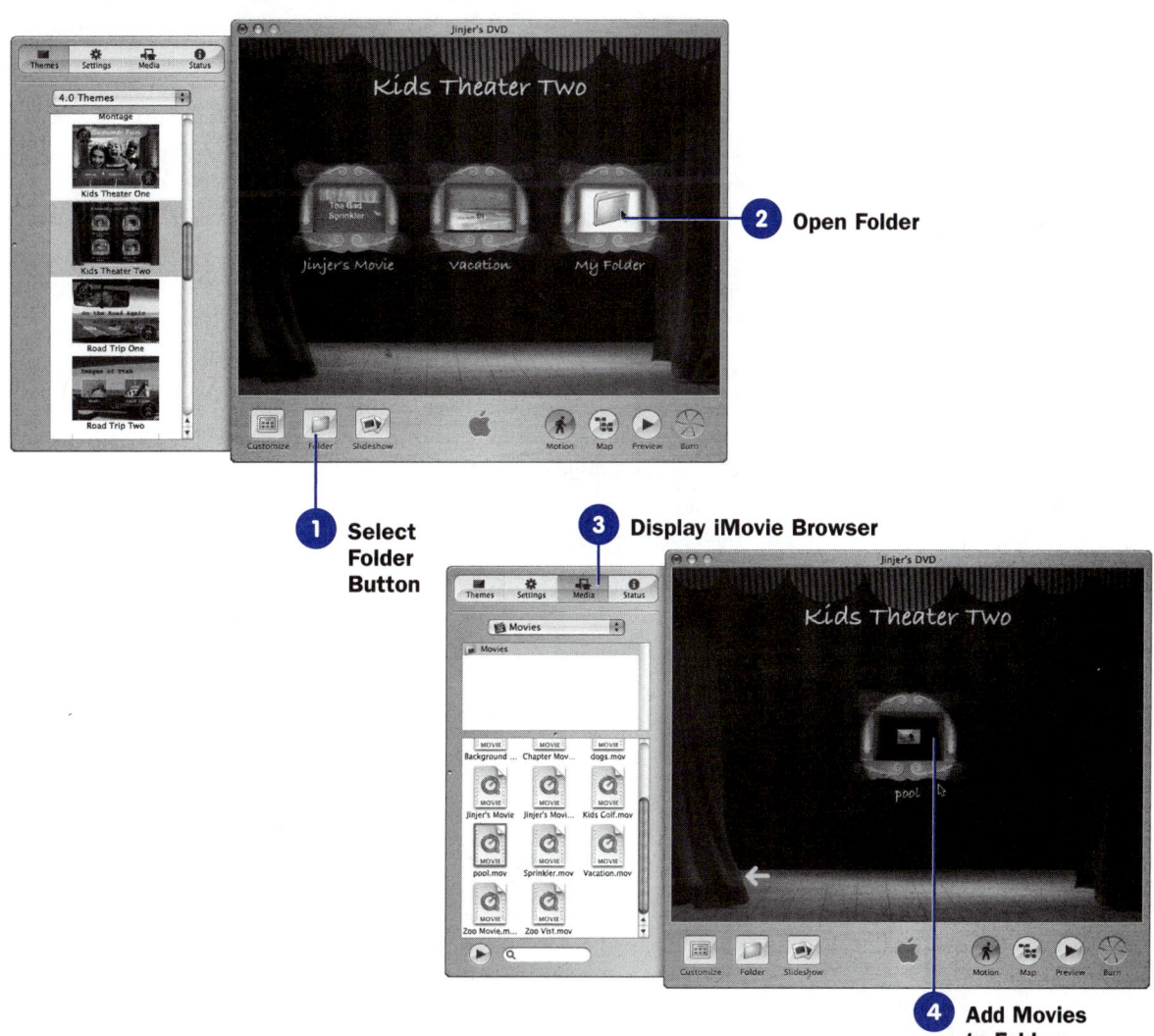

**1** Select Folder Button
**2** Open Folder
**3** Display iMovie Browser
**4** Add Movies to Folder

**CHAPTER 17:** Laying Out a DVD

## 139  Create a Menu from a Movie with Chapter Markers

**Before You Begin**

✔ **132** Add Chapter Markers
✔ **135** About DVDs

**See Also**

→ **138** Use Movie Folders
→ **145** Create a Custom Motion Menu

As you can with all menu item buttons, you can change the text of a button as described in **147** **Change Text of Buttons/Titles**.

If you have not saved the current project, iDVD displays a dialog box asking whether you want to save the current project before closing it. Make sure that you click the **Yes** button to save all your changes.

iDVD allows you to have only one DVD project open at a time. Therefore, if you create a new project, you must first close the current project.

If you created a movie in iMovie that contained chapter markers, you can add that movie to your DVD menu. *Chapter markers* indicate specific spots in a movie to which the viewer of the DVD might want to jump. For example, if you have a movie of your trip to the zoo, you can create chapter markers for each animal you visited. When the viewer clicks the **Elephants** menu item on the DVD menu, he can view the movie starting at that point in the movie.

When you add a movie with chapter markers to your DVD menu, iDVD actually places two different buttons on the menu. The menu contains one button called **Play Movie** that plays the entire movie; the other button, called **Scene Selection**, is actually a folder. When the viewer clicks the **Scene Selection** button on the menu, a submenu displays containing all the chapter markers specified for the movie.

You can add a movie containing chapter markers to an existing DVD project or you can create a new project using the **New Project** option. Each project you create is placed on a different DVD. If you add the movie with chapter markers to an existing project, a folder is created in the existing menu with the name of the movie you add. When you click that folder, you see the **Play Movie** and **Scene Selection** submenu buttons.

### ❶ Create a New Project

Choose **File**, **New Project** to display the **New Project** dialog box. If you don't want to create a new project (and instead want to add your movie with chapter markers to the existing project), skip to step 3.

### ❷ Specify Project Name

Type the name you want to assign to the new project in the **Save as** field. By default, iDVD stores the project in your **Documents** folder; to place it in a different location, click the arrow button next to the **Where** field and select the desired folder. Click the **Create** button to create the new project.

PART IV:   iDVD

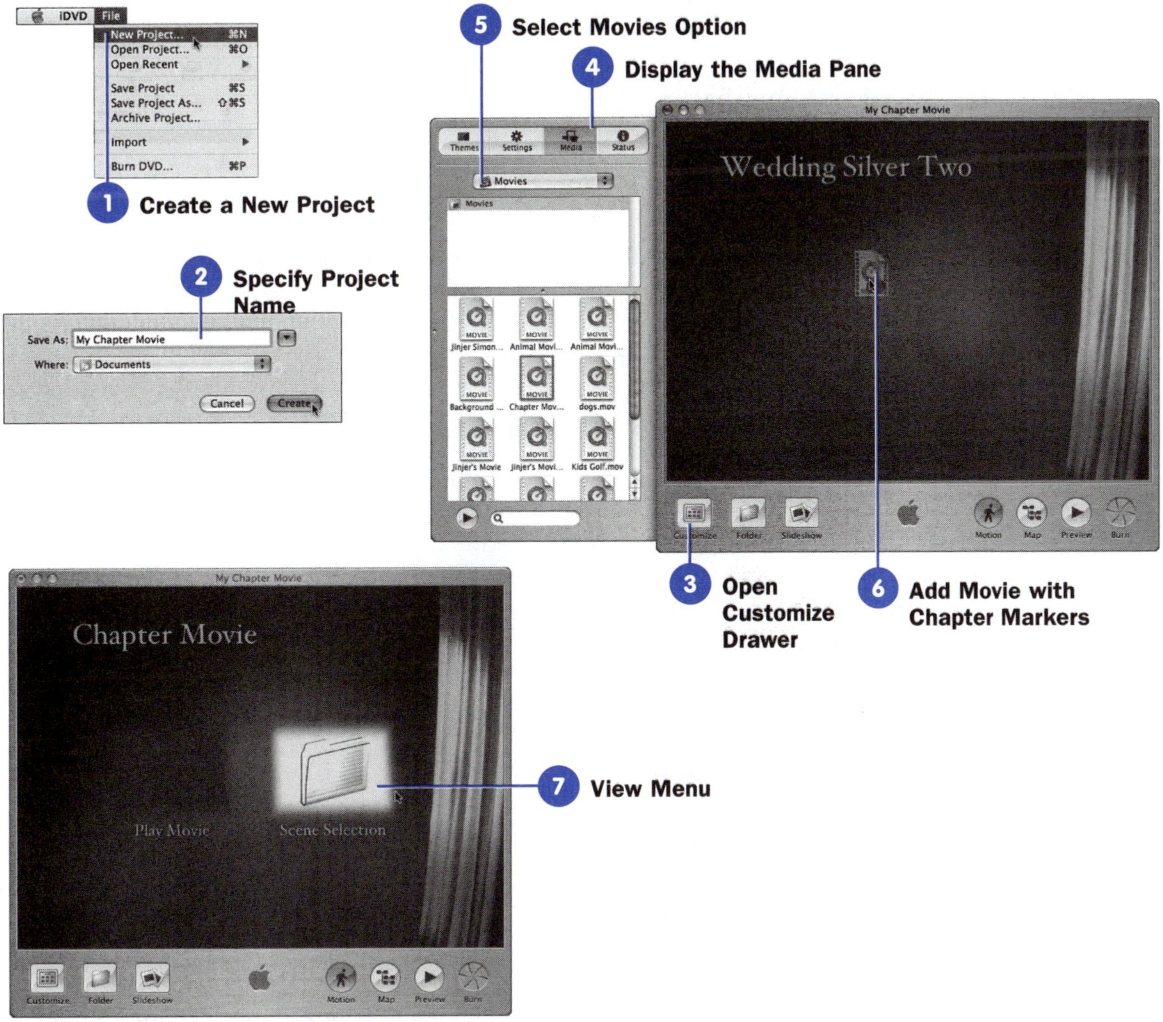

Create a Menu from a Movie with Chapter Markers  139

① Create a New Project

② Specify Project Name

③ Open Customize Drawer

④ Display the Media Pane

⑤ Select Movies Option

⑥ Add Movie with Chapter Markers

⑦ View Menu

③ **Open Customize Drawer**

Click the **Customize** button in the bottom-left corner of the iDVD window to display the **Customize** drawer.

**NOTE**

If desired, you can select a different theme for the new DVD project by clicking the **Themes** button to see the available themes. See ⑬⑥ **Select a DVD Theme** for more information on applying a theme to the DVD.

CHAPTER 17:  Laying Out a DVD      381

### 139  Create a Menu from a Movie with Chapter Markers

#### ④ Display the Media Pane

If it's not selected already, click the **Media** button to display the **Media** pane.

#### ⑤ Select the Movies Option

From the drop-down list at the top of the **Media** pane, choose the **Movies** option. When the **Movies** option is selected, the **Media** pane displays all the movies currently in the **Movies** folder. The **Movies** folder is the default location where iMovie places all the movies you create.

#### ⑥ Add Movie with Chapter Markers

Click the movie that contains the chapter markers and drag it into the menu area. iDVD creates two menu item buttons. The first one, **Play Movie**, plays the entire movie from start to finish. The second one, **Scene Selection**, is a folder that opens a new submenu containing the chapter markers specified in iMovie. When you click a button created from a chapter marker, the movie starts playing at that location.

The title of the DVD menu becomes the name of the selected movie file. For example, if the selected movie file is **Chapter Movie.mov**, the title of the menu becomes **Chapter Movie**. You can change the menu titles by altering the text as described in **146 Change Menu Title**.

#### ⑦ View Menu

View the DVD menu. You can customize the text and look of the menu items. See **147 Change Text of Buttons/Titles** for information on changing the text. See **149 Change Image Displayed on the Button** for information on changing the look of the menu item button.

## 140 About Drop Zones

When you select many of the themes provided with iDVD, you see an area of the DVD menu marked with the text **Drag photos or movies here**. This area of the DVD menu is called the *drop zone*. This special area on the DVD menu background provides a location where you can add photos or movies to customize the look of the theme. For example, the **Projector** theme has a drop zone that resembles a movie screen. When you drop movies or photos on that drop zone, the DVD menu plays them in the background.

You can add any movie to the drop zone. Keep in mind that, although the movie displays in the drop zone, it cannot be selected. If you want the same movie to be available to view, you must also add it to the DVD menu.

You can also add up to 30 different photos to the drop zone from your iPhoto **Library**. If the drop zone contains multiple photos, they are displayed one at a time as a slideshow.

- **Why can't I view the entire movie I placed in the drop zone?** When you add a movie to the drop zone, the movie plays as part of the menu that displays for the DVD. Although you might have placed a movie you want to access from the DVD menu in the drop zone, the movie is not accessible from the drop zone. If you want to select that movie from the DVD menu, you must also add the movie to your DVD menu.

    Only a portion of the movie you dropped into the drop zone displays in the drop zone. The duration of the movie can be anywhere between 0 and 30 seconds. You specify the length on the **Settings** pane of the **Customize** drawer. The **Motion Duration** slider controls the length of all motion and audio on the DVD menu. See **142 Customize the Image or Movie in the Drop Zone** for more information on customizing the length of the motion.

- **How do I know if I am adding a movie to the drop zone or to a menu?** When you drag a movie from the **iMovie** browser to the drop zone, a dotted line displays around the edges of the drop zone to indicate that the movie will be placed there.

### Before You Begin

✔ **135** About DVDs
✔ **136** Select a DVD Theme

### See Also

→ **141** Add Images to Drop Zones
→ **142** Customize the Image or Movie in the Drop Zone
→ **143** Remove Images from the Drop Zone

### KEY TERM

*Drop zone*—A portion of a DVD menu to which you can add photos and movies that display as part of the menu. Drop zones allow you to customize a DVD menu theme to match the contents of the DVD.

If you are placing the movie in the DVD menu, a solid blue line appears around the edge of the DVD menu window.

- **Why doesn't my movie play when I add it to the drop zone?** As with any of the motion on a DVD menu, the **Motion** button must be selected before you can view a movie in the drop zone. If the **Motion** button is not selected, only the first frame of the movie displays in the drop zone.

  If you click the **Motion** button and the movie still does not play, the **Motion Duration** slider might be set to **Off**. On the **Settings** panel of the **Customize** drawer, drag the **Motion Duration** slider to the desired length of time for the movie duration (up to 30 seconds in length). At the end of the specified time frame, the motion repeats.

## 141 Add Images to Drop Zones

**Before You Begin**

✔ **140** About Drop Zones

**See Also**

→ **142** Customize the Images or Movie in the Drop Zone

→ **143** Remove Images from the Drop Zone

If you have selected a theme that has a *drop zone*, you can add movies or photos to display in the drop zone. You add movies or photos to the drop zone by dragging them from the corresponding browser in the **Customize** drawer. For example, to add a movie, drag it from the **iMovie** browser to the drop zone.

You can add up to 30 different photos to the drop zone from the **iPhoto** browser and they will be displayed one at a time, similar to a slideshow. To add a series of different photos, you must add them all to the drop zone at the same time. You can either drag an entire photo album to the drop zone or select multiple photos and drag them as a group to the drop zone. If you drag one photo at a time, each new photo replaces the current photo in the drop zone.

To view a movie or a series of photos that you have placed in the drop zone, the **Motion** option must be turned on by clicking the **Motion** button. Most of the drop zones on the different themes have special effects that are applied to the movies or photos displayed in the drop zone. For example, the **Projector** theme makes the content of the drop zone look like an old movie by muting the colors and adding a scratchy appearance. You cannot alter the effects applied to the drop zone by the theme. If you do not like the effects applied to the drop zone images, select a different theme.

## Add Images to Drop Zones

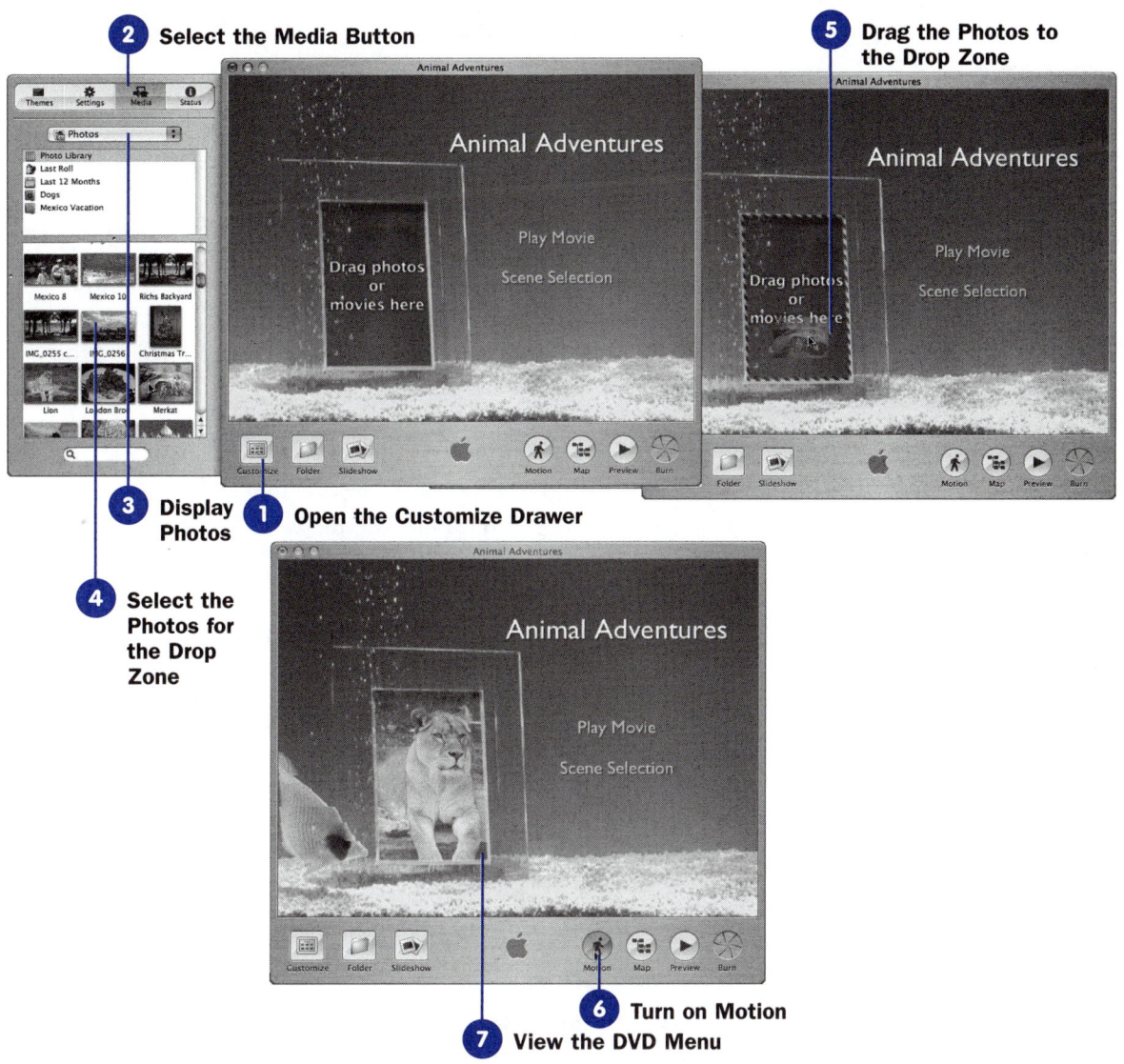

### 1 Open the Customize Drawer

Click the **Customize** button in the bottom-left corner of the iDVD window to display the **Customize** drawer.

**CHAPTER 17:** Laying Out a DVD

## Add Images to Drop Zones

### TIPS

By default, the **Library** option is selected in the **iPhoto** browser, displaying all photos in your iPhoto **Library**. If you want to see specific photos, you can select one of the albums listed.

To add a movie instead of still photos to the drop zone, click the **Movies** button to display the **iMovie** browser.

### NOTE

As you drag the selected photos to the drop zone, the number of selected photos displays in the bottom-right corner of the thumbnail. For example, if you selected five photos in the **iPhoto** browser, a **5** displays in a red circle in the corner of the thumbnail image you are dragging.

**② Select the Media Button**

If it's not selected already, click the **Media** button to display the **Media** pane.

**③ Display Photos**

From the drop-down list at the top of the **Media** pane, choose **Photos**. The **Media** pane displays the photos from your **iPhoto Library**. The top portion of the pane lists each of the iPhoto albums along with the **Library**. The bottom portion of the pane displays the photos in the entire **Library** or the selected album.

**④ Select the Photos for the Drop Zone**

Hold down the ⌘ key when you click each of the photos you want to add to the drop zone. As you select each photo, a blue box displays around the photo thumbnail image to indicate that that image is selected.

To add the photos from an entire album, click to select the desired album in the list at the top of **iPhoto** browser. Keep in mind that iDVD will add only the first 30 photos in that album to the drop zone.

**⑤ Drag the Photos to the Drop Zone**

Drag the selected photos from the **iPhoto** browser to the drop zone. As you drag the photos into the drop zone, a dotted line displays around the outside of the drop zone. Make sure that the dotted line displays before releasing the mouse button.

**⑥ Turn on Motion**

Click the **Motion** button to turn on all motion for the DVD menu. If the menu includes music, the music will also play when you click the **Motion** button.

**⑦ View the DVD Menu**

View the DVD menu with the additions to the drop zone. Make sure that you like the additions. You can customize the settings for the drop zone as explained in **142 Customize the Image or Movie in the Drop Zone**. See **143 Remove Images from a Drop Zone** for information on removing the contents of the drop zone.

386  PART IV:  iDVD

# 18

# Customizing the DVD

## IN THIS CHAPTER:

- **142** Customize the Image or Movie in the Drop Zone
- **143** Remove Images from the Drop Zone
- **144** Create a Custom Background
- **145** Create a Custom Motion Menu
- **146** Change Menu Title
- **147** Change Text of Buttons/Titles
- **148** Set the Start Frame for a Motion Button
- **149** Change Image Displayed on the Button
- **150** Change Button Locations
- **151** Create a Custom Button
- **152** Move Buttons to Other Menus
- **153** Change the Audio that Plays for the DVD Menu
- **154** Save a Custom Theme
- **155** Remove the Apple Watermark

### 142 Customize the Image or Movie in the Drop Zone

Although iDVD provides several different themes you can use to lay out your DVD menu, you are not limited to the default settings for each theme. iDVD allows you to customize nearly every element of the menu. You can create your own background, modify the text formatting, customize the look of the buttons, move the buttons, add your own audio, and even remove the Apple watermark that displays in the bottom-right corner of the menu.

After you have created your own custom theme, you can save those settings so that you can apply them to a submenu or a separate DVD menu project.

## 142 Customize the Image or Movie in the Drop Zone

**Before You Begin**
- ✔ 140 About Drop Zones
- ✔ 141 Add Images to Drop Zones

**See Also**
- → 143 Remove Images from the Drop Zone
- → 144 Create a Custom Background
- → 153 Change the Audio that Plays for the DVD Menu
- → 154 Save a Custom Theme

**KEY TERM**

*Aspect ratio*—The relationship between the height and width of an image. For example, the ratio for standard television is 4×3, which means that for every 4 units of width, there are 3 units of height.

When you add photos and movies to the *drop zone* of your DVD movie, iDVD resizes the image so that it fits within the edges of the drop zone. iDVD resizes the image by making it larger or smaller to fit within the drop zone while maintaining the same *aspect ratio*. Depending on the shape of the drop zone, your image might appear warped or stretched.

If you are not happy with the positioning of the image, you can adjust the image so that only a specific portion is visible. To do so, you drag the image within the drop zone to achieve the desired positioning. As soon as you move the image, the entire image may no longer display in the drop zone, depending on the original size of the image.

The type of positioning you can use on the image is based on the original image size. If you placed a narrow image in the drop zone, you can reposition the image by moving it up or down. If you placed a wide image in the drop zone, you can reposition the image by moving it from side to side.

**① Select the Drop Zone Contents**

Click the image in the drop zone. The mouse pointer changes to a hand to indicate that you are over the drop zone.

**② Move to Make Desired Portion Visible**

Drag the image in the drop zone to the desired positioning. If the original image is vertical (taller than wide), you can drag it up and down to position it. If the original image is horizontal (wider than tall), you can drag it from side to side to position it.

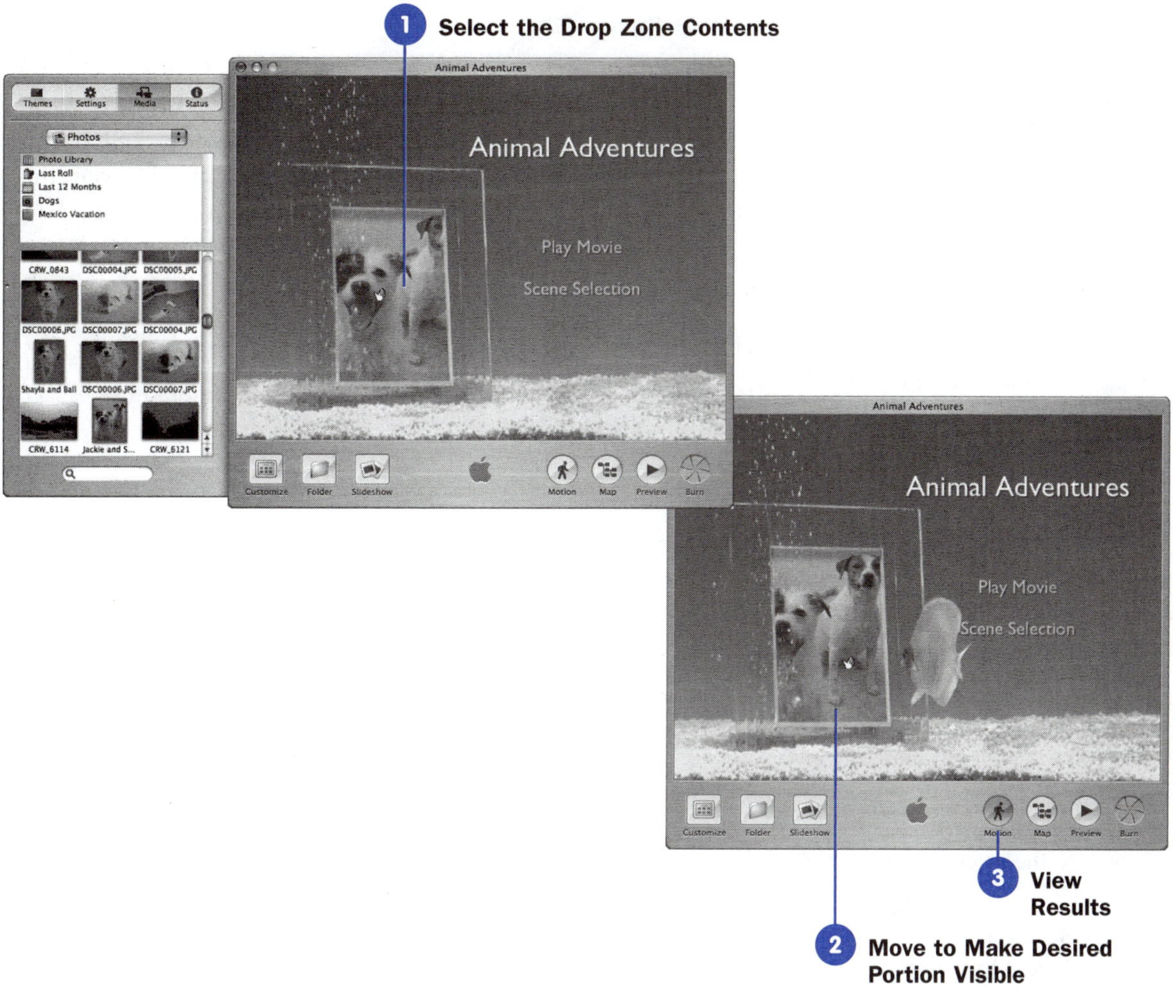

## Customize the Image or Movie in the Drop Zone   142

**1** Select the Drop Zone Contents

**3** View Results

**2** Move to Make Desired Portion Visible

---

### 3  View Results

If not selected, click the **Motion** button to make sure that the positioning is correct for the entire image. This is especially important if you have a series of photos or a movie in the drop zone.

**NOTE**

When you have a series of photos in the drop zone, you can adjust the positioning of only the first photo. iDVD applies the adjustments to all photos in the drop zone.

**CHAPTER 18:** Customizing the DVD

## 143 Remove Images from the Drop Zone

**Before You Begin**

✔ **140** About Drop Zones
✔ **141** Add Images to Drop Zones

**See Also**

→ **142** Customize the Image or Movie in the Drop Zone
→ **144** Create a Custom Background
→ **153** Change the Audio that Plays for the DVD Menu
→ **154** Save a Custom Theme

**NOTE**

If you simply want to replace the contents of the drop zone, you do not have to delete the first image. Simply drag the new image from the **Customize Drawer** to the drop zone. iDVD replaces whatever is currently in the drop zone with the new selection. If you don't want to put anything in the drop zone, you can turn off the text that appears there. Open the **Preferences** dialog box by choosing **iDVD, Preferences** and click the **General** button. Disable the **Show Drop Zones** check box.

If you no longer want the photos or movies to display in the drop zone, you can remove them. You remove the contents of the drop zone by dragging them out of the drop zone. If you have multiple photos in the drop zone, all the photos are removed when you drag a photo out. You can remove the contents of the drop zone while the **Motion** button is selected.

**1 Select the Drop Zone Contents**

Click the image in the drop zone. The mouse pointer changes to a hand to indicate that you are over the drop zone.

**2 Drag Pointer Out of Drop Zone**

Drag the mouse pointer out of the drop zone.

**3 Release the Mouse Button**

Release the mouse button. The contents of the drop zone disappear in a puff of smoke.

## Remove Images from the Drop Zone  143

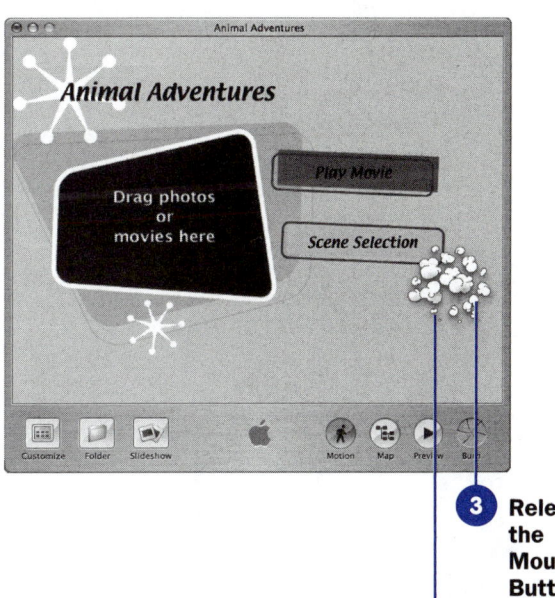

**1** Select the Drop Zone Contents

**2** Drag Pointer Out of Drop Zone

**3** Release the Mouse Button

## 144  Create a Custom Background

When you select a theme for your DVD menu, you get a default background image. For example, when you select the **Book** theme, you get a background image of a book. If you want to customize your DVD menu, you can insert your own photo as the background for the DVD menu.

To modify the background image of the DVD menu, you drag a photo from the **iPhoto Browser** to the background of the menu. If your DVD menu theme has a drop zone, make sure that you drop the photo in the background and not in the drop zone.

**1** Open the Customize Drawer

Click the **Customize** button in the bottom-left corner of the iDVD window to display the **Customize** drawer.

**Before You Begin**

✔ **136** Select a DVD Theme

**See Also**

→ **145** Create a Custom Motion Menu

→ **146** Change Menu Title

→ **149** Change Image Displayed on the Button

→ **153** Change the Audio that Plays for the DVD Menu

→ **154** Save a Custom Theme

CHAPTER 18:  Customizing the DVD

### 144 Create a Custom Background

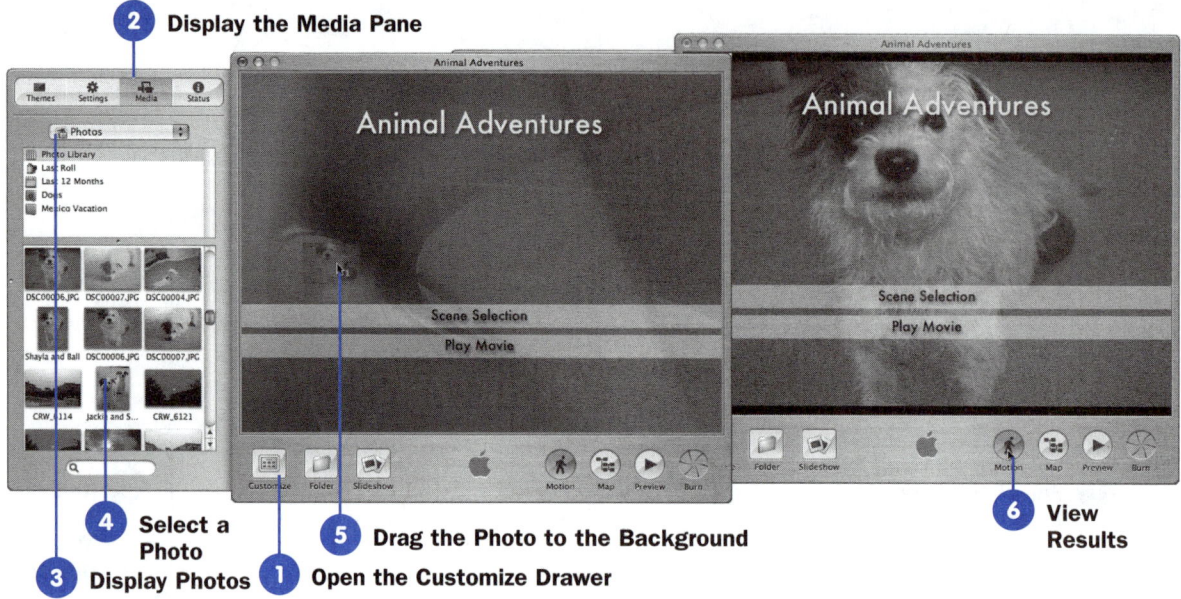

#### 2 Display the Media Pane

If it is not already selected, click the **Media** button to display the **Media** pane.

#### 3 Display Photos

From the drop-down menu at the top of the **Media** pane, choose **Photos**. The **Media** pane displays the photos from your **iPhoto Library**. The top portion of the pane lists each of the iPhoto albums along with the **Library**. The bottom portion of the pane displays the photos in the entire **Library** or the selected album.

#### 4 Select a Photo

Click to select the photo you want to use as the background for your DVD menu. You can use the scrollbar at the right side of the **Media** pane to scroll through the images and locate the desired photo.

If you want to look in a specific photo album, click the album name in the top portion of the **Media** pane.

**NOTE**

Photos with an aspect ratio of 4×3 work best as the background for your DVD menu. You can set the aspect ratio of your photos in iPhoto by enabling the **Constrain** option when you crop the photo. See **12 Crop Photos** for information on cropping photos in iPhoto.

## 5 Drag the Photo to the Background

Drag the selected photo to the background of the DVD menu. As you drag the photo onto the background, a blue box displays around the outside of the DVD menu, indicating that the photo will be placed on the background. If a dotted line displays around the drop zone, iDVD will place the photo in the drop zone and not in the background. Move the mouse pointer until the background is selected.

## 6 View Results

If it is not already selected, click the **Motion** button to view the current DVD menu with the motion turned on. Make sure that the menu buttons and title are still visible with your new background.

## 145 Create a Custom Motion Menu

When you select a theme for your DVD menu, you get a default background image. For example, when you select the **Theater** theme, you get a background of curtains opening for a movie. This type of animated background is referred to as a *motion menu*. You can create your own motion menu for any of the default themes by adding a movie to the background.

To add a movie to the background of the DVD menu, you drag a movie from the **Finder** to the background well on the **Settings** pane in the **Customize** drawer. If your DVD menu has a drop zone, the motion menu replaces both the background and the drop zone for the DVD menu.

After selecting the movie, you can specify the desired length of time you want the movie to play in the background by adjusting the **Motion Duration** slider on the **Settings** pane. The time you specify applies to all motion on the DVD menu, including the music. The motion plays for the specified length of time before repeating. For example, if you specify a duration time of 20 seconds, iDVD inserts the first 20 seconds of the movie in the background and loops the playback of that 20 seconds of video and audio. You can specify a duration time between 0 and 30 seconds.

**Before You Begin**

✔ 136 Select a DVD Theme

**See Also**

→ 144 Create a Custom Background

→ 146 Change Menu Title

→ 149 Change Image Displayed on the Button

→ 153 Change the Audio that Plays for the DVD Menu

→ 154 Save a Custom Theme

### KEY TERM

*Motion menu*—In a DVD movie menu, a background that is not a still image, but rather a movie.

## 145 Create a Custom Motion Menu

**KEY TERM**

*Finder*—A program included with Mac OS X that allows you to locate files on different drives (including all drives on your computer and any network drives to which you have access).

**TIP**

To open **Finder**, click the **Finder** icon in the Mac OS X Dock.

**① Open the Customize Drawer**

Click the **Customize** button in the bottom-left corner of the iDVD window to display the **Customize** drawer.

**② Display the Settings Pane**

Click the **Settings** button to display the **Settings** pane. The **Settings** pane provides options for customizing such settings on the DVD menu as the look of the buttons and the text. See **147 Change Text of Buttons/Titles** for information on customizing the buttons on the DVD menu and **154 Save a Custom Theme** for information on saving a DVD menu theme.

**③ Locate Movie in Finder**

In *Finder*, select the movie you want to add to the DVD menu as the background motion. If you stored your iMovie movies in the default location, you will find them in your **Movies** folder when you click the **Home** button. If the movie you want is located in a different folder, open that folder and select the movie.

**④ Drag Movie to the Background**

Drag the selected movie to the **Background** well on the **Settings** pane in the **Customize** drawer. When you release the mouse button, the DVD menu updates to include the selected movie as the background.

**⑤ Set Duration of Motion**

Drag the **Motion Duration** slider to set the desired length for the background movie and any other motion and audio on the DVD menu. At the end of the specified time frame, the motion will repeat. You can specify a duration time between 0 and 30 seconds.

**⑥ View Results**

If it is not already selected, click the **Motion** button to view the current DVD menu with the selected movie playing in the background. Make sure that the menu buttons and title are still visible with your new background.

## Create a Custom Motion Menu 145

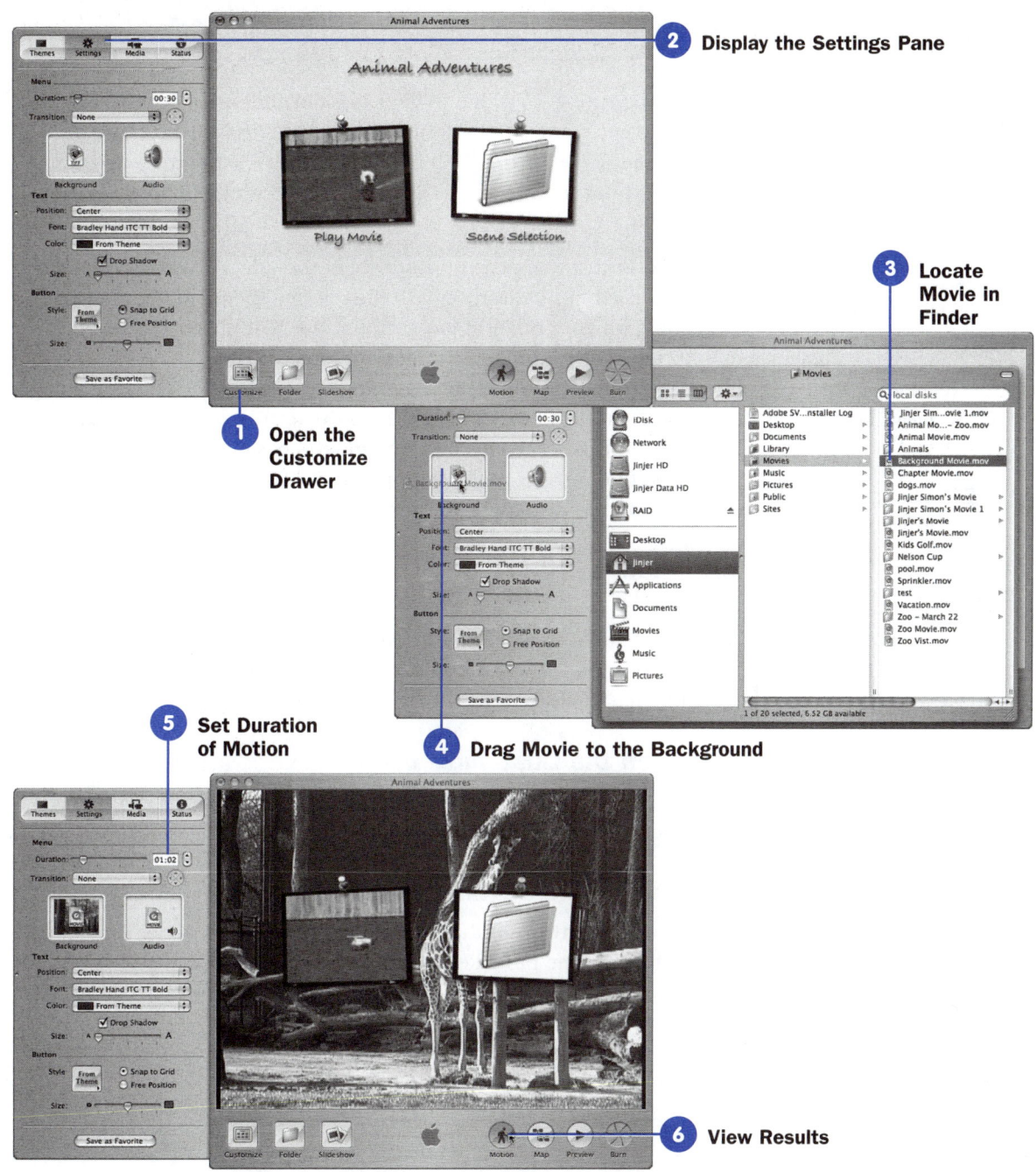

**1** Open the Customize Drawer
**2** Display the Settings Pane
**3** Locate Movie in Finder
**4** Drag Movie to the Background
**5** Set Duration of Motion
**6** View Results

**CHAPTER 18:** Customizing the DVD

## 146  Change Menu Title

**Before You Begin**

✔ **136** Select a DVD Theme

**See Also**

→ **144** Create a Custom Background

→ **145** Create a Custom Motion Menu

→ **149** Change Image Displayed on the Button

→ **153** Change the Audio that Plays for the DVD Menu

→ **154** Save a Custom Theme

When you create a DVD menu, iDVD assigns the name of the project as the DVD menu name. You might want to customize the text that displays on the screen as the DVD menu title. If this is the case, you can edit the text directly within iDVD by selecting the title and typing the desired text.

You can also customize the appearance of the title. As you know, iDVD applies the settings associated with the selected theme to the menu title. Depending on your other menu settings, those settings might not be appropriate. For example, if you have added a custom background image, the title text might not be visible on the new background. Using the options on the **Settings** pane in the **Customize** drawer, you can customize the title text settings by changing the position, font, color, and size of the title. As you make changes on the **Settings** pane, the DVD menu updates to display the current settings.

**① Change Title Text**

Click to select the title text on the DVD menu. The selected text is highlighted in blue, indicating that it is selected. Type the desired text for the DVD menu title. As you type, the text updates on the menu.

**② Open the Customize Drawer**

Click the **Customize** button in the bottom-left corner of the iDVD window to display the **Customize** drawer.

**③ Display the Settings Pane**

Click the **Settings** button to display the **Settings** pane. The **Settings** pane provides options for customizing such settings on the DVD menu as the look of the buttons and the text. See **147** **Change Text of Buttons/Titles** for information on customizing the buttons on the DVD menu and **154** **Save a Custom Theme** for information on saving a DVD menu theme.

Change Menu Title **146**

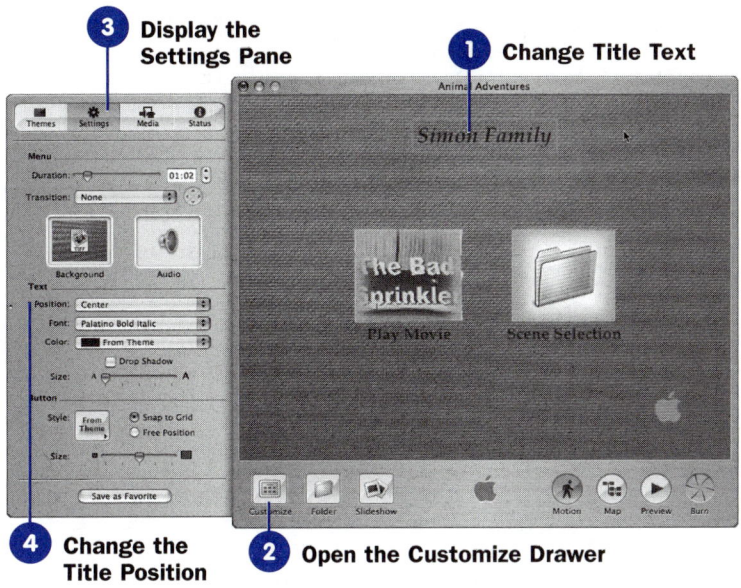

3. Display the Settings Pane
1. Change Title Text
4. Change the Title Position
2. Open the Customize Drawer

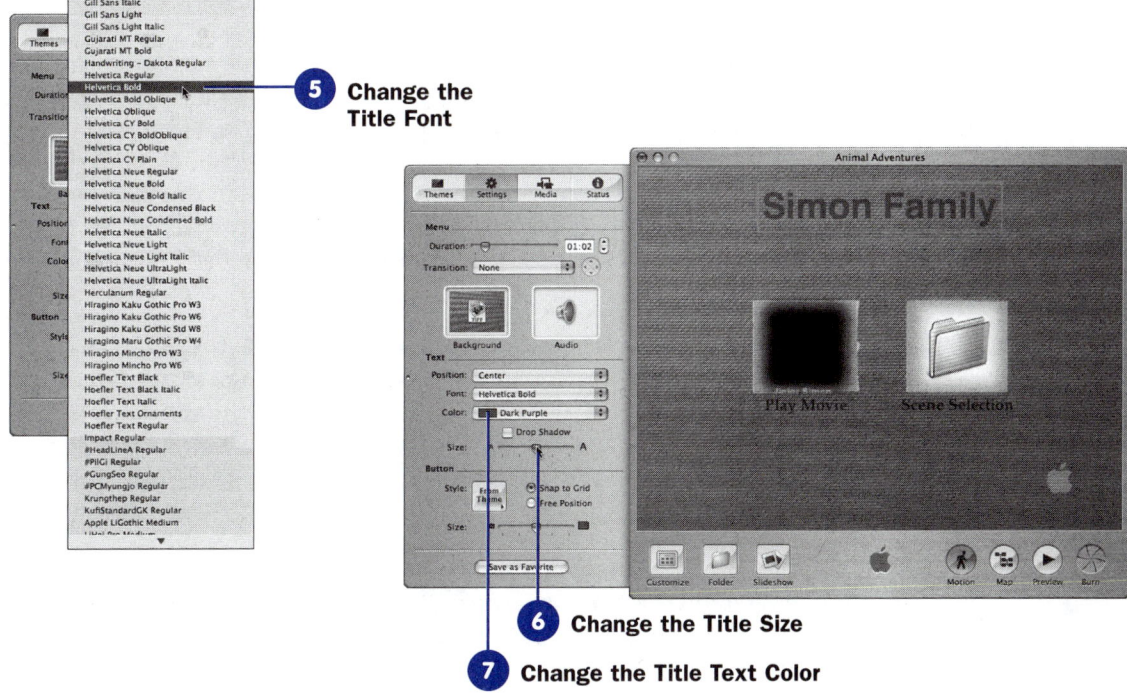

5. Change the Title Font
6. Change the Title Size
7. Change the Title Text Color

**CHAPTER 18:** Customizing the DVD

# Change Text of Buttons/Titles

**TIP**

If you select the **No Title** option from the **Title Position** drop-down list, iDVD removes the title from the DVD menu altogether.

**TIP**

You can make the title stand out more by clicking the **Drop Shadow** check box.

### ④ Change the Title Position

If desired, select the desired position for the title for the DVD menu from the **Title Position** drop-down list. You can select from five different options: **No Title**, **Top Left**, **Top Center**, **Top Right**, and **Custom**. If you select the **Custom** option, you can click the title and drag it to the desired location on the menu. If you select one of the other three options, iDVD positions the title in the indicated position on the menu.

### ⑤ Change the Title Font

If desired, select the desired font from the list of available font types in the **Title Font** drop-down list.

### ⑥ Change the Title Text Color

If desired, select the desired color for the title text from the **Title Color** drop-down list. Make sure that you select a color that will stand out well against your background.

### ⑦ Change the Title Size

If desired, drag the **Title Size** slider to the right to increase the size of the title text or to the left to decrease the size of the title text.

## 147   Change Text of Buttons/Titles

**Before You Begin**

✔ **136** Select a DVD Theme

✔ **137** Add a Movie to the DVD Menu

**See Also**

➜ **145** Create a Custom Motion Menu

➜ **146** Change Menu Title

➜ **149** Change Image Displayed on the Button

➜ **150** Change Button Locations

When you add movies to your DVD menu, iDVD creates a label for the button that is added to the menu for each movie. For example, when you add a movie to the menu, the name of the movie is assigned to the button as the label. If the movie has *chapter markers*, the label of the button becomes **Play Movie**. See **139** **Create a Menu from a Movie with Chapter Markers** for more information on adding movies with chapter markers.

You can customize the text label of each button by selecting the individual button and typing new text. You can also customize the font settings for all the buttons on the **Settings** pane of the **Customize** drawer. If you change the font settings for the buttons, those modifications affect all the buttons on the current DVD menu. For example, if you decide to set the button label color to red, all button labels will be red.

## Change Text of Buttons/Titles

**① Change Button Label Text**

Click to select the text of the desired button label on the DVD menu. The selected text is highlighted in blue to indicate that it is selected. Type the desired text for the selected button.

Repeat the process for each button with a text label you want to change on the DVD menu.

**② Open Customize Drawer**

Click the **Customize** button in the bottom-left corner of the iDVD window to display the **Customize** drawer.

**③ Display Settings Pane**

Click the **Settings** button to display the **Settings** pane. The **Settings** pane provides options for customizing such settings on the DVD menu as the look of the buttons and the text. See **154 Save a Custom Theme** for information on saving a DVD menu theme.

**④ Change Button Label Position**

From the **Button Position** drop-down list, select the desired position for the button labels in relation to the buttons. You can select from six different options: **Top, Center, Bottom, Left, Right**, and **No Text**. If you select the **Center** option, iDVD places the text title across the center of the button, across the image that appears there. If you use the **Center** option, make sure that you change the text options to make the label visible on top of the image.

**⑤ Change Button Label Font**

From the **Button Font** drop-down list, select the desired font for the button labels from the list of available font types.

**⑥ Change Button Label Color**

From the **Button Color** drop-down list, select the desired color for the button labels. Make sure that you select a color that will stand out well against your background.

→ **152** Move Buttons to Other Menus
→ **154** Save a Custom Theme

**NOTE**

When you click a button, a scroll bar and check box display above the button. The check box indicates whether the button is animated. The scrollbar allows you to select the start frame for the button. See **148 Set the Start Frame for a Motion Button** for more information on setting the button images.

**NOTE**

The **Position, Font, Color,** and **Size** options you select here will affect all buttons on the current DVD menu.

**CHAPTER 18:** Customizing the DVD

## 147 Change Text of Buttons/Titles

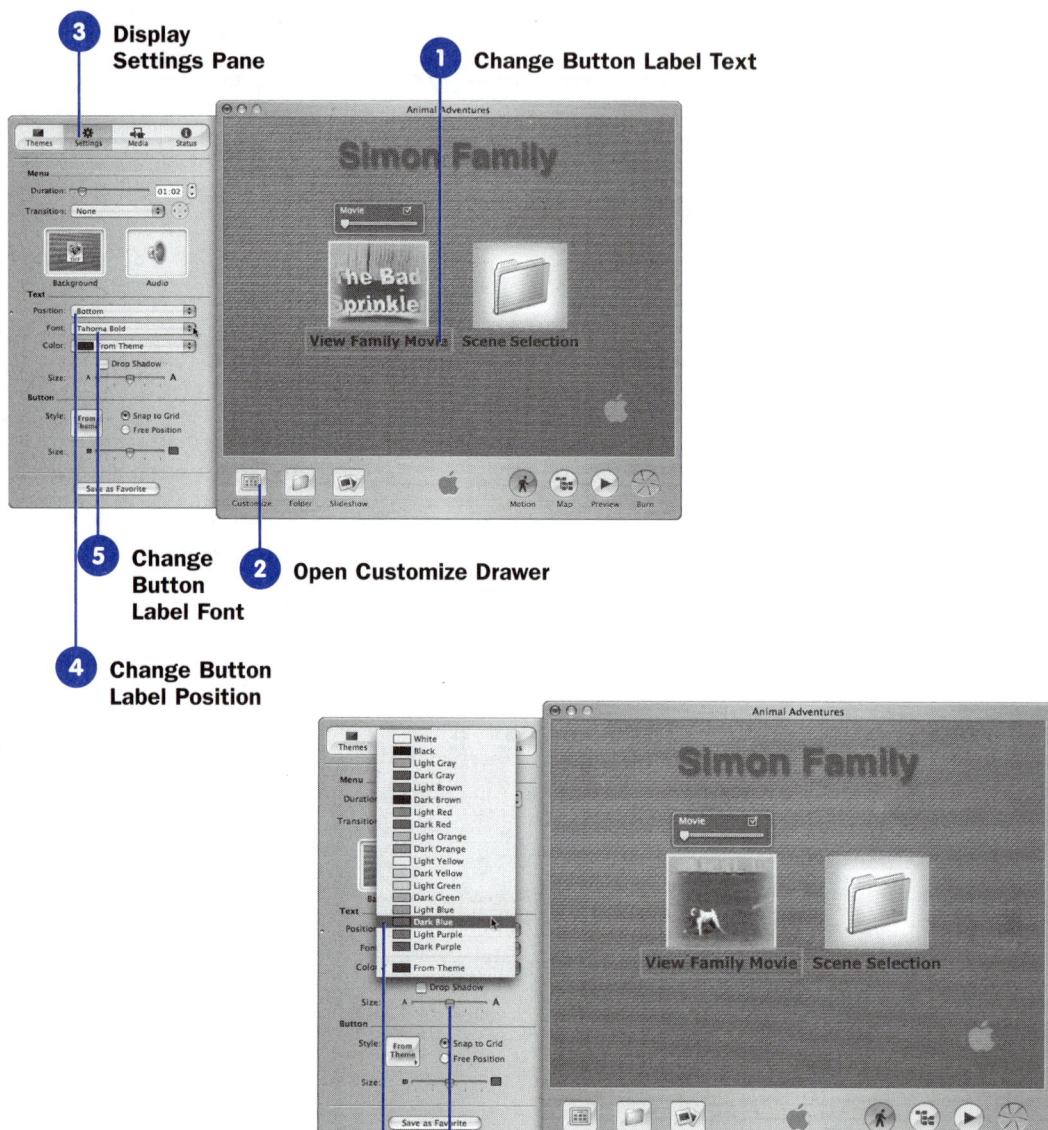

① Change Button Label Text
② Open Customize Drawer
③ Display Settings Pane
④ Change Button Label Position
⑤ Change Button Label Font
⑥ Change Button Label Color
⑦ Change Button Label Text Size

### ⑦ Change Button Label Text Size

Drag the **Button Size** slider to the right to increase the size of the button labels or to the left to decrease the size of the button labels.

## 148  Set the Start Frame for a Motion Button

When you add a movie to a DVD menu, iDVD automatically creates a menu button for the movie. Depending on the theme selected, the button will either be a picture button or a text button. If you have a picture button and the **Motion** option is selected, a portion of the movie will play on the button. The movie starts playing with the first frame and plays for the amount of time specified by the **Motion Duration** slider on the **Settings** panel in the **Customize** drawer. For example, if the **Motion Duration** slider is set to 20 seconds, the first 20 seconds of the movie play on the button and then loop back to repeat.

If you want to have the movie on the button start playing from a different frame, you can select the appropriate frame. To set the start frame, you select the button and then adjust the slider that appears until you find the frame you want to start with.

If the theme you have selected does not include picture buttons, you can add them to your DVD menu by selecting the desired button shape on the **Settings** panel. See **151 Create a Custom Button** for more information on selecting a button shape.

### ① Select the Button

Click a picture button on the DVD menu to select it. When the button is selected, a box displays for the picture button to specify the movie settings.

### ② Select Start Frame

Drag the slider to select the start frame for the portion of the movie that displays on the button.

### ③ View Results

Click the **Motion** button to view the results of adjusting the start frame for the selected button.

**Before You Begin**

✔ **136** Select a DVD Theme

✔ **137** Add a Movie to the DVD Menu

**See Also**

→ **149** Change Image Displayed on the Button

→ **150** Change Button Locations

→ **151** Create a Custom Button

→ **152** Move Buttons to Other Menus

→ **154** Save a Custom Theme

**NOTE**

The **Movie** check box must be selected if you want the movie to play for the selected button. If the **Movie** check box is not selected, only the selected frame of the movie will display on that button, even when the **Motion** button is clicked.

### 148  Set the Start Frame for a Motion Button

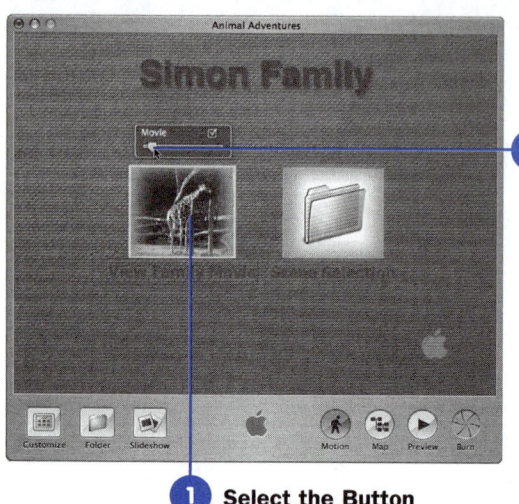
**1** Select the Button

**2** Select Start Frame

**3** View Results

---

### 149  Change Image Displayed on the Button

**Before You Begin**

✔ **136** Select a DVD Theme

✔ **137** Add a Movie to the DVD Menu

**See Also**

→ **147** Change Text of Buttons/Titles

→ **148** Set the Start Frame for a Motion Button

→ **151** Create a Custom Button

→ **152** Movie Buttons to Other Menus

When you add a movie to a DVD menu, iDVD automatically creates a button for the movie. The type of button created is based on the theme selected for the DVD menu. Your DVD menu has either text buttons or picture buttons with text labels. If your DVD menu has picture buttons, by default iDVD assigns the movie as the image that displays on the button. If you want, you can customize each button to display a still photo rather than the movie.

To customize the picture button, you select the button and then drag the desired photo to the button from the **Media** pane. When you do this, you replace the current button image with the new photo.

If the menu theme you have selected does not include picture buttons, you can add them to your DVD menu by selecting the desired button shape on the **Settings** pane. See **151 Create a Custom Button** for more information on selecting a button shape.

PART IV:  iDVD

## Change Image Displayed on the Button  149

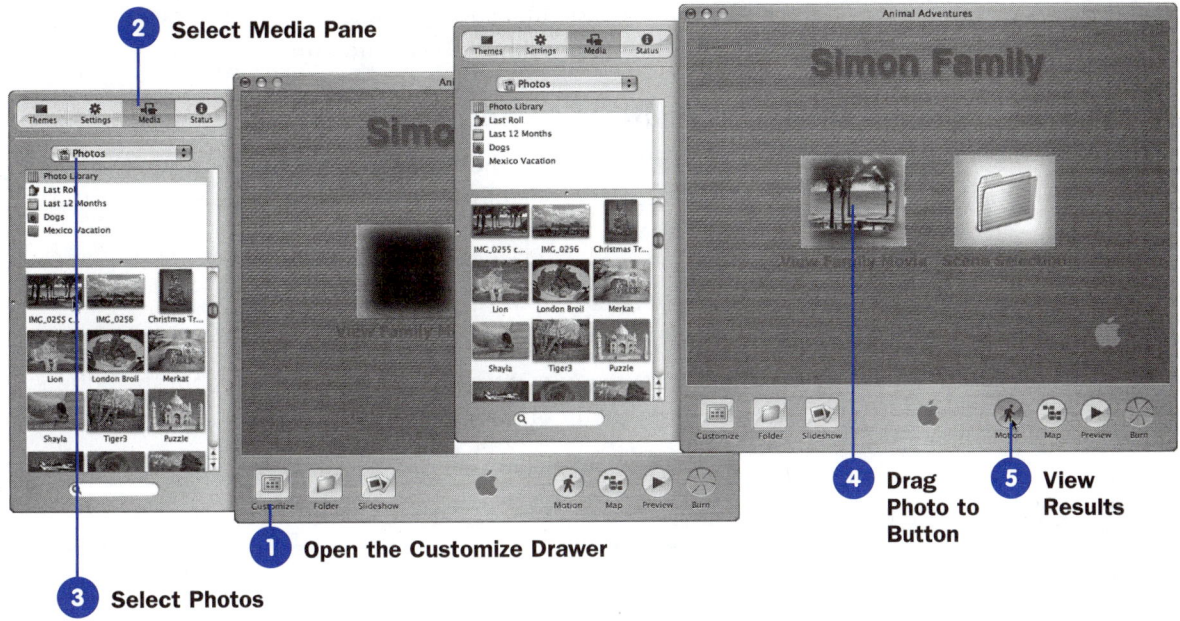

① Open the Customize Drawer

② Select Media Pane

③ Select Photos

④ Drag Photo to Button

⑤ View Results

---

### ① Open the Customize Drawer

Click the **Customize** button in the bottom-left corner of the iDVD window to display the **Customize** drawer.

### ② Select Media Pane

If not selected, click the **Media** button to display the **Media** pane. Choose the **Photos** option from the drop-down list to display the photos from your iPhoto **Library**. The top portion of the browser lists each of the iPhoto albums along with the **Library**. The bottom portion of the browser displays the photos in the entire **Library** or the selected album.

### ③ Select Photo

Click to select the photo you want to use as the image for a specific button on the DVD menu. You can use the scrollbar at the right side of the **Media** pane to scroll through your photos and locate the desired photo.

**NOTE**

When you add a picture to a button, the new image replaces the current image on the button. You can immediately undo the change by choosing **Edit, Undo Custom Set Image**. You can also replace the button image with a new movie or photo by dragging the desired selection from the **Customize** drawer to the button.

---

CHAPTER 18:   Customizing the DVD        403

### 150 Change Button Locations

If you want to look in a specific photo album, click the album name in the top portion of the **Media** pane.

#### 4 Drag Photo to Button

Drag the selected photo to the button you want to change. A white line outlines the inside of the button where iDVD will paste the selected photo.

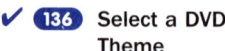

**TIP**

To change the image for another button on the menu, repeat steps 3 through 5.

#### 5 View Results

If it is not already selected, click the **Motion** button to view the current DVD menu with motion turned on. Note that the button containing the still photo will not have motion.

### 150 Change Button Locations

**Before You Begin**

✔ 136 Select a DVD Theme

**See Also**

→ 149 Change Image Displayed on the Button

→ 151 Create a Custom Button

When you add buttons to your DVD menu by inserting a movie, adding a new folder, or creating a slideshow, iDVD inserts the menu buttons based on the default layout settings of the current theme. For example, if you add a menu button to the **Fun** theme, the buttons are added vertically down the right side of the menu; if you add buttons to the **Family** theme, the buttons are added as picture buttons horizontally across the menu. By default, the **Snap to Grid** option is selected for each DVD theme. The **Snap to Grid** option means that you can change the order of the buttons by dragging one in front of the other, but you cannot move them outside of the layout.

As with the other features of the DVD menu, you can customize the location of the buttons on the menu by manually moving them to the desired locations. To move the buttons manually, you select the **Free Position** option on the **Settings** pane. With this option selected, you can drag each button to any location on the menu, instead of being limited to the gridded positions set up by the menu theme.

#### 1 Open the Customize Drawer

Click the **Customize** button in the bottom-left corner of the iDVD window to display the **Customize** drawer.

**Change Button Locations** 150

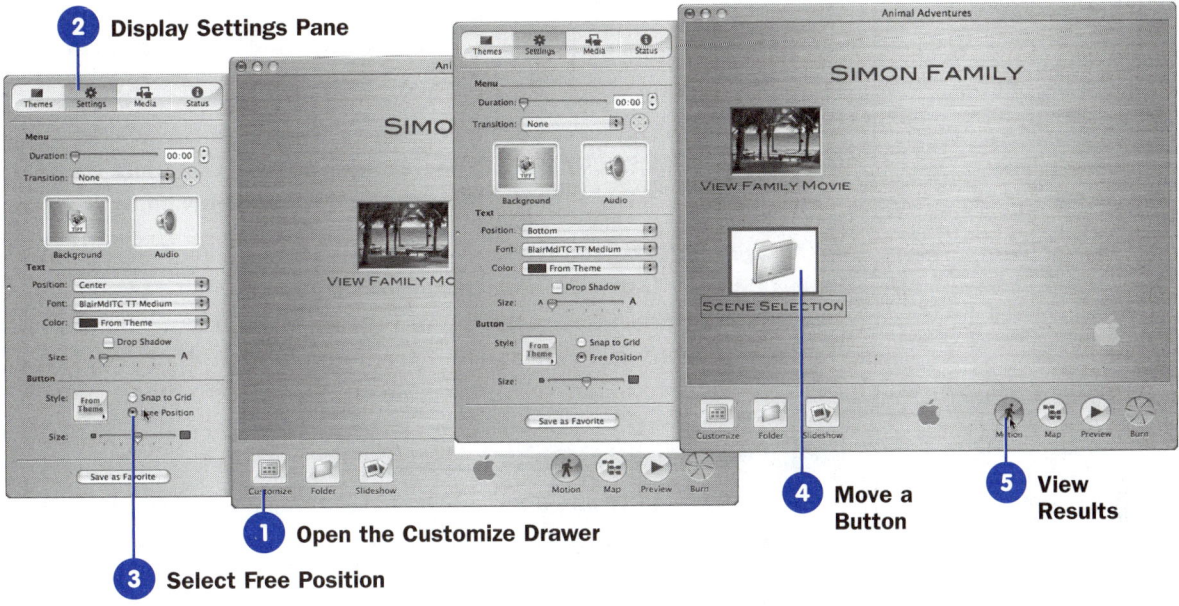

② **Display Settings Pane**

① **Open the Customize Drawer**

③ **Select Free Position**

④ **Move a Button**

⑤ **View Results**

---

② **Display Settings Pane**

Click the **Settings** button to display the **Settings** pane. The **Settings** pane provides options for customizing such settings on the DVD menu as the look of the buttons and the text. See 154 **Save a Custom Theme** for information on saving a DVD menu theme.

③ **Select Free Position**

Click to select the **Free Position** option in the **Button** portion of the **Settings** panel.

④ **Move a Button**

Click a menu button and drag it to the desired location on the menu. Repeat this step for each button on the menu.

⑤ **View Results**

Review the menu to make sure that the positions of the buttons is appropriate. If you are using motion on your DVD menu, click the **Motion** button to ensure that you have the desired results.

**NOTE**

If the **Snap to Grid** option is selected, you can change the order of the menu buttons on the menu, but you cannot reposition them.

**TIPS**

If you are moving picture buttons, you might want to change the text settings of the button label based on the button positioning. See 147 **Change Text of Buttons/Titles** for more information on customizing the labels.

To return to the original positioning of the buttons, click the **Snap to Grid** option on the **Settings** panel on the **Customize** drawer.

CHAPTER 18: Customizing the DVD    405

## 151 Create a Custom Button

**Before You Begin**

✓ **136** Select a DVD Theme

**See Also**

→ **145** Create a Custom Motion Menu

→ **149** Change Image Displayed on the Button

When you add menu buttons to a DVD menu, iDVD sets the button shape based on the selected theme. For example, for the **Fish Two** theme, iDVD creates square picture buttons. You can customize the button shape by selecting the desired option on the **Settings** pane.

When you select a button shape, the new shape applies to all the buttons on the DVD menu. If the current theme does not have picture buttons, you can select one of the buttons shapes to add picture buttons. If you want to remove the picture buttons, select the **Text** button option to remove the picture buttons and keep the text labels as buttons.

### 1 Open the Customize Drawer

Click the **Customize** button in the bottom-left corner of the iDVD window to display the **Customize** drawer.

### 2 Display the Settings Pane

Click the **Settings** button to display the **Settings** pane. The **Settings** pane provides options for customizing such settings on the DVD menu as the look of the buttons and the text. See **154** **Save a Custom Theme** for information on saving a DVD menu theme.

### 3 Display the Button List

Click the **From Theme** button at the bottom of the **Settings** panel to display a list of available button shapes.

> **NOTE**
>
> If the current menu theme does not have picture buttons, choose a shaped button to change all the text buttons to picture buttons. If you want to change all the picture buttons to text buttons, select the **Text** button (the big letter **T**); the text labels become the buttons themselves.

### 4 Select the Desired Button Shape

Click the desired button shape from the list. The buttons on the DVD menu change to match the selection.

### 5 View Results

Review the menu to make sure that the button shapes are appropriate. If you are using motion on your DVD menu, click the **Motion** button to ensure that you have the desired results.

Create a Custom Button  151

**2** Display the Settings Pane

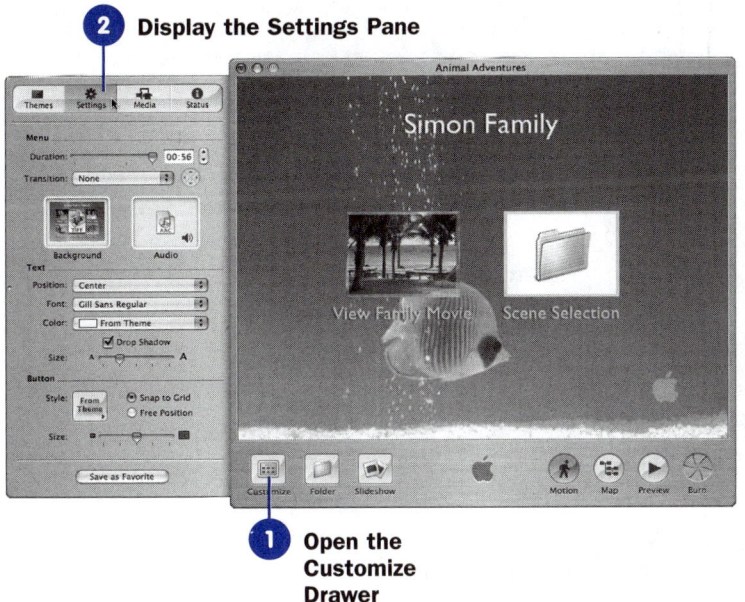
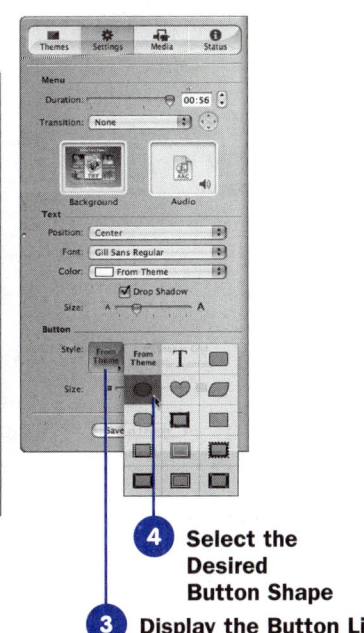

**1** Open the Customize Drawer

**4** Select the Desired Button Shape

**3** Display the Button List

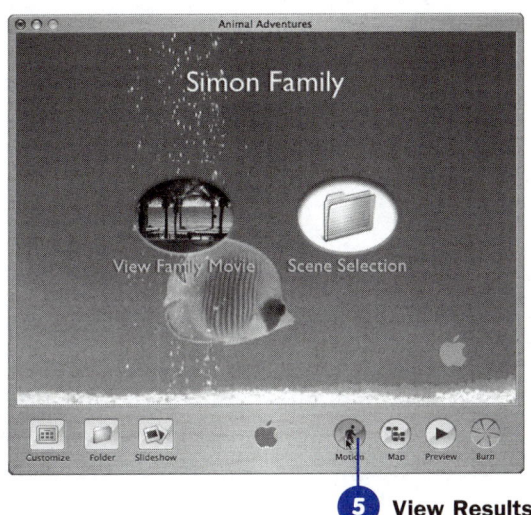

**5** View Results

CHAPTER 18: Customizing the DVD

## 152 Move Buttons to Other Menus

### Before You Begin

✔ **136** Select a DVD Theme

✔ **137** Add a Movie to the DVD Menu

### See Also

→ **147** Change Text of Buttons/Titles

→ **150** Change Button Locations

→ **151** Create a Custom Button

→ **154** Save a Custom Theme

 **TIP**

If you want to keep the menu button on the current menu *and place a copy of it* on a submenu, choose **Edit, Copy** to copy the button instead.

If you decide you want to move a button to another menu or a submenu, you can use the **Cut** and **Paste** options available on the **Edit** menu. When you move a button from one menu to another, the button takes on the attributes of the menu in which you paste it. For example, if the original menu had picture buttons but the submenu had just label buttons, the pasted menu buttons will have only labels.

**① Select the Button to Move**

Click to select the button you want to move to another menu on your DVD.

**② Cut the Button from Current Menu**

Choose **Edit, Cut** to remove the selected button from the current menu. iDVD displays a poof of smoke as it removes the selected menu button from the current DVD menu.

**③ Open the Submenu**

Double-click the submenu folder button to open it. By default, all the submenus display the folder image icon, but you can change that button image. See **149** **Change Image Displayed on the Button** for more information.

**④ Paste the Menu Button**

Choose **Edit, Paste** to paste the selected menu button on the current menu. The menu button is pasted using the current theme button settings. That is, the new button takes on the font, position, color, and font size options specified for the current menu; if the current menu uses text buttons and the button you are pasting is a picture button, the new button no longer has a picture.

**⑤ View Results**

Review the menu to make sure that the new button is placed in the desired location. You can reorganize the buttons by dragging them to the desired locations.

## Move Buttons to Other Menus 152

**1** Select the Button to Move

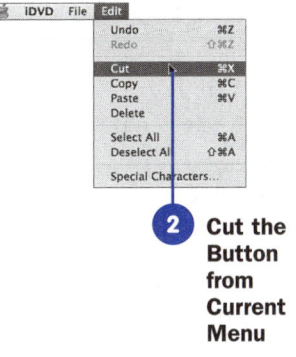

**2** Cut the Button from Current Menu

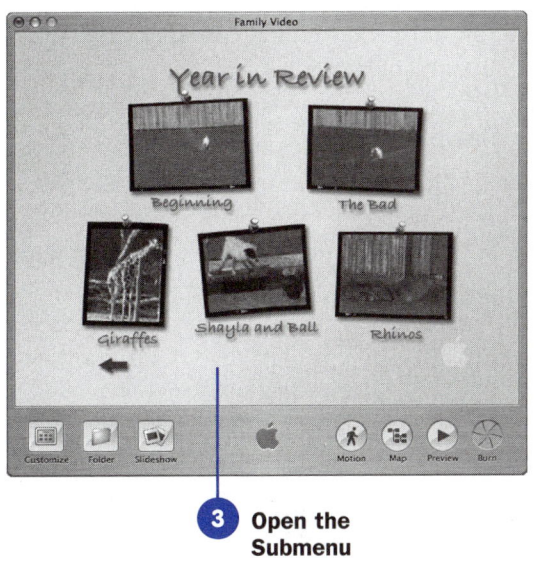

**3** Open the Submenu

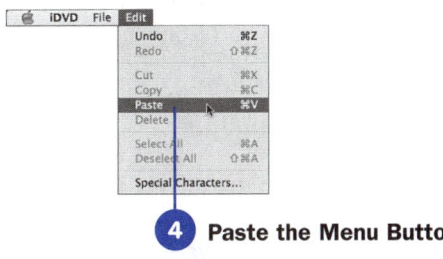

**4** Paste the Menu Button

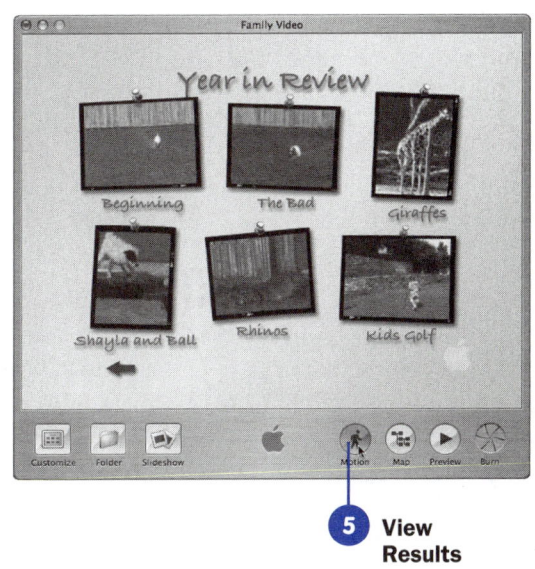

**5** View Results

**CHAPTER 18:** Customizing the DVD     409

## 153 Change the Audio that Plays for the DVD Menu

**Before You Begin**

✔ **136** Select a DVD Theme

✔ **137** Add a Movie to the DVD Menu

**See Also**

→ **144** Create a Custom Background

→ **145** Create a Custom Motion Menu

→ **146** Change Menu Title

→ **147** Change Text of Buttons/Titles

→ **154** Save a Custom Theme

When you create a DVD menu, the menu uses any audio assigned to the selected theme to play whenever the **Motion** button is selected. Audio is also assigned to the DVD menu if you create a motion menu using a movie file. See **145 Create a Custom Motion Menu** for more information on creating a motion menu for your DVD menu.

You can add custom audio to the DVD menu by selecting any of your iTunes audio files from the **Audio Browser**. When you select an audio file, iDVD adds the portion of the audio specified by the **Motion Duration** slider on the **Settings** panel. For example, if the **Motion Duration** slider is set to 25 seconds, iDVD adds the first 25 seconds of the audio file to the DVD menu. The audio repeats as long as the menu is displayed.

### ❶ Open the Customize Drawer

Click the **Customize** button in the bottom-left corner of the iDVD window to display the **Customize** drawer.

### ❷ Display the Media Pane

If it is not already selected, click the **Media** button to display the **Media** pane. From the drop-down list at the top of the **Media** pane, select **Audio**. When the **Audio** option is selected, the **Media** pane displays the audio files from your iTunes **Library**. The top portion of the pane lists each of the iTunes playlists. The bottom portion of the pane displays the audio files in the **Library** or the selected playlist.

### ❸ Select an Audio File

Click to select the audio file you want to use as the audio for the selected DVD menu. You can use the scrollbar at the right side of the **Media** pane to scroll through your iTunes **Library** and locate the desired audio file.

If you want to look at a specific playlist, click the playlist name in the top portion of the **Media** pane, and the playlist of individual audio files will display in the bottom portion of the pane.

## Change the Audio that Plays for the DVD Menu

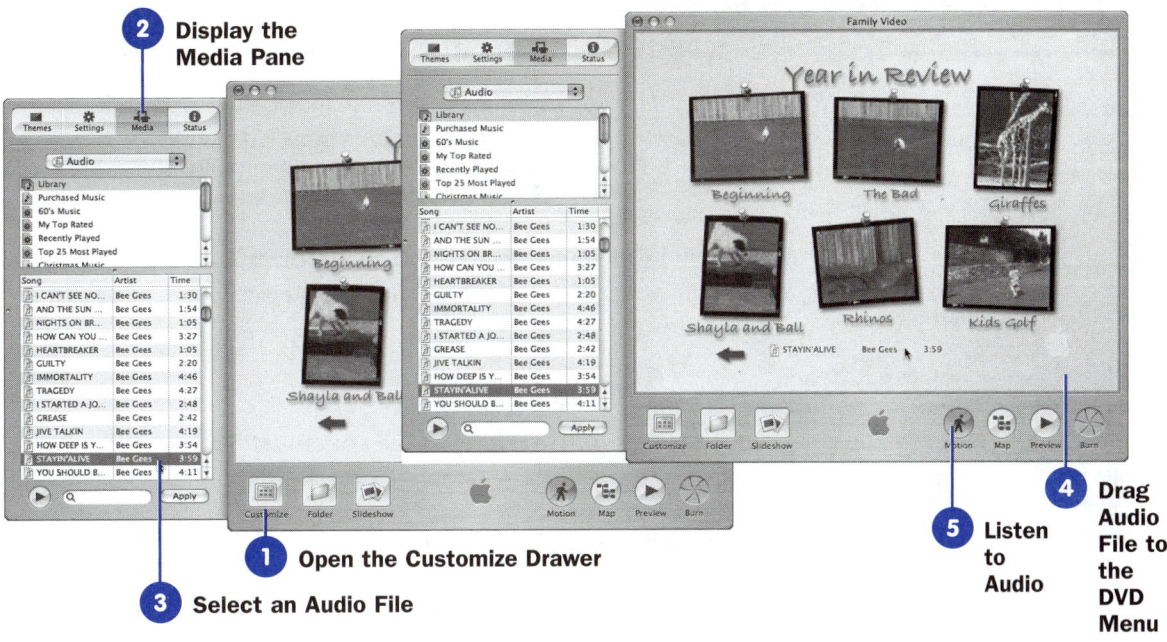

① Open the Customize Drawer
② Display the Media Pane
③ Select an Audio File
④ Drag Audio File to the DVD Menu
⑤ Listen to Audio

### ④ Drag Audio File to the DVD Menu

Drag the selected audio file to the DVD menu. As you drag, the name of the selected audio file displays under the mouse pointer. Release the mouse button to add the audio to the menu.

### ⑤ Listen to Audio

If it is not already selected, click the **Motion** button to view the motion of the menu and listen to the assigned audio.

If you don't like the audio selection, you can repeat steps 1 through 5 to add a different audio file to the DVD menu.

**TIP**

If you selected a theme that has default audio, you can switch back to the original audio by removing the new audio from the DVD menu. To remove the audio, click the **Settings** button to display the **Settings** pane on the **Customize** drawer. Click the icon in the **Audio** well and drag it out of the well to remove the audio you added so that it doesn't play on the DVD menu.

**CHAPTER 18:** Customizing the DVD    411

## 154 Save a Custom Theme

**Before You Begin**

✔ 136 Select a DVD Theme
✔ 137 Add a Movie to the DVD Menu

**See Also**

→ 144 Create a Custom Background
→ 145 Create a Custom Motion Menu
→ 146 Change Menu Title
→ 147 Change Text of Buttons/Titles
→ 149 Change Image Displayed on the Button
→ 151 Create a Custom Button

You can save the customizations you make to a DVD menu so that you can apply them again to another menu. When you save the custom theme options, iDVD creates the new theme and saves it as one of your **Favorites**.

After the custom theme is created, you can apply it to other DVD menus by selecting it from the **Favorites** list on the **Themes** panel of the **Customize** drawer.

### ❶ Open the Customize Drawer

Click the **Customize** button in the bottom-left corner of the iDVD window to display the **Customize** drawer.

### ❷ Display the Settings Pane

Click the **Settings** button to display the **Settings** pane. The **Settings** pane provides options for customizing different settings on the DVD menu, such as the look of the buttons and the text. See 151 **Create a Custom Button** for information on customizing the buttons on the DVD menu.

### ❸ Click the Save as Favorite Button

Click the **Save as Favorite** button to save the current button, title, background, and audio settings for your DVD menu. A dialog box displays in which you can specify the desired name for the new theme.

### ❹ Specify Theme Name

Type the name for the custom theme in the text box and click the **OK** button. iDVD creates a new theme and adds it to your list of favorite themes.

### ❺ Display Themes Pane

Click the **Themes** button to display the **Themes** pane in the **Customize** drawer.

**TIPS**

If you want to allow other users who use your computer to use this theme, enable the **Shared for all users** check box.

If you want to overwrite another theme with the same name, enable the **Replace existing** check box.

PART IV: iDVD

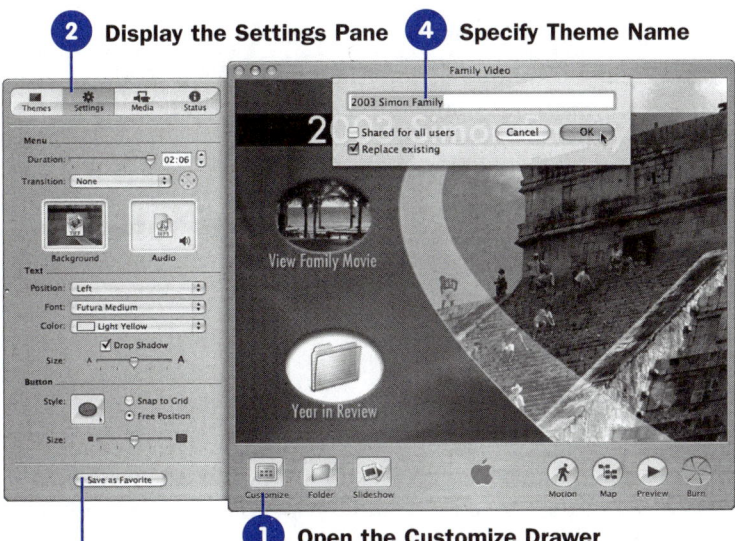

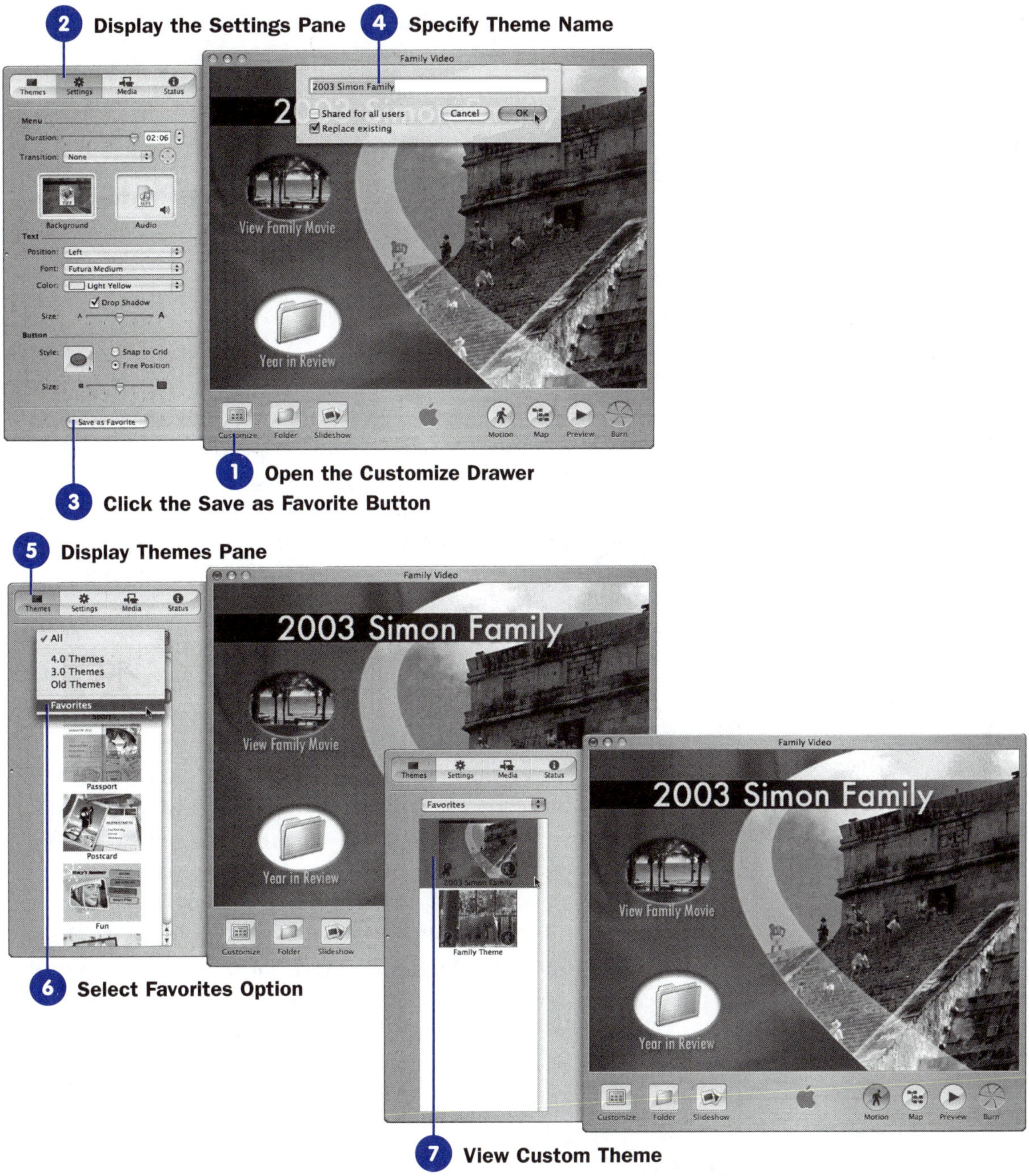
2 Display the Settings Pane
4 Specify Theme Name
Family Video
2003 Simon Family
Shared for all users
Replace existing
Cancel
OK
Themes
Settings
Media
Status
Menu
Duration:
02:06
Transition:
None
Background
Audio
Text
Position:
Left
Font:
Futura Medium
Color:
Light Yellow
Drop Shadow
Size:
Button
Style:
Snap to Grid
Free Position
Save as Favorite
View Family Movie
Year in Review
Customize
Folder
Slideshow
Motion
Map
Preview
Burn
1 Open the Customize Drawer
3 Click the Save as Favorite Button
5 Display Themes Pane
All
4.0 Themes
3.0 Themes
Old Themes
Favorites
Passport
Postcard
Fun
Family Theme
6 Select Favorites Option
7 View Custom Theme

**TIP**

You cannot remove a custom theme from within iDVD. To delete a custom theme, open **Finder** and locate your **Favorites** folder in the **iDVD** folder of your **Home** folder. Select the custom theme you want to delete and drag it to the **Trash**.

### ⑥ Select Favorites Option

From the **Themes** drop-down list at the top of the pane, select the **Favorites** option to view all the custom themes you have saved.

### ⑦ View Custom Theme

Review the list of custom themes to make sure that the new theme was created and saved.

## 155  Remove the Apple Watermark

**See Also**

→ 144 Create a Custom Background
→ 145 Create a Custom Motion Menu
→ 146 Change Menu Title
→ 147 Change Text of Buttons/Titles
→ 154 Save a Custom Theme

When you create a DVD menu in iDVD, the Apple logo is placed in the bottom-right corner of the menu by default. Depending on your intended use of the DVDs, you might not want that logo to display on your menus. Luckily, iDVD lets you remove that logo from the menu by disabling the **Show Apple logo watermark** check box on the **Preferences** dialog box.

### ① Display the Preferences Dialog Box

Choose **iDVD**, **Preferences** to display the **Preferences** dialog box.

### ② Display the General Options

If it is not selected already, click the **General** button to display the options for changing the **Project Settings** and **Video Standard** for DVDs. The name of the **Preferences** dialog box changes to reflect the button selected.

### ③ Disable the Show Apple Logo Watermark Option

Click the **Show Apple logo watermark** check box to remove the check mark. When this option is disabled, the Apple logo will not appear on your DVD menu.

Click the red **Close** button in the upper corner of the **Preferences** dialog box to close the dialog box.

### ④ View Results

Review the DVD menu to make sure that the Apple logo has been removed.

Remove the Apple Watermark  155

① **Display the Preferences Dialog Box**

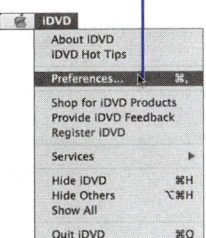

Apple Logo Watermark

② **Display the General Options**

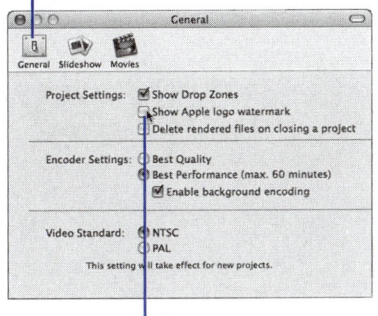

③ **Disable the Show Apple Logo Watermark Option**

④ **View Results**

CHAPTER 18: Customizing the DVD   415

# 19

# Adding a Slideshow to a DVD

## IN THIS CHAPTER:

- **156** Create a Slideshow Using an iPhoto Album
- **157** Manually Create a Slideshow Using the Media Pane
- **158** Create a Slideshow in iDVD with the Finder
- **159** Add Audio to a Slideshow in iDVD
- **160** Reorganize Images in a Slideshow
- **161** Control Slideshow Advancing

## 156 Create a Slideshow Using an iPhoto Album

Movies aren't the only things you can put on the DVDs you create in iDVD; you can also create slideshows that display on the DVD. When you create a slideshow, a **Slideshow** button is created on the DVD menu. When the **Slideshow** button is selected, the photos display in typical slideshow fashion. You can customize the slideshow display options in iDVD.

You can create a slideshow using the photos in an existing iPhoto album, or you can manually select the individual photos for the slideshow from iDVD. The photos you add to your iDVD slideshow do not have to exist within iPhoto (as must be the case when you create an slideshow in iPhoto). When you create the slideshow in iDVD, you can access photos in any folder you can open with Finder.

After the photos are selected for your slideshow, you can customize the slideshow by adding audio that plays as the slideshow is viewed. You can also change the order of the photos in the slideshow and control the way the photos are advanced by specifying the amount of time to display each photo and whether the viewer can manually advance the slides.

## 156 Create a Slideshow Using an iPhoto Album

**Before You Begin**

- ✓ **3** About Photo Libraries and Albums
- ✓ **4** Create New Albums
- ✓ **5** Create a Smart Album

**See Also**

- → **6** Organize Photos in an Album
- → **157** Manually Create a Slideshow Using the Media Pane
- → **159** Add Audio to a Slideshow in iDVD
- → **160** Reorganize Images in a Slideshow
- → **161** Control Slideshow Advancing

You can use a photo album created in iPhoto as a slideshow available on your DVD menu. To accomplish this, you must first create a photo album within iPhoto that contains all the photos you want to appear in your slideshow. Keep in mind that all the photos in the selected album will become part of the slideshow.

After creating the photo album in iPhoto, you can add it to your DVD menu using the **iPhoto Browser** in the **Customize** drawer of iDVD. When you add the photo album to your DVD menu, iDVD creates a **Slideshow** menu button and labels it to match the name of the selected photo album. For example, if the photo album you add to your DVD menu is named **Dogs**, the slideshow button is given the label **Dogs**. As with other buttons on the DVD menu, you can customize the button for slideshows. See **147 Change Text of Buttons/Titles** for more information on customizing the button labels on a DVD menu. See **149 Change Image Displayed on the Button** for information on changing the image on a slideshow button.

**Create a Slideshow Using an iPhoto Album** 156

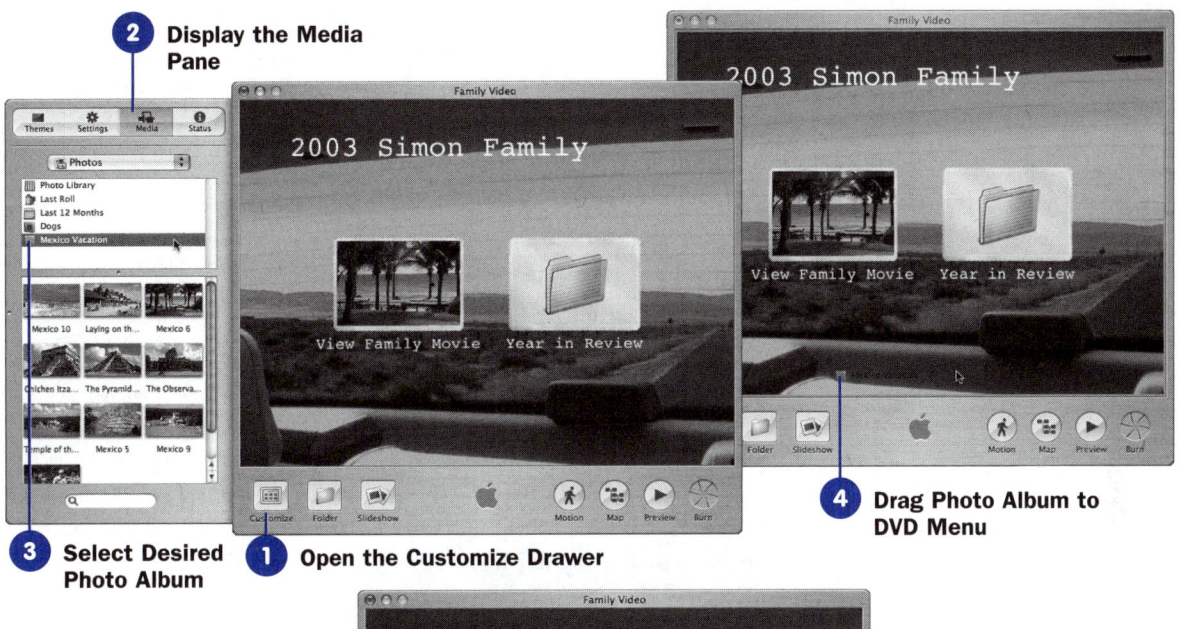

② Display the Media Pane
③ Select Desired Photo Album
① Open the Customize Drawer
④ Drag Photo Album to DVD Menu

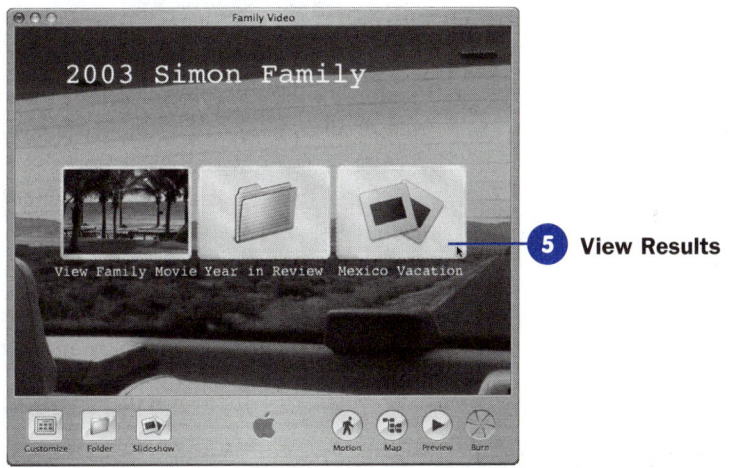

⑤ View Results

When iDVD creates the slideshow, the photos are added to the slideshow in the order they are listed in the photo album. You can change the order of the photos for the slideshow in the **Slideshow Editor**. See 160 **Reorganize Images in a Slideshow** for more information on changing the order of photos in your slideshow. iDVD also creates the slideshow to advance through the slides manually. This means that the slides change

**CHAPTER 19:** Adding a Slideshow to a DVD 419

## 156  Create a Slideshow Using an iPhoto Album

only when the **Next** button is selected. If you want to customize how the slideshow advances through the photos, you can do so with the **Slideshow Editor**. See **161** **Control Slideshow Advancing** for more information on customizing how a slideshow advances.

### ① Open the Customize Drawer

Click the **Customize** button in the bottom-left corner of the iDVD window to display the **Customize** drawer.

### ② Display the Media Pane

If it is not already selected, click the **Media** button to display the **Media** pane. From the drop-down list at the top of the **Media** pane, choose the **Photos** option. The **Media** pane displays photos from your **iPhoto Library**. The top portion of the pane lists each of the iPhoto albums along with the **Library**. The bottom portion of the pane displays the photos in the selected album.

### ③ Select Desired Photo Album

In the top portion of the **Media** pane, click to select the desired photo album. The thumbnail images of the photos in that selected album display in the bottom portion of the **Media** pane. The photos display in the order they are currently listed in iPhoto.

### ④ Drag Photo Album to DVD Menu

Drag the selected photo album to the DVD menu. As you drag the album, a blue box displays around the edge of the iDVD menu, and the name of the album displays under the cursor. Release the mouse button to create a **Slideshow** button that matches the name of the photo album.

If the theme you selected contains a *drop zone*, avoid dropping the photo album in the drop zone. If you place the photo album in the drop zone, you cannot select the slideshow. See **141** **Add Images to Drop Zones** for more information on working with a drop zone.

### ⑤ View Results

View the results of adding a slideshow to your DVD menu. A new slideshow button is created that matches the button settings for the current menu theme.

**TIPS**

If you want, you can use iPhoto to change the order of the photos in the album (see **6** **Organize Photos in an Album**). You can also change the order of the photos after creating the slideshow in iDVD on the **Slideshow Editor** (see **160** **Reorganize Images in a Slideshow**).

iDVD slideshows can have up to 99 photos. If your album contains more photos, only the first 99 are included in the slideshow.

If you want to customize the order of the slides or the way the slides advance in the slideshow, you can do that on the **Slideshow Editor**. See **160 Reorganize Images in a Slideshow** and **161 Control Slideshow Advancing**.

If you want to preview the slideshow, click the **Preview** button at the bottom of the iDVD window. iDVD displays a preview of how the DVD menu will appear. See **162 Preview the DVD Content** for information on previewing a DVD menu before burning a DVD.

## 157 Manually Create a Slideshow Using the Media Pane

You can create a slideshow in iDVD using photos you have stored in iPhoto. You can create the slideshow using the **Slideshow Browser** by adding the desired photos from the **Media Browser**.

Before you can add photos to a slideshow, you must first create the slideshow menu button on the DVD menu. When you create the slideshow button, iDVD assigns the label **My Slideshow** to the button.

When you add photos to the slideshow, they are placed in the slideshow in the order you add them to the list. If you want to add a photo in front of an existing photo, you must drag it above the current photo as you add it. You can also change the order of the photos after they have been added to the slideshow as explained in **160 Reorganize Images in a Slideshow**.

### 1 Create Slideshow Menu Button

Click the **Slideshow** button on the bottom of the iDVD window to create a new menu button for a slideshow.

iDVD uses the current theme to create a button for a slideshow. See **136 Select a DVD Theme** for information on selecting a theme for your DVD menu. If your current theme uses button labels, iDVD assigns the label **My Slideshow** to the button. As with other menu buttons, you can change the text of the label. See **147 Change Text of Buttons/Titles** for more information on customizing button labels for a DVD menu.

**Before You Begin**

✔ **3** About Photo Libraries and Albums

**See Also**

→ **156** Create a Slideshow Using an iPhoto Album

→ **158** Create a Slideshow in iDVD with the Finder

→ **159** Add Audio to a Slideshow in iDVD

→ **160** Reorganize Images in a Slideshow

→ **161** Control Slideshow Advancing

### 157  Manually Create a Slideshow Using the Media Pane

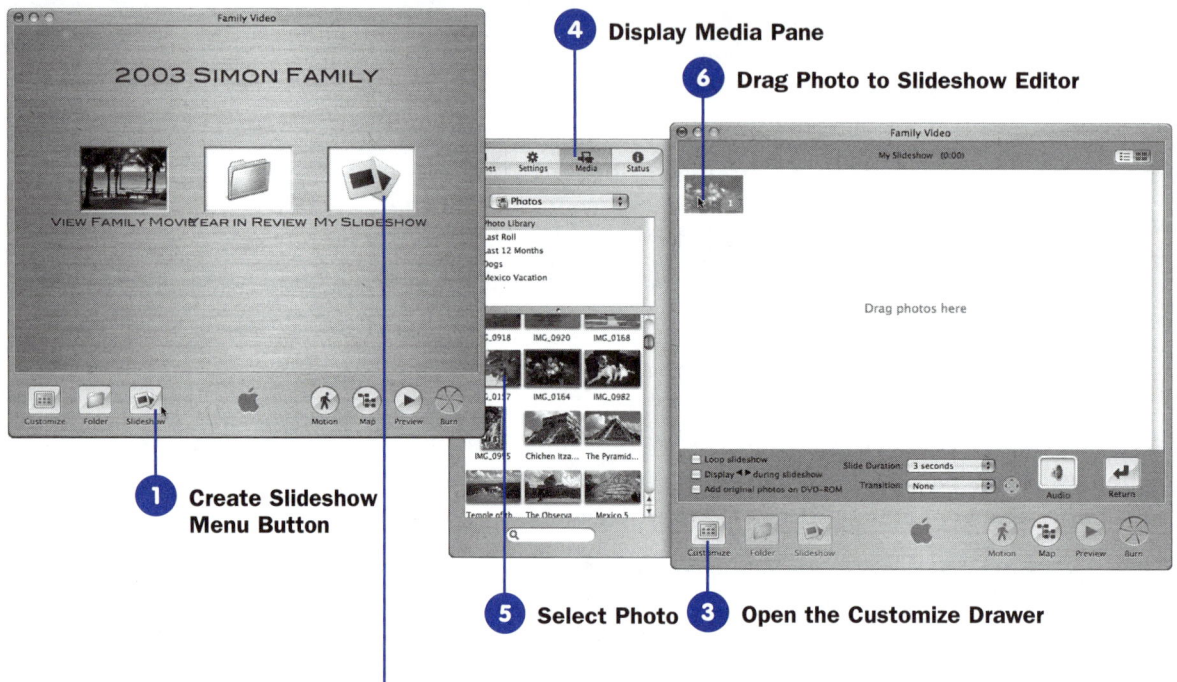
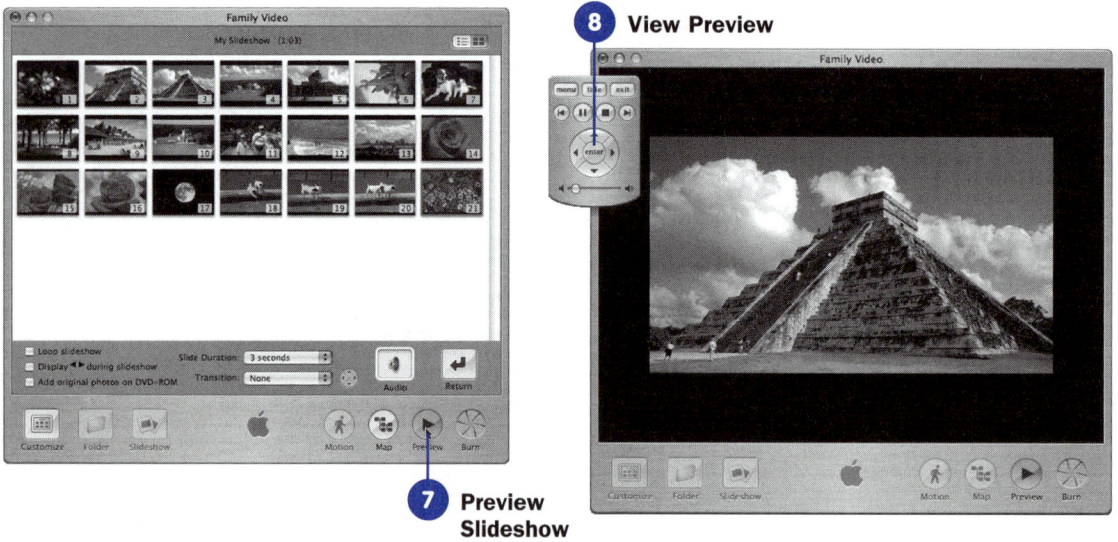

PART IV:  iDVD

## Manually Create a Slideshow Using the iPhoto Browser  157

### ② Display Slideshow Editor

Click the new slideshow button on the DVD menu to display the **Slideshow Editor** so that you can add photos to the slideshow.

### ③ Open the Customize Drawer

Click the **Customize** button in the bottom-left corner of the iDVD window to display the **Customize** drawer.

### ④ Display Media Pane

If it is not already selected, click the **Media** button to display the **Media** pane. From the drop-down list at the top of the **Media** pane, choose the **Photos** option. The **Media** pane displays photos from your **iPhoto Library**. The top portion of the pane lists each of the iPhoto albums along with the **Library**. The bottom portion of the pane displays the photos in the selected album.

### ⑤ Select Photo

Click to select the first photo you want to add to the slideshow. You can use the scrollbar at the right side of the **iPhoto Browser** to scroll through your photo library and locate the desired photo.

If you want to look in a specific photo album, click the album name in the top portion of the **iPhoto Browser**.

### ⑥ Drag Photo to Slideshow Editor

Drag the selected photo to the **Slideshow Editor**. As you drag the photo, the photo thumbnail displays under the mouse pointer. When you release the mouse button, the photo is added to the list.

### ⑦ Preview Slideshow

Click the **Preview** button to view the slideshow as it will appear on the DVD. iDVD displays the photos from the slideshow on a black background.

### ⑧ View Preview

View the preview of the slideshow that will be added to the DVD. You can use the remote control that displays on the screen to control the play of the slideshow. See  **Preview the DVD Content** for more information on previewing the DVD menu that will be created.

> **TIP**
> Repeat steps 5 and 6 to add additional photos to the slideshow. To change the order of the photos in the slideshow, see  **Reorganize Images in a Slideshow**.

> **NOTE**
> By default, the slides do not automatically advance. You must click the **Next** and **Previous** buttons on the remote control to advance the slides. See **161 Control Slideshow Advancing** for information on automatically advancing the slides.

> **TIP**
> To cancel the preview and view the DVD menu, click the **Preview** button again to deselect it.

CHAPTER 19:  Adding a Slideshow to a DVD

## 158 Create a Slideshow in iDVD with the Finder

**Before You Begin**

✓ ③ About Photo Libraries and Albums

**See Also**

→ ⑮⑥ Create a Slideshow Using an iPhoto Album

→ ⑮⑦ Manually Create a Slideshow Using the Photo Browser

→ ⑮⑨ Add Audio to a Slideshow in iDVD

→ ⑯⓪ Reorganize Images in a Slideshow

→ ⑯① Control Slideshow Advancing

You can create a slideshow in iDVD using photos located in any folder you can access from your computer. The photos you use do not have to be located in your iPhoto **Library**. You add the photos to a slideshow in iDVD using **Finder**.

Before you can add photos to a slideshow, you must first create the slideshow menu button on the DVD menu. When you create this slideshow button, iDVD assigns the label **My Slideshow**.

After creating the slideshow menu button, you open the **Slideshow Editor** and drag the photos you want to add to the slideshow into the editor from **Finder**. You can add individual photos or an entire folder of photos to the **Slideshow Editor** to create the slideshow. After you add the photos to the slideshow, you can change the order of the photos as explained in ⑯⓪ **Reorganize Images in a Slideshow**.

### ❶ Create Slideshow Menu Button

Click the **Slideshow** button on the bottom of the iDVD window to create a new menu button for a slideshow.

iDVD uses the current menu theme to create a button for a slideshow. See ⑬⑥ **Select a DVD Theme** for information on selecting a theme for your DVD menu. If your current theme uses button labels, iDVD assigns the label **My Slideshow** to the button. As with other menu buttons, you can change the text of the label as explained in ⑭⑤ **Change Text of Buttons/Titles**.

### ❷ Display Slideshow Editor

Click the new slideshow button on the DVD menu to display the **Slideshow Editor** so that you can add photos to the slideshow.

### ❸ Locate Photos in Finder

Click the **Finder** icon in the Dock to open a Finder window. In Finder, open the folder containing the photos you want to use for the slideshow. In the folder, select the photo you want to add to the slideshow. To select multiple photos, hold down the ⌘ button while you click each photo.

**TIP**

You can use photos of any size or in any orientation. iDVD will size the photos to fit the slideshow. If the photos are vertically oriented, black bars will appear on the sides of the photo.

**Create a Slideshow in iDVD with the Finder** 158

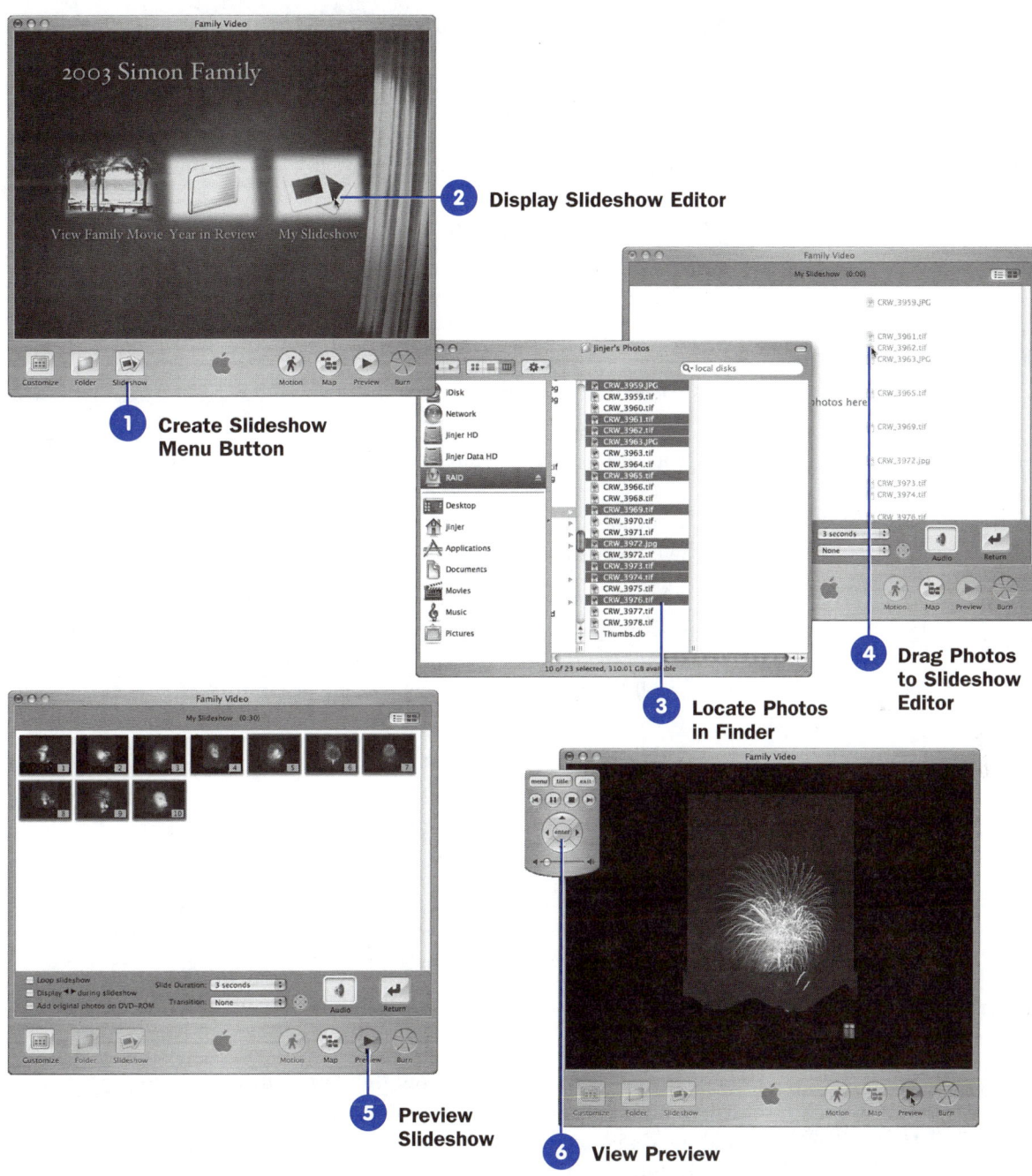

**CHAPTER 19: Adding a Slideshow to a DVD** 425

## 159  Add Audio to a Slideshow in iDVD

**NOTE**

Repeat steps 3 and 4 to add additional photos to the slideshow. You can add up to 99 different photos to your slideshow.

**④ Drag Photos to Slideshow Editor**

Drag the selected photos to the **Slideshow Editor**. As you drag the photo to the **Slideshow Editor**, the photo thumbnails display under the mouse pointer. When you release the mouse button, the photos are added to the list in the **Slideshow Editor**.

**⑤ Preview Slideshow**

Click the **Preview** button at the bottom of the iDVD window to view the slideshow as it will appear on the DVD. iDVD displays the photos from the slideshow on a black background.

**⑥ View the Preview**

View the preview of the slideshow that will be added to the DVD. You can use the remote control that displays on the screen to control the play of the slideshow. See **162 Preview the DVD Content** for more information on previewing the DVD menu that will be created.

By default, iDVD creates a slideshow that you must manually advance. If the slideshow does not advance, click the **Next** and **Previous** buttons on the remote control displayed onscreen to scroll through the slideshow. See **161 Control Slideshow Advancing** for information on switching between manual and automatic advancement of the slideshow.

To cancel the preview and view the DVD menu, click the **Preview** button again to deselect it and return to the **Slideshow Editor**.

## 159  Add Audio to a Slideshow in iDVD

**Before You Begin**

✔ **156** Create a Slideshow Using an iPhoto Album
✔ **157** Manually Create a Slideshow Using the iPhoto Browser
✔ **158** Create a Slideshow in iDVD with the Finder

You can add audio to a slideshow that you create in iDVD. You add audio to the slideshow using the **Slideshow Editor**, and you can use any of the audio files listed in the **iTunes Browser**.

After you select an audio file from the **iTunes Browser**, you drag the selected audio to the **Audio** well on the **Slideshow Editor**. When you add the audio to the slideshow, iTunes automatically adjusts the length of the slideshow to match the length of the selected audio file. The duration option displays in the **Slide Duration** field. You can modify this option as explained in **161 Control Slideshow Advancing**.

426        PART IV:   iDVD

## Add Audio to a Slideshow in iDVD

**See Also**
→ **160** Reorganize Images in a Slideshow
→ **161** Control Slideshow Advancing

### ❶ Open the Customize Drawer

Click the **Customize** button in the bottom-left corner of the iDVD window to display the **Customize** drawer.

### ❷ Display the Media Pane

If it is not already selected, click the **Media** button at the top of the **Customize** drawer to display the **Media** pane. If your iTunes audio files are not displayed, select the **Audio** option from the drop-down list at the top of the **Media** pane. The **Media** pane displays the audio files from your iTunes **Library**. The top portion of the pane lists each of the iTunes playlists in your library. The bottom portion of the pane displays the audio files in the library or the selected playlist.

### ❸ Open Slideshow Editor

Click the slideshow button on the DVD menu to display the **Slideshow Editor** so that you can add audio to the selected slideshow.

### ❹ Select Audio File

In the **Media** pane, click to select the audio file you want to use as the audio the slideshow. Use the scrollbar at the right side of the browser to scroll through your iTunes library and locate the desired audio file.

If you want to look at a specific playlist, click the playlist name in the top portion of the **Media** pane, and the playlist will display in the bottom portion of the browser.

### ❺ Drag Audio File to Audio Well

Drag the selected audio file to the **Audio** well on the iDVD window. As you drag, the name of the selected audio file displays under the mouse pointer. Release the mouse button to add the audio to the **Audio** well.

### ❻ Preview Slideshow

Click the **Preview** button to view the slideshow as it will appear on the DVD. iDVD displays the photos from the slideshow on a black background and plays the selected audio file.

### 💡 TIPS

You can also add audio to the slideshow by dragging the audio file from Finder or from your iTunes window into the **Audio** well at the bottom of the iDVD window.

To remove the audio file from a slideshow, drag the file out of the **Audio** well. When you release the mouse button, the song will disappear in a poof of smoke.

**CHAPTER 19:** Adding a Slideshow to a DVD

### 159  Add Audio to a Slideshow in iDVD

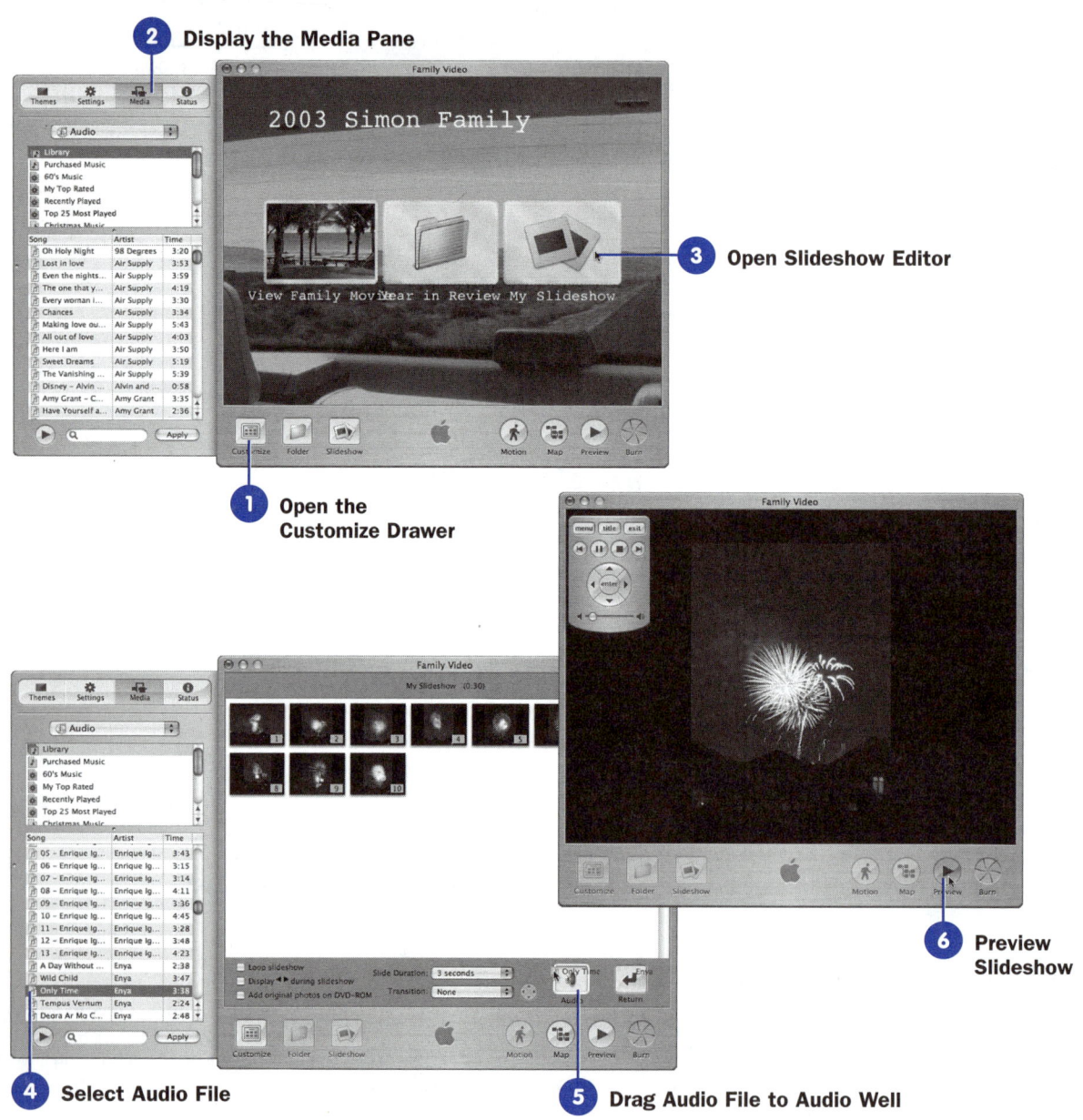

View the preview of the slideshow that will be added to the DVD. You can use the remote control that displays on the screen to control the play of the slideshow. See **162 Preview the DVD**

**Content** for more information on previewing the DVD menu that will be created.

By default, iDVD creates a slideshow that you must manually advance. If the slideshow does not advance, click the **Next** and **Previous** buttons on the remote control that appears onscreen to scroll through the slideshow. See **161 Control Slideshow Advancing** for information on switching between manual and automatic advancement of the slideshow.

To cancel the preview and view the DVD menu, click the **Preview** button again to deselect it and return to the **Slideshow Editor**.

## 160 Reorganize Images in a Slideshow

When you create a slideshow in iDVD, the photos are placed in the slideshow in the same order in which you add them to the slideshow. The order in which the photos are listed in the **Slideshow Editor** is the same order used to view the slideshow. Before burning the DVD, you can change the display order of the photos using the **Slideshow Editor**.

To change the order of photos for a slideshow, you drag a photo in the list and drop it in the desired location in the list. When you have reordered the photos, you can use the **Preview** option to check the new order of the slideshow.

### 1 Display the Slideshow Editor

Click the slideshow button on the DVD menu to display the **Slideshow Editor** so that you can customize the slideshow.

### 2 Select Photo to Move

The **Slideshow Editor** lists the photos in the slideshow in the order in which they display. A number appears to the left of each photo specifying its order in the slideshow. Click to select a photo you want to move on the list.

### 3 Drag Photo

Drag the photo to the desired location in the list. As you drag, the photo's thumbnail and filename display under the mouse pointer, and a black box outlines where the photo will be inserted when you release the mouse button.

**Before You Begin**

✔ **156** Create a Slideshow Using an iPhoto Album

✔ **157** Manually Create a Slideshow Using the iPhoto Browser

✔ **158** Create a Slideshow in iDVD with the Finder

**See Also**

→ **159** Add Audio to a Slideshow in iDVD

→ **161** Control Slideshow Advancing

### TIP

When you open the **Slideshow Editor**, it displays thumbnail images of the slides. To view the slides in list view, click the **List** button in the upper right corner of the **Slideshow Editor**. You can click the **Thumbnail** button to switch back to thumbnail view.

**CHAPTER 19:** Adding a Slideshow to a DVD

## Reorganize Images in a Slideshow

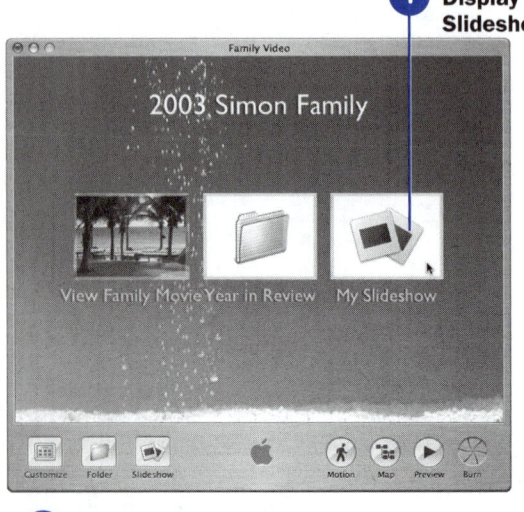

**1** Display the Slideshow Editor

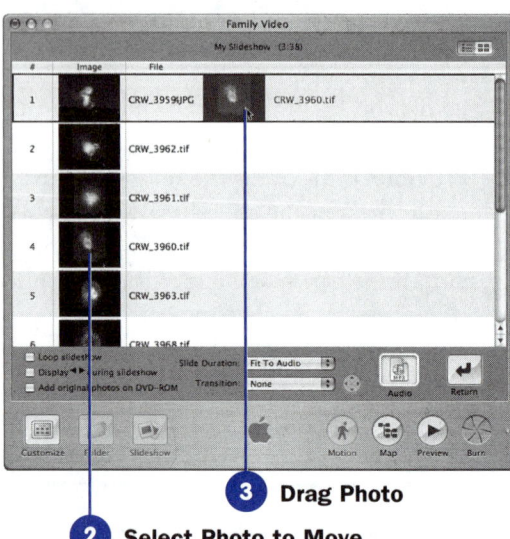

**2** Select Photo to Move

**3** Drag Photo

**4** Place Photo

**5** Preview Slideshow

**6** View the Preview

### TIP

Repeat steps 2 through 4 to move additional photos within the list.

**4** **Place Photo**

When the photo is positioned in the desired location in the list, release the mouse button to insert the photo at the outlined location.

430    PART IV:   iDVD

iDVD adjusts the photo list by inserting the photo at the specified location and adjusting the location and numbers of the remaining photos.

## ⑤ Preview Slideshow

Click the **Preview** button to view the slideshow as it will appear on the DVD. iDVD displays the photos from the slideshow on a black background in the specified order.

## ⑥ View the Preview

View the preview of the slideshow that will be added to the DVD. You can use the remote control that displays on the screen to control the play of the slideshow. See **163 Preview the DVD Content** for more information on previewing the DVD menu that will be created.

By default, iDVD creates a slideshow that you must manually advance. If the slideshow does not advance, click the **Next** and **Previous** buttons on the remote control that appears onscreen to scroll through the slideshow. See **161 Control Slideshow Advancing** for information on switching between manual and automatic advancement of the slideshow.

**NOTE**

Click the **Preview** button again to return to the **Slideshow Editor** and make further modifications to the slideshow.

## 161 Control Slideshow Advancing

When you create a slideshow, iDVD automatically sets the slideshow to manually advance through the photos. This means that the photos do not advance automatically; you must use the **Forward** and **Back** buttons on the remote control palette that appears to move through the photos.

Instead of advancing manually through the photos, you can have the photos change automatically after a specific length of time by selecting a slide duration.

You can also place arrows on the slideshow that can be used to advance forward or move back through the slideshow.

**Before You Begin**

✔ **156** Create a Slideshow Using an iPhoto Album

✔ **157** Manually Create a Slideshow Using the iPhoto Browser

✔ **158** Create a Slideshow in iDVD with the Finder

**See Also**

→ **159** Add Audio to a Slideshow in iDVD

→ **160** Reorganize Images in a Slideshow

**CHAPTER 19:** Adding a Slideshow to a DVD

## 161  Control Slideshow Advancing

### ① Display the Slideshow Editor

Click the slideshow button on the DVD menu to display the **Slideshow Editor** so that you can set the duration of the photos in the slideshow.

### ② Set Slideshow Duration

From the **Slide Duration** drop-down list, select how long you want each slide to display in the slideshow. You can display each slide for **1 second, 3 seconds, 5 seconds, 10 seconds,** or you can choose **Fit to Audio**.

You can select the **Fit to Audio** option only if you have an audio file that plays when you watch the slideshow. If so, iDVD adjusts the timing of each slide based on the length of the audio file. If you have a lot of photos, the photos might display quickly to ensure that they all display before the end of the audio. You might want to choose a longer audio file in such a case.

### ③ Display Advance Arrows

If desired, enable the **Display arrows during slideshow** check box to display arrows on the slideshow that can be used to scroll through the slides manually. If you enable the **Display arrows during slideshow** check box, you can still use the remote control buttons to advance through the slides.

### ④ Preview Slideshow

Click the **Preview** button to view the slideshow as it will appear on the DVD. iDVD displays the photos from the slideshow on a black background.

### ⑤ View the Preview

View the preview of the slideshow that will be added to the DVD. You can use the remote control that displays on the screen to control the play of the slideshow. See **163 Preview the DVD Content** for more information on previewing the DVD menu that will be created.

---

**TIPS**

You can select the method used to switch between slides by assigning a transition. Click the arrow button next to the **Transition** list box and select the desired transition.

To have the slideshow continue to repeat, enable the **Loop Slideshow** check box.

**NOTE**

Even if you have set the slideshow advance method, you can still manually advance through the slideshow by clicking the **Advance Arrow** buttons or by clicking the buttons on the remote control.

## Control Slideshow Advancing 161

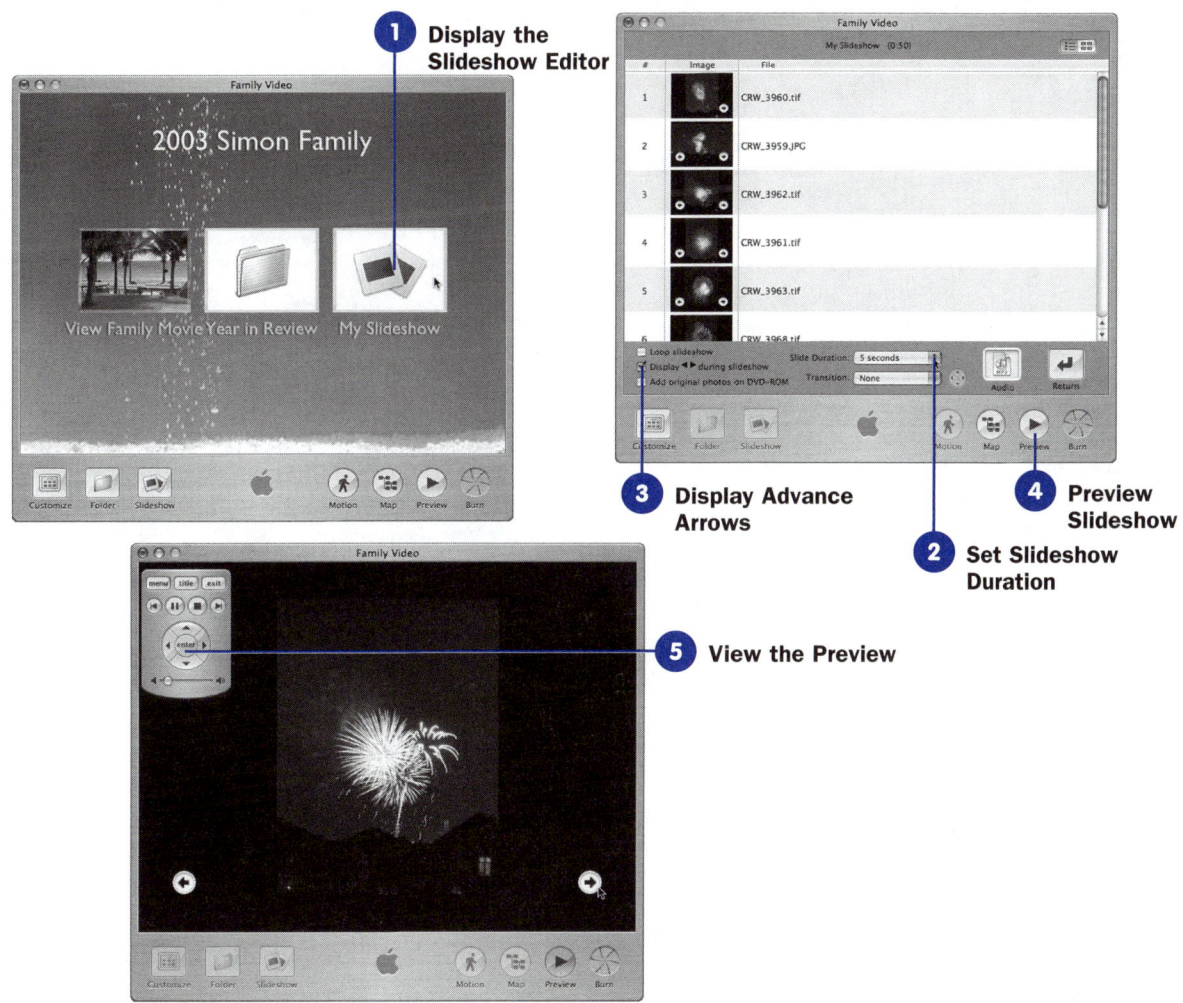

1. Display the Slideshow Editor
2. Set Slideshow Duration
3. Display Advance Arrows
4. Preview Slideshow
5. View the Preview

**CHAPTER 19:** Adding a Slideshow to a DVD 433

# 20

# Creating a DVD

**IN THIS CHAPTER:**

- **162** Add an Autoplay Movie to the DVD
- **163** Preview the DVD Content
- **164** Control the Playback Quality
- **165** Burn a Test Version on a DVD-RW
- **166** Burn a DVD

### 162  Add an Autoplay Movie to the DVD

The main purpose for using iDVD is to burn a commercial-quality movie on a DVD complete with menus. After creating the DVD menus and adding the desired movies and slideshows, you are ready to burn the contents of your iDVD project to a DVD. You can burn a DVD only if you have a DVD burner connected to your computer. Most new Apple computers come with a *SuperDrive* that allows you to burn DVDs using DVD-R and DVD-RW media. See **135 About DVDs** for more information about DVD burners and the DVD media you can purchase to create a DVD in iDVD.

Before you burn your DVD, you should use the **Preview** option to ensure that you will get the desired results when you burn the DVD. Keep in mind, when you burn a DVD-R, you cannot erase the disc if you later decide you don't like the contents. Previewing helps to make sure that what you burn to the DVD will be what you want. If you have DVD-RW media, you can perform a "test burn" on a DVD-RW that you can erase if you're not happy with the results. However, because iDVD does not recognize DVD-RW discs as valid media, you'll have to take a couple extra steps to burn to a DVD-RW.

### 162  Add an Autoplay Movie to the DVD

**You Should Know**

- ✔ **128** Preview the Completed Movie in iMovie
- ✔ **137** Add a Movie to the DVD Menu

**See Also**

- → **163** Preview the DVD Content
- → **166** Burn a DVD

By default, when a user uses iDVD to view a DVD you have created, the DVD menu is the first thing she sees. If you want to have a movie start playing automatically when the DVD is inserted in the DVD player, you must specify an autoplay movie.

You use the **Map** option in iDVD to specify which movie you want to autoplay when the DVD is inserted. When you click the **Map** button at the bottom of the iDVD window, you see a layout, or *map*, of your DVD project. The very first icon on the map is called the **Project** icon. If you want to have a movie autoplay, you must drag that movie from the **Media** pane to the **Project** icon.

When you have designated an autoplay movie, the movie plays until it is complete; iDVD then displays the DVD menu you created. If the user doesn't want to watch the autoplay movie, she can click the **Menu** button on the remote to display the DVD menu.

# Add an Autoplay Movie to the DVD 162

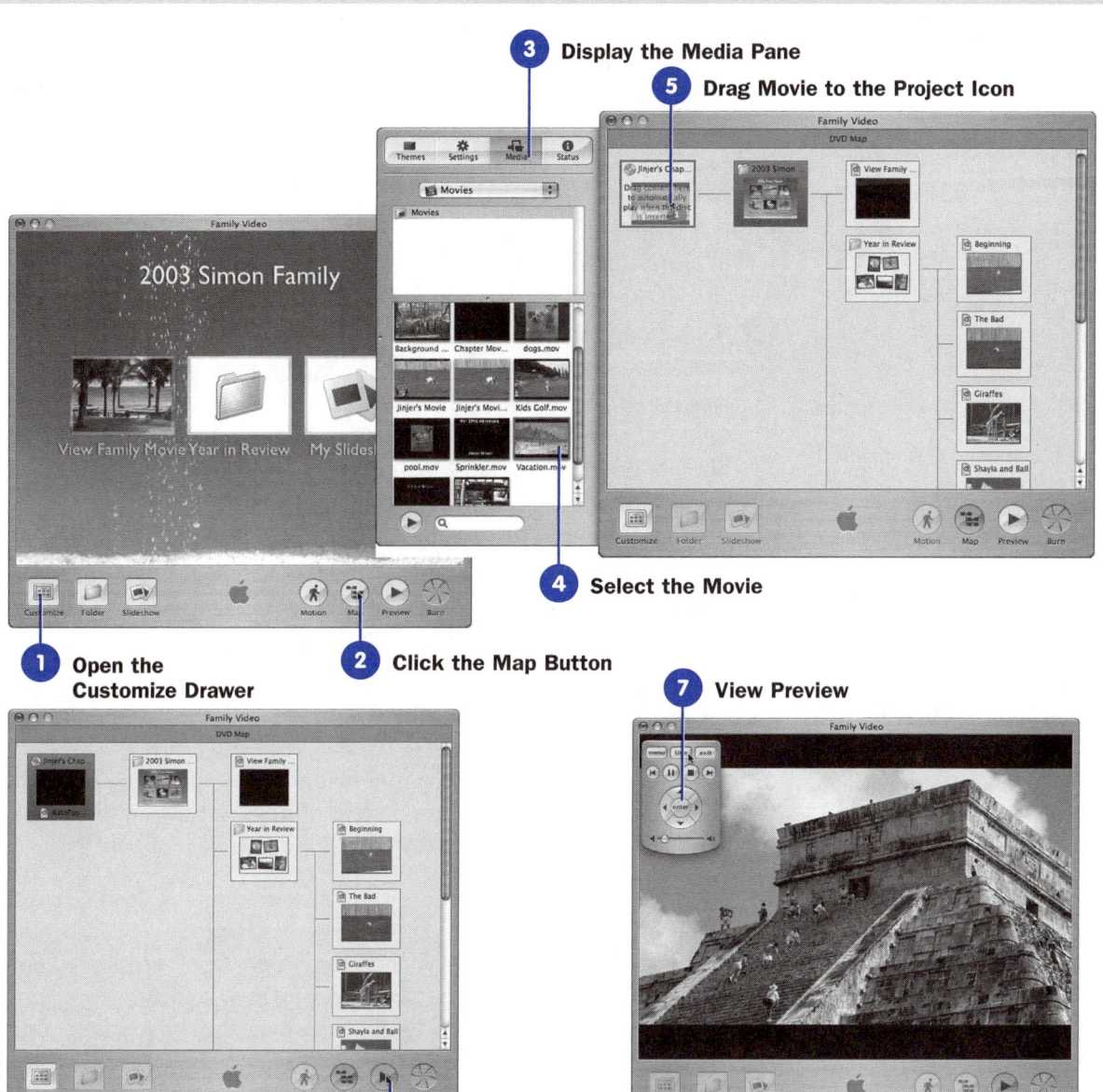

**3** Display the Media Pane
**5** Drag Movie to the Project Icon
**1** Open the Customize Drawer
**2** Click the Map Button
**4** Select the Movie
**7** View Preview
**6** Preview Project

**CHAPTER 20:** Creating a DVD    437

## 162  Add an Autoplay Movie to the DVD

### ① Open the Customize Drawer
Click the **Customize** button in the bottom-left corner of the iDVD window to display the **Customize** drawer.

### ② Click the Map Button
Click the **Map** button at the bottom of the iDVD window to display a graphical map of your DVD project.

### ③ Display the Media Pane
If it is not already selected, click the **Media** button to display the **Media** pane. From the drop-down list at the top of the **Media** pane, choose the **Movies** option. The **Media** pane displays all movies currently in your **Movies** folder. The **Movies** folder is the default location where iMovie places all movies that you create.

### ④ Select the Movie
Click to select the movie you want to use as the autoplay movie for your DVD. You can use the scrollbar on the right side of the **Media** pane to scroll through the list of movies.

### ⑤ Drag Movie to the Project Icon
Drag the selected movie from the **Media** pane to the **Project** icon. When you release the mouse button, an icon appears at the bottom of the **Project** icon indicating that an autoplay movie exists.

### ⑥ Preview Project
Click the **Preview** button to view the DVD project with the new autoplay movie.

### ⑦ View Preview
View the preview of the autoplay movie for the DVD. You can click the **Title** button on the remote control to display the DVD menu.

## TIPS

You can also create an autoplay slideshow by dragging a photo album from the **Media** pane to the **Project** icon.

If you want the movie to continuously play until the user clicks the **Menu** button on the remote control, you must make the movie loop. To set looping, select the **Project** icon and then choose **Advanced, Loop Movie**.

## 163 Preview the DVD Content

Before you burn a DVD, you should preview the entire DVD in iDVD to make sure that it is laid out as planned. You preview a DVD menu by clicking the **Preview** button at the bottom of the iDVD window. Not only can you preview the menu, you can also preview the content of the DVD by clicking the different menu buttons.

Before clicking the **Preview** button, make sure that you turn on the motion effects for the DVD by clicking the **Motion** button. This allows you to review any motion and audio you have added to the DVD menu and make sure that you achieved the desired results.

When you preview a DVD, iDVD displays a small remote control palette on the window that provides options for viewing the entire DVD. The remote resembles a remote that comes with any standalone DVD player. The remote control palette is provided only when you are viewing your DVD menu in iDVD; it is not burned on the DVD.

### Before You Begin
✔ **135** About DVDs
✔ **136** Select a DVD Theme
✔ **137** Add a Movie to the DVD Menu

### See Also
→ **164** Control the Playback Quality
→ **165** Burn a Test Version on a DVD-RW
→ **166** Burn a DVD

### 1 Turn on Motion

If it is not already selected, click the **Motion** button to make sure that any motion you have applied to the DVD menu is active when you preview the DVD menu.

You might have added motion to the DVD menu background, a drop zone, or a button. Selecting the **Motion** button also plays any audio you might have added to the DVD menu. See **145 Create a Custom Motion Menu** for information on adding motion to the background of a movie and **141 Add Images to Drop Zones** for information on adding a movie or photo to the *drop zone*. See **149 Change Image Displayed on the Button** for information on customizing the images on a menu button and **153 Change the Audio that Plays for the DVD Menu** for more information on adding or changing the audio for the DVD menu.

**NOTE**

When you are previewing a DVD menu, you cannot make any changes to the DVD menu.

**CHAPTER 20:** Creating a DVD

**163** Preview the DVD Content

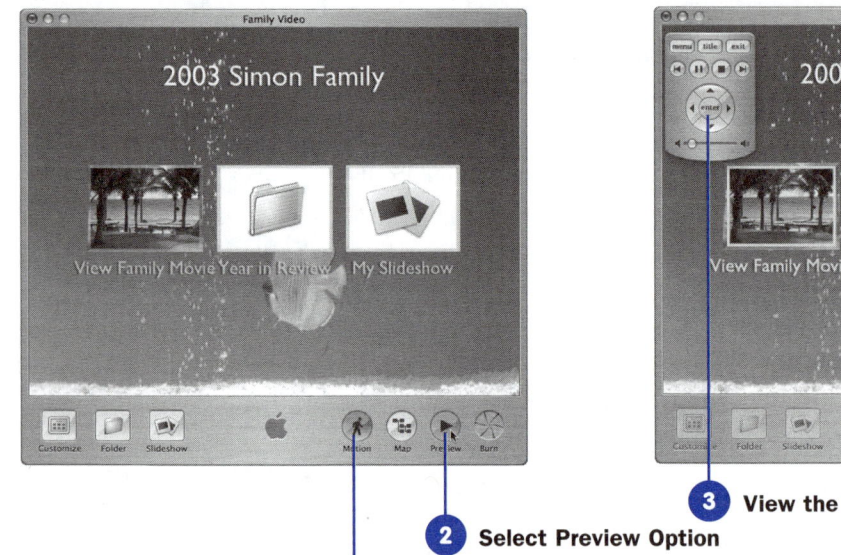

**1** Turn on Motion

**2** Select Preview Option

**3** View the Preview

**NOTE**

Click the **Enter** button on the remote control to play the currently selected menu option.

Click the **Preview** button again to cancel the preview mode.

**2** **Select Preview Option**

Click the **Preview** button to display a preview of how the DVD menu will appear when you burn the DVD. iDVD opens the DVD menu in the iDVD window and displays the iDVD remote control palette that you can use to step through the DVD menu.

**3** **View the Preview**

View the preview of the DVD menu. You can use the mouse to click menu buttons, or you can use the options on the iDVD remote control palette. Use the menu buttons to access all the movies, slideshows, and so on that comprise the DVD.

PART IV:  iDVD

## 164 Control the Playback Quality

Although several factors control the quality of the DVD you create from iDVD (such as the quality of the movies and photos you add to the DVD), you can also control the quality of the output from iDVD by specifying whether you want to use **Best Performance** or **Best Quality** to create the DVD.

When you create a DVD in iDVD, the DVD project can contain up to 90 minutes of movies, slideshows, and photos. The longer the DVD project, the higher the compression rate required to fit the entire contents of the project on the DVD. To ensure the lowest compression rate—and the highest quality output—you want to keep the length of your DVD under 60 minutes.

If your movie is less than 60 minutes, you can select between **Best Performance** and **Best Quality** as the encoding option for the DVD you will burn. By default, iDVD selects the **Best Performance** option, which means that the DVD is created using all the computer's resources. You have the option of having the movie files encoded in the background, allowing you to continue working on your computer while it's busy encoding movie and photo files for the DVD. When you create the DVD, iDVD burns the DVD faster than it does if you choose the **Best Quality** option, and the DVD is created with a compression rate of about 8Mbps.

If you have a DVD project that is longer than 60 minutes—or you just want to ensure the highest quality—select the **Best Quality** encoding option. When this option is selected, iDVD determines the length of the DVD and then finds the best compression rate to ensure that all the contents will fit on the DVD.

To determine the number of minutes of video in your DVD project, check the **DVD Capacity** option on the **Status** pane. If the capacity exceeds 60 minutes, you must use the **Best Quality** option to burn the DVD. If the capacity is less than 60 minutes, you can choose either **Best Quality** or **Best Performance**.

If the capacity of the DVD is less than 60 minutes, you might want to consider using the **Best Performance** option to burn a test version of the DVD and then use the **Best Quality** option to create the final DVD. See 165 **Burn a Test Version on a DVD-RW** for more information on creating a test DVD. See 166 **Burn a DVD** for more information on creating a final DVD.

### You Should Know

✔ 135 About DVDs
✔ 136 Select a DVD Theme
✔ 137 Add a Movie to the DVD Menu

### See Also

→ 163 Preview the DVD Content
→ 165 Burn a Test Version on a DVD-RW
→ 166 Burn a DVD

**TIP**

DVDs created using the **Best Quality** option take longer to burn but are optimized to use the best possible quality.

## 164  Control the Playback Quality

**① Display the Customize Drawer**

Click the **Customize** button in the bottom-left corner of the iDVD window to display the **Customize** drawer.

**② Display the Status Pane**

Click the **Status** button at the top of the **Customize** drawer to display the contents of the DVD project. The **Status** pane indicates the names of the files that will be placed on the DVD. It also indicates the final time length for the DVD.

**③ Check the DVD Capacity**

Check the **DVD Capacity** field at the top of the **Status** pane to see the current length of your DVD. If the field displays a total disc size instead of a time length, click the size to view the length displayed in minutes.

**④ Display the Preferences Dialog Box**

Choose **iDVD, Preferences** from the menu bar to display the **Preferences** dialog box.

**⑤ Display the General Options**

If it is not already selected, click the **General** icon at the top of the **Preferences** dialog box to display the **General** options. The name of the icon you click displays as the title of the **Preferences** dialog box.

**⑥ Select Encoder Settings**

If your DVD project is less than 60 minutes, select either **Best Performance** or **Best Quality** as the encoding option.

If the project is over 60 minutes, select **Best Quality** as the encoding option.

**⑦ Enable Background Encoding**

If you selected **Best Performance** as your encoding option, click the **Enable background encoding** check box to have iDVD perform all the encoding of movies in the background as you continue to make changes to the DVD layout.

**TIP**
If the length of your project exceeds 60 minutes, you must select **Best Quality** as your encoding option.

**TIP**
If your DVD includes a slideshow, you can adjust the length of the DVD by reducing the amount of time between each photo. See **161 Control Slideshow Advancing** for more information on reducing the amount of time between photos.

**TIP**
After deleting a movie from your DVD, you might want to rearrange the menu buttons in a more pleasing way. See **150 Change Button Locations** for more information on moving the buttons on your DVD menu.

PART IV:  iDVD

**Control the Playback Quality** `164`

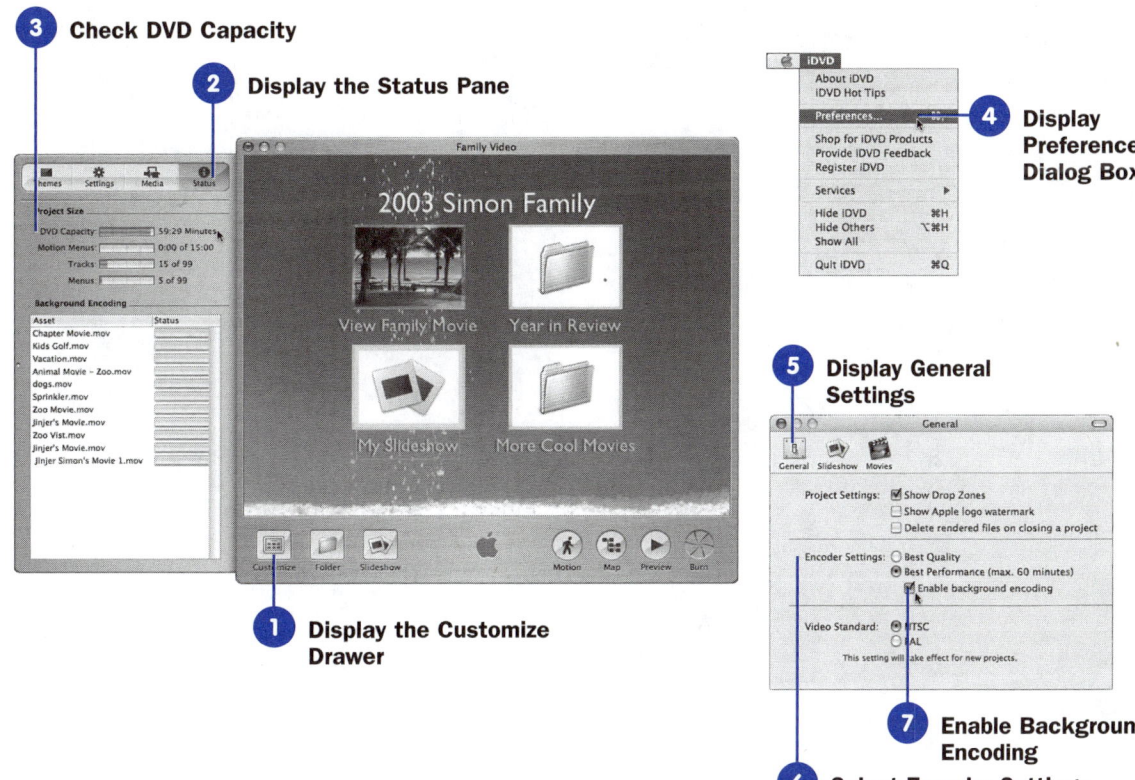

---

### `165` Burn a Test Version on a DVD-RW

You can burn a test version of your DVD on a DVD-RW to ensure that everything works correctly and that you are happy with the end result. It is always nice to be able to test something out before making the production version, and burning DVDs is no exception. By burning a test version of your DVD onto a DVD-RW, you can view the DVD on your TV and make sure that the project plays the way you want. Because it is on a rewritable disc, you can erase the DVD-RW and reburn it as needed until you achieve the desired results. This helps to save the frustration of burning a DVD-R only to find you forgot to add something.

**Before You Begin**

✔ `135` About DVDs
✔ `136` Select a DVD Theme
✔ `137` Add a Movie to the DVD Menu

**See Also**

→ `163` Preview the DVD Content
→ `164` Control the Playback Quality
→ `166` Burn a DVD

**CHAPTER 20:** Creating a DVD        443

### 165  Burn a Test Version on a DVD-RW

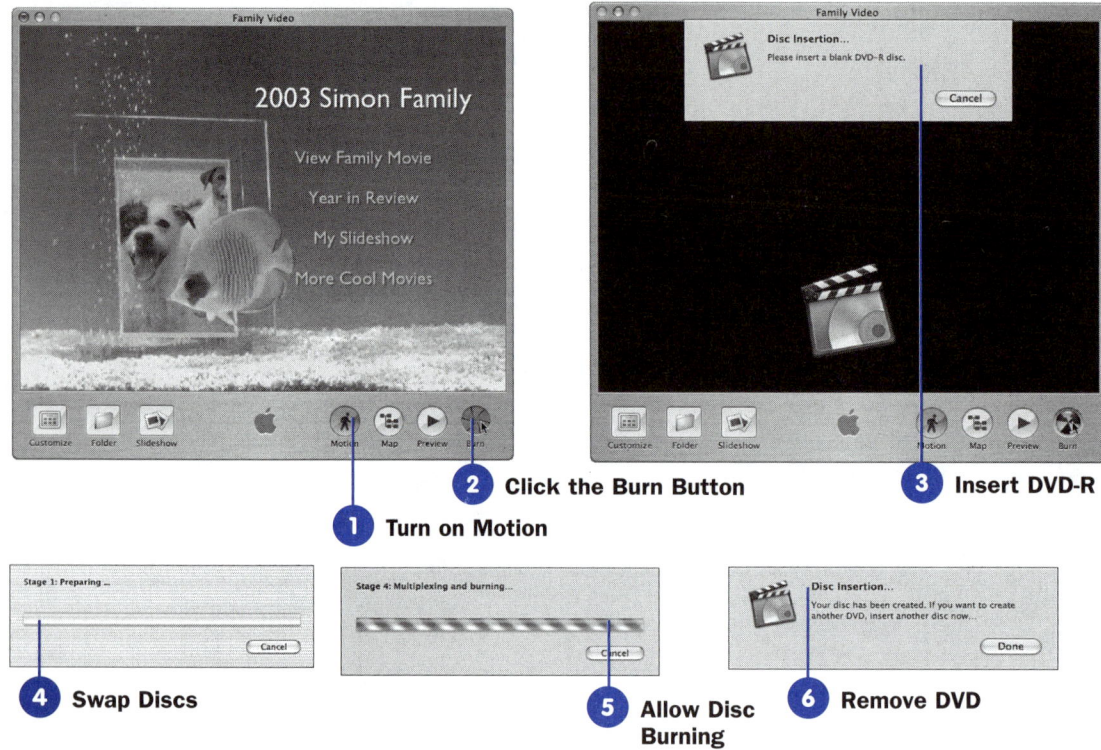

If your Apple computer has a *SuperDrive*, that drive is capable of burning a DVD-RW, even though that fact is not openly publicized by Apple. The only issue is that iDVD does not recognize a DVD-RW disc as valid media. Therefore, burning a DVD-RW requires a little extra work to trick iDVD into thinking it is burning a DVD-R disc: You must first insert a blank DVD-R disc; after iDVD has recognized that disk, you can switch and insert your DVD-RW disc.

When you are sure that the DVD project is the way you want it, you can burn the DVD project again on a DVD-R that can be played in regular DVD players. The final version on the DVD-R will look exactly the same as the test DVD-RW, but the DVD-R can be viewed in regular DVD players, whereas many DVD players cannot read DVD-RW discs.

**Burn a Test Version on a DVD-RW** (165)

**① Turn on Motion**

If it is not already selected, click the **Motion** button to make sure that any motion you have applied to the DVD menu is active when you burn the DVD.

You might have added motion to the DVD menu background, a drop zone, or a button. Selecting the **Motion** button also plays any audio you might have added to the DVD menu. See (145) **Create a Custom Motion Menu** for information on adding motion to the background of a movie and (141) **Add Images to Drop Zones** for information on adding a movie or photo to the *drop zone*. See (149) **Change Image Displayed on the Button** for information on customizing the images on a menu button and (153) **Change the Audio that Plays for the DVD Menu** for more information on adding or changing the audio for the DVD menu.

**② Click the Burn Button**

Click the **Burn** button twice to start the process of burning the current DVD project to a DVD.

**③ Insert DVD-R**

If the DVD burner does not contain a DVD-R, iDVD displays a message box indicating that you must insert a DVD-R to continue the process. Insert the DVD-R (not the DVD-RW disc) into your DVD burner and close the drive. iDVD starts the process of burning the DVD.

**④ Swap Discs**

When the **Stage 1: Preparing** message displays on the dialog box, eject the DVD-R disc and insert your DVD-RW disc in the DVD burner.

**⑤ Allow Disc Burning**

Depending on the length of the DVD you are creating, the DVD burning process might take several minutes. Because this process requires a lot of system resources, if possible, avoid running other programs while you are burning the disc.

iDVD displays the status of the burn process as the DVD is created.

### TIP

You must eject the DVD-R disc from your computer before iDVD starts writing. If you don't eject the DVD-R during **Stage 1**, you can also do it during **Stage 2: Menu rendering and encoding** or **Stage 3: Asset encoding**. If iDVD starts writing on the DVD-R before you eject the disc, you will not be able to write to the DVD-R disc again.

### NOTES

If you are burning multiple DVDs, insert the next DVD in your DVD burner and do not click **Done**. See  **Burn a DVD** for more information on burning DVDs to distribute.

To erase the contents of a DVD-RW so that you can use it again, use the **Disk Utility** program that comes with Mac OS X. You can find the program in **Finder** by clicking the **Applications** folder and then opening the **Utilities** subfolder.

**CHAPTER 20:** Creating a DVD 445

## 166  Burn a DVD

### ⑥ Remove DVD

When the DVD burning process is complete, iDVD ejects the disc and displays a dialog box indicating the process is complete. Because you are burning a test copy of the DVD, click the **Done** button to end the burning process.

If you have a DVD player that can read DVD-RW discs, test the DVD on your television. If your DVD player will not read DVD-RW discs, you must test the DVD-RW on your computer. When you insert the DVD back in your DVD burner, the **DVD Viewer** automatically loads and plays the DVD.

Remember that not all standard DVD players can play a DVD-RW disc.

## 166  Burn a DVD

**Before You Begin**

- ✔ ⑬⑤ About DVDs
- ✔ ⑬⑥ Select a DVD Theme
- ✔ ⑬⑦ Add a Movie to the DVD Menu

**See Also**

- → ⑯③ Preview the DVD Content
- → ⑯④ Control the Playback Quality
- → ⑯⑤ Burn a Test Version on a DVD-RW

After you have created your DVD menus and added the desired movies to your iDVD project, you are ready to burn the project to DVD. Although iDVD can burn both DVD-R and DVD-RW formatted discs (see ⑯⑤ **Burn a Test Version on a DVD-RW**), for distributing the DVD to other people, you want to use DVD-R discs. DVD-R discs can be read by nearly all DVD players, both those attached to televisions and those in computers. Not all DVD players, however, can read DVD-RW discs. Therefore, when your iDVD project is ready for distribution, you'll want to burn it on DVD-R to ensure that everyone can see the contents of the DVD.

If you didn't burn a test version on a DVD-RW disc, make sure that you review the iDVD project using the **Preview** option to ensure that it is laid out as desired (see ⑯③ **Preview the DVD Content**). Remember, after you burn anything on a DVD-R, you cannot change or modify the disc.

When you select the **Burn** option, iDVD encodes the DVD and then copies the entire DVD file it creates to the DVD-R. Depending on the size of the project, it can take some time to burn the DVD. During the process, you should limit the CPU usage on your computer.

Burn a DVD **166**

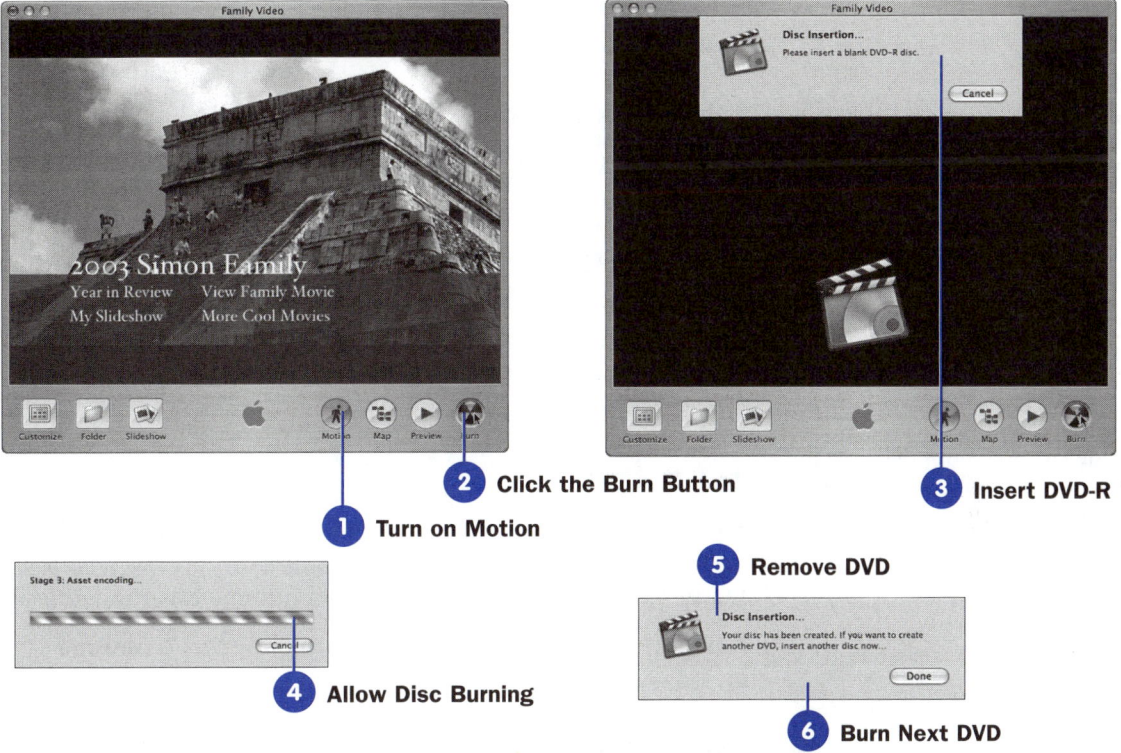

### ① Turn on Motion

If it is not already selected, click the **Motion** button to make sure that any motion you have applied to the DVD menu is active when you burn the DVD. If you don't turn on the motion, it will not be added to the DVD.

You might have added motion to the DVD menu background, a drop zone, or a button. Selecting the **Motion** button also ensures that any audio you might have added to the DVD menu is included on the DVD you are burning. See **145 Create a Custom Motion Menu** for information on adding motion to the background of a movie and **141 Add Images to Drop Zones** for information on adding a movie or photo to the *drop zone*. See **149 Change Image Displayed on the Button** for information on customizing the images on a menu button and **153 Change**

**CHAPTER 20: Creating a DVD** 447

### 166 Burn a DVD

the Audio that Plays for the DVD Menu for more information on adding or changing the audio for the DVD menu.

**② Click the Burn Button**

Click the **Burn** button twice to start the process of burning the current iDVD project to a DVD.

**③ Insert DVD-R**

If the DVD burner does not contain a DVD-R, iDVD displays a message box indicating that you must insert a DVD-R to continue the process. Insert the DVD-R into your DVD burner and close the drive. iDVD starts the process of burning the DVD.

**④ Allow Disc Burning**

Depending on the length of the DVD project, the DVD burning process might take several minutes. Because this process requires a lot of system resources, if possible, avoid running other programs.

iDVD displays a status dialog box showing the progress as the DVD is created.

**⑤ Remove DVD**

When the DVD burning process is complete, iDVD ejects the disc and displays a dialog box indicating that the process is complete.

**⑥ Burn Next DVD**

To burn an additional DVD, do not click the **Done** button when the dialog box appears. Instead, insert a new DVD-R into the DVD burner and close the drive. iDVD recognizes that you want to burn an additional disc and creates another DVD with the same DVD project.

Because the DVD project is already encoded, any additional DVDs that you burn at this point are created much more quickly than the first DVD.

**TIP**

If you want to cancel the DVD creation, you can click the **Cancel** button. However, if iDVD has already begun to burn the DVD-R, you will not be able to reuse that disc for any other purpose.

**NOTE**

If you want to create only one DVD, click the **Done** button when the **Disc insertion** dialog box appears.

# PART V

# GarageBand

**IN THIS PART:**

**CHAPTER 21** Creating a New Song — 451

**CHAPTER 22** Fine-Tuning Your Song — 477

**CHAPTER 23** Sharing Your Song — 499

# 21

# Creating a New Song

## IN THIS CHAPTER:

- **167** About Synthesized Music and Loops
- **168** Build a Song from Loops
- **169** Adjust the Repeat Length of a Loop
- **170** Add a New Music Track
- **171** Record a Track Using a MIDI/USB Keyboard
- **172** Record a Track Using the Virtual Keyboard
- **173** Record a Live Guitar or Voice Track
- **174** Play Using a Metronome
- **175** Repeat (Cycle) Part of the Song Forever

### 167  About Synthesized Music and Loops

Music is a big part of iLife; it's crucial to the functions of all the other applications in the suite. You now know how to take an existing song, listen to it in iTunes, take it with you on your iPod, burn it to a CD, add it as the soundtrack for a home movie in iMovie or photo slideshow, or create a DVD with the song playing in the background in iDVD. But what about the last link in the chain—actually making a new song from scratch yourself?

Well, there's good news. Gone are the days when, to make music of your own, you had to assemble a band of like-minded musicians, all with their own instruments (and varying skill levels), set up your amps and microphones in the garage, and falteringly play your own compositions at high volume until the neighbors called the cops.

GarageBand, the newest addition to the iLife jigsaw, is an application that bundles all the equipment you need to coax a tune out of your head and onto a recording: instruments, mixing gear, editing tools, even your backup band. You can use an inexpensive electronic keyboard (available at most music stores) to compose music for any instruments you care to put into the song, instead of having to own and know how to play the instruments themselves. You can record multiple tracks for different instruments and mix them together yourself. You can even build up background riffs using the musical equivalent of spare parts: Apple Loops (ready-made sequences of music), over a thousand of which come with GarageBand for you to use free of charge or royalty. The only thing missing is your own creativity—you don't even have to know how to read music to be able to make your Mac sing.

> **NOTE**
>
> To get the most out of GarageBand, you will want to pick up a MIDI or USB keyboard so that you can input your own original melodies. Apple sells a very capable keyboard made by M-Audio, the Keystation 49e, for about $100 through the online Apple Store or any Apple retail location. Additionally, if you play the guitar or other instruments that you want to record into GarageBand the old-fashioned way, you'll need to get adapters and junction boxes to direct their sound into your Mac. Consult your local music store for tips on the right gear to buy.

### 167  About Synthesized Music and Loops

> **KEY TERM**
>
> **MIDI (Musical Instrument Digital Interface)**—A technology for describing and storing music to be synthesized (re-created through software rather than a recording).

For many years, it has been possible for computer users to create very complex synthesized music using **MIDI (Musical Instrument Digital Interface)** technology. The idea behind MIDI is that synthesized music is a great deal more flexible than digitized music, or music stored on your computer as a simple stream of audio samples. A digitized song, for example, might sound crisp and realistic—but it takes up many megabytes of space on your disk and cannot be easily transferred over the Internet. The MP3 and AAC files used in iTunes are digitized music files, and even though they're compressed (losing some of their original sound quality), they're quite large. Nobody would ever want to stick an entire MP3 file into the background of a Web page, as it would bring a modem user's Internet connection to a standstill. And what if the musician wanted to go back and change a bit of instrumentation, or fix a sour note? That kind of editing is not possible with digitized music. What's recorded is pretty much what you're stuck with.

Synthesized music, however, gives Web authors and digital musicians many more options. Instead of comprising millions of samples of audio data at high frequency to build up the desired sound (as with digitized music files), a MIDI file consists of simple commands for the computer to play each note at a specified time, along with information about what synthesized instrument should be used to play it. Thus, a song that weighs in at 6.5 megabytes in a digitized version might take up only a svelte 50 kilobytes in synthesized MIDI. Plus you can go back into a MIDI file at any time, adjust the timing or instrumentation, add or subtract notes, or change just about anything else.

The only downside to synthesized music is that it depends on whatever software is trying to play the song to supply the music-generating software code that turns the digital "sheet music" into realistic sound. Some such software is better than others. To your dismay, you might find that the beautiful grand piano piece you recorded in your favorite MIDI application, when you send it to your cousin as an email attachment, comes out sounding like a touchtone phone on *her* computer.

It's more difficult for a computer to produce synthesized music than to play back digitized music; playing back digitized music requires far less processing power. If you use a lot of synthesized loops in your song, your computer might start to perform sluggishly, whereas it won't have as much trouble with those huge digitized loops.

GarageBand helps you solve the problems of computer-generated music by marrying the benefits of synthesized music to those of digitized music. You get the best of both worlds: the consistency of playback from the digitized files and the flexibility of synthesized files. GarageBand starts with a library of very realistic synthesized instruments, from pianos to horns to guitars to drums. It then adds *loops*, or prerecorded instrumental riffs (some synthesized, some digitized), which you can use to build up the background of your song. Finally, it lets you record your own digitized input, using a microphone, a line-in jack, or your own synthesized input using a MIDI or USB keyboard. When you're all done, your song is mixed using Apple's best synthesizers and recorded into a digitized and uncompressed audio file, which you can then send to all

## TIP

Think of a MIDI file as being like a piece of sheet music. A whole song fits on several pieces of paper. The paper contains nothing more than notes, or instructions for which instruments should play which sounds and when. But to store a *recording* of a performance, you'd need truckloads of paper and the language of a computer—or, more efficiently, a tape or CD. On the other hand, to turn a piece of sheet music into a song, you've got to get a good band together....

## NOTE

GarageBand is not, strictly speaking, a MIDI editor. You can use a MIDI keyboard to record your songs, true; but the final output you produce is digitized music in uncompressed AIFF format, not a MIDI file. After you compress it, your song is generally suitable for email or for downloading, but you don't want to use it as the background music for your Web page because it's too big. Refer to  **About Audio Formats** for more information on these formats and how they differ in size and editability.

CHAPTER 21: Creating a New Song

## 168  Build a Song from Loops

your friends (as an AAC file, as used in iTunes), transfer to your iPod, or burn onto a CD.

In GarageBand, synthesized instruments are known as **Software Instruments**; digitized instruments, which you must play yourself, are henceforth **Real Instruments**.

## 168  Build a Song from Loops

**Before You Begin**

✔ 167 About Synthesized Music and Loops

**See Also**

→ 171 Record a Track Using a MIDI/USB Keyboard

→ 173 Record a Live Guitar or Voice Track

### KEY TERM

*Loop*—A ready-made sequence of music, usually featuring a single instrument, which can be combined with other loops and repeated to form background riffs.

### TIP

The virtual keyboard appears floating over the GarageBand window when you open a new project; if you don't want to use it, dismiss it by clicking its red **Close** button. See 172 **Record a Track Using the Virtual Keyboard** for more.

The simplest way to create new music in GarageBand—and the way that requires the least musical ability on your part—is to take advantage of the library of *loops* that comes with the application. More than 1,000 loops are available for you to use, each one featuring a certain instrument and designed for a certain mood or musical style. GarageBand lets you add any of these loops into your song, blend them all together, and modify them to your taste to create an original and complex song all your own.

The GarageBand Jam Pack, available from Apple for $99, adds more than 2,000 additional loops to GarageBand—as well as more than 100 additional **Software Instruments**, and more than 100 new presets for your audio effects. The Jam Pack also adds 15 new simulated guitar amps to the 6 that come with the basic GarageBand.

### ① Open a New Song Project

When you first launch GarageBand, you are prompted to open a new song project. In the **New Project** dialog box, enter a name for the new song, a location (the default is the **GarageBand** folder inside the **Music** folder in your **Home** folder), a *tempo*, a *time signature*, and a *key*. It's okay to leave these options at their default values for now; you can change them later at any time. See 176 **Change the Song's Title, Time Signature Measurement, Tempo, and Key** for details on what these terms mean and how to change them.

You can always start over with a new project from within GarageBand by selecting **File**, **New**. Like iMovie and iDVD, GarageBand can work with only one project at a time, and it must always have a project open. If you open a new project, your old one must be saved or discarded.

454    PART V:   GarageBand

## Build a Song from Loops

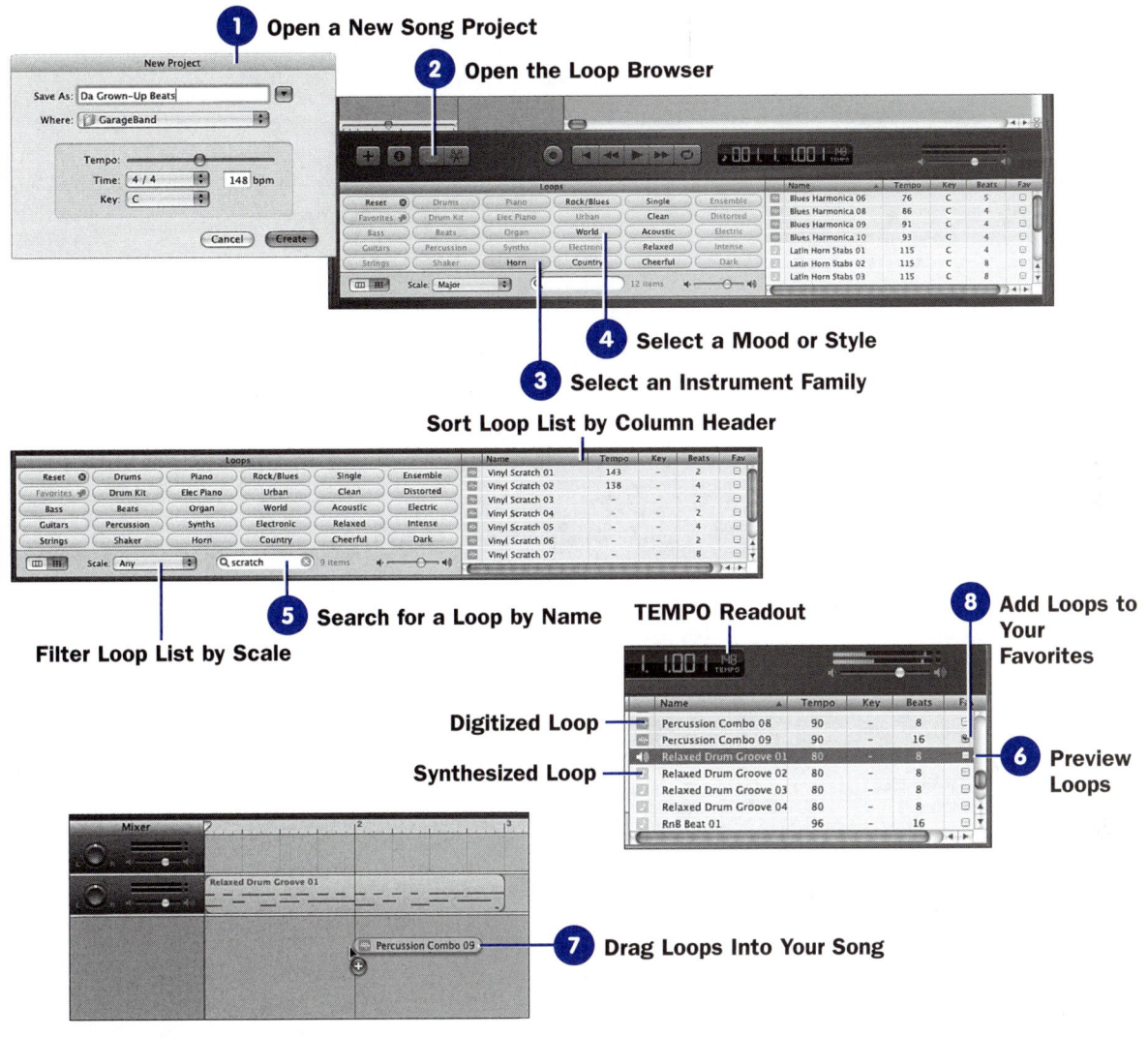

### Open the Loop Browser

Click the **Loop Browser** button to display the **Loop Browser** panel at the bottom of the GarageBand window.

The **Loop Browser** consists of a large array of buttons on the left and an (initially empty) list of loops on the right. This layout

CHAPTER 21: Creating a New Song

## 168  Build a Song from Loops

provides a mechanism for you to zero in on the loop you want by specifying its instrument family, a desired genre or musical style, a mood, its scale (major or minor), or even directly using the loop's name. As you click the buttons on the left, a filtered list of loops appears on the right, showing only the loops that match the buttons you click. The order in which you click buttons doesn't matter, and steps 3 and 4 can be reversed if you like.

Each loop has a native tempo (speed) and a native key. These are the settings under which each loop was recorded, and in which it's designed to sound best. However, GarageBand saves you a lot of hassle by automatically *transposing* each loop and adjusting its tempo to match the settings you've chosen for the song. Also, only loops that are compatible with your song's time signature are shown in the loop list.

### ❸ Select an Instrument Family

Click one of the buttons on the left side of the **Loop Browser**, matching an instrument you like. For example, click **Horn** to produce a list of loops with horn instruments.

**TIP**

Click a button again to deselect it, or click **Reset** to return all the buttons to their deselected state.

Notice that some buttons become grayed out; this means that they're incompatible with the first button you clicked. For instance, if you click **Horn**, the **Piano** button (and others) becomes disabled because there's no instrument loop that can be both a piano *and* a horn.

### ❹ Select a Mood or Style

From the buttons in the fourth, fifth, and sixth columns on the left side of the **Loop Browser**, narrow down the list of loops further into the style you're looking for by clicking the names of genres or moods. Only the loops matching the buttons you click are visible in the right pane.

The loops are listed by title, in alphabetical order. You can also sort them by their native tempo, their native key, their number of beats (the length of the loop), and whether they're in your **Favorites**. Click one of the column headers in the right pane to sort the loop list by that column; click the column header again to reverse the sort order.

456    PART V:    GarageBand

To further filter your results to your needs, select an entry from the **Scale** drop-down menu. The **Scale** options let advanced musicians zoom in on the most appropriate loops and view only the ones in a major key, a minor key, neither key (as with drums), or loops that will work equally well in a major or minor song. Be sure that you don't put a minor-key loop into a major-key song, or it'll sound really weird!

### 5 Search for a Loop by Name

Using the **Search** box at the bottom of the left pane of the **Loop Browser**, type a title (or part of a title) and press **Return**. Only the loops that match your search text *and* that match the filter buttons you've already clicked appear in the loop list on the right.

### 6 Preview Loops

Click any of the loops listed on the right side of the **Loop Browser** to play it and hear what it sounds like. Click the loop again to stop it playing. GarageBand automatically transposes the loop to match your song's tempo and key; if you click a loop in the list while playing your in-progress song, GarageBand begins playing the loop at a suitable point in the timeline so that it matches your music's pattern.

Both synthesized (**Software Instrument**) and digitized (**Real Instrument**) loops are available in the loop list, and both behave the same in the **Loop Browser**. You can even adjust the key and tempo of digitized loops, and GarageBand will make the necessary (difficult) transformations on the fly.

Synthesized loops are indicated in green with a "note" icon, and digitized loops are shown in blue with a "waveform" icon.

### 7 Drag Loops Into Your Song

When you find a loop that you want to add to your song, drag it from the **Loop Browser** list into the timeline. Your mouse position becomes the point where the loop begins, and the loop immediately renders itself into a visual track represented by a colored rectangle. (Remember that **Software Instrument** loops are green and show the individual notes, while **Real Instrument** loops are blue and show a digital waveform.) Be sure to place the loop at a point

**TIP**

Click the **Reset** button to clear out all the instrument and style filters and return the **Loop Browser** to its original state. If you don't reset the buttons and try to search for a loop by name, unless the loop you're looking for matches the buttons you've selected, the desired loop won't be shown.

**TIP**

Some loops are specifically intended to be played at a certain tempo and might sound very strange if the song's tempo is much faster or slower than the number of beats per minute shown in the **Tempo** column for that loop. To hear the loop properly, and to change the song's overall speed to match that of the loop, click and hold the **TEMPO** readout in the time display window above the **Loop Browser**; use the pop-up slider to select a tempo more suitable for the loop.

## 169  Adjust the Repeat Length of a Loop

in the song where it sounds appropriate, using the timing marks at the top of the window. For instance, place the loop at measure marker 5 or 9 to allow for four or eight full measures before the loop starts, respectively.

If you drag the loop to an unused area of the timeline (below any existing tracks), the loop is added to the song using its native instrument, which appears as a new track. However, if you drag the loop into an existing track, it uses that track's instrument instead of its own.

Move a loop back and forth in the timeline, or from track to track (and instrument to instrument), by simply dragging the colored rectangle representing the loop to its new position.

Continue adding loops, using the playhead and the playback control buttons to play your song as you work on it. Experiment until you have a complex tune constructed to your liking.

### 8  Add Loops to Your Favorites

You can quickly access certain loops by adding them to your **Favorites** list. To do this, locate a frequently used loop as described in steps 3–6, and then click its **Fav** check box. The loop is now in your **Favorites** list, which you can access immediately by clicking the **Favorites** button at the far left of the **Loop Browser**.

## 169  Adjust the Repeat Length of a Loop

**Before You Begin**

✔ **168** Build a Song from Loops

**See Also**

→ **175** Repeat (Cycle) Part of the Song Forever

→ **178** Transpose a Track Up or Down in Pitch

The beauty of loops is that they're designed to be played over and over again, without a break, until the end of the song (or until they're not needed anymore). The end of the loop leads back into the beginning of the loop, lending to a seamless musical ambiance for each instrument in your song.

When you drag a loop into your song, you're only dragging in a single repetition of it. To lengthen the loop's role in your song, don't simply drag more and more copies of the loop into the track; instead, extend the loop you already have to the length you need. GarageBand automatically repeats the loop for as long as you need it to do so.

## Adjust the Repeat Length of a Loop

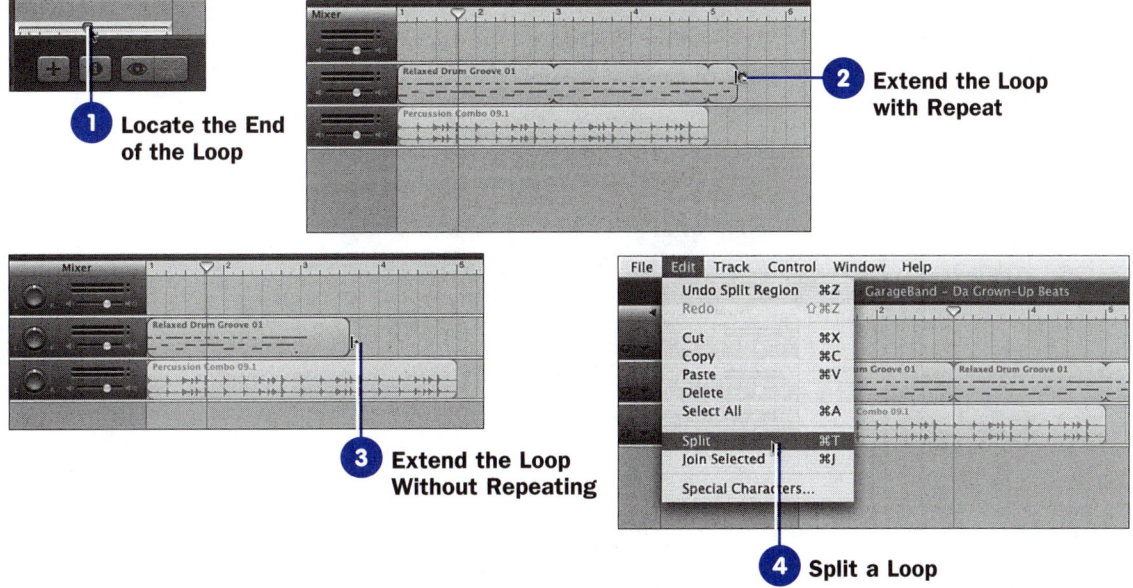

① **Locate the End of the Loop**

② **Extend the Loop with Repeat**

③ **Extend the Loop Without Repeating**

④ **Split a Loop**

### ① Locate the End of the Loop

In the timeline area, find the track with the loop you want to extend. Depending on your current zoom level, you may not be able to see the end of the loop. Adjust the zoom slider to fit more of the song's length into the timeline area, or use the horizontal scrollbar to scroll through the song and find the end of the loop. (It might be easier to zoom out because you must drag the mouse along the whole length of the song.)

### ② Extend the Loop with Repeat

Position the mouse on the upper-right edge of the *region* representing the loop you want to extend. The mouse pointer should turn into a vertical bar with a circular arrow, indicating the **repeat extender** function. Click the region's edge and drag to the right. As you drag, notice that the loop's contents are filled out with a repeat of the notes from the original loop. Continue dragging until the loop is extended for as many repetitions as you need.

**TIP**

It's generally best to create full repetitions (dragging the region until the exact end of the loop sequence, shown by the rounded corners on the region), but you can leave a repetition partway completed if you want—it just might sound a little strange. You can always tidy up your repetitions later using this same technique.

CHAPTER 21: Creating a New Song 459

**169  Adjust the Repeat Length of a Loop**

### KEY TERMS

***Region***—The colored rectangle in the timeline that represents a loop or a length of recorded music.

***Measure***—A division of time within a song, consisting of a fixed number of beats (most commonly four) and used to help you find your place in the song and align musical phrases.

### NOTE

You can only extend or contract the loop without repeating its contents if the loop has not already had repetitions added. To extend the loop without repeating, shorten the loop so that it contains only a single repetition.

At the endpoint of each repetition of the loop, the region indicates a new loop's beginning by showing rounded, joined "corners"; each of these divots in the region's outline should correspond to a *measure* division appropriate for where a new repetition of the loop should begin.

Shorten a repeated loop by clicking the upper-right edge of the region and dragging to the left.

### ③ Extend the Loop Without Repeating

You can extend a loop's length without repeating its contents; instead, the remainder of the loop becomes blank. This approach is primarily useful if you want to modify the loop by adding your own creative touches with a keyboard, and the length of the loop as it is isn't exactly what you need.

Click the lower-right edge of the loop region. The mouse pointer turns into a vertical line and right-pointing arrow. Click and drag to the right to lengthen the loop and add silence, or drag to the left to shorten the loop.

### ④ Split a Loop

Splitting a loop allows you to perform modifications (such as transpositions) to a certain section of the loop without affecting the rest of the loop. First move the *playhead* to the point where you want to split the loop; then select **Edit**, **Split**. The loop is now split into two separate regions, which remain attached to each other if you move them, but which can be edited separately.

Undo a split by selecting both regions (click and drag to form a selection rectangle or **Shift**+click one region after another) and then selecting **Edit**, **Join Selected**.

460        PART V:    GarageBand

## 170 Add a New Music Track

To add your own creative talent to your song, you start by creating a new track for your musical input. This new track can be a **Real Instrument**, if you want to lay down a guitar track or sing a vocal line; or it can be a **Software Instrument**, if you want to use a MIDI or USB keyboard to play a line for a virtual instrument of your choice.

The more tracks you add to your song, the more your computer's performance will be taxed. Bear in mind that **Real Instruments** are comparatively easy for the computer to handle (although their file sizes are larger), while **Software Instruments** require more processing power (although their file sizes are smaller). A song with a lot (eight or more, depending on your computer and the kinds of instruments) of **Software Instruments** might push the computer beyond its capabilities. So don't get too carried away adding tracks!

If you have an older Mac with limited processing power, adjust GarageBand's buffer handling by going to the **Preferences** dialog box (choose **GarageBand**, **Preferences** from the menu bar) and experimenting with different settings in the **Audio/MIDI** pane. (A larger buffer makes GarageBand respond more slowly, but play more smoothly, on slower machines.) Also, on the **Advanced** tab of the **Preferences** dialog box, limit the maximum number of tracks you can add using the drop-down menus.

### 1 Click the New Track Button

Click the **New Track** button to create a new instrument for your song. Alternatively, select **Track**, **New Track** from the menu bar. The **New Track** window appears.

### 2 Select a Software Instrument

Use the tabs at the top of the floating window to select whether you want to create a new **Real Instrument** or a new **Software Instrument**. Whichever you select, two columns show you all the available instruments to choose from—the left column shows the instrument families, and the right shows the individual instruments in each family.

### Before You Begin

✔ 168 Build a Song from Loops

### See Also

→ 171 Record a Track Using a MIDI/USB Keyboard

→ 172 Record a Track Using the Virtual Keyboard

→ 173 Record a Live Guitar or Voice Track

### TIP

Tests show that pianos are among the least processor-intensive **Software Instruments**, whereas drums can be as much as four times as taxing on the computer.

### 170  Add a New Music Track

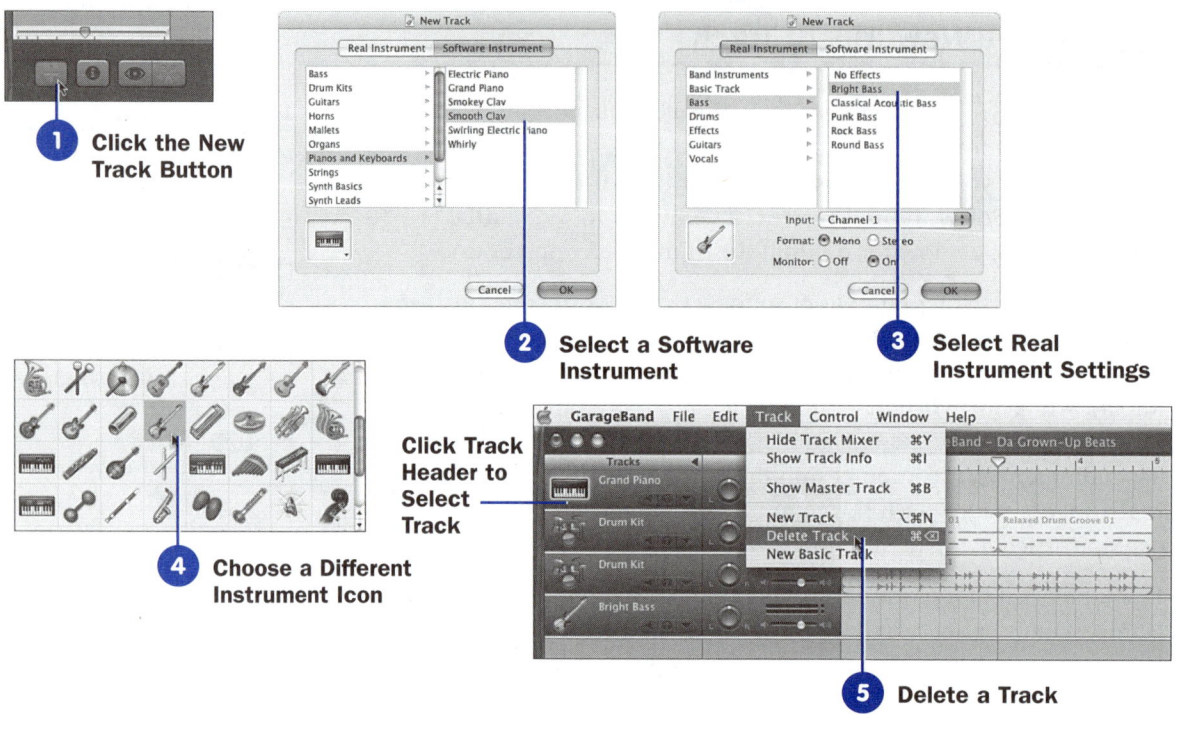

If you select **Software Instrument**, choose both a family and an instrument. Now play your MIDI keyboard (or the virtual keyboard, accessible from the **Window** menu) to hear what the selected instrument sounds like. (See **172 Record a Track Using the Virtual Keyboard** for details about the virtual keyboard.)

### ③ Select Real Instrument Settings

If you select a **Real Instrument**, you're not actually creating a unique "instrument" for the track; instead, you're selecting a set of post-processing effects to apply to your musical input. Guitars, for instance, have six different simulated amps through which you can run your axe's wail, depending on the sound you're going for. Bass guitars have their own simulated amp settings. Even band instruments (such as horns, woodwinds, choruses, and so on), which you can record using a microphone, have their own sets of effects that are added to the audio stream as it's captured by GarageBand, each one tuned to the kind of instrument you're using (flute, trumpets, violin, and so on). Select the instrument and the effect that matches your needs, and then play your instrument into the microphone or line-in channel to hear what the effects sound like.

Select additional options, such as the input channels to use (this setting varies depending on what audio input jacks your computer has), whether the input should be mono or stereo, and whether "monitoring" should be on. If the **Monitor** feature is **On**, the input from your **Real Instrument** is played through the speakers or headphones as you play it. If the **Monitor** feature is **Off**, the instrument's input is omitted until you finish recording and go back to review what you've played. You may want to leave monitoring off to reduce feedback from your microphone, if this causes a problem. You must, however, have monitoring turned on to preview the selected **Real Instrument** effects.

Remember that a **Real Instrument** track is a digitized recording and thus (aside from some very basic modifications) after you've made a recording using a **Real Instrument**, that's what you're going to get. You can't go back after you've laid down a live track and fiddle with different amp settings to see how it might have sounded. Be sure to pick the right settings and practice before recording your final track!

**TIP**

You can add a track that has no audio effects added at all; this is known as a *basic track*, and you can get one by selecting the **Real Instrument** tab, then **Basic Track**, **No Effects**. More easily, simply select **Track**, **New Basic Track** from the menu bar.

### ④ Choose a Different Instrument Icon

If a lot of your tracks use similar instruments, you might find that many of the instrument icons look the same. You can choose a different icon for any track, either in the **New Track** window or in the **Track Info** window later, by clicking the instrument's icon in the well. A palette opens showing all the instrument icons in GarageBand. Scroll up and down the list using the scrollbar on the right, and click the icon you want to use for the track. The icon you assign to the track does not affect the **Software Instrument** settings or the **Real Instrument** effects used by the track.

### ⑤ Delete a Track

To remove a track from the song—and to delete all the music in that track—first click the *header* for the track (the box containing the instrument's name and icon) and then select **Track**, **Delete Track** from the menu bar.

## 171 Record a Track Using a MIDI/USB Keyboard

**Before You Begin**

✔ 168 Build a Song from Loops
✔ 170 Add a New Music Track

**See Also**

→ 172 Record a Track Using the Virtual Keyboard
→ 174 Play Using a Metronome
→ 182 Fix the Timing on a Live Software Music Track

If you have a MIDI or USB keyboard, you have what you need to begin using GarageBand to its full potential as a tool for creating your own original music. All the simulated instruments are there in GarageBand's library; all you have to provide is the music for those virtual instruments to play.

Many modern keyboards come with USB ports, which you can connect directly to your Mac. Those keyboards that don't have a USB port, however, as long as they're not terribly inexpensive, have a MIDI-out port that carries all the information GarageBand needs to capture your musical commands: attack velocity, sustain, modulation, pitch bend, and so on—all of which GarageBand understands. If your keyboard has only a MIDI port, though, you must get an adapter to connect your keyboard to your Mac's USB port. These adapters can be had for $30–$60, although larger adapters and mixing devices that accept many more inputs can cost significantly more. Start small!

### ❶ Connect the Keyboard

If your keyboard is not already plugged in, connect it to a free USB port on your computer. You might have to quit and restart GarageBand to make it recognize the keyboard after you connect it to your Mac; to determine whether the keyboard is recognized, open the **Preferences** dialog box (choose **GarageBand**, **Preferences** from the menu bar) and look at the **MIDI Status** line under the **Audio/MIDI** tab. (Alternatively, select **Window**, **Audio/MIDI** to open that **Preferences** box to the **Window** tab directly.) If the dialog box correctly reports your keyboard's model, you're good to go.

### ❷ Select the Software Instrument Track to Use

If you have not yet created a **Software Instrument** track to use for recording your new musical line, do so now. (Refer to 170 **Add a New Music Track** for details.)

Click the track *header* (the box containing the instrument's name and icon) to select the track you want to use for recording.

PART V: GarageBand

## Record a Track Using a MIDI/USB Keyboard  171

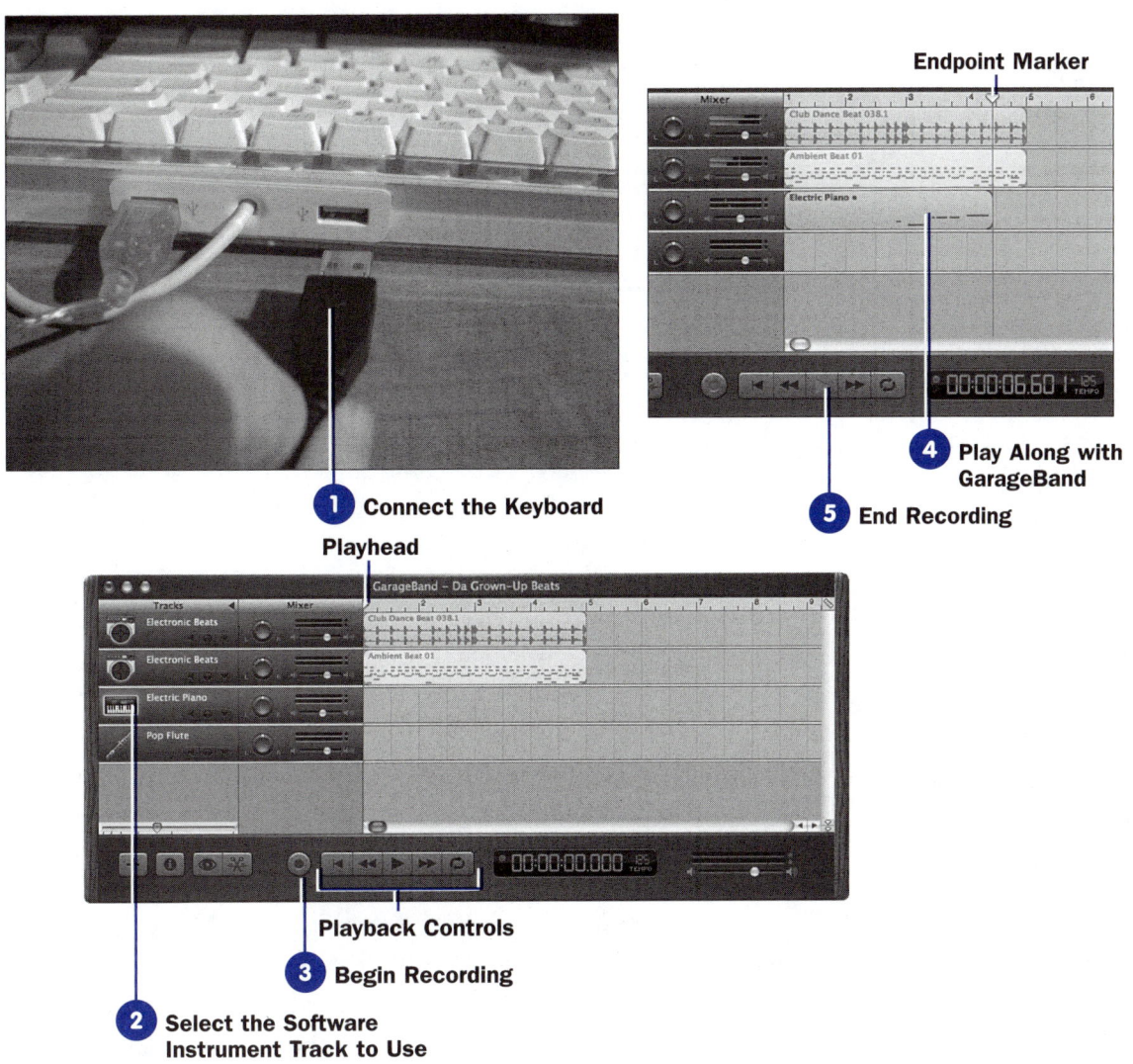

### 3 Begin Recording

Move the playhead to the beginning of the piece (using the leftmost playback control button); you can also begin recording at any position in the song—just move the playhead to that position. When you are ready to begin recording, click the **Record** button.

CHAPTER 21: Creating a New Song  465

**172** Record a Track Using the Virtual Keyboard

**TIP**
As you play the keyboard, the MIDI activity indicator—a small blue light in the time display, to the left of the **TEMPO** readout—flashes each time you press a key. This can be helpful in troubleshooting if your keyboard doesn't seem to be working.

**④ Play Along with GarageBand**

GarageBand begins playing the piece's existing tracks and additionally opens a new region to capture any notes you play on your keyboard. The music you play is incorporated into GarageBand's output to the speakers or headphones, and the *region* keeps growing and marking down your notes as long as you keep recording.

**⑤ End Recording**

GarageBand automatically stops recording when the playhead reaches the *endpoint marker* (the left-facing triangle at the far right end of the timeline ruler, which you can drag right or left to extend or shorten the song). If you want to stop recording sooner, click the **Play** button. (If you simply click the **Record** button, GarageBand stops recording, but the playhead continues through the song.)

If you don't start playing immediately after you begin recording, or if you stop playing before you stop recording, GarageBand automatically clips the recorded region to the beginning and end (rounded to the nearest full measure) of where you played.

**TIP**
After a track is recorded, you can extend or repeat it just as you can with any built-in loop. Refer to **169 Adjust the Repeat Length of a Loop** for details.

Your **Software Instrument** track is now recorded. You can go back and edit the captured music, fix sour notes, adjust the timing, or even change the instrument used to play the track. See **181 Modify an Existing Loop's Notes** for more on how to do this.

---

**172** **Record a Track Using the Virtual Keyboard**

**Before You Begin**

✔ **168** Build a Song from Loops
✔ **170** Add a New Music Track

**See Also**

→ **174** Play Using a Metronome
→ **181** Modify an Existing Loop's Notes
→ **182** Fix the Timing on a Live Software Music Track

If you don't have a MIDI or USB keyboard to use to create **Software Instrument** tracks, don't worry—GarageBand comes with an onscreen virtual keyboard you can use to enter notes. It isn't as easy to manage as a real keyboard, and you can't play more than one note at a time (so it isn't suitable for complex chord-filled piano tracks), but with patience, you can construct a fine-sounding music track using no extra hardware beyond what came with your computer.

**① Enable the Virtual Keyboard**

Choose **Window**, **Keyboard** from the menu bar. The virtual keyboard—a small floating window—appears. Move it to whatever position on the screen is comfortable for you.

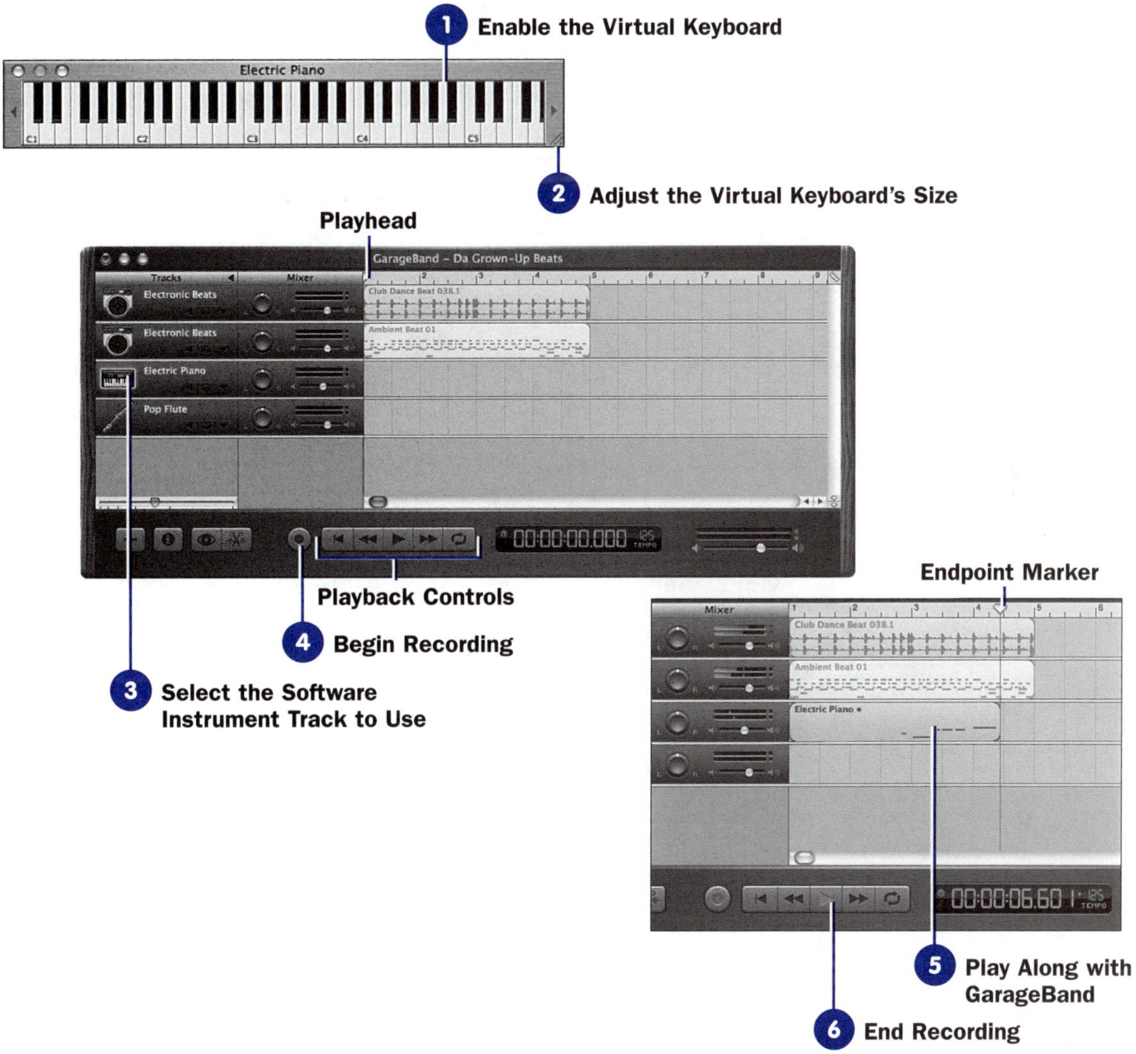

# Record a Track Using the Virtual Keyboard

**1** Enable the Virtual Keyboard

**2** Adjust the Virtual Keyboard's Size

Playhead

Playback Controls

**4** Begin Recording

**3** Select the Software Instrument Track to Use

Endpoint Marker

**5** Play Along with GarageBand

**6** End Recording

## **2** Adjust the Virtual Keyboard's Size

The key marked **C3** is "middle C." From this starting point, you can find your bearings on the virtual keyboard. Only four octaves are shown by default; however, you can scroll back and forth (using the left and right arrows on the side borders of the keyboard

**CHAPTER 21:** Creating a New Song     467

## 172  Record a Track Using the Virtual Keyboard

**TIP**
Depending on the **Software Instrument** track you plan to use, make sure that the keyboard is centered on the middle of the useful range of the instrument. For instance, an electric bass is probably most usefully centered on the two or three octaves below middle C (**C3**).

window) to see additional keys above or below the displayed four octaves.

To see more (or less) of the keyboard at all times, resize the window by clicking the bottom-right corner and dragging it left or right.

### 3  Select the Software Instrument Track to Use

If you have not yet created a **Software Instrument** track to use for recording your new musical line, do so now. (Refer to **170 Add a New Music Track** for details.)

Click the track *header* (the box containing the instrument name and icon) to select the track you want to use for recording.

### 4  Begin Recording

Move the playhead to the beginning of the piece (using the leftmost playback control button); you can also begin recording at any position in the song—just move the playhead to that position. When you are ready to begin recording, click the **Record** button.

### 5  Play Along with GarageBand

GarageBand begins playing the piece's existing tracks and additionally opens a new region to capture any notes you play on the virtual keyboard. The music you play is incorporated into GarageBand's output to the speakers or headphones, and the *region* keeps growing and marking down your notes as long as you keep recording.

Use the mouse to click the keys on the virtual keyboard to create notes. The higher up on the key you click, the lower the velocity and volume of the note recorded; the lower on the key you click, the higher the velocity. You can also click and drag up and down the notes to create "glissando" effects.

### 6  End Recording

GarageBand automatically stops recording when the playhead reaches the endpoint marker (the left-facing triangle at the far right end of the timeline ruler, which you can drag right or left to extend or shorten the song). If you want to stop recording sooner, click the **Play** button. (If you simply click the **Record** button again,

PART V:   GarageBand

GarageBand stops recording, but the playhead continues through the song.)

Your **Software Instrument** track is now recorded. Because you can play only one note at a time on the virtual keyboard, you will probably want to add more notes manually in the **Track Editor** panel by copying and pasting existing notes. See 181 **Modify an Existing Loop's Notes** for more on how to do this.

After a track is recorded, you can extend or repeat it just as you can for any built-in loop. Refer to 169 **Adjust the Repeat Length of a Loop** for details.

> **NOTE**
> If you don't start playing immediately after you begin recording, or if you stop playing before you stop recording, GarageBand automatically clips the recorded region to the beginning and end (rounded to the nearest full measure) of where you played.

## 173 Record a Live Guitar or Voice Track

To record a real, physical musical instrument—whether it's a guitar or other electrical instrument with a line-out cable, or an old-fashioned instrument such as a trumpet, violin, or human voice—you record into a **Real Instrument** track. This kind of track captures a digitized sample of your performance on the instrument, runs it through some predefined filters and effects that you can select, and incorporates the adapted recording into your song. You cannot go back and modify individual notes or effects in a **Real Instrument** track the way you can with a **Software Instrument** track; aside from some basic pitch and tempo modifications, what you record is what you get.

If you have an expensive MIDI keyboard—one that has a lot more musical "voices" than the **Software Instruments** in GarageBand's library—you can still put them to good use. Instead of using your keyboard as a MIDI or USB input device, simply plug its output audio cable into your computer's **Line In** jack and play it as you would any **Real Instrument**. GarageBand captures your performance on the keyboard using the keyboard's own native voices, just as they come out of the keyboard itself. Thus your investment in a high-end keyboard isn't wasted with GarageBand!

**Before You Begin**
- ✔ 168 Build a Song from Loops
- ✔ 170 Add a New Music Track

**See Also**
- → 174 Play Using a Metronome
- → 180 Add Audio Effects to a Track

> **TIP**
> Make sure that you plug the cable (from the guitar, microphone, or mixing box) into the **Line In** jack and not into the headphone or speaker jack. The **Line In** jack is marked with a symbol that looks like two triangles pointing to the inside of a circle.

### 1 Connect the Instrument or Microphone

A **Real Instrument** must be connected to your computer through the Mac's **Line In** jack. Guitar plugs are 1/4 inch in diameter, but you can get adapters that convert this kind of plug to the 1/8 inch diameter needed for the Mac's mini-stereo jack.

**Record a Live Guitar or Voice Track**

**① Connect the Instrument or Microphone**

**② Select the Real Instrument Track to Use**

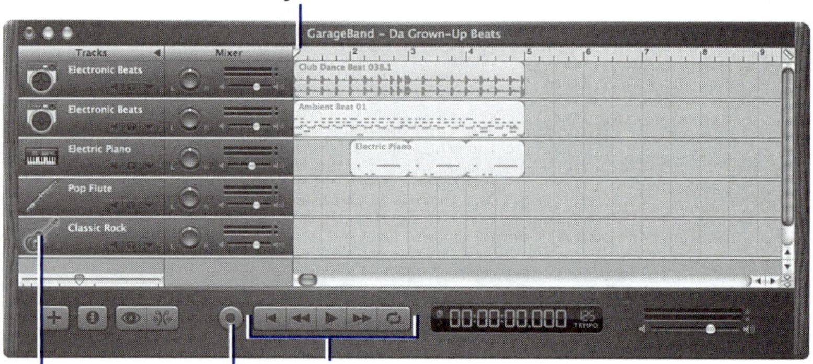

**③ Begin Recording**

**Playback Controls**

**Playhead**

**④ Play Along with GarageBand**

**⑤ End Recording**

For other instruments (including a vocal performance or band instruments that have no electrical output), set up a microphone to capture the sound. Plug the microphone into the **Line In** jack.

# Record a Live Guitar or Voice Track

## ② Select the Real Instrument Track to Use

If you have not yet created a **Real Instrument** track to use for recording your new musical line, do so now. (Refer to **170 Add a New Music Track** for details.)

Click the track *header* (the box containing the instrument's name and icon) to select the track you want to use for recording.

## ③ Begin Recording

Move the playhead to the beginning of the piece (using the leftmost playback control button); you can also begin recording at any position in the song—just move the playhead to that position. When you are ready to begin recording, click the **Record** button.

## ④ Play Along with GarageBand

GarageBand begins playing the piece's existing tracks and additionally opens a new region to capture the music you play on your instrument. If the **Monitor** feature is enabled in the **Real Instrument** track, the captured sound is incorporated into GarageBand's output to the speakers or headphones. The recorded region keeps growing and registering the sampled waveform as long as you keep recording.

## ⑤ End Recording

GarageBand automatically stops recording when the playhead reaches the *endpoint marker* (the left-facing triangle at the far right end of the timeline ruler, which you can drag right or left to extend or shorten the song). If you want to stop recording sooner, click the **Play** button. (If you simply click the **Record** button again, GarageBand stops recording, but the playhead continues through the song.)

Your **Real Instrument** track is now recorded. You cannot edit individual notes or change the instrument filters or effects, but you *can* make changes such as transposing the entire track or changing its tempo. See **181 Modify an Existing Loop's Notes** for more on how to do this.

**TIP**

After a track is recorded, you can extend or repeat it just as you can with any built-in loop. Refer to **169 Adjust the Repeat Length of a Loop** for details.

## 174 Play Using a Metronome

### Before You Begin

✔ **171** Record a Track Using a MIDI/USB Keyboard

✔ **173** Record a Live Guitar or Voice Track

### See Also

→ **176** Change the Song's Title, Time Signature Measurement, Tempo, and Key

→ **182** Fix the Timing on a Live Software Music Track

**NOTE**

GarageBand's metronome doesn't need to have its tempo set; it automatically uses the tempo your song is set to. Refer to **176** **Change the Song's Title, Time Signature Measurement, Tempo, and Key** for more information on changing the song's tempo.

**TIP**

You can turn off the metronome altogether by selecting **Control, Metronome** from the menu bar, so that the check mark is turned off.

A *metronome*, in the musical world, is a device that produces a regular clock-like *tick* at a specified *tempo* to help keep you on the beat as you play. GarageBand features a built-in metronome for this purpose. It's a simple thing, but one that can be indispensable in a complex project with lots of live performances.

The metronome's sound is never captured as part of the final recording in GarageBand; someone listening to the final product would never know you'd used it.

### ① Enable the Metronome for Playback and Recording

By default, GarageBand's metronome is activated whenever you're recording a new track. However, it can be useful to have the metronome available when you're just practicing along with your loops before you're ready to record.

Open the **Preferences** dialog box (choose **GarageBand, Preferences**) and click the **General** tab. Enable the **During playback and recording** radio button under **Metronome**. This option allows you to hear the metronome even when you're simply playing your existing tracks.

### ② Enable the Count-In Measure

Normally, when playing back or recording new music, the metronome kicks in at the same time the music does: at the very beginning, *measure* 1. However, you can get an extra few moments to psych yourself up for the performance by enabling the **Count-In** measure. When you enable this option, the metronome plays for a complete measure before the music starts, giving you time to get into the groove.

To enable the **Count-In** measure, choose **Control, Count In** from the menu bar.

## Play Using a Metronome  174

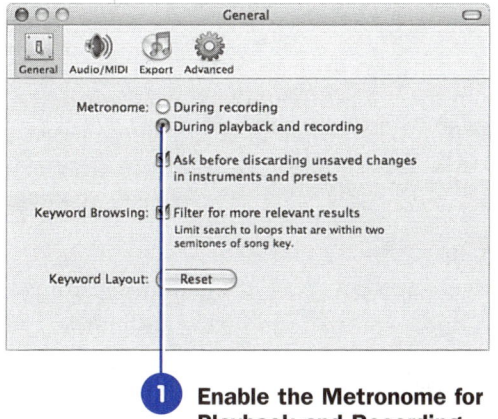

① Enable the Metronome for Playback and Recording

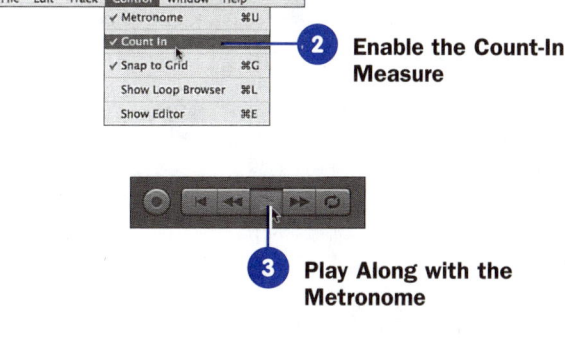

② Enable the Count-In Measure

③ Play Along with the Metronome

### ③ Play Along with the Metronome

As you play, listen to the ticks of the metronome. In a typical 4/4 *time signature* (four beats to the measure, with the quarter note getting a full beat), the metronome ticks four times per measure. The first beat's tick is at a higher pitch than the rest of the ticks; this way you always know when you're at the top of the measure, even if your music is made up of long and featureless atmospheric sounds that leave no clues as to your position in the measure.

The metronome stops playing when the song ends—either when it reaches the endpoint marker or you click the **Play** button to stop it.

## 175  Repeat (Cycle) Part of the Song Forever

As you compose your masterwork, you might find yourself agonizing over a particular short segment of music that you just can't get right. You want to make sure that you have it fully internalized before you record a live track over it, or you might want to figure out just which troublesome note it is that's out of place in the musical canvas. To do this, you might want to select a small portion of the song and play it repeatedly.

**Before You Begin**

✔ 168 Build a Song from Loops

✔ 169 Adjust the Repeat Length of a Loop

**See Also**

→ 179 Mix Your Song's Tracks

→ 181 Modify an Existing Loop's Notes

CHAPTER 21:   Creating a New Song            473

**Repeat (Cycle) Part of the Song Forever**

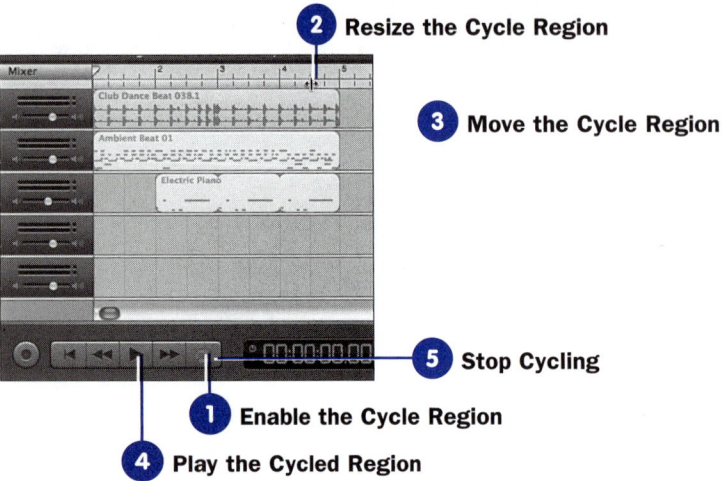

**KEY TERM**

*Cycle region*—A yellow bar at the top of the timeline that indicates a segment of the song that will repeat endlessly when you play the song; helpful for fine-tuning a specific musical passage.

Fortunately, you don't have to keep moving the playhead and clicking **Play** to accomplish this. You can enable the *cycle region*, a segment of the song that the playhead cannot escape from as long as it's active. It just keeps repeating until you tell it to stop.

When you export your completed song to an audio file, if the cycle region is active, only the cycle region—and only one repetition of it—is exported. Generally, make sure that the cycle region is turned off before exporting your final song.

### 1 Enable the Cycle Region

Click the rightmost playback control button (the two arrows chasing each other) to activate the cycle region. This region appears as a yellow bar at the top of the timeline window, just below the timing ruler and playhead. The area under and inside the cycle region is the music that will be repeated.

### 2 Resize the Cycle Region

You must adjust the size (duration) of the cycle region to make sure that it matches the part of the song you're interested in. Move the mouse pointer over the right edge of the cycle region; the

474    PART V:    GarageBand

pointer should turn into a vertical bar with left and right arrows. Click and drag the right edge of the cycle region to the left or right according to where you want the cycle region to end. Do the same for the left edge, the beginning of the region.

### ③ Move the Cycle Region

To select another part of the song entirely, click and drag the yellow bar left or right along the timeline.

### ④ Play the Cycled Region

Click the **Play** button. The playhead begins at the beginning of the cycle region and returns to that point when it reaches the end of the region.

### ⑤ Stop Cycling

When you're done repeating that segment of the song and working out any problems in the music, simply click the rightmost playback control button again to deactivate the cycle region.

# 22

# Fine-Tuning Your Song

## IN THIS CHAPTER:

- **176** Change the Song's Title, Time Signature Measurement, Tempo, and Key
- **177** Rename Your Loops and Tracks
- **178** Transpose a Track Up or Down in Pitch
- **179** Mix Your Song's Tracks
- **180** Add Audio Effects to a Track
- **181** Modify an Existing Loop's Notes
- **182** Fix the Timing on a Live Software Music Track
- **183** Add an External Audio Track
- **184** Copy a Track from One Song to Another

## 176 Change the Song's Title, Time Signature Measurement, Tempo, and Key

Great! You've mastered the basics of creating music in GarageBand. You can add prerecorded loops to your song; you can add a synthesized track using your keyboard; and you can record a live track from a guitar or microphone. But that's only the beginning.

Just laying down a few raw tracks might sound nice—but to make your production sound really top-notch and professional, you'll want to sand down a few rough edges, add some creative flourishes, and do some final buffing and polishing to take your music to the next level. After your composing skills have reached the point where you're ready to take them up a notch, you can start to explore some of the additional features of GarageBand's editing suite.

## 176 Change the Song's Title, Time Signature Measurement, Tempo, and Key

**Before You Begin**

✔ **168** Build a Song from Loops

**See Also**

→ **179** Mix Your Song's Tracks

→ **181** Modify an Existing Loop's Notes

As you work with the built-in Apple Loops, you might find that you like the sound of a lot of the loops, but they're all intended for a much slower or much faster *tempo* (speed) than what you specified when initially creating the project. Although GarageBand automatically *transposes* the loops and adjusts their tempo on the fly to match the song's settings (and only shows you the loops that are compatible with your selected *time signature*), this means that to hear the loops the way they were meant to be played, you must change the song's overall tempo to match the loops.

These global adjustments to timing and *key* are made in the **Master Track** information window, which you can summon at any time.

### ❶ Change the Song's Title

Changing the song's name, or title, as in iMovie, is a matter of changing the name of the song file in the Finder. Simply navigate to the song's location (the default folder in which GarageBand saves your files is **GarageBand**, inside the **Music** folder, in your **Home** folder). Rename the file by simply selecting the filename and typing a new name. You can do this even while GarageBand is running and the project file is open.

## Change the Song's Title, Time Signature Measurement, Tempo, and Key  176

### 2  Show the Master Track

The most direct way to get to the master track information is to summon it from the master track, the way you call up the **Track Info** window from an individual instrument track. The master track sits at the bottom of the workspace, giving you control over the song's master volume controls. See  179  **Mix Your Song's Tracks** for more on how to use this volume track.

Choose **Track**, **Show Master Track** from the menu bar to make the master track visible and gain access to its fine-tuning controls.

### 3  View the Master Track Info

Select the master track by clicking its header (as you do to select any other track). Then click the **Track Info** button to bring up the **Track Info** window.

### 4  Adjust the Tempo

The tempo is the absolute speed of the beats in your song, ranging from slow (80 beats per minute) to very fast (160 or more). You can adjust the tempo of your song to any number of beats per minute, depending on how fast you feel the song should move.

Use the horizontal slider to select a new tempo, which is indicated in the window under the slider in beats per minute (bpm). This slider is similar in function to the slider that appears if you click the **TEMPO** readout on the **Time Display** window.

### 5  Select a New Time Signature

Whereas the tempo signifies how fast the beats in your song are played, the time signature dictates the architecture of the song by describing how many beats are in each measure (the first number) and what kind of note, in musical notation, gets a full beat. The most common beat is **4/4**, meaning four beats per measure, with the quarter note getting the value of one beat.

To select another time signature, such as **3/4** (waltz time), **6/8**, or **2/4** (the "two-step" rhythm), select that timing value from the **Time** drop-down menu.

---

### KEY TERMS

*Tempo*—The speed of the song, measured in beats per minute.

*Time signature*—The musical notation describing the structure of the song's rhythm; it consists of two numbers: the number of beats in the measure and the type of note that is valued at a full beat.

*Key*—The native pitch of the song. A key consists of a series of chords and scales, which can be used to build up the song's music.

### TIP

An alternative way to get to the master track information is to select any instrument track, click the **Track Info** button, and then select **Master Track** from the drop-down menu at the top of the **Track Info** window.

### NOTE

In GarageBand, you can't arbitrarily switch from one time signature to another during the course of a song. You have to choose one time signature and stick to it.

---

CHAPTER 22:  Fine-Tuning Your Song

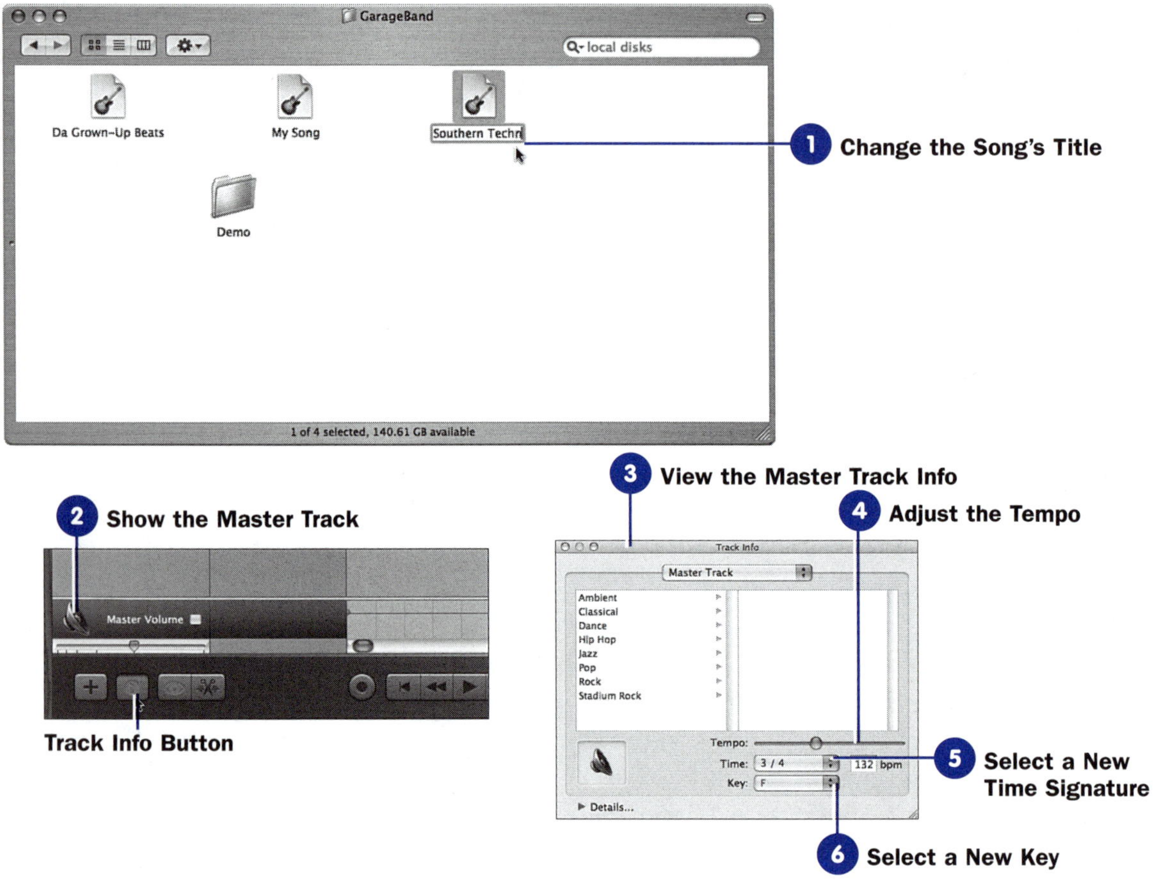

## 176 Change the Song's Title, Time Signature Measurement, Tempo, and Key

**1** Change the Song's Title

**2** Show the Master Track

**Track Info Button**

**3** View the Master Track Info

**4** Adjust the Tempo

**5** Select a New Time Signature

**6** Select a New Key

---

**TIP**

If you deliberately want to put a discordant loop into your song, you can transpose a loop yourself to a different key; see **178 Transpose a Track Up or Down in Pitch** for more information on how to do this.

**6 Select a New Key**

The key of your song is the musical note that sits at the foundation of all the chords you play; the key is important only when you're recording using a keyboard or a real instrument, because some keys are easier to play in than others. Your finely tuned musical ear will tell you which key is appropriate for your song.

To change the key, simply select it from the **Key** drop-down menu; all loops (even the ones you've moved into the timeline) automatically transpose themselves to play in the new key.

## 177 Rename Your Loops and Tracks

As you add more and more tracks to your song, you will notice that GarageBand adds names to each music region that reflects the name of the loop or the name of the **Real Instrument** or **Software Instrument** you used. If you record several tracks, the names can become confusing. You can assign names of your choice to each of the loops and tracks in your song, allowing you to keep them all straight even as you move them around, duplicate them, delete them, and split them into fragments.

**Before You Begin**
- ✔ **168** Build a Song from Loops

**See Also**
- → **178** Transpose a Track Up or Down in Pitch
- → **185** Customize Your Export Information

### 1 Select a Music Region

In the timeline area, click the colored rectangle representing any music *region*—whether a loop, a synthesized recording, or a **Real Instrument** audio stream.

### 2 Open the Track Editor

Click the **Track Editor** button (the "scissors" icon) to open the **Track Editor** pane at the bottom of the window. Alternatively, double-click the region you want to edit.

### 3 Change the Track's Name

The **Name** field at the far left of the **Track Editor** pane shows the region's name. Select the text in the field and type a new, descriptive name for your track or loop.

**TIP**

Repeat steps 1–3 for all your music regions. Be sure to choose names that usefully reflect the contents of each region, so that you can tell what is to be played at which points in the timeline—even without listening to the song.

### 178  Transpose a Track Up or Down in Pitch

1. Select a Music Region
2. Open the Track Editor
3. Change the Track's Name

---

### 178  Transpose a Track Up or Down in Pitch

**Before You Begin**

- ✓ 168  Build a Song from Loops
- ✓ 169  Adjust the Repeat Length of a Loop
- ✓ 176  Change the Song's Title, Time Signature Measurement, Tempo, and Key

**See Also**

- → 180  Add Audio Effects to a Track
- → 181  Modify an Existing Loop's Notes

Although GarageBand automatically adjusts each built-in loop to play correctly in your song's native key, occasionally you will want to vary the track's pitch by a few notes. This isn't just being avant-garde; it's how chord progressions are constructed.

For example, if your song is in the key of C, you might want to take your bass guitar line and spend four measures repeating the same riff with a C chord, followed by B flat, then by F, then by G, before finally returning to C. This common chord progression can be achieved in GarageBand by repeating an appropriate loop four times, splitting it into four separate regions, and then *transposing* each region down by a different amount.

**1  Select the Region to Transpose**

In the timeline area, click the colored rectangle representing any music region—whether a loop, a synthesized recording, or a **Real Instrument** audio stream.

PART V:    GarageBand

**Transpose a Track Up or Down in Pitch** 178

### 2 Split the Region

*This step is optional; it's only used here as part of the example in which we're creating a chord progression.*

Position the playhead at the measure marker between the first and second repetition of the loop. Then choose **Track**, **Split** from the menu bar. The region splits into two new regions, which can be selected and edited independently.

For this example, I repeated this step to divide the region into four independent riffs, one after another.

### 3 Open the Track Editor

Select any of the regions by clicking it, and then click the **Track Editor** button (the "scissors" icon) to open the **Track Editor** pane. (Alternatively, double-click the region.) In this example, the first repetition of the loop doesn't have to be transposed, but the second one does, so I opened the second region in the **Track Editor**.

### 4 Transpose the Region

Regardless of whether you're working with a **Software Instrument** or **Real Instrument** track, the **Track Editor** has a **Transpose** slider. Use the slider to select how far up or down the chromatic scale you want to move the notes in the track. Each unit on the slider represents a half-step on the scale. For instance, to change a loop in the key of C to one in the key of B flat, set the **Transpose** slider to –2.

In this example, I repeated this step for the third and fourth regions (setting them to –7 for the key of F and –5 for the key of G, respectively) to get a chord progression I can use to build up a much more complex piece than by using bare loops alone!

> **KEY TERM**
>
> *Transpose*—To convert a piece of music from its native key into a higher or lower key, giving the whole piece a higher or lower pitch.

> **WEB RESOURCE**
>
> Visit this site to learn more about chord progression and scales, as well as a great deal more about fundamental music theory.

http://www.chordwizard.com/hmw.asp

CHAPTER 22: Fine-Tuning Your Song

## 178  Transpose a Track Up or Down in Pitch

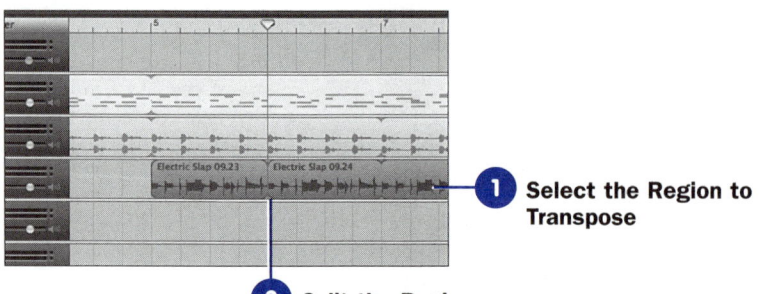

1. Select the Region to Transpose
2. Split the Region

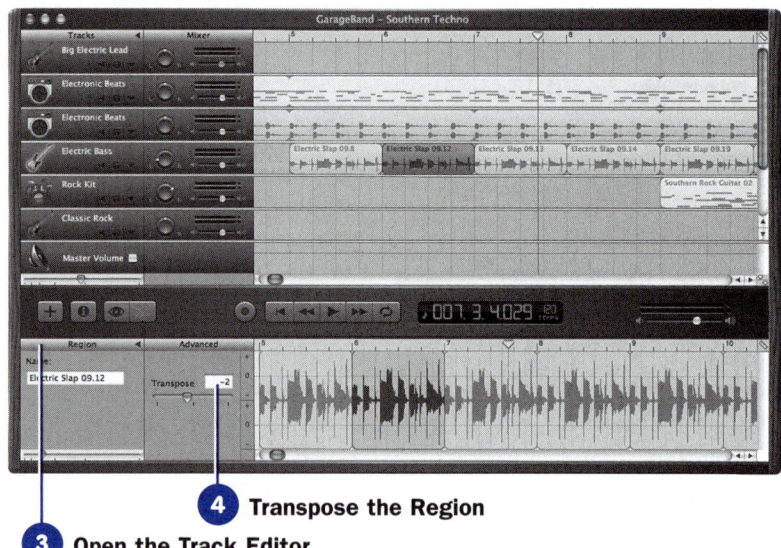

3. Open the Track Editor
4. Transpose the Region

## 179  Mix Your Song's Tracks

**Before You Begin**

✔ 168  Build a Song from Loops

**See Also**

→ 178  Transpose a Track Up or Down in Pitch

→ 180  Add Audio Effects to a Track

So your song sounds great—except for that one scratchy bass line, which you wish was just a little bit quieter. Or maybe you want the shaker to be over on the right side in your stereo headphones. Furthermore, your song just isn't complete without a fade-out at the end. How can you tackle all these problems?

484    PART V:    GarageBand

# Mix Your Song's Tracks  179

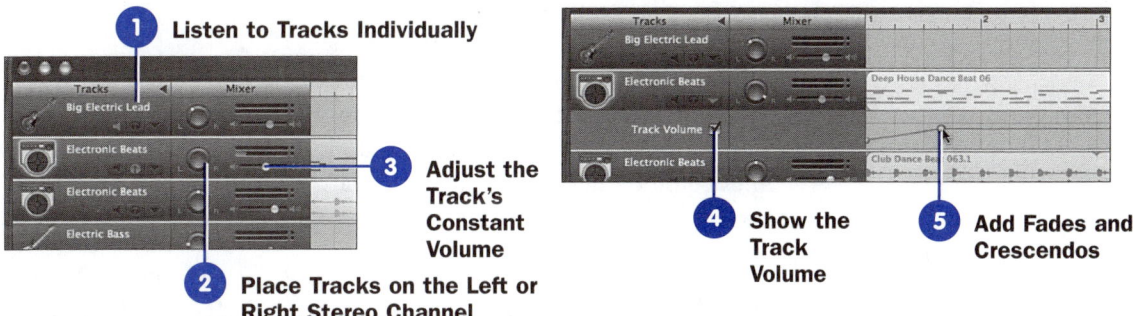

1. Listen to Tracks Individually
2. Place Tracks on the Left or Right Stereo Channel
3. Adjust the Track's Constant Volume
4. Show the Track Volume
5. Add Fades and Crescendos

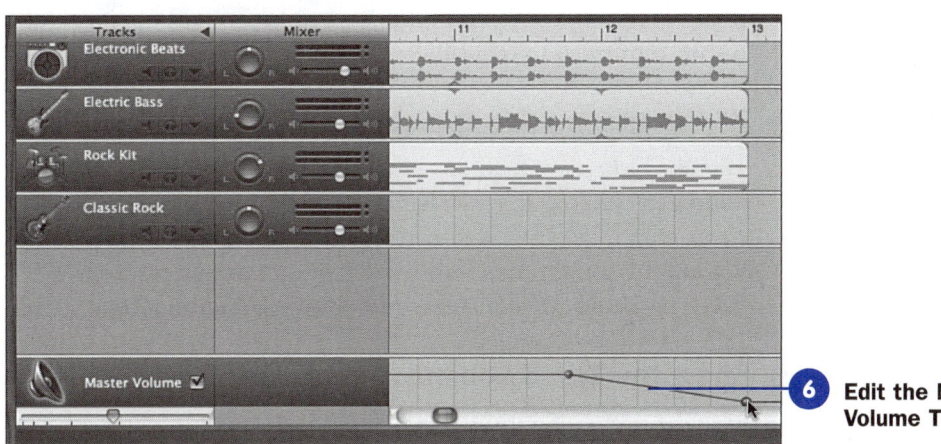

6. Edit the Master Volume Track

GarageBand gives you control over all your tracks' individual volume settings. You can make an entire track louder or softer from beginning to end, or you can step in and make finer-grained adjustments—just as you can in iMovie—over the course of the song. You can use the **Balance** knob to shift tracks to the left or right stereo channel. Finally, you can use the **Master Track** to edit the volume levels over the course of the whole song, for all instruments at once. All these controls give you the professional mixing edge that proves that the power to take raw recorded sound and massage it into smooth, listenable music is no longer the sole province of those guys in soundproof booths at recording studios.

CHAPTER 22: Fine-Tuning Your Song

## 179  Mix Your Song's Tracks

### ① Listen to Tracks Individually

As you edit your song, you can use the **Mute** and **Solo** buttons (found in each track's header) to better hear how your tracks work with each other. Click the **Mute** button (a speaker with no sound lines coming out of it) to silence a track; click the **Solo** button (the headphones) to silence all tracks except the one (or ones) you select.

### ② Place Tracks on the Left or Right Stereo Channel

Click the **Balance** knob on a track's header and drag left or right to shift that track to one side or the other of the stereo channels.

### ③ Adjust the Track's Constant Volume

Use the volume slider in any track's **Mixer** to adjust the relative volume of that track, while leaving the volume of all the other tracks alone. Use the level meters above the volume slider while playing the song to determine whether an instrument is "clipping," or losing coherence because it's turned up too high.

### ④ Show the Track Volume

To make more fine-grained adjustments to an individual track's relative volume, you must enable the **Track Volume** editing region. To do this, click the down-pointing triangle on any track's header. Enable the **Track Volume** check box to allow editing of the track's volume over time.

### ⑤ Add Fades and Crescendos

Editing the volume of a track over the course of the song is much like editing the volume of an audio file in iMovie (see **125 Mix Audio Track Levels** for details on how this works). In short, click at any point along the line and drag up or down to create a *control point* for defining regions of fade or growth in volume. Drag control points left or right to change where volume changes begin or end; drag one control point on top of another to remove an unwanted one.

---

**NOTE**

If the **Mixer** column is not visible, choose **Track, Show Track Mixer** from the menu bar, or click the right-pointing triangle above the track headers (the triangle points left if the **Mixer** column is visible).

## 6 Edit the Master Volume Track

You can control the overall volume behavior of the entire song in the same way you control the volume for an individual track. Choose **Track**, **Show Master Track** from the menu bar to display the master track; enable the **Master Volume** check box to allow editing of the song's overall volume track.

To make the song fade out at the end, for example, scroll to that point in the song and click once to create a control point where you want the fade to begin. Then click again further to the right, where you want the fade to end, and drag downward to create a downward slope in the volume track line.

## 180 Add Audio Effects to a Track

There's a lot more to GarageBand's music synthesizers than just playing back notes that sound like a certain instrument when you play a keyboard. Each **Software Instrument** can be further tuned using a variety of sliders and presets that simulate various kinds of amps and other equipment; you can experiment with echo, reverb, cutoff, release, and many more aspects of how the sound is generated. This book certainly can't aspire to cover all the audio effects possible—that's a task for a book focused on music engineering. If music engineering isn't how you want to spend your time, you can much more easily explore and experiment with the settings in the **Track Info** window. Feel free to play with the settings on any instrument to find the style you like best!

**Real Instruments** have the same sliders and presets as **Software Instruments** do; however, because a recording from a **Real Instrument** is merely a stream of samples and not a list of "notes" (as is true with a **Software Instrument**), any effects you change after recording are applied to what's recorded, not to a pure or "clean" signal. For best results with **Real Instruments**, experiment with the settings to get the sound right *before* you begin recording.

The sliders and presets in the **Track Info** window are what define the built-in simulated guitar amps, by the way, such as "British Invasion" or "Classic Rock." You can develop your own unique amp sounds by simply playing with the sliders and observing how the existing presets are configured.

### Before You Begin
✔ 168 Build a Song from Loops
✔ 171 Record a Track Using a MIDI/USB Keyboard
✔ 173 Record a Live Guitar or Voice Track

### See Also
→ 178 Transpose a Track Up or Down in Pitch
→ 181 Modify an Existing Loop's Notes

## 180  Add Audio Effects to a Track

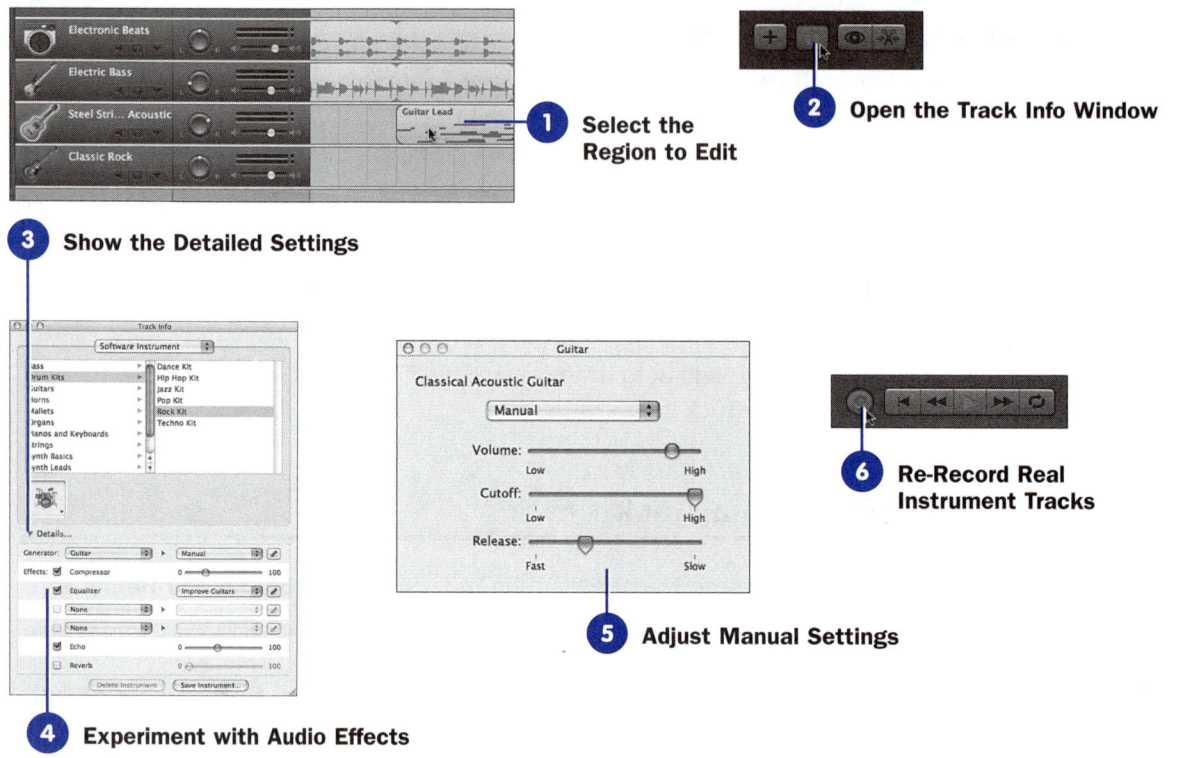

### ❶ Select the Region to Edit

In the timeline area, click the colored rectangle representing any music region—whether a loop, a synthesized recording, or a **Real Instrument** audio stream.

### ❷ Open the Track Info Window

Click the **Track Info** button (the "i" icon) to open the **Track Info** window.

### ❸ Show the Detailed Settings

Click the triangle next to **Details** to expand the **Track Info** window so that it shows the advanced controls for your instruments.

488   PART V:   GarageBand

Add Audio Effects to a Track

**4  Experiment with Audio Effects**

Adjust any of the settings that look interesting to you. **Echo** and **Reverb** create a hollow or sustained sound; **Equalizer** can be used to select certain useful presets from the drop-down lists under the **Equalizer** check box. Presets include one that reduces sibilant "S" sounds, another that suppresses excess bass, and another that enhances snare drums. Some of these presets are clearly intended for certain instruments, but if you apply them to other instruments, the results can be quite bizarre—maybe even in a good way!

**5  Adjust Manual Settings**

For sliders and selectors with a **Manual** setting, click the "pencil" button to the right of the drop-down menu to open another window, which gives you access to still more fine-grained control over your instrument's sound.

If you are prompted to save the changes to the instrument you're working with, click **Don't Save**. By not saving the changes at this point, you can experiment freely, allowing you to return to the original instrument's settings at any time by selecting the instrument from the **Track Info** window. If you want to keep your existing settings and not discard them, however, click **Save** and enter the name for a new preset, which is added to the instrument list for the menu you are working with. Regardless of which button you select, the original instrument settings built into GarageBand are not affected, and you can always choose a fresh instrument from the list.

**6  Re-Record Real Instrument Tracks**

If you're working on a **Real Instrument** track, after you have found the right sound, you can begin recording a new track that uses those settings.

While experimenting with audio settings for a **Real Instrument**, turn on the **Monitor** feature so that you can hear how the instrument sounds with the effects applied. The **Monitor** check box can be found in the **Track Info** window for any **Real Instrument**.

**NOTE**

**Software Instruments** have a drop-down menu called **Generator** from which you can select the basic instrument family (such as **Piano**) that you can then fine-tune using the other menus. Changing the **Generator** setting, however, does not change your instrument's icon or name in the track header.

**TIP**

For a **Software Instrument** track that's already recorded or a loop that's already in place, turn on the cycle region (see  Repeat (Cycle) Part of the Song Forever) and play the track over and over again as you experiment with the audio settings. This approach lets you compare the different sounds easily.

CHAPTER 22:  Fine-Tuning Your Song    489

## 181 Modify an Existing Loop's Notes

**Before You Begin**

✓ 168 Build a Song from Loops

✓ 171 Record a Track Using a MIDI/USB Keyboard

**See Also**

→ 178 Transpose a Track Up or Down in Pitch

→ 180 Add Audio Effects to a Track

### TIP

The **Track Editor** has its own playhead; as you play the song, the editor's playhead moves along with the main playhead to show your progress through the song, even when you're zoomed in much further in the **Track Editor** than in the main timeline area. If you click the playhead lock button (in the lower right of the timeline area), you can toggle GarageBand between keeping the two playheads in sync (so that both panes scroll to keep up with the playhead as it plays) and allowing the playheads to move separately (so that the contents of the **Track Editor** don't move even when the playhead moves out of frame).

### KEY TERM

*Pitch*—The soundwave frequency of a note, manifested in how high or how low it sounds.

As you play your **Software Instruments** and create new tracks, you will confront the realities of live performance—nobody can play absolutely perfectly. You might find sour notes here and there, or you might want to see how the track would have sounded with a certain note in a different place, or with a few extra notes at a certain point. GarageBand lets you make these experiments using the **Track Editor**.

**① Select a Software Instrument Region to Edit**

In the timeline area, click the colored rectangle representing a **Software Instrument** music region. (**Real Instruments** cannot be edited using the **Track Editor**.)

**② Open the Track Editor**

Click the **Track Editor** button (the "scissors" icon) to open the region in the **Track Editor**. Make sure that **Notes** is selected from the **Display** drop-down menu.

**③ Zoom In**

Use the **Zoom** slider at the lower left of the timeline area to change the zoom level of the contents of the **Track Editor** pane independently of the zoom level in the main timeline area. Because the **Track Editor** allows you to change the fine details of the track's notes, you will want to zoom in fairly closely, so that you can easily distinguish the notes.

**④ Move Notes Up and Down in Pitch**

Notes are shown in a "matrix" against a vertical keyboard, indicating their *pitch*; notes higher in the matrix are higher in pitch. Click and drag any note up or down to change its pitch. GarageBand plays the note as soon as you click or move it, so you can tell what it sounds like in its final position.

**⑤ Adjust Note Position and Duration**

Click and drag any note left or right to change where it appears in the timeline. Use the grid lines in the matrix to line the notes up with the beats where you want them.

PART V: GarageBand

### Modify an Existing Loop's Notes

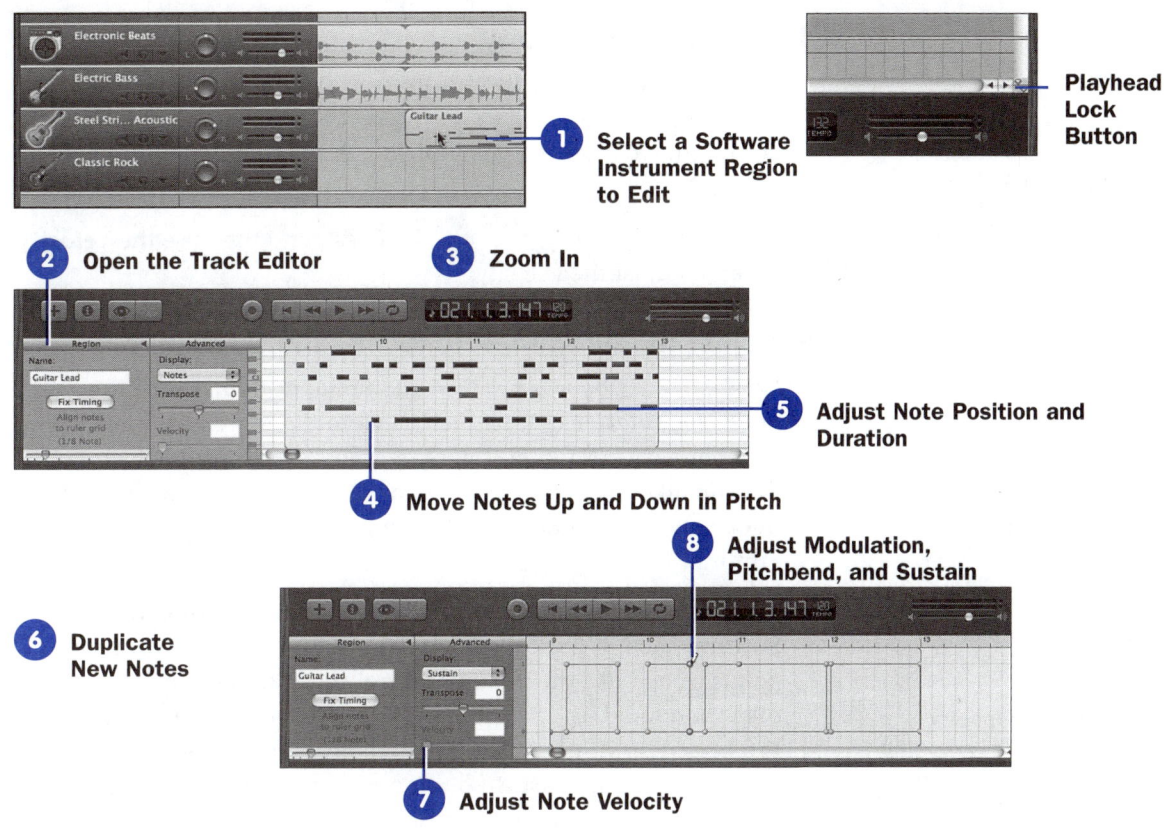

To lengthen or shorten a note, click its rightmost edge and then drag left or right.

**⑥ Duplicate New Notes**

You can create new notes in the track that were never part of what you played on the keyboard. Simply click to select a note, copy it (choose **Edit**, **Copy**), and then paste the note into the matrix again (choose **Edit**, **Paste**). The new note appears nearby, selected. You can then move it to whatever position you need it in, change its duration and pitch, and make any other necessary changes. If you don't like it there after all, simply press **Delete** to remove it.

CHAPTER 22: Fine-Tuning Your Song

**Modify an Existing Loop's Notes**

> **TIP**
> If you adjust multiple notes' velocities at once, they all are shifted by the same amount, even if they all started with different velocities.

**Modulation**—Instrument-specific effects such as vibrato and tremolo, depending on what each instrument is capable of producing.

**Pitchbend**—Temporary "bending" of a note a small amount up or down from its native pitch, used for "grace note" effects.

**Sustain**—An effect that keeps a note playing continuously instead of damping (stopping) it when the note or key is released.

### 7  Adjust Note Velocity

Each note has a "velocity" attribute, which is the energy with which the note was played on the keyboard. The higher a note's velocity, the darker the note appears in the matrix and the louder it sounds.

Click to select a note (or multiple notes), and then use the **Velocity** slider to adjust the velocity.

### 8  Adjust Modulation, Pitchbend, and Sustain

Good MIDI keyboards produce additional attributes with their notes: *modulation* (effects such as vibrato and tremolo), *pitchbend* (a slight temporary adjustment of a note's pitch up or down), and *sustain* (like the pedal on a piano). GarageBand captures all this information and allows you to edit it manually in the **Track Editor**.

From the **Display** menu, choose **Modulation**, **Pitchbend**, or **Sustain**. Each of these display modes shows you lines with control points (much like the volume control tracks in the timeline) that allow you to adjust the specifics of these effects. For instance, the **Pitchbend** display lets you fine-tune how far a note's pitch should be bent, while the **Sustain** display gives you control over how long the sustain pedal should be pushed.

Hold down the ⌘ key to turn the mouse pointer into a "pencil" pointer; click with this pointer to create new control points, which you can then drag to new positions to form lines that dictate how these audio effects apply to the notes in the region.

Remember that you can turn on the cycle region (see **175 Repeat (Cycle) Part of the Song Forever**) while you're working with these audio effects so that you can hear the music continuously as you experiment.

## 182 Fix the Timing on a Live Software Music Track

There's an inescapable reality about an application like GarageBand that lets you mix your human performing talents with the precision of computer-generated loops—what you play will be a tiny bit off the beat, almost without exception. The tracks you play on your keyboard might sound pretty good indeed, but they'll never be absolutely perfect, no matter who you are.

Generally, human imprecision is so slight as to be unnoticeable. But there will be times when the music is off the beat just enough that you can't help noticing it. If you're playing a **Real Instrument**, there isn't really anything that can be done to correct this problem; what you record is the final product. However, **Software Instruments**—because they record the actual *notes* you play rather than simply the collection of waveforms they generate—are much more flexible. GarageBand provides a handy function that corrects any timing imperfections in your recorded **Software Instrument** tracks.

### Before You Begin

✔ **171** Record a Track Using a MIDI/USB Keyboard

✔ **172** Record a Track Using the Virtual Keyboard

### See Also

→ **181** Modify an Existing Loop's Notes

### ① Select a Software Instrument Recorded Region

In the timeline area, click the colored rectangle representing a **Software Instrument** music region that you recorded live from a keyboard. (You can't use this technique to fix the timing on **Real Instrument** tracks.)

### ② Open the Track Editor

Click the **Track Editor** button (the "scissors" icon) to open the region in the **Track Editor**. Make sure that **Notes** is selected in the **Display** drop-down menu.

### ③ Select the Alignment Scale

In the **Track Editor** window, use the **Zoom** slider at the lower left of the timeline area to adjust the fineness of the matrix grid. The guide lines shown are where the notes will snap to when you fix the timing, and the spacing of the grid is reflected in the label under **Align notes to ruler grid**.

### ④ Align the Notes

When the correct grid fineness is shown, click the **Fix Timing** button. The notes in the region all become aligned to the grid.

### TIP

Make sure to zoom in to a fine-enough level that you don't lose intentional detail on your notes timing when you correct it. For instance, if you're playing sixteenth notes, but your grid is zoomed in far enough to show only eighth notes, your notes will become aligned to the eighth-note boundaries, which certainly isn't what you want.

### 183  Add an External Audio Track

1. Select a Software Instrument Recorded Region

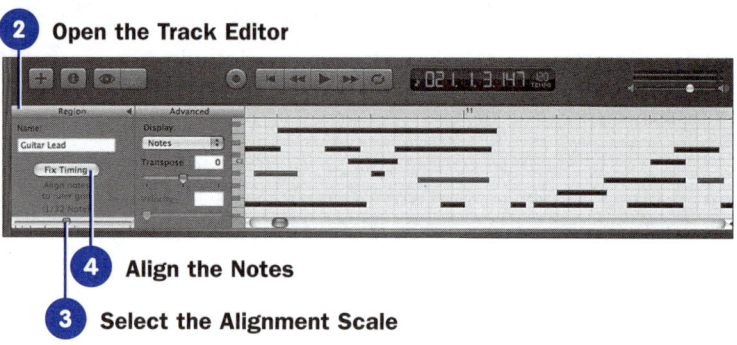

2. Open the Track Editor
3. Select the Alignment Scale
4. Align the Notes

You can't fix the timing of only certain selected notes; you must deselect all notes in the **Track Editor** before the **Fix Timing** button becomes available; the button applies the "fix notes" function to all the notes in the region.

## 183  Add an External Audio Track

**Before You Begin**

✔ 168 Build a Song from Loops

**See Also**

→ 184 Copy a Track from One Song to Another

→ 187 Convert the Song to MP3 or AAC Format for Sharing

Let's face it—some of the most fun that it's possible to have in creating music is in adding amusing sound effects, whether recorded from TV shows, movies, video games, or political campaign speeches. After you've put together all your loops in the background, all that you often need to finish it off is a well-placed sound bite.

Fortunately, to add such a piece of media into your GarageBand song is a matter of a single drag-and-drop maneuver—as long as the clip is in MP3 or AIFF format to begin with.

## Add an External Audio Track

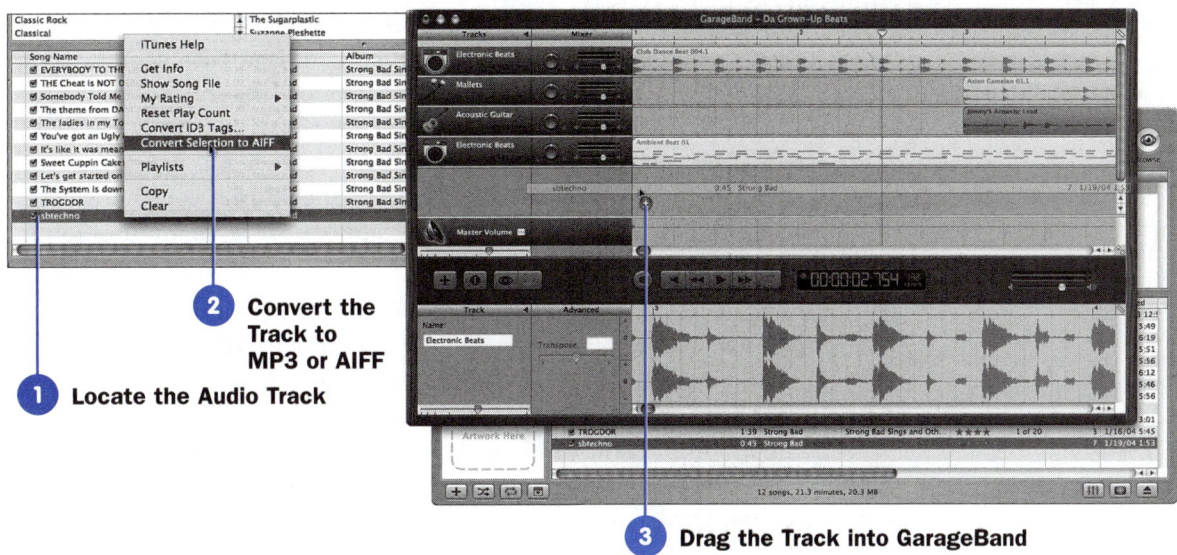

① Locate the Audio Track
② Convert the Track to MP3 or AIFF
③ Drag the Track into GarageBand

### ① Locate the Audio Track

Find the audio track you want to use. It might be on your Desktop, after you downloaded it from the Internet; on the other hand, it might be a track in your iTunes **Library**. Whether it's accessible in the **Finder** or in iTunes, you can drag it directly into GarageBand.

In this example, I have a song file called **sbtechno** in my iTunes **Library** that I want to use in my current GarageBand song.

### ② Convert the Track to MP3 or AIFF

First, determine the format the track is in. Most audio recordings found on the Internet these days are in MP3 format; but a song in iTunes, whether it's one you ripped from a CD or bought through the iTunes **Music Store**, might instead be in AAC format, which cannot be imported directly into GarageBand.

To use iTunes to convert a song into AIFF format, first add the song to your iTunes **Library** if it's not already in it (simply drag the music file into the **iTunes** window). Then select **AIFF Encoder** from the **Import Using** drop-down menu on the **Importing** tab of the iTunes **Preferences** dialog box. Then select the song you want to

iTunes does not allow you to convert songs that you have purchased through the iTunes **Music Store** to AIFF format; this is part of the built-in copy-protection scheme. In other words, you can't create a new song that includes an existing copyrighted song if you bought that copyrighted song online.

**CHAPTER 22:** Fine-Tuning Your Song 495

**Copy a Track from Ono Song to Another**

## TIP

In Mac OS X Panther, you can put the Exposé feature to good use here. First click and begin dragging the file; then press **F9** to tile all open windows. Still dragging the file, hover the mouse over the GarageBand window until the window flashes and pops to the front. Then drop the audio track into place.

convert, and choose **Advanced, Convert selection to AIFF** from the menu bar. Alternatively, right-click (or **Control**+click) the song and choose **Convert selection to AIFF** from the contextual menu that appears. (You can also use the MP3 format in place of the AIFF format, but the sound quality of the track is somewhat reduced in an MP3 file, depending on the settings you choose. See  **Set Custom MP3 Quality Options** for more information.)

###  Drag the Track into GarageBand

Click and drag the converted file from its current location (either in the **Finder** or in the iTunes **Library**) into the GarageBand window. As with any built-in loop, the track is inserted beginning at the point in the timeline where you release the mouse. The track becomes a **Real Instrument** recording, under the header name **New Track**. You can then move the track around, shorten it, loop it, copy it to multiple places in the song—whatever makes the song match your vision.

## WEB RESOURCE

The Dent du Midi shareware by Bery Rinaldo allows you to take regular MIDI files that you obtain from the Internet and convert them to AIFF format for use in GarageBand.

http://homepage.mac.com/beryrinaldo/ddm/

---

 **Copy a Track from One Song to Another**

### Before You Begin

✔ **168** Build a Song from Loops

### See Also

→ **183** Add an External Audio Track

Copying a track or region from one part of the timeline to another is fairly simple—*within the same song*. Just select, copy, and paste as you do with any application.

However, because of the way GarageBand (like other iLife applications) is designed, one project—and only one project—can be open at any time. If you open a second project, you must close the first. This makes copying media from one song/project to another fairly tricky.

PART V: GarageBand

# Copy a Track from One Song to Another  184

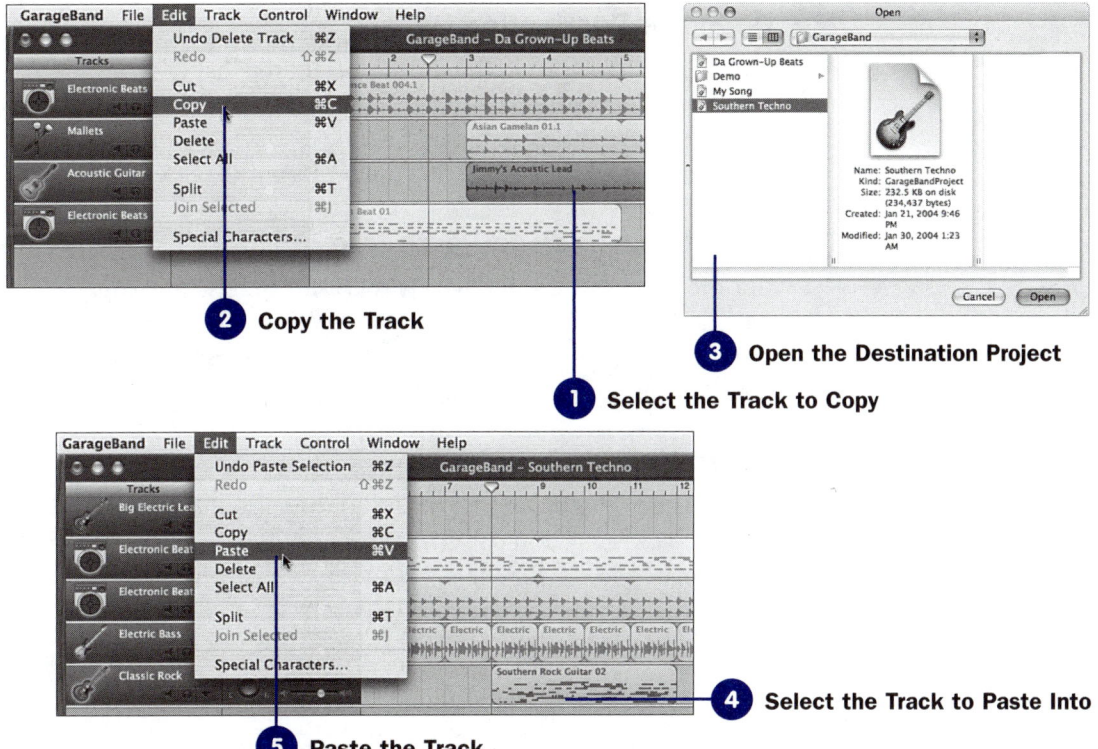

② **Copy the Track**

③ **Open the Destination Project**

① **Select the Track to Copy**

④ **Select the Track to Paste Into**

⑤ **Paste the Track**

---

① **Select the Track to Copy**

Click to select any single music region, or click the header of a track to select the entire track. You can also click and drag a rectangle to select multiple regions at once; however, if you select across several adjoining tracks, note that you cannot paste the multiple tracks into the destination project. Instead, make sure to select and copy each track individually.

② **Copy the Track**

Choose **Edit**, **Copy** from the menu bar to copy the selected regions to the Clipboard.

CHAPTER 22: Fine-Tuning Your Song    497

**184** Copy a Track from One Song to Another

**③ Open the Destination Project**

Choose **File**, **Open** from the menu bar. If there are changes to save in your current project/song, you are prompted to save them. Select the second song project (the song into which you want to paste the copied track) from the file browser and click **Open**.

**④ Select the Track to Paste Into**

Click to select a track into which you want to paste the copied regions. These regions are added *to the end* of the track you select, as close to the playhead as possible. If an appropriate track is not present, create one and select it.

**⑤ Paste the Track**

Choose **Edit**, **Paste** from the menu bar to paste the copied regions into the new song. You can then click and drag the regions to a new location in the timeline, whether to adjust where in time they occur or what music tracks they're part of.

**NOTE**

If you are copying an entire track, you must still select an existing destination track into which to paste it. You're really only copying all the regions in that track, not the entire track entity, with instrument and volume settings intact.

# 23

# Sharing Your Song

### IN THIS CHAPTER:

- **185** Customize Your Export Information
- **186** Export the Song to iTunes
- **187** Convert the Song to MP3 or AAC Format
- **188** Locate the Audio File in the Finder

# 185 Customize Your Export Information

As with any creation, what good is composing your own musical masterwork if you can't share it with your friends, family, and the rest of the world? It's fun to play back your song in GarageBand, watching each instrument coming in where the visual indicators say it should; but not everybody has GarageBand—or a Mac. When you're done creating your song, you'll want to get it out into the world in the same form that everybody uses to listen to music these days: a stream of digitized audio in MP3 or AAC format.

After your song is *exported*—or saved in a format that everybody can read, as you do with an iMovie project—you can burn it to a CD, send it in email, or upload it to the Web where everybody can enjoy it.

Because GarageBand exports music as a digitized bitstream rather than a collection of synthesized instruments (as is the case with a MIDI file), an exported GarageBand song cannot be directly edited by someone who simply downloads the final MP3 or AAC file. A person must have access to your saved GarageBand project file to make changes to the song. Unless you share that project file with someone (which is, incidentally, in its own proprietary file format, an uncompressed raw-media "bundle" format that cannot be easily transmitted across the Internet because of both its size and its structure), you can rest assured, knowing that no one is likely to pirate your exported masterpiece and make adjustments to it.

## 185 Customize Your Export Information

**See Also**
→ **186** Export the Song to iTunes
→ **187** Convert the Song to MP3 or AAC Format

When you export your song from GarageBand, the music is saved in an AIFF file, which is a format that contains very little supplementary information (such as the ID3 tags that appear in MP3 files; see **46** **About Audio Formats** for more about these technical details). AIFF files are uncompressed, meaning they are of pristine studio quality and suitable for the highest-grade multimedia work; but they're also much too large to transfer over the Internet. AIFF files also don't carry with them any supplementary data, such as the composer name, the track title, or what playlists the song should be part of.

## Customize Your Export Information 185

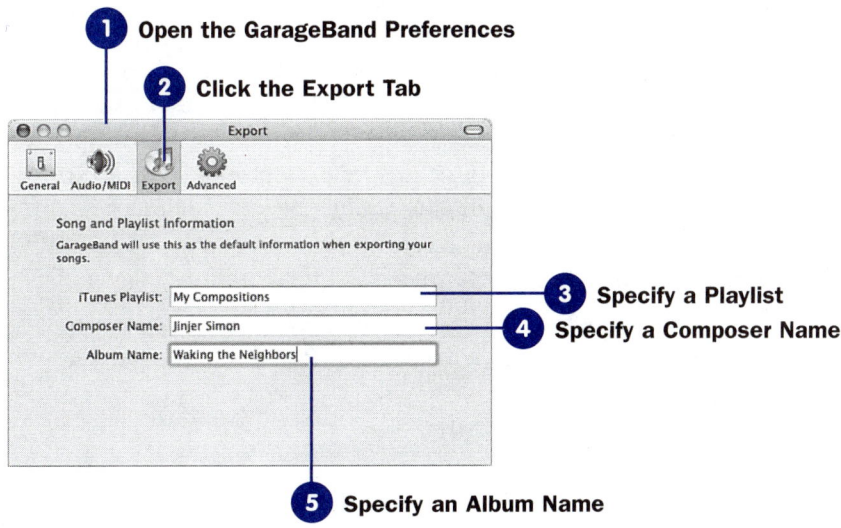

GarageBand solves this problem by using iTunes as an intermediary application for storing the song file. Your song becomes an AIFF file, but it's entered into your iTunes **Library** as well, under your name and with album and playlist information you specify. From within iTunes, as you will see in this chapter's remaining tasks, you can then create an MP3 or AAC file for sharing with the rest of the world. You can, of course, use the uncompressed AIFF file if you need that kind of audio quality (for instance, to create a studio-quality CD).

This task describes how to specify the information that appears in iTunes associated with each of your songs: the album name, composer name, and playlist.

 **NOTE**

GarageBand exports in AIFF because it's reasonably easy to convert from AIFF to compressed formats such as MP3 or AAC; but it's impossible to go from MP3 or AAC back to AIFF without losing audio quality.

**① Open the GarageBand Preferences**

Choose **GarageBand**, **Preferences** from the menu bar to bring up the **Preferences** window.

**② Click the Export Tab**

Click the **Export** tab to view the exporting options available in GarageBand.

CHAPTER 23: Sharing Your Song 501

## 186  Export the Song to iTunes

**TIP**

The **iTunes Playlist** field is not optional; if you leave the field blank, GarageBand creates a playlist with a blank name and puts the song in it. If you delete or rename this blank playlist (you can select it in the **Source** pane), you can still access the song through the **Browse** lists in iTunes.

### 3  Specify a Playlist

When GarageBand exports your song into iTunes, it automatically puts the song into a playlist of your choice or creates a new one if the playlist you specify doesn't exist. For instance, you can specify a playlist called **My Compositions**, and each song you export from then on is added to the **My Compositions** playlist.

### 4  Specify a Composer Name

The name you put into the **Composer Name** field is what appears in both the **Composer** and **Artist** fields for the song in iTunes.

### 5  Specify an Album Name

The **Album Name** field allows you to associate the song with a certain album, primarily so that you can find it more easily in iTunes. Feel free to get creative here; just imagine what you'd like to see as the name on the album cover when your song goes platinum!

Remember that you can always change the name of the album (or any other informational field) in iTunes, as described in 52 **Change Song Information**.

Close the **Preferences** window. Each song that you export from GarageBand from now on will take on the organizational information you have specified in this window.

## 186  Export the Song to iTunes

**Before You Begin**

✔ 185 Customize Your Export Information

**See Also**

→ 187 Convert the Song to MP3 or AAC Format

→ 188 Locate the Audio File in the Finder

After you have configured GarageBand to export your song using the organizational information you want, exporting your song is a matter of a single click. However, there are a few checklist items to look at before you create the final product.

### 1  Make Sure That the Song Is Ready to Play

Play the song one last time in GarageBand to ensure that everything is the way you want it. If there are any muted tracks you want to be included in the final cut, be sure to unmute them.

# Export the Song to iTunes  186

② Export the Song        ① Make Sure That the Song Is Ready to Play

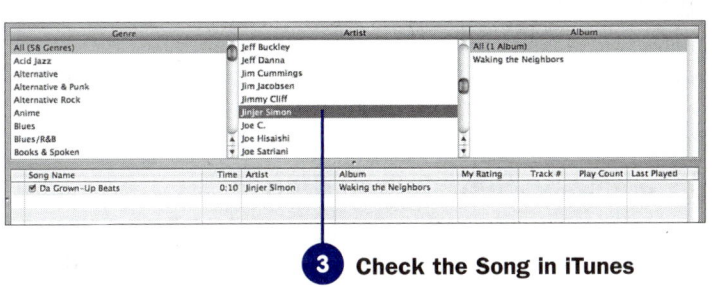

③ Check the Song in iTunes

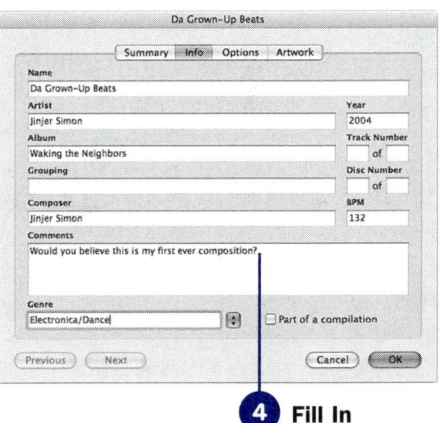

④ Fill In Remaining Song Information

Make sure that the cycle region is turned off (see **175 Repeat (Cycle) Part of the Song Forever** for more information); if it's on, GarageBand exports only the part of the song within the cycle region, and only one repetition of it.

Check the volume and the balance. If either the left or right channel is too loud (the level meters are too full or the red dots to the right of the level meters light up), adjust the **Master Track** master volume control to bring the levels to where their dynamic range stays cleanly within the level meter.

 **NOTE**

Try playing a song in iTunes to get an idea of the volume level of your existing songs. Adjust GarageBand's master volume control to match them.

**CHAPTER 23:  Sharing Your Song**  503

**187 Convert the Song to MP3 or AAC Format**

> **KEY TERM**
> **Mixdown**—The process of compiling a multi-track song into a single track with two stereo channels, as stored in the final AIFF file.

**② Export the Song**

When you're satisfied with how the song sounds, choose **File**, **Export to iTunes** from the menu bar. GarageBand begins saving the song to an AIFF file, creating the *mixdown* and transferring your export information into iTunes.

**③ Check the Song in iTunes**

iTunes launches automatically, if it is not already running, when GarageBand finishes the export process. Browse to your song in the iTunes song list using the **Search** bar, the **Browse** view (where you can scroll to your own name), or the playlist that contains all your GarageBand-exported songs.

Double-click to play the song and make sure that it sounds the way you want it before you convert it to a portable format (MP3 or AAC) and send it off to all your friends!

**④ Fill In Remaining Song Information**

Choose **File**, **Get Info** from the menu bar. Under the **Info** tab, fill in the rest of the information about the song that you think is relevant: track number, genre, and any comments you want to add. GarageBand automatically fills in fields such as the year, the composer, and the tempo (in bpm, or beats per minute).

---

**187 Convert the Song to MP3 or AAC Format**

**Before You Begin**
✔ **186** Export the Song to iTunes

**See Also**
→ **54** Set Import Format for Audio Files
→ **55** Set Custom MP3 Quality Options
→ **188** Locate the Audio File in the Finder

With your song exported into iTunes, you can immediately do such things as burn it onto a CD, transfer it to your iPod, or simply play and enjoy it with the visualizer. However, the song you exported into iTunes from GarageBand is still in AIFF format; although the format doesn't really matter as far as iTunes itself is concerned, the AIFF file is really large and takes up a lot of disk space (one minute of AIFF audio consumes 8–10MB). If you're going to upload the song to the Web or send it to a friend in email, you should convert the song to a compressed format: MP3 or AAC, either of which only uses about 1MB per minute (AAC compresses somewhat better than MP3 does). Fortunately, this functionality is built right in to iTunes.

## Convert the Song to MP3 or AAC Format

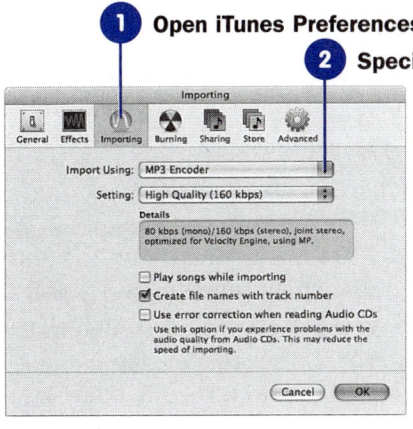

**1** Open iTunes Preferences

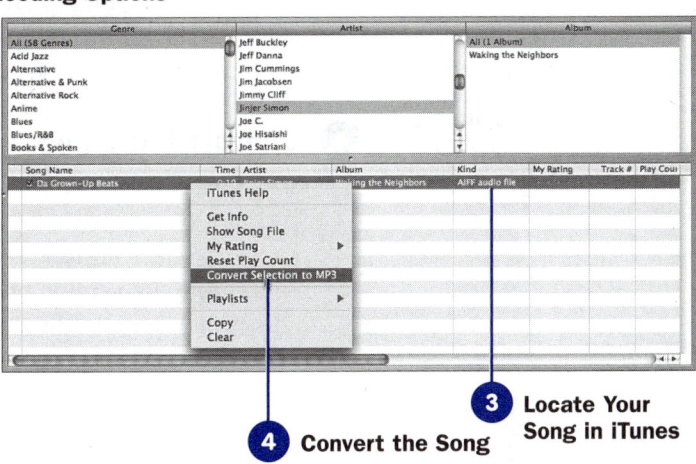

**2** Specify Encoding Options

**3** Locate Your Song in iTunes

**4** Convert the Song

### 1 Open iTunes Preferences

Launch iTunes and open the iTunes **Preferences** window (select **Preferences** from the **iTunes** menu). Click the **Importing** tab to access the importing and encoding options.

### 2 Specify Encoding Options

From the **Import Using** drop-down list, select either the **MP3 Encoder** or **AAC Encoder**, depending on which format you want to use. Remember that MP3 files can be played on a wider variety of computers (whether those computers have iTunes or not) and on all portable audio players; AAC files, on the other hand, can be played only in iTunes and on the iPod, but their sound quality is considerably better than MP3 for the same file size. See **54** **Set the Import Format for Audio Files** and **55** **Set Custom MP3 Quality Options** for more information on how to choose a suitable encoding format.

**NOTE**

You can transfer AIFF files to your iPod and listen to them there; however, because of their size, you can fit only a fraction of the number of AIFF songs on an iPod as you can MP3 or AAC files.

## 188 Locate the Audio File in the Finder

**TIP**

The **Kind** column, if shown, should display **AIFF audio file** for your GarageBand song. This is how you know, in part, that the song was exported from GarageBand.

**3 Locate Your Song in iTunes**

Browse to your song in iTunes, using the **Search** bar, the **Browse** view (where you can scroll to your own name), or the playlist that contains all your GarageBand-exported songs.

**4 Convert the Song**

Select the song in the list. From the **File** menu (alternatively, right-click or **Control**+click the file to display the context menu), select **Convert Selection to MP3** or **Convert Selection to AAC** (whichever is shown, depending on the format you selected in step 1). iTunes performs the conversion, which should take only a few seconds. The new song, in MP3 or AAC format, has all the same song information as the original AIFF file, so it should appear in the same listings or search results as the original file (which is still in the iTunes **Library** and has not been replaced by the new file).

After converting the song, you can transfer the resulting MP3 or AAC file to your iPod (see **67 Sync Playlists with iPod**), attach it to an email message to send to a friend, upload it to your Web site, import it into an iMovie project (see **119 Add Music from iTunes**), or simply turn on your visualizer and enjoy the final product of your creative labors.

## 188 Locate the Audio File in the Finder

**Before You Begin**

✔ **186** Export the Song to iTunes

✔ **187** Convert the Song to MP3 or AAC Format

**See Also**

→ **183** Add an External Audio Track

If you exported your GarageBand song into iTunes, filled out its song information, and converted it into MP3 or AAC format, congratulations—there's only one step left before you can show your song to the world. Because your email application or uploading software can't see into your iTunes **Library** and can instead only work with the more cumbersome system of files and folders in which your music is actually stored behind the scenes, you must first locate your MP3 or AAC song file on the computer's hard disk before you can send it out into the world. When you have done this, you can put the file in an email, drop it in someone else's public **Drop Box** folder, or upload it to the Web.

PART V: GarageBand

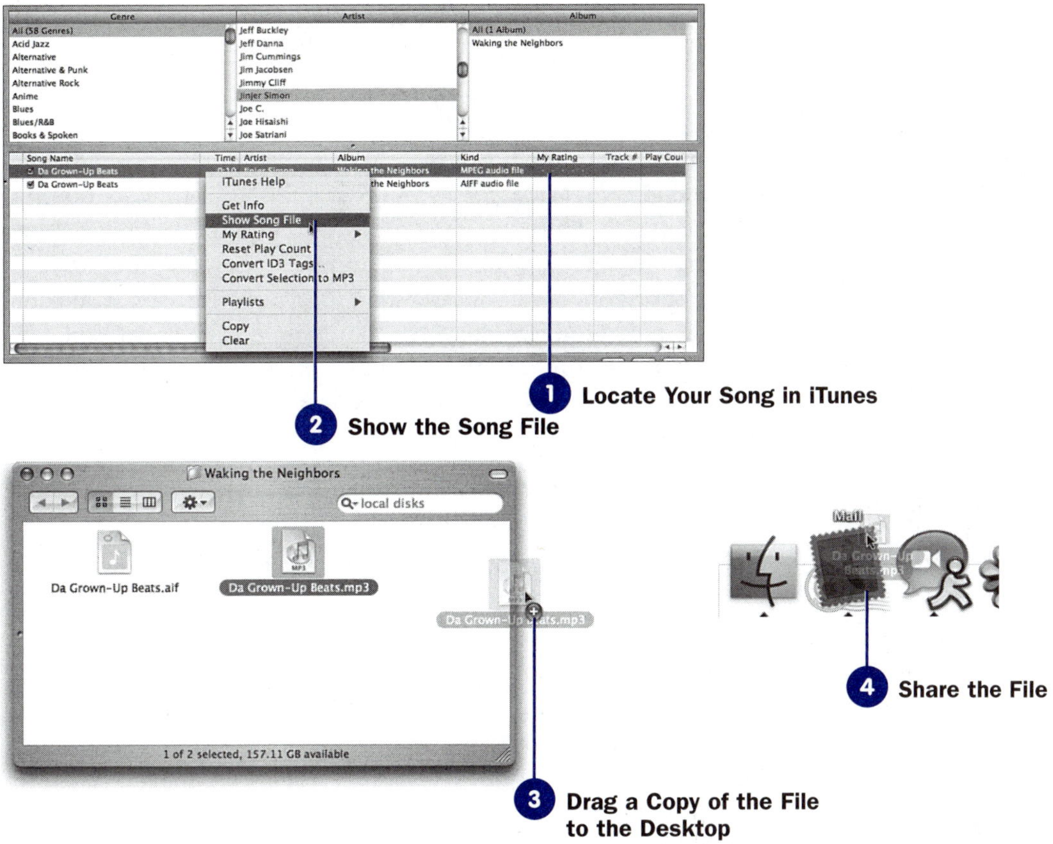

## Locate the Audio File in the Finder  188

① **Locate Your Song in iTunes**
② **Show the Song File**
③ **Drag a Copy of the File to the Desktop**
④ **Share the File**

### ① Locate Your Song in iTunes

Browse to your song in iTunes, using the **Search** bar, the **Browse** view (where you can scroll to your own name), or the playlist that contains all your GarageBand-exported songs. Make sure that you find the version of the song that's in MP3 or AAC format, not the original AIFF file.

### ② Show the Song File

Select the MP3 or AAC version of your song from the song list. From the **File** menu (alternatively, right-click or **Control**+click the song to display the context menu), select **Show Song File**. A

> **TIP**
> Make sure that the **Kind** column is shown in the iTunes song list so that you can tell what format each song is in. Choose **Edit**, **View Options** and select the column names to specify which columns are visible.

**CHAPTER 23:** Sharing Your Song    507

**Locate the Audio File in the Finder**

MP3 files are listed in the iTunes **Kind** column as **MPEG audio file**, reflecting the fact that "**MP3**" is an abbreviation of "**MPEG-1 layer 3**," the proper full name of the compression algorithm.

**Finder** window appears, showing the folder where the MP3 or AAC file is stored, with the appropriate file selected.

### 3 Drag a Copy of the File to the Desktop

You can skip this step if you're an expert at using the **Finder**, spring-loaded folders, Exposé, and other power-user navigational tricks. However, for many users, it's easiest to make a duplicate of the song file and put it on the Desktop before sending it off to its final destination. If you put the song file on the Desktop, you can close the file's **Finder** window and don't have to mess with the location where iTunes expects to find the file (if you accidentally delete the file or move it across volumes, iTunes won't be able to find it anymore).

Hold down the **Option** key while dragging the file to the Desktop; this action creates a duplicate of the song file, leaving the original in its folder. You can then close the **Finder** window.

### 4 Share the File

Using whatever method you like, send the song file on its merry way. You can drag it into an email message; you can drop it into your **Sites** folder to share it using **Personal Web Sharing**, or your Mac's **Public** folder to share it with other Mac users on your network; you can upload it to a remote Web site or add it to the **Public** folder on your iDisk, so that anybody can download your song and enjoy the results of your hard work. Stardom is only a few clicks away!

 **WEB RESOURCE**

MacJukebox is a public clearinghouse site where GarageBand musicians all over the world can upload their creations. Add your own compositions to the database or browse others' songs in search of inspiration!

http://www.macjukebox.net

PART V:   GarageBand

# Index

## A

AAC format (Advanced Audio Coding), 141
    importing as (iTunes), 141
    songs, converting to (iTunes), 504-506
    streaming audio, 211
adding
    audio to slideshows (iDVD), 426-429
    audio files to CD-RW discs, 240
    chapter markers to movies (iMovie), 359
    effects in movies (iMovie), 314-316
    fade-in/out effects (iMovie), 317-319
    images to drop zones (iDVD), 384-386
    keywords to photographs (iPhoto), 64-66
    motions effects to photos (Timeline viewer), 298-300
    movies to DVD menu (iDVD), 375-378
    music
        to movies from CDs, 332-334
        to movies from iTunes, 330-332
    music tracks (GarageBand), 461-463
    photos (Timeline viewer), 294

## adding

pictures to albums (iPhoto), 32

sound effects to movies (iMovie), 328-330

still images from other applications (Timeline viewer), 300-302

video clips (Timeline viewer), 290-292

adjusting

CD burner speeds, 240-242

loops, repeat lengths (GarageBand), 458-460

Advanced menu commands (iMovie)

Lock Audio Clip, 347

Unlock Audio Clip, 347

AIFF (Audio Interchange File Format) audio format, 141, 327

music CDs, creating (iTunes), 141

versus WAV format, 142

albums (iPhoto)

creating, 32

naming, 32

organizing, 36-38

photo books

comment additions, 78-80

creating, 70-71

page design, 74-76

page reordering, 76-78

themes selection, 71-74

pictures

adding, 32

removing, 38-40

slideshows

customization, 94-96

exporting to iDVD, 99-101

exporting to QuickTime, 96-99

playing, 90-92

settings, 92-94

thumbnail images, background appearance, 9

analog video, 261

importing (iMovie), 267-268

Apple iPod. *See* iPod

Apple Music Store

account setup, 150

music

computer authorization, 150

copyright protection features, 152

cost information, 148

purchasing, 148-152

shopping cart option, 152

Apple watermarks, removal of (iDVD), 414

Apple Web site

CD drive resources, 240

DVD player compatibility listing, 372

iPhoto digital camera compatibility listing, 12, 28

QuickTime viewer, downloading, 357

Apple.com Web site, third-party effects software availability, 310, 316

aspect ratios, 388

assigning keywords to photographs (iPhoto), 64-66

Audible.com Web site

audio book files, downloading, 160-162

audio CDs, burning guidelines, 250

audio

copyright issues, 18

DVD menus, changing (iDVD), 410-411

formats, 140
slideshows, adding (iDVD), 426-429
video clips, extracting (iMovie), 336-338

audio CDs
- Audible.com Web site, burning guidelines, 250
- burning with segmented audio files (iTunes), 249-252
- burning (iTunes), 244-246
- creation overview, 238
- gap lengths, setting between files (iTunes), 242-244
- playing/troubleshooting CD-RW discs, 239
- playlists, song selection for burning, 244
- time capacities, 244
- versus MP3 CDs, storage capacities, 238

audio effects, music tracks (GarageBand), 487-489

audio files
- bit rates, quality levels, 163
- books, downloading (Audible.com), 160-162
- CD-RW discs, troubleshooting additions/retrievals, 240
- CDs
  - burning with segmented files (iTunes), 249-252
  - capturing (iTunes), 143-145
  - information, changing (CDDB), 157-159
- clips
  - fade effects (iMovie), 344-346
  - locking to video clips (iMovie), 347
  - splitting (iMovie), 338-340
  - volume adjustments (iMovie), 340-341
- copying to Music folder (iTunes), 192-194
- crossfades, creating (iTunes Equalizer), 230-231
- format conversion (iTunes), 140
- formats, 141
  - AAC (Advanced Audio Coding), 141
  - AIFF (Audio Interchange File Format), 141-142
  - AU, 141
  - MOV (QuickTime), 142
  - MP3, 142
  - WAV (Windows Audio), 141
- frequency levels
  - adjusting (iTunes Equalizer), 222-224
  - decibels, 222
  - presets (iTunes Equalizer), 222-223
  - saving (iTunes Equalizer), 226-228
- gap lengths, setting (iTunes), 242-244
- import formats
  - MP3 custom settings (iTunes), 165-169
  - setting (iTunes), 163-165
- importing (iTunes), 140-141
- iPod
  - anti-piracy systems, 196
  - deleting, 206
  - manual updates, 203-206
- Library (iTunes), creation of backups, 253-255
- linking (iTunes), 153-155
- organizing (iTunes), 174
- removing from Library (iTunes), 188-190
- ripping (iTunes), 145
- searching Library (iTunes), 190-192

## audio files

storage location, 169-171
streaming audio, 210
supported formats, 211
visual effects, applying (iTunes Equalizer), 232-234

audio formats (iMovie), 326-327

Audio pane (iMovie)
iTunes music, 330-332
music CD tracks, adding, 332-334
songs, adding through iTunes, 326
sound effects, 328-330
voiceover effects, 334-336

audio tracks
mixing capabilities (iMovie), 342-344
movies, number of (iMovie), 326
Timeline viewer, 286
playing, 287
volume adjustments, 288
volume adjustments (iMovie), 342-344

AVI format (Audio Video Interleave), 266

## B

B & W tool, photographic black-and-white effects (iPhoto), 60
backgrounds in DVD menus, creating (iDVD), 391-393
backups, Library (iTunes), 253-255
bit rates
audio streams, 211
MP3s, selecting, 165-169
quality levels, 163

bitmap (BMP) file format, 11
black-and-white photographs, converting from color types, 60
BMP (bitmap) file format, 11
Book pane (iPhoto), photo books
creating, 70-71
page design, 74-76
printing, 81-83
themes selection, 71-74
books, audio files, downloading (Audible.com), 160-162
breaks, video clips, importing (iMovie), 268-270
brightness in photographs, changing (iPhoto), 52
buffered play, streaming audio, 210
burners (CDs)
CD-RW drive, 238
speeds, 239
SuperDrive, 238
burners (DVDs), 370
burning
audio CDs
iTunes, 244-246
segmented audio files (iTunes), 249-252
CDs
external drives, 239
speed adjustments, 240-242
DVDs
final versions to DVD-Rs (iDVD), 446-448
iDVD, 370
test versions to DVD-RWs (iDVD), 443-446

images to photo CDs (iPhoto), 131-133
MP3 CDs (iTunes), 247-248
buttons in DVD menus (iDVD)
    changing images of, 402-404
    changing location of, 404-405
    custom creation, 406
    label changes, 398-401
    moving, 408

## C

capturing
    audio files from CDs (iTunes), 143-145
    video clips (iMovie), 262-265
CCDs (charge-coupled devices), 46, 261
CD players, compatibility with CD-RW discs, 239
CD-R discs, burn speeds, 239
CD-RW discs, 239
    audio files, troubleshooting, 240
    burn speeds, 239
    burning CDs, 238
    compatibility with older CD players, 239
    contents, erasing, 240
CDDB (CD Database), 143
    changing information, 157-159
    retrieving information, 155-157
CDs
    audio
        burning (iTunes), 244-246
        burning with segmented audio files (iTunes), 249-252

creation overview, 238
time capacities, 244
versus MP3 storage, 238
audio files
    capturing (iTunes), 143-145
    gap lengths between files (iTunes), 242-244
    ripping (iTunes), 145
burners
    CD-RW drive, 238
    external drives, 239
    speed adjustments, 240-242
    SuperDrive, 238
CDDB (CD Database), 143
data, creation overview, 238
drive resources, Apple Web site, 240
MP3
    burning (iTunes), 247-248
    creation overview, 238
    number of songs per disc, 239
    versus audio storage, 238
photos, creating (iPhoto), 131-133
track information
    changing (CDDB), 157-159
    retrieving (CDDB), 155-157
tracks, 143
chapter markers
    adding (iMovie), 359
    creating Scene Selection menu (iDVD), 380-382
ChordWizard Web site, 483
Clip Info dialog box, 274

Clips pane

Clips pane (iMovie), 272
    Monitor playback, 272
    video clips
        cropping, 277-279
        freeze frame images, 281-283
        naming, 274
        setting direction of, 279-281
        splitting, 275-277
Clips Viewer (iMovie), 15-16
    versus Timeline viewer, 287
colors, enhancing in photographs (iPhoto), 56-58
commands
    Advanced menu (iMovie)
        Lock Audio Clip, 347
        Unlock Audio Clip, 347
    Edit menu (iMovie)
        Create Still Frame, 283
        Crop, 279
        Split, 340
        Split Clip at Playhead, 277
        Undo Crop, 279
        Undo Split, 340
    Edit menu (iPhoto), Rotate, 49
    File menu (iMovie)
        Empty Trash, 277
        Preferences, 269
        Save Frame As, 283
        Show Info, 274
    File menu (iPhoto)
        Export, 97
        Import, 29

        New Album, 32
        Remove from Album, 38
        Revert to Original, 62
        Show Photo Info, 44
comments in photo books, adding (iPhoto), 78-80
composing songs from loops (GarageBand), 454-458
composite video cables for analog video transfers, 267-268
compression of images, 281
computers
    digital video cameras, FireWire connections, 260-261
    pictures, importing (iPhoto), 29
    USB cables, connection process, 28
    video clips
        capturing (iMovie), 262-265
        importing (iMovie), 260-265
contact sheets, printing (iPhoto), 110-112
contrast in photographs, changing (iPhoto), 52
controlling
    DVDs, playback quality (iDVD), 442
    slideshows, navigation settings (iDVD), 431-432
converting
    audio file formats (iTunes), 140
    photographs, color to black-and-white (iPhoto), 60
    songs
        to AAC format (iTunes), 504-506
        to MP3 format (iTunes), 504-506

copying
- music tracks to other songs (GarageBand), 496-498
- playlists to iPod (iTunes), 174
- songs to iTunes Library, 192-194

copyrights, multimedia issues, 18

Create Still Frame command (Edit menu-iMovie), 283

creating
- albums (iPhoto), 32
- credits for movies (iMovie), 321-324
- custom buttons in DVD menus (iDVD), 406
- freeze frame images from video clips (iMovie), 281-283
- greeting cards (iPhoto), 107-109
- iDVD files from iMovie files, 360-362
- movies in QuickTime format (iMovie), 357-358
- photo CDs (iPhoto), 131-133
- projects (iMovie), 264
- screensavers from photos (iPhoto), 127-129
- smart playlists (iTunes Library), 180-182
- titles for movies (iMovie), 311-314
- voiceover effects for movies (iMovie), 334-336

credits, movies, creating (iMovie), 321-324

Crop command (Edit menu-iMovie), 279

Crop tool (iPhoto), 49-51

cropping
- photographs (iPhoto), 49-51
- video clips (iMovie), 273, 277-279

crossfades in songs, creating (iTunes Equalizer), 230-231

Customize drawer (iDVD), 17, 373-386

customizing
- audio in DVD menus (iDVD), 410-411
- images in drop zones (iDVD), 388-389
- iPod playlists, 206-208
- movies in drop zones (iDVD), 388-389
- playlists (iTunes Library), 177-179
- slideshow music (iPhoto), 94-96

cycle regions in songs, repeating (GarageBand), 473-475

# D

data CDs
- audio files, supported backup formats, 253-255
- creation overview, 238

deactivating screensavers, 3-5

decibels, 222

deleting
- iPod songs, 206
- music tracks (GarageBand), 463
- photos from Photo Library (iPhoto), 38
- songs
  - iTunes Library, 188-190
  - playlists, 176

Dent du Midi shareware, MIDI to AIFF conversion, 496

desktop photos, placement of (iPhoto), 129-130

digital cameras
- external microphones, use of, 327
- images, importing to iPhoto, 12

**digital cameras**

    iPhoto, compatibility listing, 12
    pictures, transferring from (iPhoto), 26-28
    poor audio quality, troubleshooting, 327
    resolution
        CCDs, 46
        purchasing criteria, 46
    USB cables, connection process, 28

**digital video cameras**
    CCDs, number of, 261
    computers, FireWire connections, 260-261
    video clips
        break detection during importation (iMovie), 268-270
        capturing (iMovie), 262-265
        importing (iMovie), 260-265
        importing from non-camera sources (iMovie), 265-267
    video tape, storage of movies (iMovie), 354-356

digital video recording decks, 354

digitized music versus synthesized music, 452-453

Disk Utility, CD-RW discs, erasing, 240

displaying
    movies in full-screen mode (iMovie), 350-351
    photos, time settings (Timeline viewer), 296

distributing video, iMovie options, 350

Dot Photo Web site, digital photographic print service, 113

downloading
    audio book files (Audible.com), 160-162
    iTunes, latest version, 151
    MP3s, copyright violations, 140
    music from Web sites, 147
    music files (iTunes), 145-148
    QuickTime viewer, 357
    dragging loops into songs (GarageBand), 457

drop zones
    DVD menu
        function of, 383-384
        image additions, 384-386
    images
        customizing (iDVD), 388-389
        removing (iDVD), 390
    movies, customizing (iDVD), 388-389

DSL connections, selection advice, 211

DVD-R discs, 239, 371
    burning final versions, 446-448
    time capacities, 371

DVD-RW discs, 239, 371
    burning test versions, 443-446
    player support, 371
    time capacities, 371

DVDs
    burn speeds, 239
    burning, 370
    commercial versus personal, 371
    content, previewing prior to burn process (iDVD), 439-440
    content layout (iDVD), 370
    final versions, burning to DVD-R (iDVD), 446-448
    format types, 371
    international formats
        NTSC, 372-373
        PAL, 372-373
        SECAM, 372-373

menus
- button label changes, 398-401
- changing audio, 410-411
- changing button images, 402-404
- changing button locations, 404-405
- custom background creation (iDVD), 391-393
- custom button creation, 406
- drop zones, image additions, 384-386
- motion type (iDVD), 393-394
- movie folders, adding (iDVD), 378
- movies, adding to (iDVD), 375-376
- moving buttons, 408
- removal of Apple watermark, 414
- saving custom themes, 412-414
- start frames, setting, 401
- title changes, 396-398

movies, chapter marker additions (iMovie), 359

personal versus commercial, 371

playback quality, controlling (iDVD), 442

players
- compatibility listing, 372
- format support, 372
- selection criteria, 372

slideshows, 418
- advance controls (iDVD), 431-432
- audio additions (iDVD), 426-429
- creating (iDVD), 424-426
- creating (iPhoto album), 418-421
- creating (iPhoto Browser), 421-423
- reorganizing images (iDVD), 429-431

test versions, burning on DVD-RW (iDVD), 443-446

themes
- motion options (iDVD), 375
- selecting (iDVD), 373-375

# E

Edit menu commands (iMovie)
- Create Still Frame, 283
- Crop, 279
- Split, 340
- Split Clip at Playhead, 277
- Undo Crop, 279
- Undo Split, 340

Edit menu commands (iPhoto), Rotate, 49

Edit pane (iPhoto), 7
- button options, 42
- photographs
    - black-and-white effect, 60
    - brightness adjustments, 52
    - color enhancement, 56-58
    - contrast adjustments, 52
    - cropping via Crop tool, 49-51
    - red-eye removal, 54-56
    - retouching, 58-60
    - rotating, 47-49

editing photographs (iPhoto), 42

effects

effects
- movies, adding (iMovie), 314-319
- third-party software, 316
- Timeline viewer, rendering, 288-289

Effects pane (iMovie), 308, 314-319

email, sending photographs (iPhoto), 115-118

Empty Trash command (File menu-iMovie), 277

Enhance tool, photographic adjustments (iPhoto), 56-58

enhancing colors in photographs (iPhoto), 56-58

Equalizer (iTunes)
- audio files
  - applying visual effects, 232-234
  - crossfade creation, 230-231
  - frequency levels, 222-223
    - adjusting, 224
    - presets, 222-223
    - saving, 226-228
  - presets, applying to individual songs, 228-230

erasing CD-RW discs (Disk Utility), 240

Export command (File menu-iPhoto), 97

Export Photos dialog box, 97

exporting
- photos to other applications (iPhoto), 134-136
- slideshows
  - to iDVD (iPhoto), 99-101
  - to QuickTime (iPhoto), 96-99
- songs
  - GarageBand preferences, 500-502
  - iTunes, 502-504

external audio tracks, adding (GarageBand), 494-496

external CD burners, 239

external microphones, use of, 327

extracting audio from video clips (iMovie), 336-338

# F

fade effects in audio clips (iMovie), 344-346

File menu commands (iMovie)
- Empty Trash, 277
- Preferences, 269
- Save Frame As, 283
- Show Info, 274

File menu commands (iPhoto)
- Export, 97
- Import, 29
- New Album, 32
- Remove from Album, 38
- Revert to Original, 62
- Show Photo Info, 44

file types (iPhoto)
- BMP (bitmap), 11
- Flashpix, 12
- GIF (Graphics Interchange Format), 11
- JPEG (Joint Photographic Experts Group), 11
- MacPaint, 11
- PICT (Picture File Format), 11
- PNG (Portable Network Graphics), 11

PSD (Photoshop), 11
SGI (Silicon Graphics Image Format), 11
TGA (Targa File Format), 12
TIFF (Tag Image File Format), 12
Finder, locating songs from iTunes, 506-508
FireWire (IEEE 1394), 197
    digital video cameras, connecting to computers, 260-261
    port location, 260
FlashbackRadio.com Web site, 214
Flashpix file format, 12
frames in video clips
    NTSC standard rate, 273
    PAL standard rate, 273
Freeplay Music Web site, 147
freeze frame images, creating (iMovie), 281-283
frequency levels
    adjusting (iTunes Equalizer), 222-224
    decibels, 222
    presets (iTunes Equalizer), 222-223
    saving (iTunes Equalizer), 226-228
full-screen mode (iMovie), viewing, 350-351

# G - H

gap lengths in audio files, setting (iTunes), 242-244
GarageBand
    features overview, 452
    Jam Pack, 454

live tracks, time fixes, 493-494
loops
    adding to Favorites list, 458
    defined, 454
    digitized indicator, 457
    instrument selections, 456
    mood/style selections, 456
    number of, 454
    opening Browser, 455
    previewing, 457
    purchasing additional, 454
    regions, 460
    renaming, 481
    repeat lengths, adjusting, 458-460
    searching by name, 457
    songs, building, 454-458
    songs, dragging into, 457
    splitting, 460
    synthesized indicator, 457
    tempo changes, 456-457
MacJukebox Web site, song clearinghouse, 508
metronome, activating, 472-473
MIDI keyboards, composing, 452
music tracks
    audio effects additions, 487-489
    loops, note changes, 490-492
    mixing, 484-487
    renaming, 481
    stereo channels, 486
    transposing keys, 482-483
    volume settings, 486-487

## GarageBand

note attributes
- modulation, 492
- pitchbend, 492
- sustain, 492
- velocity, 492

real instruments (digitized), 454

software instruments (synthesized), 454

songs
- export preferences, 500-502
- exporting to iTunes, 502-504
- external audio track additions, 494-496
- key changes, 478-480
- live instrument tracks, recording, 469-471
- master tracks, viewing, 479
- music tracks, adding, 461-463
- music tracks, deleting, 463
- music tracks, instrument settings, 461-463
- music tracks, recording via MIDI/USB keyboards, 464-466
- music tracks, recording via virtual keyboards, 466-469
- music tracks, system loads, 461
- renaming, 478
- repeat cycle regions, 473-475
- tempo changes, 478-480
- time signature changes, 478-480
- tracks, copying to other songs, 496-498
- voice tracks, recording, 469-471

synthesized music
- loops, 453-454
- recording process, 453-454
- USB keyboards, composing, 452

GIF (Graphics Interchange Format) file format, 11

Gracenote CDDB (CD Database), track information, 143
- changing, 157-159
- retrieving, 155-157

Graphics Interchange Format (GIF) file format, 11

greeting cards, creating (iPhoto), 107-109

hard-bound photo books, ordering (iPhoto), 86-88

Hollywood Edge Web site, sound effects downloads, 328

# I

iDisk
- photos, publishing on Internet, 118-121
- slideshows
  - setting as screensavers, 125
  - sharing over Internet, 122-124

iDVD
- Apple SuperDrive, 16
- content layout, 370
- controls, 16-18
- Customize drawer, 17

DVD menu
- drop zone additions, 383-386
- movie folder additions, 378

DVD-R discs, burning, 371

DVD-RW discs, burning, 371

DVDs
- burning, 370
- burning final versions to DVD-Rs, 446-448
- burning test versions to DVD-RWs, 443-446
- content, previewing prior to burn process, 439-440
- playback quality, 442
- theme selection, 373-375

Finder, locating slideshow images for DVDs, 424-426

images
- customizing in drop zones, 388-389
- removing from drop zones, 390

menus
- changing audio, 410-411
- changing button images, 402-404
- changing button labels, 398-401
- changing button locations, 404-405
- changing titles, 396-398
- creating custom buttons, 406
- custom backgrounds, 391-393
- motion type, 393-394
- moving buttons, 408
- removal of Apple watermark, 414
- saving custom themes, 412-414
- start frames, setting, 401
- themes, 17

movies
- adding to DVD menu, 375-376
- customizing in drop zones, 388-389
- transferring from iMovie, 360-362

MPEG-2 compression, 371

overview, 16-18

Scene Selection menu, creating from movies with chapter markers, 380-382

slideshows
- advance controls, 431-432
- audio additions, 426-429
- creating, 18
- exporting (iPhoto), 99-101
- image reorganization, 429-431

IEEE 1394 (FireWire), 197, 260

illegal downloads of MP3 files, 140

images
- aspect ratios, 388
- buttons, changing in DVD menus (iDVD), 402-404
- compression, 281
- digital cameras, importing to iPhoto, 12
- drop zones
  - adding (iDVD), 384-386
  - customizing (iDVD), 388-389
  - function of (iDVD), 383-384
  - removing (iDVD), 390
- formats, 134
- photo CDs, burning to (iPhoto), 131-133
- slideshows
  - navigation settings (iDVD), 431-432
  - reorganizing (iDVD), 429-431

## images

storage locations, setting (iPhoto), 10-11

Timeline viewer, adding from other applications, 300-302

iMovie
- audio clips
  - fade effects, 344-346
  - locking to video clips, 347
  - volume adjustments, 340-341
- audio formats, 326
  - AIFF, 327
  - MP3, 327
  - selecting for movies, 327
  - WAV, 327
- Audio pane
  - iTunes music, 330-332
  - sound effects, 328-330
- audio tracks
  - adding to movies, 326
  - mixing capabilities, 342-344
  - number of, 326
  - volume adjustments, 342-344
- Clips pane, Monitor playback, 272
- Clips Viewer, 15-16
- Clips/Timeline Viewer, 14-15
- digital video, capturing, 262-265
- digital video cameras, FireWire connections, 260-261
- Effects pane, 308, 314-319
- full-screen mode, 350-351
- interface, 14-15
- Monitor, 14-15
- movies
  - chapter marker additions, 359
  - creating in QuickTime format, 357-358
  - previewing, 350-351
  - storing on digital video tape, 354-356
- nondigital video, importing, 267-268
- overview, 14
- panes, 14-15
- projects
  - creating, 264
  - opening, 264
  - transferring to iDVD, 360-362
- Scrubber bar, 14
- Timeline Viewer, 15-16, 286-290, 296-302
- Titles pane, 308, 311-314, 321-324
- Transitions pane, 308-311, 319-321
- video clips
  - break detection during importation, 268-270
  - cropping, 273, 277-279
  - freeze frame creation, 281-283
  - full-screen mode, 273
  - importing, 260-265
  - importing from non-camera sources, 265-267
  - inserting credits, 321-324
  - inserting transitions, 308-314
  - modifying transitions, 319-321
  - naming, 274
  - setting direction, 279-281
  - splitting, 275-277
- videos, distribution options, 350

Import command (File menu-iPhoto), 29

Import Files dialog box, 266

Import pane (iPhoto), 6, 28

Import Photos dialog box, 29

# iPhoto

importing
- audio files (iTunes), 140-141
- images from digital cameras (iPhoto), 12
- Internet music files (iTunes), 145-148
- nondigital video (iMovie), 267-268
- pictures from other computers (iPhoto), 29
- video clips
  - break detection (iMovie), 268-270
  - iMovie, 260-265
  - non-camera sources (iMovie), 265-267

information, photographs, setting (iPhoto), 44

instruments, live tracks
- recording (GarageBand), 469-471
- setting (GarageBand), 461-463

Internet radio
- audio streams, loading (iTunes), 214-215
- bit rates, 211
- listening (iTunes), 212-213
- radio sites
  - adding to iTunes Library, 211
  - storing (iTunes), 215-217
- streaming audio
  - bit rate selection for DSL connections, 211
  - buffered play, 210
- supported formats (iTunes), 211

iPhoto
- albums
  - creating, 32
  - naming, 32
  - organizing, 36-38
- picture additions, 32
- picture removal, 38-40
- slideshows, creating, 418-421
- slideshows, exporting to iDVD, 99-101
- slideshows, exporting to QuickTime, 96-99
- slideshows, music customization, 94-96
- slideshows, playing, 90-92
- slideshows, settings, 92-94

Book mode, 7

Browser, creating slideshows for DVDs, 421-423

contact sheets, printing, 110-112

digital cameras
- compatibility listing, 12, 28
- picture transfers to PCs, 26-28

Edit pane, button options, 42

file types
- BMP (bitmap), 11
- Flashpix, 12
- GIF (Graphics Interchange Format), 11
- JPEG (Joint Photographic Experts Group), 11
- MacPaint, 11
- PICT (Picture File Format), 11
- PNG (Portable Network Graphics), 11
- PSD (Photoshop), 11
- SGI (Silicon Graphics Image Format), 11
- TGA (Targa File Format), 12
- TIFF (Tag Image File Format), 12

files, importing from digital cameras, 12

# iPhoto

greeting cards, creating, 107-109
images, storage locations, 10-11
Import pane, 6, 28
Organize mode, 6
    thumbnail image backgrounds, 9
    thumbnail image sizes, 7
Organize pane, 28
overview, 5
photo books
    comment additions, 78-80
    creating, 70-71
    ordering online, 86-88
    page design, 74-76
    page reordering, 76-78
    PDF format, saving as, 84-86
    printing, 81-83
    themes selection, 71-74
photo CDs, creating, 131-133
Photo Library
    organization overview, 30-31
    photo deletion, 38
photographs
    adding to Timeline viewer (iMovie), 294
    black-and-white effect (Enhance tool), 60
    brightness adjustments, 52
    color enhancement (Enhance tool), 56-58
    contrast adjustments, 52
    creating screensavers from, 127-129
    cropping, 49-51
    display times (iMovie), 296
    displaying resolution information, 47
    editing overview, 42
    exporting to other applications, 134-136
    keyword additions, 64-66
    original versions, reverting to, 62-64
    placing on desktop, 129-130
    printing, 104-107
    red-eye removal, 54-56
    retouching (Enhance tool), 58-60
    rotating, 47-49
    searching via keywords, 66-68
    sending via email, 115-118
pictures, importing from other computers, 29
prints, online ordering, 112-115
thumbnail images, 29
versus third-party editors, 43
iPod, 140
    audio files
        anti-piracy systems, 196
        deleting, 206
        manual updates, 203-206
    available disk space, monitoring, 196
    charging times, 196
    FireWire ports, 197
    interface controls, 195
    iTunes complete compatibility, 194
    playlists
        copying from iTunes, 174
        customized views, 206-208
        synchronizing, 200-203

popularity of, 194
preferences, setting, 196-200
songs, adding, 195
storage space options, 194
turning on/off, 196

iTunes
   Apple Music Store, purchasing music files, 148-152
   audio book files, downloading from Audible.com, 160-162
   audio CDs
      burning, 244-246
      burning with segmented audio files, 249-252
   audio files
      capturing from CDs, 143-145
      format conversion, 140
      import settings, 163-165
      importing, 140-141
      linking, 153-155
      organizational overview, 174
      setting gap lengths between files, 242-244
      storage location, 169-171
   audio formats
      AAC (Advanced Audio Coding), 141
      AIFF (Audio Interchange File Format), 141-142
      AU, 141
      MOV (QuickTime), 142
      MP3, 142
      WAV (Windows Audio), 141

CDDB
   audio file information modifications, 157-159
   audio file information retrieval, 155-157

CDs
   burn speed adjustments, 240-242
   CD-RW file additions, 240
   CD-RW file retrieval, 240
   creation overview, 238
   disc burn capacities, 239
   disc burn support, 238
   MP3 capacities, 239

controls, 12-14

Equalizer
   crossfade creation, 230-231
   frequency levels, 222-223
   presets, applying to individual songs, 228-230
   visual effects, 232-234

interface appearance, 12-14

Internet radio
   bit rate information, 211
   buffered play, 210
   supported formats, 211

iPod, complete compatibility, 194

latest version, downloading, 151

Library
   audio files, copying to Music folder, 192-194
   audio files, removing, 188-190
   audio files, searching, 190-192

iTunes

backup creation, 253-255
playlists, customizing, 177-179
playlists, default, 177
playlists, multiple, 176
playlists, sharing, 183-186
playlists, smart, 180-182
radio site additions, 211
songs, rating system, 186-188

MP3s
burning, 247-248
import settings, 165-169

music
adding to movies (iMovie), 330-332
downloading, 145-148

playlists
copying to iPod, 174
randomize playback, 218-219
shuffle options, 210
shuffling by album, 234-235

radio sites
genre selection, 212
listening, 212-213
loading, 214-215
storing, 215-217

songs
adding to Audio pane, 326
converting to MP3 or AAC format, 504-506
importing from GarageBand, 502-504
locating in Finder, 506-508

Source list icons, 175

streaming audio, 210
AAC format, 211
MP3 format, 211
volume levels, adjusting, 220-221

## J - K

Jam Pack (GarageBand), 454
Joint Photographic Experts Group. *See* JPEGs
Joint Stereo, 166-168
JPEGs (Joint Photographic Experts Group), 11, 134
compressed images, 281

Ken Burns effect, still images, 283
motion appearance, 298-300

keyboards
MIDI, composing (GarageBand), 452
USB, composing (GarageBand), 452

keys
music tracks, transposing (GarageBand), 482-483
songs, changing (GarageBand), 478-480

Keystation 49e keyboard, 452

keywords in photographs
adding (iPhoto), 64-66
searching via (iPhoto), 66-68

## L

Library (iPhoto), image storage, 10-11
Library (iTunes)
    audio files
        copying to Music folder, 192-194
        linking, 153-155
        removing, 188-190
        searching, 190-192
        storage location, 169-171
    audio formats, 141
        ACC (Advanced Audio Coding), 141
        AIFF (Audio Interchange File Format), 141-142
        AU, 141
        MOV (QuickTime), 142
        MP3, 142
        WAV (Windows Audio), 141
    CD track information, changing, 157-159
    data CDs, backup creation, 253-255
    playlists
        customizing, 177-179
        sharing, 183-186
        smart, 175-177, 180-182
        storing, 174-177
    songs, rating system, 186-188
linking audio files (iTunes), 153-155
listening
    Internet radio (iTunes), 212-213
    music
        random playback (iTunes), 218-219
        volume adjustments (iTunes), 220-221

live instrument tracks
    recording (GarageBand), 469-471
    time fixes (GarageBand), 493-494
loading audio streams (iTunes), 214-215
locating iTune songs
    Finder, 506-508
    iTunes Library, 190-192
Lock Audio Clip command (Advanced menu-iMovie), 347
locking audio clips to video clips (iMovie), 347
loops (GarageBand), 454
    adding to Favorites list, 458
    Browser, opening, 455
    digitized indicator, 457
    instrument selections, 456
    mood/style selections, 456
    music tracks, note changes, 490-492
    number of, 454
    previewing, 457
    purchasing, 454
    regions, 460
    renaming, 481
    repeat lengths, adjusting, 458-460
    searching by name, 457
    songs, building, 454-458
    songs, dragging into, 457
    splitting, 460
    stored, 453-454
    synthesized indicator, 457
    tempo changes, 456-457
lossless compression (PICT), 281
lossy compression (JPEG), 134, 281

.Mac accounts

# M

.Mac accounts
   HomePage option, photo publishing, 118-121
   slideshows
      setting as screensavers, 125
      sharing over Internet, 122-124

MacJukebox Web site, GarageBand song repository, 508

MacPaint file format, 11

master tracks, viewing (GarageBand), 479

measures in songs, composing, 460

Media pane, 374-378, 382, 386, 392

megapixels, digital cameras, 46

menus, DVDs (iDVD)
   audio changes, 410-411
   button label changes, 398-401
   buttons, moving, 408
   changing button images, 402-405
   custom backgrounds, creating, 391-393
   custom button creation, 406
   custom themes, saving, 412-414
   motion type, creating, 393-394
   removal of Apple watermark, 414
   start frame settings, 401
   title changes, 396-398
   themes, 17

metronome, activating (GarageBand), 472-473

MIDI (Musical Instrument Digital Interface), 452
   Dent du Midi shareware, AIFF conversion, 496
   keyboards
      composing (GarageBand), 452
      recording tracks (GarageBand), 464-466
   synthesized music
      disadvantages, 453
      versus digitized music, 452-453

mixing
   audio tracks (iMovie), 342, 344
   music tracks (GarageBand), 484-487

modifying
   brightness in photographs (iPhoto), 52
   CD information (iTunes), 157-159
   contrast in photographs (iPhoto), 52
   slideshow settings (iPhoto), 92-94
   video clips, speed of (Timeline viewer), 292-293
   volume levels (iTunes), 220-221

modulation attributes (musical notes), 492

Monitor (iMovie)
   clips, viewing, 272
   Playhead bar, 272-273
   Scrubber bar, 272-273, 279

monitors, screensavers, 2

motion effects, adding to photos (iMovie), 298-300

motion menus, custom creation (iDVD), 393-394

MOV format (QuickTime), 142, 266, 357

movies
- audio clips
  - fade effects (iMovie), 344-346
  - locking to video clips (iMovie), 347
  - splitting (iMovie), 338-340
  - volume adjustments (iMovie), 340-341
- audio files, extracting (iMovie), 336-338
- audio tracks
  - adding (iMovie), 326
  - number of (iMovie), 326
  - volume adjustments (iMovie), 342-344
- chapter markers
  - adding (iMovie), 359
  - creating Scene Selection menu (iDVD), 380-382
- credits, creating (iMovie), 321-324
- digital video tape, storing on (iMovie), 354-356
- drop zones
  - customizing (iDVD), 388-389
  - function of (iDVD), 383-384
- DVDs
  - burning final versions to DVD-Rs (iDVD), 446-448
  - burning test versions on DVD-RWs (iDVD), 443-446
  - commercial time capacities, 371
  - menus, adding to (iDVD), 375-376
  - monitoring time lengths (iDVD), 442
  - motion menus, creating, 393-394
- effects, adding (iMovie), 314-316
- fade-in/out effects, adding (iMovie), 317-319
- iDVD files
  - saving as (iMovie), 360, 362
  - start frame settings, 401
- music
  - adding from CDs, 332-334
  - adding from iTunes, 330-332
- poor audio quality, troubleshooting, 327
- previewing (iMovie), 350-351
- QuickTime format, creating (iMovie), 357-358
- sound effects, adding (iMovie), 328-330
- titles, creating (iMovie), 311-314
- video clip transitions
  - inserting (iMovie), 308-311
  - modifying (iMovie), 319-321
- voiceover effects, creating (iMovie), 334-336

moving buttons in DVD menus (iDVD), 408

Moving Pictures Experts Group Audio Layer 3. See MP3s

MP3.com Web site, 147

MP3s (Moving Pictures Experts Group Audio Layer 3), 140, 327
- bit rates, selecting, 165-169
- burning (iTunes), 247-248
- copyright issues, 18, 140
- creation overview, 238
- disk space requirements versus other formats, 142
- import settings, quality levels, 163-169
- iPod players, 140
- joint stereo, 165-169
- number of songs per disc, 239

# MP3s

songs, converting to (iTunes), 504-506
streaming audio, 211
variable bit rate (VBR), 165-169
versus audio CDs, storage capacities, 238

MPEG-2 compression format (DVDs), 371

multimedia
copyright issues, 18
QuickTime format, 350

music
adding to movies (iMovie), 332, 334
CD information
changing (CDDB), 157-159
retrieving (CDDB), 155-157
creating (AIFF format), 141
downloading (iTunes), 145-148
Freeplay Music Web site, 147
movies
adding from CDs, 332-334
adding from iTunes, 330-332
MP3.com Web site, 147
purchasing (Apple Music Store), 140
royalty-free sites, 145-148
slideshows, customizing (iPhoto), 94-96

music tracks (GarageBand)
audio effects, adding, 487-489
keys, transposing, 482-483
loops, note changes, 490-492
MIDI/USB keyboards, recording, 464-466
mixing, 484-487
renaming, 481
songs
adding, 461-463
copying to other songs, 496-498
deleting, 463
instrument settings, 461-463
system loads, 461
stereo channels, 486
virtual keyboards, recording, 466-469
volume settings, 486-487

Musical Instrument Digital Interface. *See* MIDI

# N - O

naming
albums (iPhoto), 32
video clips (iMovie), 274

networks, sharing playlists with other users (iTunes), 183-186

New Album command (File menu-iPhoto), 32

nondigital video, importing (iMovie), 267-268

notes (musical)
attributes
modulation, 492
pitchbend, 492
sustain, 492
velocity, 492
loops, changing on music tracks, 490-492

NTSC standard
DVD video format, 353, 372-373
frame rates, 273

opening projects (iMovie), 264
Order Prints dialog box (iPhoto), 112-115
Organize pane (iPhoto), 28
- photo books, page reordering, 76-78
- photographs, rotating, 47-49
- slideshows
  - exporting to iDVD, 99-101
  - exporting to QuickTime, 96-99
  - music customization, 94-96
  - playing, 90-92
  - settings, 92-94
- thumbnail images
  - background settings, 9
  - size settings, 7

organizing
- albums (iPhoto), 36-38
- audio files (iTunes), 174

original photographs, pre-edit changes (iPhoto)
- retrieving, 43
- reverting back to, 62-64
- storing, 42

# P

pages in photo books
- comment additions (iPhoto), 78-80
- designing (iPhoto), 74-76
- reordering (iPhoto), 76-78

PAL standard
- DVD video format, 353, 372-373
- frame rates, 273

pass-through options, analog video transfers/recordings, 267-268

PDF format, photo books, saving as, 84-86

photo album slideshows
- playing (iPhoto), 90-92
- settings (iPhoto), 92-94

photo books
- creating (iPhoto), 70-71
- ordering online (iPhoto), 86-88
- pages
  - comments, adding (iPhoto), 78-80
  - designing (iPhoto), 74-76
  - reordering (iPhoto), 76-78
- PDF format, saving (iPhoto), 84-86
- printing (iPhoto), 81-83
- themes, selecting (iPhoto), 71-74

photo CDs, creating (iPhoto), 131-133

Photo Info dialog box (iPhoto), 44

Photo Library (iPhoto)
- organization overview, 30-31
- pictures, deleting, 38

photographs (iPhoto)
- black-and-white effect, applying, 60
- brightness, changing, 52
- colors
  - enhancing, 56-58
  - retouching, 58-60
- contact sheets, creating, 110-112
- contrast, changing, 52

photographs

cropping, 49-51
desktop, placing on, 129-130
editing, 42
exporting to other applications, 134-136
formats
    JPEG, 134
    PNG, 134
    TIFF, 134
information, setting, 44
keywords
    assigning, 64-66
    searching via, 66-68
original versions
    retrieving, 43
    reverting, 62-64
    storing, 42
photo books
    comments, adding, 78-80
    creating, 70-71
    ordering online, 86-88
    page design, 74-76
    page reordering, 76-78
    printing, 81-83
    saving in PDF format, 84-86
    themes selection, 71-74
printing, 104-107
professional prints
    online ordering, 112-115
    resolutions, 114
publishing on Internet (iDisk), 118-121
red-eye, removing, 54-56

resolution
    information, displaying, 47
    modifying, 47
    pixel requirements, 46
rotating, 47-49
screensavers, creating (iPhoto), 127-129
sending via email (iPhoto), 115-118
slideshows
    setting as screensavers (iDisk), 125
    sharing over Internet (iDisk), 122-124
Timeline viewer
    adding, 294
    display time adjustments, 296
    motion additions, 298-300
Photoshop (PSD) file format, 11
PICT (Picture File Format) file format, 11
    uncompressed images, 281
pictures
    albums, removing (iPhoto), 38-40
    computers, importing (iPhoto), 29
    digital cameras, transferring (iPhoto), 26-28
    new albums
        adding to (iPhoto), 32
        naming (iPhoto), 32
        organizing (iPhoto), 36-38
    Photo Library
        deleting (iPhoto), 38
        organizing (iPhoto), 30-31
    thumbnail sizes, 29
pitchbend attributes (musical notes), 492

pixels in photographs
- changing (iPhoto), 47
- information, displaying (iPhoto), 47
- resolution, 46

placing photos on desktop (iPhoto), 129-130

players (DVDs)
- compatibility listing, 372
- selection criteria, 372

Playhead, 272-273

playing
- audio CDs, troubleshooting CD-RW discs, 239
- DVDs, quality controls (iDVD), 442
- slideshows in photo albums (iPhoto), 90-92

playlists
- audio CDs, song selection for burning, 244
- copying to iPod, 174
- customizing (iTunes), 177-179
- iPod
  - customized views, 206-208
  - synchronizing, 200-203
- iTunes
  - smart, 175
  - storing, 174-175
- radio sites, loading (iTunes), 215-217
- rating systems (iTunes), 186-188
- sharing (iTunes), 183-186
- shuffle options (iTunes), 210, 218-219, 234-235
- slideshow song selection, 94-96
- smart, creating (iTunes), 180-182

songs
- deleting, 176
- multiple additions (iTunes), 176
- organizational overview (iTunes), 174
- versus smart playlists, 176

PNG (Portable Network Graphics) file format, 11, 134

poor audio quality in digital cameras, troubleshooting, 327

preferences
- iPod, setting, 196-200, 240-242
- screensavers, setting, 3

Preferences command (File menu-iMovie), 269

presets, songs, applying individually (iTunes Equalizer), 228-230

previewing
- DVD content prior to burn process (iDVD), 439-440
- movies (iMovie), 350-351

printers, photographic quality (iPhoto), 104-107

printing
- contact sheets, 110-112
- photo books, 81-83
- photos, 104-107

prints (photographs)
- online ordering, 112-115
- resolutions, 114

projects
- existing, opening (iMovie), 264
- final DVD versions, burning to DVD-Rs (iDVD), 446-448
- new, creating (iMovie), 264

PSD (Photoshop) file format, 11
publishing photos to Web servers (iDisk), 118-121
purchasing
- digital cameras, pixel requirements, 46
- music files at Apple Music Store, 148-152
- photographic prints (iPhoto), 112-115

## Q - R

QuickTime format, 96, 350
- .mov file extension, 357
- movies, creating (iMovie), 357-358
- slideshows, exporting (iPhoto), 96-99
- viewer, downloading, 357

radio sites
- adding to iTunes Library, 211
- FlashbackRadio.com, 214
- genre selection (iTunes), 212
- listening (iTunes), 212-213
- loading (iTunes), 214-215
- Shoutcast.com, 214
- Somafm.com, 214
- storing (iTunes), 215, 217

rating songs (iTunes Library), 186-188
recording music tracks (GarageBand), 453-454
- live, 469-471
- via MIDI/USB keyboards, 464-466
- via virtual keyboards, 466-469
- voice tracks, 469-471

red-eye in photographs, removing (iPhoto), 54-56
region, 459-460
relocating buttons in DVD menus (iDVD), 404-405
Remove from Album command (File menu-iPhoto), 38
removing
- Apple watermarks from DVD menus (iDVD), 414
- images from drop zones (iDVD), 390
- pictures from albums (iPhoto), 38-40
- red-eye from photographs (iPhoto), 54-56
- songs (iTunes Library), 188-190

renaming
- loops, 481
- music tracks, 481
- songs, 478

rendering effects (Timeline viewer), 288-289
reordering pages in photo books (iPhoto), 76-78
reorganizing images in slideshows (iDVD), 429-431
repeat cycle regions, songs (GarageBand), 473-475
repeat lengths of loops (GarageBand), 458-460
resolution
- digital cameras (CCDs), 46
- photographs
    - information, displaying (iPhoto), 47
    - modifying (iPhoto), 47
    - pixel requirements, 46

retouching photographs with Retouch tool (iPhoto), 58-60

retrieving

    audio files from CD-RW discs, 240

    CD information from CDDB (iTunes), 155-157

    photographs, original versions (iPhoto), 43

Revert to Original command (File menu-iPhoto), 62

reverting photographs to original versions (iPhoto), 62-64

ripping CDs (iTunes), 145

Rotate command (Edit menu-iPhoto), 49

rotating photographs (iPhoto), 47-49

# S

S-Video cable, analog video transfers, 267-268

Save Frame As command (File menu-iMovie), 283

saving

    custom themes in DVD menus (iDVD), 412-414

    Equalizer settings (iTunes), 226-228

    photo books in PDF format (iPhoto), 84-86

Scene Selection menu, chapter markers, creating (iDVD), 380-382

screen burn-in, 2

screensavers

    activation settings, 3-5

    deactivating, 3-5

    function of, 2

    iDisk slideshows, setting, 125

    photos, creating from (iPhoto), 127-129

    preferences, setting, 3

    sleep settings, 2

Scrubber bar (iMovie), 14

searching

    photographs

        keyword additions (iPhoto), 64-66

        via keywords (iPhoto), 66-68

    slideshow images (iDVD), 424-426

    songs (iTunes Library), 190-192

SECAM standard, DVD video format, 372-373

selecting

    DVD themes (iDVD), 373-375

    playlists for CD creation, 244

sending photos via email (iPhoto), 115-118

setting

    import formats

        audio files (iTunes), 163-165

        MP3 custom settings (iTunes), 165-169

    information for photographs (iPhoto), 44

    iPod preferences, 196-200

    slideshows as screensavers (iDisk), 125

    storage locations for music files (iTunes Library), 169-171

    thumbnail images

        background appearance (iPhoto), 9

        sizes (iPhoto), 7

    video clips, direction of (iMovie), 279-281

SGI (Silicon Graphics Image) file format, 11
sharing
    playlists (iTunes Library), 183-186
    slideshows with .Mac account users (iDisk), 122-124
Shoutcast.com Web site, 214
Show Info command (File menu-iMovie), 274
Show Photo Info command (File menu-iPhoto), 44
shuffle option (iTunes)
    playlists, 218-219
    songs by album (iTunes), 234-235
Shutterfly Web site, digital photographic print service, 113
Silicon Graphics Image (SGI) file format, 11
Skywalker Sound Effects, 328-330
slideshows
    creating (iDVD), 18
    DVDs, 418
        advance controls (iDVD), 431-432
        audio additions (iDVD), 426-429
        creating (iDVD), 424-426
        creating (iPhoto album), 418-421
        creating (iPhoto Browser), 421-423
        image reorganization (iDVD), 429-431
    exporting to iDVD (iPhoto), 99-101
    exporting to QuickTime (iPhoto), 96-99
    .Mac accounts, sharing over Internet, 122-124
    music, customizing (iPhoto), 94-96
    playing (iPhoto), 90-92
    screensavers, setting (iDisk), 125
    settings, adjusting (iPhoto), 92-94

smart playlists
    creating (iTunes), 180-182
    iTunes Library, 175-177
    versus playlists, 176
Snapfish Web site, digital photographic print service, 113
Somafm.com Web site, 214
songs
    AAC format, converting to (iTunes), 504-506
    adding to Audio pane (iTunes), 326
    audio files, locating (iTunes), 506-508
    CD information
        changing (CDDB), 157-159
        retrieving (CDDB), 155-157
    ChordWizard Web site, 483
    composing from loops (GarageBand), 454-458
    copying to Music folder (iTunes Library), 192-194
    crossfades, creating (iTunes Equalizer), 230-231
    downloading (iTunes), 145-148
    Freeplay Music Web site, 147
    GarageBand
        export preferences, 500-504
        external audio track additions, 494-496
        key changes, 478-480
        live tracks, recording, 469-471
        live tracks, time fixes, 493-494
        loops, note changes, 490-492
        loops, renaming, 481
        MacJukebox Web site, 508

master tracks, viewing, 479
metronome activation, 472-473
music tracks, adding, 461-463
music tracks, audio effects additions, 487-489
music tracks, deleting, 463
music tracks, instrument settings, 461-463
music tracks, mixing, 484-487
music tracks, recording via MIDI/USB keyboards, 464-466
music tracks, recording via virtual keyboards, 466-469
music tracks, renaming, 481
music tracks, stereo channels, 486
music tracks, system loads, 461
music tracks, transposing keys, 482-483
music tracks, volume settings, 486-487
renaming, 478
repeat cycle regions, 473-475
tempo changes, 478-480
time signature changes, 478-480
tracks, copying to other songs, 496-498
voice tracks, recording, 469-471

iPod
adding, 195
anti-piracy systems, 196
available disk space, 196
charging times, 196
deleting, 206
manual updates, 203-206
playlist synchronization, 200-203
preferences, setting, 196-200
turning on/off, 196

joint stereo, 165-169
live instrument tracks, recording (GarageBand), 469-471
measures, composing, 460
MP3 format, converting to (iTunes), 504-506
MP3.com Web site, 147
playlists
customizing (iTunes Library), 177-179
deleting, 176
sharing (iTunes Library), 183-186
smart (iTunes Library), 175-182
storing (iTunes Library), 174-177
presets, applying individually (iTunes Equalizer), 228-230
purchasing (Apple Music Store), 140
random playback (iTunes), 218-219
rating system (iTunes Library), 186-188
removing (iTunes Library), 188-190
searching (iTunes Library), 190-192
shuffling by album (iTunes), 234-235
variable bit rate (VBR), 165-169
visual effects, applying (iTunes Equalizer), 232-234
voice tracks, recording (GarageBand), 469-471
volume levels, adjusting (iTunes), 220-221

sound effects
Hollywood Edge Web site, 328
movies, adding (iMovie), 328-330
Skywalker Sound Effects, 328-330

## Source list

Source list (iTunes), 175

Split Clip at Playhead command (Edit menu-iMovie), 277

Split command (Edit menu-iMovie), 340

splitting
- audio clips (iMovie), 338-340
- loops (GarageBand), 460
- video clips (iMovie), 275-277

start frames in DVD menus, setting (iDVD), 401

stereo channels, music tracks (GarageBand), 486

still images
- Ken Burns effect, 283
- Timeline viewer, adding from other applications (iMovie), 300-302

storing
- images (iPhoto Library), 10-11
- movies on digital video tape (iMovie), 354-356
- music files, location of (iTunes Library), 169-171
- photographs, original versions (iPhoto), 42
- playlists (iTunes Library), 174-177
- radio sites (iTunes), 215-217

streaming audio, 210
- AAC format, 211
- bit rates, selecting for DSL connections, 211
- loading (iTunes), 214-215
- MP3 format, 211
- Web Streaming format, 353

SuperDrive
- burning CDs, 238
- disc types
    - DVD-R, 371
    - DVD-RW, 371

sustain attributes (musical notes), 492

synchronizing iPod playlists, 200-203

synthesized music (GarageBand). *See also* MIDI
- disadvantages, 453
- loops, 453-454
- recording process, 453-454
- versus digitized music, 452-453

## T

Tag Image File Format (TIFF), 12, 134

Targa File Format (TGA) file format, 12

tempo of songs, changing (GarageBand), 478-480

themes
- DVDs
    - menus, saving (iDVD), 412-414
    - motion options (iDVD), 375
    - selecting (iDVD), 373-375
- photo books, selecting (iPhoto), 71-74

thumbnail images, 29
- background settings (iPhoto), 9
- size settings (iPhoto), 7

TIFF (Tag Image File Format) file format, 12, 134

time signatures of songs, changing (GarageBand), 478-480

Timeline viewer (iMovie), 15-16

    audio tracks, 286

        playing, 287

        volume adjustments, 288

    changing size of, 288

    clips

        adding, 290-292

        speed of, 292-293

    effects, rendering, 288-289

    images, adding from other applications, 300-302

    photos

        adding, 294

        adjusting display time, 296

        motion additions, 298-300

    ruler, 286

    versus Clips viewer, 287

    video tracks, 286

    Zoom slider, 288

timing live tracks, fixes (GarageBand), 493-494

titles

    DVD menus, changing (iDVD), 396-398

    movies, creating (iMovie), 311-314

Titles pane (iMovie), 308-314, 321-324

tracks (CDs), 143

transferring pictures from digital cameras (iPhoto), 26-28

transitions

    movies

        inserting (iMovie), 308-311

        modifying (iMovie), 319-321

    third-party software, 310

Transitions pane (iMovie), 308-311, 319-321

transposing music tracks (GarageBand), 482-483

two-layer DVDs (commercial), 371

# U - V

Undo Crop command (Edit menu-iMovie), 279

Undo Split command (Edit menu-iMovie), 340

Universal Serial Bus. *See* USB

Unlock Audio Clip command (Advanced menu-iMovie), 347

updating iPod manually, 203-206

USB (Universal Serial Bus)

    cables

        computers, connection process, 28

        digital cameras, picture transfers to PCs, 26-28

    keyboards

        composing (GarageBand), 452

        recording tracks (GarageBand), 464-466

variable bit rate (VBR), 165-168

VBR (variable bit rate), 165-168

velocity attributes (musical notes), 492
video clips
    audio, extracting (iMovie), 336-338
    break detection, importing (iMovie), 268-270
    capturing (iMovie), 262-265
    copyright issues, 18
    credits, creating (iMovie), 321-324
    cropping (iMovie), 273, 277-279
    direction, setting (iMovie), 279-281
    distribution options (iMovie), 350
    effects, adding (iMovie), 314-316
    fade-in/out effects, adding (iMovie), 317-319
    formats
        .avi (Audio Video Interleave), 266
        .mov (QuickTime), 266
    frame rates
        NTSC standard, 273
        PAL standard, 273
    free frame images, creating (iMovie), 281-283
    full-screen mode (iMovie), 273
    importing (iMovie), 260-266
    locking to audio clips (iMovie), 347
    naming (iMovie), 274
    poor audio quality, troubleshooting, 327
    QuickTime format, 350
    splitting (iMovie), 275-277
    Timeline viewer
        adding, 290-292
        speed of, 292-293
    titles, creating (iMovie), 311-314
    transitions
        inserting (iMovie), 308-311
        modifying (iMovie), 319-321
    viewing (Clips pane), 272
viewer (Timeline)
    audio tracks, 286
        playing, 287
        volume adjustments, 288
    changing size of, 288
    clips
        adding, 290-292
        speed of, 292-293
    effects, rendering, 288-289
    images, adding from other applications, 300-302
    photos
        adding, 294
        display time adjustments, 296
        motion additions, 298-300
    ruler, 286
    versus Clips viewer, 287
    video tracks, 286
    Zoom slider, 288
viewing
    DVD themes (iDVD), 374
    movies in full-screen mode (iMovie), 350-351
virtual keyboards, recording tracks (GarageBand), 466-469
visual effects in audio files, applying (iTunes Equalizer), 232-234
voice tracks, recording (GarageBand), 469-471
voiceover effects, creating (iMovie), 334-336

volume
- audio tracks, adjusting (iMovie), 341-344
- music tracks, adjusting (GarageBand), 486-487
- songs, adjusting (iTunes), 220-221

## W - Z

watermarks (Apple logo), removal of (iDVD), 414

WAV (Windows Audio) audio format, 141, 327
- versus AIFF format, 142

Web pages, publishing photos to Apple HomePage, 118-121

Web servers, photos, publishing (iDisk), 118-121

Web sites
- Apple
    - CD drive resources, 240
    - DVD player compatibility listing, 372
    - iPhoto digital camera compatibility listing, 12, 28
    - QuickTime viewer downloads, 357
- Apple Music Store, 148-152
- Apple.com, 310, 316
- Audible.com
    - audio book file downloads, 160-162
    - Audio CD burning guidelines, 250
- ChordWizard, 483
- Dot Photo, digital photographic print service, 113
- FlashbackRadio.com, 214
- Freeplay Music, 147
- Hollywood Edge, 328
- MacJukebox, GarageBand song repository, 508
- MP3.com, 147
- Shoutcast.com, 214
- Shutterfly, digital photographic print service, 113
- Snapfish, digital photographic print service, 113
- Somafm.com, 214

Web Streaming format, 353

## Jump In Anywhere!

Organized into a series of **short**, **clearly written**, **well-illustrated** lessons, all *In a Snap* books in the Sams Teach Yourself series let you **zero right in** on that one particular task you need to accomplish right now—and then they let you get back to work.

Learning how to do new things with your computer shouldn't be tedious or time-consuming. It *should* be quick, easy, and maybe even a little bit fun.

### Digital Photography with Adobe Photoshop Album in a Snap

*Jennifer Fulton and Scott M. Fulton III*
0-672-32568-3
$24.99 US/$37.99 CAN

**Mac OS X Panther in a Snap**
*Brian Tiemann*
ISBN: 0-672-32612-4
$24.99 US • $37.99 CAN

**Digital Video with Windows XP in a Snap**
*Greg Perry*
ISBN: 0-672-32569-1
$24.99 US • $37.99 CAN

**Creating Web Pages with Macromedia Contribute in a Snap**
*Ned Averill-Snell*
ISBN: 0-672-32516-0
$24.99 US • $37.99 CAN

**eBay in a Snap**
*Preston Gralla*
ISBN: 0-672-32646-9
$19.99 US • $30.99 CAN

When you only have time for the answers™

www.samspublishing.com

# Key Terms

Don't let unfamiliar terms discourage you from learning all you can about iLife. If you don't completely understand what one of these words means, flip to the indicated page, read the full definition there, and find techniques related to that term.

**.avi (Audio Video Interleave)** *A multimedia format common to Microsoft Windows programs.* **Page 266**

**.mov** *A file extension used for QuickTime multimedia files.* **266**

**AAC (Advanced Audio Coding)** *A new standard in compressing audio while maintaining high sound quality (better than MP3 files).* **141**

**AIFF (Audio Interchange File Format)** *An uncompressed audio file format used by Macintosh computers to create CD-quality audio.* **141**

**Analog video** *A format that stores a recording of sound and light fluctuations. This format loses quality each time the video tape is copied or viewed.* **261**

**Aspect ratio** *The relationship between the height and width of an image.* **388**

**AU** *An audio format commonly used to create sound files you can download from the Internet and play on most operating systems.* **141**

**Bit rate** *A compression measurement indicating the average number of bits required for one second of sound. The higher the bit rate, the higher the sound quality.* **163**

**Buffer** *A temporary storage location for data during a transfer process between computers.* **210**

**CCD (charge-coupled device)** *A device in a digital camera that captures the light from an image and converts it into a digital image.* **46**

**CDDB** *A database maintained by a company called Gracenote containing track information about all commercial audio CDs.* **143**

**Chapter marker** *A marker inserted in a movie to indicate a specific point that can be indexed from a menu. Each marker becomes a button in an iDVD menu.* **359**

**Compression** *The process of reducing the size of a graphic image or audio file so that it requires less disk space to store.* **281**

**Contact sheet** *A printed sheet that contains thumbnail images of all the photos in a group to allow the photographer to select the photos to develop.* **110**

**Crop marks** *Triangular marks that display on the ruler under the Scrubber bar below the Monitor that indicate the frames to remove from a video clip.* **279**

**Crossfade** *The process of fading out one song as another song fades in, eliminating breaks in the audio.* **230**

**Cycle region** *A yellow bar at the top of the timeline that indicates a segment of the song that will repeat endlessly when you play the song.* **474**

**Decibel (dB)** *A measurement to determine the intensity of each sound frequency.* **Page 222**

**Drop zone** *A portion of a DVD menu to which you can add photos and movies that display as part of the menu.* **383**

**DVD-R** *A DVD to which you can copy files once. The disc cannot be erased and no more files can be added to it after the initial burn.* **239**

**DVD-RW** *A DVD that is rewritable. You can erase the disc or add additional files if the disc is not full. DVD-RW discs do not play in many standalone DVD players.* **239**

**Equalizer** *A hardware or software device that allows you to adjust the frequency ranges of the audio.* **222**

**External microphone** *A wired or wireless microphone attached to a video camera through a special jack.* **327**

**FireWire** *A small six-pin cable that connects a computer and an external device and provides a high-speed connection for transferring data.* **197**

**Frame** *A single image or picture within a video clip or movie.* **273**

**Hertz (Hz)** *A measurement used to represent a sound frequency.* **222**

**iDisk** *100 megabytes of personal storage on Apple's .Mac service online servers.* **118**

**iPod** *A portable MP3 player developed by Apple that has a large storage space and can interface directly with iTunes.* **140**

**Joint stereo** *The process of combining high frequency stereo sounds into a single channel to make them easier to detect.* **166**

**JPEG (Joint Photographics Experts Group)** *A graphics file format standard for creating a compressed image using a lossy compression format that shrinks the file size by eliminating elements from the picture.* **134**

**Ken Burns effect** *A method created by film documentary specialist Ken Burns for adding motion to a photograph by panning across the image or by zooming in and out on the image.* **298**

**Key** *The native pitch of the song. A key consists of a series of chords and scales, which can be used to build up the song's music.* **479**

**Loop** *A ready-made sequence of music, usually featuring a single instrument, which can be combined with other loops and repeated to form background riffs.* **454**

**Media pane** *Options available on the Customize drawer in iDVD that allow you to import files directly from iTunes, iMovie, and iPhoto.* **375**